SOMETHING ABOUT THE AUTHOR®

Something about
the Author *was named
an "**Outstanding
Reference Source,**"
the highest honor given
by the American
Library Association
Reference and Adult
Services Division.*

ISSN 0276-816X

FLORIDA STATE
UNIVERSITY LIBRARIES

JUN 2 3 2005

TALLAHASSEE, FLORIDA

SOMETHING ABOUT THE AUTHOR®

**Facts and Pictures about Authors
and Illustrators of Books for Young People**

volume 157

THOMSON
GALE

Detroit • New York • San Francisco • San Diego • New Haven, Conn. • Waterville, Maine • London • Munich

LSC
REF
PN
451
.S6
V.157
2005

THOMSON
™
GALE

Something About the Author, Volume 157

Project Editor
Maikue Vang

Editorial
Katy Balcer, Sara Constantakis, Michelle Kazensky, Julie Keppen, Joshua Kondek, Lisa Kumar, Tracey Matthews, Mary Ruby, Lemma Shomali

Permissions
Margaret Chamberlain-Gaston, Lori Hines, Shalice Shah-Caldwell

Imaging and Multimedia
Leitha Etheridge-Simms, Lezlie Light, Mike Logusz

Composition and Electronic Capture
Carolyn Roney

Manufacturing
Drew Kalasky

Product Manager
Chris Nasso

© 2005 Thomson Gale, a part of the Thomson Corporation.

Thomson and Star Logo are trademarks and Gale is a registered trademark used herein under license.

For more information, contact
Thomson Gale, Inc.
27500 Drake Rd.
Farmington Hills, MI 48331-3535
Or you can visit our internet site at
http://www.gale.com

ALL RIGHTS RESERVED
No part of this work covered by the copyright herein may be reproduced or used in any form or by any means —graphic, electronic, or mechanical, including photocopying, recording, taping, Web distribution, or information storage retrieval systems — without the written permission of the publisher.

This publication is a creative work fully protected by all applicable copyright laws, as well as by misappropriation, trade secret, unfair competition, and other applicable laws. The authors and editors of this work have added value to the underlying factual material herein through one or more of the following: unique and original selection, coordination, expression, arrangement, and classification of the information.

For permission to use material from the product, submit your request via the Web at http://www.gale-edit.com/permissions, or you may download our Permissions Request form and submit your request by fax or mail to:

Permissions Department
Thomson Gale
27500 Drake Rd.
Farmington Hills, MI 48331-3535
Permissions Hotline:
248-699-8006 or 800-877-4253, ext. 8006
Fax 248-699-8074 or 800-762-4058

Since this page cannot legibly accommodate all copyright notices, the acknowledgments constitute an extension of the copyright notice.

While every effort has been made to secure permission to reprint material and to ensure the reliability of the information presented in this publication, Thomson Gale neither guarantees the accuracy of the data contained herein nor assumes any responsibility for errors, omissions or discrepancies. Thomson Gale accepts no payment for listing; and inclusion in the publication of any organization, agency, institution, publication, service, or individual does not imply endorsement of the editors or publisher. Errors brought to the attention of the publisher and verified to the satisfaction of the publisher will be corrected in future editions.

LIBRARY OF CONGRESS CATALOG CARD NUMBER 62-52046

ISBN 0-7876-8781-2
ISSN 0276-816X

Printed in the United States of America
10 9 8 7 6 5 4 3 2 1

Contents

Authors in Forthcoming Volumes

Below are some of the authors and illustrators that will be featured in upcoming volumes of SATA. These include new entries on the swiftly rising stars of the field, as well as completely revised and updated entries (indicated with *) on some of the most notable and best-loved creators of books for children.

*David Almond ▌ When Almond penned his first YA novel, awards committees took notice. *Skellig,* which is inspired by the stories and small towns of the author's native England, mixes fantasy and a dash of the supernatural in its story of a boy coping in the midst of a family tragedy. The novel earned its author several prestigious awards, including Whitbread and Carnegie honors, and Almond has continued to impress critics with books such as *Kit's Wilderness* and *The Fire Eaters,* which draws readers into the life of a teen growing up under the threat of the cold war.

*Sandra Fenichel Asher ▌ A multi-award-winning playwright, Asher has devoted her career to introducing children to the magic of theatre. While her plays, such as *Dancing with Strangers* and *In the Garden of the Selfish Giant,* have been produced throughout the United States, Asher is better known as the author of picture books, middle-grade novels that draw on the author's Jewish cultural heritage, and short-story anthologies such as *On Her Way: Stories and Poems about Growing up Girl.* In addition to an active teaching career, Asher has devoted much of her time to youth theatre groups.

*Ian Bone ▌ Bone began his career working for the Australian Broadcasting System producing, writing, and directing children's programming for a decade before taking on the role of children's book author. His young-adult novels, such as *Fat Boy Saves World* and *The Song of an Innocent Bystander,* have earned him a number of top Aussie awards as well as praise for compelling plots which focus on teens placed in unusual and emotionally challenging situations. Bone has also endeared himself to younger readers with books such as *The Virus That Ate Barry* and *The Yuckiest Wish,* and is the author of the "VIDZ" series of middle-grade novels.

Shari Graydon ▌ From government press secretary to journalist to college teacher, Graydon has spent her career working with words. Understanding the power of words to influence decision-making—particularly among style-conscious teens—inspired her to begin a book-writing career. In books such as *Made You Look: How Advertising Works and Why You Should Know,* Graydon shows readers how to navigate in a sea of hype directed at separating young people from their allowance. She has become a sort of advertising activist in her native Canada, where, in addition to writing newspaper columns and presenting workshops in schools, Graydon has been active in media watch groups.

*Joyce Hansen ▌ Like many authors, Hansen was inspired to begin writing children's books through her work as a teacher. She also draws on her cultural background as an African American, combining it with her interest in the past to pen historical novels as well as highly praised nonfiction that reveals the diverse roles people of color have played throughout history. In *African Princesses* Hansen spans the centuries in her profile of talented women, while her fascination with the historical record has resulted in books such as *Freedom Roads: Searching for the Underground Railway,* which show modern archeologist at work revealing mysteries about black America's roots.

Wendy Mass ▌ Synesthesia may not be a household word for most teen readers, but that didn't stop Mass from making the condition—in which senses such as smell and color become neurologically "cross-wired"—the focus of her award-winning novel *A Mango-shaped Space.* Mass continues to exhibit her own knack for interpreting things in new ways in novels such as *Leap Day,* in which a variety of perspectives on a teen's eventful sixteenth birthday are interwoven in a compelling story. Coming from a varied career in publishing and film, Mass now alternates fiction with a range of nonfiction titles, and has produced several literature guides.

*Daniel Pinkwater ▌ While Pinkwater's books may be as quirky and eccentric as their author, his many awards attest to the fact that their themes resonate with parents. From *The Big Orange Splot,* a simple story that conveys a crucial lesson about uniqueness, to the totally for-fun *The Wuggie Norple Story* and *Fat Camp Commandos Go West,* Pinkwater often peoples his whimsical world with emboldened underdogs who often mete out a gentle justice. Pinkwater is also known to adults through his radio commentaries, which have been collected in several volumes, and *Chicago Days, Hoboken Nights,* in which he describes the childhood that has inspired much of his fiction.

*Robert D. San Souci ▌ Folktale reteller par excellence, San Souci has racked up a long list of awards due to his talent for spinning a captivating tale. Stories from around the world provide the fodder for his picture books, which range from *Little Gold Star,* a Latin fairy tale, to *Callie Ann and Mistah Bear,* a story with its roots firmly planted in American soil. Whether drawn from Asian, American, European, British, or African folklore, San Souci's many books show young readers that, wherever they live, all people share similar hopes, fears, dreams, and joys.

Geronimo Stilton ▌ Who Geronimo Stilton actually is may be a mystery, but this pseudonymous Italian-born writer has become one of the top-selling children's-book authors in Europe. Mimicking the high adventure, drama, and pathos of old-time movie serials, Stilton's books, which include *Too Fond of My Fur* and *Watch Your Whiskers, Stilton!,* follow the adventures of a journalist mouse who, when not busy working at the *Rodent's Gazette,* travels the world in search of adventure, often accompanied by his loyal friends as well as the occasional nemesis.

*Rich Wallace ▌ The world of high-school sports is central to the young-adult fiction penned by Wallace. A former sportwriter who now works in magazine publishing, Wallace writes both novels and short stories, consistently focusing on young male athletes whose competitive nature and single-mindedness sometimes cause problems in their lives off the field, court, or track. In *Losing Is Not an Option* Wallace follows a teen athlete growing up in a working-class town and hoping for more from life, while his novel *Wrestling Sturbridge* finds a second stringer attempting to turn his going-nowhere life around by challenging the top athlete on his varsity wrestling team. While family and romantic relationships play important roles, for Wallace's protagonists winning means more than just winning the game; it means winning at life.

Introduction

Something about the Author (*SATA*) is an ongoing reference series that examines the lives and works of authors and illustrators of books for children. *SATA* includes not only well-known writers and artists but also less prominent individuals whose works are just coming to be recognized. This series is often the only readily available information source on emerging authors and illustrators. You'll find *SATA* informative and entertaining, whether you are a student, a librarian, an English teacher, a parent, or simply an adult who enjoys children's literature.

What's Inside *SATA*

SATA provides detailed information about authors and illustrators who span the full time range of children's literature, from early figures like John Newbery and L. Frank Baum to contemporary figures like Judy Blume and Richard Peck. Authors in the series represent primarily English-speaking countries, particularly the United States, Canada, and the United Kingdom. Also included, however, are authors from around the world whose works are available in English translation. The writings represented in *SATA* include those created intentionally for children and young adults as well as those written for a general audience and known to interest younger readers. These writings cover the entire spectrum of children's literature, including picture books, humor, folk and fairy tales, animal stories, mystery and adventure, science fiction and fantasy, historical fiction, poetry and nonsense verse, drama, biography, and nonfiction. Obituaries are also included in *SATA* and are intended not only as death notices but also as concise overviews of people's lives and work. Additionally, each edition features newly revised and updated entries for a selection of *SATA* listees who remain of interest to today's readers and who have been active enough to require extensive revisions of their earlier biographies.

Autobiography Feature

Beginning with Volume 103, *SATA* features two or more specially commissioned autobiographical essays in each volume. These unique essays, averaging about ten thousand words in length and illustrated with an abundance of personal photos, present an entertaining and informative first-person perspective on the lives and careers of prominent authors and illustrators profiled in *SATA*.

Two Convenient Indexes

In response to suggestions from librarians, *SATA* indexes no longer appear in every volume but are included in alternate (odd-numbered) volumes of the series, beginning with Volume 57.

SATA continues to include two indexes that cumulate with each alternate volume: the Illustrations Index, arranged by the name of the illustrator, gives the number of the volume and page where the illustrator's work appears in the current volume as well as all preceding volumes in the series; the Author Index gives the number of the volume in which a person's biographical sketch, autobiographical essay, or obituary appears in the current volume as well as all preceding volumes in the series.

These indexes also include references to authors and illustrators who appear in *Gale's Yesterday's Authors of Books for Children, Children's Literature Review,* and *Something about the Author Autobiography Series.*

Easy-to-Use Entry Format

Whether you're already familiar with the *SATA* series or just getting acquainted, you will want to be aware of the kind of information that an entry provides. In every *SATA* entry the editors attempt to give as complete a picture of the person's life and work as possible. A typical entry in *SATA* includes the following clearly labeled information sections:

PERSONAL: date and place of birth and death, parents' names and occupations, name of spouse, date of marriage, names of children, educational institutions attended, degrees received, religious and political affiliations, hobbies and other interests.

ADDRESSES: complete home, office, electronic mail, and agent addresses, whenever available.

CAREER: name of employer, position, and dates for each career post; art exhibitions; military service; memberships and offices held in professional and civic organizations.

MEMBER: professional, civic, and other association memberships and any official posts held.

AWARDS, HONORS: literary and professional awards received.

WRITINGS: title-by-title chronological bibliography of books written and/or illustrated, listed by genre when known; lists of other notable publications, such as plays, screenplays, and periodical contributions.

ADAPTATIONS: a list of films, television programs, plays, CD-ROMs, recordings, and other media presentations that have been adapted from the author's work.

WORK IN PROGRESS: description of projects in progress.

SIDELIGHTS: a biographical portrait of the author or illustrator's development, either directly from the biographee—and often written specifically for the *SATA* entry—or gathered from diaries, letters, interviews, or other published sources.

BIOGRAPHICAL AND CRITICAL SOURCES: cites sources quoted in "Sidelights" along with references for further reading.

EXTENSIVE ILLUSTRATIONS: photographs, movie stills, book illustrations, and other interesting visual materials supplement the text.

How a *SATA* Entry Is Compiled

A *SATA* entry progresses through a series of steps. If the biographee is living, the *SATA* editors try to secure information directly from him or her through a questionnaire. From the information that the biographee supplies, the editors prepare an entry, filling in any essential missing details with research and/or telephone interviews. If possible, the author or illustrator is sent a copy of the entry to check for accuracy and completeness.

If the biographee is deceased or cannot be reached by questionnaire, the *SATA* editors examine a wide variety of published sources to gather information for an entry. Biographical and bibliographic sources are consulted, as are book reviews, feature articles, published interviews, and material sometimes obtained from the biographee's family, publishers, agent, or other associates.

Entries that have not been verified by the biographees or their representatives are marked with an asterisk (*).

Contact the Editor

We encourage our readers to examine the entire *SATA* series. Please write and tell us if we can make *SATA* even more helpful to you. Give your comments and suggestions to the editor:

Editor
Something about the Author
Thomson Gale
27500 Drake Rd.
Farmington Hills MI 48331-3535

Toll-free: 800-877-GALE
Fax: 248-699-8070

Something about the Author Product Advisory Board

The editors of *Something about the Author* are dedicated to maintaining a high standard of excellence by publishing comprehensive, accurate, and highly readable entries on a wide array of writers for children and young adults. In addition to the quality of the content, the editors take pride in the graphic design of the series, which is intended to be orderly yet inviting, allowing readers to utilize the pages of *SATA* easily and with efficiency. Despite the longevity of the *SATA* print series, and the success of its format, we are mindful that the vitality of a literary reference product is dependent on its ability to serve its users over time. As literature, and attitudes about literature, constantly evolve, so do the reference needs of students, teachers, scholars, journalists, researchers, and book club members. To be certain that we continue to keep pace with the expectations of our customers, the editors of *SATA* listen carefully to their comments regarding the value, utility, and quality of the series. Librarians, who have firsthand knowledge of the needs of library users, are a valuable resource for us. The *Something about the Author* Product Advisory Board, made up of school, public, and academic librarians, is a forum to promote focused feedback about *SATA* on a regular basis. The nine-member advisory board includes the following individuals, whom the editors wish to thank for sharing their expertise:

Eva M. Davis
Youth Department Manager,
Ann Arbor District Library,
Ann Arbor, Michigan

Joan B. Eisenberg
Lower School Librarian,
Milton Academy,
Milton, Massachusetts

Francisca Goldsmith
Teen Services Librarian,
Berkeley Public Library,
Berkeley, California

Susan Dove Lempke
Children's Services Supervisor,
Niles Public Library District,
Niles, Illinois

Robyn Lupa
Head of Children's Services,
Jefferson County Public Library,
Lakewood, Colorado

Victor L. Schill
Assistant Branch Librarian/Children's Librarian,
Harris County Public Library/Fairbanks Branch,
Houston, Texas

Caryn Sipos
Community Librarian,
Three Creeks Community Library,
Vancouver, Washington

Steven Weiner
Director,
Maynard Public Library,
Maynard, Massachusetts

Acknowledgments

Grateful acknowledgment is made to the following publishers, authors, and artists whose works appear in this volume.

AGEE, JON ▮ Agee, Jon, illustrator. From a jacket cover of *Palindromania!*, by Jon Agee. Farrar Straus and Giroux, 2002. Copyright © 2002 by Jon Agee. Reproduced by permission of Farrar, Straus and Giroux, LLC.

ALBERT, LOUISE ▮ Spalenka, Greg, photographer. From a jacket cover of *Less Than Perfect*, by Louise Albert. Holiday House, 2003. Reproduced by permission.

ANNO, MITSUMASA ▮ Anno, Mitsumasa, illustrator. From a cover of *Anno's Mysterious Multiplying Jar*, by Masaichiro Anno and Mitsumasa Anno. Paperstar, 1983. Copyright © 1982 by Kuso Kobo. Text translation copyright © 1983 by Philomel Books. Used by permission of Philomel Books, A Division of Penguin Young Readers Group, A Member of Penguin Group (USA) Inc., 345 Hudson Street, New York, NY 10014. All rights reserved./ Mitsumasa, Anno, illustrator. From an illustration in *Anno's Magic Seeds*, by Anno Mitsumasa. Paperstar, 1995. Copyright © 1992 by Kuso Kobo. Translation copyright © 1995 by Philomel Books. Used by permission of Philomel Books, A Division of Penguin Young Readers Group, A Member of Penguin Group (USA) Inc., 345 Hudson Street, New York, NY 10014. All rights reserved./ Anno, Mitsumasa, illustrator. From an illustration in *Anno's Spain*, by Mitsumasa Anno. Philomel Books, 2003. Copyright © 2003 by Mitsumasa Anno. Used by permission of Philomel Books, A Division of Penguin Young Readers Group, A Member of Penguin Group (USA) Inc., 345 Hudson Street, New York, NY 10014. All rights reserved.

BATESON, CATHERINE ▮ From a cover of *Painted Love Letters*, by Catherine Bateson. University of Queensland Press, 2002. Reproduced by permission.

BOND, (THOMAS) MICHAEL ▮ Fortnum, Peggy, illustrator. From a jacket cover of *Paddington Treasury*, by Michael Bond. Houghton Mifflin Company, 1999. Jacket art © 1979 by Peggy Fortnum. All rights reserved. Reproduced by permission of Houghton Mifflin Company./ Bond, Michael, holding his creations, J. D. Polson (l), and Paddington Bear, photograph by Larry Ellis. Hulton Archive. Reproduced by permission.

BORTOLOTTI, DAN ▮ Bortolotti, Dan, photograph by Laura Arsie Photography. Courtesy of Dan Bortolotti.

BRANDENBERG, ALIKI (LIACOURAS) ▮ Aliki, illustrator. From a jacket of *Ah, Music!*, by Aliki. HarperCollins Publishers, 2003. Used by permission of HarperCollins Publishers./ Aliki, illustrator. From an illustration in *All By Myself!*, by Aliki. HarperCollins Publishers, 2000. Used by permission of HarperCollins Publishers./ Brandenberg, Aliki, illustrator. From a cover of *Digging Up Dinosaurs*, by Aliki Brandenberg. HarperCollins Publishers, 1988. Used by permission of HarperCollins Publishers./ Brandenberg, Aliki, illustrator. From a jacket cover of *William Shakespeare & the Globe*, by Aliki Brandenberg. HarperCollins Publishers, 1999. Copyright © 1999 by Aliki Brandenburg. Used by permission of HarperCollins Publishers./ Brandenberg, Aliki, photograph. Reproduced by permission.

BRUMBEAU, JEFF ▮ de Marcken, Gail, illustrator. From an illustration in *The Quiltmaker's Gift*, by Jeff Brumbeau. Orchard Books, a division of Scholastic Inc., 2000. Illustrations copyright © 2000 by Gail de Marcken. Reprinted by permission of Scholastic Inc.

BURGESS, MARK ▮ Burgess, Mark, illustrator. From an illustration in *Teddy Time*, by Mark Burgess. HarperCollins Publishers Ltd., 2000. Text and illustrations copyright © Mark Burgess 2000. Reprinted by permission of HarperCollins Publishers Ltd.

CHRISTENSEN, BONNIE ▮ Christensen, Bonnie, illustrator. From a jacket of *In My Grandmother's House*, by Bonnie Christensen. HarperCollins Publishers, 2003. Cover art copyright © 2003 by Tinou Le Joly Senoville. Used by permission of HarperCollins Publishers.

COOK, LISA BROADIE ▮ McCauley, Adam illustrator. From an illustration in *Martin MacGregor's Snowman*, by Lisa Broadie Cook. Walker & Company, 2003. Illustrations copyright © 2003 by Adam McCauley. Reproduced by permission./ Cook, Broadie, portrait. Photo courtesy of Lisa Broadie Cook.

COOPER, ELISHA ▮ Cooper, Elisha, illustrator. From an illustration in *Dance!*, by Elisha Cooper. Greenwillow Books, 2001. Used by permission of HarperCollins Publishers./ Cooper, Elisha, illustrator. From an illustration in *Magic Thinks Big*, by Elisha Cooper. Greenwillow Books, 2004. Text copyright © 2004 by Elisha Cooper. Illustrations copyright © 2004 by Elisha Cooper. Used by permission of HarperCollins Publishers./ Cooper, Elisha, photograph by Elise Capella. Courtesy of Elisha Cooper.

CORNELIUS, KAY ▮ From a cover of *Francis Marion: The Swamp Fox*, by Kay Cornelius. Chelsea House Publishers, 2001. Reproduced by permission of Chelsea House Publishers, a subsidiary of Haights Cross Communications./ Cornelius, Kay, photograph. Photo courtesy of Kay Cornelius.

CUSHMAN, DOUG ▮ Cushman, Doug, illustrator. From an illustration in *Inspector Hopper*, by Doug Cushman. HarperCollins Publishers, 2000. Used by permission of HarperCollins Publishers./ Cushman, Doug, photograph by John Massimino. Reproduced by permission of Doug Cushman.

de LINT, CHARLES ▮ Palencar, Jude, illustrator. From a cover of *Spirits in the Wires*, by Charles de Lint. Tor Books, 2003. Reprinted by permission of St. Martin's Press, LLC./ Palencar, Jude, illustrator. From a jacket of *Waifs and Strays*, by Charles de Lint.

xiii

Viking, 2002. Cover copyright © 2002 by John Jude Palencar. Used by permission of Viking Children's Books, A Division of Penguin Young Readers Group, A Member of Penguin Group (USA) Inc., 345 Hudson Street, New York, NY 10014. All rights reserved./ de Lint, Charles, photograph. Copyright © 2000 by Mary Ann Harris. Reproduced by permission.

DEWAN, TED ▌ Dewan, Ted, illustrator. From an illustration in *Crispin: The Pig Who Had It All,* by Ted Dewan. Dell Dragonfly Books, 2000. Copyright © 2000 by Ted Dewan. Used by permission of Random House Children's Books, a division of Random House, Inc. Reprinted in the UK by permission of The Random House Group, Ltd.

DOWELL, FRANCES O'ROARK ▌ Frost, Michael, illustrator. From a jacket cover of *The Secret Language of Girls,* by Frances O'Roark Dowell. Atheneum Books for Young Readers, 2004. Reproduced by permission./ Katz, Bruce, photographer. From a book cover of *Where I'd Like to Be,* by Frances O'Roark Dowell. Aladdin Paperbacks, 2003. Reproduced by permission./ Dowell, Frances O'Roark, photograph. Courtesy of Frances O'Roark Dowell.

FEIFFER, JULES ▌ Feiffer, Jules, illustrator. From an illustration in *Bark, George,* by Jules Feiffer. HarperCollins Publishers, 1999. Text and pictures copyright © 1999 by Jules Feiffer. All rights reserved. Used by permission of HarperCollins Publishers.

FRANK, E(MILY). R. ▌ Digital Vision, photographer. From a jacket cover of *Friction,* by E. R. Frank. Atheneum Books for Young Readers, 2003. Reproduced by permission./ Yuen, Michael, photograph. From a cover of *Life is Funny,* by E. R. Frank. Puffin Books, 2000. Copyright © 2000 by Michael Yuen. Used by permission of Puffin Books, A Division of Penguin Young Readers Group, A Member of Penguin Group (USA) Inc., 345 Hudson Street, New York, NY 10014. All rights reserved.

FROST, HELEN ▌ From a photograph in *Coming to America: German Immigrants, 1820-1920,* written by Helen Frost, image by Corbis. Immigrants crowd together on the deck of the Kroonland, September, 1920. © Bettmann/Corbis./ Christie, R. Gregory, illustrator. From a jacket cover of *Keesha's House,* by Helen Frost. Frances Foster Book, 2003. Copyright © 2003 Helen Frost. Reproduced by permission of Farrar, Straus and Giroux, LLC.

GILBERT, SHERI L. ▌ Wubbels, Wendy Schultz, illustrator. From a jacket of *The Legacy of Gloria Russell,* by Sheri Gilbert. Alfred A. Knopf, 2004. Copyright © 2004 by Sheri Gilbert. Jacket cover illustration copyright © 2004 by Wendy Schultz Wubbels. Used by permission of Alfred A. Knopf, an imprint of Random House Children's Books, a division of Random House, Inc./Gilbert, Sheri L., photograph. Photo courtesy of Sheri L. Gilbert.

HAHN, MARY DOWNING ▌ All photos courtesy of Mary Downing Hahn.

HARLOW, JOAN HIATT ▌ Day, Larry, illustrator. From a jacket cover of *Joshua's Song,* by Joan Hiatt Harlow. Margaret K. McElderry Books, 2001. Illustrations copyright © 2001 by Larry Day. Reproduced by permission./ Yuen, Sammy J., illustrator. From a jacket cover of *Shadows on the Sea,* by Joan Hiatt Harlow. Margaret K. McElderry Books, 2003. Reproduced by permission./ Harlow, Joan Hiatt, photograph by Barbara Banks. Courtesy of Joan Hiatt Harlow.

HARMON, DANIEL E(LTON) ▌ Harmon, Daniel, photograph by Courtney Danielle Harmon. Courtesy of Daniel Elton Harmon.

HASELEY, DENNIS ▌ Sano, Kazuhiko, illustrator. From a jacket of *The Amazing Thinking Machine,* by Dennis Haseley. Dial Books, 2002. Cover copyright © 2002 by Kazuhiko Sano. Used by permission of Dial Books for Young Readers, A Division of Penguin

Young Readers Group, A Member of Penguin Group (USA) Inc., 345 Hudson Street, New York, NY 10014. All rights reserved./ Green, Jonathan, illustrator. From an illustration in *Crosby,* by Dennis Haseley. Harcourt, 1996. Illustrations © 1996 by Jonathan Green. Reproduced by permission of Harcourt, Inc./ Vermeer, Johannes, illustrator. From "Girl Interrupted at Her Music," cover art from *Trick of the Eye,* by Dennis Haseley. Dial Books, 2004. Cover art copyright the Frick Collection, New York. Used by permission of Dial Books for Young Readers, A Division of Penguin Young Readers Group, A Member of Penguin Group (USA) Inc., 345 Hudson Street, New York, NY 10014. All rights reserved./ Haseley, Dennis, photograph. Reproduced by permission.

HIÇYILMAZ, GAYE ▌ From a cover of *Pictures from the Fire,* by Gaye Hicyilmaz. Dolphin Paperbacks, 2004. Reproduced by permission.

HIRSCH, ODO ▌ Hall, August, illustrator. From a jacket cover of *Antonio S & the Mysterious Theodore Guzman,* by Odo Hirsch. Hyperion Books for Children, 1997. Illustrations © 2001 by August Hall. All rights reserved. Reprinted by permission of Hyperion Books for Children./ McLean, Andrew, illustrator. From a jacket cover of *Hazel Green,* by Odo Hirsch. Bloomsbury, 2000. Reproduced by permission.

KELLER, HOLLY ▌ Keller, Holly, illustrator. From an illustration in *Farfallina and Marcel,* by Holly Keller. Greenwillow Books, 2002. Used by permission of HarperCollins Publishers./ Keller, Holly, illustrator. From an illustration in *Snow Is Falling,* by Franklyn M. Branley. HarperCollins Publishers, 1986. Copyright © 1996 by Holly Keller. Used by permission of HarperCollins Publishers./ Keller, Holly, illustrator. From an illustration in *That's Mine, Horace,* by Holly Keller. Greenwillow Books, 2000. Used by permission of HarperCollins Publishers./ Keller, Holly, photograph by Corey Keller. Reproduced by permission of Holly Keller.

KOLLER, JACKIE FRENCH ▌ Guay, Rebecca, illustrator. From a cover of *The Keepers Book One: A Wizard Named Nell,* by Jackie French Koller. Aladdin Paperbacks, 2003. Reproduced by permission./ Cockcroft, Jason, illustrator. From a cover jacket of *Someday,* by Jackie French Koller. Orchard Books, a division of Scholastic Inc., 2002. Copyright © 2002 by Jackie French Koller. Reprinted by permission of Scholastic, Inc./ Koller, Jackie French, with dog, photograph. Reproduced by permission.

KRAFT, BETSY HARVEY ▌ Library of Congress, photograph. From a photograph in *Theodore Roosevelt: Champion of the American Spirit,* by Betsy Harvey Kraft. Houghton Mifflin Company, 2003.

LASKY, KATHRYN ▌ Harrington, Glenn, illustrator. From a cover of *My America: An American Spring: Sofia's Immigrant Diary,* by Kathryn Lasky. Scholastic Inc., 2004. Jacket illustration copyright © 2004 by Scholastic, Inc. Reprinted by permission of Scholastic, Inc./ O'Brien, Tim, illustrator. From a cover of *Marie Antoinette, Princess of Varsailles, Austria-France, 1769,* by Kathryn Lasky. Scholastic, Inc., 2000. Painting by Tim O'Brien. Copyright © 2000 by Kathryn Lasky. Reprinted by permission of Scholastic, Inc./ La Brosse, Darcia, illustrator. From an illustration in *Mommy's Hands,* by Kathryn Lasky and Jane Kamine. Hyperion Books for Children, 2002. Illustrations © 2002 by Darcia La Brosse. Reproduced by permission of Hyperion Books For Children.

LASSITER, RHIANNON ▌ Young, Paul, illustrator. From a cover of *Hex,* by Rhiannon Lassiter. Archway Paperback, 1998. Reproduced by permission./ Gerber, Mark, illustrator. From a cover of *Shadows,* by Rhiannon Lassiter. Simon Pulse, 1999. Reproduced by permission.

LESTER, JULIUS ▌ Brown, Rod, illustrator. From an illustration in *From Slave Ship to Freedom Road,* by Julius Lester. Puffin Books, 1998. Illustrations copyright © 1998 by Rod Brown. Used by permission of Dial Books for Young Readers, A Division of Penguin

Young Readers Group, A Member of Penguin Group (USA) Inc., 345 Hudson Street, New York, NY 10014. All rights reserved./ Feelings, Tom, illustrator. From a cover of *To Be a Slave,* by Julius Lester. Copyright © 1968 by Tom Feelings, illustrations. Used by permission of Dial Books for Young Readers, A Division of Penguin Young Readers Group, A Member of Penguin Group (USA) Inc., 345 Hudson Street, New York, NY 10014. All rights reserved./ Irby, Kevin and Ellen Dooley, photographers. From a cover of *When Dad Killed Mom,* by Julius Lester. Harcourt, Inc., 2001. Reproduced by permission of Harcourt, Inc.

LONDON, JONATHAN ▌ Rex, Michael, illustrator. From an illustration in *Crunch Munch,* by Jonathan London. Harcourt Inc., 2001. Illustrations copyright © 2001 by Michael Rex. Reproduced by permission of Harcourt, Inc./ Remkiewicz, Frank, illustrator. From an illustration in *Froggy Goes to the Doctor,* by Jonathan London. Puffin Books, 2002. Illustrations copyright © 2002 Frank Remkiewicz. Used by permission of Viking Children's Books, A Division of Penguin Young Readers Group, A Member of Penguin Group (USA) Inc., 345 Hudson Street, New York, NY 10014. All rights reserved./ Souci, Daniel San, illustrator. From an illustration in *Mustang Canyon,* by Jonathan London. Candlewick Press, 2002. Illustrations copyright © 2002 by Daniel San Souci. Text copyright © 2002 Jonathan London. Reproduced by permission of the publisher Candlewick Press, Inc., Cambridge, MA.

LOTTRIDGE, CELIA BARKER ▌ Fitzgerald, Joanne, illustrator. From *The Little Rooster and the Diamond Button,* by Celia Barker Lottridge. Groundwood Books, 2001. Illustrations copyright © 2001 by Joanne Fitzgerald. Reproduced by permission of Groundwood Books Ltd./ Fitzgerald, Joanne, illustrator. From *Ten Small Tales: Stories from around the World,* by Celia Barker Lottridge. Groundwood Books, 1993. Illustrations copyright © 1993 by Joanne Fitzgerald. All rights reserved. Reproduced by permission of Groundwood Books, Ltd.

LUND, DEB ▌ Nakata, Hiroe, illustrator. From an illustration in *Tell Me My Story, Mama,* by Deb Lund. HarperCollins Publishers, 2004. Illustrations copyright © 2004 by Hiroe Nakata. All rights reserved. Used by permission of HarperCollins Publishers./ Lund, Deb, photograph by Celeste Mergens. Courtesy of Deborah Lund.

MENDES, VALERIE ▌ Fletcher, Claire, illustrator. From an illustration in *Look at Me, Grandma!,* by Valerie Mendes. Scholastic Inc., 2001. Illustrations © Claire Fletcher 2001. All rights reserved. Reproduced by permission of Scholastic, Inc./ Mendes, Valerie, photograph by Eamonn McCabe. Courtesy of Valerie Mendes.

MURPHY, STUART J. ▌ Bendall-Brunello, John, illustrator. From an illustration in *100 Days of Cool,* by Stuart J. Murphy. HarperCollins Publishers, 2004. Copyright © 2003 by John Bendall-Brunello. Used by permission of HarperCollins Publishers./ Tusa, Tricia, illustrator. From an illustration in *Lemonade for Sale,* by Stuart J. Murphy. HarperCollins Publishers, 1998. Copyright © 1998 by Tricia Tusa. All rights reserved. Mathstart(TM) is a trademark of HarperCollins Publishers, Inc. Used by permission of HarperCollins Publishers./ Murphy, Stuart J., photograph by Evanston Photographic Studios, Inc. Courtesy of Stuart J. Murphy.

MYERS, WALTER DEAN ▌ Johnson, Joel P., illustrator. From a cover of *It Ain't All for Nothing,* by Walter Dean Myers. Harper Trophy, 1978. Cover art copyright © 2003 by Joel Johnson. Used by permission of HarperCollins Publishers./ From a cover of *The Glory Field,* by Walter Dean Myers. Scholastic Inc., 1994. Copyright © 1994 by Walter Dean Myers. Reprinted by permission of Scholastic, Inc./ Jenkins, Leonard, illustrator. From an illustration in *I've Seen the Promised Land: The Life of Dr. Martin Luther King, Jr.,* by Walter Dean Myers. HarperCollins Publishers, 2004. Text copyright © 2004 by Walter Dean Myers. Illustrations copyright © 2004 by Leonard Jenkins. Used by permission of HarperCollins Publishers./ Beck, Robert, artist. From a jacket of *Shooter,* by Walter Dean Myers, HarperTempest, 2004. Cover art copyright © 2004 by Robert Beck. Used by permission of HarperCollins Publishers.

NAMIOKA, LENSEY ▌ Namioka, Lensey. From a cover of *An Ocean Apart, A World Away,* by Lensey Namioka. Laurel-Leaf Books, 2002. Copyright © 2002 by Lensey Namioka. Used by permission of Random House Children's Books, a division of Random House, Inc./ Frost, Michael, photographer. From a cover of *Ties that Bind, Ties that Break,* by Lensey Namioka. Laurel-Leaf Books, 1999. Copyright © 1999 by Lensey Namioka. Used by permission of Random House Children's Books, a division of Random House, Inc./ Namioka, Lensey, photograph by Don Perkins. Courtesy of Lensey Namioka.

NEUSCHWANDER, CINDY ▌ Geehan, Wayne, illustrator. From an illustration in *Sir Cumference and the Sword in the Cone: A Math Adventure,* by Cindy Neuschwander. Charlesbridge Publishing, 2003. Text copyright © 2003 by Cindy Neuschwander. Illustrations copyright © 2003 by Wayne Geehan. All rights reserved. Used with permission by Charlesbridge Publishing, Inc./ Neuschwander, Cindy, photograph. Courtesy of Cindy Neuschwander.

NOLAN, HAN ▌ Hoffman, A./Photonica. From a cover of *Born Blue,* by Han Nolan. Harcourt, Inc., 2001. Reproduced by permission of Harcourt, Inc./ Howe, Alex, photographer. From a jacket cover of *When We Were Saints,* by Han Nolan. Harcourt, Inc., 2003. Reproduced by permission of Harcourt, Inc.

NOLEN, JERDINE ▌ Buehner, Mark, illustrator. From an illustration in *Harvey Potter's Balloon Farm,* by Jerdine Nolen. Lothrop, Lee & Shepard Books, 1994. Illustrations copyright © 1994 by Mark Buehner. All rights reserved. Used by permission of HarperCollins Publishers./ Nelson, Kadir, illustrator. From an illustration in *Thunder Rose,* by Jerdine Nolen. Silver Whistle, Harcourt, Inc., 2003. Illustrations copyright © 2003 by Kadir Nelson. Reproduced by permission of Harcourt, Inc./ Nolen, Jerdine, photograph. Reproduced by permission.

O'MALLEY, KEVIN ▌ O'Malley, Kevin, illustrator. From an illustration in *Miss Malarkey's Field Trip,* by Judy Finchler, Kevin O'Malley. Walker & Company, 2004. Illustrations copyright © 2004 by Kevin O'Malley. All rights reserved. Reproduced by permission.

ONYEFULU, IFEOMA ▌ Onyefulu, Ifeoma, photographer. From a cover of *A is for Africa,* by Ifeoma Onyefulu. Puffin Books, 1993. Copyright © 1993 by Ifeoma Onyefulu, text and photographs. Used by permission of Cobblehill Books, an affiliate of Dutton Children's Books, A Division of Penguin Young Readers Group, A Member of Penguin Group (USA) Inc., 345 Hudson Street, New York, NY 10014. All rights reserved./ Onyefulu, Ifeoma, photographer. From a photograph in *Here Comes Our Bride!: An African Wedding Story,* by Ifeoma Onyefulu. Frances Lincoln Children's Books, 2004. All rights reserved. Text and photographs copyright © Ifeoma Onyefulu 2004. Reproduced by permission of Frances Lincoln Ltd., 4 Torriano Mews, Torriano Avenue, London NW5 2RZ. Distributed in the USA by Publishers Group West./ Onyefulu, Ifeoma, photograph by Mamta Kapoor. Courtesy of Ifeoma Onyefulu.

ORENSTEIN, DENISE GOSLINER ▌ Harris, Craig, photographer. From a jacket of *Unseen Companion,* by Denise Gosliner Orenstein. Katherine Tegen Books, 2003. Cover art copyright © 2003 by Craig Harris. Used by permission of HarperCollins Publishers.

PAOLINI, CHRISTOPHER ▌ Palencar, John Jude, illustrator. From a jacket of *Eragon: Inheritance (Book One),* by Christopher Paolini. Alfred A. Knopf, 2003. Text copyright © 2003 by Christopher Paolini. Jacket art copyright © 2003 by John Jude Palencar. Illustrations on endpapers, pages ii-iii, iv, 514 copyright © 2002 by Christopher Paolini. Used by permission of Alfred A. Knopf, an imprint of Random House Children's Books, a division of Random House, Inc.

PARKER, BARBARA KEEVIL ∎ McIntyre, Rick, photographer. From a photograph in *North American Wolves,* by Barbara Keevil Parker. Carolrhoda Books, Inc., 1998. Reproduced by permission./ Parker, Barbara Keevil, photograph. Photo courtesy of Barbara K. Parker.

PEYTON, KATHLEEN WENDY (HERALD) ∎ Kelly, Pete, illustrator. From a cover of *Blind Beauty,* by K.M. Peyton. Dutton Children's Books, 1999. Cover copyright © 2001 by Pete Kelly. Used by permission of Dutton Children's Books, A Division of Penguin Young Readers Group, A Member of Penguin Group (USA) Inc., 345 Hudson Street, New York, NY 10014. All rights reserved./ Sayles, Elizabeth, illustrator. From a cover of *Snowfall,* by K.M. Peyton. Houghton Mifflin Company, 1994. Reproduced by permission./ Wyatt, David, illustrator. From a jacket of *Stealaway,* by K.M. Peyton. Cricket Books, 2001. Illustrations © 2001 by David Wyatt. All rights reserved. Reproduced by permission.

RAKE, JODY ∎ Rake, Jody, photograph. Photo courtesy of Jody Rake.

RATHMANN, PEGGY ∎ Rathmann, Peggy, illustrator. From a cover of *The Day the Babies Crawled Away,* by Peggy Rathmann. G.P. Putnam's Sons, 2003. Copyright © 2003 by Peggy Rathmann. Used by permission of G.P. Putnam's Sons, A Division of Penguin Young Readers Group, A Member of Penguin Group (USA) Inc., 345 Hudson Street, New York, NY 10014. All rights reserved./ Rathmann, Peggy, illustrator. From an illustration in *Officer Buckle and Gloria,* by Peggy Rathmann. G. P. Putnam's Sons, 1995. Copyright © 1995 by Peggy Rathmann. Used by permission of G.P. Putnam's Sons, a Division of Penguin Young Readers Group, A Member of Penguin Group (USA) Inc., 345 Hudson Street, New York, NY 10014. All rights reserved./ Rathmann, Peggy, illustrator. From an illustration in *Ten Minutes till Bedtime,* by Peggy Rathmann. G.P. Putnam's Sons, 1998. Copyright © 1998 by Peggy Rathmann. Used by permission of G.P. Putnam's Sons, A Division of Penguin Young Readers Group, A Member of Penguin Group (USA) Inc., 345 Hudson Street, New York, NY 10014. All rights reserved.

ROTTMAN, S(USAN) L(YNN) ∎ Rottman, S. L., photograph. Reproduced by permission.

SHANGE, NTOZAKE ∎ Nelson, Kadir, illustration. From an illustration in *Ellington Was Not a Street,* by Ntozake Shange. Simon & Schuster Books for Young Readers, 1983. Illustrations copyright © 2004 by Kadir Nelson. All rights reserved. Reproduced by permission of Simon & Schuster Children's Publishing Division./ From a production still for *For Colored Girls Who Have Considered Suicide/ When The Rainbow is Enuf,* by Ntozake Shange. Photograph by Martha Swope. © Martha Swope. Reproduced by permission./ Shange, Ntozake, photograph. AP/Wide World Photos. Reproduced by permission.

STANLEY, GEORGE EDWARD ∎ Murdocca, Salvatore, illustrator. From an illustration in *The Mystery of the Hairy Tomatoes,* by George Edward Stanley. Aladdin, 2001. Illustrations copyright ©

2001 Salvatore Murdocca. Reproduced by permission of Aladdin, an imprint of Simon & Schuster Children's Publishing Division./ Lee, Jared, illustrator. From an illustration in *Snake Camp,* by George Edward Stanley. Golden Books, 2000. Illustrations copyright © 2000 by Jared D. Lee Studio, Inc. Used by permission of Golden Books, an imprint of Random House Children's Books, a division of Random House, Inc./ Stanley, George Edward, photograph. Courtesy of George Edward Stanley.

SUEN, ANASTASIA ∎ Smith, Elwood H., illustrator. From an illustration in *Raise the Roof,* by Anastasia Suen. Viking, 2003. Illustrations copyright © 2001 by Elwood H. Smith. Used by permission of Viking Children's Books, A Division of Penguin Young Readers Group, A Member of Penguin Group (USA) Inc., 345 Hudson Street, New York, NY 10014. All rights reserved.

SZEKERES, CYNDY ∎ All photos courtesy of Cyndy Szekeres.

TUNNELL, MICHAEL O. ∎ Roman, Barbara J., illustrator. From a cover of *School Spirits,* by Michael O. Tunnell. Holiday House, 1997. Copyright © 1997 Michael O. Tunnell. Reproduced by permission of Holiday House, Inc./ Tronc, Jo, illustrator. From a jacket of *Wishing Moon,* by Michael O. Tunnell. Dutton Children's Books, 2004. Jacket copyright © 2004 by Jo Tranc. Used by permission of Dial Books for Young Readers, A Division of Penguin Young Readers Group, A Member of Penguin Group (USA) Inc., 345 Hudson Street, New York, NY 10014. All rights reserved./ Tunnell, Michael O., photograph. Photo courtesy of Michael O. Tunnell.

WADSWORTH, GINGER ∎ Anderson, G. E., photographer. From a jacket cover of *Words West,* by Ginger Wadsworth. Clarion Books, 2003. Reproduced by permission of L. Tom Perry Special Collections/Harold B. Lee Library, Brigham Young University./ Wadsworth, Ginger, photograph. Reproduced by permission.

WAGNER, MICHELE R. ∎ Wagner, Michele R., photograph. Photo courtesy of Michele Wagner.

WELLINGTON, MONICA ∎ Wellington, Monica, illustrator. From an illustration in *Apple Farmer Annie,* by Monica Wellington. Dutton Children's Books, 2001. Copyright © 2001 by Monica Wellington. Used by permission of Dutton Children's Books, A Division of Penguin Young Readers Group, A Member of Penguin Group (USA) Inc., 345 Hudson Street, New York, NY 10014. All rights reserved./ Wellington, Monica, illustrator. From an illustration in *Crepes by Suzette,* by Monica Wellington. Dutton Children's Books, 2004. Copyright © 2004 by Monica Wellington. Used by permission of Dutton Children's Books, A Division of Penguin Young Readers Group, A Member of Penguin Group (USA) Inc., 345 Hudson Street, New York, NY 10014. All rights reserved./ Wellington, Monica, illustrator. From an illustration in *Squeaking of Art: The Mice Go to the Museum,* by Monica Wellington. Dutton Children's Books, 2000. Copyright © 2000 by Monica Wellington. Used by permission of Dutton Children's Books, A Division of Penguin Young Readers Group, A Member of Penguin Group (USA) Inc., 345 Hudson Street, New York, NY 10014. All rights reserved./ Wellington, Monica, photograph. Photo courtesy of Monica Wellington

SOMETHING ABOUT THE AUTHOR

AGEE, Jon 1960-

Personal

Born 1960, in Nyack, NY; son of a teacher and an artist; married June, 2002; wife's name, Audrey. *Education:* Cooper Union School of Art, B.F.A.

Addresses

Home—San Francisco, CA. *Agent*—c/o Author Mail, Hyperion Books, 114 Fifth Ave., New York, NY 10011.

Career

Author and illustrator of children's books.

Awards, Honors

Best illustrated Children's Book designation, *New York Times,* and Notable Book selection, American Library Association (ALA), both for *The Incredible Painting of Felix Clousseau;* Best Illustrated Children's Book designation, *New York Times,* for *The Return of Freddy LeGrand;* Best Illustrated Children's Book designation, *New York Times,* for *Dmitri the Astronaut; Los Angeles Times* Best Book of the Year selection, and ALA Notable Children's Book selection, both for *Milo's Hat Trick.*

Writings

SELF-ILLUSTRATED

If Snow Falls: A Story for December, Pantheon (New York, NY), 1982.

Ellsworth, Pantheon (New York, NY), 1983.
Ludlow Laughs, Farrar, Straus & Giroux (New York, NY), 1985.
The Incredible Painting of Felix Clousseau, Farrar, Straus & Giroux (New York, NY), 1988.
Go Hang a Salami! I'm a Lasagna Hog! and Other Palindromes, Farrar, Straus & Giroux (New York, NY), 1991.
The Return of Freddy Legrand, Farrar, Straus & Giroux (New York, NY), 1992.
Flapstick: Ten Ridiculous Rhymes with Flaps, Dutton (New York, NY), 1993.
So Many Dynamos! and Other Palindromes, Farrar, Straus & Giroux (New York, NY), 1994.
Dmitri the Astronaut, HarperCollins (New York, NY), 1996.
Who Ordered the Jumbo Shrimp? and Other Oxymorons, HarperCollins (New York, NY), 1998.
Sit on a Potato Pan, Otis!: More Palindromes, Farrar, Straus & Giroux (New York, NY), 1999.
Elvis Lives!: and Other Anagrams, Farrar, Straus & Giroux (New York, NY), 2000.
Milo's Hat Trick, Hyperion (New York, NY), 2001.
Palindromania!, Farrar, Straus & Giroux (New York, NY), 2002.
Z Goes Home, Hyperion (New York, NY), 2003.
Terrific, Hyperion (New York, NY), 2005.

ILLUSTRATOR

Lucia Monfried, *Dishes All Done,* Dutton (New York, NY), 1989.

1

Dee Lillegard, *Sitting in My Box,* Dutton (New York, NY), 1989.

Mary H. Heyward, *The Toy Box,* Dutton (New York, NY), 1989.

(With others) *The Big Book for Peace,* Dutton (New York, NY), 1990.

Jennifer Jacobson, *Mr. Lee,* Open Court (Chicago, IL), 1995.

Erica Silverman, *The Halloween House,* Farrar, Straus & Giroux (New York, NY), 1997.

Tor Seidler, *Mean Margaret,* HarperCollins (New York, NY), 1998.

William Steig, *Potch and Polly,* Farrar, Straus & Giroux (New York, NY), 2002.

OTHER

Also author of book and lyrics to musicals *B.O.T.C.H.* and *Flies in the Soup,* produced at TADA! Theater, New York, NY.

Sidelights

Jon Agee is an author and illustrator of such children's books as *The Incredible Painting of Felix Clousseau, The Return of Freddy LeGrand,* and *Dmitri the Astronaut.* In addition, Agee's fascination with language has inspired him to create a series of books on wordplay as well as the books and lyrics for two musicals produced off-off Broadway. A cartoonist, he has also had several of his cartoons published in the *New Yorker.*

Agee grew up along the Hudson River in Nyack, New York. He developed an interest in art at a young age: as a child he created picture books, detective comics, and flip books he constructed from train ticket stubs. Agee's mother, who had studied art during her college years, was an inspiration to him. "My mom is a wonderful artist, and she made it kind of irresistible for my sister and me," Agee told Heather Vogel Frederick in a *Publishers Weekly* interview. "The dining room table was her studio space, and there were always art supplies around for us to get into."

After graduating from high school, Agee enrolled at the Cooper Union School of Art in New York City, where he studied painting, dabbled in animation, and made an "art" film. It was at Cooper Union that he also discovered his knack for storytelling. As Agee commented to Frederick, "There was a point in college where I was painting and I was also doing animated cartoons and writing comic strips. I found a lot of joy in creating a story line, and after a while the idea of doing a picture without any narrative or sequence–of just an individual image–dropped away."

Agee eventually moved to Brooklyn, where his work caught the attention of editor Frances Foster who agreed to publish a holiday tale. Agee's debut picture book, *If Snow Falls: A Story for December,* concerns a young boy whose dreams of his grandfather transform the elderly man into Santa Claus. A reviewer for *Publishers Weekly* found *If Snow Falls* to be "an extraordinary visual treat" that "unfolds like a lullaby."

Ellsworth relates the story of a dog who works as a university professor. Acting true to his doggy nature outside of the classroom, the academic pup soon loses the respect of his colleagues and students when he is observed chasing cats, burying bones, and lifting his leg near trees and signposts. Ellsworth spends much of his energy worrying about his career until he meets a poodle who is quite comfortable just being a dog. *Horn Book* reviewer Karen Jameyson noted, in particular, Agee's "textured, shadowy illustrations," which she maintained produce "a slightly comical, pleasing effect." A "lighthearted gem" was Debra Hewitt's summation of *Ellsworth* in *School Library Journal,* while a *Publishers Weekly* reviewer concluded that the author/illustrator "scores a hit," adding that Agee's "big, lusty, full-color pictures illustrate this frolic perfectly."

Ludlow Laughs tells the tale of a grumpy man with an enormous frown and a perpetually sour demeanor. One day, however, the man's tedious daily routine is shaken up by an amusing dream. On waking, Ludlow begins to laugh, and his laughter becomes contagious as it spreads throughout his neighborhood and then throughout the world. *Ludlow Laughs* was a featured selection narrated by Phyllis Diller on the PBS children's show *Reading Rainbow.*

Agee spent more than two years completing *The Incredible Painting of Felix Clousseau.* A contributor to *Publishers Weekly* described the resulting volume as "an unusual picture book that works on several levels: as a work of art, as an inventive fantasy, and as a satirical comment on the academic art world." The artist Clousseau wins a grand prize when his entry, a painting of a duck, quacks. His other paintings, including a waking snake, an erupting volcano, a firing cannon, and a flowing river and waterfall, also come to life. While Clousseau is jailed because of the chaos his paintings cause, he is eventually released when a dog jumps from one of his canvasses to stop a thief attempting to steal the king's crown from the royal palace. Upon returning to his studio, the artist opts for a more benign world and enters one of his own pictures. Reviewing *The Incredible Painting of Felix Clousseau,* Raymond Briggs wrote in the *Times Educational Supplement* that Agee's style "is a bizarre mixture of Peter Arno and Magritte." "Agee's pictures make even the most ordinary objects appear just strange enough to be worth our most wide-eyed attention," opined Leonard Marcus in the *New York Times Book Review,* adding that, "in their intensely quirky way, the author's paintings are every bit as lifelike as Clousseau's." In a review for the *Times Literary Supplement,* Jan Dalley wrote of the book that Agee's "monochromatic, block-like figures" provide "a counterweight to its whimsy."

The Return of Freddy Legrand is Agee's tale of an early twentieth-century pilot who crosses the Atlantic in his biplane, the *Golden Gull,* only to crash in the French countryside. Unhurt, Freddy stays at the farm of Sophie and Albert, who put the broken plane in their barn and begin working to repair it. Meanwhile, Freddy bicycles to Paris and is declared a hero. He embarks on another trip in the *Silver Swan* and flies over the Great Wall of China, the pyramids, the Golden Gate Bridge, and the Panama Canal. Freddy again crashes, this time in the Alps. With survival skills he learned from the French couple, he builds a shelter. Once again Sophie and Albert are his rescuers as they fly the repaired *Golden Gull* to the peak where Freddy is marooned. "Delightful entertainment," was Linda Phillips Ashour's description of *The Return of Freddy Legrand* in her *New York Times Book Review* appraisal. *Horn Book* reviewer Mary M. Burns wrote that Agee "knows how to woo the comic spirit so that various elements are exaggerated but stop short of heavy-handed caricature." "High-flying text and art convey the effervescent spirits of this simpler era," added a *Publishers Weekly* reviewer.

Agee's picture book *Dmitri the Astronaut* relates the story of a space explorer who has returned from the moon after an absence of more than two years. He soon realizes that the world has forgotten him and that his moon rocks are insignificant. Rejected, Dmitri throws his rocks into a trash can. Unknown to Dmitri, his friend Lulu, a pink polka-dotted alien, is hiding in the bag. Revealing her alien origins to the public, Lulu quickly becomes a sensation, bringing Dmitri back into the limelight. "The wry humor of Agee's clever book springs in equal measure from the minimal, tongue-in-cheek text and adroitly exaggerated cartoon illustrations," wrote a *Publishers Weekly* reviewer. Writing in the *New York Times Book Review,* Christopher Lehmann-Haupt called the pictures "exuberant" and the story "deliciously nonsensical." "Agee scores again," wrote a *Kirkus Reviews* critic, dubbing *Dmitri the Astronaut* "a charmer."

A bumbling magician is the subject of *Milo's Hat Trick.* After Milo the Magnificent gives yet another disastrous performance, his frustrated stage manager delivers an ultimatum: pull a rabbit out of your hat or lose your job. Milo heads to the nearest meadow and attempts to snare a rabbit, but instead he meets a brown bear that can dive into Milo's top hat with ease, having learned the trick from a friendly bunny. The pair soon develop a wildly popular act, much to the delight of the stage manager, until winter arrives and the bear returns to his cave to hibernate, leaving Milo to perform the trick solo. "The tough, cigar-smoking theater manager is the perfect foil for droopy haired, short-trousered Milo, and Milo's unlikely savior, the generous-hearted and uncannily graceful bear, is a natural for situation comedy," observed a critic in *Horn Book.* Other reviewers praised Agee for his artwork in *Milo's Hat Trick.* In *School Library Journal,* Helen Foster James noted that the "amusing illustrations use interesting perspectives and

close-up crops to focus on the characters and action," while a *Publishers Weekly* reviewer wrote that "Agee sets off the delectably farfetched story line with pared-down charcoal-and-watercolor illustrations, and the strong planes and diagonals of his cityscapes recall Ben Katchor's comics."

In addition to story books, Agee has crafted and illustrated a number of books that play with words and language. *Go Hang a Salami! I'm a Lasagna Hog! and Other Palindromes* was called "delightful visual and verbal fun" by a *Kirkus Reviews* commentator. The book's approximately sixty entries are a collection of palindromes: phrases and words that, when read left to right or right to left, say the same thing. Illustrating one such phrase, Agee paints a parking lot filled with animals: a "Llama Mall." In another, a cook yells: "Stop pots!" "Hilarious," was Michael Steinberg's description in the *New York Times Book Review,* while a *Publishers Weekly* contributor concluded: "It all adds up to plenty of fun."

Susan Sullivan, writing in the *Los Angeles Times Book Review,* called Agee's second collection of palindromes, *So Many Dynamos! and Other Palindromes,* "even better" than his first. Sullivan noted the example of two owls sitting on a tree limb in the sun. Because of the heat, one falls, unable to even flap its wings. Calling the caption under the illustration—"Too hot to hoot,"—"pure whimsy," Sullivan called the more-than-sixty entries in the book "a truly inspired marriage of cartooning and wordplay." A *Publishers Weekly* reviewer noted that while some entries are slightly off-color, they are nonetheless "likely to please kids." An example is a dog lifting his leg by a tree as he says to a man painting the Tower of Pisa, "As I pee, sir, I see Pisa!"

Agee serves up a new offering of palindromes titled *Sit on a Potato Pan, Otis!: More Palindromes.* As Deborah Stevenson commented in *Bulletin of the Center for Children's Books,* "this is more of the same, but when the same is fine entertainment it is hard to quibble." As in Agee's previous collections, each palindrome appears as either a caption or the punch line to a pen-and-ink cartoon joke, such as two cowpokes pondering the wanted poster of a big wildcat who kidnapped the deputy sheriff. One cowboy says to the other: "Darn ocelots stole Conrad." "The book hits some hilarious heights," enthused Stevenson, while a critic for *Kirkus Reviews* stated that "readers will enjoy [this book] backwards and forwards." In *Palindromania!,* the author "continues his love affair with the English language," commented *School Library Journal* reviewer Linda Wadleigh. The work contains some 170 palindromes, from the familiar ("Madam, I'm Adam") to the unexpected ("Stacy, must I jujitsu my cats?") Agee uses both single-page cartoons and four-panel strips in the volume; according to Roger Leslie in *Booklist,* the author/illustrator's "expressive, black-and-white illustrations enhance the humor, sometimes creating meaning where

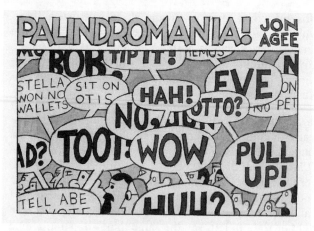

Readers honing their word-reversal skills will enjoy Jon Agee's many books that toy with words and set each palindrome—a word or phrase that reads the same forward or backward—in a cartoon setting.

the palindromes alone do not." Calling the work a "comical, visual, and verbal train ride through the land of palindromes," Wadleigh noted that Agee whimsically mentions "aibohphobia," defined as an unusual fear of palindromes. "Good at least for several minutes of chuckles, these spirited cartoons may inspire readers young and old to find linguistic and artistic opportunity in gnu dung," wrote a critic in *Kirkus Reviews,* while Peter D. Sieruta, reviewing *Palindromania!* for *Horn Book,* stated that "readers who enjoy the clever wordplay and zany art . . . may be so amused they won't know whether they're coming or going."

Agee turns his attention to a different form of wordplay in *Elvis Lives!: and Other Anagrams.* "In this latest effort to unravel and reconstitute language," remarked a *Publishers Weekly* contributor, Agee "demonstrates how letters can he rearranged to produce new meanings and pumps up the humor with pen-and-ink cartoons." The collection includes some sixty anagrams, each accompanied by one of Agee's illustrations. Peter D. Sieruta, reviewing *Elvis Lives!* in *Horn Book,* stated that the anagrams "generally make amazingly apt connections between each set of rearranged words, coupling 'the eyes' with 'they see' and 'astronomer' with 'moonstarer.'" According to Lucinda Snyder Whitehurst in *School Library Journal,* "the black-and-white cartoons are an integral aspect of the humor," as in the cartoon for "Nice seat/I can't see," which shows a hulking figure blocking the view of a smaller man at a movie theater. As *Booklist* critic Carolyn Phelan observed, "Agee's cartoonlike drawings bring out the most in every phrase."

According to a *Publishers Weekly* contributor, the four-line rhymes in Agee's *Flapstick: Ten Ridiculous Rhymes with Flaps* "range from the sublimely slapstick to the mundanely silly. . . . Both children and adults . . . will giggle at the sight gags." In this interactive lift-the-flap book, Agee hides the last word of each rhyme under a flap. Edward Sorel wrote in the *New York Times*

Book Review that Agee's illustrations "are loose as a goose. . . . Drawn with a brush, they have a spontaneous, unlabored look." Sorel felt they are "childlike enough to inspire children to try their own hand with brush and paint." *School Library Journal* reviewer Kathleen Whalin called *Flapstick* "a genuine delight" as well as "a salute to the zaniness in all of us."

Abbott Combes wrote in the *New York Times Book Review* that *Who Ordered the Jumbo Shrimp? and Other Oxymorons* is an "almost perfect collection." A *Publishers Weekly* reviewer seconded that assessment, noting that Agee's sixty sayings and illustrations demonstrate that "his pleasure from oxymorons depends on observational humor, à la George Carlin or Jerry Seinfeld." *School Library Journal* reviewer Pamela K. Bomboy noted that some of the themes are sophisticated—for example, "stiff drink" and "Great Depression"—and called the book "highly amusing."

In his alphabet book *Z Goes Home* Agee "brings a fresh eye to a classic genre," wrote *Horn Book* contributor Lauren Adams. At the end of a long day, the letter Z heads for home, passing an alien, crossing a bridge, and munching on some cake along the way. Each letter of the alphabet is represented by an object that the Z encounters, "but to make matters more interesting, the object is also shaped like the letter," noted *Booklist* critic Karin Snelson. When the Z goes for a swim at the seashore, for example, the beachfront curves in an S-shape. "Agee's clean graphic design energizes and dramatizes the bordered pages," stated a critic in *Kirkus Reviews.*

In addition to creating artwork to accompany his own stories, Agee sometimes illustrates texts by other authors. In *Sitting in My Box,* by Dee Lillegard, a young boy shares a box with an assortment of jungle animals. "Agee's distinctive pictures are full of lush vegetation and lively detail," noted a *Publishers Weekly* reviewer. *Booklist* reviewer Susan Dove Lempke called Agee's artwork for *The Halloween House,* written by Erica Silverman, "hilarious," adding that the illustrator's work is "reminiscent of *New Yorker* cartoons." Agee also provided illustrations for *Mean Margaret,* Tor Seidler's story of woodchuck couple Fred and Phoebe, who adopt a human child. *Booklist* reviewer Michael Cart noted that Agee's drawings "match the text in wit and boundless good humor." M. P. Dunleavey, reviewing Seidler's book for the *New York Times Book Review,* maintained that Agee "infuses his black-and-white drawings with great comic energy. He nails poor Fred's hapless expression, and his Bunyanesque depiction of Margaret, who dwarfs her woodchuck caretakers, is hilarious." Agee also served as illustrator for *Potch and Polly,* William Steig's humorous look at an unlikely romance. "The balding, paunchy Potch and orange-haired, pencil-thin Polly make quite an eye-catching couple, and Agee makes the most of their antics," remarked *School Library Journal* reviewer Joy Fleishhacker.

Biographical and Critical Sources

PERIODICALS

Book, November-December, 2001, review of *Milo's Hat Trick,* p. 75.

Booklist, December 15, 1990, p. 836; November 1, 1992, p. 517; February 1, 1993, p. 978; December 15, 1994, p. 747; April 1, 1995, p. 1412; October 15, 1996, p. 429; September 1, 1997, Susan Dove Lempke, review of *The Halloween House,* p. 141; December 1, 1997, Michael Cart, review of *Mean Margaret,* p. 619; March 1, 1999, Carolyn Phelan, review of *Sit on a Potato Pan, Otis!,* p. 1206; February 1, 2000, Carolyn Phelan, review of *Elvis Lives! and Other Anagrams,* p. 1017; July, 2001, Gillian Engberg, review of *Milo's Hat Trick,* p. 2016; October 15, 2002, Roger Leslie, review of *Palindromania!,* p. 402; September 1, 2003, Karin Snelson, review of *Z Goes Home,* p. 127.

Bulletin of the Center for Children's Books, October, 1992, p. 34; January, 1995, p. 156; February, 1999, Deborah Stevenson, review of *Sit on a Potato Pan, Otis!,* p. 194.

Horn Book, April, 1984, Karen Jameyson, review of *Ellsworth,* pp. 179-180; January-February, 1993, Mary M. Burns, review of *The Return of Freddy Legrand,* p. 71; spring, 1993, pp. 18, 101; January, 1994, p. 59; spring, 1994, p. 24; spring, 1995, p. 112; spring, 1997, p. 17; September, 1997, p. 564; January-February, 1998, Martha V. Parravano, review of *Mean Margaret,* pp. 80-81; March, 1999, Peter D. Sieruta, review of *Sit on a Potato Pan, Otis!,* p. 183; March, 2000, Peter D. Sieruta, review of *Elvis Lives!,* p. 179; May, 2001, review of *Milo's Hat Trick,* p. 306; September-October, 2002, Peter D. Sieruta, review of *Palindromania!,* p. 547; November-December, 2003, Lauren Adams, review of *Z Goes Home,* p. 727.

Kirkus Reviews, August 1, 1992, review of *Go Hang a Salami! I'm a Lasagna Hog!,* p. 996; October 1, 1992, p. 1251; October 1, 1993, p. 1268; July 15, 1996, review of *Dmitri the Astronaut,* p. 1044; January 15, 1999, review of *Sit on a Potato Pan, Otis!,* p. 142; October 1, 2002, review of *Palindromania!,* p. 1462; July 1, 2003, review of *Z Goes Home,* p. 905.

Los Angeles Times Book Review, June 4, 1995, Susan Sullivan, review of *So Many Dynamos! and Other Palindromes,* p. 6.

New York Times Book Review, November 27, 1988, Leonard Marcus, review of *The Incredible Painting of Felix Clousseau,* p. 37; June 21, 1992, Michael Steinberg, review of *Go Hang a Salami! I'm a Lasagna Hog;* January 10, 1993, Linda Phillips Ashour, review of *The Return of Freddy Legrand,* p. 18; November 14, 1993, Edward Sorel, "What's under the Hood?," p. 22; December 9, 1996, Christopher Lehmann-Haupt, "Turning Pages to Children's Pleasure," p. C18; March 2, 1997, p. 25; November 16, 1997, M. P. Dunleavey, "Woodchuck Nation," p. 34; November 15, 1998, Abbott Combes, review of *Who Ordered the Jumbo Shrimp? and Other Oxymorons,* p. 48.

Publishers Weekly, July 23, 1982, review of *If Snow Falls: A Story for December,* p. 132; December 2, 1983, review of *Ellsworth,* p. 89; July 29, 1988, review of *The Incredible Painting of Felix Clousseau,* pp. 133-136; March 24, 1989, review of *The Toy Box* and *Dishes All Done,* p. 66; September 29, 1989, review of *Sitting in My Box,* p. 66; October 26, 1990, p. 71; July 20, 1992, review of *Go Hang a Salami! I'm a Lasagna Hog!,* p. 247; September 14, 1992, review of *The Return of Freddy Legrand,* p. 123; August 23, 1993, review of *Flapstick: Ten Ridiculous Rhymes with Flaps,* p. 68; April 18, 1994, p. 65; August 8, 1994, p. 450; November 14, 1994, p. 65; July 29, 1996, review of *Dmitri the Astronaut,* p. 87; February 24, 1997, p. 93; August 18, 1997, p. 93; October 6, 1997, review of *The Halloween House,* p. 49; March 23, 1998, p. 102; August 17, 1998, review of *Who Ordered the Jumbo Shrimp? and Other Oxymorons,* pp. 72-73; March 22, 1999, review of *Sit on a Potato Pan, Otis!,* p. 90; September 27, 1999, review of *The Halloween House,* p. 48; April 17, 2000, review of *Elvis Lives!,* p. 80; April 30, 2001, review of *Milo's Hat Trick,* p. 76; February 10, 2003, Heather Vogel Frederick, "Jon Agee: The ABC's of Picture Books," pp. 157-159.

School Library Journal, January, 1990, p. 83; November, 1992, pp. 65, 125; December, 1992, p. 19; March, 1994, Kathleen Whalin, review of *Flapstick: Ten Ridiculous Rhymes with Flaps,* p. 224; April, 1994, Debra Hewitt, review of *Ellsworth,* p. 97; November, 1996, p. 76; November, 1997, pp. 40, 99-100; March, 1998, p. 119; November, 1998, Pamela K. Bomboy, review of *Who Ordered the Jumbo Shrimp? and Other Oxymorons,* p. 133; March, 1999, p. 216; April, 2000, Lucinda Snyder, review of *Elvis Lives!: and Other Anagrams,* p. 144; May, 2001, Helen Foster James, review of *Milo's Hat Trick,* p. 108; June, 2002, Teresa Bateman, review of *Milo's Hat Trick* (video review) p. 63; August, 2002, Joy Fleishhacker, review of *Potch & Polly,* p. 170; November, 2002, Linda Wadleigh, review of *Palindromania!,* pp. 180-181; September, 2003, Sophie R. Brookover, review of *Z Goes Home,* p. 166; June, 2004, Steven Engelfried, review of *Elvis Lives!,* p. 55.

Times Educational Supplement, Raymond Briggs, "The Logic of Nonsense," September 6, 1989.

Times Literary Supplement, April 7, 1989, Jan Dalley, "Adult Assumptions," p. 380.

ONLINE

Pippin Properties, Inc. Web site, http://www.pippin properties.com/ (January 11, 2005), "Jon Agee."

*   *   *

ALBERT, Louise 1928-

Personal

Born May 20, 1928, in White Plains, NY; daughter of Benjamin Leopold (an electrical engineer) and Esther (a psychotherapist and writer; maiden name, Pfeffer) Spitzer; married Floyd Albert (a manufacturer of dental education aids), April 15, 1951; children: Elizabeth, David, Alice. *Education:* Cornell University, B.A. (honors), 1949; University of Michigan, M.A., 1950. *Politics:* "Liberal/Radical–if that means anything." *Hobbies and other interests:* Reading (adult and juvenile fiction), music.

Addresses

Home—35 Park Rd., Scarsdale, NY 10583. *Agent*— Richard Huttner, 330 East 33rd St., New York, NY 10016.

Career

Elementary school teacher in Poughkeepsie, NY, 1950-52, and White Plains, NY 1952-53; private remedial reading teacher, 1953-60; writer, 1968—.

Member

Authors Guild, Authors League of America, Phi Beta Kappa.

Writings

But I'm Ready to Go, Bradbury Press (Scarsdale, NY), 1976.
Less than Perfect, Holiday House (New York, NY), 2003.

Sidelights

Louise Albert is the author of the novels *But I'm Ready to Go* and, more recently, *Less than Perfect,* the latter a story about a fifteen-year-old girl named Laura Gould, who is attempting to deal with her mother's diagnosis of breast cancer while also starting a new romantic relationship with a neighborhood boy. *School Library Journal* reviewer Roxanne Myers Spencer commented that in her story of how tragedy affects a well-to-do suburban New York family "Albert creates believable situations, and . . . portrays typical adolescent reactions realistically." While noting that the character of Laura did not seem altogether believable, Spencer went on to praise the novel for treating a serious family illness "candidly and sensitively." More impressed with the novel was a *Publishers Weekly* reviewer, who wrote of *Less than Perfect* that, "With great insight, the author develops Laura's fear and suppressed anger as her mother undergoes a mastectomy, and readers who have shared some of Laura's experiences are likeliest to appreciate Albert's knowing portrayal."

Albert once told *Something about the Author:* "I write out of my own experience and deep emotional needs. Although [I write] . . . fiction with characters

In Louise Albert's 2003 novel fifteen-year-old Laura finds her emotions divided between concern over her mother's failing health and a young man who threatens to steal her heart. (Cover illustration by Greg Spalenka.)

and events made up, . . . my imagination, so far, is fueled by the deepest and most tragic parts of my life. . . . Writing helps me, and I hope others, learn to accept and understand and go beyond these things in life."

Biographical and Critical Sources

PERIODICALS

Kirkus Reviews, October 15, 2003, review of *Less than Perfect,* p. 1267.
Publishers Weekly, December 15, 2003, review of *Less than Perfect,* p. 74.
School Library Journal, February, 2004, Roxanne Myers Spencer, review of *Less than Perfect,* p. 141.

*   *   *

ALIKI
See BRANDENBERG, Aliki (Liacouras)

ANNO, Mitsumasa 1926-

Personal

Born March 20, 1926, in Tsuwano, Japan; son of Yojiro and Shikano Anno; married Midori Suetsugu, April 1, 1952; children: Masaichiro (son), Seiko (daughter). *Education:* Graduated from Yamaguchi Teacher Training College, 1948.

Addresses

Home—3-8-14 Midoricho, Koganei Shi, Tokyo 184, Japan. *Agent*—c/o Author Mail, Philomel, Putnam Berkley Group, 200 Madison Ave., New York, NY 10016.

Career

Artist, educator, essayist, and author and illustrator of children's books. Taught mathematics at elementary schools in Tokyo for ten years. *Exhibitions:* Has exhibited in major galleries and museums in Japan, Canada, the United States, and Great Britain. *Military service:* Japanese army; served during World War II.

Awards, Honors

Best Illustrated Books of the Year citation, *New York Times,* 1970, Spring Book Festival Award, *Chicago Tribune Book World,* 1970, Brooklyn Art Books for Children citation, 1973, German Children's and Youth Book award, 1973, Notable Book citation, American Library Association (ALA), and *Horn Book* honor list, all for *Topsy-Turvies: Pictures to Stretch the Imagination;* Brooklyn Art Books for Children citation, 1973, for *Upside-Downers: More Pictures to Stretch the Imagination;* named among best fifty books of the year, American Institute of Graphic Arts, and Kate Greenaway Medal commendation, both 1974, *Boston Globe/Horn Book* award for illustration, and Best Illustrated Books of the Year citation, *New York Times,* both 1975, Christopher Award, and Children's Book Showcase selection, both 1976, Brooklyn Art Books for Children citation, 1976, 1977, 1978, and ALA Notable Book citation, all for *Anno's Alphabet: An Adventure in Imagination;* Golden Apple Award, Bratislava International Biennale, 1977; Outstanding Science Books for Children citation, New York Academy of Sciences, 1978, and *Horn Book* honor list, both for *Anno's Counting Book;* Brooklyn Art Books for Children citation, 1979, ALA Notable Book citation, and *Horn Book* honor list, all for *Anno's Journey;* ALA Notable Book citation, for *The King's Flower;* first prize for graphic excellence, Bologna Children's Book Fair, 1978, for *The Unique World of Mitsumasa Anno;* Parent's Choice Award for illustration in children's books, 1980, for *Anno's Italy;* first prize for graphic excellence, Bologna Children's Book Fair, 1980, for *Nippon no uta;* Best Illustrated Books of the Year citation, *New York Times,* 1982, for *Anno's Britain;* prize from Bologna Children's Book Fair, 1982, and Notable Book citation, both for *Anno's Counting House;* Hans Christian Andersen Medal, 1985; Jane Ad-

dams Children's Book honorary award, 1987, for *All in a Day;* the Mitsumasa Anno Museum was established in Tsuwano, 2001, Japan, to honor Anno.

Writings

SELF-ILLUSTRATED

Fushigi na E (title means "Mysterious Pictures"), Fukuinkan Shoten (Tokyo, Japan), 1968, translated as *Topsy-Turvies: Pictures to Stretch the Imagination,* Walker/Weatherhill (New York, NY), 1970, reprinted, 1989.

Sakasama, Fukuinkan Shoten (Tokyo, Japan), 1969, translated by Meredith Weatherby and Suzanne Trumbull as *Upside Downers: More Pictures to Stretch the Imagination,* Weatherhill (New York, NY), 1971.

Dr. Anno's Magical Midnight Circus, translated by Meredith Weatherby, Weatherhill (New York, NY), 1972.

ABC no Hon: hesomagari no afurabatto (title means "Book of ABCs: A Twisted Alphabet"), Fukuinkan Shoten (Tokyo, Japan), 1974, translated as *Anno's Alphabet: An Adventure in Imagination,* Crowell (New York, NY), 1975.

Kazoetemiyou, Kodansha (Tokyo, Japan), 1975, translated as *Anno's Counting Book,* Crowell (New York, NY), 1977.

Okina Monono Sukina Osama, Kodansha (Tokyo, Japan), 1976, translated as *The King's Flower,* Collins (New York, NY), 1979.

Tabi no Ehon (title means "Journey Book"), Fukuinkan Shoten (Tokyo, Japan), 1977, translated as *Anno's Journey,* Collins (New York, NY), 1978.

Mori no Ehon, Fukuinkan Shoten (Tokyo, Japan), 1977, translated as *Anno's Animals,* Collins (New York, NY), 1979.

Tabi no Ehon II (title means "Journey Book II"), Fukuinkan Shoten (Tokyo, Japan), 1978, translated as *Anno's Italy,* Bodley Head (London, England), 1979.

Tendo setsu no hon, Fukuinkan Shoten (Tokyo, Japan), 1979, translated as *Anno's Medieval World,* Philomel (New York, NY), 1980.

Nippon no uta (title means "Anno's Song Book"), Kodansha (Tokyo, Japan), 1979.

Anno Mitsumasa no Gashu, Kodansha (Tokyo, Japan), 1980, translated as *The Unique World of Mitsumasa Anno: Selected Works (1968-1977),* Philomel (New York, NY), 1980.

(With son, Masaichiro Anno) *Mahotsukai no ABC,* Kusokobo, 1980, translated as *Anno's Magical ABC: An Anamorphic Alphabet,* Philomel (New York, NY), 1981.

(With Masaichiro Anno) *10-nin no yukai na hikkoshi,* Dowaya (Tokyo, Japan), 1981, translated as *Anno's Counting House,* Philomel (New York, NY), 1982.

Tabi no Ehon III (title means "Journey Book III"), Fukuinkan Shoten (Tokyo, Japan), 1981, translated as *Anno's Britain,* Philomel (New York, NY), 1982.

Tsubo no Naka, Dowaya (Tokyo, Japan), 1982.

Tabi no Ehon IV (title means "Journey Book IV"), Fukuinkan Shoten (Tokyo, Japan), 1982, translated as *Anno's USA,* Philomel (New York, NY), 1983.

(With Masaichiro Anno) *Anno's Mysterious Multiplying Jar,* Philomel (New York, NY), 1983, reprinted, 2004.

Nomi no Ichi, Dowaya (Tokyo, Japan), 1983, translated as *Anno's Flea Market,* Philomel (New York, NY), 1984.

(With others) *Marui Chikyu no Maru Ichinichi* (title means "Around the Clock in a Round World"), Dowaya (Tokyo, Japan), 1986, translated as *All in a Day,* Philomel (New York, NY), 1986.

Inai Inai Baa no Ehon, Dowaya (Tokyo, Japan), 1987 translated as *Anno's Peekaboo,* Philomel (New York, NY), 1987.

Anno's Math Games, Philomel (New York, NY), 1987.

Anno's Sundial, Putnam (New York, NY), 1987.

Niko Niko Kabocha, Dowaya (Tokyo, Japan), 1988, translated as *Anno's Faces,* Philomel (New York, NY), 1988.

In Shadowland, Orchard (New York, NY), 1988.

Anno's Math Games II, Putnam (New York, NY), 1989.

(Editor) *Anno's Aesop: A Book of Fables by Aesop and Mr. Fox,* Orchard (New York, NY), 1989.

Omen no Ehon, Dowaya (Tokyo, Japan), 1989, translated as *Anno's Masks,* Philomel (New York, NY), 1989.

(Reteller) Jacob and Wilhelm Grimm, *Kitsune ga hirotta Gurimu dowa,* Iwanami Shoten (Tokyo, Japan), 1991, translated as *Anno's Twice-Told Tales: The Fisherman and His Wife and The Four Clever Brothers,* Philomel (New York, NY), 1993.

Anno's Counting Book Big Book, HarperCollins (New York, NY), 1992.

Fushigina tane, [Japan], translated as *Anno's Magic Seeds,* Putnam (New York, NY), 1994.

Tabi no Ehon V (title means "Journey Book V"), Fukuinkan Shoten (Tokyo, Japan), 2003, translated as *Anno's Spain,* Philomel (New York, NY), 2004.

Seishun no Bungotai, Chikuma Shobo (Tokyo, Japan), 2003.

Also author of *Maze, Dr. Stone-Brain's Computer,* and *The Theory of Set.*

Anno's books have been translated into Danish, Dutch, Spanish, French, Italian, Taiwanese, and Swedish.

ILLUSTRATOR

Akihiro Nozaki, *Akai Boshi,* Dowaya (Tokyo, Japan), 1984, translated as *Anno's Hat Tricks,* Philomel (New York, NY), 1985.

Tsuyoshi Mori, *Sanbiki no Kobuta,* Dowaya (Tokyo, Japan), 1985, translated as *Socrates and the Three Little Pigs,* Philomel (New York, NY), 1986.

Michio Mado, *The Animals: Selected Poems,* translated by Empress Michiko of Japan, Philomel (New York, NY), 1992.

Michio Mado, *Fushigi na poketto,* [Japan], translated by Empress Michiko of Japan as *The Magic Pocket: Selected Poems,* Margaret K. McElderry Books (New York, NY), 1998.

Contributor of illustrations to *All in a Day,* PaperStar, 1999.

Adaptations

Anno's Journey was adapted as an animated filmstrip, Weston Woods, 1983; *Anno's Math Games,* an interactive CD-ROM, was produced by Putnam New Media, 1994.

Work in Progress

A sixth volume in his "journey" series, to be titled *Anno's Denmark.*

Sidelights

Japanese illustrator and author Mitsumasa Anno has been praised as one of the most original and accomplished picture-book artists in the field of children's books. Using pen-and-ink and watercolor, as well as collage and woodcuts, Anno is known for creating highly detailed illustrations that display his love of mathematics and science, as well as his interest and appreciation for foreign cultures. His drawings, which have been compared to those of Dutch graphic artist M. C. Escher, abound with visual trickery and illusions, and also display the artist's playful sense of humor.

Many of Anno's books contain hidden jokes and pranks that are intended to amuse and lead readers into imaginative thinking about numbers, counting, the alphabet, or more complex concepts involving time and space. Addressing readers of various levels of sophistication, Anno's books appeal to both children and adults, and his universal approach has made him popular around the world. He has received numerous awards, including the Kate Greenaway award and the prestigious Hans Christian Andersen Medal for illustration, the latter awarded every two years for the most outstanding accomplishment in international illustration.

Born in 1926, Anno grew up in western Japan in the town of Tsuwano, a small, isolated community located in a valley surrounded by mountains. As a child he had a strong desire to experience places beyond the mountains surrounding his village. "On the other side of the mountains were villages with rice fields, and beyond these rice fields was the ocean, which seemed to be very, very far away," the author/illustrator recalled in an interview with Hisako Aoki for *Horn Book.* "When I reached the ocean for the first time in my life, I tasted it to see if it was really salty. Because my world was cut off from the outside world, first by the mountains and then by the ocean, the desire to go and see what lay on the other side grew stronger." Anno began drawing as a young boy, and also showed an early aptitude for mathematics. From a young age onward, as he explained in the *Fourth Book of Junior Authors,* he "earnestly desired to become an artist."

Anno finally had the chance to leave Tsuwano when he attended a regional high school. In addition to studying art and drawing, he also became an avid reader, and was influenced by German author Hermann Hesse. Anno described to Aoki his return to Tsuwano after graduation: "I got off the train at the station, feeling happy and proud and a bit shy at the same time, thinking how much I had matured being away from Tsuwano but that the town would accept me as I was. . . . When I read how Hermann Hesse, as a student, went home to Calw, getting off the train at the end of the town, walking by the river, and crossing the bridge, my heart ached because everything was exactly the same with me." Years later, when Anno traveled to German and sketched scenes in Hesse's home town of Calw, he was startled to discover that his renderings were very similar to sketches he'd made of his own home town of Tsuwano. He maintains that his sketches of the two places represented "the world as seen through my eyes, and they are my own compositions—which other people may see differently. I believe that this is one of the reasons for . . . expressing oneself in any form. Through a creative work, people may experience something which they may not have experienced before."

During World War II Anno was drafted into the Japanese army; following the war he earned a degree in 1948 from the Yamaguchi Teacher Training College. Before engaging in an art career, Anno taught mathematics at an elementary school in Tokyo for several years. As he commented to Aoki: "As a teacher I tried to present material to pupils so that they could widen their scope of understanding and self-expression. At the same time I learned a lot from them. Children's way of seeing is actually different from that of adults. . . . For example, children's sense of perspective is different from ours, partly because their faces are smaller and their eyes are closer together. In addition, their experience is more restricted, so they have less to base their judgement on."

Anno's first two picture books reflect his love of playing with visual perception. *Topsy-Turvies: Pictures to Stretch the Imagination,* was published in Japan in 1968, and was followed the next year by *Upside Downers: More Pictures to Stretch the Imagination. Topsy-Turvies* plays visual tricks on perspective and logic, while *Upside Downers* contains illustrations that convey different images depending on the angle or direction from which they are viewed. In presenting such illustrations, Anno hopes to stimulate the powers of young people's imaginations. He wrote in a postscript to *Topsy-Turvies:* "One professor of mathematics claims that in a single picture he has found twelve different 'impossibilities' . . . . Nothing is impossible to the young, not until we become caught in the problems of living and forget to make-believe. Perhaps these pictures of mine will keep all of us young a little longer, will stretch our imaginations enough to help keep us magically human. I hope so, I believe so—for nothing is impossible."

Anno's more innovative picture books include *Anno's Alphabet: An Adventure in Imagination,* which features "impossible" wood-grain letters that are framed within

Mitsumasa Anno is joined by his son in penning this fascinating introduction to factorials, illustrating the concept by creating one island on which there are two countries, each of which contain three mountains, and so on up to the number ten.

decorative borders containing objects beginning with each letter. Interestingly, the book was in the running for the 1974 Kate Greenaway Medal until the judges of the British award realized that the author was Japanese, and that the book had originally been published in Japan, not Great Britain. Although the publishing history disqualified it for the Medal, the judges were so impressed with the work that it was awarded a special commendation. Anno provides the illustrations, while his son, Masaichiro, adds the lettering in another imaginative alphabet book, *Anno's Magical ABC: An Anamorphic Alphabet,* in which letters and their corresponding objects are viewed through a reflective cylinder that is provided with the book. Many of Anno's books illustrate abstract mathematical concepts for young readers. *Anno's Mysterious Multiplying Jar,* also co-written with son Masaichiro, demonstrates the concept of factorials through a series of interconnected illustrations that make the ever-expanding quantities concrete: one island contains two countries, each of which contains three mountains, each mountain being divided into four kingdoms, and so on until ten factorial is reached. In *School Library Journal,* Janet Dawson Hamilton praised *Anno's Mysterious Multiplying Jar* for "cleverly" portraying factorials in what the critic described as "deceptively simple" and "meticulously detailed" artwork by Anno.

Focusing on the mathematical discoveries that have advanced scientific knowledge, *Anno's Medieval World* chronicles the discovery in Western Europe of the fact that the Earth is a round planet that revolves around the sun. Leonard S. Marcus, writing in *The Lion and the Unicorn,* noted that the book, like Anno's other works, demonstrates the author/illustrator's belief that "an interest in science and mathematics is compatible with an interest in art" and that "art and science represent different approaches to the common end of exercising human perception beyond known limits."Another history lesson of sorts is related in *Anno's Magic Seeds,* which Ann A. Flowers praised as a "charming story" that presents the history of agriculture and basic conservation while engaging readers in math games, thereby creating "a tour de force from a most original author-illustrator." Told in folk-tale style, Anno's story of a young man who is given two seeds by a wizard and increases his annual yield of seeds by planting more than he eats was praised by a *Publishers Weekly* contributor who dubbed *Anno's Magic Seeds* as "another worthy addition" to the author/illustrator's "collection of playful stories with mathematical themes." Anno published the first in a series of acclaimed, wordless "journey" books in the mid-1970s, and has since taken readers on picture-book travels throughout Europe, Great Britain, and the United States. The first volume, *Anno's Journey* arose from travels the author made in 1963 to Scandinavia, Germany, and England; it has been followed by *Anno's Italy, Anno's Britain, Anno's U.S.A.,* and *Anno's Spain;* a sixth volume, *Anno's Denmark,* was planned for 2005,

to honor the 200th birthday of Hans Christian Andersen. *Anno's Journey* features "a mass of colorful detail, a picture narrative, and a poetic meditation in narrative form," wrote Marcus, adding that "without a written text as a guide, readers are left to invent stories of their own, which may or may not concern the little man whose journey by boat and on horseback forms the one narrative lifeline or thread running through the book." Calling *Anno's Spain* "a voyage to savor—and embark on again and again," a *Publishers Weekly* contributor noted that the artist's "innovative, often playful presentation, every spread tells a story—and encourages readers to interpret it for themselves." Throughout each of his "journey" books, Anno continues this technique: communicating wordless, universal messages that can be understood by people of many cultures. In his postscript to *Anno's Italy,* he comments: "Although it is difficult for me to understand the languages of the western world, still I can understand the hearts of the people. This book has no words, yet I feel sure that everyone who looks at it can understand what the people in the pictures are doing, and what they are thinking and feeling."

While Anno most frequently illustrates his own concept books, he has also provided illustrations for works by several Japanese authors, including the award-winning poet Michio Mado. Featuring English texts translated by Japan's Empress Michiko alongside Mado's original Japanese verse, *The Animals: Selected Poems* and *The*

The power of one small seed in generating a field of crops through seasonal reproduction is just one of the magical events explored in **Anno's Magic Seeds.**

Inspired by his travels around the world, Anno created a series of wordless picture books, including Anno's Spain, *which introduces children to the history, art, and landscape of that corner of southern Europe.*

Magic Pocket both feature Anno's artwork, and both proved to be somewhat of a challenge, despite the artist's extensive experience as an illustrator. "It's very difficult to draw illustrations for poems," he explained in an interview for *Japanese Children's Books Online.* "For example, [Mado's] . . . elephant poem goes 'Little elephant, little elephant what a long nose you have.' You can't just draw a picture of an elephant with a long nose for a poem like that. I think descriptive illustrations for a poem would really show a lack of taste." Reviewing *The Magic Pocket* in *Booklist,* Carolyn Phelan noted that Anno's "artwork never overwhelms the verse, but instead softly reflects it and makes it more accessible."

In addition to writing and illustrating picture books, Anno is also an accomplished painter and graphic artist known for creating images that challenge the visual and cultural perceptions of the viewer. His work has been honored in his native Japan, where the Mitsumasa Anno Museum was established in the author's home town of Tsuwano. For fans unable to travel to Asia, *The Unique World of Mitsumasa Anno: Selected Works (1968-1977)* includes forty of Anno's most acclaimed works of graphic art. In a postscript to the book, Anno comments: "Once someone said, upon seeing my pictures, 'You amuse yourself by fooling people; you can't draw without a mischievous spirit.'. . . My pictures are like maps, which perhaps only I can understand. Therefore, in following my maps there are some travellers who get lost. There are those who become angry when they discover they have been fooled; but there are also those who enter into the maze of my maps willingly, in an attempt to explore their accuracy for themselves."

Biographical and Critical Sources

BOOKS

Anno, Mitsumasa, *Anno's Italy,* Collins (London, England), 1980.

Anno, Mitsumasa, *The Unique World of Mitsumasa Anno: Selected Works (1968-1977),* Philomel (New York, NY), 1980.

Anno, Mitsumasa, *Topsy-Turvies: Pictures to Stretch the Imagination,* Walker/Weatherhill (New York, NY), 1970.

Children's Literature Review, Gale (Detroit, MI), Volume 2, 1976, Volume 14, 1988.

Fourth Book of Junior Authors and Illustrators, edited by Doris de Montreville and Elizabeth D. Crawford, H. W. Wilson (Bronx, NY), 1978.

PERIODICALS

Bookbird, Volume 2, 1984; Volume 4, 1984; October, 1987.

Booklist, April 1, 1995, Carolyn Phelan, review of *Anno's Magic Seeds,* p. 1394; February 1, 1999, Carolyn Phelan, review of *The Magic Pocket,* p. 977.

Bulletin of the Center for Children's Books, November, 1983; June, 1984; December, 1984; December, 1987; May, 1988; June, 1988.

Horn Book, April, 1983, Hisako Aoki, "A Conversation with Mitsumasa Anno," pp. 137-145; September-October, 1995, Ann A. Flowers, review of *Anno's Magic Seeds,* p. 585.

Lion and the Unicorn, Volume 7-8, Leonard S. Marcus, "The Artist's Other Eye: The Picture Books of Mitsumasa Anno," pp. 24-46.

Publishers Weekly, December 5, 1994, review of *Anno's Magic Seeds,* p. 76; November 23, 1998, review of *The Magic Pocket,* p. 65.

School Library Journal, September, 2004, Janet Dawson Hamilton, review of *Anno's Mysterious Multiplying Jar,* p. 57.

ONLINE

Japanese Children's Books Online, http://www.yameneko. org/einfo/mgzn/ (May 5, 2005), interview with Anno.*

B

BATESON, Catherine 1960-

Personal
Born 1960; married; two children.

Addresses
Home—Central Victoria, Australia. *Agent*—c/o Author Mail, University of Queensland Press, Staff House Rd., P.O. Box 6042, St. Lucia, Queensland 4067, Australia.

Career
Creative writing teacher and writer.

Awards, Honors
Book of the Year designation, Children's Book Council of Australia (CBCA), for *Rain May and Captain Daniel;* CBCA Honour Book for Older Readers designation, and Australian Family Therapists' Award, both 2003, both for *Painted Love Letters;* New South Wales Premier's Literary Award, and Queensland Premier's Literary Award, both 2003, both for *Painted Love Letters,* and *Rain May and Captain Daniel;* John Shaw Neilson Award.

Writings

FOR YOUNG ADULTS

A Dangerous Girl, University of Queensland Press (St. Lucia, Queensland, Australia), 2000.

The Year It All Happened, University of Queensland Press (St. Lucia, Queensland, Australia), 2001.

Painted Love Letters, University of Queensland Press (St. Lucia, Queensland, Australia.), 2002.

Rain May and Captain Daniel, University of Queensland Press (St. Lucia, Queensland, Australia), 2002.

The Airdancer of Glass, 2004.

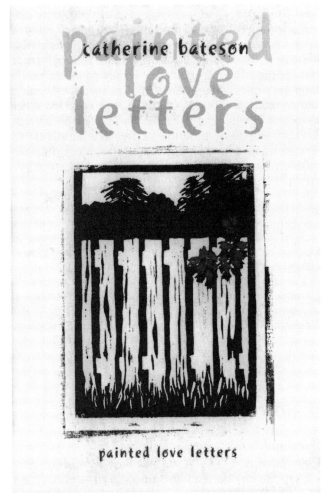

Catherine Bateson's 2002 young-adult novel focuses on a sensitive twelve-year-old girl who watches as her beloved artist father slowly wastes away from lung cancer, then dies following a long-awaited exhibit of his paintings.

OTHER

Pomegranates from the Underworld (poetry), Pariah Press, 1990.

The Vigilant Heart (poetry), University of Queenland Press (St. Lucia, Queensland, Australia), 1998.

Also author of short fiction.

Work in Progress

A junior fiction novel, *Millie and the Night Heron;* the young-adult novel *His Name in Fire;* a new volume of poetry.

Sidelights

Award winning Australian author Catherine Bateson credits a childhood spent in a used bookstore with sparking her career as a poet and author of young-adult fiction. A published poet, Bateson made the transition to fiction by creating *A Dangerous Girl* and its sequel, *The Year It All Happened,* verse novels that reflect the concerns and speech of modern Australian teens. In *Painted Love Letters* she tells the story of Chrissie, a teen who must deal with the death of her mother to lung cancer and the tragedy's effect on other family members, while *Rain May and Captain Daniel* finds an inner-city mother and daughter adapting to platypus, fruit bats, and other quirks of life in rural Australia. In addition to writing novels and poetry, Bateston has worked as a creative writing teacher for over a decade. In her spare time she hosts writing workshops for students and appears at poetry and writing festivals.

Biographical and Critical Sources

ONLINE

Catherine Bateson Web site, http://www.catherine-bateson. com (October 22, 2004).
University of Queensland Press Web site, http://www.uqp. edu.au/ (July 23, 2004), "Catherine Bateson."*

*   *   *

BOND, (Thomas) Michael 1926-

Personal

Born January 13, 1926, in Newbury, Berkshire, England; son of Norman Robert (a civil servant) and Frances Mary (Offer) Bond; married Brenda Mary Johnson, June 29, 1950 (divorced, 1981); married Susan Marfrey Rogers, 1981; children: Karen Mary Jankel, Anthony Thomas Barwell. *Ethnicity:* "White." *Education:* Attended Presentation College, 1934-40. *Hobbies and other interests:* "Food, wine, theater, photography and things French."

Addresses

Home—22 Maida Avenue, London W2 1SR, England.
Agent—Stephen Durbridge, The Agency, 24-32 Pottery Lane, Holland Park, London W11 4LZ, England.

Michael Bond

Career

British Broadcasting Corp. (BBC), Reading, England, engineer's assistant, 1941-43; BBC, Caversham, England, with monitoring service, 1947-50; BBC, London, England, television cameraman, 1950-65; full-time writer, 1965–. *Military service:* Royal Air Force, 1943-44, air crew; British Army, Middlesex Regiment, 1944-47.

Awards, Honors

American Library Association Notable Book citation for *Tales of Olga Da Polga;* named to Order of the British Empire, 1997, for services to children's literature.

Writings

"PADDINGTON" SERIES

A Bear Called Paddington (also see below), illustrations by Peggy Fortnum, Collins (London, England), 1958, Houghton Mifflin (Boston, MA), 1960, revised edition, Houghton Mifflin, 1998.
More about Paddington (also see below), illustrations by Peggy Fortnum, Collins (London, England), 1959, Houghton Mifflin (Boston, MA), 1962, revised edition, Houghton Mifflin, 1997.
Paddington Helps Out (also see below), illustrations by Peggy Fortnum, Collins (London, England), 1960, Houghton Mifflin (Boston, MA), 1961.
Paddington Abroad, illustrations by Peggy Fortnum, Collins (London, England), 1961, Houghton Mifflin (Boston, MA), 1972.

Paddington at Large (also see below), illustrations by Peggy Fortnum, Collins (London, England), 1962, Houghton Mifflin (Boston, MA), 1963.

Paddington Marches On, illustrations by Peggy Fortnum, Collins (London, England), 1964, Houghton Mifflin (Boston, MA), 1965, reprinted, Fontana (Huntington, NY), 1986.

Adventures of Paddington (also see below), Collins (London, England), 1965.

Paddington at Work (also see below), illustrations by Peggy Fortnum, Collins (London, England), 1966, Houghton Mifflin (Boston, MA), 1967, revised edition, Houghton Mifflin, 2001.

Paddington Goes to Town, illustrations by Peggy Fortnum, Collins (London, England), 1968, Houghton Mifflin (Boston, MA), 1969, revised edition, Houghton Mifflin, 2001.

Paddington Takes the Air, illustrations by Peggy Fortnum, Collins (London, England), 1970, Houghton Mifflin (Boston, MA), 1971.

Paddington Bear, illustrations by Fred Banbery, Collins (London, England), 1972, Random House (New York, NY), 1973, revised with new illustrations by R. W. Alley, HarperCollins (New York, NY), 1998.

Paddington's Garden, illustrations by Fred Banbery, Collins (London, England), 1972, Random House (New York, NY), 1973, reprinted, HarperFestival (New York, NY), 1993.

Paddington at the Circus, illustrations by Fred Banbery, Collins (London, England), 1973, Random House (New York, NY), 1974, revised with new illustrations by R. W. Alley, HarperCollins (New York, NY), 2000.

Paddington Goes Shopping, illustrations by Fred Banbery, Collins (London, England), 1973, published as *Paddington's Lucky Day,* Random House (New York, NY), 1974.

Paddington's "Blue Peter" Story Book, illustrations by Ivor Wood, Collins (London, England), 1973, published as *Paddington Takes to T.V.,* Houghton Mifflin (Boston, MA), 1974, reprinted, Houghton Mifflin, 2000.

Paddington Goes to School, Caedmon (New York, NY), 1974.

Paddington on Top, illustrations by Peggy Fortnum, Collins (London, England), 1974, Houghton Mifflin (Boston, MA), 1975, revised edition, Houghton Mifflin, 2000.

(With Albert Bradley) *Paddington on Stage* (play; adapted from Bond's *Adventures of Paddington*), illustrations by Peggy Fortnum, Collins (London, England), 1974, Houghton Mifflin (Boston, MA), 1977, acting edition, Samuel French (New York, NY), 1976.

Paddington at the Tower, illustrations by Fred Banbery, Collins (London, England), 1975, Random House (New York, NY), 1978.

Paddington at the Seaside, illustrations by Fred Banbery, Collins (London, England), 1975, Random House (New York, NY), 1976, published as *Paddington at the Seashore,* HarperCollins (New York, NY), 1992.

Paddington Takes a Bath, Collins (London, England), 1976.

Paddington Goes to the Sales, Collins (London, England), 1976.

Paddington's New Room, Collins (London, England), 1976.

Paddington at the Station, Collins (London, England), 1976.

The Great Big Paddington Book, illustrations by Fred Banbery, Collins & World (London, England), 1976.

Paddington's Loose-End Book: An ABC of Things to Do, illustrations by Ivor Wood, Collins (London, England), 1976.

Paddington's Party Book, illustrations by Ivor Wood, Collins (London, England), 1976.

Paddington's Pop-up Book, Collins (London, England), 1977.

Fun and Games with Paddington, Collins & World (London, England), 1977.

Paddington's Birthday Party, Collins (London, England), 1977.

Paddington Carpenter, Collins (London, England), 1977.

Paddington Conjurer, Collins (London, England), 1977.

Paddington Cook, Collins (London, England), 1977.

Paddington Golfer, Collins (London, England), 1977.

Paddington Hits Out, Collins (London, England), 1977.

Paddington Does It Himself, Collins (London, England), 1977.

Paddington in the Kitchen, Collins (London, England), 1977.

Paddington's First Book, Collins (London, England), 1978.

Paddington's Picture Book, Collins (London, England), 1978.

Paddington's Play Book, Collins (London, England), 1978.

Paddington's Counting Book, Collins (London, England), 1978.

Paddington's Cartoon Book, illustrations by Ivor Wood, Collins (London, England), 1979.

Paddington Takes the Test, illustrations by Peggy Fortnum, Collins (London, England), 1979, Houghton Mifflin (Boston, MA), 1980, revised edition, Houghton Mifflin, 2002.

Paddington: A Disappearing Trick and Other Stories (anthology; also see below), Collins (London, England), 1979.

Paddington for Christmas (also see below), Collins (London, England), 1979.

Paddington Goes Out, Collins (London, England), 1980.

Paddington at Home, Collins (London, England), 1980.

Paddington and Aunt Lucy, illustrations by Barry Wilkinson, Collins (London, England), 1980.

Paddington in Touch, illustrations by Barry Wilkinson, Collins (London, England), 1980.

Paddington and the Snowbear, Collins (London, England), 1981.

Paddington at the Launderette, Collins (London, England), 1981.

Paddington's Shopping Adventure, Collins (London, England), 1981.

Paddington's Birthday Treat, Collins (London, England), 1981.

Paddington on Screen: The Second "Blue Peter" Story Book, illustrations by Barry Macey, Collins (London, England), 1981, Houghton Mifflin (Boston, MA), 1982.

Paddington Has Fun, Collins (London, England), 1982.

Paddington Works Hard, Collins (London, England), 1982.

Paddington's Storybook, illustrations by Peggy Fortnum, Collins (London, England), 1983, Houghton Mifflin (Boston, MA), 1984.

Paddington on the River, illustrations by Barry Wilkinson, Collins (London, England), 1983.

Paddington Weighs In, illustrations by Barry Wilkinson, Collins (London, England), 1983.

Paddington's Suitcase (includes *Paddington's Notebook* and *Paddington's Birthday Book,* Collins (London, England), 1983.

Great Big Paddington Bear Picture Book, Pan (London, England), 1984.

Paddington at the Zoo, illustrations by David McKee, Collins (London, England), 1984, Putnam (New York, NY), 1985, revised edition with new illustrations by R. W. Alley, HarperCollins (New York, NY), 1998.

Paddington and the Knickerbocker Rainbow, illustrations by David McKee, Collins (London, England), 1984, Putnam (New York, NY), 1985.

Paddington's Art Exhibition, illustrations by David McKee, Collins (London, England), 1985, published as *Paddington's Painting Exhibition,* Putnam (New York, NY), 1986.

Paddington at the Fair, illustrations by David McKee, Collins (London, England), 1985, Putnam (New York, NY), 1986, revised with new illustrations by R. W. Alley, HarperCollins (New York, NY), 1998.

Paddington at the Palace, illustrations by David McKee, Putnam (New York, NY), 1986, revised with new illustrations by R. W. Alley, HarperCollins (New York, NY), 1999.

Paddington Minds the House, illustrations by David McKee, Collins (London, England), 1986, revised with new illustrations by R. W. Alley, HarperCollins (New York, NY), 1999.

Paddington Spring Cleans, Collins (London, England), 1986, published as *Paddington Cleans Up,* Putnam (New York, NY), 1986.

The Hilarious Adventures of Paddington (boxed set; contains *A Bear Called Paddington, More about Paddington, Paddington at Large, Paddington at Work,* and *Paddington Helps Out*), Dell (New York, NY), 1986.

(With daughter, Karen Bond) *Paddington at the Airport,* illustrations by Toni Goffe, Hutchinson (London, England), 1986.

(With Karen Bond) *Paddington Mails a Letter,* illustrations by Toni Goffe, Macmillan (New York, NY), 1986, published as *Paddington Bear Posts a Letter,* Hutchinson (London, England), 1986.

(With Karen Bond) *Paddington's Clock Book,* Hutchinson (London, England), 1986.

(With Karen Bond) *Paddington's London,* Hutchinson (London, England), 1986.

(With Karen Bond) *Paddington's First Puzzle Book,* Crocodile (New York, NY), 1987.

(With Karen Bond) *Paddington's Second Puzzle Book,* Crocodile (New York, NY), 1987.

Paddington's Busy Day, illustrations by David McKee, Collins (London, England), 1987, revised with new illustrations by R. W. Alley, HarperCollins (New York, NY), 1999.

Paddington and the Marmalade Maze, illustrations by David McKee, Collins (London, England), 1987, revised with new illustrations by R. W. Alley, HarperCollins (New York, NY), 1999.

Paddington's ABC, HarperCollins (New York, NY), 1990.

Paddington's 123, HarperCollins (New York, NY), 1990.

Paddington's Colors, HarperCollins (New York, NY), 1990.

Paddington's Opposites, HarperCollins (New York, NY), 1990.

Paddington's Jar of Jokes, Carnival (London, England), 1992.

Paddington Breaks the Peace, Young Lions (London, England), 1992.

Paddington Does the Decorating, Young Lions (London, England), 1993.

Paddington's Disappearing Trick, Young Lions (London, England), 1993.

Paddington's Picnic, illustrations by Nick Ward, Young Lions (London, England), 1993.

Paddington Meets the Queen, HarperCollins (New York, NY), 1993.

Paddington Rides On!, HarperCollins (New York, NY), 1993.

Paddington's Magical Christmas, HarperCollins (New York, NY), 1993.

Paddington Book and Bear Box (includes plush toy), Viking (New York, NY), 1993.

Paddington's First Word Book, HarperCollins (New York, NY), 1993.

Paddington's Things I Do, HarperCollins (New York, NY), 1994.

Paddington's Things I Feel, HarperCollins (New York, NY), 1994.

Paddington's Christmas Treat, illustrations by R. W. Alley, HarperCollins (New York, NY), 1997.

Paddington Bear and the Christmas Surprise, illustrations by R. W. Alley, HarperCollins (New York, NY), 1997.

Paddington "A Classic Collection" (collection), illustrations by Peggy Fortnum, HarperCollins UK, 1998.

Paddington and the Tutti Frutti Rainbow, illustrations by R. W. Alley, HarperCollins (New York, NY), 1998.

Paddington Bear All Day, illustrations by R. W. Alley, HarperFestival (New York, NY), 1998.

Paddington Bear and the Busy Bee Carnival, illustrations by R. W. Alley, HarperCollins (New York, NY), 1998.

Paddington Goes to Market, illustrations by R. W. Alley, HarperCollins (New York, NY), 1999.

Paddington My Scrapbook, illustrations by R. W. Alley, HarperCollins (New York, NY), 1999.

Paddington Treasury (collection), illustrations by Peggy Fortnum, colored by Caroline Nuttall-Smith, Houghton Mifflin (Boston, MA), 1999.

Paddington up and About, illustrations by R. W. Alley, HarperCollins (New York, NY), 1999.

Paddington's Party Tricks, illustrations by R. W. Alley, HarperCollins (New York, NY), 2000.

(With Karen Jankel) *Paddington Goes to Hospital,* illustrations by R. W. Alley, Collins (London, England), 2001, published as *Paddington Bear Goes to the Hospital,* HarperCollins (New York, NY), 2001.

Paddington Bear in the Garden, illustrations by R. W. Alley, Collins (London, England), 2001, HarperCollins (New York, NY), 2002.

Paddington's Grand Tour, illustrations by R. W. Alley, Collins (London, England), 2003.

Also author of fifty-six episodes of animated "Paddington" films and three half-hour "Paddington" television specials for Home Box Office.

"THURSDAY" SERIES

Here Comes Thursday!, illustrations by Daphne Rowles, Harrap (London, England), 1966, Lothrop (New York, NY), 1967.

Thursday Rides Again, illustrations by Beryl Sanders, Harrap (London, England), 1968, Lothrop (New York, NY), 1969.

Thursday Ahoy!, illustrations by Leslie Wood, Harrap (London, England), 1969, Lothrop (New York, NY), 1970.

Thursday in Paris, illustrations by Ivor Wood, Harrap (London, England), 1971.

"OLGA DA POLGA" SERIES

Tales of Olga da Polga (omnibus volume), illustrated by Hans Helweg, Penguin (Harmondsworth, England), 1971, Macmillan (New York, NY), 1973.

Olga Meets Her Match, illustrated by Hans Helweg, Penguin (Harmondsworth, England), 1973, Hastings House (New York, NY), 1975.

Olga Counts Her Blessings, Penguin (Harmondsworth, England), 1975.

Olga Makes a Friend, Penguin (Harmondsworth, England), 1975.

Olga Makes a Wish, Penguin (Harmondsworth, England), 1975.

Olga Makes Her Mark, Penguin (Harmondsworth, England), 1975.

Olga Takes a Bite, Penguin (Harmondsworth, England), 1975.

Olga's New Home, Penguin (Harmondsworth, England), 1975.

Olga's Second House, Penguin (Harmondsworth, England), 1975.

Olga's Special Day, Penguin (Harmondsworth, England), 1975.

Olga Carries On, illustrated by Hans Helweg, Penguin (Harmondsworth, England), 1976, Hastings House (New York, NY), 1977.

Olga Takes Charge, illustrated by Hans Helweg, Penguin (Harmondsworth, England), 1982, Dell (New York, NY), 1983.

The Complete Adventures of Olga da Polga (omnibus volume), illustrated by Hans Helweg, Delacorte (New York, NY), 1982.

First Big Olga da Polga Book, illustrated by Hans Helweg, Longman (Harlow, England), 1983.

Second Big Olga da Polga Book, illustrated by Hans Helweg, Longman (Harlow, England), 1983.

Olga Moves House, illustrated by Hans Helweg, Oxford University Press (Oxford, England), 2001.

"PARSLEY" SERIES

Parsley's Tail, illustrations by Esor, BBC Publications (London, England), 1969.

Parsley's Good Deed, illustrations by Esor, BBC Publications (London, England), 1969.

Parsley's Last Stand, BBC Publications (London, England), 1970.

Parsley's Problem Present, BBC Publications (London, England), 1970.

Parsley's Parade [and] *Parsley the Lion,* Collins (London, England), 1972.

Parsley and the Herbs, edited by Sheila M. Lane and Marion Kemp, Ward, Lock (London, England), 1976.

Also author of *The Herbs* (thirteen-episode puppet series) and *The Adventures of Parsley* (thirty-two-episode puppet series).

MYSTERIES; FOR ADULTS

Monsieur Pamplemousse, Hodder (London, England), 1983, Beaufort (New York, NY), 1985.

Monsieur Pamplemousse and the Secret Mission, Hodder (London, England), 1984, Beaufort (New York, NY), 1986.

Monsieur Pamplemousse on the Spot, Hodder (London, England), 1986, Beaufort (New York, NY), 1987.

Monsieur Pamplemousse Takes the Cure, Hodder (London, England), 1987.

Monsieur Pamplemousse Aloft, Hodder (London, England), 1989.

Monsieur Pamplemousse Investigates, Hodder (London, England), 1990.

Monsieur Pamplemousse Rests His Case, Hodder Headline (London, England), 1991.

Monsieur Pamplemousse Stands Firm, Hodder Headline (London, England), 1992.

Monsieur Pamplemousse on Location, Hodder Headline (London, England), 1992.

Monsieur Pamplemousse Takes the Train, Hodder Headline (London, England), 1993.

Monsieur Pamplemousse Afloat, Alison & Busby (London, England), 1998.

Monsieur Pamplemousse on Probation, Alison & Busby (London, England), 2000.

Monsieur Pamplemousse on Vacation, Alison & Busby (London, England), 2002.

Monsieur Pamplemousse Hits the Headlines, Alison & Busby (London, England), 2003.

Contributor of short stories to *Strand* magazine and *Malice Domestic 7.*

OTHER

(Editor) *Michael Bond's Book of Bears,* Purnell (London, England), 1971.

The Day the Animals Went on Strike (picture book), illustrations by Jim Hodgson, American Heritage (New York, NY), 1972.

(Editor) *Michael Bond's Book of Mice,* Purnell (London, England), 1972.

(Translator with Barbara von Johnson) *The Motormalgamation,* Studio-Vista (Eastbourne, England), 1974.

Windmill, illustrations by Tony Cattaneo, Studio-Vista (Eastbourne, England), 1975.

How to Make Flying Things (nonfiction), photographs by Peter Kibble, Studio-Vista (Eastbourne, England), 1975.

Mr. Cram's Magic Bubbles, illustrations by Gioia Fiammenghi, Penguin (West Drayton, England), 1975.

Picnic on the River, Collins (London, England), 1980.

J. D. Polson and the Liberty Head Dime, illustrations by Roger Wade Walker, Mayflower (London, England), 1980.

J. D. Polson and the Dillogate Affair, illustrations by Roger Wade Walker, Hodder (London, England), 1981.

The Caravan Puppets, illustrations by Vanessa Julian-Ottie, Collins (London, England), 1983.

(With Paul Parnes) *Oliver the Greedy Elephant,* Methuen (London, England), 1985, Western Publishing (New York, NY), 1986.

(And photographer) *The Pleasures of Paris* (guidebook), Pavilion (London, England), 1987.

A Day by the Sea, illustrations by Ross Design, Young Lions (London, England), 1992.

Something Nasty in the Kitchen, Young Lions (London, England), 1992.

Bears and Forebears: A Life So Far, HarperCollins (New York, NY), 1996.

Also author of radio and television plays for adults and children, including *Simon's Good Deed, Napoleon's Day Out, Open House,* and *Paddington* (various short- and full-length animated films), which have been shown in Great Britain, the United States, France, Germany, Scandinavia, Canada, South Africa, the Netherlands, Hong Kong, Italy, Ceylon, and many other countries. Contributor to British periodicals.

SOUND RECORDINGS

A Bear Called Paddington, Caedmon (New York, NY), 1978.

Paddington: A Disappearing Trick and Other Stories, Caedmon (New York, NY), 1979.

Paddington for Christmas, Caedmon (New York, NY), 1979.

Paddington Turns Detective, Caedmon (New York, NY), 1979.

Also author of audio version of *Paddington's Storybook.*

Adaptations

Many of the "Paddington Bear" works have been adapted to videocassette, filmstrip, and cassette tape.

Sidelights

English author Michael Bond has delighted children all over the world with his stories of Paddington the Bear. He began his series with *A Bear Called Paddington* in 1958, and has continued writing for decades about the bear from Peru who lives with the Brown family. Bond's "Paddington" projects have ranged from picture and pop-up books for younger children to activity books, and Paddington has been featured in plays as well as television series and specials. The bear's appeal, according to critics, is his ability to get into trouble and then manage to come out of it without any major harm being done. Bond has also created such memorable children's characters as the lovable guinea pig Olga da Polga, Thursday the mouse, Parsley the lion, and J. D. Polson the armadillo. In the early 1980s Bond also began publishing works for adults, most notably the "Monsieur Pamplemousse" mysteries. Bond was born January 13, 1926, in Newbury, Berkshire, England. He grew up in a home where he was surrounded by books, and he began to read at an early age. His mother enjoyed English mystery writers, but young Bond's favorite books were *Bulldog Drummond* and *The Swiss Family Robinson.*

Unfortunately, Bond enjoyed reading at home more than he liked attending school. Though his family was Anglican, he went to a Catholic school, and feeling like an outsider, he often faked illnesses to avoid attending class.

Completing his schooling at the age of fourteen, Bond went to work in a lawyer's office. Soon afterward, he responded to a newspaper job advertisement for radio work, won the position because he had handled radio sets as a hobby, and began his career at the British Broadcasting Corporation (BBC). One of his colleagues at the BBC supplemented his income by writing short stories. This coworker inspired Bond to attempt something creative, and he submitted a cartoon to *Punch.* It was rejected, but the editor had written favorable comments on it, so Bond was not discouraged.

Bond took time out during the 1940s to serve in the British Armed Forces, beginning with the Royal Air Force until airsickness forced him to transfer to the British Army. While serving in Egypt, Bond wrote an adult short story and submitted it to *London Opinion.* To his delight, it was accepted. From that time on, he continued to write and submit stories and plays, making occasional sales.

On Christmas Eve in 1957, Bond stopped in a London store to find a present for his wife. "On one of the shelves I came across a small bear looking, I thought,

The original illustrations from the "Paddington Bear" books are collected in this compilation volume, which includes selections from Bond's books published between 1958 and 1979.

very sorry for himself as he was the only one who hadn't been sold," Bond recalled in *Something about the Author Autobiography Series.* "I bought him and because we were living near Paddington station at the time, we christened him Paddington. He sat on a shelf of our one-roomed apartment for a while, and then one day when I was sitting in front of my typewriter staring at a blank sheet of paper wondering what to write, I idly tapped out the words 'Mr. and Mrs. Brown first met Paddington on a railway platform. In fact, that was how he came to have such an unusual name for a bear, for Paddington was the name of the station.' It was a simple act, and in terms of deathless prose, not exactly earth shattering, but it was to change my life considerably. . . . Without intending it, I had become a children's author." *A Bear Called Paddington* was published in 1958.

Since his first appearance on the literary scene, Paddington has "become part of the folklore of childhood," wrote Marcus Crouch in *The Nesbit Tradition: The Children's Novel in England 1945-70.* The now-world-famous bear is recognized, despite his diverse representation at the hand of a variety of illustrators, by his unkempt appearance, Wellington boots, and duffel coat. A foreigner from Peru, Paddington exhibits both innocence and a knack for trouble. "The humour of Pad-

dington is largely visual; it is not what he is but what he does and how he does it that is funny," observed Crouch. In the *New York Times Book Review,* Ellen Lewis Buell cited the bear's "endearing combination of bearishness and boyishness" as one reason for his popularity. According to Pico Iyer in the *Village Voice,* "Paddington is a resolute little fellow of strong principles and few prejudices, full of resourcefulness and free of rancor: both the bear next door and something of a role model."

With sequels such as *Paddington Helps Out, Paddington Abroad,* and *Paddington at Work,* Bond has continued to add to his creation's popularity. Eric Hudson wrote in *Children's Book Review* that "one is immensely impressed by the way each collection of stories comes up so fresh and full of humorous and highly original situations." Bond has also adapted his Paddington stories for even younger readers in a series of picture books that include *Paddington Bear* and *Paddington at the Circus,* and he has written several Paddington activity books, some with the assistance of his daughter, Karen Bond.

In the late 1960s Bond began experimenting with other children's characters, such as Thursday the mouse and Parsley the lion. The latter was a feature of a stop-action animation show on the BBC television network in addition to being the subject of children's books. Bond's most successful children's character, after Paddington, is perhaps Olga da Polga, the guinea pig he began writing about in the early 1970s. Though Olga is restricted to the hutch her owners keep her in, she entertains herself and her animal friends by telling imaginative stories. *Horn Book* contributor Virginia Haviland asserted that in Olga, Bond "has drawn another beguiling creature with a distinct personality—a guinea pig whose cleverness equals that of Paddington." Olga is featured in books such as *Tales of Olga da Polga, Olga Meets Her Match,* and *Olga Moves House.*

In the early 1980s, Bond branched out into the field of adult mystery books with the "Monsieur Pamplemousse" books. The hero of these, Monsieur Pamplemousse, is a French food inspector who solves mysteries with the aid of his dog, Pommes Frites. For the works, Bond draws on his knowledge of France, a country he enjoys visiting frequently. Sybil Steinberg, writing in *Publishers Weekly,* noted, "Pamplemousse and his faithful hound are an appealing pair and offer an evening of civilized entertainment."

Despite Bond's varied literary output, he will always be remembered for the character of Paddington. "Most critics agree . . . that to think of Michael Bond is to think of Paddington Bear," observed Dictionary of Literary Biography contributor Charles E. Matthews. And Bond enjoys his role as a children's author. In *Something about the Author Autobiography Series,* he remarked: "One of the nice things about writing for children is their total acceptance of the fantastic. Give a child a stick and a patch of wet sand and it will draw the outline of a boat and accept it as such. I did learn though, that to make fantasy work you have to believe in it yourself. If an author doesn't believe in his inventions and his characters nobody else will. Paddington to me is, and always has been, very much alive."

Over the years, Paddington has become something of a cottage industry. Bond's creation has been reproduced as a stuffed animal and as a float balloon in the Macy's Thanksgiving Day Parade, and his image has appeared on a British postage stamp. In 2000 a life-sized bronze statue of the bear was unveiled in Paddington Station in London, and the official Paddington Bear Web site debuted in 2003.

Reflecting on his characters and life as a writer, Bond mused in the *Something about the Author Autobiography Series,* "Writing is a lonely occupation, but it's also a selfish one. When things get bad, as they do for everyone from time to time, writers are able to shut themselves away from it, peopling the world with their characters, making them behave the way they want them to behave, saying the things they want to hear. Sometimes they take over and stubbornly refuse to do what you tell them to do, but usually they are very good. Sometimes I am Paddington walking down Windsor Gardens en route to the Portobello Road to buy his morning supply of buns, but if I don't fancy that I can always be Monsieur Pamplemousse, sitting outside a cafe enjoying the sunshine over a baguette split down the middle and filled with ham, and a glass of red wine. I wouldn't wish for anything nicer."

Biographical and Critical Sources

BOOKS

Blount, Margaret, *Animal Land,* Hutchinson (London, England), 1974.
Children's Literature Review, Volume 1, Gale (Detroit, MI), 1976.
Crouch, Marcus, *The Nesbit Tradition: The Children's Novel in England, 1945-70,* Benn (London, England), 1972.
Dictionary of Literary Biography, Volume 161: *British Children's Writers since 1960,* Gale (Detroit, MI), 1996.
St. James Guide to Children's Writers, 5th edition, St. James Press (Detroit, MI), 1999.
Something about the Author Autobiography Series, Volume 3, Gale (Detroit, MI), 1986.

PERIODICALS

Armchair Detective, summer, 1991.
Booklist, December 1, 1990; September 15, 1991; December 15, 1991; September 15, 1997, Carolyn Phelan, review of *Paddington Bear and the Christmas Sur-* *prise,* p. 239; April, 1998, Carolyn Phelan, review of *Paddington Bear All Day* and *Paddington Bear Goes to Market,* p. 1329; May 15, 1998, Carolyn Phelan, review of *Paddington Bear and the Busy Bee Carnival,* pp. 1629-1630; August, 1998, Shelle Rosenfeld, review of *Paddington at Large,* p. 2002; January 1, 1999, Carolyn Phelan, review of *Paddington Bear,* p. 886; April 15, 2002, Carolyn Phelan, review of *Paddington Bear in the Garden,* p. 1405.
Books and Bookmen, February, 1985.
Books for Keeps, March, 1991; January, 1992.
Bulletin of the Center for Children's Books, November, 1973, p. 38; February, 1974, p. 90.
Children's Book Review, February, 1971.
Christian Science Monitor, November 3, 1960; May 6, 1965; May 2, 1973.
Contemporary Review, November, 1971; January, 1984.
Horn Book, February, 1961, p. 53; October, 1961, p. 443; December, 1967, p. 748; April, 1973; June, 1973; June, 1980, p. 335.
Kirkus Reviews, December 1, 2001, review of *Paddington Bear in the Garden,* p. 1681.
Los Angeles Times Book Review, June 9, 1985.
New Yorker, December 4, 1971; December 1, 1975.
New York Times Book Review, August 27, 1961, p. 22; May 9, 1965, p. 24; November 9, 1969; March 1, 1987.
Observer (London, England), March 10, 1985.
Publishers Weekly, July 29, 1988; June 23, 1989; July 28, 1989; October 12, 1990, Sybil Steinberg, review of *Monsieur Pamplemousse Investigates,* p. 48; September 6, 1991, review of *Monsieur Pamplemousse Rests His Case,* p. 97; November 8, 1999, "Together for the First Time," p. 70.
Saturday Review, November 9, 1968; April 17, 1971.
School Librarian, August, 1992.
School Library Journal, March, 1968, p. 127; December, 1973, p. 41; September, 1989; February, 1992; December, 1992.
Times Literary Supplement, November 24, 1966, p. 1087; November 12, 1970; October 22, 1971, p. 1333; November 3, 1972; December 6, 1974; October 1, 1976; September 30, 1983.
Village Voice, July 16, 1985.
Washington Post Book World, December 15, 1991.
Wilson Library Bulletin, January, 1974, p. 381.

ONLINE

Official Paddington Bear Web Site, http://www.paddington bear.co.uk (January 11, 2005).*

*   *   *

BORTOLOTTI, Dan 1969-

Personal

Born July 27, 1969, in Toronto, Ontario, Canada. *Education:* University of Waterloo, B.A. (English; with honors), 1992.

Dan Bortolotti

Addresses

Home—27 Twelve Oaks Dr., Aurora, Ontario, Canada L4G 6J5. *Agent*—Don Sedgwick, Transatlantic Literary Agency, 1603 Italy Cross Rd., Petite Riviere, Nova Scotia, Canada B0J 2P0. *E-mail*—dan@danbortolotti. com.

Career

Writer and journalist.

Awards, Honors

Science in Society Book Award shortlist, both 2003, both for *Exploring Saturn* and *Panda Rescue*.

Writings

Exploring Saturn, Firefly Books (Buffalo, NY), 2003.
Panda Rescue: Changing the Future for Endangered Wildlife, Firefly Books (Buffalo, NY), 2003.
Tiger Rescue: Changing the Future for Endangered Wildlife, Firefly Books (Buffalo, NY), 2003.
Hope in Hell: Inside the World of Doctors without Borders (adult nonfiction), Firefly Books (Buffalo, NY), 2004.

Sidelights

Canadian journalist Dan Bortolotti is the author of several nonfiction books for young readers. His 2004 book, *Exploring Saturn*, helps readers position the sixth planet within the solar system, then examines the ringed planet's unique characteristics, including its many moons. Tracing the known history of Saturn for young researchers, Bortolotti follows human understanding about the planet, from the ancient models of Ptolemy to the photographs captured by modern space probes such as the Hubble satellite, and even up to the preparations for the 2004 Cassini-Hygens probe's trip into the Saturnian planetary system. In *Resource Links* Heather Empey described *Exploring Saturn* as a "fantastic" resource that is "absolutely packed with information" useful to amateur astronomers. Noting the timeliness of Bortolotti's book, John Peters predicted in *School Library Journal* that "serious students and casual browsers alike will have trouble putting this down."

Moving to earthbound studies, Bortolotti contributed *Panda Rescue* and *Tiger Rescue* to the "Firefly Animal Rescue" series, which focuses on wildlife trouble spots on our own planet. After profiling the animal under study, the author then discusses the factors that threaten each species, some involving long-held local customs and others a result of an expanding human population. With the threat to each species recognized, some conservation measures have already been enacted, and Bortolotti includes an overview of these programs, while also focusing on ways in which specific threats might also be averted. Praising Bortolotti's "engaging writing style" as well as the photographs in each book, *School Library Journal* contributor Kathy Piehl dubbed the series "fascinating" and "readable." In *Booklist* Gillian Engberg also noted the author's "accessible, lively language" and Bortolotti's inclusion of useful information and reference sources, while Linda Irvine praised both *Tiger Rescue* and *Panda Rescue* in a *Resource Links* review, citing their realistic depiction of animal species and the inclusion of information "on the cultural and economic issues around protection of species."

Biographical and Critical Sources

PERIODICALS

Booklist, December 1, 2003, Carolyn Phelan, review of *Exploring Saturn,* p. 674; January 1, 2004, Gillian Engberg, review of *Panda Rescue: Changing the Future for Endangered Wildlife,* p. 850; September 15, 2004, Donna Chavez, review of *Hope in Hell: Inside the World of Doctors without Borders,* p. 188.
Kliatt, January, 2004, Janet Julian, review of *Exploring Saturn,* p. 35.
Library Journal, October 1, 2004, Tina Neville, review of *Hope in Hell,* p. 103.
Publishers Weekly, August 9, 2004, review of *Hope in Hell,* p. 237.
Resource Links, February, 2004, Heather Empey, review of *Exploring Saturn,* p. 20; February, 2004, Linda Irvine, review of *Panda Rescue* and *Tiger Rescue,* p. 43.
School Library Journal, April, 2004, Kathy Piehl, review of *Panda Rescue:,* p. 166; May, 2004, John Peters, review of *Exploring Saturn,* p. 164.

BOUDELANG, Bob
See PELL, Ed(ward)

*   *   *

BRANDENBERG, Aliki (Liacouras)
(Aliki)

Personal

Born September 3, 1929, in Wildwood Crest, NJ; daughter of James Peter and Stella (Lagakos) Liacouras; married Franz Brandenberg (an author), March 15, 1957; children: Jason, Alexa, Demetria. *Education:* Graduated from Philadelphia Museum School of Art (now Philadelphia College of Art), 1951. *Hobbies and other interests:* Macrame, weaving, music, baking, traveling, reading, gardening, theater, films, museums.

Addresses

Home—17 Regent's Park Terrace, London NW1 7ED, England.

Career

Muralist and commercial artist in Philadelphia, PA, and New York, NY, 1951-56, and in Zurich, Switzerland, 1957-60; commercial artist, writer, and illustrator of children's books in New York, NY, 1960-77, and London, England, 1977—. Has also taught art and ceramics.

Awards, Honors

Boys' Clubs of America Junior Book Award, 1968, for *Three Gold Pieces: A Greek Folk Tale;* American Institute of Graphic Arts for the Children's Book Show includee, 1976, and Children's Book Council Children's Book Showcase includee, 1977, both for *At Mary Bloom's;* New York Academy of Sciences Children's Science Book Award, 1977, for *Corn Is Maize: The Gift of the Indians;* Dutch Children's Book Council Silver Slate Pencil Award, and Garden State (NJ) Children's Book Award, both 1981, both for *Mummies Made in Egypt;* Omar's Book Award, 1986, for *Keep Your Mouth Closed, Dear;* Prix du Livre pour Enfants (Geneva, Switzerland), 1987, for *Feelings;* World of Reading Readers' Choice Award, 1989, for *The Story of Johnny Appleseed;* Drexel University/Free Library of Philadelphia citation, 1991; Pennsylvania School Librarians Association Award, 1991, for outstanding contributions in field of literature; Garden State Children's Book Award, 1996, for *My Visit to the Aquarium;* Honor Book Award, *Boston Globe/Horn Book,* 1999, for *William Shakespeare and the Globe;* Jane Addams Peace Prize, 1999, for *Marianthe's Story.*

Writings

AUTHOR AND ILLUSTRATOR; UNDER NAME ALIKI

The Story of William Tell, Faber & Faber (London, England), 1960, A. S. Barnes, 1961.
My Five Senses, Crowell (New York, NY), 1962.

Aliki Brandenberg

My Hands, Crowell (New York, NY), 1962.
The Wish Workers, Dial (New York, NY), 1962.
The Story of Johnny Appleseed, Prentice-Hall (Englewood Cliffs, NJ), 1963.
George and the Cherry Tree, Dial (New York, NY), 1964.
The Story of William Penn, Prentice-Hall (Englewood Cliffs, NJ), 1964.
A Weed Is a Flower: The Life of George Washington Carver, Prentice-Hall (Englewood Cliffs, NJ), 1965.
Keep Your Mouth Closed, Dear, Dial (New York, NY), 1966.
Three Gold Pieces: A Greek Folk Tale, Pantheon (New York, NY), 1967.
New Year's Day, Crowell (New York, NY), 1967.
(Editor) *Hush Little Baby: A Folk Lullaby,* Prentice-Hall (Englewood Cliffs, NJ), 1968.
My Visit to the Dinosaurs, Crowell (New York, NY), 1969, reprinted, 1985.
The Eggs: A Greek Folk Tale, Pantheon (New York, NY), 1969.
Diogenes: The Story of the Greek Philosopher, Prentice-Hall (Englewood Cliffs, NJ), 1969.
Fossils Tell of Long Ago, Crowell (New York, NY), 1972.
June 7!, Macmillan (New York, NY), 1972.
The Long Lost Coelacanth and Other Living Fossils, Crowell (New York, NY), 1973.
Green Grass and White Milk, Crowell (New York, NY), 1974.
Go Tell Aunt Rhody, Macmillan (New York, NY), 1974.
At Mary Bloom's, Greenwillow (New York, NY), 1976.
Corn Is Maize: The Gift of the Indians, Crowell (New York, NY), 1976.
The Many Lives of Benjamin Franklin, Prentice-Hall (Englewood Cliffs, NJ), 1977.
Wild and Woolly Mammoths, Crowell (New York, NY), 1977.
The Twelve Months, Greenwillow (New York, NY), 1978.

Mummies Made in Egypt, Crowell (New York, NY), 1979.
The Two of Them, Greenwillow (New York, NY), 1979.
Digging up Dinosaurs, Crowell (New York, NY), 1981, released with audiocassette, HarperAudio (New York, NY), 1991.
We Are Best Friends, Greenwillow (New York, NY), 1982.
Use Your Head, Dear, Greenwillow (New York, NY), 1983.
A Medieval Feast, Harper (New York, NY), 1984.
Feelings, Greenwillow (New York, NY), 1984.
Dinosaurs Are Different, Crowell (New York, NY), 1985.
How a Book Is Made, Crowell (New York, NY), 1986.
Jack and Jake, Greenwillow (New York, NY), 1986.
Overnight at Mary Bloom's, Greenwillow (New York, NY), 1987.
Welcome, Little Baby, Greenwillow (New York, NY), 1987.
Dinosaur Bones, Crowell (New York, NY), 1988.
King's Day: Louis XIV of France, Crowell (New York, NY), 1989.
My Feet, Crowell (New York, NY), 1990.
Manners, Greenwillow (New York, NY), 1990.
Christmas Tree Memories, HarperCollins (New York, NY), 1991.
I'm Growing!, HarperCollins (New York, NY), 1992.
Milk: From Cow to Carton, HarperCollins (New York, NY), 1992.
Aliki's Dinosaur Dig: A Book and Card Game, HarperCollins (New York, NY), 1992.
My Visit to the Aquarium, HarperCollins (New York, NY), 1993.
Communication, Greenwillow (New York, NY), 1993.
Gods and Goddesses of Olympus, HarperCollins (New York, NY), 1994.
Tabby: A Story in Pictures, HarperCollins (New York, NY), 1995.
Best Friends Together Again, Greenwillow (New York, NY), 1996.
Hello! Good-bye!, Greenwillow (New York, NY), 1996.
My Visit to the Zoo, HarperCollins (New York, NY), 1997.
Those Summers, HarperCollins (New York, NY), 1997.
Marianthe's Story (contains *Painted Words* and *Spoken Memories*), Greenwillow (New York, NY), 1998.
William Shakespeare and the Globe, HarperCollins (New York, NY), 1999.
All by Myself!, HarperCollins (New York, NY), 2000.
One Little Spoonful, HarperCollins (New York, NY), 2000.
Ah, Music!, HarperCollins (New York, NY), 2003.
A Play's the Thing, HarperCollins (New York, NY), 2005.

Aliki's books have been translated into Chinese, Portuguese, Spanish, Catalan, Danish, Dutch, Finnish, French, German, Hebrew, Japanese, Norwegian, Swedish, and Braille.

ILLUSTRATOR; UNDER NAME ALIKI

Pat Witte and Eve Witte, *Who Lives Here?,* Golden Press, 1961.
Joan M. Lexau, *Cathy Is Company,* Dial (New York, NY), 1961.
Paul Showers, *Listening Walk,* Crowell (New York, NY), 1961.
Margaret Hodges, *What's for Lunch, Charley?,* Dial (New York, NY), 1961.

Mickey Marks, *What Can I Buy?,* Dial (New York, NY), 1962.
Dorothy Les Tina, *A Book to Begin On: Alaska,* Holt (New York, NY), 1962.
James Holding, *The Lazy Little Zulu,* Morrow (New York, NY), 1962.
Joan M. Heilbronner, *This Is the House Where Jack Lives,* Harper (New York, NY), 1962.
Vivian L. Thompson, *The Horse That Liked Sandwiches,* Putnam (New York, NY), 1962.
Arthur Jonas, *Archimedes and His Wonderful Discoveries,* Prentice-Hall (Englewood Cliffs, NJ), 1962.
Bernice Kohn, *Computers at Your Service,* Prentice-Hall (Englewood Cliffs, NJ), 1962.
Arthur Jonas, *New Ways in Math,* Prentice-Hall (Englewood Cliffs, NJ), 1962.
Eugene David, *Television and How It Works,* Prentice-Hall (Englewood Cliffs, NJ), 1962.
Eugene David, *Electricity in Your Life,* Prentice-Hall (Englewood Cliffs, NJ), 1963.
James Holding, *Mister Moonlight and Omar,* Morrow (New York, NY), 1963.
Joan M. Lexau, *That's Good, That's Bad,* Dial (New York, NY), 1963.
Judy Hawes, *Bees and Beelines,* Crowell (New York, NY), 1964.
Arthur Jonas, *More New Ways in Math,* Prentice-Hall (Englewood Cliffs, NJ), 1964.
James Holding, *Sherlock on the Trail,* Morrow (New York, NY), 1964.
Bernice Kohn, *Everything Has a Size* (also see below), Prentice-Hall (Englewood Cliffs, NJ), 1964.
Bernice Kohn, *Everything Has a Shape* (also see below), Prentice-Hall (Englewood Cliffs, NJ), 1964.
Bernice Kohn, *One Day It Rained Cats and Dogs,* Coward (New York, NY), 1965.
Helen Clare, *Five Dolls in a House,* Prentice-Hall (Englewood Cliffs, NJ), 1965.
Rebecca Kalusky, *Is It Blue As a Butterfly?,* Prentice-Hall (Englewood Cliffs, NJ), 1965.
Mary K. Phelan, *Mother's Day,* Crowell (New York, NY), 1965.
Betty Ren Wright, *I Want to Read!,* A. Whitman, 1965.
Sean Morrison, *Is That a Happy Hippopotamus?,* Crowell (New York, NY), 1966.
Bernice Kohn, *Everything Has a Shape and Everything Has a Size,* Prentice-Hall (Englewood Cliffs, NJ), 1966.
Helen Clare, *Five Dolls in the Snow,* Prentice-Hall (Englewood Cliffs, NJ), 1967.
Helen Clare, *Five Dolls and the Monkey,* Prentice-Hall (Englewood Cliffs, NJ), 1967.
Helen Clare, *Five Dolls and Their Friends,* Prentice-Hall (Englewood Cliffs, NJ), 1968.
Helen Clare, *Five Dolls and the Duke,* Prentice-Hall (Englewood Cliffs, NJ), 1968.
Wilma Yeo, *Mrs. Neverbody's Recipes,* Lippincott (Philadelphia, PA), 1968.
Esther R. Hautzig, *At Home: A Visit in Four Languages,* Macmillan (New York, NY), 1968.
Polly Greenberg, *Oh Lord, I Wish I Was a Buzzard,* Macmillan (New York, NY), 1968.
Roma Gans, *Birds at Night,* Crowell (New York, NY), 1968.

Jane Jonas Srivastava, *Weighing and Balancing,* Crowell (New York, NY), 1970.

Joanne Oppenheim, *On the Other Side of the River,* Franklin Watts (New York, NY), 1972.

Philip M. Sherlock and Hilary Sherlock, *Ears and Tails and Common Sense: More Stories from the Caribbean,* Crowell (New York, NY), 1974.

Jane Jonas Srivastava, *Averages,* Crowell (New York, NY), 1975.

Joanna Cole, *Evolution,* Crowell (New York, NY), 1987.

Alice Low, *Mommy's Briefcase,* Scholastic (New York, NY), 1995.

Polly Greenberg, *O Lord, I Wish I Was a Buzzard,* SeaStar (New York, NY), 2002.

ILLUSTRATOR, UNDER NAME ALIKI; BY HUSBAND, FRANZ BRANDENBERG

I Once Knew a Man, Macmillan (New York, NY), 1970.

Fresh Cider and Pie, Macmillan (New York, NY), 1973.

No School Today!, Macmillan (New York, NY), 1975.

A Secret for Grandmother's Birthday, Greenwillow (New York, NY), 1975.

A Robber! A Robber!, Greenwillow (New York, NY), 1976.

I Wish I Was Sick, Too!, Greenwillow (New York, NY), 1976, published as *I Don't Feel Well,* Hamish Hamilton (London, England), 1977.

What Can You Make of It?, Greenwillow (New York, NY), 1977.

Nice New Neighbors, Greenwillow (New York, NY), 1977.

A Picnic, Hurrah!, Greenwillow (New York, NY), 1978.

Six New Students, Greenwillow (New York, NY), 1978.

Everyone Ready?, Greenwillow (New York, NY), 1979.

It's Not My Fault!, Greenwillow (New York, NY), 1980.

Leo and Emily, Greenwillow (New York, NY), 1981.

Leo and Emily's Big Idea, Greenwillow (New York, NY), 1982.

Aunt Nina and Her Nephews and Nieces, Greenwillow (New York, NY), 1983.

Aunt Nina's Visit, Greenwillow (New York, NY), 1984.

Leo and Emily and the Dragon, Greenwillow (New York, NY), 1984.

The Hit of the Party, Greenwillow (New York, NY), 1985.

Cock-a-Doodle-Doo, Greenwillow (New York, NY), 1986.

What's Wrong with a Van?, Greenwillow (New York, NY), 1987.

Aunt Nina, Good Night!, Greenwillow (New York, NY), 1989.

Sidelights

In her many books for children, Greek-American author-illustrator Aliki Brandenberg—known to readers simply as Aliki—has proven a rare talent in imparting information to children and newly minted readers. Sometimes using comic book-style illustrations incorporating word bubbles, and at others times using elaborate frieze pictures or styling pages to resemble an illuminated manuscript, Aliki is well known for adapting her illustrations to content. Gearing her texts to a preschool to middle-grade audience, she fills her nonfiction, picture books, and story books with warmth, humor, and enthusiasm. As she once told *Children's Books and Their Creators,* "I write fiction out of a need to express myself. I write nonfiction—out of curiosity and fascination. And I draw in order to breathe." In addition to the books she has written herself, Aliki has also illustrated dozens of books written by other writers, including her husband, Franz Brandenberg.

Aliki's generational tales include *The Two of Them, At Mary Bloom's,* and *Marianthe's Story;* while her picture books *We Are Best Friends, Best Friends Together Again,* and *Hello! Good-bye!* detail the emotional lives of young children. Her Greek heritage and family memories surface in still other books, among them *Christmas Tree Memories* and *Those Summers.* Moving to nonfiction, Aliki has produced award-winning biographies, including books that relate the life stories of William Tell, Benjamin Franklin, and King Louis XIV of France, as well as British playwright William Shakespeare. Aliki's other nonfiction ranges in subject matter from dinosaurs to natural history and anatomy, each book featuring her own illustrations.

Aliki was born in Wildwood Crest, New Jersey, where her parents, who lived in Philadelphia, were vacationing at the time. Starting to draw from an early age, she exhibited her first two portraits—one of her family and another of Peter Rabbit's family—in kindergarten. "Such a fuss was made over them," she remembered in the *Third Book of Junior Authors,* "that the course of my life was decided that day." Aliki thereafter attended art classes on Saturdays and also pursued a secondary interest in music by taking piano lessons.

After she graduated from high school, she enrolled in the Philadelphia Museum School of Art. After graduating in 1951, she took a job working in the display department of the J. C. Penney Company in New York City. After a year she moved back to Philadelphia and worked as a freelance advertising and display artist. She also painted murals, started her own greeting card company, and taught classes in art and ceramics.

Aliki's parents were natives of Greece and had taught her to speak Greek before she learned to speak English. In 1956 she decided to use her language skills on a visit to that country, and also included Italy and other European locations in her trip. While traveling, painting, sketching, and learning about her heritage, she also met Franz Brandenberg, the man she would marry. After wedding in 1957, the couple settled in Brandenberg's native Switzerland, where Aliki continued her freelance art career. When she learned that William Tell was Swiss, she and Franz visited the territory where he lived. That experience inspired her to write and illustrate her first book, *The Story of William Tell,* which was published in 1960. Reviewing this debut book in *School Librarian,* H. Millington wrote that "Aliki has taken [the old tale] and dressed it up as fresh as the daisies with some of the most gorgeous illustrations I have seen." The characters in Aliki's biography "jump off the page," Millington continued, "with the sheer audacious simplicity of their representation." Later that same year Aliki and her husband moved to New York City, where she was asked to illustrate several books written by other authors. While working as an illustrator, she also

The author/illustrator best known to readers as Aliki introduces young people to the work of scientists who hunt for and study the bones of prehistoric beasts.

got an idea for a second book, titled *My Five Senses.* From this point she has gone on to write and illustrate dozens more nonfiction titles, many of them in association with the "Let's Read and Find Out" science book series for Crowell. Some of her most popular titles deal with dinosaurs, a topic of great interest to young children. Reviewing *My Visit to the Dinosaurs,* a *Kirkus Reviews* writer commented that "what this dinosaur book has that others don't is what might be called human interest—also a sense of humor." Praising Aliki's popular *Digging up Dinosaurs,* Susan Bolotin noted in the *New York Times Book Review* that the book's "main text and energetic drawings will appeal to any child who hungers for extra information on those endlessly fascinating 'bags of bones.'" Aliki has continued to follow her personal fascination for ancient reptiles in *Dinosaurs Are Different, Dinosaur Bones,* and *Aliki's Dinosaur Dig.*

Like her books on dinosaurs, Aliki's other nonfiction books are inspired by her fascination with a certain topic. She then researches the subject, usually over an extended period of time. "The pleasure of these books," she once wrote of her nonfiction work, "is writing complicated facts as clearly and simply as possible, so readers (and I) who know nothing about a subject learn a great deal by the time we are finished." *Publishers Weekly* reviewer Dulcy Brainard observed that the resulting "science primers inform, entertain and delight in a way that is particularly Aliki's, using script and different typefaces, with frieze frames and borders. One doesn't have to be a kid to devour each page, intent on not missing a single bit of information it contains." Aliki spoke about her science books with Margaret Carter in *Books for Your Children,* remarking, "It's best for me to know nothing about a subject when I begin . . . that way I have to get it right. Because I am not a scientist I can perhaps approach the subject with fresh eyes."

Aliki has developed a text-within text style that uses dialogue or thought bubbles to express her characters'

speech alongside a main text that presents much of the information. Among the subjects that have prompted Aliki's pen are fossils, natural cycles, manufacturing, and history. Reviewing *Fossils Tell of Long Ago,* Mary Neale Rees commented in *School Library Journal* that this "factually accurate, clearly written text will be welcomed by primary graders who are usually captivated by fossils and dinosaurs." Combining both science and history, Aliki studies the significance of corn in America in *Corn Is Maize: The Gift of the Indians,* in which the author/illustrator's "engaging" text presents a "successful blend of social studies, science, and history," according to Diane Holzheimer in *School Library Journal.*

Food also serves as the subject of *Green Grass and White Milk, Milk: From Cow to Carton,* and *A Medieval Feast,* the last which blends history and sociology to allow readers to experience what a feast of the year 1400 must have been like. Although the book took Aliki two years to produce, *A Medieval Feast* "seems to spring from the copy," Brainard maintained. Creating illustrations that mimic an illuminated manuscript of the period and using a lush prose style, "Aliki has provided us with a veritable feast of a book," concluded Patricia Dooley in *School Library Journal.* History is also at the heart of the popular *Mummies Made in Egypt,* which contains "stunning" art "adapted from the real article and rendered frieze-style," according to Nora Magid in the *New York Times Book Review.* The book's text "is uncompromisingly informative and clear," Magid added.

Aliki tackles a manufacturing process in *How a Book Is Made,* which uses a comic-strip format and step-by-step illustrations to "make the information easily accessible," according to Zena Sutherland, reviewing the book for the *Bulletin of the Center for Children's Books.* "Yes, there are other good books on how a book is made," noted Sutherland, "but probably none better for younger readers." A more creative process is the subject of *Ah, Music!,* in which "the indefatigable Aliki takes on the whole of music—its origins, its history, its necessity to the human spirit," according to *Booklist* contributor GraceAnne A. DeCandido. After discussing the component parts—harmonics, rhythm, tempo, melody, pitch, and the function and range of instruments—she moves into different types of music, such as orchestral, jazz, pop, and different folk songs, all described within a multicultural context. The interrelation of music and dance, the use of music as therapy, and the dedication required of professional musicians are also covered in a book that "should lead young music lovers to the shelves to find out more about a type of music or composer who has piqued their curiosity," according to *School Library Journal* critic Jane Marino. Praising the author/illustrator's "clear, child-friendly illustrations," a *Kirkus* reviewer dubbed *Ah, Music!* a "comprehensive examination" of a broad subject, while in *Horn Book* Lolly Robinson wrote that Aliki breaks her topic "down into child-sized portions with a masterful sense of pacing, humor, and page design."

The art of being human is also the subject of several books by Aliki. In *Communication* she presents the many ways people communicate—both verbally and non-verbally—and illustrates her text using children of many races, who are linked by their efforts to write, talk, listen, and read, thereby sharing knowledge, expressing feelings, and opinions, and solving problems. Praising Aliki's text as "clear" and "succinct," *Horn Book* contributor Margaret A. Bush concluded that the "empathy, humor, and insight proffer very satisfying reading," making *Communication* "a masterful accomplishment in simple nonfiction. Emotions are the focus of *Feelings,* in which Aliki again uses the comic-strip format to create a "lighthearted mood," according to *Booklist* contributor Denise M. Wilms, who concluded that Aliki's "fresh, colorful execution lends grace beyond what often passes for bibliotherapy." With *Manners* Aliki presented a short course in etiquette designed to be useful for both parents and teachers, according to Cathryn A. Camper writing in *Five Owls.* "The playful cartoon dialogue and the funny 'good manners' quiz on the endpapers help keep the tone of the book nondidactic and lighthearted," concluded Camper.

A biography, *The Story of William Tell,* began Aliki's career, and she has continued to produce acclaimed life stories throughout her long career in children's books. Her award-winning *The Story of Johnny Appleseed* and *The Story of William Penn* were praise for their relaxed style and humor. Reviewing Aliki's biography of Ameri-

Aliki shares her lifelong love of music with young readers in this ambitious picture book, which surveys the long and varied history of Western music, from classical to folk to rock, pop, and jazz.

ca's apple-tree planter, Millicent J. Taylor commented in the *Christian Science Monitor* that the author/illustrator "has a remarkable way of capturing the spirit of a small child's paintings and lighting them up with the genius of the adult painter of true primitives." The life of George Washington Carver is profiled in *A Weed Is a Flower,* "a simplified biography true both to its subject and the interests of early childhood," according to a *Kirkus Reviews* writer.

Following her own interest, Aliki continues to seek out fascinating individuals as subjects of her biographies. In *The King's Day* she details the life of the "Sun King," Louis XIV of France, whose long reign lasted from 1643 to 1715. In a book full of fascinating details and fine artwork, she recreates the baroque opulence of the king's royal court at Versailles. "Color is the most striking element in Aliki's drawings," observed Shirley Wilton in a *School Library Journal* review of the book. "The richness of the king's costumes, his wigs, lace, red stockings, and high-heeled shoes are echoed by the attire of his courtiers."A famous English playwright also gets the Aliki treatment in *William Shakespeare and the Globe,* "one of the most appealing and responsible biographies of Shakespeare" produced for middle-grade readers according to Sally Margolis in *School Library Journal.* While noting facts about Shakespeare's life, Aliki concentrates on his work as a playwright, includes quotes from his plays, and even structures her book in the five "acts" the Bard used in his plays. She recounts the history of the Globe Theatre and the role of drama in Elizabethan England, then moves ahead to the twentieth century to profile the successful effort by American actor/director Sam Wanamaker to construct a new Globe in Stratford-on-Avon. Margolis called *William Shakespeare and the Globe* a "thoroughly enjoyable and reliable introduction to the Bard." while a *Kirkus Reviews* contributor wrote that in the book "Aliki creates a cascade of landscapes, crowd scenes, diminutive portraits, and sequential views, all done with her trademark warmth and delicacy of line." Calling the book "an ambitious project," *Booklist* reviewer Carolyn Phelan commended Aliki for a successful story that contains "a pervasive sense of history and fine sense of style."

In addition to her nonfiction books and her work as an illustrator for other writers—including her husband—Aliki is also noted for creating fiction. Many of her books are inspired by day-to-day incidents, particularly those relating to the raising of her own two children. Human anatomy becomes the central joke of *Keep Your Mouth Closed, Dear,* an "altogether winning creation," according to Richard Kluger in *Book Week,* while in *All by Myself* a young boy strives to be independent, wrestling with buttons, zippers, faucets, and other everyday hurdles facing small humans. In *School Library Journal* Sharon R. Pearce called the book "jubilant" while in *Publishers Weekly* Aliki's "brightly hued" illustrations were praised for "convincingly convey[ing] . . . the protagonists's high energy and enthusiasm."

Babies—both mouse and human—beckon in *At Mary Bloom's* and *Welcome, Little Baby.* The former title, a

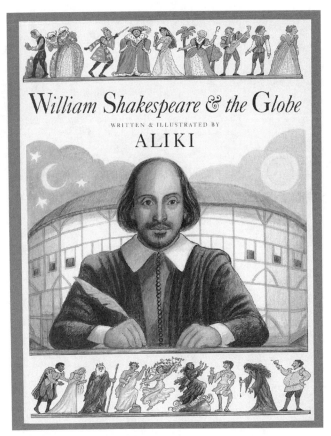

With captivating, detailed illustrations and engaging text, Aliki introduces the life and work of one of the most enduring writers of the Western world and follows the colorful history of the English theater in which his works were first performed.

generational story about a little girl and an older neighbor, was praised as "great fun," by Sutherland in a review for the *Bulletin of the Center for Children's Books.* Another powerful generational tale is *The Two of Them,* a story inspired by Aliki's own father that recounts the mutual love between an old man and his granddaughter. A *Publishers Weekly* reviewer called the tale "a moving but unsentimental story," and concluded that *The Two of Them* is a book "parents who read to their children will probably appreciate even more than will the young." In the two-part book *Marianthe's Story* a young immigrant girl learns a new language sufficiently to tell her school class the story of how her family came to this new land. "The words and illustrations combine to tell a powerful story of growth, acceptance and overcoming adversity," commented Kristi Steele in *Children's Book Review Service,* while a *Kirkus* reviewer called the "storytelling . . . vivid and exquisitely emotional, making Aliki's story painfully personal, yet resonant, in very few pages."

Aliki's story of the Greek philosopher in *Diogenes* underlines her interest in her Greek heritage. Adapting the style of the Greek fresco for this biography, she introduces young readers to someone they might not otherwise know. In her retelling of Greek myth and folktales, she also has introduced new and less typical informa-

tion to young readers. In her award-winning *Three Gold Pieces,* she retells the story of a submissive Greek peasant and the meager pay he receives for ten years of work. Eleanor Dienstag noted the "almost Biblical quality" of the story in her appraisal of *Three Gold Pieces* for the *New York Times Book Review,* and also praised Aliki's "rich, Oriental illustrations." More folktales are presented in *The Twelve Months* and *The Eggs,* while in *The Gods and Goddesses of Olympus* Aliki moves to Greek myth, presenting a winning introduction to an endlessly fascinating subject.

Aliki's personal memories of friends and family are gathered in several books, including *Christmas Tree Memories, June 7!,* and *Those Summers.* Reviewing the birthday party book, *June 7!,* Edward Hudson noted in *Children's Book Review* that Aliki "has a simplicity of line and an eye for detail that children seek out," while Judith Gloyer observed in *School Library Journal* that Aliki's *Those Summers* "offers vivid memories of childhood summers spent at the ocean with her cousins, parents, aunts, and uncles." Gloyer concluded that the book provided a "delightful glimpse of a cherished childhood."

Due to the many topics she has covered throughout her long career, and the wealth of information she packs into each of her illustrated nonfiction picture books, Aliki's books are a staple in the recommended reading lists of preschool to middle-grade readers. The simplicity of her approach belies the fact of the expertise and research that go into each title. As Aliki noted in an essay for the *St. James Guide to Children's Writers,* "Much of my work involves intricate and time-consuming research—made doubly difficult because I both write and illustrate. I spend long hours at my desk. Some books take three years to complete. That is why I call what I do 'hard fun.' But I love the challenge of a new idea, and finding out something I don't know about a subject—or even myself."

Living and working in England since 1977, Aliki continues to produce new titles. "I'm one of those lucky people who love what they do," she once commented. "I also love my garden, music, theater, museums, and traveling. But I'm happiest when I'm in my studio on the top floor of our tall house in London, alone with the book I'm working on, and Mozart."

Biographical and Critical Sources

BOOKS

Children's Books and Their Creators, edited by Anita Silvey, Houghton (Boston, MA), 1995, p. 16.
Children's Literature Review, Volume 9, Gale (Detroit, MI), 1985, pp. 15-32.
St. James Guide to Children's Writers, 5th edition, edited by Sara Pendergast and Tom Pendergast, St. James Press (Detroit, MI), 1999, pp. 17-20.
Third Book of Junior Authors, H. W. Wilson (Bronx, NY), 1972, pp. 8-9.

A young, energetic boy is determined to gain independence from his helpful parents, and even tries to help out with household activities, in the entertaining picture book All by Myself!, *published in 2000.*

PERIODICALS

Booklist, December 1, 1994, Denise M., Wilms, review of *Feelings,* p. 520; August, 1995, p. 94; May 1, 1996, p. 1511; July, 1996, p. 1827; June 1, 1999, Carolyn Phelan, review of *William Shakespeare and the Globe,* p. 1824; November 1, 2000, Carolyn Phelan, review of *All by Myself!,* p. 544; July, 2001, Hazel Rochman, review of *One Little Spoonful,* p. 2022; June 1, 2003, GraceAnne A. DeCandido, review of *Ah, Music!,* p. 1781.

Books for Your Children, spring, 1984, Margaret Carter, "Cover Artist—Aliki," p. 9.

Book Week, October 30, 1966, Richard Kluger, "Crocodile Smiles," pp. 4-5, 8.

Bulletin of the Center for Children's Books, November, 1976, Zena Sutherland, review of *At Mary Bloom's,* p. 37; November, 1986, Zena Sutherland, review of *How a Book Is Made,* p. 41.

Child-Life, May-June, 2003, review of *Ah, Music!,* p. 26.

Children's Book Review Service, summer, 1975, Edward Hudson, review of *June 7!,* p. 55; October, 1998, Kristi Steele, review of *Marianthe's Story,* p. 19.

Christian Science Monitor, November 14, 1963, Millicent J. Taylor, "Peopling the Past," p. 7B.

Five Owls, February, 1991, Cathryn, A. Camper, review of *Manners,* p. 53.

Horn Book, May-June, 1993, Margaret A. Bush, review of *Communications,* p. 342; March-April, 1994, p. 198;

July-August, 1995, p. 446; September-October, 1997, p. 589; September-October, 1998, p. 595; January, 2000, review of *William Shakespeare and the Globe,* p. 50; September, 2000, review of *All by Myself,* p. 545; May-June, 2003, Lolly Robinson, review of *Ah, Music!,* p. 366.

Kirkus Reviews, October 1, 1965, review of *A Weed Is a Flower: The Life of George Washington Carver,* p. 1039; September 1, 1969, review of *My Visit to the Dinosaurs,* pp. 930-931; September 1, 1998, review of *Marianthe's Story,* p. 1282; May 1, 1999, review of *William Shakespeare and the Globe,* p. 718; April 1, 2003, review of *Ah, Music!,* p. 530.

New York Times Book Review, April 30, 1967, Eleanor Dienstag, review of *Three Gold Pieces,* p. 26; November 18, 1979, Nora Magid, review of *Mummies Made in Egypt,* pp. 30-31; March 8, 1981, Susan Bolotin, *Digging up Dinosaurs,* p. 30; October 16, 1983.

Publishers Weekly, September 10, 1979, review of *The Two of Them,* p. 65; July 22, 1983, Dulcy Brainard, interview with Aliki, pp. 134-135; August 8, 1994, p. 434; June 3, 1996, p. 82; August 19, 1996, p. 66; August 11, 1997, p. 402; July 20, 1998, p. 219; May 31, 1999, p. 91; August 21, 2000, review of *All by Myself!,* p. 71; February, 24, 2003, review of *Ah, Music!,* p. 70.

School Librarian, H. Millington, review of *The Story of William Tell,* December, 1961, p. 567.

School Library Journal, November, 1962, Allie Beth Martin, review of *The Wish Workers,* p. 39; September, 1972, Mary Neale Rees, review of *Fossils Tell of Long Ago,* p. 111; April, 1976, Diane Holzheimer, review of *Corn Is Maize,* p. 58; September, 1983, Patricia Dooley, review of *A Medieval Feast,* p. 114; October, 1989, Shirley Wilton, review of *The King's Day, Louis XIV of France,* p. 99; April, 1993, p. 104; May, 1995, Sally Margolis, review of *William Shakespeare and the Globe,* p. 134; August, 1996, Judith Gloyer, review of *Those Summers,* p. 115; October, 1998, p. 86; September, 2000, Sharon R. Pearce, review of *All by Myself,* p. 184; September, 2001, Karen land, review of *One Little Spoonful,* p. 182; May, 2003, Jane Marino, review of *Ah, Music!,* p. 133; February, 2004, Nancy Menaldi-Scanlan, review of *William Shakespeare and the Globe,* p. 81.*

BRUMBEAU, Jeff 1955-

Personal

Born June 1, 1955, in New York, NY; son of John (a carpenter) and Dorothy Marie (an administrator; maiden name Doud) Brumbeau; married Marcia Koplon (in advertising), May 4, 1994. *Ethnicity:* "Caucasian." *Education:* Attended City College of New York. *Politics:* "Independent."

Addresses

Home—Chicago, IL. *Agent*—Author Mail, Scholastic Educational Publishing, 557 Broadway, New York, NY 10012. *E-mail*—Brumbeau.rodman@sbcglobal.net.

Jeff Brumbeau's picture book **The Quiltmaker's Gift** *celebrates creativity in its story of a woman who teaches a king the joy in simple things. (Illustration by Gail de Marcken.)*

Career

Writer.

Awards, Honors

Children's Book of the Year, *Book Sense,* 2000, for *The Quiltmaker's Gift;* Logos Book Award; *Publishers Weekly* Cuffy Award; Parent's Choice Silver Honor designation.

Writings

The Man-in-the-Moon in Love, illustrated by Greg Couch, Stewart, Tabori & Chang (New York, NY), 1992.
The Quiltmaker's Gift, illustrated by Gail de Marcken, Pfeifer-Hamilton (Duluth, MN), 2000.
Miss Hunnicutt's Hat, illustrated by Gail de Marcken, Orchard Books (New York, NY), 2003.
The Quiltmaker's Journey, illustrated by Gail de Marcken, Orchard Books (New York, NY), 2004.

Adaptations

Brumbeau's *The Quiltmaker's Gift* inspired several quilt pattern books by Joanne Larsen Line and Nancy Loving Tubesing: *Quilts from The Quiltmaker's Gift: Twenty Traditional Patterns for a New Generation of Generous Quiltmakers,* Pfeifer-Hamilton, 2000, and *More Quilts from The Quiltmaker's Gift: Nineteen Traditional Patterns for a Generation of Generous Quiltmakers,* Orchard Books, 2003.

Sidelights

Jeff Brumbeau is the author of several children's books, among them *Miss Hunnicutt's Hat, The Quiltmaker's Gift,* and *The Man-in-the-Moon in Love.* Joining illustrator Greg Couch for his picture-book debut, Brumbeau spins what a *Publishers Weekly* reviewer praised as a "straightforward" tale with "storybook charm" in relating the reason for the Man-in-the-Moon's on-again, off-again appearances in the night sky. Also told in folklore fashion, Brumbeau's *The Quiltmaker's Gift* finds an unhappy king learning that true happiness cannot be purchased with money, as with each possession he willingly gives away a talented seamstress adds another patch to a beautiful and intricately patterned quilt. In her review of *The Quiltmaker's Gift, Booklist* contributor Shelley Townsend-Hudson praised the book as "a delightful moral tale," noting that the "lush, colorful" artwork by illustrator Gail de Marcken includes a quilting puzzle as well as illustrations about many traditional quilting patterns.

Also enhanced with watercolor illustrations by de Marcken, *Miss Hunnicutt's Hat* presents readers with a silly tale featuring the townspeople of Littleton, who go crazy one day when they receive news that their queen may be stopping by for a visit. Shortly after preparations begin to make the town fit for a queen, an uproar is created over Miss Hunnicutt's new hat, which prominently features a live chicken. Littleton townspeople, who want everything to be perfect as well as perfectly normal, try to convince the wayward citizen that she simply cannot wear the hat and disgrace them all. However, by obsessing on the hat, they neglect to take care of other, more pressing, matters and before they know it the whole town has fallen into disrepair. "Endpapers filled with outlandish hats and many visual jokes will keep youngsters amused for some time," wrote Marianne Saccardi in *School Library Journal* in praise of the book's illustrations, while a *Publishers Weekly* reviewer dubbed the humorous story "over the top."

Biographical and Critical Sources

PERIODICALS

Booklist, January 1, 2000, Shelley Townsend-Hudson, review of *The Quiltmaker's Gift,* p. 935; January 1, 2003, Kay Weisman, review of *Miss Hunnicutt's Hat,* p. 904.
Childhood Education, spring, 2003, review of *The Quiltmaker's Gift,* p. 150.
Kirkus Reviews, February 15, 2003, review of *Miss Hunnicutt's Hat,* p. 301.
People, August 10, 1992, Susan Toepfer, review of *The Man-in-the-Moon in Love,* p. 33.
Publishers Weekly, March 23, 1992, review of *The Man-in-the-Moon in Love,* p. 71; October 11, 1999, review of *The Quiltmaker's Gift,* p. 75; January 6, 2003, review of *Miss Hunnicutt's Hat,* p. 58.
School Library Journal, March, 2003, Marianne Saccardi, review of *Miss Hunnicutt's Hat,* p. 178.*

*   *   *

BURGESS, Mark

Personal

Born in England; married. *Education:* Attended Slade School (London, England). *Hobbies and other interests:* Reading, gardening, walking.

Addresses

Home—Southwest England. *Agent*—c/o Author Mail, Dutton/Penguin Putnam, 375 Hudson St., New York, NY 10014. *E-mail*—mark@markburgess.co.uk.

Career

Writer and illustrator. Designer of Web sites, greeting cards, and animation.

Writings

SELF-ILLUSTRATED

The Cat's Pajamas, Doubleday (New York, NY), 1990.
One Little Teddy Bear, Collins (London, England), 1991.

In Teddy Time *British author/illustrator Mark Burgess weaves a lesson in time-telling into an engaging tale that follows the birthday-party preparations of a group of teddy bears.*

Winnie-the-Pooh's Pop-up Theatre Book (based on books by A. A. Milne and Ernest H. Shepard), Dutton Children's Books (New York, NY), 1993.

Night, Night, HarperCollins (London, England), 1994.

Hello, Day, Collins (London, England), 1994.

Mutiny at Crossbones Bay, Usborne (London, England), 1997.

Teddy and Rabbit's Picnic Outing, Picture Lions (London, England), 1999.

Peek-a-Pooh! (based on books by A. A. Milne and Ernest H. Shepard), Dutton Children's Books (New York, NY), 2001.

"HANNAH'S HOTEL" SERIES; SELF-ILLUSTRATED

Beside the Sea, Collins (London, England), 1994.

Rainy Weather, Collins (London, England), 1994.

Late Arrivals, Collins (London, England), 1994.

Many Happy Returns, Collins (London, England), 1994.

ILLUSTRATOR

Martin Waddell, *Harriet and the Haunted School,* Atlantic Monthly Press (Boston, MA), 1984, reprinted, Harper-Trophy (New York, NY), 2001.

Martin Waddell, *Harriet and the Crocodiles,* Little, Brown (Boston, MA), 1984.

Martin Waddell, *Harriet and the Robot,* Joy Street Books (Boston, MA), 1987.

Richard Groves, *Surprise, Surprise Queen Loonia!,* Barron's (Hauppauge, NY), 1992.

Anna Nilsen, *Follow the Kite,* Picture Lions (London, England), 1998.

Hardie Gramatky, *Little Toot,* abridged edition, Grosset & Dunlap (New York, NY), 1999.

(With Allan Curless) Meredith Hooper, *Dogs' Night,* Millbrook Press (Brookfield, CT), 2000.

Sidelights

British-based graphic artist, author, and illustrator Mark Burgess began his career in the early 1980s, creating artwork for several volumes in Martin Waddell's popular series about a young protagonist named Harriet. While he has continued to work as an illustrator, producing a newly illustrated edition of Hardie Gramatky's classic childhood favorite, *Little Toot* and designing pop-up adaptations of A. A. Milne's "Winnie the Pooh" books, Burgess has also collaborating with author Meredith Hooper and fellow illustrator Allen Curless on *Dog's Night,* a humorous story that finds the dogs depicted on paintings in London's National Gallery freed from their canvases and running through the museum in riotous fashion, only to return, at night's end, to the wrong paintings. In *School Library Journal* Patricia Mahoney Brown praised the book's illustrations as "comical and whimsical as the tale itself," while Ken Marantz wrote in *School Arts* that the "colored drawings set the stage" for Hooper's quirky tale. In addition to illustration, Burgess has also expanded into the writer's realm with *The Cat's Pajamas,* which uses a rhyme wheel to relate the adventures of a seagoing feline; the lift-the-flap counting book *One Little Teddy Bear;* and the pirate adventure *Mutiny at Crossbow Bay.* Praising Burgess's *Teddy Time,* a *Publishers Weekly* reviewer noted that the book "encourages telling time" through a simple, repetitive rhyming text. His other self-illustrated books include the four-part "Hannah's Hotel" series, about a holiday establishment run by Hannah Hedge-hog, Mollie Mouse, Sam Squirrel, and hardworking handyman Rodney Rabbit.

Biographical and Critical Sources

PERIODICALS

Publishers Weekly, March 12, 2001, review of *Teddy Time,* p. 93.

School Arts, October, 2000, Ken Marantz, review of *Dog's Night,* p. 64.

School Library Journal, July, 2000, Patricia Mahoney Brown, review of *Dog's Night,* p. 80.

ONLINE

Mark Burgess Web site, http://www.markburgess.co.uk (October 22, 2004).*

C

CHRISTENSEN, Bonnie 1951-

Personal

Born January 23, 1951, in Saranac Lake, NY; daughter of Wallace (a forest economist) and Theo (a homemaker) Christensen; children: Emily Herder. *Education:* University of Vermont, B.A. *Hobbies and other interests:* Travel, printing history, playing violin.

Addresses

Home—601C Dalton Dr., Colchester, VT 05446. *Agent*—Marcia Wernick, Sheldon Fogelman Agency, 10 East 40th St., New York, NY 10016. *E-mail*—btc@together.net.

Career

Author, illustrator, and playwright. Formerly worked for New York theatre, then Screen Actors Guild and Paramount Pictures. St. Michael's College, Colchester, VT, drawing instructor, 1995—. *Exhibitions:* Work shown at Society of Illustrators, New York, NY; Scuola Internazionale di Grafica, Venice, Italy; Line Gallery, Linlithgow, Scotland; Firehouse Gallery, Burlington, VT; and International Youth Library, Munich, Germany.

Member

Society of Children's Book Writers and Illustrators.

Writings

FOR CHILDREN; SELF-ILLUSTRATED

An Edible Alphabet, Dial (New York, NY), 1994.
Rebus Riot, Dial (New York, NY), 1997.
Woody Guthrie: Poet of the People, Knopf (New York, NY), 2001.
The Daring Nelly Bly: America's Star Reporter, Knopf (New York, NY), 2003.

(Editor) *In My Grandmother's House: Award-winning Authors Tell Stories about Their Grandmothers* (for young adults), HarperCollins (New York, NY), 2003.

ILLUSTRATOR

Joseph A. Citro, *Green Mountain Ghosts, Ghouls, and Unsolved Mysteries* (for adults), Houghton Mifflin (Boston, MA), 1994.
Shelley Moore Thomas, *Putting the World to Sleep,* Houghton Mifflin (Boston, MA), 1995.
Stephen Krensky, *Breaking into Print: Before and after the Invention of the Printing Press,* Little, Brown (Boston, MA), 1996.
John Steinbeck, *The Grapes of Wrath* (for adults), Folio Society (London, England), 1998.
Craig Crist-Evans, *Moon over Tennessee: A Boy's Civil War Journal,* Houghton Mifflin (Boston, MA), 1999.

OTHER

Author of plays produced off-off-Broadway, c. 1970s, Contributor to periodicals, including *Vermont Life, Vermont, National Gardening,* and *LadyBug,* among other periodicals. Contributor to *Endgrain: Contemporary Wood Engraving in North America,* 1994.

Sidelights

Author and illustrator Bonnie Christensen began her career in children's literature in the mid-1990s, and since 2000 has brought the life of enigmatic Americans into focus for younger readers through such self-illustrated picture books as *Woody Guthrie: Poet of the People* and *The Daring Nelly Bly: America's Star Reporter.* Her first book for young readers was *An Edible Alphabet,* which appeared in 1994. The work is an abecedarium, or alphabet book, for primary graders in which each of the twenty-six letters are represented by a food item. The book is also unusual in that Christensen borrows terms from other languages for the more unusual letters—instead of the usual xylophone or X-ray for the letter X, she introduces Xanthorhiza, the term for an edible root used in homeopathic medicine. Her colored woodcut illustrations depict both the item itself and a way in which people might use it. The apple page, for instance, shows an adult and a child using a cider press. Many illustrations are set in gardens, such as the urban rooftop garden that is home to the fig tree she draws for the letter F. In another section Christensen explains the process of woodcut printing and its origins in the seventeenth century. She also includes an appendix with a brief entry for each plant, and cautions her young readers that not all plants and berries are edible.

An Edible Alphabet won Christensen praise for her imaginative visuals. "The effect is striking," maintained Carolyn Jenks in *School Library Journal,* dubbing the volume "beautiful as well as interesting." Writing for *Booklist,* Hazel Rochman described Christensen's debut effort as a work "with an extraordinary sense of depth," and particularly rife with "images [that] celebrate our connection with food that grows on the land." A *Publishers Weekly* commentator also praised Christensen's efforts, terming *An Edible Alphabet* "thoughtfully designed and masterfully executed."

Another work written and illustrated by Christensen is *Rebus Riot,* which contains fifteen poems in rebus form. A rebus is a riddle in which the reader must decipher a series of images whose sounds represent a different word or syllable. Some of the rhymes featured involve food, while others center around other themes such as transportation or animals. Christensen introduces difficult words to her young readers—"shallot" and "tapir" among them—and also provides nearby solutions for her riddles as well. In the *School Library Journal,* Patricia Pearl Dole termed the verse "clever, imaginative, and hilarious," and the illustrations "full of action and humor," and predicted that even adult readers will derive enjoyment from *Rebus Riot.* In a critique for *Horn Book,* Nancy Vasilakis praised Christensen's "deft visual puns and sprightly rhymes," as well as for images that are "as inviting as the verses themselves."

Christensen has also provided pictures for texts by other writers, including Joseph A. Citro's *Green Mountain Ghosts, Ghouls, and Unsolved Mysteries* and *Putting the World to Sleep,* by Shelley Moore Thomas. In Thomas's bedtime story, the author relates the tale of a child being lulled to sleep by his mother's song, while a little girl does the same for her teddy bear nearby. Ruth K. MacDonald, reviewing the book in *School Library Journal,* offered particular praise for the watercolor hues and variegated images ranging from indoor coziness to a majestic night sky that, the critic asserted, provide a "sense of movement, of stately rejoicing in the coming of night."

For the pages of Stephen Krensky's *Breaking into Print: Before and after the Invention of the Printing Press,* Christensen created wood engravings and painted borders. Aimed at ages seven to ten, this title explains and illustrates how books were painstakingly copied by hand before the invention of the printing press by Johann Gutenberg in the 1400s. The author and illustrator then detail just how radically that innovation impacted the world. Reviews of *Breaking into Print* commended the quality of its design and execution. *School Library Journal* contributor Shirley Wilton maintained that the author and illustrator's talents blend to create a handsomely designed and highly successful introduction to what is generally viewed as Western civilization's most significant achievement.

In 2001 Christensen published her first self-illustrated biography, *Woody Guthrie: Poet of the People.* "This picture-book biography masterfully blends the elements of two genres," Betty Carter declared in *Horn Book,* adding that the book "is well told, perfectly paced, and beautifully illustrated." As Christensen's text and illustrations depict the noted folk musician's life, the words to all seven verses of Guthrie's most famous song, "This Land Is Your Land" frame the spreads in a hand-lettered border. Christensen's "dramatic mixed media, woodcut-like illustrations," as a *Kirkus Reviews* contributor described them, were perhaps the most-praised aspect of this book. Writing in *Booklist,* GraceAnne A. DeCandido called them "sinewy and emotionally compelling," while a *Publishers Weekly* reviewer wrote that, with their earth tones, Christensen's works "creatively evoke the period and the variegated landscapes" through which Guthrie moved.

The Daring Nellie Bly: America's Star Reporter profiles the famous journalist, who was born Elizabeth Jane Cochran in 1864. As Nellie Bly, she traveled the world breaking important stories at a time when any type of female newspaper reporter, even a much less serious one, was an oddity. Christensen explains some of Bly's more famous work, including her tour as a war correspondent in World War I and her efforts to expose the deplorable conditions in which female factory workers and insane asylum inmates were forced to survive. (She actually had herself committed to an asylum to get the latter story!) In 1889 she set out to travel around the world in under eighty days and succeeded, completing the circuit in seventy-two. "Appropriately enough" in light of these exploits, Sue Morgan wrote in *School Library Journal,* "this terrific biography reads like an adventure story." "Younger readers may lack the historical context to appreciate the nature of Bly's crusades," thought a *Publishers Weekly* critic, but they "will come away with an appreciation of her many feats." Christensen has also edited a book for older readers. Featuring original illustrations, *In My Grandmother's House: Award-winning Authors Tell Stories about Their Grandmothers* includes personal essays by twelve famous writers, among them Beverly Cleary, author of the "Ramona" books; Native American author Cynthia Leitich Smith; Minfong Ho, creator of *Sing to the Dawn* and *Rice without Rain;* Cuban picture-book author Alma Flor Ada; and author/illustrator Pat Cummings. Each woman takes a different perspective on her grandmother

In this 2003 work Christensen collects autobiographical stories from noted authors such as Beverly Cleary, Alma Flor Ada, and Beverley Naidoo that focus on the special relationship between children and their grandparents.

and the older woman's role in her life. Some write from a child's perspective, while others view their grandmother through the eyes of an adult woman. Interestingly, many of the writers, looking back as adults, see their grandmothers, not as variations on a simple, cookie-baking stereotype, but as complex women who were once young themselves. *Booklist* reviewer Gillian Engberg termed *In My Grandmother' House* "a fine collection that will encourage teens to reflect on their own families and recognize the individuals behind the family roles." A *Kirkus Reviews* critic, while also praising the tales as "deeply moving," noted that most "require an adult perspective to be appreciated fully."

Discussing her career, Christensen once explained to *Something about the Author:* "After college I worked in New York theater including Joe Papp's Public Theatre, New York Shakespeare Festival, Actor's Studio, Chelsea Theater, and Stella Adler Studio. Eventually playwriting became my main focus. A few of the plays actually saw the light of day off-off Broadway. During that time, I worked for Screen Actors Guild and then Paramount Pictures.

"While in New York I studied wood engraving with John Depol and attended classes at Parsons School of Design and Center for Book Arts. I returned to Vermont and focused on wood engraving, exhibiting prints locally, and was offered my first illustration work. Through a keen interest in printmaking and letterpress printing I eventually hand-printed and bound a limited-edition book. Desire to see that book reach a wider audience eventually led me to trade publishers and initiated my career."

Biographical and Critical Sources

PERIODICALS

Booklist, January 15, 1994, Hazel Rochman, review of *An Edible Alphabet,* p. 932; October 15, 1996, Ilene Cooper, review of *Breaking into Print: Before and after the Invention of the Printing Press,* pp. 426-27; May 15, 1997, Susan Dove Lempke, review of *Rebus Riot* p. 1577; September 1, 2001, GraceAnne A. DeCandido, review of *Woody Guthrie: Poet of the People,* p. 98; June 1, 2003, Gillian Engberg, review of *In My Grandmother' House: Award-winning Authors Tell Stories about Their Grandmothers,* p. 1757; September 1, 2003, GraceAnne A. DeCandido, review of *The Daring Nellie Bly: America's Star Reporter,* p. 117.

Horn Book, January-February, 1996, Elizabeth S. Watson, review of *Putting the World to Sleep,* pp. 68-69; May-June, 1997, Nancy Vasilakis, review of *Rebus Riot,* pp. 336-337; January-February, 2002, Betty Carter, review of *Woody Guthrie,* p. 93; September-October, 2003, Betty Carter, review of *The Daring Nellie Bly,* pp. 626-627.

Kirkus Reviews, October 15, 2001, review of *Woody Guthrie,* p. 1480; March 1, 2003, review of *In My Grandmother's House,* pp. 380-381; September 15, 2003, review of *The Daring Nellie Bly,* p. 1172.

Publishers Weekly, December 13, 1993, review of *An Edible Alphabet,* p. 69; September 11, 1995, review of *Putting the World to Sleep,* p. 85; October 8, 2001, review of *Woody Guthrie,* p. 62; November 10, 2003, review of *The Daring Nellie Bly,* p. 61.

School Library Journal, May, 1994, Carolyn Jenks, review of *An Edible Alphabet,* p. 107; October, 1995, Ruth K. MacDonald, review of *Putting the World to Sleep,* pp. 120-121; October, 1996, Shirley Wilton, review of *Breaking into Print,* pp. 114-115; March, 1997, Patricia Pearl Dole, review of *Rebus Riot,* p. 149; October, 2001, Kathleen Simonetta, review of *Woody Guthrie,* pp. 136-137; May, 2003, Susan Oliver, review of *In My Grandmother's House,* p. 164; October, 2003, Sue Morgan, review of *The Daring Nellie Bly,* p. 146.

Teacher Librarian, September, 1998, Jessica Higgs, review of *Rebus Riot,* p. 51.

Teaching Music, October, 2003, review of *Woody Guthrie,* p. 76.

ONLINE

Bonnie Christensen Home Page, http://www.bonnie christensen.com (February 4, 2005).

In Lisa Broadie Cook's **Martin MacGregor's Snowman**, *a young boy who holds the record for making the largest snowman in town is forced to hone his snowman-making skills with substitute materials when the real show refuses to fall. (Illustration by Adam McCauley.)*

* * *

COFFIN, M. T.
See STANLEY, George Edward

* * *

COOK, Lisa Broadie

Personal
Female.

Addresses
Home—Boone, IA. *Agent*—c/o Author Mail, Walker & Company, 104 Fifth Ave., New York, NY 10011.

Career
Teacher and writer.

Writings

The Author on My Street, illustrated by Jeanne Friar, Richard C. Owen Publishers (Katonah, NY), 2001.
Martin MacGregor's Snowman, illustrated by Adam Mc-Cauley, Walker Books (New York, NY), 2003.

Sidelights
Lisa Broadie Cook is a teacher who has two published children's books to her credit. In *The Author on My Street* she shows young readers that writers are regular, everyday people who have a knack for seeing stories in even the most commonplace things.Cook's second book, *Martin MacGregor's Snowman,* was inspired by a life spent in northern climes—Cook reported on her Web site that she has lived in Kansas, Ohio, Pennsylvania, and Iowa—and introduces readers to a young boy named Martin. Known throughout the neighborhood for building the biggest snowman the year before, Martin can't wait for the winter snow to fall so he can once again start building. He so intensely anticipates the season's first snowfall, in fact, that he creates snow-like scenes wherever he can, even gluing cotton balls to the family dog and arranging the marshmallows in his hot chocolate in the shape of a snowman. Cook "humorously conveys the intensity of longing for something elusive" by depicting Martin "as a suffering artist who (until the last moment) works in everything but his desired medium" commented a reviewer for *Publishers Weekly,* while Joy Fleishhacker called *Martin MacGregor's Snowman* "a fun choice for snow dreamers."

Biographical and Critical Sources

PERIODICALS

Kirkus Reviews, October 1, 2003, review of *Martin MacGregor's Snowman,* p. 1221.
Publishers Weekly, November 24, 2003, review of *Martin MacGregor's Snowman,* p. 64.

Lisa Broadie Cook

School Library Journal, October, 2003, Joy Fleishhacker, review of *Martin MacGregor's Snowman,* p. 116.

ONLINE

Lisa Broadie Cook Web site, http://www.lisabroadiecook. com (October 22, 2004).

*   *   *

COOPER, Elisha 1971-

Personal

Born February 22, 1971, in New Haven, CT; son of Peter (a lawyer and farmer) and Diana (a writer and farmer) Cooper. *Education:* Yale College, B.A., 1993.

Addresses

Home—77-A Tamalpais Rd., Berkeley, CA 94708. *Agent*—Darhansoff & Verrill Literary Agency, 179 Franklin St., 4th Fl., New York, NY.

Career

New Yorker magazine, messenger, 1993-95; writer and artist, 1995—.

Writings

FOR CHILDREN; SELF-ILLUSTRATED

Country Fair, Greenwillow (New York, NY), 1997.
Ballpark, Greenwillow (New York, NY), 1998.
Building, Greenwillow (New York, NY), 1999.
Henry, Chronicle Books (San Francisco, CA), 1999.
Dance!, Greenwillow (New York, NY), 2001.
Ice Cream, Greenwillow (New York, NY), 2002.
Magic Thinks Big, Greenwillow (New York, NY), 2004.
A Good Night Walk, Orchard Books (New York, NY), 2005.

OTHER

A Year in New York, City and Company (New York, NY), 1995.
Off the Road: An American Sketchbook, Villard (New York, NY), 1997.
A Day at Yale, Yale Bookstore (New Haven, CT), 1998.
California: A Sketchbook, Chronicle Books (San Francisco, CA), 2000.
Paris Night and Day: From the Marais to the Café, Impressions from the City of Lights, Artisan (New York, NY), 2002.

Sidelights

Author and illustrator Elisha Cooper once told *Something about the Author* (*SATA*): "I grew up drawing cows. In the fields below our house there was a herd of

Elisha Cooper

Cooper's energetic watercolor-and-ink illustrations reflect the excitement and dedication of a group of dance students in his 2001 picture book Dance!

Jerseys, and when I was three or four I sat on our porch with pencils and paper and tried to sketch them. The results were pretty lousy, or so I thought at the time, and I remember having tantrums and ripping up the drawings when they didn't look exactly right.

"When I got older, my best friend and I started a lawn-mowing business; we took the money we made and went on trips. I disliked cameras—more accurately, I disliked the loud, splashy tourists who used them—so I kept notebooks and wrote down things we saw, what we ate, smells. My mother gave me a tin of watercolors (the same one I use now) and I took that on my trips, too. At home I read a lot, especially *Tintin* and *Asterix*. I took books and newspapers on walks with my goats.

"When I was at Yale and playing football, I brought sketch books with me on road trips. I also wrote for the *New Journal,* a magazine, usually about things I had done, like bottling beer at a factory or playing in a game. I spent the summer before my senior year in Idaho working for the Forest Service—inspired by Norman Maclean's short stories—and wrote in a notebook and missed my friends. When I graduated and came to New York, I took a sketchbook along on the subway when I made deliveries as a messenger for the *New Yorker* magazine. That became my first book, *A Year in New York.* I think at this time I fell in love with books, and with New York. They both have a richness to them. Then I quit my job and drove around the country, sleep-

ing in the front seat, showering in rivers, and seeing what I could find. That book was called *Off the Road: An American Sketchbook.*

"I think most kids' books are stories. I like reading stories, but can't write them. I write what I see. For my first two kids' books, I spent a fall hanging out at country fairs and ballparks. I like nosing around and looking for the weird, something that hits me, a goofy gesture."

Cooper's penchant for "nosing around" has paid off for readers of *Country Fair,* his illustrated look at one day in the life of the popular rural event, from corn-shucking to award-winning cows. *Booklist* reviewer Susan Dove Lempke called the work "as removed from big, splashy preschool books as it can be. It is brimming with tiny, precisely described moments." Lolly Robinson wrote in *Horn Book:* "The small size of this book and the quiet honesty of text and art indicate a book that will be shared one-on-one and frequently revisited by children who enjoy an amiable ramble." A *Kirkus Reviews* critic called Cooper's work "a quirky, engaging look at the sights, sounds, and scents of a country fair."

Cooper next turned his gaze to baseball, for his book *Ballpark.* A *Kirkus Reviews* critic noted the author/ illustrator's attention to detail and his ability to evoke the baseball experience and share it with everyone, writing that, "Sports fan or not, spectators or athletes, children will be engaged for the full nine innings."

Elizabeth Bush, reviewing the book for the *Bulletin of the Center for Children's Books,* noted Cooper's "tidy phrasing . . . and restrained humor" in recommending *Ballpark* as "an elegant visual presentation."

Cooper acknowledges his penchant for reporting on a particular event—be it a fair or a ballgame—but only up to a point. "I think of myself as a lazy journalist," he once told *SATA.* "If I were more serious, I'd write long pieces with lots of facts. I read too much, the *New York Times* and *Calvin and Hobbes.*

"In some way, I've never evolved. I'm most happy when I'm about to set off on a trip with a sketchbook in my back pocket. There's a lot of cool stuff out there. For me, books are a way of looking. I still have tantrums when I can't draw cows."

In *Building* Cooper depicts a vacant lot's transformation into a building. He combines simple illustrations of construction workers and equipment with text that at times reads sideways or upside down. A *Publishers Weekly* reviewer praised Cooper's "signature pleasing balance between the factual and the whimsical," describing the book as a "cheerful tribute" to building construction. *Horn Book* contributor Lolly Robinson described the "measured pace and detail-oriented approach" as akin to that of the author/illustrator's previous works, but found the illustrations somewhat lacking, noting that, "Occasionally, Cooper's loose style makes it difficult to decipher objects." While Lauren Peterson of *Booklist* concluded that the book is well written and presents the information in easily understood language, she noted that because of the small

text, the book's "overall design doesn't particularly lend itself to a young audience." Critics embraced *Dance!* for its expressive illustrations, simple text, and introduction to the process of rehearsal and training. The book focuses not on the performance and the costumes, but instead on the dancers as they learn new steps and practice new routines. K. C. Patrick, writing in *Dance* magazine, commented that the illustrations "almost move." In *Horn Book,* Robinson wrote, "With an economy of line and color, Cooper conjures up pain and grace, hard work and camaraderie, stillness and velocity." While applauding Cooper's delightful illustrations, Kelly Milner Halls observed in *Booklist* that this "sensitive" treatment of dance is more than the "usual dreams of pink tutus and toe shoes." Most critics enjoyed the creative text placement throughout the book, as Cooper's words wind and meander across the pages. Catherine Threadgill of *School Library Journal* however, found it distracting. Still, she concluded that overall, *Dance!* "successfully provides inquisitive children with a believable vicarious experience." In *Publishers Weekly,* a reviewer noted Cooper's "spontaneous, lyrical narrative," adding that the portrayal of "the many steps leading up to the grand event are deserving of enthusiastic applause."

Ice Cream centers on another favorite subject of childhood. Here, Cooper explains how ice cream is made, from grazing cows to a truck loaded with packed gallons of ice cream. Reviews of the book were favorable, applauding the book's playful text and illustrations, along with Cooper's engaging use of language. In *Publishers Weekly,* a reviewer commented that not only is the book informative as it relates "specifics that may

Magic the cat may be a little overweight, but that doesn't stop him from aspiring to acts of cat-greatness in Cooper's sly and engaging picture book **Magic Thinks Big.**

surprise even the most ardent aficionados," but it is fun to read. The reviewer observed that "readers can hear the sounds in the barn at milking time" and that the "small-scale art precisely follows each step." Blair Christolon, writing in *School Library Journal,* praised both the appearance of the book and the content; he noted that the author's "sense of humor finds its way into the pages" and that it is "an excellent vocabulary enhancer." In *Horn Book,* Robinson wrote that "Cooper balances the relevant facts with his folksy, child-centered descriptions of minutiae." *Booklist* reviewer Diane Foote found that while the drawings are "appealing," they lack sufficient "detail for curious readers." nonetheless, she added, "Creative type placement in spirals, loops, and curves adds interest." Offering a completely different look and feel from Cooper's standard picture-book fare, *Magic Thinks Big* is about a large housecat whose imagination takes him on adventures he is too contented to pursue. Praising the book's fun story, *Horn Book* reviewer Susan Dove Lempke also commented, "In contrast to Elisha Cooper's previous picture books, with their tiny pictures and copious white space, the pictures here fill each page almost to the edges." In a review for *School Library Journal,* Julie Roach commented on the strength of the book's story and illustrations: "The simple text is full of dry humor and whimsy. The dreamy pencil-and-watercolor illustrations are a pleasing mixture of soft colors and thick lines." In *Publishers Weekly,* a reviewer described the illustrations as "spare [and] wryly understated," while also praising "Cooper's clever use of the hypothetical and his story's fittingly languid tone." "Cooper has captured feline behavior and attitude to a T in both story and art," declared a *Kirkus Reviews* contributor, who dubbed *Magic Thinks Big* "totally charming."

Biographical and Critical Sources

PERIODICALS

Booklist, September 1, 1997, Susan Dove Lempke, review of *Country Fair,* p. 240; June 1, 1999, Lauren Peterson, review of *Building,* p. 1832; September 15, 2001, Kelly Milner Halls, review of *Dance!* p. 217; May 15, 2002, Diane Foote, review of *Ice Cream,* p. 1598.

Bulletin of the Center for Children's Books, March 1998, Elizabeth Bush, review of *Ballpark,* p. 239.

Dance, December, 2001, K. C. Patrick, review of *Dance!* p. 77.

Horn Book, September-October, 1997, Lolly Robinson, review of *Country Fair,* p. 554; May 1999, Lolly Robinson, review of *Building,* p. 312; November-December, 2001, Lolly Robinson, review of *Dance!* pp. 733-734; May-June, 2002, Lolly Robinson, review of *Ice Cream,* p. 343; May-June, 2004, Susan Dove Lempke, review of *Magic Thinks Big,* p. 309.

Kirkus Reviews, June 15, 1997, review of *Country Fair,* pp. 947-948; February 15, 1998, review of *Ballpark,* p. 265; April 1, 2004, review of *Magic Thinks Big,* p. 326.

Publishers Weekly, March 15, 1999, review of *Building,* p. 57; July 30, 2001, review of *Dance!* p. 84; February 18, 2002, review of *Ice Cream,* p. 96; April 12, 2004, review of *Magic Thinks Big,* p. 64.

School Library Journal, September, 2001, Catherine Threadgill, review of *Dance!* p. 212; May, 2002, Blair Christolon, review of *Ice Cream,* p. 136; April, 2004, Julie Roach, review of *Magic Thinks Big,* pp. 103-104.*

*   *   *

CORNELIUS, Kay 1933-

Personal

Born January 14, 1933, in Memphis, TN; married an aerospace contracts specialist; children: two. *Ethnicity:* "Caucasian." *Education:* George Peabody College of Vanderbilt University, B.A.; Alabama A & M University, M.Ed. *Politics:* "Independent." *Religion:* "Southern Baptist." *Hobbies and other interests:* Knitting, travel.

Addresses

Agent—c/o Author Mail, Chelsea House Publishers, 1974 Sproul Rd., Ste. 400, Broomall, PA 19008. *E-mail*—kaycorn@hiwaay.net.

Career

Teacher in Huntsville, AL, 1956-86; teacher at a magnet school, 1986-90; writer.

Member

Romance Writers of America, Authors Guild, National League of American PEN Women, Novelists, Inc., Alabama Writers Conclave, Alabama Writers Forum, Phi Delta Kappa, Delta Kappa Gamma.

Awards, Honors

Sullivan Award, Peabody College, 1952.

Writings

A Matter of Security, Barbour Publishing Co. (Ulrichsville, OH), 1995.

A Nostalgic Noel, Barbour Publishing Co. (Ulrichsville, OH), 1998.

Twin Willows, Barbour Publishing Co. (Ulrichsville, OH), 1999.

The Supreme Court, Chelsea House Publishers (Philadelphia, PA), 2000.

Francis Marion: The Swamp Fox, Chelsea House Publishers (Philadelphia, PA), 2001.

Chamique Holdsclaw, Chelsea House Publishers (Philadelphia, PA), 2001.

Kay Cornelius

Edgar Allan Poe, Chelsea House Publishers (Philadelphia, PA), 2002.

Emily Dickinson, Chelsea House Publishers (Philadelphia, PA), 2002.

Pennsylvania, Barbour Publishing Co. (Ulrichsville, OH), 2002.

Love's Gentle Journey, Barbour Publishing Co. (Ulrichsville, OH), 2002.

Toni's Vow, Heartsong Presents (Uhrichsville, OH), 2003.

Anita's Fortune, Heartsong Presents (Ulrichsville, OH), 2004.

Mary's Choice, Barbour Publishing Co. (Ulrichsville, OH), 2004.

Alabama (novel collection), Barbour Publishing Co. (Ulrichsville, OH), 2004.

The Bell Witch Phenomenon, Barbour Publishing Co. (Ulrichsville, OH), 2005.

Contributor to anthology *Promises and Prayers for the Military,* Barbour Publishing, 2004. Contributor to periodicals, including *Alabama Heritage, Tennessee Historical Quarterly, Tennessee Encyclopedia of History, Alabama Writing Teacher, Alabama Writers' Forum, Journal of Doublespeak, Event, Daily Blessing, Peabody Post,* and *Alabama Alitcom.*

Work in Progress

Summons to the Chateau d'Arc, for Five Star.

Sidelights

Young-adult author Kay Cornelius has had a passion for words ever since she was a little girl growing up in the south. Today she is the author of novels for both adults and younger readers as well as works of nonfiction reflecting her interest in history. Her books include the juvenile biographies *Francis Marion; The Swamp Fox* and *Chamique Holdsclaw* as well as the historical novels *Love's Gentle Journey, Anita's Fortune,* and *Twin Willows,* all of which are Christian romances. Carolyn Janssen, writing in *School Library Journal,* praised *Francis Marion* for its "lively" narrative focusing on the man who led the British cavalry into the muck and mire of a South Carolina swamp during the American Revolution.

Prior to writing full time, Cornelius worked as an English teacher up until her retirement in 1990. She also wrote test units for the PSAT and College Board specialized-subject achievement tests, as well as reviewing the Board's English literature examination. As she told *Something about the Author:* "Like most authors, I was read to long before I started to school. Born Southern, I was surrounded by natural storytellers,

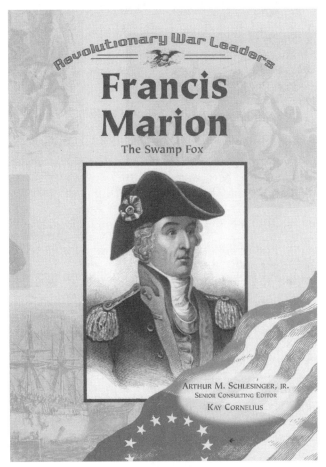

Drawing on letters and other original documents, Cornelius introduces readers to Revolutionary War leader General Francis Marion, who led the South Carolina militia to victory against the British in sometimes difficult terrain and gained the name "the swamp fox."

and since my father ran the local 'picture show,' I also absorbed hundreds of movies. I loved working with words and finding new ways to express myself, so it was only natural that after winning a four-year college scholarship for a 750-word essay in a national contest, I should major in English and become a teacher.

"While I continued to write sporadically, my present writing career grew out of my participation in the National Writing Project at Auburn University in 1981. The intensive writing led me to combine my love of historical research and story-telling to produce my first novel, *Love's Gentle Journey.* Since its publication in 1985, it has been almost constantly in print. After I retired from teaching in 1990, I started writing full-time. I approach each new project with prospective readers in mind. I want my work to be entertaining as well as informative and inspiring.

"It's satisfying to conduct writing workshops and mentor authors. I tell them writing is hard work, but seeing their name in print on something that will live on after they are gone is well worth the effort."

Biographical and Critical Sources

PERIODICALS

Publishers Weekly, January 18, 1999, review of *Twin Willows,* p. 336.
School Library Journal, July, 2001, Carolyn Janssen, review of *Francis Marion: The Swamp Fox,* p. 118.

ONLINE

Heartsong Presents Web site, http://www.heartsong presents.com/ (October 22, 2004).

*   *   *

CROSBY, Margaret
See RATHMANN, Peggy

*   *   *

CUSHMAN, Doug 1953-

Personal

Born May 4, 1953, in Springfield, OH. *Education:* Attended Paier School of Art, 1971-75. *Hobbies and other interests:* Cooking, kayaking, reading.

Addresses

Home—Redding, CA, and Paris, France. *Agent*—c/o HarperCollins Children's Books, 1350 Avenue of the Americas, New York, NY 10019. *E-mail*—aunteater@ aol.com.

Doug Cushman

Career

Apprentice to book illustrator Mercer Mayer, 1975-77; writer and illustrator, 1977—. Instructor at Paier College of Art, 1980, and Southern Connecticut State University, 1981—.

Member

Society of Children's Book Writers and Illustrators, National Cartoonists Society, Mystery Writers of America.

Awards, Honors

Reuben Award for Book Illustration, National Cartoonists Society, 1996; Christopher Award, 2005.

Writings

FOR CHILDREN; SELF-ILLUSTRATED

(Compiler) *Giants* (stories and poems), Platt & Munk (New York, NY), 1980.
(Compiler) *Trolls* (stories), Platt & Munk (New York, NY), 1981.
(Compiler) *Once upon a Pig,* Platt & Munk (New York, NY), 1982.
Nasty Kyle the Crocodile, Grosset & Dunlap (New York, NY), 1983.
Mickey Takes a Bow, Little, Brown (Boston, MA), 1986.
Aunt Eater Loves a Mystery, Harper & Row (New York, NY), 1987.
The Missing Mystery, Checkerboard (New York, NY), 1987.
Uncle Foster's Hat Tree, Dutton (New York, NY), 1988.
Mouse and Mole, Grosset & Dunlap (New York, NY), 1989.

Possum Stew, Dutton (New York, NY), 1990.

Camp Big Paw, Harper & Row (New York, NY), 1990.

Aunt Eater's Mystery Vacation, HarperCollins (New York, NY), 1992.

The ABC Mystery, HarperCollins (New York, NY), 1993.

Mouse and Mole and the Year-Round Garden, Scientific American Books for Young Readers (New York, NY), 1994.

Mouse and Mole and the Christmas Walk, Scientific American Books for Young Readers (New York, NY), 1994.

Mouse and Mole and the All-Weather Train Ride, Scientific American Books for Young Readers (New York, NY), 1995.

Aunt Eater's Mystery Christmas, HarperCollins (New York, NY), 1995.

The Mystery of King Karfu, HarperCollins (New York, NY), 1996.

Aunt Eater's Mystery Halloween, HarperCollins (New York, NY), 1998.

The Mystery of the Monkey's Maze, HarperCollins (New York, NY), 1999.

Inspector Hopper, HarperCollins (New York, NY), 2000.

Inspector Hopper's Mystery Year, HarperCollins (New York, NY), 2003.

Space Cat, HarperCollins (New York, NY), 2004.

Mystery at the Club Sandwich, Clarion (New York, NY), 2004.

ILLUSTRATOR

H. L. Ross, *Not Counting Monsters,* Platt & Munk (New York, NY), 1978.

Lillie Patterson, *Haunted Houses on Halloween,* Garrard (Champaign, IL), 1979.

Elizabeth Norine Upham, *Little Brown Bear,* Platt & Munk (New York, NY), 1979.

F. Kaff, *Monster for a Day; or, The Monster in Gregory's Pajamas,* Gingerbread House (Westhampton Beach, NY), 1979.

Leonard Kessler, *The Silly Mother Hubbard,* Garrard (Champaign, IL), 1980.

Leonard Kessler, *Hickory Dickory Dock,* Garrard (Champaign, IL), 1980.

Michaela Muntean, *Bicycle Bear,* Parents Magazine Press (New York, NY), 1983.

The Pudgy Fingers Counting Book, Grosset & Dunlap (New York, NY), 1983.

Ida Luttrell, *Tillie and Mert,* Harper (New York, NY), 1985.

Suzanne Gruber, *Chatty Chipmunk's Nutty Day,* Troll (Mahwah, NJ), 1985.

Michael J. Pellowski, *Benny's Bad Day,* Troll (Mahwah, NJ), 1986.

Jack Long, *The Secret of the Nile,* Checkerboard (New York, NY), 1987.

Jack Long, *The Sunken Treasure,* Checkerboard (New York, NY), 1987.

Jack Long, *The Vanishing Professor,* Checkerboard (New York, NY), 1987.

Rose Greydanus, *Bedtime Story,* Troll (Mahwah, NJ), 1988.

C. S. White, *The Monsters' Counting Book,* Platt & Munk (New York, NY), 1988.

Sharon Gordon, *The Jolly Monsters,* Troll (Mahwah, NJ), 1988.

Terry Webb Harshman, *Porcupine's Pajama Party,* Harper & Row (New York, NY), 1988.

Melanie Martin, *Itsy-Bitsy Giant,* Troll (Mahwah, NJ), 1989.

Michael J. Pellowski, *Mixed-up Magic,* Troll (Mahwah, NJ), 1989.

Dorothy Corey, *A Shot for Baby Bear,* Albert Whitman (Morton Grove, IL), 1989.

Thomas P. Lewis, *Frida's Office Day,* Harper & Row (New York, NY), 1989.

Michaela Munteen, *Bicycle Bear Rides Again,* Parents Magazine (New York, NY), 1989.

Marcia Leonard, *The Three Little Pigs,* Silver Press (Parsippany, NJ), 1990.

Marcia Leonard, *The Elves and the Shoemaker,* Silver Press (Parsippany, NJ), 1990.

Teresa Noel Celsi, *The Fourth Little Pig,* Raintree (Milwaukee, WI), 1990.

Michael Berenstain, *1 + 1 Take Away Two!,* Western (Racine, WI), 1991.

Lois G. Grambling, *An Alligator Named Alligator,* Barron's (Hauppauge, NY), 1991.

Joan Davenport Carris, *Aunt Morbelia and the Screaming Skulls,* Little, Brown (Boston, MA), 1992.

William H. Hooks, *How Do You Make a Bubble?,* Bantam (New York, NY), 1992.

William H. Hooks, *Feed Me! An Aesop Fable,* Bantam (New York, NY), 1992.

Gary Richmond, *The Early Bird,* Word Publishing (Dallas, TX), 1992.

Naomi Baltuck, *Crazy Gibberish: And Other Story-Hour Stretches from a Storyteller's Bag of Tricks,* Linnets Books (Hamden, CT), 1993.

Mary Packard, *The Witch Who Couldn't Fly,* Troll (Mahwah, NJ), 1994.

Patricia Lakin, *Get Ready to Read,* Raintree Steck-Vaughn (Austin, TX), 1995.

Patricia Lakin, *A Good Sport,* Raintree Steck-Vaughn (Austin, TX), 1995.

Patricia Lakin, *A True Partnership,* Raintree Steck-Vaughn (Austin, TX), 1995.

Bethany Roberts, *Halloween Mice!,* Clarion (New York, NY), 1995.

Gail Herman, *Teddy Bear for Sale,* Scholastic (New York, NY), 1995.

Patricia Lakin, *The Mystery Illness,* Raintree Steck-Vaughn (Austin, TX), 1995.

Patricia Lakin, *Trash and Treasure,* Raintree Steck-Vaughn (Austin, TX), 1995.

Patricia Lakin, *Up a Tree,* Raintree Steck-Vaughn (Austin, TX), 1995.

Patricia Lakin, *Where There's Smoke,* Raintree Steck-Vaughn (Austin, TX), 1995.

Patricia Lakin, *Signs of Protest,* Raintree Steck-Vaughn (Austin, TX), 1995.

Patricia Lakin, *Aware and Alert,* Raintree Steck-Vaughn (Austin, TX), 1995.

Patricia Lakin, *A Summer Job,* Raintree Stack-Vaughn (Austin, TX), 1995.

Patricia Lakin, *Information, Please,* Raintree Steck-Vaughn (Austin, TX), 1995.

Patricia Lakin, *Red Letter Day,* Raintree Steck-Vaughn (Austin, TX), 1995.

Alice Cary, *Nat the Crab,* Open Court (Chicago, IL), 1995.

Robin Dexter, *Frogs,* Troll (Mahwah, NJ), 1996.

William H. Hooks, reteller, *Feed Me! An Aesop Fable,* Gareth Stevens (Milwaukee, WI), 1996.

Bethany Roberts, *Valentine Mice!,* Clarion (New York, NY), 1997.

Susan Goldman Rubin, *The Whiz Kids Plugged In,* Scholastic (New York, NY), 1997.

Rita Balducci, *Halloween Pigs,* WhistleStop/Troll (Mahwah, NJ), 1997.

Shelagh Canning, *The Turkey Saves the Day,* Troll (Mahwah, NJ), 1997.

Susan Goldman Rubin *The Wiz Kids Take Off!,* Scholastic (New York, NY), 1997.

Douglas Wood, *What Dads Can't Do,* Simon & Schuster (New York, NY), 2000.

Bethany Roberts, *Christmas Mice!,* Clarion (New York, NY), 2000.

Douglas Wood, *What Moms Can't Do,* Simon & Schuster (New York, NY), 2001.

Lilian Moore, *Little Raccoon,* Henry Holt (New York, NY), 2001.

Bethany Roberts, *Thanksgiving Mice!,* Clarion (New York, NY), 2001.

Joan M. Lexau, *Crocodile and Hen: A Bakongo Folktale,* HarperCollins (New York, NY), 2001.

Jane Yolen, *Animal Train,* Little Simon (New York, NY), 2002.

Douglas Wood, *What Teachers Can't Do,* Simon & Schuster (New York, NY), 2002.

Kay Winters, *But Mom, Everybody Else Does,* Dutton Children's Books (New York, NY), 2002.

Bethany Roberts, *Birthday Mice!,* Clarion Books (New York, NY), 2002.

Barbara Williams, *Albert's Impossible Toothache,* Candlewick Press (Cambridge, MA), 2003.

Bethany Roberts, *Easter Mice!,* Clarion Books (New York, NY), 2003.

John Schindel, *What Did They See?,* Henry Holt (New York, NY), 2003.

Bethany Roberts, *Halloween Mice!,* Clarion (New York, NY), 2003.

Katherine Brown Tegen, *Dracula and Frankenstein Are Friends,* HarperCollins (New York, NY), 2003.

Douglas Wood, *What Santa Can't Do,* Simon & Schuster (New York, NY), 2003.

Jacklyn Williams, *Happy Valentine's Day, Gus!,* Picture Window Books (Minneapolis, MN), 2004.

Jacklyn Williams, *Happy Easter, Gus!,* Picture Window Books (Minneapolis, MN), 2004.

Judy Sierra, *What Time Is It, Mr. Crocodile?,* Gulliver Books (Orlando, FL), 2004.

Bethany Roberts, *Fourth of July Mice!,* Clarion (New York, NY), 2004.

Karma Wilson, *Never Ever Shout in a Zoo,* Little, Brown (New York, NY), 2004.

Jacklyn Williams, *Happy Halloween, Gus!,* Picture Window Books (Minneapolis, MN), 2004.

Matt Mitter, *ABC: Alphabet Rhymes,* Gareth Stevens (Milwaukee, WI), 2004.

Matt Mitter, *1, 2, 3, Counting Rhymes,* Gareth Stevens (Milwaukee, WI), 2004.

Jacklyn Williams, *Merry Christmas Gus!,* Picture Window Books (Minneapolis, MN), 2004.

Douglas Wood, *What Grandmas Can't Do,* Simon & Schuster (New York, NY), 2005.

Susan Schafer, *Where's My Tail?,* Marshall Cavendish (New York, NY), 2005.

Shirley Mozelle, *The Bear Upstairs,* Henry Holt (New York, NY), 2005.

ILLUSTRATOR; "HANDS-ON EARLY-LEARNING SCIENCE ACTIVITIES" SERIES

Seymour Simon and Nicole Fauteux, *Let's Try It out in the Water,* Simon & Schuster (New York, NY), 2001.

Seymour Simon and Nicole Fauteux, *Let's Try It out in the Air,* Simon & Schuster (New York, NY), 2001.

Seymour Simon and Nicole Fauteux, *Let's Try It out on the Playground,* Simon & Schuster (New York, NY), 2002.

Sidelights

In the many well-received picture books that California-based author Doug Cushman has written and illustrated, his emphasis on character is evident in both text and artwork. As he once commented: "A good character will almost write a book by himself with a little nudge or two from the author." Indeed, vivid characters abound in books such as *Possum Stew,* wherein mischievous Possum ties together Bear and Gator's fishing lines, tricking the friends into believing they've hooked the "Big Catfish." When the two fall into the water trying to pull in their enormous catch, Possum sneaks off with their full baskets of fish. Wanting to even the score, Bear and Gator plan a surprise of their own for Possum. Beth Herbert, writing in *Booklist,* called *Possum Stew* a "knee-slapping tale," while a reviewer for *Kirkus Reviews* noted that the story's humor is enhanced by the "expressive faces" in Cushman's "uncluttered illustrations." *School Library Journal* contributor Sally R. Dow also commented favorably on the author/illustrator's fictional creations, maintaining that Cushman's "light-hearted" illustrations "capture the mischievous spirit of the animals."

The ABC Mystery, another of Cushman's self-illustrated stories, is an alphabet primer charged with a mystery. The letter "A" states the crime—stolen Art—and the mystery, told in rhyming couplets, continues to unfold as Detective McGroom, a badger, pursues clues attached to successive letters of the alphabet. Calling the book a "fresh approach to the ABC's," *School Library Journal* contributor Jody McCoy claimed that *The ABC Mystery* would attract children with its "bright cartoon creatures skillfully rendered." *Booklist* reviewer Deborah Abbott suggested the book be used as a "kickoff for mystery units in the primary grades," and praised Cushman's illustrations for their "touches of melodrama and humor." A *Publishers Weekly* commentator stated that repeated readings would give "budding detectives" more chances to "spot new clues," describing the picture book as a "cunning twist on the traditional ABC" primer.

Cushman has followed the success of his *ABC Mystery* with more tales of intrigue, among them *Aunt Eater's Mystery Christmas, The Mystery of King Karfu,* and *Aunt Eater's Mystery Halloween. Booklist* reviewer Linda Perkins offered high praise for *The Mystery of King Karfu,* declaring that it will "delight mystery aficionados." In this story, wombat detective Seymour Sleuth investigates a stolen stone chicken in Egypt. Seymour and Abbott Muggs, his sidekick, catch the thief after uncovering a critical clue. Cushman designed the book as an actual detective's casebook, with investigative notes, photographs, coffee stains, and business receipts (including a camel rental) all related to the investigation. Perkins noted that the illustrated details add "silliness, suspense, and intrigue." Steven Engelfried, a *School Library Journal* contributor, described the notebook as a "clear and insightful look at how a detective puts evidence together." Engelfried also noted a "clue-filled plot, plenty of humor, and an innovative presentation" that he predicted will create a demand for more "Seymour Sleuth" mysteries. In *Inspector Hopper* Cushman introduces two new sleuths, the dapperly dressed grasshopper Inspector Hopper and his sidekick, the bowler hat-wearing beetle McBugg. The book, intended for early elementary students who are just beginning to read independently, features three separate mystery tales. Mr. Ladybug's wife disappears in the first story, and does not return when he calls her: "Ladybug, Ladybug, fly away home!" However, with the help of Inspector Hopper and McBugg she is soon found, safe and sound. In the second tale, "A Boat Disappears," a mosquito named Skeet loses his leaf boat. Inspector Hopper interrogates several other insects, including the Eensy Weensy Spider and a snail who jogs, before finding the culprit: Conrad the caterpillar, who ate the small vessel. In the final installment, Inspector Hopper and McBugg track down a rat—literally—with the help of the moon. Reviewers praised the book; Maura Bresnahan, writing in *School Library Journal,* thought that "the short sentences, catchy dialogue, and repetitive vocabulary are just right for beginning readers." Other critics praised Cushman's "handsome watercolors," as Gillian Engberg described them in *Booklist,* that "will draw children in with their bug's-eye view of the world."

Inspector Hopper and McBugg return to solve another four conundrums in 2003's *Inspector Hopper's Mystery Year.* Here Cushman presents one mystery per season. First, in the fall, Emma Worm asks the detectives to help her figure out who is apparently haunting a

A super-sleuth grasshopper and his low-to-the-ground assistant, Detective McBugg, solve three cases for their insect friends in Doug Cushman's beginning chapter book Inspector Hopper.

pumpkin. In the winter a doctor disappears, rather inconveniently for Inspector Hopper as he has a cold that he would like to be treated. A young beetle-child goes missing in the spring, and in the summer, a cricket named Holly loses her sheet music; as it turns out, it was stolen by a wasp who needed materials to help him paper over a hole in his nest. Each of these four stories "is just the right length for sharing aloud or independent reading," wrote *School Library Journal* contributor Wanda Meyers-Hines, who also called the book "a fun selection for units on insects." Plus, as a *Kirkus Reviews* contributor noted, "Cushman drops visual clues to let readers participate in the solutions to the mysteries [and] sight gags to keep the stories lively."

An elephant named Nick Trunk is the detective in *Mystery at the Club Sandwich.* The book openly spoofs classic film noir detective stories such as *The Maltese Falcon;* it is even dedicated to "Sam, Phil and Dashiell"—as in the famous noir detective Sam Spade, his creator Dashiell Hammett, and Philip Marlowe, the detective created by author Raymond Chandler. As with all good noir tales, *Mystery at the Club Sandwich* opens with "trouble" walking through the door: Maggie Trouble, a cat who works at the Club Sandwich as an assistant to its star cabaret singer, Lola Gale. Gale's lucky marbles have been stolen, and she wants Nick Trunk's help in recovering them. "Readers will guess the villain early on," commented *School Library Journal* reviewer Marie Orlando, "but that won't interfere with their enjoyment of the droll story."

Cushman has also received favorable notice for the pictures he has provided for scores of works by many different authors. Among these efforts is *Valentine Mice!*, written by Bethany Roberts. In this tale, four mice celebrate a wintery Valentine's Day by passing out holiday cards to all the woodland animals. Amid all the excitement, hardly anyone notices that the youngest mouse has disappeared. "Motion-filled, festive watercolors humorously document the rescue of the missing mouse," asserted a *Publishers Weekly* reviewer. Praising the successful union of words and pictures, a *Kirkus Reviews* critic claimed the "rhythmic text and action-packed line and watercolor illustrations will draw young readers in."

Biographical and Critical Sources

PERIODICALS

Booklist, March 1, 1990, Beth Herbert, review of *Possum Stew,* p. 1338; September 15, 1990, p. 177; April 1, 1992, p. 1459; November 15, 1993, Deborah Abbott, review of *The ABC Mystery,* p. 629; April 1, 1994, Denia Hester, review of *Mouse and Mole and the Year-Round Garden,* p. 1458; January 1 & 15, 1997, Linda Perkins, review of *The Mystery of King Karfu,* p. 869; April 15, 2000, Gillian Engberg, review of *Inspector Hopper,* p. 1555; July, 2004, Carolyn Phelan, review of *Space Cat,* p. 1850; September 15, 2004, Lauren Peterson, review of *What Time Is It, Mr. Crocodile?,* p. 254.

Horn Book, July, 2000, review of *Inspector Hopper,* p. 454.

Instructor, November-December, 2001, Judy Freeman, review of *Inspector Hopper,* pp. 12-14.

Junior Bookshelf, October, 1983, p. 206.

Kirkus Reviews, January 15, 1990, review of *Possum Stew,* p. 103; March 1, 1994, p. 301; December 1, 1997, review of *Valentine Mice!,* p. 1778; March 1, 2003, review of *Inspector Hopper's Mystery Year,* p. 381; May 15, 2004, review of *Space Cat,* p. 489; September 1, 2004, review of *Mystery at the Club Sandwich,* p. 863.

Publishers Weekly, March 21, 1994, p. 71; December 1, 1997, review of *Valentine Mice!,* p. 52; August 2, 1998, review of *The ABC Mystery,* p. 78; December 13, 2004, review of *Mystery at the Club Sandwich,* p. 68.

School Library Journal, February, 1990, Sally R. Dow, review of *Possum Stew,* p. 72; July, 1992, p. 58; February, 1994, Jody McCoy, review of *The ABC Mystery,* p. 83; February, 1997, Steven Engelfried, review of *The Mystery of King Karfu,* pp. 74-75; January, 1998, p. 91; July, 2000, Maura Bresnahan, review of *Inspector Hopper,* p. 70; May, 2003, Wanda Meyers-Hines, review of *Inspector Hopper's Mystery Year,* pp. 110-111; January, 2005, Marie Orlando, review of *Mystery at the Club Sandwich,* p. 89.

ONLINE

Doug Cushman Home Page, http://www.doug-cushman.com (February 4, 2005).

D

de LINT, Charles (Henri Diederick Höefsmit) 1951-
(Samuel M. Key)

Personal

Born December 22, 1951, in Bussum, Netherlands; immigrated to Canada, 1952, naturalized citizen, 1961; son of Frederick Charles (a navigator and survey project manager) Hoefsmit and Gerardina Margaretha (a high school teacher) Hoefsmit-de Lint; married MaryAnn Harris (an artist), September 15, 1980. *Education:* Attended Aylmer and Philemen Wright high schools. *Hobbies and other interests:* Music, fine arts.

Addresses

Home and office—P.O. Box 9480, Ottawa, Ontario, Canada K1G 3V2. *Agent*—Russell Galen, Scovil Chichak Galen Literary Agency, Inc., 381 Park Avenue South, Suite 1020, New York, NY 10016. *E-mail*—cdl@cyberus.ca.

Career

Worked in various clerical and construction positions, 1967-71, and as retail clerk and manager of record stores, 1971-83; writer in Ottawa, Ontario, Canada, 1983—. Owner and editor of Triskell Press; juror for William L. Crawford Award, Canadian SF/Fantasy Award, World Fantasy Award, Theodore Sturgeon Memorial Short Fiction Award, Horror Writers of America Award, and Nebula Short Fiction Award; member of Wickentree (traditional Celtic folk music band), Ottawa, 1972-85, and Jump at the Sun (Celtic/Americana folk band).

Member

Science Fiction Writers of America, SF Canada.

Awards, Honors

William L. Crawford Award for best new fantasy author, International Association for the Fantastic in the Arts, 1984; Canadian SF/Fantasy Award ("Casper")

Charles de Lint

nominations, 1986, for *Mulengro,* and 1987, for *Yarrow;* Casper Award for best work in English, 1988, for *Jack the Giant-Killer;* Readercon Small Press Award for Best Short Work, 1989, for short story, "The Drowned Man's Reel"; Reality I Commendations, Best Fantasy Author Award, 1991; Best Books for the Teen Age list, New York Public Library, and CompuServe Science Fiction and Fantasy Forum Homer Award for Best Fantasy Novel, both 1992, both for *The Little Country;* Prix Ozone for Best Foreign Fantasy Short

Story, 1997, for "Timeskip"; Best Books for Young Adults selection, American Library Association, 1998, for *Trader;* World Fantasy Award for best collection, 2000, for *Moonlight and Vines.*

Writings

FICTION

De Grijze Roos (title means "The Grey Rose"; short stories), Een Exa Uitgave (Belgium), 1983.

The Riddle of the Wren, Ace Books (New York, NY), 1984.

Moonheart: A Romance, Ace Books (New York, NY), 1984.

The Harp of the Grey Rose, Starblaze, 1985.

Mulengro: A Romany Tale, Ace Books (New York, NY), 1985.

Yarrow: An Autumn Tale, Ace Books (New York, NY), 1986.

Ascian in Rose (novella), Axolotl Press (Eugene, OR), 1987.

Jack the Giant-Killer: A Novel of Urban Faerie, Armadillo-Ace, 1987.

Greenmantle, Ace Books (New York, NY), 1988.

Wolf Moon, New American Library (New York, NY), 1988.

Westlin Wind (novella), Axolotl Press (Eugene, OR), 1988, Tor (New York, NY), 1993.

(With others) *Philip Jose Farmer's The Dungeon: Book Three* (shared series), Byron Preiss/Bantam (New York, NY), 1988.

(With others) *Philip Jose Farmer's The Dungeon: Book Five* (shared series), Byron Preiss/Bantam (New York, NY), 1988.

Svaha, Ace Books (New York, NY), 1989, Tor (New York, NY), 1994.

Berlin (novella), Fourth Avenue Press, 1989, published in *Life on the Border,* Tor (New York, NY), 1991.

The Fair in Emain Macha, Tor (New York, NY), 1990.

Drink down the Moon: A Novel of Urban Faerie, Ace, 1990.

The Dreaming Place, illustrated by Brian Froud, Atheneum (New York, NY), 1990.

Ghostwood, illustration by Donna Gordon, Axolotl Press (Eugene, OR), 1990.

Paperjack (novella), illustrated by Judy J. King, Cheap Street (New Castle, VA), 1991.

Ghosts of Wind and Shadow (novella), Axolotl Press (Eugene, OR), 1991.

The Little Country, Morrow (New York, NY), 1991.

Spiritwalk, Tor (New York, NY), 1992.

Into the Green, Tor (New York, NY), 1993.

Dreams Underfoot: The Newford Collection, Tor (New York, NY), 1993.

The Wild Wood, Bantam Books (New York, NY), 1994.

Memory and Dream, Tor (New York, NY), 1994.

The Ivory and the Horn, Tor (New York, NY), 1995.

Jack of Kinrowan, Tor (New York, NY), 1995.

Trader, Tor (New York, NY), 1997.

Someplace to Be Flying, Tor (New York, NY), 1998.

Moonlight and Vines, Tor (New York, NY), 1999.

The Newford Stories, SF Book Club, 1999.

Triskell Tales, Subterranean Press (Burton, MI), 2000.

Forests of the Heart, Tor (New York, NY), 2000.

The Road to Lisdoonvarnia, Subterranean Press (Burton, MI), 2001.

Seven Wild Sisters, illustrated by Charles Vess, Subterranean Press (Burton, MI), 2001.

The Onion Girl, Tor (New York, NY), 2001.

Tapping the Dream Tree (stories), Tor (New York, NY), 2002.

A Handful of Coppers; Collected Early Stories, Volume One: *Heroic Fantasy,* Subterranean Press (Burton, MI), 2003.

Waifs and Strays (stories), Viking (New York, NY), 2003.

A Circle of Cats, illustrated by Charles Vess, Viking (New York, NY), 2003.

Spirits in the Wind, Tor (New York, NY), 2003.

The Blue Girl, Viking (New York, NY), 2004.

Medicine Road, illustrated by Charles Vess, Subterranean Press (Burton, MI), 2004.

Author of "The Fane of the Grey Rose" (novelette), published in *Swords against Darkness IV,* edited by Andrew J. Offutt, Zebra, 1979; *Stick,* (novella), published in *Borderland,* edited by Terri Windling and Mark Arnold, Signet (New York, NY), 1986; and coauthor of *Death Leaves an Echo* (novella) published in *Café Purgatorium,* Tor Horror (New York, NY), 1991. Work represented in anthologies, including *The Year's Best Fantasy Stories: 8,* edited by Arthur W. Saha, DAW, 1982; *Dragons and Dreams* and *Spaceships and Spells,* both edited by Jane Yolen, Martin H. Greenberg, and Charles G. Waugh, Harper, 1986 and 1987; and *The Annual Review of Fantasy and Science Fiction,* Meckler Publishing, 1988. Author of columns in horror and science-fiction magazines, including a monthly book review column in the *Magazine of Fantasy and Science Fiction;* "Urban Thrills: Reviews of Short Horror and Contemporary Fantasy Fiction," in *Short Form,* "Behind the Darkness: Profiles of the Writers of Horror Fiction," in *Horrorstruck,* "Scattered Gold," in *Other-Realms,* "Night Journeys," in *Mystery Scene,* and "The Eclectic Muse," in *Pulphouse.* Contributor to periodicals, including *Isaac Asimov's Science Fiction Magazine.*

FICTION; UNDER PSEUDONYM SAMUEL M. KEY

Angel of Darkness, Jove (New York, NY), 1990.

From a Whisper to a Scream, Berkley (New York, NY), 1992.

I'll Be Watching You, Jove (New York, NY), 1994.

Sidelights

Canadian author Charles de Lint is a pioneer of modern fantasy, melding the world of faerie with the modern inner city. No fey, upland greenery for him; no cavorting elves or fire-breathing dragons. Instead, de Lint blends a potent brew of contemporary realism, characters that live and breathe right off the page, fast-paced plotting, and thought-provoking messages that has captured a wide and loyal readership as well as critical raves. Gary Westfahl, in a _Los Angeles Times Book Review_ piece on de Lint's _The Little Country,_ warned the reader off easy assumptions vis-a-vis fantasy: "In a genre choking to death on regurgitated [J. R. R.] Tolkien, de Lint does research and imbues his story with an unusual, authentic atmosphere." Westfahl continued, "In a genre of elaborately mapped Neverlands," de Lint's tales take place in a "contemporary world" that is "no less magical." De Lint has created an intricately mapped region of his own, described in the "Newford" books; not dew-filled nature, but an urban environment peopled by folks like us, and others not quite like us—crow people, shape-changers, tricksters, and grifters gussied up in fantastical finery.

"If . . . de Lint didn't create the contemporary fantasy," announced Tanya Huff in _Quill and Quire,_ "he certainly defined it. . . . Unlike most fantasy writers who deal with battles between ultimate good and evil, de Lint concentrates on smaller, very personal conflicts." This may be the reason he appeals to all types of readers, both devoted fans and other audiences. De-

This 2002 story collection by de Lint includes supernatural tales such as "Fairy Dust," "One Chance," and "Ghosts of Wind and Shadow" most of which were originally published in fiction anthologies. (Cover illustration by John Jude Palencar.)

scriptives like "master of the genre" and "gifted storyteller" pepper reviews of de Lint's work, but de Lint himself is low-key about his achievements; he describes himself simply as a writer of mythic fiction. As he told _Locus_ interviewer Richard B. Brignall, "'Mythic fiction' works because it has broader resonances and alludes to the heart of this fiction, which is, of course, myth. It has the right tonality because these are stories that have modern sensibilities, dealing with contemporary people and issues, but they utilize the material of folklore, fairy tale, and myth to help illuminate that."

Beginning with his 1979 debut, the novelette "The Fane of the Grey Rose," de Lint has proven himself to be a versatile and prolific author, with dozens of books and an arm's-length list of awards and honors to his credit, including a Canadian SF/Fantasy award and the Prix Ozone from France. Apart from a few early books in the standard high-fantasy format, de Lint's output has been mainly in urban fantasy or mythic fiction, bringing magic to the streets of contemporary North America. Folk tales and myths inform his novels and short stories, which often include themes of music—de Lint himself is a musician—and artists and other creative people as bridges to a deeper insight into the world.

Many of de Lint's tales are set in the fictional city of Newford: novels such as _Someplace to Be Flying, Trader,_ and _The Onion Girl,_ and the inter-connected short-story collections _Dreams Underfoot, Moonlight and Vines,_ and _Tapping the Dream Tree._ De Lint is also known for the cult classic _Moonheart,_ as well as for _Yarrow_ and _The Little Country,_ books that, as he stated on his Web site, convey "an everyday sort of magic— the inexplicable connectedness we sometimes experience with places, people, works of art and the like; the eerie appropriateness of moments of synchronicity; the whispered voice, the hidden presence, when we think we're alone. These are magics that many of us experience, parts of a Mystery that can't—and perhaps shouldn't—be explained."

Born in Bussum, Netherlands, on December 22, 1951, de Lint immigrated with his family to Canada when he was four months old. His father worked with a surveying company, a job that took the family from Ontario to Western Canada to Quebec and on to Turkey and Lebanon until they finally settled near Ottawa. During these years of uprootedness, de Lint found stability in books, reading widely in myth and folklore. He lists E. B. White, Tolkien, H. P. Lovecraft, William Morris, and Mervyn Peake among the authors whose works he delighted in reading. But though he loved books, he never thought of becoming a writer. For the young de Lint, it was music that beckoned, and growing up he formed a love for Celtic music long before it became a fashionable address on the world-beat map. Leaving high school two credits short of graduation, de Lint took a variety of jobs to support his music, primary among them working as a clerk at a record store.

Increasingly, de Lint began concentrating on fiction, writing fantasy short stories that a friend illustrated. Initially this was a pastime; but when a writer saw the stories and recommended submission, avocation quickly turned to vocation. "I sold these first stories for the princely sum of $10.00 each and the proverbial light went on in my head," de Lint wrote on his Web site. "Here was something that I loved to do and people would actually pay me to do it." Over the next six or seven years de Lint continued to play gigs on the weekend and write stories that he submitted to small magazines. His first success with a larger market came with publication of "The Fane of the Grey Rose" in a Zebra collection, and de Lint later expanded this short story into the novel *The Harp of the Grey Rose.*

Married in 1980 to MaryAnn Harris, de Lint continued clerking, playing music—now often with his wife—and writing. When he lost his job at the record shop in 1983, his wife encouraged him to write full time. It was wise advice: de Lint sold three manuscripts that first year of full-time writing. One of these early books, *Riddle of the Wren,* won the author critical attention despite the fact that it plows the Tolkien furrow, as did his re-worked short story *The Harp of the Grey Rose.* Writing in *Twentieth-Century Science-Fiction Writers,* Maureen Speller commented that in these derivative novels "de Lint's fascination for the humbler creatures of folktale and legend, and for the darker side of magic, is also evident, and this mitigates against the more sentimental aspects."

With publication of *Moonheart,* de Lint was already moving away from the typical imaginary landscape of fantasy to an urban environment. Working on further advice from his wife, he decided to set his fantasy fiction in a realistic environment, opting for modern Ottawa, as it was the locale he knew best. With this novel de Lint began also his peculiar blending of Canadian mythologies, using traditions found in Native Indian shamanism and in Welsh Druidism. Called "a milestone of modern fantasy writing" by Speller, *Moonheart* also blends suspense, horror, and romance in the tale of an Ottawa mansion that proves to be linked to an old battle between good and evil. Tamson House is actually a gate between our world and a magical realm. De Lint's cast of characters ranges from a mage's apprentice, a reformed biker, and an inspector for the Canadian Mounted Police to the magical little people called manitous and legendary figures out of Welsh and Celtic myth.

Writing in *Voice of Youth Advocates,* David Snider called *Moonheart* "a fascinating and enthralling work that should be in every YA collection," while *Booklist*'s Roland Green dubbed the book "very good and distinctly unconventional." De Lint had found his territory and his voice. Over the next several years he wrote several more loosely linked novels and stories in the "Moonheart" series: *Ascian in Rose, Westlin Wind,* and *Ghostwood,* later collected in *Spiritwalk.* Reviewing

that collection in *Quill and Quire,* Michelle Sagara noted that de Lint explores not only the "brightness of magic," but also "its shadow," and that with his multilayered characters thrown into the mix, "magic becomes choice and consequence, an echo of reality, not an escape from it." Sagara concluded that "there are very few fantasists today who write with such poetic simplicity and skill."

De Lint turned his fictional eye to Romany culture for *Mulengro,* a hybrid of the horror and fantasy genres. Set among Canada's modern-day gypsy communities, the novel tells the story of a series of bizarre murders that have police baffled. The gypsies, however, know they are dealing with the mythic Mulengro, "He Who Walks with Ghosts." It is up to a reclusive gypsy man and a young woman to get to the heart of this mythic threat and eliminate it. Gary Farber commented in *S.F. Chronicle* that *Mulengro* is "suspenseful, original, and extremely well written." While some other critics did not find the novel to be as successful in blending magic with urban reality as was *Moonheart, Booklist* reviewer Green noted that de Lint "deserves high marks for his research, storytelling," and for his character descriptions.

Other early books considered notable in the development of de Lint's mythic fiction include *Yarrow* and *Jack the Giant-Killer.* The former deals with a young fantasy writer whose work comes from her nightly dreamscape; when her dreams are increasingly being stolen by a telepathic vampire-type creature, she loses the ability to create. Nancy Choice noted in *Voice of Youth Advocates* that *Yarrow* "is filled with suspense and tension from beginning to end." The protagonist of the novel, Cat, is one of a long line of appealing female characters de Lint has created, a "just plain nice person you would like to have living next door," according to Choice. *Jack the Giant-Killer* continues the two-fold trend of strong female characters and a blend of urban setting with faerie legend. Part of a series of modern retellings of fairy tales, the novel centers on Jacky Rowan, who develops magical powers through the use of a red cap with which are revealed the giant in the city park and the elves in the oaks. Jacky learns that the good elves are dwindling in number, the bad ones prospering. The only way to stop this process is to set the princess free and recapture the Horn for the forces of good. Identifying with the elves as part of the Kinrowan clan, Jacky takes on the task with a little help from her friends, in a "very satisfying" tale, according to Tom Easton of *Analog Science Fiction/Science Fact,* who also dubbed de Lint "one of Canada's modern masters of fantasy." De Lint reprises the character Jacky in *Drink down the Moon,* another blend of fairy-tale motifs and modern settings; both books have also been published in the omnibus *Jack of Kinrowan.*

De Lint once again combines Native American mythology with Celtic story in his 1990 novel *The Dreaming Place,* with illustrations by Brian Froud. Featuring teenage cousins, Nina and Ashley, and emphasizing realism, this book "might . . . encourage some realistic fiction fans to give . . . fantasy a try," according to Kathryn Pierson in a review for the *Bulletin of the Center for Children's Books.*

De Lint's novel *The Little Country* is one of his most complex. It is also one of his favorites, a story within a story and a loving exposition of de Lint's own affection for folk music. Set in modern Cornwall, the novel tells the story of Janey Little, a successful musician who comes back to the village of Mousehole in England. Apart from her music, a major influence on her life is the writings of Billy Dunthorn, and she soon discovers an unpublished manuscript of Dunthorn's in the family attic. This manuscript tells the story of Jodi and her friend Denzil, who lives in the fictional village of Bodbury. As Janey gets further into the book, parallels develop between real life and that of the story in the found manuscript. Outside forces conspire in the form of John Madden of the Order of the Grey Dove, a man who desires the magical Dunthorn manuscript because it can provide the possessor with ultimate power. As Peter Crowther noted in the *St. James Guide to Fantasy Writers,* the book is filled with "charm, excitement, and above all, complete believability." According to Crowther, "it is [de Lint's] unerring knack of concentrating on his characters and filling them out, making them so real, that places his work at the forefront of the field." A *Publishers Weekly* contributor commented that de Lint's "rendering of the small Cornish town of Mousehole and the life of a folk musician rings true."

One of de Lint's most popular fictional conceits has been his creation of a fantasy world for an ensemble cast of characters. True to de Lint form, this imaginary world is a compilation of urban settings, from London to Los Angeles. "Much of what I write about requires a root in the real world," the author noted in an interview with Lawrence Schimel for *Marion Zimmer Bradley's Fantasy Magazine.* When he was asked to contribute a story to a fantasy anthology, the author "decided to set it in an unnamed big city. This way, while I could get the 'feel' of the place from having visited many such cities over the years, I wouldn't be tied down to figuring out the details of which way a street went, what store was on what corner, that sort of thing." After writing several other tales, de Lint stated, "I realized that I'd been setting all these stories in the same unnamed city, using a repertory company of characters that I knew I would continue to visit in the future, so I gave the place a name, started a map to keep locations straight, started a concordance to keep track of things . . . and never quite kept up with any of it." The city of Newford has since become the locale for more than a dozen of de Lint's books.

The first collection of "Newford" tales, *Dreams Underfoot,* gathers stories published in magazines over several years, and introduces the ensemble cast of characters that flow in and out of all the "Newford" stories. There is Jilly, the artist; Lorio, part gypsy and part

punk; Lesli, who sets free the faerie with her music; and a rich assortment of other urban types. One of the outstanding stories in *Dreams Underfoot,* "Timeskip," won France's Prix Ozone. Elizabeth Hand, writing in the *Washington Post Book World,* called this work "a genuinely chilling ghost story as poignant as it is creepy." Further additions to the "Newford" saga include *The Ivory and the Horn,* a "fanciful and moving collection," according to a *Publishers Weekly* critic, and *Moonlight and Vines,* a collection of stories that demonstrates de Lint to be, according to *Booklist*'s Green, "the most literate and ingenious purveyor of urban fantasy." In 2000, de Lint received the World Fantasy Award for *Moonlight and Vines.*

De Lint has also used his fictional town of Newford as the setting for several novels, among them *Memory and Dream, Trader, Someplace to Be Flying,* and *Forests of the Heart.* In the first of these, artist Isabelle learns to paint amazing creatures that unleash ancient spirits into the modern world. "It is hard to imagine urban fantasy done better than it is by de Lint at his best," remarked *Booklist*'s Green. Jodi L. Israel, writing in *Kliatt,* commented that "de Lint is a master of contemporary fantasy," and that the author's "literate and flowing style makes his words a pleasure to read."

Trading places is at the heart of de Lint's 1997 *Trader,* in which a man named Trader awakes to discover he has traded bodies with a reprobate named Johnny Devlin. Trying to reclaim his own life, Trader becomes involved in the lives of all those whom Devlin has injured. Along the way, readers are re-introduced to stock characters out of Newford, including Jilly Coppercorn and street musician Geordie Riddell, as well as the shaman, Bones. "Readers familiar with de Lint's work know that he is a master of imagery and trenchant detail," wrote Donna Scanlon in a *Voice of Youth Advocates* review of *Trader.* "He continues to demonstrate his remarkable ability here," Scanlon concluded, "never los[ing] control of his myriad plot threads or deftly drawn characters."

One of the most popular "Newford" novels, and one of de Lint's personal favorites, is *Someplace to Be Flying,* featuring freelance photographer Lily Carson and a gypsy cab driver, Hank Walker. Once again, de Lint draws the reader into a parallel otherworld, a city beneath the city in the Tombs, and into the realm of the shape-shifting animal people who were the original inhabitants of the earth. The original animal people, as de Lint has it, ultimately turned into the separate animals and people we know today, and in his book, the author focuses specifically on corvids: crows and ravens. *Library Journal* contributor Jackie Cassada praised de Lint's "elegant prose and effective storytelling" and his "unique" blend of "magical realism" and "multicultural myths." Brian Jacomb concluded a laudatory *Washington Post Book World* review by noting that "*Someplace to Be Flying* is . . . a solid thriller, full of suspense and peppered with villains of various talents and their adversaries, the decent folk who constantly try to thwart their evil intentions."

De Lint's novel *Forests of the Heart* "weaves a complex story of intrigue and suspense while exploring the power of spirituality and friendship," observed a contributor in *Resource Links*. Set in and around Newford, the work concerns four individuals—a sculptor with psychic powers, a music-store owner, a New Mexican healer, and a musician—who join together to combat the Gentry, a force of ancient, amoral spirits who traveled to the New World with early Irish immigrants and who seek to displace the native spirits, the manitou. According to *Library Journal* critic Jackie Cassada, de Lint convincingly portrays "the relationship between artistic creation and the magical energies that permeate the world these characters inhabit," and a *Publishers Weekly* reviewer called *Forests of the Heart* "a leisurely, intriguing expedition into the spirit world, studded with Spanish and Gaelic words and an impressive depth of imagination."

Artist Jilly Coppercorn, a recurring character in de Lint's "Newford" tales, is the protagonist of the 2001 novel *The Onion Girl*. Hospitalized after a devastating hit-and-run accident, Jilly visits manido-aki, a spirit world she enters through her dreams and in which she must face her personal demons in order to heal her physical self. Jilly's recovery is complicated by the sudden appearance of a troubled figure from her past, her sister Raylene. "De Lint's novels are driven not so much by destinations as by journeys, and *The Onion Girl* is no exception," observed *Booklist* contributor Regina Schroeder. A critic in *Kirkus Reviews* called the work an "absorbing tale, as believable and insightful as they come," and a *Publishers Weekly* reviewer stated, "This crazy-quilt fantasy moves from the outer to the inner world with amazing ease." In *Spirits in the Wires* de Lint creates "a magical otherworld, where spirits of faerie and folklore occupy modern technology and cyberspace is a fantasy realm in which imagination fuels artificial intelligence," wrote a critic in *Publishers Weekly*. In the work, a popular research Web site known as Wordwood is disrupted by a virus, causing everyone visiting the site to disappear and prompting a group of Newford residents to journey to the technological otherworld, hoping to rescue their missing friends. According to Jackie Cassada, writing in *Library Journal, Spirits in the Wires* "combines world mythologies with cyber-culture to produce a new vision of interwoven realities.

De Lint has also collaborated with award-winning illustrator Charles Vess on a number of fantasy works, including *Seven Wild Sisters, Medicine Road,* and *A Circle of Cats*. The rambunctious, red-haired Dillard sisters are introduced in *Seven Wild Sisters,* "a gentle and at times humorous enchantment," in the words of a *Publishers Weekly* reviewer. In *Medicine Road,* twins Laurel and Bess Dillard encounter a pair of restless spirits who

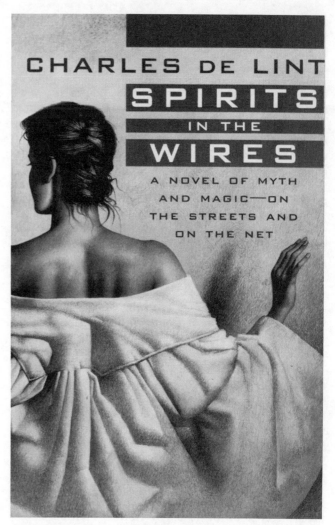

This 2003 novel transports readers to de Lint's fictional town of Newford, where the lines between reality and illusion become blurred after a computer virus brings the humanity of many town residents into question. (Cover illustration by John Jude Palencar.)

seek human soul mates. *Medicine Road* is "well-laced with humor, romance, and Native American mythology," observed Sally Estes in *Booklist*. The children's book *A Circle of Cats* concerns a young girl's transformation from a human into a kitten. "De Lint's sonorous, ingenuous language is complemented beautifully by Vess's full-color line-and-watercolor illustrations," noted a contributor in *Kirkus Reviews*.

De Lint has described his writing style as "organic." In an interview with Mike Timonin for *Wordsworth,* the author stated, "I write a lot of material to get the character's voice right, sometimes hundreds of pages, but not all of that goes into the novel." He added, "I guess I lose a lot of time that way, unlike someone who uses an outline, but it's what works for me." De Lint concluded, "It's strange, when I started writing, I thought it would get easier as I went on, but it doesn't. It actually gets harder, each novel I write. I have to find something new to say, and because I don't want to repeat what I've said before, I have to go deeper, further."

Biographical and Critical Sources

BOOKS

Authors and Artists for Young Adults, Volume 33, Gale (Detroit, MI), 2000.

Clute, John, and Peter Nicholls, editors, *The Encyclopedia of Science Fiction,* St. Martin's Press (New York, NY), 1993.

St. James Guide to Fantasy Writers, St. James Press (Detroit, MI), 1996.

St. James Guide to Young-Adult Writers, 2nd edition, St. James Press (Detroit, MI), 1999.

Science Fiction and Fantasy Literature, 1975-1991, Gale, (Detroit, MI), 1992.

Twentieth-Century Science-Fiction Writers, 3rd edition, St. James Press (Detroit, MI), 1991, pp. 196-198.

PERIODICALS

Analog Science Fiction/Science Fact, September, 1987, pp. 159-162; August, 1988, pp. 137-138; November, 1993, pp. 162-169.

Booklist, December 15, 1984, Roland Green, review of *Moonheart,* p. 558; November 15, 1985, Roland Green, review of *Mulengro,* p. 468; May 15, 1992, p. 1666; October 1, 1994, Roland Green, review of *Memory and Dreams,* p. 246; February 1, 1995, p. 993; January 1, 1997, p. 826; December 1, 1998, Roland Green, review of *Moonlight and Vines,* p. 655; May 1, 2000, Patricia Monaghan, review of *Forests of the Heart,* p. 1655; November 15, 2000, Roland Green review of *Triskell Tales: Twenty-two Years of Chapbooks,* p. 625; October 1, 2001, Regina Schroeder, review of *The Onion Girl,* p. 304; October 1, 2002, Sally Estes, review of *Waifs and Strays,* p. 312; November 15, 2002, Roland Green, review of *Tapping the Dream Tree,* p. 584; February 1, 2003, review of *A Handful of Coppers; Collected Early Stories,* pp. 978-979; August, 2003, Frieda Murray, review of *Spirits in the Wires,* p. 1967; April 15, 2004, Sally Estes, review of *Medicine Road,* p. 1431.

Bulletin of the Center for Children's Books, January, 1991, Kathryn Pierson, review of *The Dreaming Place,* p. 114.

Kirkus Reviews, September 1, 2001, review of *The Onion Girl,* p. 1252; August 15, 2002, review of *Waifs and Strays,* p. 1221; September 15, 2002, review of *Tapping the Dream Tree,* pp. 1357-1358; June 1, 2003, review of *A Circle of Cats,* p. 802; October 1, 2004, review of *The Blue Girl,* p. 959.

Kliatt, January, 1996, Jodi L. Israel, review of *Memory and Dreams,* p. 14; November, 2002, Deirdre B. Root, review of *The Onion Girl,* p. 24; January, 2004, review of *Tapping the Dream Tree,* p. 22.

Library Journal, May 15, 1992, p. 123; January, 1998, Jackie Cassada, review of *Someplace to Be Flying,* p. 148; February 15, 1999, Jackie Cassada, review of *Moonlight and Vines,* p. 188; May 15, 2000, Jackie Cassada, review of *Forests of the Heart,* p. 128; November 15, 2002, Jackie Cassada, review of *Tapping the Dream Tree,* p. 106; August, 2003, Jackie Cassada, review of *Spirits in the Wires,* p. 140.

Locus, October, 1993, p. 33; November, 1994, pp. 52, 68; June, 2003, Richard B. Brignall, "Charles de Lint: Mythic Fiction," p. 6.

Los Angeles Times Book Review, February 3, 1991, Gary Westfahl, "Orange County Apple and Other Aberrations," p. 11.

Marion Zimmer Bradley's Fantasy Magazine, summer, 1996, Lawrence Schimel, interview with de Lint.

Publishers Weekly, December 7, 1990, review of *The Little Country,* p. 74; October 3, 1994, p. 54; March 27, 1995, review of *The Ivory and Horn,* p. 77; January 26, 1998, p. 74; December 21, 1998, review of *Moonlight and Vines,* p. 60; May 1, 2000, review of *Forests of the Heart,* p. 54; April 30, 2001, review of *The Road to Lisdoonvarna,* p. 59; October 22, 2001, M. M. Hall, interview with de Lint, and review of *The Onion Girl,* p. 53; February 18, 2002, review of *Seven Wild Sisters,* p. 81; October, 28, 2002, review of *Tapping the Dream Tree,* p. 56; January 27, 2003, review of *A Handful of Coppers,* p. 241; July 7, 2003, review of *Spirits in the Wires,* p. 57; March 29, 2004, review of *Medicine Road,* p. 43.

Quill and Quire, July, 1992, Michelle Sagara, review of *Spiritwalk,* pp. 37-38; May, 1993, Tanya Huff, "Rising Stars in Fantasy Worlds," p. 26; January, 1995, p. 35; January, 1997, p. 18; February, 1997, p. 49; February, 1998, p. 35.

Resource Links, October, 2000, review of *Forests of the Heart,* pp. 48-49; October, 2002, Gail de Vos, review of *Seven Wild Sisters* and *The Onion Girl,* pp. 55-56; October, 2003, p. 62.

School Library Journal, February, 1991, p. 93; December, 1993, p. 29; November, 2002, Vicki Reutter, review of *Waifs and Strays,* pp. 160-161; October, 2003, Teri Markson and Stephen S. Wise, review of *A Circle of Cats,* p. 116.

Science Fiction Chronicle, July, 1986, Gary Farber, review of *Mulengro,* p. 41.

Voice of Youth Advocates, February, 1985, David Snider, review of *Moonheart,* pp. 335-336; February, 1987, Nancy Choice, review of *Yarrow,* p. 291; April, 1994, p. 36; August, 1997, Donna Scanlon, review of *Trader,* p. 192; April, 1998, pp. 12, 36.

Washington Post Book World, May 30, 1993, Elizabeth Hand, review of *Dreams Underfoot,* p. 9; March 15, 1998, Brian Jacomb, review of *Someplace to Be Flying,* p. 9.

Wordsworth, January, 1998, Mike Timonin, interview with de Lint.

ONLINE

Charles de Lint Home Page, http://www.sfsite.com/charles delint (June 14, 2004).*

* * *

DEWAN, Ted 1961-

Personal

Born 1961, in Boston, MA; married Helen Cooper (an author/illustrator); children: Pandora. *Education:* Brown

University, degree (engineering and electronic music); studied art with author/illustrator David Macaulay. *Hobbies and other interests:* Music.

Addresses

Home—Oxford, England. *Agent*—c/o Author Mail, David Fickling Books, 31 Beaumont St., Oxford OX1, England. *E-mail*—ted.dewan@wormworks.com.

Career

Milton Academy, Boston, MA, physics instructor for five years; illustrator and cartoonist, 1988—.

Member

Society of Authors (former chairman, Children's Writers and Illustrators Group), Royal Institution.

Awards, Honors

Mother Goose Award, and *Times Educational Supplement* Information Award shortlist (for foreign editions), both 1992, both for *Inside the Whale and Other Animals;* Kurt Maschler Award shortlist, 1997, for *The Sorcerer's Apprentice.*

Writings

SELF-ILLUSTRATED; FOR CHILDREN

(Reteller) *Three Billy Goats Gruff,* Andre Deutsch (London, England), 1994, Scholastic (New York, NY), 1995.

Top Secret: Don't Breathe a Word, Andre Deutsch (London, England), 1996, Doubleday (New York, NY), 1997.

(Reteller) *The Sorcerer's Apprentice and Music of Magic and Electricity* (based on *Der Zauberhling* by Wolfgang von Goethe; includes audiotape), Corgi (London, England), 1997, Doubleday (New York, NY), 1998.

The Weatherbirds (nonfiction), Puffin (London, England), 1999.

Crispin, the Pig Who Had It All, Doubleday (New York, NY), 2000.

Baby Gets the Zapper, Transworld (London, England), 2001, Random House (New York, NY), 2002.

Crispin and the Three Little Piglets, Transworld (London, England), 2002, Doubleday (New York, NY), 2003.

"BING BUNNY" SERIES; SELF-ILLUSTRATED; FOR CHILDREN

Bing: Something for Daddy, David Fickling (New York, NY), 2003.

Bing: Paint Day, David Fickling (New York, NY), 2003.

Bing: Get Dressed, David Fickling Books (New York, NY), 2003.

Bing: Bed Time, David Fickling Books (New York, NY), 2003.

Bing: Go Picnic, David Fickling Books (New York, NY), 2004.

Bing: Make Music, David Fickling Books (New York, NY), 2004.

ILLUSTRATOR; FOR CHILDREN

Grace L. Mitchell and Harriet Chmela, *I Am, I Can: A Preschool Curriculum,* Telshare, 1977.

Steve Parker, *Inside the Whale and Other Animals,* Dorling Kindersley (London, England), 1992.

Steve Parker, *Inside Dinosaurs and Other Prehistoric Creatures,* Dorling Kindersley (London, England), 1993, Delacorte (New York, NY), 1994.

Kit Wright, *Rumpelstiltskin,* Hippo (London, England), 1998.

Helen Cooper, *Sandmare,* Corgi (London, England), 2001, Farrar, Straus & Giroux (New York, NY), 2004.

Elizabeth Kay, *The Divide,* Chicken House, 2003.

Elizabeth Laird, *The Ice Cream Swipe,* Oxford University Press (Oxford, England, 2003.

Elizabeth Kay, *The Half Twist,* Chicken House, 2005.

ILLUSTRATOR; FOR ADULTS

Robert Ornstein, *The Evolution of Consciousness,* Prentice-Hall (Englewood Cliffs, NJ), 1991.

Robert Ornstein, *The Roots of the Self: Unraveling the Mystery of Who We Are,* HarperCollins (San Francisco, CA), 1993.

James Burke and Robert Ornstein, *The Axemaker's Gift,* Putnam (New York, NY), 1995.

Marc D. Hauser, *Wild Minds,* Henry Holt (New York, NY), 1999.

Dewan's illustrations have appeared in British newspapers, including as regular features in London *Times,* and *Guardian.*

Sidelights

An American-born artist who now makes his home in Great Britain, Ted Dewan has been praised for creating book illustrations that feature his characteristic quirky, engaging style. Using his artistic skills, timely marketing, and creative concepts, Dewan encourages readers to find new appreciation for familiar material. *Books for Keeps* contributor Pam Harwood admired the author's "'cool' language" and "bright, lively pictures," which bring Dewan's adaptation of the time-honored story *Three Billy Goats Gruff* back to life. Among original tales, Dewan has also authors the self-illustrated picture books *Baby Gets the Zapper* and *Crispin and the Three Little Piglets,* as well as several volumes in the ongoing "Bing Bunny" series of picture books for the toddler set. Praising *Bing: Get Dressed* from the series, Ilene Cooper wrote in *Booklist* that "it's hard to know what's more fun here, the computer-collage art or the satisfying way Dewan captures a child's world."

After studying engineering at Brown University and teaching physics at Milton Academy in Boston, Massachusetts, Dewan decided to make a career change. He began illustrating nonfiction books for both children and adults, including several volumes by science writer Steve Parker. Published in 1992, *Inside the Whale* showcases Dewan's pen-and-ink and watercolor drawings alongside Parker's examination of the morphology of the world's largest mammals. Similar in format, *Inside Dinosaurs and Other Prehistoric Creatures* investigates the processes used by modern scientists to recreate detailed models of dinosaurs. *School Library Journal* contributor Cathryn A. Camper praised both books for using "humor and imagination, instead of knives" to examine the anatomy of these creatures.

With the success of his illustrations for Parker, Dewan moved on to create his own stories for children, and he attempts to explain one of the great mysteries of childhood in *Top Secret*. Published in 1996, *Top Secret* reveals, in a comic-book format, the complex technology and heroic bravery responsible for the legend of the tooth fairy. In Dewan's book, the "new kid," one of seven turtle-like creatures, describes the dangerous mission with which his crew has been charged. Their goal: undetected tooth extraction from beneath the pillow of a sleeping girl and replacement of said tooth with a shiny coin. *School Library Journal* contributor Karen James noted Dewan's humorous peppering of technical jargon, such as "zip cable" and "Slumber Zone," to augment the text. Citing the combination of "catchy lingo of the narration and the Lego-like machines," a *Kirkus Reviews* critic called *Top Secret* "adventurous fun, especially for the mechanically inclined," while *Booklist* reviewer Carolyn Phelan wrote that "Children will enjoy the visual wit and pizzazz that characterizes this original picture book."

The Sorcerer's Apprentice, Dewan's next endeavor, is an original story based on a ballad by eighteenth-century German writer Johann Wolfgang von Goethe. It is doubtful, however, that Goethe could have imagined a robot cast in the title role. In a workshop that *School Librarian* contributor Anne Rowe described as "a cross between a metal workshop and Dr. Frankenstein's laboratory," Dewan's modern-day sorcerer puts together gears, wires, bulbs, transistors, and other mechanical things to create new inventions. Because his workshop has becoming cluttered with bits of left-over stuff, he wires together a savvy robot apprentice to clean up after him. The first robot, who quickly becomes addicted to technology himself in the form of television, accumulates enough stuff to build a successor to perform all the hard work; the new robot does the same. So it goes, until the robots revolt against the sorcerer, forcing the inventor to flip the "off" switch on the entire mechanical crew, all except his original apprentice. A *Publishers Weekly* contributor called *The Sorcerer's Apprentice* a "post-modern melodrama" that "cautions against cloning, environmental depletion and television," while a *Kirkus* reviewer dubbed the work a "rollicking remake of the classic tale." Drawing on his interest in electronic music, Dewan also created a musical accompani-

The star of Ted Dewan's slyly humorous picture book **Crispin: The Pig Who Had It All** *learns that he has been a hog in more ways than one after Santa delivers an unusually light-weight package one year.*

ment to compliment his visual story, arranging compositions by Paul-Abraham Dukas and Camille Saint-Saëns and including his own, titled "The March of the Robots."

Wealthy young porker Crispin Tamworth is introduced in Dewan's *Crispin: The Pig Who Had It All,* which focuses on what *Booklist* reviewer Ilene Cooper called "a familiar theme, made fresh and funny thanks to a witty yet heartfelt text and eye-popping art." Getting anything and everything he wants, Crispin values next to nothing, and his room soon becomes a dumping ground for broken and discarded toys of all sorts. Still, there is always something new to want, and when Santa leaves him nothing but an empty box one Christmas, the pig is more than a little petulant. Fortunately, with the help of resourceful new friends Penny and Nick, he learns that a toy's real value is having someone to share it with. The flip side of sharing, sharing his family with a new sibling, is the focus of *Crispin and the Three Little Piglets,* which finds Crispin out of the limelight when his mother brings home three new siblings. In *School Library Journal* Barbara Buckley praised Dewan's "cleverness," noting that the illustrations of Crispin and his endlessly exercising mother in their upper-middle-class home "give real personalities to all of the characters." Also enjoying Dewan's humorous twist on the classic story about the three little pigs, Julie Cummins wrote in *Booklist* that *Crispin and the Three Little Piglets* is enlivened by "puckish, humorous illustrations . . . burst[ing] with details that reflect real life with a twist."

Each of Dewan's books takes up to eight months to create, from idea to finished art, and most of that time is spent on the illustrations. Noting on his Web site that he chose not to major in art during college because "I didn't think I was groovy enough to fit in with the other art students (I didn't have any black clothes)," Dewan offered this encouragement to aspiring illustrators: "The best way to become good at drawing is to do a lot of it. Too many people stop drawing when they're ten because suddenly they get worried that they're not good enough. You have to keep practicing if you want to get better."

Biographical and Critical Sources

PERIODICALS

Booklist, July, 1992, p. 1935; March 15, 1994, p. 1345; April 1, 1997, Carolyn Phelan, review of *Top Secret,* p. 1337; November 15, 2000, Ilene Cooper, review of *Crispin: The Pig Who Had It All,* p. 638; April 1, 2003, Julie Cummins, review of *Crispin and the Three Little Piglets,* p. 1401; February 15, 2004, Ilene Cooper, review of *Bing: Get Dressed,* p. 1062.
Books for Keeps, September, 1995, Pam Harwood, review of *Three Billy Goats Gruff,* p. 10; May, 1996, p. 24.
Kirkus Reviews, January 15, 1997, review of *Top Secret,* p. 140; December 1, 1997, review of *The Sorcerer's Apprentice,* p. 1774; January 1, 2002, review of *Baby Gets the Zapper,* p. 43; December 15, 2002, review of *Crispin and the Three Little Piglets,* p. 1849.
New York Times Book Review, June 28, 1992, p. 26.
Publishers Weekly, February 7, 1994, p. 88; February 24, 1997, review of *Top Secret,* p. 90; January 12, 1998, review of *The Sorcerer's Apprentice,* p. 59; January 19, 2004, review of *Bing: Get Dressed* and *Bing: Paint Day,* p. 74.
School Librarian, November, 1997, Anne Rowe, review of *The Sorcerer's Apprentice,* p. 185.
School Library Journal, July, 1992, p. 81; April, 1994, Cathryn A. Camper, review of *Inside Dinosaurs and Other Prehistoric Creatures,* p. 144; March, 1997, Karen James, review of *Top Secret,* p. 150; March, 2003, Barbara Buckley, review of *Crispin and the Three Little Piglets,* p. 191; July, 2004, Olga R. Kuharets, review of *Bing: Get Dressed,* p. 69.
Times Educational Supplement, September 29, 1995, p. 10; October 25, 1996, p. 12; October 3, 1997, p. 9; November 7, 1997, p. 11.

ONLINE

Ted Dewan Web site, http://www.homepage.ntlworld.com/ted.dewan/tedpages/ (February 1, 2005).*

* * *

DIXON, Franklin W.
See STANLEY, George Edward

DOWELL, Frances O'Roark

Personal

Female. *Education:* Wake Forest University, B.A.; University of Massachusetts, M.F.A.

Addresses

Home—8 Briarfield Rd., Durham, NC 27713. *E-mail*—fdowell@mindspring.com.

Career

Worked variously as paralegal, college English instructor, and arts administrator. Former editor and copublisher of *Dream/Girl* (arts magazine for girls).

Awards, Honors

Edgar Allan Poe Award for Best Juvenile Novel, 2001, and William Allen White Award, 2003, both for *Dovey Coe.*

Writings

FOR CHILDREN

Dovey Coe, Atheneum (New York, NY), 2000.
Where I'd Like to Be, Atheneum (New York, NY), 2003.
The Secret Language of Girls, Atheneum (New York, NY), 2004.
Chicken Boy, Atheneum (New York, NY), 2005.

Contributor of poetry to periodicals, including *Poetry East, Shenandoah,* and *New Delta Review.*

Work in Progress

Two novels.

Sidelights

Frances O'Roark Dowell's novels for young adult readers explore issues of growing up, family and friend relationships, and overcoming adversity. Reviewing her novels, which include *Dovey Coe* and *The Secret Language of Girls,* critics have praised her well-developed and believable protagonists. While Dowell's subjects range from the ordinary to the dramatic, the female protagonists at the center of her stories are girls to whom teen readers can relate.

Dowell's acclaimed debut novel *Dovey Coe* features a spunky young heroine who is outspoken, assertive, and protective of her family. Dovey does not like Parnell, her older sister's suitor, particularly the way he disrespects her family, and she is not afraid to say so. When Parnell takes her dog one night and threatens to kill it, Dovey tries to save her pet by attacking Parnell and is

Frances O'Roark Dowell

knocked unconscious. When she wakes up, both her dog and Parnell are dead, and Dovey must face a courtroom battle to prove her innocence. Betsy Fraser, writing in *School Library Journal,* noted that the novel "maintains a very fast pace, and Dovey is an original character," adding, "The background and characters are carefully developed and appealing." *Booklist* contributor Frances Bradburn added that "Dowell has created a memorable character in Dovey, quick-witted and honest to a fault."

In an interview for *DreamGirl* online, Dowell answered questions about the inspiration behind *Dovey Coe.* "The reasons I wanted to set a book in the past is because I'm very interested in folklore and folkways—the ways people lived before we had so many time-saving devices and big grocery stores and all of our modern conveniences. I had been reading a lot of books about life in the Blue Ridge mountains in earlier times, and I thought it would be fun to write a book using some of the knowledge I'd picked up." As for critics who draw comparisons between *Dovey Coe* and Harper Lee's classic novel *To Kill a Mockingbird,* Dowell commented, "It's a little embarrassing, to be honest. . . . Don't get me wrong, I like my own book a lot, but nothing will ever truly compare to *To Kill a Mockingbird.* There are similarities, it's true. Both Scout, the narrator of *To Kill*

a Mockingbird, and Dovey are tomboys, they're both outspoken and honest, and they're both loyal to the people they love." *Where I'd Like to Be* is set in a home where orphaned children await foster homes. The protagonist is a girl named Maddie who makes the best of her bad situation and has a strong sense of herself. When a new girl, Murphy, arrives, Maddie is captivated by the girl's story as well as her imaginative personality. Dowell creates a cast of diverse children who create a family among themselves as they dream of becoming part of a permanent family. In *Booklist,* Linda Perkins wrote that Maddie's "voice and views are consistently those of a perceptive eleven-year-old," and added that the novel provides "ample discussion possibilities." The characters in the novel were particularly impressive to Faith Brautigam of *School Library Journal,* who commented that "the foster children's backgrounds are believable, diverse, and engaging," creating "unique and memorable characters." A contributor to *Kirkus Reviews* also praised Dowell's characterizations, concluding: "The talky pie-in-the-sky resolution mars the tightness of the narrative that precedes it, but taken as a whole, this is a lovely, quietly bittersweet tale of friendship and family." And a *Publishers Weekly* reviewer deemed *Where I'd Like to Be* "a celebration of friendship and the powers of the imagination."

The way teenage girls grow apart from their friends is the subject of *The Secret Language of Girls.* Kate and Marilyn have been friends since childhood, but as they enter the sixth grade, their paths diverge. While Marilyn gains access to the popular crowd, becomes a cheerleader, and is increasingly preoccupied by make-up and boys, Kate worries about her father's health and shies away from being noticed by her peers. In the end, the two girls find that their different lifestyles have not forced them as far apart as they thought. Martha P. Par-

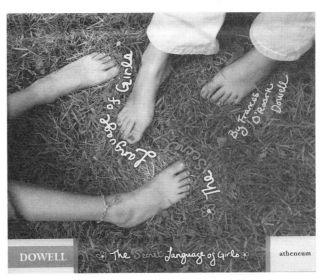

Best friends Kate and Marylin find their strong friendship put to the test when they begin to focus on different interests during middle school. (Cover illustration by Michael Frost.)

Dowell tells the story of a group of foster children who band together to create a secure family in this 2003 novel. (Cover illustration by Bruce Katz.)

ravano, reviewing the novel for *Horn Book,* observed that "Dowell's development of this familiar situation is

refreshingly nonjudgmental," and noted that the thoughtful tone of the novel is balanced by "supersonic pacing—a perspective that swings freely between Kate and Marylin, and vivid characterization." A *Publishers Weekly* reviewer described the book as a "perceptive slice-of-life novel" that will leave readers feeling "encouraged by the author's honest and sympathetic approach." B. Allison Gray of *School Library Journal* maintained that *The Secret Language of Girls* will ring true to young readers because of "excellent characterization, an accurate portrayal of the painful and often cruel machinations of preteens, and evocative dialogue."

Biographical and Critical Sources

PERIODICALS

Booklist, April 15, 2000, review of *Dovey Coe,* p. 1537; May 15, 2003, Linda Perkins, review of *Where I'd Like to Be,* pp. 1660-1661.

Horn Book, July-August, 2004, Martha P. Parravano, review of *The Secret Language of Girls,* p. 450.

Kirkus Reviews, March 1, 2003, review of *Where I'd Like to Be,* p. 382.

Publishers Weekly, February 24, 2003, review of *Where I'd Like to Be,* p. 73; May 31, 2004, review of *The Secret Language of Girls,* p. 74.

School Library Journal, May, 2000, review of *Dovey Coe,* p. 171; April, 2003, Faith Brautigam, review of *Where I'd Like to Be,* p. 158; May, 2004, B. Allison Gray, review of *The Secret Language of Girls,* p. 146.

ONLINE

DreamGirl Online, http://www.dgarts.com/ (February 2, 2005), interview with Dowell.

F

FEIFFER, Jules (Ralph) 1929-

Personal

Born January 26, 1929, in Bronx, NY; son of David (a dental technician, then salesman) and Rhoda (a fashion designer; maiden name, Davis) Feiffer; married Judith Sheftel (a motion picture executive), September 17, 1961 (divorced 1983); married Jennifer Allen (a journalist), September 11, 1983; children: (first marriage) Kate; (second marriage) Halley. *Education:* Attended Art Students' League, 1946, and Pratt Institute, 1947-48, 1949-51.

Addresses

Home—New York, NY; Martha's Vineyard, MA. *Agent*—Royce Carlton Inc., 866 United Nations Plaza, New York, NY 10017. *E-mail*—info@julesfeiffer.com.

Career

Playwright, cartoonist, and author/illustrator. Assistant to cartoonist Will Eisner, 1946-51; drew syndicated cartoon series "Clifford," 1949-51; held various art jobs, 1953-56, including making slide films, as writer for Terrytoons, and as designer of booklets for an art film; freelance cartoonist, with work published in *Village Voice,* New York, NY, 1956-97, in *Observer,* London, England, 1958-66, 1972-2000, and in *Playboy,* 1959–; cartoons syndicated by Publishers-Hall Syndicate and distributed to more than one hundred newspapers in the United States and abroad, 1956-2000. Member of faculty at Yale University School of Drama, 1972-73, Northwestern University, 1996, and Southampton College, 1999–; senior fellow of national arts journalism program, Columbia University, 1997. *Exhibitions:* Retrospective staged at University of Wisconsin-Milwaukee, 2003. *Military service:* U.S. Army, Signal Corps, 1951-53; worked in cartoon-animation unit.

Member

Authors League of America, Dramatists Guild (member of council), PEN, Writers Guild of America, East.

Awards, Honors

Academy Award for Best Short-Subject Cartoon, Academy of Motion Picture Arts and Sciences, 1961, for *Munro;* Special George Polk Memorial Award, 1961; most promising playwright, New York Drama Critics, 1966-67, Best Foreign Play of the Year, London Theatre Critics, 1967, and Outer Critics Circle Award, and Off-Broadway Award, *Village Voice,* both 1969, all for *Little Murders;* Outer Critics Circle Award, 1970, for *The White House Murder Case;* Pulitzer Prize, 1986, for editorial cartooning; best screenplay honor, Venice Film Festival, 1989, for *I Want to Go Home;* elected to American Academy of Arts & Letters, 1995; honorary D.H.L., Long Island University, 1999; Red Colver Children's Choice Picture Book Award, 2000, for *Bark, George;* Milton Caniff Lifetime Achievement Award, National Cartoonists Society, 2003; Ian McLellan Hunter Award for Lifetime Achievement in Writing, Writers Guild of America, East, 2004; Harold Washington Literary Award, 2004; Patricia A. Barr Shalom Award, Americans for Peace Now, 2004.

Writings

FOR CHILDREN; SELF-ILLUSTRATED

(Illustrator) Norton Juster, *The Phantom Tollbooth,* Random House (New York, NY), 1961, published with an appreciation by Maurice Sendak, Random House (New York, NY), 1996.

The Man in the Ceiling, HarperCollins (New York, NY), 1993.

A Barrel of Laughs, a Vale of Tears, HarperCollins (New York, NY), 1995.

Meanwhile . . . , HarperCollins (New York, NY), 1997.

I Lost My Bear, Morrow (New York, NY), 1998.

Bark, George, HarperCollins (New York, NY), 1999.

(Illustrator) Florence Parry Heide, *Some Things Are Scary,* Candlewick Press (Cambridge, MA), 2000.

I'm Not Bobby!, Hyperion (New York, NY), 2001.

By the Side of the Road, Hyperion (New York, NY), 2002.

The House across the Street, Hyperion (New York, NY), 2002.

The Daddy Mountain, Hyperion (New York, NY), 2004.

FOR ADULTS; CARTOONS, UNLESS OTHERWISE NOTED

Sick, Sick, Sick: A Guide to Non-confident Living, McGraw (New York, NY), 1958, with introduction by Kenneth Tynan, Collins (London, England), 1959.

Passionella and Other Stories, McGraw (New York, NY), 1959.

(Illustrator) Robert Mines, *My Mind Went All to Pieces,* Dial (New York, NY), 1959.

The Explainers, McGraw (New York, NY), 1960.

Boy, Girl, Boy, Girl, Random House (New York, NY), 1961.

Feiffer's Album, Random House (New York, NY), 1963.

Hold Me!, Random House (New York, NY), 1963.

Harry, the Rat with Women (novel), McGraw (New York, NY), 1963.

(Compiler and annotator) *The Great Comic Book Heroes,* Dial (New York, NY), 1965, revised edition, Fantagraphics Books (Seattle, WA), 2003.

The Unexpurgated Memories of Bernard Mergendeiler, Random House (New York, NY), 1965.

The Penguin Feiffer, Penguin (London, England), 1966.

Feiffer on Civil Rights, Anti-Defamation League (New York, NY), 1966.

Feiffer's Marriage Manual, Random House (New York, NY), 1967.

Pictures at a Prosecution: Drawings and Text from the Chicago Conspiracy Trial, Grove (New York, NY), 1971.

Feiffer on Nixon: The Cartoon Presidency, Random House (New York, NY), 1974.

Ackroyd (novel), Simon & Schuster (New York, NY), 1977.

Tantrum: A Novel-in-Cartoons, Knopf (New York, NY), 1979.

Feiffery: Jules Feiffer's America from Eisenhower to Reagan, Knopf (New York, NY), 1982.

Marriage Is an Invasion of Privacy, and Other Dangerous Views, Andrews & McMeel (Kansas City, MO), 1984.

Feiffer's Children: Including Munro, Andrews & McMeel (Kansas City, MO), 1986.

Ronald Reagan in Movie America: A Jules Feiffer Production, Andrews & McMeel (Kansas City, MO), 1988.

Feiffer: The Collected Works, Volume 1, Fantagraphics Books (Seattle, WA), 1989.

Feiffer: The Collected Works, Volume 3, Fantagraphics Books (Seattle, WA), 1991.

Feiffer: The Collected Works, Volume 4, Fantagraphics Books (Seattle, WA), 1997.

Ghost-scripted comic-book series "The Spirit," 1949-51. Contributor to periodicals, including *Ramparts.*

Feiffer's books have been translated into German, Swedish, Italian, Dutch, French, and Japanese.

PLAYS

The Explainers (satirical review), first produced in Chicago, IL, 1961.

The World of Jules Feiffer, first produced in New Jersey, 1962.

Crawling Arnold (one-act; first produced in Spoleto, Italy, 1961; produced by WEAV-TV, 1963), Dramatists Play Service (New York, NY), 1963.

The Unexpurgated Memoirs of Bernard Mergendeiler (first produced in Los Angeles, CA, 1967; produced with other plays as *Collision Course,* off-Broadway, 1968), published in *Collision Course,* edited by Edward Parone, Random House (New York, NY), 1968.

Little Murders (two-act comedy; first produced on Broadway, 1967; produced by Royal Shakespeare Company in London, England, 1967; revived off-Broadway, 1969), Random House (New York, NY), 1968.

God Bless, first produced at Yale School of Drama, New Haven, CT, 1968; produced by Royal Shakespeare Company, 1968.

Dick and Jane: A One-Act Play (also see below; first produced in New York, NY, as part of *Oh! Calcutta!,* revised by Kenneth Tynan, 1969), published in *Oh! Calcutta!,* edited by Tynan, Grove (New York, NY), 1969.

The White House Murder Case: A Play in Two Acts [and] *Dick and Jane: A One-Act Play* (*The White House Murder Case* first produced in New York, NY, 1970), Grove (New York, NY), 1970.

Feiffer's People: Sketches and Observations Dramatists Play Service (New York, NY), 1969. (first produced in Edinburgh, Scotland, 1968; produced in Los Angeles, CA,)1971.

(With others) *The Watergate Classics,* first produced at Yale Repertory Theatre, 1973.

Knock-Knock (first produced in New York, NY, 1974), Hill & Wang (New York, NY), 1976.

Hold Me! (first produced in New York, NY, 1977), Dramatists Play Service (New York, NY), 1977.

Grown-ups (first produced in New York, NY, 1981), Samuel French (New York, NY), 1982.

A Think Piece, first produced in Chicago, IL, 1982.

Feiffer's America, first produced in Evanston, IL, 1988.

Carnal Knowledge, first produced in Houston, TX, 1988.

Elliot Loves (first produced in Chicago, IL, 1988), Grove (New York, NY), 1990.

Anthony Rose, first produced in Philadelphia, PA, 1989.

E-mail (one-act play), first produced as part of *Short Talks on the Universe,* produced in New York, NY, 2002.

A Bad Friend, first produced in New York, NY, 2003.

SCREENPLAYS

Little Murders, Twentieth Century-Fox, 1971.

(With Israel Horovitz) *VD Blues* (produced by Public Broadcasting Service, 1972), Avon (New York, NY), 1974.

Popeye, Paramount, 1980.

(Adapter) *Puss in Boots,* Columbia Broadcast System/Fox Video, 1984.

I Want to Go Home, Marvin Karmitz Productions, 1989.

Contributor of sketches to productions of DMZ Cabaret, New York; writer for *Steve Allen Show,* 1964; author of episode "Kidnapped" for *Happy Endings* (series), American Broadcasting Company, Inc., 1975.

Adaptations

Munro, an animated cartoon based on Feiffer's story, was produced by Rembrandt Films, 1961; *The Apple Tree,* a musical by Jerry Bock and Sheldon Harnick, contains a playlet based on Feiffer's "Passionella," and was produced in New York, NY, 1966; *Harry, the Rat with Women* was adapted as a play produced at the Detroit Institute of Arts, 1966; *Carnal Knowledge* was adapted as a motion picture, Avco Embassy, 1971; *Grown-Ups* was adapted for film and produced by PBS-TV, 1986; *Popeye, the Movie Novel,* based on Feifer's screenplay, was edited and adapted by Richard J. Anobile, Avon, 1980; *Bark, George* was adapted as an animated film narrated by John Lithgow, Weston Woods, 2003.

Work in Progress

A full-length animated film for Sony Pictures.

Sidelights

Decades before he published his first self-illustrated children's book in 1993, Pulitzer Prize-winning cartoonist Jules Feiffer was well known to young readers as the illustrator of Norman Juster's classic 1961 novel *The Phantom Tollbooth.* During the intervening years, he was known to adult readers as the creator of satiric cartoons published in hundreds of newspapers, while his plays have appeared on numerous stages and several, with the artist/playwright's screenplays, have been adapted for film. In the early 1990s Feiffer came full circle, beginning a new phase of his career as a children's book author, and with books such as *By the Side of the Road* and *The House across the Street,* has won new fans through his sketchy pen-and-ink drawings and quirky texts.

Born in the Bronx, New York, in 1929, Feiffer was the son of a Polish mother and a father whose unsuccessful business ventures caused money worries to haunt the Feiffer household. The trials of the Great Depression did not help matters in the Feiffer home, and young Jules reacted by escaping into books—more specifically comic books such as "Detective Comics"—and drawing. When Feiffer was approximately seven years of age, he won a gold medal in an art contest sponsored by a New York department store. Knowing that a good job would help him avoid the financial plight of his parents, he decided to become a cartoonist. As Feiffer recalled in *The Great Comic Book Heroes:* "I . . . drew sixty-four pages in two days, sometimes one day, stapled the product together, and took it out on the street where kids my age sat behind orange crates selling and trading comic books. Mine went for less because they weren't real."

Feiffer studied the comic strips in the pages of the *New York Times* and the *World-Telegram* his father brought home after work, salvaged newspapers from garbage cans, and got friends to bring him the comics sections from the newspapers their parents discarded. "To see 'Terry and the Pirates,'" Feiffer explained, "we'd have to get the *Daily News,* which my family wouldn't allow in the house." The reason: his parents–both Jewish and both Democrats–believed that the publisher of the New York *Daily News* was anti-Semitic.

At age fifteen Feiffer enrolled at the Art Students' League, then studied at the Pratt Institute for a year, taking night courses. Meanwhile, in 1946, through a stroke of luck, he became an assistant to noted cartoonist Will Eisner. "He said I was worth absolutely nothing, but if I wanted to hang out there, and erase pages or do gofer work, that was fine," Feiffer recalled to Gary Groth in *Comics Journal.* Eisner eventually assigned Feiffer the writing and layout for the comic strip "The Spirit," and in exchange let his young apprentice cartoonist have the space on the last page of his current strip. Thus, the "Clifford" comic strip was born.

"Clifford" came to a close in 1951, when Feiffer was drafted into the U.S. Army during the Korean War. His experiences as part of the military provided Feiffer with the subject he would satirize for most of his remaining career: the workings of the U.S. government. "It was the first time I was truly away from home for a long period of time," Feiffer explained to Groth, "and thrown into a world that was antagonistic to everything I believed in, on every conceivable level. In a war that I was out of sympathy with, and in an army that I despised; [an army that] displayed every rule of illogic and contempt for the individual and mindless exercise of power. [That] became my material."

Released from duty in 1953, Feiffer was at work creating a weekly comic strip for the *Village Voice* by 1956. "We cut a stiff deal," the cartoonist recalled to a writer for *Dramatists Guild Quarterly* of his early attempt to get published. "They would publish anything I wrote and drew as long as I didn't ask to be paid." As he planned, Feiffer got a call from an editor at a different publication, who, as the cartoonist recalled, "said, 'oh boy, this guy is good, he's in the *Voice,* ' and accepted the same stuff his company had turned down when I had come to their offices as an unpublished cartoonist."

With the security of regular cartoon assignments, Feiffer could now refine his style, which was already influenced by the work of illustrator William Steig. By the late 1950s, his cartoons appeared regularly in *Playboy,* the London *Observer,* and in newspapers across the United States. Many of these strips have been collected in books such as *Feiffer's Album, Feiffer on Nixon,* and *Feiffer's Children.* In 1986 Feiffer was honored with a Pulitzer Prize for editorial cartooning. He continued to create comic strips on a regular basis for several decades, finally ending his syndicated comic strip in the summer of 2000.

In the humorously illustrated **Bark, George,** *a young dog who finds his bark straying from "Quack" to "Meow," makes a trip to the doctor's office seeking relief.*

While working as a syndicated cartoonist, Feiffer also began penning plays, and his first drama, *Little Murders,* was produced on Broadway in 1967. The play was a popular and critical success, winning an Outer Critics Circle Award and a *Village Voice* Off-Broadway Award, among others. Through the 1980s Feiffer wrote a number of other plays, as well as several screenplays that were produced as major motion pictures. His film *Popeye,* starring Robin Williams, was released in 1980, and his stage works, which include the autobiographical *Grown-ups, The White House Murder Case,* and with *A Bad Friend,* have been produced both in the United States and in Europe.

Feiffer's debut as a children's author came in the early 1990s with *The Man in the Ceiling,* a story about ten-year-old Jimmy Jibbett and his efforts to win the friendship of the popular Charlie Beemer by expressing a willingness to translate Charlie's stories into cartoons. Cathryn M. Camper noted in *Five Owls* that *The Man in the Ceiling* "recognizes that a large part of the for-

mation of an artist takes place in his or her youth. . . . Feiffer conveys . . . this with a sense of humor, combining samples of Jimmy's comics to help tell the tale."

Some of Feiffer's children's books feature their creator's characteristic mature satire even as they entertain younger readers with a humorous tale. His *A Barrel of Laughs, a Vale of Tears* was described by a *Publishers Weekly* contributor as "a sophisticatedly silly fairy tale that relaxes storytelling conventions." The topic of road rage prompted by long-distance family auto trips is the focus of *By the Side of the Road,* which finds the parents of an unruly eight year old making good on their threat: "If you don't stop that now you'll end up on the side of the road." Actually deposited on the side of the road and abandoned, the boy makes a new life for himself, is joined by another abandoned child, and grows to adulthood, occasionally visited by his family and becoming the subject of envy by his stay-at-home brother. While noting that *By the Side of the Road* is "really for parents," *New York Times Book Review* contributor Cynthia Zarin wrote that Feiffer "is in top form here."

Feiffer turns to more traditional tales for children with *Meanwhile . . .* , *The Daddy Mountain*, and *Bark, George*, the last a reversal of the old-lady-who-swallowed-a-fly story. *Meanwhile . . .* draws on a fantasy tradition of a modern sort, as comic-book fan Raymond, pursued by his angry mother, decides to pull the "Meanwhile. . ." dialogue balloon out of his comic book to see if it will transport him somewhere else in a hurry. "Frantic action and the clever theme make this a great read-aloud," concluded *School Library Journal* contributor Lisa S. Murphy. In *The Daddy Mountain*, which narrates a small girl's successful attempt at a daunting ascent up onto her father's shoulders, the author captures what *Booklist* reviewer Jennifer Mattson described as "daddies' special fondness for roughhousing" in illustrations that "are vintage Feiffer," according to Grace Oliff in *School Library Journal*. A young dog who goes "meow" instead of "arf" is the focus of Feiffer's award-winning *Bark, George*, which finds the pup's distressed mother hurrying her son off to the local vet to find the source of the problem: he has swallowed a cat. Praising *Bark George* as the "pairing of an ageless joke with a crisp contemporary look," a *Publishers Weekly* contributor dubbed Feiffer's simply drawn illustrations "striking" and "studies in minimalism and eloquence." *Booklist* reviewer Stephanie Zvirin praised Feiffer's "easy to follow" text and added that the author/illustrator's "characters are unforgettable . . . and the pictures burst with the sort of broad physical comedy that a lot of children just love."

I'm Not Bobby finds a young boy determined to be someone else. Refusing to respond to calls for Bobby, he pretends to be a horse, a car, a dinosaur, a giant, and even a space ship in an effort to tune out his mother's calls. Finally, dinner time and fatigue make being Bobby by far the best option, in a book that features "Feiffer's exuberantly drawn signature illustrations," according to a *Horn Book* contributor.

Dissatisfaction is also the subject of *The House across the Street*, which finds a young boy wishing he lived in the larger house of a neighborhood friend. While imagining that a wealth of wonderful toys, fabulous dogs, and even a dolphin-filled swimming pool must exist in that amazing house, the boy also conjures up a family in which parents never fight, happy friends come and go, and the house rings with laughter, giving *The House across the Street* a poignant note while it also captures the whining note of many a "common childhood tune," according to a *Kirkus* reviewer. Noting that Feiffer captures "a child's anger about . . . adult authority," *Booklist* contributor Hazel Rochman praised the book for also expressing "a child's loneliness and his soaring imaginative power."

Biographical and Critical Sources

BOOKS

Cohen, Sarah Blacher, editor, *From Hester Street to Hollywood: The Jewish-American Stage and Screen*, Indiana University Press (Bloomington, IN), 1983.

Contemporary Dramatists, 5th edition, St. James Press (Detroit, MI), 1993.

Contemporary Literary Criticism, Volume 64, Gale (Detroit, MI), 1991.

Dictionary of Literary Biography, Gale (Detroit, MI), Volume 7: *Twentieth-Century American Dramatists*, 1981, Volume 44: *American Screenwriters*, 1986.

DiGaetani, John L., editor, *A Search for a Postmodern Theater: Interviews with Contemporary Playwrights*, Greenwood Press (New York, NY), 1991.

Encyclopedia of World Biography, 2nd edition, Gale (Detroit, MI), 1998.

Feiffer, Jules, *The Great Comic Book Heroes*, Dial (New York, NY), 1965.

PERIODICALS

American Theatre, May-June, 2003, "Twenty Questions: Jules Feiffer," p. 88.

Back Stage, June 27, 2003, Irene Backalenick, review of *A Bad Friend*, p. 48.

Booklist, November 15, 1993, Elizabeth Bush, review of *The Man in the Ceiling*, p. 620; December 1, 1997, Stephanie Zvirin, review of *Meanwhile . . .* , p. 636; August 19, 1999, Stephanie Zvirin, review of *Bark, George*, p. 2052; June 1, 2002, Hazel Rochman, review of *By the Side of the Road*, p. 1742; December 1, 2002, Hazel Rochman, review of *The House across the Street*, p. 673; May 1, 2004, Jennifer Mattson, review of *The Daddy Mountain*, p. 1562.

Bulletin of the Center for Children's Books, December, 1993, pp. 120-121; February, 1996, p. 189.

Comics Journal, August, 1988, Gary Groth, "Memories of a Pro Bono Cartoonist"; winter, 2004, "A Thirst for Storytelling."

Dramatists Guild Quarterly, winter, 1987, Christopher Duran, "Jules Feiffer, Cartoonist-Playwright."

Editor & Publisher, May 31, 1986, David Astor, "An Unexpected Pulitzer for Jules Feiffer;" May 29, 2000, Dave Astor, "Feiffer Focus No Longer on Syndication," p. 35.

Five Owls, January-February, 1994, Cathryn M. Camper, review of *The Man in the Ceiling*, pp. 66-67.

Horn Book, September-October, 1997, p. 557; March-April, 1998, Lauren Adams, review of *I Lost My Bear*, p. 212; January, 2001, review of *Some Things Are Scary*, p. 83; November-December, 2001, review of *I'm Not Bobby!*, pp. 735-736; May-June, 2002, Kristi Beavin, review of *The Man in the Ceiling*, p. 353; May-June, 2004, Joanna Rudge Long, review of *The Daddy Mountain*, pp. 310-311.

Kirkus Reviews, July 15, 1997, p. 1110; March 15, 1998, p. 402; November 1, 2002, review of *The House across the Street*, p. 1611; April 1, 2004, review of *The Daddy Mountain*, p. 328.

Library Journal, July, 2003, Steve Raiteri, review of *The Great Comic Book Heroes*, pp. 69-70.

Los Angeles Times, September 30, 1993, Lawrence Christon, "Jules Feiffer Fine-toons His Career," p. E1; June 17, 2000, John J. Goldman, "Swan Song for Feiffer's Dancer," p. D1.

New Leader, July-August, 2003, Stefan Kanfer, "Family Affairs," pp. 41-43.

New York Post, May 26, 2002, "Still Quick on the Draw," p. 62.

New York Times, May 29, 1997, Elisabeth Bumiller, "Jules Feiffer Draws the Line at No Pay from *The Voice,* " p. B1; January 23, 2000, Josh Schonwald, "Laughs and Learning with Jules Feiffer," p. P2; June 17, 2000, Sarah Boxer, "Jules Feiffer, at Seventy-one, Slows down to a Gallop," p. B1; March 4, 2003, Mel Gussow, "Jules Feiffer, Freed of His Comic Strip Duties, Finds a New Visibility," p. E1; June 10, 2003, Bruce Weber, "Uncle Joe Smiles down on a Family of Old Lefties," p. E1.

New York Times Book Review, November 14, 1993, Jonathan Fast, review of *The Man in the Ceiling,* p. 57; December 31, 1995, Daniel Pinkwater, review of *A Barrel of Laughs, a Vale of Tears;* March 15, 1998, Constance L. Hays, review of *Meanwhile . . . ,* p. 24; May 17, 1998, Krystyna Poray Goddu, review of *I Lost My Bear,* p. 22; August 15, 1999, review of *Bark, George,* p. 24; November 19, 2000, Jeanne P. Binder, "Things That Go Squish in the Night," p. 44; November 18, 2001, Dwight Garner, "'Better Not Call Me Again. I'm a Monster,'" p. 25; September 29, 2002, Cynthia Zarin, "The Boy Who Willed One Thing," p. 27; October 29, 2002, Cynthia Zarin, review of *By the Side of the Road;* June 8, 2003, Andrea Stevens, "Jules Feiffer's Communist Manifesto," p. 5; June 27, 2004, p. 14.

New York Times Magazine, May 16, 1976, Robin Brantley, "'Knock Knock' 'Who's There?' 'Feiffer'"; June 15, 2003, Deborah Solomon, "Playing with History," p. 13.

Print, May-June, 1998, Steven Heller, interview with Feiffer, pp. 40-41; May-June, 1999, Carol Stevens, "Baby Teeth," p. 50; September, 2000, Steven Heller, "Feiffer's Last Dance," p. 26.

Publishers Weekly, October 25, 1993, review of *The Man in the Ceiling,* p. 62; November 27, 1995, review of *A Barrel of Laughs, a Vale of Tears,* p. 70; January 26, 1998, review of *I Lost My Bear,* p. 91; June 21, 1999, review of *Bark, George,* p. 66; October, 2000, review of *Some Things Are Scary,* p. 76; August 20, 2001, review of *I'm Not Bobby,* p. 78; May 13, 2002, review of *By the Side of the Road,* p. 69; October 14, 2002, review of *The House across the Street,* p. 82; June 30, 2003, review of *The Great Comic Book Heroes,* p. 59; April 5, 2004, review of *The Daddy Mountain,* p. 60.

Quill & Quire, November, 1993, p. 40.

School Library Journal, January, 1996, p. 108; September, 1997, Lisa S. Murphy, review of *Meanwhile . . . ,* p. 180; March, 1998, Julie Cummins, review of *I Lost My Bear,* p. 179; September, 1999, p. 182; January 1, 2001, Maryann H. Owen, review of *Some Things Are Scary,* p. 101; November, 2001, review of *I'm Not Bobby!,* pp. 119-120; May, 2002, Wendy Lukehart, review of *By the Side of the Road,* p. 152; February, 2003, Wendy Lukehart, review of *The House across the Street,* p. 111; May, 2003, Steve Weiner, "A Found Feiffer," p. 33; June, 2004, Grace Oliff, review of *The Daddy Mountain,* p. 108.

Time, May 21, 2001, Francine Russo, "A Matter of Medium," p. G8.

ONLINE

Jules Feiffer Online, http://www.julesfeiffer.com (February 1, 2005).

Public Broadcasting System Web site, http://www.pbs.org/ (March 15, 1998), "The Art of Jules Feiffer"; (August 10, 2000) "Power of the Pen."*

* * *

FRANK, E(mily) R. 1967-

Personal

Born 1967, in Richmond, VA; married. *Education:* College graduate; attended writing class at New School of Social Research (now New School University).

Addresses

Home—Montclair, NJ. *Agent*—Charlotte Sheedy Literary Agency, 65 Bleecker St., New York, NY 10012.

Career

Psychotherapist and clinical social worker in New York, NY; author of young adult novels.

Awards, Honors

Quick Picks for Reluctant Young Adult Readers selection, American Library Association (ALA), 2001, for *Life Is Funny;* Best Books for Young Adults selection, ALA, and *Los Angeles Times* Book Award finalist, both 2003, both for *America;* Best Books for Young Adults selection, ALA, 2004, for *Friction.*

Writings

Life Is Funny, DK Ink (New York, NY), 2000.
America, Atheneum (New York, NY), 2002.
Friction, Atheneum (New York, NY), 2003.
Wave, Atheneum (New York, NY), 2005.

Contributor to *Rush Hour.*

Sidelights

E. R. Frank has worked in prisons, day treatment centers, a middle school, and an outpatient mental health clinic. A clinical social worker who also established a psychotherapy practice in Manhattan, Frank has had many troubled youths pass her way; in fact, a full third of her caseload has been adolescents. Frank brings her experience and expertise in the area of teen problems to bear in her novels about young New Yorkers at risk and dealing with trauma. Beginning with *Life Is Funny,* and continuing in *America, Friction,* and *Wave,* Frank presents non-sensationalized yet haunting evocations of adolescents and teenagers confronted with daunting situations, including recognizing and surviving sexual abuse.

"All of my characters are complete fiction," Frank assured Holly Atkins in an interview for the *St. Petersburg Times.* Although inspired by the experiences she has had as a clinical psychologist, the author maintains that "the characters in those books are not based on any one person." Rather they are a composite of many of the adolescents she has worked with over the years. Speaking with Jean Westmoore in the *Buffalo News,* Frank reiterated this point: "I do not write or talk about my clients at all. After so many years of working with kids, adolescents, [and] adults within the criminal justice system, I had this cumulative emotion of so many people who had been lost in the system and hadn't had the one kind of relationship that might have saved them."

Born into a family of "voracious readers," as Jason Britton noted in a *Publishers Weekly* profile of the author, Frank gravitated to writing at an early age. She spent a lot of time during her childhood around her grandfather, writer Gerold Frank, author of *The Boston Strangler, American Death,* and *Judy.* "When I was very young, it was because of [my grandfather] . . . that I realized that a writing career was a possibility," Frank told Britton. A clinical social worker who sometimes used writing as a form of therapy with her clients, Frank finally began writing herself in 1996.

Frank did not have a particular audience in mind when composing her first book, a tale of eleven kids that is composed of interlocking stories. Her young protagonists narrate their misadventures over a seven-year period, each in his or her distinctive voice. When she was finished with the manuscript, Frank took the advice of friends and submitted it to a literary agent who liked the story and sent it on to Richard Jackson at DK Ink. Jackson also appreciated the story and gave Frank a call, during which he began the editorial process. "It was like a dream come true," Frank told Britton. "I felt honored to be working with him." Published in 2000, Frank's debut novel, *Life Is Funny,* drew praise from critics. Alice Casey Smith, writing in *School Library Journal,* called the book a "choral piece of writing that sings of coming-of-age in a multiracial Brooklyn community." Dysfunctional families, racism, drugs, violence, divorce, death, molestation, violence, and abandonment all mar the lives of the book's seven adolescents, but they greet their predicaments with more than anger. As Smith noted, the characters "are boisterous and full of laughter, because after all is said and done, life is funny, isn't it?" According to *Booklist* critic Hazel Rochman, "Each chapter, each vignette within a chapter, builds to its own climax, and the stories weave together to surprise you." More praise came from a contributor for *Publishers Weekly,* who remarked that "the language is gritty, and some of the story lines will be intense for young readers, but this is ultimately an uplifting book about resilience, loyalty and courage." Paula Rohrlick, reviewing the title in *Kliatt,* pronounced *Life Is Funny,* "an arresting, accomplished first novel."

Taking place over seven years, E. R. Frank's 2000 novel focuses on a group of teens living in Brooklyn, New York, who find their lives weaving together in surprising ways despite their diverse circumstances. (Cover illustration by Michael Yuen.)

Frank continues her gritty investigations of adolescence and young adulthood with 2002's *America,* a "heartbreaking story of survival, forgiveness, and redemption," in the opinion of *School Library Journal* contributor Jennifer Ralston. In the book Frank tells the story of America, a confused fifteen-year-old boy of mixed race who is lost in the labyrinthine system of foster care and hospitalization. So damaged is America by abandonment and abuse that he has tried to kill himself. When he becomes a patient in a residential psychiatric program, he is lucky enough to meet up with Dr. B, who slowly teaches him the lessons of survival.

Frank's second book was greeted with wide critical acclaim. A contributor for *Kirkus Reviews* called *America* a "wrenching tour de force" as well as a "work of sublime humanity," while *Booklist* reviewer Gillian Engberg found it a "piercing, unforgettable novel." Kathleen Isaacs, writing in *School Library Journal,* felt that Frank's "control of this story is impressive." For

Horn Book contributor Jennifer M. Brabander, "it's the strong, deeply felt connection created between protagonist and audience that makes this such a moving novel." Kristen R. Crabtree, writing in the *Journal of Adolescence & Adult Literacy,* commented that *America* "is not for the immature reader" because its complex plot makes it "sophisticated in delivering disturbing experiences." Crabtree went on to note, though, that mature "adolescents will find a connection to [America's] voice and self-acceptance. America is worth finding and getting to know." In *Friction* Frank again deals with teen trauma and abuse. In this novel, she focuses on an eighth-grade classroom, a microcosm in which friction can arise between students and teacher and between individual students. The book is told in the present tense from the point of view of twelve-year-old Alex, a student in an alternative school. A happy tomboyish kid on the cusp of adolescence, Alex loves soccer, her buddy, Tim, and her teacher, Simon, who she considers to be the best teacher in the school. Simon has managed, in fact, to win over the entire class with his unorthodox teaching style and his friendliness. But all this changes with the arrival of a new student in class, Stacy. The new girl has real attitude and at first Alex is drawn to her. But soon Stacy begins spreading rumors that Simon has more than a friendly interest in Alex. Stacy ac-

cuses the teacher of being a "pervert," and soon the whole class, including Alex, is re-thinking their relationship with him. The police enter the picture, and Alex is confused when they ask her if Simon has ever touched her. Ultimately, through the intercession of Alex's psychiatrist father, things are straightened out, and it becomes apparent that in fact it is Stacy's father who is doing the abusing.

Again reviewers responded warmly to Frank's hard-hitting theme. A reviewer for *Publishers Weekly* noted that the author "insightfully addresses topics of teen sexuality and child abuse" in a "provocative novel" that is "sure to spark heated discussions." *Kliatt* reviewer Rohrlick also observed that Frank "doesn't shy away from difficult topics," and that *Friction* serves as an "excellent way for teachers, counselors, and parents to open up discussions of what constitutes sexual abuse." Rohrlick also thought the novel would be a "gripping read for younger adolescent girls." A critic for *Kirkus Reviews* praised Frank for a "subtly done" approach to a "combustible" subject, and *Horn Book* contributor Bridget T. McCaffrey commended Alex's narrative voice as "genuine" and "believable."

Speaking with Westmoore, Frank summed up her approach to writing for young adults. "I don't write to make a point," she noted. "If people read [one of my novels] and take away from it some new information or feelings about action they want to take, that would be wonderful." In her interview with Atkins, Frank commented that she does not write with an "agenda." Instead, "what's important to me is that readers are moved or touched in some way and that when they finish a book, they feel they've been transported into the world of the characters for a short while."

Biographical and Critical Sources

PERIODICALS

Book, May-June, 2002, review of *America,* p. 29.

Booklist, February 15, 2001, Hazel Rochman, review of *Life Is Funny,* p. 1152; February 15, 2002, Gillian Engberg, review of *America,* p. 1013; July, 2003, Gillian Engberg, review of *Friction,* p. 1886; January 1, 2004, Lolly Gepson, review of *Friction* (audiobook), p. 893.

Buffalo News, February 11, 2002, Jean Westmoore, "The Story of a Boy Named 'America,'" p. A7.

Horn Book, May, 2000, Jennifer M. Brabander, review of *Life Is Funny,* p. 313; March-April, 2002, Jennifer M. Brabander, review of *America,* pp. 211-212; July-August, 2003, Bridget T. McCaffrey, review of *Friction,* p. 455; March-April, 2004, Kristi Elle Jemtegaard, review of *America* (audiobook), p. 199.

Journal of Adolescent and Adult Literacy, September, 2002, Kristen R. Crabtree, review of *America,* p. 83.

Kirkus Reviews, December 1, 2001, review of *America,* p. 1684; May 1, 2003, review of *Friction,* p. 676.

When accusations of sexual abuse are raised by a new student at Alex's posh private school, Alex and her fellow students are torn between loyalty to a popular teacher and the need to discover the truth.

Kliatt, January, 2002, Paula Rohrlick, review of *America,* pp. 5-6; July, 2002, Paula Rohrlick, review of *Life Is Funny,* p. 18; May, 2003, Paula Rohrlick, review of *Friction,* p. 8; November, 2003, Sherri F. Ginsberg, review of *Friction* (audiobook), p. 48.

New York Times, May 19, 2002, Mary Harris Russell, "Lost Boy," p. 24L.

Publishers Weekly, March 13, 2000, review of *Life Is Funny,* p. 85; June 26, 2000, Jason Britton, "E. R. Frank," p. 32; January 7, 2002, review of *America,* p. 66; April 7, 2003, review of *Friction,* p. 68; June 16, 2003, review of *Friction* (audiobook), p. 25.

St. Petersburg Times (St. Petersburg, FL), February 16, 2004, Holly Atkins, interview with Frank, p. E6.

School Library Journal, May, 2000, Alice Casey Smith, review of *Life Is Funny,* p. 172; March, 2002, Kathleen Isaacs, review of *America,* p. 230; October, 2003, Lynn Evarts, review of *Friction* (audiobook), p. 91, and Jennifer Ralston, review of *America,* p. 99.*

* * *

FROST, Helen 1949-

Personal

Born 1949, in Brookings, SD; married Chad Thopson; children: Lloyd, Glen. *Education:* Syracuse University, B.A. (elementary education); Indiana University, M.A. (English), 1994. *Hobbies and other interests:* Hiking, cross-country skiing, raising and releasing monarch butterflies, geneaology.

Addresses

Home—Fort Wayne, IN. *Agent*—Capstone Press, 151 Good Counsel Dr., P.O. Box 669, Mankato, MN 56002. *E-mail*—helenfrost@comcast.net.

Career

Educator and author. Kilquhanity House School (boarding school), Scotland, teacher; elementary school teacher/principal in Telida, AK, for three years, then Ketchican, AK; Indiana University/Purdue University at Fort Wayne, instructor. Fort Wayne Dance Collective, member of inderdisciplinary artistic team, beginning 1994.

Awards, Honors

Robert H. Winner Memorial Award, Poetry Society of America, 1992; Mary Carolyn Davies Award, Poetry Society of America, 1993; Women Poets Series Competition winner, Ampersand Press, 1993; Michael Printz Honor Book designation, American Library Association, 2004, for *Keesha's House; several other awards and honors.*

Writings

JUVENILE FICTION

Keesha's House, Frances Foster Books (New York, NY), 2003.

Spinning through the Universe: A Novel in Poems from Room 214, Frances Foster Books (New York, NY), 2004.

"BIRDS" SERIES: JUVENILE NONFICTION

Bird Eggs, Pebble Books (Mankato, MN), 1999.
Bird Nests, Pebble Books (Mankato, MN), 1999.
Baby Birds, Pebble Books (Mankato, MN), 1999.
Bird Families, Pebble Books (Mankato, MN), 1999.

"BUTTERFLIES" SERIES: JUVENILE NONFICTION

Butterfly Eggs, Pebble Books (Mankato, MN), 1999.
Caterpillars, Pebble Books (Mankato, MN), 1999.
Butterfly Colors, Pebble Books (Mankato, MN), 1999.
Monarch Butterflies, Pebble Books (Mankato, MN), 1999.

"DENTAL HEALTH" SERIES: JUVENILE NONFICTION

Your Teeth, Pebble Books (Mankato, MN), 1999.
Going to the Dentist, Pebble Books (Mankato, MN), 1999.
Food for Healthy Teeth, Pebble Books (Mankato, MN), 1999.
Brushing Well, Pebble Books (Mankato, MN), 1999.

"FOOD GUIDE PYRAMID" SERIES; JUVENILE NONFICTION

The Fruit Group, Pebble Books (Mankato, MN), 2000.
Eating Right, Pebble Books (Mankato, MN), 2000.
The Vegetable Group, Pebble Books (Mankato, MN), 2000.
The Dairy Group, Pebble Books (Mankato, MN), 2000.
Fats, Oils, and Sweets, Pebble Books (Mankato, MN), 2000.
Drinking Water, Pebble Books (Mankato, MN), 2000.
The Grain Group, Pebble Books (Mankato, MN), 2000.
The Meat and Protein Group, Pebble Books (Mankato, MN), 2000.

"WATER" SERIES: JUVENILE NONFICTION

Keeping Water Clean, Pebble Books (Mankato, MN), 2000.
The Water Cycle, Pebble Books (Mankato, MN), 2000.
Water as a Solid, Pebble Books (Mankato, MN), 2000.
Water as a Liquid, Pebble Books (Mankato, MN), 2000.
Water as a Gas, Pebble Books (Mankato, MN), 2000.
We Need Water, Pebble Books (Mankato, MN), 2000.

Author's titles have been translated into Spanish.

"NATIONAL HOLIDAYS" SERIES; JUVENILE NONFICTION

Memorial Day, Pebble Books (Mankato, MN), 2000.
Independence Day, Pebble Books (Mankato, MN), 2000.
Martin Luther King, Jr., Day, Pebble Books (Mankato, MN), 2000.
Presidents' Day, Pebble Books (Mankato, MN), 2000.

"SENSES" SERIES; JUVENILE NONFICTION

Your Senses, Pebble Books (Mankato, MN), 2000.
Smelling, Pebble Books (Mankato, MN), 2000.
Touching, Pebble Books (Mankato, MN), 2000.
Tasting, Pebble Books (Mankato, MN), 2000.
Seeing, Pebble Books (Mankato, MN), 2000.
Hearing, Pebble Books (Mankato, MN), 2000.

"EMOTIONS" SERIES; JUVENILE NONFICTION

Feeling Sad, Pebble Books (Mankato, MN), 2001.
Feeling Angry, Pebble Books (Mankato, MN), 2001.
Feeling Scared, Pebble Books (Mankato, MN), 2001.
Feeling Happy, Pebble Books (Mankato, MN), 2001.

"HUMAN BODY SYSTEMS" SERIES; JUVENILE NONFICTION

The Circulatory System, Pebble Books (Mankato, MN), 2001.
The Respiratory System, Pebble Books (Mankato, MN), 2001.
The Nervous System, Pebble Books (Mankato, MN), 2001.
The Muscular System, Pebble Books (Mankato, MN), 2001.
The Skeletal System, Pebble Books (Mankato, MN), 2001.
The Digestive System, Pebble Books (Mankato, MN), 2001.

"LOOKING AT SIMPLE MACHINES" SERIES: JUVENILE NONFICTION

What Are Inclined Planes?, Pebble Books (Mankato, MN), 2001.
What Are Levers?, Pebble Books (Mankato, MN), 2001.
What Are Screws?, Pebble Books (Mankato, MN), 2001.
What Are Wedges?, Pebble Books (Mankato, MN), 2001.
What Are Wheels and Axles?, Pebble Books (Mankato, MN), 2001.
What Are Pulleys?, Pebble Books (Mankato, MN), 2001.

"OUR WORLD" SERIES: JUVENILE NONFICTION

A Look at China, Pebble Books (Mankato, MN), 2002.
A Look at France, Pebble Books (Mankato, MN), 2002.
A Look at Kenya, Pebble Books (Mankato, MN), 2002.
A Look at Russia, Pebble Books (Mankato, MN), 2002.
A Look at Japan, Pebble Books (Mankato, MN), 2002.
A Look at Canada, Pebble Books (Mankato, MN), 2002.
A Look at Australia, Pebble Books (Mankato, MN), 2002.
A Look at Mexico, Pebble Books (Mankato, MN), 2002.
A Look at Egypt, Pebble Books (Mankato, MN), 2003.
A Look at Cuba, Pebble Books (Mankato, MN), 2003.
A Look at Germany, Pebble Books (Mankato, MN), 2003.
A Look at Vietnam, Pebble Books (Mankato, MN), 2003.

"ALL ABOUT PETS" SERIES; JUVENILE NONFICTION

Cats, Pebble Books (Mankato, MN), 2001.
Fish, Pebble Books (Mankato, MN), 2001.
Hamsters, Pebble Books (Mankato, MN), 2001.

Dogs, Pebble Books (Mankato, MN), 2001.
Rabbits, Pebble Books (Mankato, MN), 2001.
Birds, Pebble Books (Mankato, MN), 2001.

"INSECTS" SERIES; JUVENILE NONFICTION

Praying Mantises, Pebble Books (Mankato, MN), 2001.
Walkingsticks, Pebble Books (Mankato, MN), 2001.
Water Bugs, Capstone Press (Mankato, MN), 2001.
Moths, Capstone Press (Mankato, MN), 2001.
Wasps, Capstone Press (Mankato, MN), 2001.
Cicadas, Capstone Press (Mankato, MN), 2001.

"RAIN FOREST ANIMALS" SERIES; JUVENILE NONFICTION

Jaguars, Pebble Books (Mankato, MN), 2002.
Boa Constrictors, Pebble Books (Mankato, MN), 2002.
Gorillas, Capstone Press (Mankato, MN), 2002.
Tree Frogs, Pebble Books (Mankato, MN), 2002.
Tarantulas, Pebble Books (Mankato, MN), 2002.
Parrots, Capstone Press (Mankato, MN), 2002.
Lemurs, Pebble Books (Mankato, MN), 2003.
Chimpanzees, Pebble Books (Mankato, MN), 2003.
Leaf-cutting Ants, Pebble Books (Mankato, MN), 2003.
Tigers, Pebble Books (Mankato, MN), 2003.

"COMING TO AMERICA" SERIES; JUVENILE NONFICTION

German Immigrants, 1820-1920, Blue Earth Books (Mankato, MN), 2002.
Russian Immigrants, 1860-1949, Blue Earth Books (Mankato, MN), 2003.

"FAMOUS AMERICANS" SERIES; JUVENILE NONFICTION

John F. Kennedy, Pebble Books (Mankato, MN), 2003.
Sojourner Truth, Pebble Books (Mankato, MN), 2003.
Betsy Ross, Pebble Books (Mankato, MN), 2003.
Thurgood Marshall, Pebble Books (Mankato, MN), 2003.

"LET'S MEET" SERIES; JUVENILE NONFICTION

Let's Meet Jackie Robinson, Chelsea Clubhouse Books (Philadelphia, PA), 2004.
Let's Meet Booker T. Washington, Chelsea Clubhouse (Philadelphia, PA), 2004.
Let's Meed Ida B. Wells-Barnett, Chelsea Clubhouse Books (Philadelphia, PA), 2004.

"WEATHER" SERIES; JUVENILE NONFICTION

Ice, Capstone Press (Mankato, MN), 2004.
Fog, Capstone Press (Mankato, MN), 2004.
Snow, Capstone Press (Mankato, MN), 2004.
Wind, Capstone Press (Mankato, MN), 2004.

"DINOSAURS AND PREHISTORIC ANIMALS" SERIES; JUVENILE NONFICTION

Woolly Mammoth, Capstone Press (Mankato, MN), 2004.
Tyrannosaurus Rex, Capstone Press (Mankato, MN), 2004.
Triceratops, Capstone Press (Mankato, MN), 2004.

Sabertooth Cat, Capstone Press (Mankato, MN), 2004.
Allosaurus, Capstone Press (Mankato, MN), 2004.
Stegosaurus, Capstone Press (Mankato, MN), 2004.

"HELPERS IN OUR COMMUNITY" SERIES; JUVENILE NONFICTION

We Need Auto Mechanics, Capstone Press (Mankato, MN), 2004.
We Need Plumbers, Capstone Press (Mankato, MN), 2004.
We Need School Bus Drivers, Pebble Books (Mankato, MN), 2004.
We Need Pharmacists, Capstone Press (Mankato, MN), 2005.

FOR ADULTS

(Editor) *Season of Dead Water* (poetry and prose anthology), Breitenbush Books (Portland, OR), 1990.
Skin of a Fish, Bones of a Bird: Poems, Ampersand Press (Bristol, RI), 1993.
(Editor) *Why Darkness Seems So Light: Young People Speak out about Violence* (also see below), Pecan Grove Press, 1998.
(With Harvey Cocks) *Why Darkness Seems So Light* (play; based on the book of the same title), Pioneer Drama, 1999.
When I Whistle, Nobody Listens: Helping Young People Write about Difficult Issues, Heinemann (Portsmouth, NH), 2001.

Work in Progress

Monarch and Milkweed, for Atheneum, and the novel *The Braid,* for Frances Foster Books, 2006.

Sidelights

In addition to her work as a teacher—she has taught students in Scotland, Alaska, and the American Midwest—poet, and playwright, Helen Frost is a prolific author of fiction and nonfiction for young readers. Frost's fictional works include the award-winning young-adult novel *Keesha's House* and the novel *Spinning through the Universe: A Novel in Poems from Room 214,* while nonfiction contributions to informative series for elementary-grade students reflect her interest in science and biology. In addition to her work for young people, Frost is also the author of *When I Whisper, Nobody Listens: Helping Young People Write about Difficult Issues,* a book which, according to *Journal of Adolescent and Adult Literacy* contributor M. P. Cavanaugh, is designed to "prepare teachers to work with students on sensitive issues and to provide nonviolent solutions to some of their problems." A novel-in-verse for older readers, *Keesha's House* focuses on seven inner-city teens whose lives are currently in turmoil and who find refuge in a home owned by a caring adult named Joe. Dubbed "Keesha's House" in honor of the first person to be welcomed there, the home becomes a haven for pregnant teen Stephie; Katie, who is

escaping her stepfather's sexual molestation; gay teen Harris, whose parents do not accept his sexual orientation; unhappy foster child Dontay; Carmen, who is battling an addiction to drugs; high school basketball star Jason, who struggles between college and his responsibility as the father of Stephie's baby; and Keesha herself. Praised as a "moving" work containing "dramatic monologues that are personal, poetic, and immediate," by *Booklist* contributor Hazel Rochman, *Keesha's House* features sonnet and sestina verse forms that reflect contemporary speech, making the book easy going for those unfamiliar with poetry. In *Publishers Weekly* a reviewer found the work "thoughtfully composed and ultimately touching," while Michele Winship wrote in *Kliatt* that the poems in *Keesha's House* "weave together stories that depict the harsh reality of teenage life."

A book that "brings to life the voices and spirit of a fifth-grade classroom," according to a *Publishers Weekly* contributor, *Spinning through the Universe* contains poems that reflect the dreams, worries, enthusiasms, and day-to-day lives of Mrs. Williams's twenty-six fifth graders, each of whom composes a poem in a different poetic form. The fictional preteen writers wax poetic about subjects ranging from a lost bicycle to the death of a parent, in what the *Publishers Weekly* critic de-

In Frost's 2003 young-adult novel-in-verse, seven teens find a temporary refuge from problems ranging from pregnancy and abusive relationships to discrimination based on their sexual identity through the help of homeless teen Keesha. (Cover illustration by R. Gregory Christi.)

In Helen Frost's nonfiction title Coming to America: German Immigrants *the author profiles the experiences of the many Europeans who left their families to create a new life in America after 1820.* (Photograph by Corbis.)

scribed as "brief, deceptively casual poetic monologues" that Frost follows with a concluding chapter about reading and writing verse. Forms include haiku, blank verse, sonnets, sestinas, rondelets, and other less-familiar schemes; an entire section devoted to acrostics prompted *School Library Journal* contributor Lee Bock to note that "readers will enjoy decoding them to reveal an additional thought about each character." Bock dubbed *Spinning through the Universe* a "boon for poetry classes," while in *Kirkus Reviews* a critic wrote that Frost's use of "original imagery and understated, natural voices make these poems sensitive and insightful." Many of Frost's series nonfiction are short books presenting basic facts and information in a minimal text well-illustrated with photographs, maps, diagrams, and other artwork. With approximately twenty sentences per book, volumes such as *A Look at France* in the "Our World" series and *What Are Levers?* in the "Looking at Simple Machines" series are designed for beginning scholars, and incorporate large print and a simple vocabulary to convey rudimentary information. More de-

tail is provided in Frost's contributions to the "Coming to America" series, designed for older readers. Praising Frost's research in *German Immigrants, 1820-1920* as "solid," *Booklist* reviewer Rochman added that the book serves young readers of German and Scandinavian descent as "a good place to start researching family history."

Biographical and Critical Sources

PERIODICALS

Booklist, October 15, 2001, Hazel Rochman, review of *German Immigrants, 1820-1920,* p. 406; March 1, 2003, Hazel Rochman, review of *Keesha's House,* p. 1192; April 1, 2004, Hazel Rochman, review of *Spinning through the Universe: A Novel in Poems from Room 214,* p. 1363.

Journal of Adolescent & Adult Literacy, November, 2002, M. P. Cavanaugh, review of *When I Whisper, Nobody*

Listens: Helping Young People Write about Difficult Issues, p. 275.

Kirkus Reviews, March 1, 2004, review of *Spinning through the Universe,* p. 221.

Kliatt, March, 2003, Michele Winship, review of *Keesha's House,* p. 10.

Publishers Weekly, May 25, 1990, Penny Kaganoff, review of *Season of Dead Water,* p. 54; April 21, 2003, review of *Keesha's House,* p. 63; April 5, 2004, review of *Spinning through the Universe,* p. 63.

School Library Journal, August, 2000, Pamela K. Bombay, review of *Martin Luther King, Jr. Day,* p. 169; October, 2000, Carolyn Jenks, review of *Drinking Water,* p. 147; January, 2001, Judith Constantinides, review of *Feeling Angry,* p. 117; April, 2001, Dona J. Helmer, review of *The Circulatory System,* p. 130; August, 2001, Blair Christolon, review of *What Are Levers?,* p. 168; September, 2001, Karey Wehner, review of *Moths,* p. 214; December, 2001, Elizabeth Talbot, review of *A Look at Russia,* p. 121; June, 2002, Ann W. Moore, review of *A Look at France,* p. 120; October, 2002, Linda Ludke, review of *A Look at Canada,* p. 144; October, 2003, Jennifer Ralston, review of *Keesha's House,* p. 99; November, 2003, Michele Shaw, review of *Betsy Ross,* p. 125; April, 2004, Lee Bock, review of *Spinning through the Universe,* p. 154; April, 2004, review of *Keesha's House,* p. 64.

ONLINE

Helen Frost Web site, http://helenfrost.com (December 30, 2004).

G-H

GILBERT, Sheri L.

Personal

Married; children: one son.

Addresses

Home—AZ. *Agent*—c/o Author Mail, Knopf Publishing Group, Random House, 299 Park Avenue, New York, NY 10171-0002. *E-mail*—sherilgilbert@qwest.net.

Career

Writer.

Writings

The Legacy of Gloria Russell, Alfred A. Knopf (New York, NY), 2004.

Sidelights

Beginning her authorial career after dedicating several years to her family, Sheri L. Gilbert approached the craft of writing children's books seriously. She studied, wrote, and connected with other writers, ultimately publishing her first book, *The Legacy of Gloria Russell,* in 2004. Taking place in the Ozarks of Missouri, Gilbert's debut recounts the affect small-town's prejudice has on an unfortunate outsider with the Eastern European last name Satan. After twelve-year-old Billy James Wilkins' best friend, Gloria Russell, dies of an aneurysm, Billy decides to follow the outgoing girl's example and befriends Mr. Satan, a reclusive woodcarver who had also been a friend of Gloria's prior to her death. While his friendship is at first motivated by curiosity as much as anything, Billy gradually comes to appreciate his new friend, as Gloria did, and defends the foreign-born craftsman when suspicions start to circulate among neighbors. "Billy James' grief over the loss of his friend

Sheri L. Gilbert

is palpable, and young readers will admire his determination" to defend his friend's memory, stated *Booklist* reviewer Jennifer Mattson, while a *Publishers Weekly* reviewer praised Gilbert's prose as "skillful." In a review for *School Library Journal,* Connie Tyrrell Burns praised the book as an effective coming-of-age novel, adding that *The Legacy of Gloria Russell* is "lyrically written."

Biographical and Critical Sources

PERIODICALS

Booklist, May 1, 2004, Jennifer Mattson, review of *The Legacy of Gloria Russell,* p. 1559.
Kirkus Reviews, April 1, 2004, review of *The Legacy of Gloria Russell,* p. 329.

In Sheri Gilbert's coming-of-age novel a boy living in the Ozarks learns to deal with the death of a young friend named Gloria Russell by creating relationships with others who shared his affection for her. (Cover illustration by Wendy Schultz Wubbels.)

Publishers Weekly, April 5, 2004, review of *The Legacy of Gloria Russell,* p. 62.
School Library Journal, April, 2004, Connie Tyrrell Burns, review of *The Legacy of Gloria Russell,* p. 154.

ONLINE

Sheri L. Gilbert Web site, http://www.sherigilbert.com (January 25, 2005).

*   *   *

HAHN, Mary Downing 1937-

Personal

Born December 9, 1937, in Washington, DC; daughter of Kenneth Ernest (an automobile mechanic) and Anna Elisabeth (a teacher; maiden name, Sherwood) Downing; married William E. Hahn, October 7, 1961 (divorced, 1977); married Norman Pearce Jacob (a librar-

ian), April 23, 1982; children: (first marriage) Katherine Sherwood, Margaret Elizabeth. *Education:* University of Maryland at College Park, B.A., 1960, M.A., 1969, doctoral study, 1970-74. *Politics:* Democrat. *Hobbies and other interests:* Reading, walking, photography, bicycling.

Addresses

Home—6525 Smokehouse Court, Columbia, MD 21045. *E-mail*—mdh12937@aol.com.

Career

Novelist and artist. Art teacher at junior high school in Greenbelt, MD, 1960-61; Hutzler's Department Store, Baltimore, MD, clerk, 1963; correspondence clerk for Navy Federal Credit Union, 1963-65; homemaker and writer, 1965-70; English instructor, University of Maryland, 1970-75; freelance artist for *Cover to Cover,* WETA-TV, 1973-75; Prince George's County Memorial Library System, Laurel Branch, Laurel, MD, children's librarian associate, 1975-91; full-time writer, 1991—.

Member

Society of Children's Book Writers and Illustrators, Washington Children's Book Guild.

Awards, Honors

American Library Association (ALA) Reviewer's Choice, Library of Congress Children's Books, and *School Library Journal* Best Books citations, all 1983, Child Study Association of America Children's Books of the Year and National Council of Teachers of English Teachers' Choice citations, both 1984, and William Allen White Children's Choice Award, 1986, all for *Daphne's Book;* Dorothy Canfield Fisher Award, 1988, and children's choice awards from ten other states, all for *Wait till Helen Comes;* Child Study Association Book Award, 1989, Jane Addams Children's Book Award Honor Book, 1990, and California Young Reader's Medal, 1991, all for *December Stillness;* ALA Books for Reluctant Readers designation, 1990, and children's choice awards from five states, all for *The Dead Man in Indian Creek;* children's choice awards from seven states, all for *The Doll in the Garden;* ALA Notable Book citation, Scott O'Dell Award for Historical Fiction, and Joan G. Sugarman Award, all 1992, Hedda Seisler Mason Award, 1993, and children's choice awards from three states, all for *Stepping on the Cracks;* Best Book for Young Adults citation, Young Adult Library Services Association (YALSA), 1993, and New York Public Library Books for the Teen Age citation, 1994, both for *The Wind Blows Backward;* YALSA pick, 2001, for *Look for Me by Moonlight.*

Writings

FOR CHILDREN

The Sara Summer, Clarion (Boston, MA), 1979.
The Time of the Witch, Clarion (New York, NY), 1982.

Mary Downing Hahn

Daphne's Book, Clarion (New York, NY), 1983.

The Jellyfish Season, Clarion (New York, NY), 1985.

Wait till Helen Comes: A Ghost Story, Clarion (New York, NY), 1986.

Tallahassee Higgins, Clarion (New York, NY), 1987.

December Stillness, Clarion (New York, NY), 1988.

Following the Mystery Man, Clarion (New York, NY), 1988.

The Doll in the Garden, Clarion (New York, NY), 1989.

The Dead Man in Indian Creek, Clarion (New York, NY), 1990.

The Spanish Kidnapping Disaster, Clarion (New York, NY), 1991.

Stepping on the Cracks, Clarion (New York, NY), 1991.

The Wind Blows Backward (young adult), Clarion (New York, NY), 1993.

Time for Andrew: A Ghost Story, Clarion (New York, NY), 1994.

Look for Me by Moonlight, Clarion (New York, NY), 1995.

The Gentleman Outlaw and Me—Eli: A Story of the Old West, Clarion (New York, NY), 1996.

Following My Own Footsteps, Clarion (New York, NY), 1996.

As Ever, Gordy, Clarion (New York, NY), 1998.

Anna All Year Round, illustrated by Diane de Groat, Clarion (New York, NY), 1999.

Promises to the Dead, Clarion (New York, NY), 2000.

Anna on the Farm, illustrated by Diane de Groat, Clarion (New York, NY), 2001.

Hear the Wind Blow, Clarion (New York, NY), 2003.

The Old Willis Place: A Ghost Story, Clarion (New York, NY), 2004.

Janey and the Famous Author, Clarion (New York, NY), 2005.

Witch Trap, Clarion (New York, NY), 2006.

Hahn's books have been translated into Danish, Swedish, Italian, German, Japanese, and French. Contributor to anthologies, including *Don't Give up the Ghost,* 1993, *Bruce Coville's Book of Ghost Stories,* 1994, and *Bruce Coville's Book of Nightmares,* 1995.

Sidelights

A former librarian and artist, Mary Downing Hahn has drawn upon her own childhood, as well as that of her parents and children, to write closely detailed stories that explore family issues. The themes in her books include loss of a parent or loved one, the struggle for identity and acceptance, and the blending of families. Hahn's novels have been successful, winning not only awards for novels such as *Daphne's Book, Wait till Helen Comes: A Ghost Story, The Jellyfish Season, December Stillness, Stepping on the Cracks,* and *Hear the Wind Blow,* but also a large and loyal readership whom Hahn regularly visits on her school speaking tours. Hahn once told *Something about the Author (SATA)* that she strives to create "real life" in her novels. "Like the people I know, I want my characters to be a mixture of strengths and weaknesses, to have good and bad qualities, to be a little confused and unsure of themselves." Like in real life, a happy ending is not always guaranteed. "At the same time, however," Hahn remarked, "I try to leave room for hope."

However, not all of Hahn's work is serious, as she explained in an interview with *Authors and Artists for Young Adults (AAYA).* "Some of my books I call entertainments, and they are often among my most popular. In those I use elements of fantasy and the supernatural, elements I can't employ in the serious fiction. You can't simply have a ghost come along in real life and change the course of a story. Or have the main character time travel out of trouble. But with my entertainments, that is not only possible but demanded." Many of the books Hahn has created in this vein feature supernatural elements, such as time travel, witches, ghosts, and vampires. Though not of a supernatural bent, one of her "entertainments" is *The Gentleman Outlaw and Me–Eli,* in which Hahn was finally able to indulge her own childhood fantasies of running off to the Wild West.

Reading to her daughters gave Hahn the encouragement she needed to try her hand at writing. When her first attempts were rejected, Hahn enrolled in graduate school, working toward a doctorate in English literature. She didn't complete her degree, instead working in the library system and beginning to write for children. Her first book, *The Sara Summer*—the story of a twelve-year-old girl who does not feel comfortable in the world around her—was published in 1979 after three years of writing and revision.

The Sara Summer exhibits an "intimate knowledge of subteens and a well-tuned ear," according to a *Publishers Weekly* contributor. The work centers on the developing friendship between Emily, who is often teased about her height, and Sara, who just moved in next door and is even taller than Emily. Unfortunately, Sara's brash, independent demeanor has a cruel side, exhibited in her treatment of her younger sister. Through a confrontation over this issue, Sara and Emily come to a new understanding of each other and themselves. Although Cyrisse Jaffee, writing in *School Library Journal,* faulted the book's "lack of plot," she noted that "kids will find [it] easy to read and relate to" the "ups and downs" of the girls' friendship. "The vivid characterizations of the two girls make the author's first novel a worthwhile venture," Richard Ashford concluded in *Horn Book.*

Hahn first exhibited her aptitude for including elements of the supernatural in her second book, *The Time of the Witch,* a novel that centers on a young girl's desire for her parents to stay together. "Sulky and opinionated, Laura is not a particularly attractive character," wrote Ann A. Flowers in *Horn Book;* nevertheless, "her problems are real and understandable." In her quest to halt the divorce of her parents, Laura seeks help from a local witch, who uses the opportunity to settle an old score with the unsuspecting family. Barbara Elleman in *Booklist* described the witch as one "readers won't soon forget," and *School Library Journal* contributor Karen Stang Hanley remarked that the "elements of mystery, suspense and the occult are expertly balanced against the realistic dimensions" of the story.

Hahn returns to the subjects of being an outsider and acting responsibly in her third novel, *Daphne's Book,* which a *Publishers Weekly* critic dubbed "a meaningful, gently humorous novel about characters the author endows with humanity." Jessica is dismayed when her English teacher assigns "Daffy" Daphne to be her partner in a school project, but over time the two girls form a friendship that must withstand Jessica's betrayal of Daphne's dangerous living situation to the authorities. "The characters, even secondary ones," stated Audrey B. Eaglen in *School Library Journal,* "are completely believable and very likable." Despite the "happy" ending, Barbara Cutler Helfgott commented in the *New York Times Book Review,* the book's "vitality derives from a convincing respect for hopeful beginnings and hard choices—two conditions for growth, no matter what your age."

Hahn's next work, *The Jellyfish Season,* "is a very realistic look at family stress and the permanent changes it can make," according to a *Bulletin of the Center for Children's Books* reviewer. When thirteen-year-old Kathleen's father loses his job, she, her mother, and her three younger sisters must move in with relatives in a new town. *Horn Book* critic Mary M. Burns commented: "The well-defined characters are the key ingredients in an appealing, first-person narrative which ably conveys the tensions created by economic hardships." Although a reviewer in *Publishers Weekly* stated that at times Kathleen expresses herself "in words too adult for belief," *School Library Journal* writer Marjorie Lewis praised the author's resolution of "almost insurmountable problems in a most satisfying, realistic and reassuring way" and predicted *The Jellyfish Season* "should be a favorite among young teens."

The supernatural reappears in Hahn's next novel, *Wait till Helen Comes,* a tale Cynthia Dobrez described in Chicago's *Tribune Books* as "suspenseful and often terrifying." Molly and her brother move with their mother into a converted church near a graveyard with their new stepfather and his daughter, Heather, whose troublemaking includes her increasingly ominous friendship with a ghost. *Wait till Helen Comes* was widely praised for its effective pacing, realistic characterizations, and convincing supernatural elements. While Elizabeth S. Watson in *Horn Book* found the novel's opening "rather slow," she observed that Hahn "has written a gripping and scary ghost story that develops hauntingly." Judy Greenfield concluded in *School Library Journal,* "This is a powerful, convincing, and frightening tale," that should produce "a heavy demand from readers who are not 'faint at heart.'" Hahn herself found the book to be scary; she explained to *AAYA* "I don't think I would have been able to read it when I was ten. It has remained one of my most popular titles and was one of the quickest and easiest I've written. I have no idea why some books are so hard and some so easy."

Hahn's young characters often live in unusual family situations. In *Tallahassee Higgins,* for instance, Talley must move in with her childless aunt and uncle when her irresponsible mother takes off for Hollywood in search of stardom. *Bulletin of the Center for Children's Books* critic Zena Sutherland praised the "strong characters, good pace, and solid structure" of the novel, while *Voice of Youth Advocates* contributor Dolores Maminski found the story "sad, humorous, believable and readable." In *Following the Mystery Man* the young protagonist convinces herself that her grandmother's new tenant is the father she has never known—then finds herself in a lot of trouble when she discovers he is really a criminal. While Watson, writing in *Horn Book,* found that "there are no really frightening moments in this rather gentle, occasionally sad story," other reviewers concurred with *School Library Journal* contributor Elizabeth Mellett's assessment: "This is a suspenseful book that will keep readers interested and entertained until the last page."

Hahn takes on the subject of war and its consequences in *December Stillness,* in which a girl, Kelly, becomes emotionally involved with the homeless Vietnam vet she interviews for a school project. Kelly's ultimately tragic interference with the man eventually brings her closer to her Vietnam vet-father in what Nancy Vasilakis remarked "could have been a maudlin ending" that is saved by "the author's skillful use of dialogue in defining her characters" in *Horn Book*. Though several critics found the story preachy at times, *Bulletin of the Center for Children's Books* writer Roger Sutton remarked that "Hahn's practiced handling of suspense serves her well here." Hahn introduced the subject of war in a more sophisticated manner in 1991's *Stepping on the Cracks*, set during World War II. In this work, two patriotic twelve-year-old girls risk the wrath of their parents and the ostracism of their community when they befriend a conscientious objector. A *Kirkus Reviews* writer called the result "suspenseful, carefully wrought, and thought-provoking—a fine achievement." While acknowledging these strengths, critic Sutherland added that "what makes [the novel] outstanding is the integrity of the plot and the consistency of the characterization." *Horn Book* reviewer Maeve Visser Knoth similarly concluded: "The engrossing story handles the wide range of issues with grace and skill."

Hahn returns to ghost stories with *The Doll in the Garden,* a work Sutton dubbed "not as straight-ahead-scary" as *Wait till Helen Comes,* but which nonetheless benefits from "a direct style and smooth storytelling." After the death of her father, Ashley and her mother move into an apartment in a house owned by a hostile woman. Ashley and a new friend discover a doll buried in the garden and encounter the ghost of a dying child, which leads them back in time to discover the landlady's old secret. Although *Horn Book* critic Ethel R. Twichell found the ending "a little too pat," she nonetheless concluded: "Ashley's intriguing although never really scary experiences should hold most readers' attention to the end." *Time for Andrew,* published in 1994, is similarly spooky time-travel story distinguishes. While spending the summer with relatives in Missouri, twelve-year-old Drew becomes switched in time with his namesake, Andrew, who lived in the house eighty years before. Andrew refuses to return to his own time for fear he will die of diphtheria, and so the two join forces to change family history. While Virginia Golodetz, writing in *School Library Journal,* characterized the ending as "humorous but somewhat contrived," *Bulletin of the Center for Children's Books* reviewer Sutton dubbed *Time for Andrew* an "assured work from a deservedly popular writer, who, while gifted with the instincts of a storyteller, doesn't let her narrative get away from her characters."

Hahn branches out into adventure fiction with *The Dead Man in Indian Creek,* the story of two boys who suspect a local antique dealer of being behind the murder of the man they find in a nearby creek. Reviewers praised the fast-paced action and high suspense of this novel. Although Carolyn Noah in *School Library Journal* found several "illogical gaps" in the plot, other crit-

ics agreed with a contributor to *Publishers Weekly* that the "combination of crackling language and plenty of suspense" found here makes *The Dead Man in Indian Creek* "likely to appeal to even the most reluctant readers." Similarly, in *The Spanish Kidnapping Disaster,* three children are thrown together by the marriage of their parents, whom they are unexpectedly forced to join on their honeymoon in Spain. When one of them lies to the wrong person about their wealth, the three are kidnapped, which "creates action, danger, and suspense," commented Sutherland. The critic nevertheless faulted the book for "an undue amount of structural contrivance." Other reviewers, however, focused on Hahn's superb characterizations, including what a critic described in *Publishers Weekly* as "a surprisingly understanding look at what impels people to terrorist activity."

In *Look for Me by Moonlight* Hahn creates a supernatural romance for teen readers. In this "deliciously spine-tingling story," as it was described by a reviewer for *Publishers Weekly,* Hahn tells the story of sixteen-year-old Cynda as she spends some time with her father at his inn, called Underhill, on the coast of Maine. Reputedly haunted by a ghost of a woman who was murdered there many years ago, the inn is also the place where Cynda encounters Vincent Morthanos, a guest and vampire. Cynda falls in love with the mysterious and forbidding stranger in a book that "takes the traditional elements . . . [and] places them in a setting that is alternately cozy and frightening" to create a perfect blend for readers who appreciate "danger with a dash of romance," noted Linda Perkins in *Wilson Library Bulletin.* Similarly, a critic for *Publishers Weekly* remarked that although some elements of the story are clichéd, "in Hahn's able hands, they add up to a stylish supernatural thriller."

Hahn has also written the young adult novel *The Wind Blows Backward,* which *Bulletin of the Center for Children's Books* contributor Sutton called "a lavishly romantic novel, with all the moody intensity anyone could want." Lauren's junior high crush on Spencer is revived in their senior year in high school, but Spencer is haunted by his father's suicide and by his behavior seems tempted to follow in his father's footsteps. In portraying Lauren's relationships, a *Publishers Weekly* critic commented, "Hahn makes excellent use of contrasting family situations to illustrate her theme of perseverance." Although *Booklist* critic Stephanie Zvirin found the plot "so predictable that it's only Hahn's rich, occasionally inspired prose that saves it from becoming mournfully melodramatic," *School Library Journal* writer Gerry Larson felt that "nonetheless, YA readers will identify with the pressures, conflicts, and concerns facing these teens." And Marilyn Bannon praised Hahn's handling of the subject of teen suicide, noting in *Voice of Youth Advocates* that "because [Hahn] has crafted such interesting, well rounded characters, her message is delivered effectively."

In *The Gentleman Outlaw and Me—Eli: A Story of the Old West* Hahn presents younger readers with the story of twelve-year-old Eliza and her dog Caesar as they make their way to Colorado in search of Eli's father. Accompanying Eli and Caesar on their quest is Calvin, a gentleman outlaw they encounter in the woods after Eli escapes her abusive guardians. At the end of many adventures, the three reach Colorado and finally locate Eli's Papa, a sheriff. Lola Teubert, writing in *Voice of Youth Advocates* characterized *The Gentleman Outlaw and Me* as a "rollicking read, full of the true flavor of the old West," while *Horn Book* reviewer Elizabeth S. Watson called it "tailor-made to satisfy a youngster's ache for high adventure." In addition to garnering praise for her storytelling abilities, Hahn once again also elicited praise for the historical background presented in the story. For example, Susan Dove Lempke was particularly impressed with the "fine job" Hahn did in "recreating the atmosphere of the days of cowboys and miners." As a child, Hahn had dreamed of running off to join cowboys, but as she told *AAYA*, "Growing up in College Park, there was not much opportunity for such high adventure."

Known for writing about difficult subjects, Hahn tackles an abusive family situation in her series of books featuring young Gordy Smith and his family, previously introduced to readers in *Stepping on the Cracks*. In her next book featuring Gordy, titled *Following My Own Footsteps,* Hahn's young protagonist finds himself living in North Carolina with his grandmother after his father has been imprisoned for being abusive. As he adjusts to life in a new place, Gordy struggles with doubt that he will escape the violence that surrounds him, especially after his mother accepts his father's apology and decides to give the troubled man a second chance.

Praising the honesty with which the book deals with "the pain of some insoluble problems," Deborah Stevenson wrote in the *Bulletin of the Center for Children's Books* that Hahn has created a "telling and believable portrait of a boy on the cusp of major changes in his life." Maeve Visser Knoth also lauded Hahn for the difficulty of the subject she tackles in this work, noting her deft handling of such issues as alcoholism and domestic abuse. Additionally, critics were also appreciative of Hahn's skillful re-creation of the mid-1940s. *Booklist* reviewer Susan Dove Lempke felt that setting Gordy's story against World War II-America is a masterful touch by Hahn, and that the writer presents a "terrific rendering of day-to-day life" of the setting, with each "detail integral to the story."

In her third book of the series, *As Ever, Gordy,* the young boy's life is beset with turmoil once again; this time the death of his grandmother forces Gordy to return to his hometown with his younger sister. As he struggles to establish a relationship with his old rival, Liz, Gordy at first relapses into his old ways until he realizes that his father and older brother are not the best role models. Reviewing this book for *Booklist,* Linda

Perkins wrote that although the historical background of *As Ever, Gordy* seems incidental to the story, Hahn has done a masterful job of creating a "painfully believable adolescent" character in Gordy Smith.

In *Anna All Year Round* Hahn uses the backdrop of pre-World War I America against which she sets the world of eight-year-old Anna. Based on recollections by Hahn's own mother, the writing in this book has been praised once again for its poignant evocation of the past, as well as the author's realistic depiction of her young protagonist. Several critics remarked on the accuracy of the portrait Hahn draws, noting especially her skillful use of the historical background. Anna is a tomboy, much to the dismay of her very proper mother, who speaks in German to Anna's aunt when the pair of them want to keep her from understanding. Anna's adventures include roller-skating down a cobblestone road and falling so that her chin needs stitches, throwing herself a "surprise" birthday party without telling her mother, learning long division, and trying to convince her mother that she should have a bright-colored coat for the winter. Stephanie Zvirin, writing in *Booklist,* noted particularly the accuracy of Hahn's research, praising the author for her skill in capturing the "flavor of early 1900s setting[s]." A reviewer for *Horn Book* noted that "All the chapters are informed by Hahn's able evocation of time and place."

In *Anna on the Farm,* the second novel featuring Anna Sherwood, Hahn tells the story of one summer spent by Anna on her uncle's farm in Maryland. Unfortunately, Anna is not the only guest; her uncle's nephew Theodore is staying there as well. The two spark immediately, Theodore calling Anna a "city slicker" and Anna considering him a "country bumpkin"; it doesn't take long for the pranks to start and quickly get out of hand. However, through their competition, the cousins see each other as friends. In a tale that is "rollicking fun" according to *Voice of Youth Advocates* contributor Debbie Whitbeck, Hahn provides "a great glimpse of pre-World War I America." As a *Horn Book* reviewer wrote, "Hahn defies nostalgia with both the immediacy and the honesty of her up-close, present-tense telling."

Although it might sound like a ghost story, *Promise to the Dead* is actually a story about slavery at the beginning of the U.S. Civil War. Jesse makes a promise to a dying slave that he will deliver her son Perry to his aunt in Baltimore. This is complicated by the fact that Perry's aunt is white, and is the sister to the deceased slave-owner who used to own both Perry and his mother. The two boys—Jesse at age fourteen and Perry at only seven—make a desperate flight; what keeps Jesse going is that he knows he cannot break a promise to someone who is dead. "This piece of historical fiction will be a hit," predicted Michele Baker in a review for *Book Report.* Cyrisse Jaffee, writing in *School Library Journal,* called *Promise to the Dead* "an involving story that raises many of the issues that led to the

Civil War," while Ilene Cooper, in her *Booklist* review, commented "Obviously there's a lot going on here, but the plot never seems too overwhelming.

With *Hear the Wind Blow,* Hahn again tackles the difficulties of war. Set, like *Promise to the Dead,* during the U.S. Civil War, the novel centers around Haswell Magruder, a teen whose father has died fighting against the Union forces and whose brother is still out in the field. When a wounded Confederate soldier seeks to hide at the Magruder farm, the Magruders take him in and attempt to nurse him back to health, even though if they are discovered by the Union soldiers they will be punished. Unfortunately for the Magruders, the Union forces do come; they kill the soldier and raze the Magruder farm. Haswell's mother becomes ill and dies, and Haswell takes his sister and flees to the home of their relatives. After seeing her to safety, he then travels to find his brother, discovering the realities of war along the way. In her review for *Horn Book,* Betty Carter called the novel "a strong adventure inextricably bound to a specific time and place, but one that resonates with universal themes." Hahn presents "a picture of ordinary men who are not at all sure why they are fighting" according to Hazel Rochman in *Booklist.* "The drama of the Civil War and the fine storytelling and characterization hook readers from the outset," praised Renee Steinberg in her review for *School Library Journal,* while a reviewer for *Publishers Weekly* noted: "With his bravery and his honest grapplings with complex issues, Haswell will win readers' interest and sympathy from the outset."

Like several previous titles, *The Old Willis Place: A Ghost Story* deals with ghosts, but not in the expected way. The main character, Diana, lives with her brother in the woods behind a mansion; they have seen caretakers come and go, but they never reveal themselves to the people taking care of the property. They must never let themselves be seen and must never go into the house. Diana does not explain to readers why these are the rules–perhaps she does not know herself. However, when Lissa, the new caretaker's daughter, who is about Diana's age, arrives, the lonely girl hopes to have a friend, even though it is against the rules. As a complement to Diana's narration, readers also have access to Lissa's diary. "Hahn is a master at stretching the suspense," praised Ilene Cooper in her *Booklist* review, and a critic for *Children's Bookwatch* called the novel "another satisfying ghost story." Maria B. Salvadore noted, "This riveting novel is a mystery and a story of friendship and of redemption," and a critic for *Kirkus Review* characterized *The Old Willis Place* as "spooky, but with an underlying sweetness."

In her interview with *AAYA,* Hahn talked about her goals in writing: "I want to tell a good story, first and foremost. I don't think about theme. If it comes, great. But that is not my focus. I want readers to come away from my books feeling that they have read a story that sticks with them, with characters that linger on the

mind. They might also gain a bit more understanding about people and realize that everyone has a story inside of them."

Biographical and Critical Sources

BOOKS

Authors and Artists for Young Adults, Volume 23, Gale (Detroit, MI), 1998.

PERIODICALS

Booklist, October 15, 1982, Barbara Elleman, review of *The Time of the Witch,* p. 311; May 1, 1993, Stephanie Zvirin, review of *The Wind Blows Backward,* pp. 1580, 1582; April 1, 1994, Stephanie Zvirin, review of *Time for Andrew: A Ghost Story,* p. 1446; March 15, 1995, Ilene Cooper, review of *Look for Me by Moonlight,* p. 1322; April 1, 1996, Susan Dove Lempke, review of *The Gentleman Outlaw and Me— Eli,* p. 1364; September 15, 1996, Susan Dove Lempke, review of *Following My Own Footsteps,* p. 240; May 1, 1998, Linda Perkins, review of *As Ever, Gordy,* p. 1518; March 15, 1999, Stephanie Zvirin, review of *Anna All Year Round,* p. 1329; April 1, 2000, Ilene Cooper, review of *Promises to the Dead,* p. 1473; February 15, 2001, Kay Weisman, review of *Anna on the Farm,* p. 1136; May 15, 2003, Hazel Rochman, review of *Hear the Wind Blow,* p. 1663; September 1, 2004, Ilene Cooper, review of *The Old Willis Place: A Ghost Story,* p. 124.

Book Report, January, 2001, Michele Baker, review of *Promises to the Dead,* p. 57.

Bulletin of the Center for Children's Books, February, 1986, review of *The Jellyfish Season,* p. 108; April, 1987, Zena Sutherland, review of *Tallahassee Higgins,* p. 146; September, 1988, Roger Sutton, review of *December Stillness,* p. 9; March, 1989, Roger Sutton, review of *The Doll in the Garden,* p. 171; May, 1991, Zena Sutherland, review of *The Spanish Kidnapping Disaster,* p. 218; December, 1991, Zena Sutherland, review of *Stepping on the Cracks,* p. 91; May, 1993, Roger Sutton, review of *The Wind Blows Backward,* pp. 281-282; April, 1994, Roger Sutton, review of *Time for Andrew,* pp. 259-260; October, 1996, Deborah Stevenson, review of *Following My Own Footsteps,* p. 61.

Children's Bookwatch, December, 2004, review of *The Old Willis Place.*

Horn Book, October, 1979, Richard Ashford, review of *The Sara Summer,* p. 534; February, 1983, Ann A. Flowers, review of *The Time of the Witch,* p. 44; March-April, 1986, Mary M. Burns, review of *The Jellyfish Season,* p. 201; November-December, 1986, Elizabeth S. Watson, review of *Wait till Helen Comes,* pp. 744-45; July-August, 1988, Elizabeth S. Watson, review of *Following the Mystery Man,* p. 493; November-December, 1988, Nancy Vasilakis, review of *December Stillness,* pp. 786-787; May/June, 1989, Ethel R. Twichell, review of *The Doll in the Garden,* p. 370; November-December, 1991, Maeve Visser Knoth, review of *Stepping on the Cracks,* p. 736; September, 1996, Maeve Visser Knoth, review of *Following My Own Footsteps,* pp. 595-596; September, 1996, Elisabeth S. Watson, review of *The Gentleman Outlaw and Me—Eli,* p. 596; July, 1999, review of *Anna All Year Round,* p. 465; May, 2001, review of *Anna on the Farm,* p. 324; May-June, 2003, Betty Carter, review of *Hear the Wind Blow,* pp. 346-347.

Kirkus Reviews, October 15, 1991, review of *Stepping on the Cracks,* p. 1343; April 1, 1995, review of *Look for Me by Moonlight,* p. 468; June 15, 1996, review of *Following My Own Footsteps,* p. 899; May 15, 2003, review of *Hear the Wind Blow,* p. 751; September 1, 2004, review of *The Old Willis Place,* p. 866.

Kliatt, July, 2003, Claire Rosser, review of *Hear the Wind Blow,* p. 12.

New York Times Book Review, October 23, 1983, Barbara Cutler Helfgott, review of *Daphne's Book,* p. 34.

Publishers Weekly, November 19, 1979, review of *The Sara Summer,* p. 79; August 5, 1983, review of *Daphne's Book,* p. 92; December 6, 1985, review of *The Jellyfish Season,* p. 75; February 9, 1990, review of *The Dead Man in Indian Creek,* p. 62; March 1, 1991, review of *The Spanish Kidnapping Disaster,* p. 73; November 1, 1991, review of *Stepping on the Cracks,* p. 81; April, 26, 1993, review of *The Wind Blows Backward,* pp. 80-81; April 10, 1995, review of *Look for Me by Moonlight,* p. 63; July 8, 1996, review of *Following My Own Footsteps,* p. 84; April 19, 1999, review of *Anna All Year Round,,* p. 74; April 17, 2000, review of *Promises to the Dead,* p. 81; May 19, 2003, review of *Hear the Wind Blow,* p. 75.

School Library Journal, December, 1979, Cyrisse Jaffee, review of *The Sara Summer,* p. 86; November, 1982,

Karen Stang Hanley, review of *The Time of the Witch,* p. 84; October 1983, Audrey B. Eaglen, review of *Daphne's Book,* p. 168; October, 1985, Marjorie Lewis, review of *The Jellyfish Season,* p. 172; October, 1986, Judy Greenfield, review of *Wait till Helen Comes,* p. 176; April, 1988, Elizabeth Mellett, review of *Following the Mystery Man,* p. 100; April, 1990, Carolyn Noah, review of *The Dead Man in Indian Creek,* p. 118; May, 1993, Gerry Larson, review of *The Wind Blows Backward,* p. 124; May, 1994, Virginia Golodetz, review of *Time for Andrew,* p. 114; July 8, 1996, review of *Following My Own Footsteps,* p. 84; May, 1999, Linda Bindner, review of *Anna All Year Round,* p. 90; June, 2000, Cyrisse Jaffee, review of *Promises to the Dead,* p. 146; March, 2001, Debbie Whitbeck, review of *Anna on the Farm,* p. 209; May, 2003, Renee Steinberg, review of *Hear the Wind Blow,* pp. 152-153; December, 2004, Maria B. Salvadore, review of *The Old Willis Place,* p. 146.

Tribune Books (Chicago, IL), April 5, 1987, Cynthia Dobrez, review of *Wait till Helen Comes,* sec. 14, p. 4.

Voice of Youth Advocates, August, 1993, Marilyn Bannon, review of *The Wind Blows Backward,* p. 152; June, 1987, Dolores Maminski, review of *Tallahassee Higgins,* p. 78; June, 1996, Lola Teubert, review of *The Gentleman Outlaw and Me—Eli,* pp. 95-96; March, 2001, Debbie Whitbeck, review of *Anna on the Farm,* p. 209.

Wilson Library Bulletin, June, 1995, Linda Perkins, review of *Look for Me by Moonlight,* p. 135.

OTHER

A Visit with Mary Downing Hahn (video), Kit Morse Productions, Houghton Mifflin (New York, NY), 1994.*

Autobiography Feature

Mary Downing Hahn

Mary Downing Hahn contributed the following autobiographical essay to *SATA:*

Writing an autobiography is a difficult task for novelists. Although we use personal experiences in our books, we don't like to be hemmed in by facts. It's so boring to describe events as they actually occurred. For instance, each time I tell a story about my past, my family accuses me of adding something new. "That's not how you told it last time," they say, or worse, "That's not how it happened. I was there, remember?"

Worse than their objections, though, is the uncertainty I feel when they voice them. Although my changes make the story funnier, sadder, or scarier than the event itself, they also make me wonder about my own life. Did it really happen the way I remember it? Or did I alter my history bit by bit over the years until my memory of it bears little resemblance to the truth?

Some things, of course, are irrefutable, and that's probably why so many autobiographies begin with a boring statement of undeniable fact. Here is mine: I was born Mary Elizabeth Downing on the ninth of December in the year 1937, the first child of Anna Elisabeth Sherwood Downing and Kenneth Ernest Downing. My mother was an elementary school teacher. My father was first and foremost an English citizen, but he supported himself as an automobile mechanic in Washington, D.C.

I mention my father's nationality because that was his biggest distinction, the keystone of his personality, what he most wanted people to notice about him. Although he was only ten years old when he came to this country, he clung to his heritage and spoke with a proper English accent until the day he died at the age of fifty-eight.

My father's Anglophilia had its roots in the contrast between his life in England and his life in America. My grandparents' families were both wealthy. My great-grandfathers, William Alexander Downing and James Pettengill, were barristers in London. At one time they practiced law together, but they had a falling out of some sort and parted ways. In an act of defiance, my grandparents married against their parents' wishes. Grandfather further rebelled by refusing to enter his father's law practice. His desire to go to America and become a gentleman farmer outraged his father, who had worked his way up to a position of wealth and respectability and wanted his children to live lives of upper-middle-class comfort.

In 1915 the Downings sailed to America on the *Lusitania.* In danger of being torpedoed by German submarines, my father, his five brothers, and one sister, as well as the other passengers, spent most of the journey in lifeboats, prepared for the worst.

Although my father remembered the voyage as a great adventure, I'm sure my grandmother felt very differently about it. Unfortunately, the *Lusitania* was, in fact, sunk by the Germans on her return trip, and several months later America entered the First World War.

Just as his father had predicted, my grandfather failed completely in his new endeavor. Stubbornly using the farming methods he'd learned in New Zealand years before, he lost all his money, and managed to reverse the American dream. He came to this country wealthy and ended up impoverished, dragging his wife and children down with him.

Thanks to my grandfather's neglect, my father's life in America was full of hardship. Looking back, he must have seen England as the lost Eden of his childhood, a place to which he longed to return but could not. America, on the other hand, was definitely east of Eden, a land of banishment. It is no wonder he kept his English citizenship until his death in 1963. Like my father, my mother's life was marked by loss, not of a place but of a person. When she was thirteen, her father, Ira Sherwood, died, leaving her and her mother, Anna Ruehr Sherwood, almost penniless. Her father's death ended my mother's childhood and her happiness as surely as my father's departure from England ended

Parents, Kenneth and Elisabeth Downing, Catonsville, Maryland, 1936

his. She was left in the hands of a cold and unloving mother who claimed she could not support a daughter. After taking Mother to a relative's farm, my maternal grandmother moved back to Baltimore, where she supported herself as a dressmaker and a housekeeper.

Mother lived with her father's sister Agnes and her husband George Armiger in Beltsville, Maryland, for several years and then moved to Catonsville, where she lived with her uncle, Harry Sherwood, a reporter for the *Baltimore Sun,* and his wife Grace. After graduating from Western High School, she enrolled in a two-year teaching program at Towson State Normal School. What she really wanted to do was go to the Maryland Institute of Art, but her relatives did not think that advisable. She needed to support herself. For a young woman in 1923, teaching was a practical and dependable career.

After completing the course, Mother took a position at College Park Elementary School when she was nineteen years old. While visiting her aunt in Beltsville, Mother met my father at a dance. In 1935, when she was twenty-nine and he was thirty-one, they married.

Shortly after my parents' honeymoon, my mother's mother moved in with them. An only child, my mother felt she was obligated to provide a home for her mother.

Unfortunately, my grandmother's presence did not contribute to the happiness of my parents' marriage. She disliked my father, and, as she grew older, she frequently accused him of stealing from her and plotting against her. To avoid the scenes her behavior provoked, Daddy spent more and more time in the company of his older brother Alfred, a bachelor.

When I was less than a year old, my mother returned to teaching and I was left in the care of my grandmother, an arrangement born of financial necessity. Already suffering from arteriosclerosis, Nanny was a strange and frightening person. Given to morbid ramblings about sin and death, she made my early childhood less than happy.

We were living in College Park then, on the second floor of a house on Guilford Road just off Route One. The school where Mother taught was less than a block away. Its playground was large and well equipped with swings, a sliding board, and seesaws. A little creek meandered across it, shaded by tall trees. By the time I was three, I learned to avoid Nanny by spending as much time as possible outside. I rode my tricycle up and down the sidewalk, played with the little boy next door, and squabbled with the girls across the street. Anything to get away from Nanny.

*

Two days before my fourth birthday, the Japanese bombed Pearl Harbor, and World War II began for us. Like many civilians, my father volunteered to be a block warden, which meant he patrolled our neighborhood at night wearing a white civil-defense helmet and making sure everyone complied with the blackout law; to protect cities from the possibility of bombing raids, no visible lights were permitted. This did not mean everyone sat around in the dark. At the sound of sirens, families simply covered their windows with opaque blinds and waited for the all clear.

Because my father had relatives in London, he took his responsibility seriously and often quarreled with the man next door, a German citizen who claimed to belong to the pro-Nazi Bund party. Our neighbor was convinced Germany would win the war. When the Nazis came to America, he assured my father that his name would be at the top of the firing squad's list. This more or less ended my friendship with his son.

Two of my father's younger brothers went to war, and my English grandmother hung two blue stars in her window signifying her sons were overseas. Although Uncle Eric survived the Battle of the Bulge, Uncle Dudley was killed in Belgium in the fall of 1944. He received the Distinguished Service Cross for "exceptional heroism in combat," and Grandmother took down his blue star and hung a gold one in its place. A gold star meant someone in the family had died in the war. That fall and winter, I saw gold stars in many windows.

The main things I remember about the war years are my uncle Dudley's departure and the news, a year

later, of his death. He was my favorite uncle, and his death saddened all of us. It was the first time I ever saw my father cry. The sight of his tears frightened me almost more than the reason for them.

Like most people my age, I also remember Victory gardens, saving scrap, waiting in long lines with Mother in nearly empty grocery stores, buying war stamps in school, watching my parents count their ration coupons, worrying about being bombed, and watching the troop trains go by. It was my job, my contribution to the war effort, to stamp tin cans flat, to mix yellow food coloring into the butter substitute, and to play "Step on a crack, break Hitler's back," a variant of the old chant in which you stamped hard on every crack in the sidewalk.

When I was three years old, one of my mother's friends gave me a four-volume set of A. A. Milne's stories and poems. Both Daddy and Mother read them to me, and Pooh, Piglet, Christopher Robin, Eeyore, Tigger, and all the others came to life as I listened. Believing every word, I was sure the Hundred Acre Wood existed, maybe not too far away. If I could find it, I'd join Pooh in his tree and play with Christopher Robin. I'd help trap the Heffalump, I'd go along on the journey to the North Pole, I'd take Eeyore a birthday present, I'd bounce with Tigger and play Pooh Sticks in the creek. The closest I came to finding the Hundred Acre Wood was the year Uncle Alfred surprised me with a big, brown teddy bear. I named him Pooh, and we spent hours acting out Christopher Robin's adventures and inventing new ones. We climbed trees, explored, rode about on my tricycle, made a little house in the lilac bushes, and slept together every night. For years, Pooh was my best friend and inseparable companion.

One rainy day I discovered a new route to the Wood. Alone in my room, I noticed the blank pages in the front and back of my Pooh books. Could they be for children to use? Happily I covered the white pages with pictures of Pooh and his friends, telling myself new stories while I drew. Not satisfied, I turned my attention to Ernest Shepard's black-and-white sketches. Why hadn't anyone colored them? Seizing my crayons, I happily went to work. Still not satisfied, I added smiling suns, extra rabbits and birds, and a little girl, thus drawing myself into the stories I loved.

When my mother (a schoolteacher, remember!) discovered what I'd done to my lovely set of books she was not happy. After explaining the difference between coloring books and real books, she made sure I had a plentiful supply of drawing paper.

In 1942, when I was four, we rented our first house on Osage Street in Berwyn, just north of College Park and halfway between Route One and the trolley tracks. Here I encountered a large gang of children, nearly all older than I was. Tall for my age, I tried desperately to keep up with them, never realizing the difference two years made in our abilities. I wanted them to like me, but they thought I was a hopeless crybaby.

Feeling like an outcast, I spent hours with Pooh and my doll Margaret in the rose garden behind our house. I was convinced that fairies lived there. Hoping to catch sight of them, I built tiny houses out of stones, covered them with twig roofs, carpeted them with moss, made beds out of rose petals, left small portions of food, and lit them with marbles, which I thought glowed after dark. Although I never actually saw a fairy in one of my houses, I was sure they slept in the moss beds and ate the bread.

In January 1943, my mother went to the hospital and returned with my sister, Constance Ann, an occasion somewhat darkened by my belief that both she and Mother were dead. Nanny was responsible for this idea. While Mother was away, Nanny convinced me she would never return. On the day Mother came home, I hid under our old-fashioned kitchen stove and refused to come out. For years, Mother thought my strange behavior was prompted by jealousy, a belief Nanny encouraged. Mother had no way of knowing I was terrified, and, at five, I was too young to explain my fear.

That fall my mother enrolled me in Holy Redeemer Catholic School. Because I would be six in December, I was old enough, but emotionally I was immature. Terrified of Sister in her long black robe, I made no friends and was frequently ill. When I came down with a particularly severe case of mumps in November, Mother gave up and took me out of school.

One good thing came out of my brief stay at Holy Redeemer—I learned to read. No longer did I have to

Mary, age five, with Pooh, Osage Street, Berwyn, Maryland, 1943

depend on the moods and whims of grown ups. Whenever I wanted a story I could read it ALL BY MYSELF.

Of the many books I loved I particularly remember *Watty Piper's Twice Told Tales,* an illustrated anthology of fairy tales, fables, and legends. One story in that book especially fascinated me. Before I learned to read, I'd ask Mother for "Hansel and Gretel," but I never let her get past the part where the witch stepped out of her gingerbread house and said, "Nibble, nibble, Mousekin." As soon as Mother read those words, I'd cover my ears and beg her to stop. The next night, I'd request "Hansel and Gretel" again, but, no matter how often Mother started, I never let her finish. The witch was simply too much for me.

Then, in bed with the mumps, I discovered I could read those stories myself. Avoiding "Hansel and Gretel," I worked my way through the whole book. Still sick, I read my Raggedy Ann and Andy books, I read *Scat, Scat, Go away Little Cat* (a favorite of mine), *The Little Engine That Could,* and any other easy book I owned at the time (Pooh was a bit too difficult for a new reader). Finally "Hansel and Gretel" was all that was left. Telling myself I could stop any time I wanted to, I began the story, reached the terrible words "Nibble, nibble, Mousekin," and kept on, straight to the happy ending. Closing the book, I felt as brave as Gretel herself.

As you can guess from the troubles I had with "Hansel and Gretel," I was a fearful child, one who saw wolves behind the bedroom door and lived in terror of the long-armed witch under my bed. Disguised as dust balls in the daytime, she lay in wait, ready to reach up over the mattress and seize me while I slept. Her presence forced me to lie in the middle of the bed with the sheets pulled up to my chin no matter how hot it was. If I needed to go to the bathroom, I'd stand up and leap as far from the bed as I could to avoid her grasp.

*

In October 1944 we moved back to College Park, where we rented a house at the end of Guilford Road. Our new home was one of several frame bungalows with dormered roofs and big front porches. In those days our street was unpaved and shaded by tall maples. On rainy days, the street was a sea of puddles, with lots of luscious mud to squeeze between your bare toes. Behind our house was a rutted alley where my father dumped the ashes from our coal furnace. Neighbors kept chickens and sold eggs, tended Victory gardens, and let their dogs run loose. You could ride the trolley into Washington, a half hour's trip away, and, if your parents weren't afraid of your catching polio, you could go to Greenbelt and swim in the pool or go to the movies in Hyattsville, a short trolley ride away. More like a Small town than a suburb, College Park was surrounded by woods and fields and creeks to explore. The University of Maryland campus was a half hour's walk away, just across Route One, and its president, Curly Byrd,

Mrs. Schindler's First Grade Reading Club, College Park Elementary School, 1945. Mary is second from right.

lived in a big house at the top of Beechwood Road and allowed us to sled ride in his backyard whenever it snowed. It was a wonderful place to grow up.

Less than a block from our house was the Baltimore and Ohio Railroad. It carried both passengers and freight up and down the eastern seaboard. The cars were pulled by smoke-spouting, cinder-spewing steam engines that caught the fields on fire on dry summer days. We lived near enough for the trains to shake my bed and make things jingle and shake in the china cupboard.

Odd as it may sound, I loved living close to the railroad. You might think the noise of the whistle and the engine would keep you awake, but you'd be amazed at how quickly you stop hearing the blast and rumble. The trains rocked me to sleep at night, and in the daytime my friends and I loved to sit on the grassy bank and count the freight cars rattling past. Lackawanna, Great Northern, Union Pacific, Lehigh, Susquehanna, Wabash, Seaboard, Southern—the very names stenciled on the boxcars had the ring of romance and the lure of distant places. They made me want to travel.

In College Park, I made my first real friend, the girl next door. Ann Sines was a year younger than I but she was in the first grade too. Her mother and mine had taught together and were delighted to see us take a liking to each other. Dark-haired and brown-eyed, Ann was shorter than I and she had wonderful dimples. Because I was tall, long-legged, and skinny, our parents kidded us about our resemblance to the old comic-strip figures Mutt and Jeff. I was as happy in public school as I'd been unhappy at Holy Redeemer. Unlike Sister, my teacher, Mrs. Schindler, encouraged me to draw and read. Impressed by my love of books, she made me a member of the Reading Club, an elite group who occupied a special corner of our classroom. Furnished with chairs and tables made from orange crates, the space was reserved for us, the best readers. I can't remember exactly what we did in the club, but we had tea parties on special occasions, and I loved belonging to it. I loved Mrs. Schindler too. Once I embarrassed myself by calling her "Mother," the ultimate compliment a child can give a teacher.

Although Mrs. Schindler graciously overlooked my obvious inability to understand arithmetic, other teachers weren't as sympathetic as she or as appreciative of my other talents. I languished in second and third grade, perked up a bit in fourth and fifth, and slumped again in sixth. Except for Mrs. Schindler and Miss Perry, my teachers saw me as a daydreamy, inattentive child who could not or would not learn her multiplication tables. I began thinking of myself as stupid and clumsy—stupid because I couldn't understand fractions, decimals, and percents or remember my nine and seven tables; clumsy because I couldn't learn to hit a ball, dodge a ball, catch a ball, play jacks, or skip rope.

During these years, Nanny's mental health deteriorated rapidly, and her dislike for my father intensified. Her attitude toward me changed also. In response to her hostility, I grew sassy and defiant. Because Mother didn't return to teaching after Connie was born, I wasn't alone with Nanny anymore. No longer afraid of her, I positively enjoyed causing scenes and making her angry. If she thought I was a wicked child, then that was what I'd be. I teased her, called her names, and ran away if she tried to slap me. I even encouraged Ann to join me in tormenting her.

Confused and disoriented, Nanny wandered the streets of College Park. The police often found her blocks from home, speaking German and trying to find her way back to Baltimore. Once we returned from the store to find the paperboy in the apple tree and Nanny keeping him there with her broom. Expecting to die in the night, she set up an altar on her dresser so the priest could administer the last rites. She used a bucket instead of the toilet and dumped its contents out the bedroom window every morning, something Ann and I found hilarious.

Finally my mother took the advice of our family doctor. Pregnant for the third time, she put Nanny in a nursing home near Baltimore. Refusing to eat, Nanny became gravely ill and died at Spring Grove State Hospital in Catonsville.

When my mother told me Nanny was dead, a thrill of elation shot through me with the force of an electrical current. My tormenter was gone for good. I would never see her again. Almost immediately, I recoiled from my own emotions. What kind of a nine-year-old child is glad when her grandmother dies? Believing myself to be just as wicked as Nanny said I was, I began to weep hysterically. This was not grief. This was guilt. But no one knew that but me.

One week later my father's mother died unexpectedly in her sleep. I loved my kind and gentle English grandmother, and my sorrow for her genuine. The tears I shed were real, but I did not cry for her as I had for Nanny.

Shortly after the deaths of my grandmothers, Ann's mother woke my sister and me in the middle the night to tell us good news. We had a brother. John Alfred Downing was born on March 1947. With no one there to prophesy death and disaster, I could hardly wait for Mother to bring him home.

Almost immediately a new crisis emerged. In midst of the postwar housing shortage, our landlord gave my father a month to find another home. His son, a recently married veteran, needed the house were renting. Finding a home in 1947 was no easy task. My father had three children, including an infant, and very little money. The houses we looked at cost too much, and apartments were too small for a family our size. At the end of the month, my father asked for an extension. When another month passed with no success, the landlord threatened to evict us.

Having nowhere else to go, we put our furniture in storage and moved into Grandfather's house in Riverdale, a few miles south of College Park. Already living there were Daddy's bachelor brother, Alfred; his youngest brother, George, and his wife Isabel; and my cousin Brenda.

Somehow the house accommodated all of us. But not graciously. There was tension among the adults and there was tension among the children. Brenda and I did not like each other. In my nine-year-old opinion, she was a spoiled brat, and I'm she thought even worse of me. At any rate, she had her own room and when we arrived she told my sister and me not to put one foot over the threshold. Left on her own, Connie would have obeyed Brenda's order. Unlike me, my sister was a sweet child who never got into trouble. Unfortunately, telling me not to do something was the surest way to make me do it.

Therefore, whenever I could, I sneaked into Brenda's room, often dragging poor Connie with me, and played with her toys. I couldn't resist. To Brenda, toys were decorative items, not playthings, and she couldn't bear to see them touched. What fun I had tossing her stuffed animals around her room and rearranging the furniture in her dollhouse.

Although Brenda was a year younger than I was, she was large for her age (fat, I called it) and not very fast. Taking advantage of my long, skinny legs and the years of practice I'd had running from Nanny, I easily escaped my cousin's wrath.

After a few weeks, however, my taunting and teasing backfired. In the interest of peace and quiet, I was exiled to a day camp run by the Girl Scouts. At Camp Conestoga I spent two miserable weeks sitting in the hot sun making misshapen pot holders.

When my session at Camp Conestoga ended, I was sent even farther away, this time to Misty Mount, an overnight Scout camp near Thurmont, Maryland, where we made more pot holders, swam in icy cold water, ate burned food, and sang dumb songs about little red cabooses. The only part I liked was eating s'mores, a dessert you made by melting marshmallows over a fire and mashing them between two graham crackers and a few squares of Hershey chocolate.

When I tell you what happened at the end of my two weeks at camp, you'll be convinced I'm rewriting my life to give myself a happy ending, but I assure you I'm not. While I was at Camp Misty Horrible Mount, the people who lived in the bungalow on the other side of Ann put a "For Sale" sign in their front yard. My parents bought the house, and we moved back to Guilford Road. Ann was still my next-door neighbor, and, when school started, I was in Miss Perry's room, right where I wanted to be.

*

I remember far too much of my elementary-school years to include it all in this essay. By the time I was in fourth grade, four girls my age lived on my block: Ann Sines, Barbara Rogers, Natalie Burdette, and Mary Slayton. In addition, Barbara had two brothers, Alan (two years older) and Curtis (one year younger), and Mary had a sister, Sally (also one year younger). At the lowest end of the scale were "the little kids": my sister Connie, Ann's brother Butch, and Natalie's sister Carol (Jack being too small to count). When the weather was nice we played old-fashioned games like "Mother, May I," Statues, Red Rover, Dodgeball, Keep Away, Follow the Leader, and, my favorite, Kick the Can, ideally

"Celebrating V-J Day": (front row) Butch Sines, Connie Downing, Jennifer McVaugh, (back row) Michael McVaugh, Mary Downing, Ann Sines

played after dark on hot summer nights. We quarreled over rules, split into warring factions, made up, and quarreled again.

We also played Cowboys with cap pistols, climbed trees, built forts and clubhouses, explored the woods in forbidden territory across the train tracks, risked polio by wading in the creek, belonged to Girl Scouts, dug for treasure in remote places, roller-skated down Beechwood Road, and cost our parents a fortune in Band-Aids for all the skinned knees and elbows we suffered. At night and on rainy days, I read, fueling my imagination. During the height of my interest in the "Nancy Drew" books, my friends and I followed people, wrote down license-plate numbers, spied from trees and bushes, and made, no doubt, pests of ourselves. Although we never found any evidence of criminal activity in College Park, two of us once came close, we thought, to catching a Russian spy.

Several blocks away lived a man who "looked" Russian and had a ham radio tower in his backyard. What else could he be? This was in 1947 or 1948, a time when people far older and wiser than we imagined they saw Russian spies everywhere.

One Saturday Mary S. and I walked past the spy's house and noticed his garage door was open and his car gone. Inside were stacks of newspapers and magazines. Mary and I looked at each other. Without a doubt, those were Russian papers and magazines, the evidence we needed. Taking a quick look at the silent house and the empty street, we dashed into the garage. Engrossed in our search, we didn't hear the spy enter the garage behind us.

"What are you kids doing?" he yelled.

I spun around and saw the man's big body blocking the door. Horrified, I looked at Mary.

Fortunately, she was much quicker than I was. Staring the spy in the eye, she said, "This is National Fire Prevention Week, and our teacher told us to search the neighborhood for fire hazards. Just look at all this newspaper! Don't you know how easily a fire could start here?"

The man stepped closer, scowling at us. "What's your name?" he asked. "Where do you live?"

Without hesitating, Mary gave him a false name and address. Swerving around the spy, she took off running with me at her heels, not daring to look back.

I'd like to be able to tell you we found *Tass* and other Russian-language publications, but all our spy had in his garage were old *National Geographics, Lifes, Saturday Evening Posts,* and *Washington Evening Stars,* the same thing you would have found in almost any garage or basement in 1948. In addition to Nancy Drew, I read dog stories by the dozens. My all-time favorite was *Lassie Come Home* by Eric Knight, but I also read a series of collie stories by Albert Payson Terhune, the "Irish Red" stories by Jim Kjelgaard, *Call of the Wild*

Mary and Pete, about 1950

and *White Fang* by Jack London, and *Grey Friars Bobby* by Atkinson. These books gave me an idealized concept of the noble dog, a loyal companion who would stay by your side even after your death. I begged my parents for a dog, pleaded, cajoled, all to no avail. No matter what I said or did or promised, my father steadily refused to consider my request. He did allow me finally have a cat, a beautiful little black kitten he insisted we name Pete after a cat he once owned, but NO DOG!

I happened to be the sort of girl whom strays recognized from afar. No doubt encouraged to do so, they followed me home. Despite heartrending scenes on our front porch, my father chased off every dog and sent me to bed to cry myself to sleep. One dreary afternoon, I rebelled against my father and ran away with a shaggy, friendly little dog I'd found in the park. With Max at my heels, I dashed off through the rain, refusing to heed my father's order to come back.

If my little sister hadn't followed me, I might not have gotten into so much trouble. When Daddy found the two of us, soaked to the skin and sharing a candy bar with Max behind a neighbor's garage, he dragged us home. In the kitchen, he pulled off his belt and whipped me. I'd had plenty of spankings with switches and hairbrushes but never one like this. He was so angry he actually broke his belt.

It was a small comfort to know it was his favorite, the one with the Union Jack buckle.

A month or so later, Daddy brought home a cocker spaniel named Binky, the biggest surprise of my life. I think he felt bad about the Max episode, and Binky was his way of saying he was sorry.

Unfortunately, Binky did not live up to the noble dog image. He bit the mailman and terrified the garbagemen, was frightened of other dogs, and loved my father best (ironic touch, that), but I adored him anyway.

In addition to mysteries and dog stories, I loved orphan stories. Among my favorites were *Anne of Green Gables, Oliver Twist, Kidnapped, Great Expectations, The Little Princess,* and *The Secret Garden.* Although I dreamed of being showered with gifts like the little princess and had an imagination to match red-haired Anne's, I identified most strongly with the heroine of *The Secret Garden.* Mary Lennox not only shared my name but most adults disliked her. Like her, I struck people as cold, selfish, and not very well-behaved. Tall, skinny, and painfully self-conscious, I avoided my parents' friends and my aunts and uncles, sure they would either ignore or criticize me. The loneliness I felt as a child probably drew me to stories about girls like Anne, Jane, and Mary. The happy endings gave me hope that someday I too would be loved and valued.

Acting out my orphan fantasies, I pretended the dollhouse my grandfather made for me was an orphanage. The little plastic dolls who lived in it were orphans, of course, and Ann and I spent hours making up adventures for them in which they ran away and sailed down the creek on rafts made from Popsicle sticks or lived in the hedge or under the forsythia bush. We built little stone houses for them, like the ones I used to make for the fairies. Once we got in trouble for almost catching a field on fire; we'd built a village, and, in the interest of verisimilitude, we lit little fires in the houses.

*

Obviously books played an important part in my life. I didn't just read them, I *lived* them. I became the hero or the heroine. I read with an absorption that deafened me to the real world and its demands. I read in the bathtub, I read under the covers with a flashlight, I read in school when I was supposed to be learning geography and often had my book taken away by angry teachers. When asked to set the table, bathe, or go to bed, my most frequent response was "Wait till I finish this page."

Second in importance to books were the radio shows I listened to faithfully. Every weekday afternoon beginning at five thirty, I sprawled in front of our big Philco to follow the adventures of Jack Armstrong, Sky King, Terry and the Pirates, and Captain Midnight. Like every other child in the 1940s, I saved box tops, hoping to be the first kid on my block to own a Sky King Glow-in-the-Dark Ring or a Captain Midnight Decoder Badge. Three nights a week, the Lone Ranger and Tonto galloped into our living room, their arrival signaled by the thrilling chords of the *William Tell* Overture and the announcer crying, "A fiery horse with the speed of light, a cloud of dust, and a hearty hi-ho Silver!"

On Sunday afternoons, I left the house to avoid hearing Lamont Cranston's eerie laughter on *The Shadow,* and on weekday evenings, I trembled at the sound of the squeaking door opening to *Inner Sanctum.* On the lighter side, I laughed at the Aldrich Family, the Great Gildersleeve, Baby Snooks, and Charlie McCarthy. When I was sick I listened to the long string of afternoon soap operas broadcast every weekday afternoon, and on Saturday mornings I tuned in to my very favorite show, *Let's Pretend.* After singing the Cream of Wheat song, Uncle Bill asked the Pretenders how they wanted to travel to the Land of Pretend. By flying carpet? By train, by plane, on the back of a bird? With appropriate sound effects, off they would go, taking me with them, a willing passenger.

Probably as a result of reading books and listening to radio shows, I began telling myself long stories while I drew pictures to illustrate them. When I look at my old drawing tablets now, I can't make much sense out of them beyond their carelessly printed titles: "The Story of an Orhanage (sic) Belived (sic) to be Haunted," "The Story of a Poor Boy," "The Story of Two Orphan Brothers," and so on.

Many of them, particularly the one about the orphan brothers, are derivative. Like most children, I didn't think of my own ordinary, everyday life as a source for books, so I imitated the authors I loved, rewriting their stories and drawing the pictures I saw in my head.

In seventh grade, I began my first diary, an illustrated account of my daily life, starting with a list of important facts about myself, such as my height and best friends and favorite color. At the bottom of the page, I wrote: "What I want to be when I grow up—a writer and illustrator."

Perhaps to prove I was serious, I bought a gray composition book and started "Small Town Life." My heroine was a twelve-year-old girl named Susan. In the illustrations, Susan is tall, skinny, freckled, and usually wearing a baseball cap, tee shirt, jeans, and tennis shoes. She bears a striking resemblance to myself. In its adherence to suburban life as I knew it, the sixty-three-page story reveals that I had abandoned my interest in orphan boys and turned to my own existence as a source of inspiration.

Unfortunately, the fictional Susan is much happier than her creator was. At twelve, I was miserably self-conscious. It wasn't just my long, skinny legs and arms that worried me. I felt uncomfortable around my friends, who were all growing up faster than I was. I didn't share their interest in boys or movie stars or makeup, and they didn't want to ride bikes or climb trees or go to the creek. I thought something must be wrong with me. I was different. Strange. Not like everybody else.

Well, that was all right, I told myself. Who wanted to be like everyone else anyway? Instead of conforming, I reveled in being different. At home, I wore baseball caps and boy's high-top basketball shoes, and at school I turned my nose up at girls who used lipstick. They might want to grow up, but I didn't. Like Peter Pan, I planned to stay a kid forever. Anyone with two eyes could see that adults led incredibly boring lives. Going to work, shopping, cooking, cleaning, taking care of kids—why was anyone eager to do that?

Eighth grade was even worse than seventh. I grew taller and taller, reaching my present height (five feet, ten inches) by the time I was fourteen. I was down to one friend, Mary S. of the famous Russian garage raid, the only other girl who wasn't trying to be a bobby-soxer. Together we roamed the streets of College Park, feeling like outsiders and looking more like boys than girls.

That spring I joined the chorus of our junior high's production of *The Pirates of Penzance,* not as one of "the sisters and the cousins whom they reckoned up by dozens and the aunts," but as a pirate. Even though I was still trying to be one of the boys, belonging to a group changed me. I lived and breathed Gilbert and Sullivan during the months we rehearsed, and I fell in love with Clarence, the male lead (who, of course, never noticed me). Up on the stage, wearing a red bandana and stamping around in boots, I wasn't the least self-conscious.

It was after the operetta ended that I made a conscious decision, one that probably affected the rest of my life. Giving up my earlier ambition to be a rebel, I decided to conform. Insecure and lonely, I vowed to hide everything about me that was weird or strange or different. Like the smiling girls in the pages of *Seventeen* magazine, I was going to be just like everybody else. A normal person.

One of the first things the new Mary did was end her friendship with Mary S. and make up with Ann, Barbara, and Natalie. Imitating them, I rolled up the legs of my jeans, wore thick white socks and saddle shoes, begged my father for his old shirts, bought lipstick, fell in love with movie stars, and swooned over Johnnie Ray, Eddie Fisher, Julius LaRosa, and Tony Bennett.

By the time I entered the tenth grade at Northwestern High School, my disguise was complete. I was a teenager, fifties style. Hidden was my sad, maladjusted adolescent self. I laughed and acted silly, dressed like everyone else, and yearned for a boyfriend. When I saw Mary S. slouch past, alone and left out, all I felt was relief that I wasn't with her.

*

My high-school years slid past in a blur, undistinguished academically or socially. Except for A's in art and B's in English, my grades were mediocre, dropping down to a few D's in unimportant subjects like Latin, chemistry, and geometry. I still daydreamed, especially in classes which bored me, and I covered my notebook pages with doodles and boys' names. Being in love was a permanent state, and I wasted time hanging around lockers and stairwells and drinking fountains, just to get glimpses of certain boys.

Unfortunately, no matter how many boys I fell in love with, not one of them reciprocated. I was tall and clumsy, and I thought I was ugly. I didn't dance well, I laughed too loud and too often, I said stupid things, I never quite understood what was going on, and I was often unhappy. Down deep inside, I worried about myself. Was I normal? Did my friends really like me? Why did they tease me so much? Was I on the verge of a nervous breakdown? I recorded all of these agonizing questions in the tear-stained pages of my diary, the surest way to remember exactly how you felt at a particular time of your life. Despite my self-doubts, I ran around with a gang of seven or eight girls. Ann, of course, was one of them, but the leader was undoubtedly Jimmy Harris Jones, a newcomer to College Park. She appeared the year we started high school. Wearing a straight skirt and thick white socks, swinging a purse by a long strap, chewing gum, she sauntered into our lives from a farm near the Chesapeake Bay. Her face was long and pointed, she brushed her short blonde hair straight up, and she spoke with a Tennessee accent. A hillbilly, my father called her, taking an instant dislike to her. Ann's parents shared his opinion and so did just about everyone else's. Of course that sort of disapproval just made Jimmy all the more fascinating. Where she went, we followed.

We hung out in People's Drugstore reading movie magazines and drinking Cherry Cokes, arguing about

"Some of the College Park gang at Breezy Point Beach on the Chesapeake Bay," 1954: *Kay Williams, Mary Downing, Ann Sines, and Jimmy Jones*

which star was cutest—Marlon Brando or James Dean, Rock Hudson or Tab Hunter. After the manager asked us to leave, we'd trudge a little farther down Route One to the record store, where the discussions would continue: Bill Haley or the Crew-cuts, Fats Domino or Chuck Berry, Carl Perkins or Elvis Presley, Dean Martin or Perry Como, Rosemary Clooney or Patti Page, Little Richard or Shirley and Lee. In those days, you could listen to records in little booths before you spent your hard-earned baby-sitting money on them. Taking advantage of the owner's patience, we spent hours there, enjoying the air-conditioning and the current top ten hits.

Jimmy introduced us to a number of things, particularly the thrill of going to Breezy Point Beach, a small resort on the Chesapeake Bay. In addition to playing slot machines, swimming in brackish salt water, burning ourselves tan, and ducking the stinging embrace of jellyfish, we discovered sailors and soldiers. I fell passionately in love with one of them, agonized over him for two years, but never managed to make any romantic progress. He insisted on treating me like his kid sister, something my parents had trouble believing when they found out about him.

Like my childhood, I remember my teens vividly, especially the agony of trying to fit in. A typical suburban high school, Northwestern had an elaborate social structure. At the top were the athletes and cheerleaders. Just below them were the Honor Society members. On the third and most difficult to define level was a variety of cliques, not true insiders but not outsiders either. Among them were the downs, the artists, the actors and actresses, the singers and dancers, the entertainers—kids who were fun to have around.

The third level was our place. Wearing identical red jackets, the College Park Gang stuck together. We decorated for dances, participated in play productions, painted posters for school events, attended football and basketball games, hung out at the Hot Shoppe, and joined clubs. Sometimes we skipped school and went to the beach or took the bus into Washington. Our grades weren't great, but most of our teachers liked us. For one reason or another, people knew who we were. The powerful ones tolerated us because we didn't threaten them. We were neither jocks nor brains—but we were funny. We didn't care whether the big wheels liked us or not. We had each other, and that was enough.

I spent my first summer away from home in 1956, right after I graduated from high school. Considering how strict my parents were, it amazes me that they allowed an eighteen year old to accept a job as a waitress in the Rideau Hotel in Ocean City. Maybe they couldn't face another summer of rock-and-roll music blasting from my bedroom, trips to Breezy Point Beach with Jimmy Jones, quarrels, tears, and slamming doors. My high-school years hadn't been easy for me or anyone else. After seeing *Rebel without a Cause,* I wrote in my diary that Natalie Wood's father was just like mine: he didn't understand me, we weren't close, he criticized

Mary (sitting on roof), Bill Hahn (in door), and friends, "fooling around in our tomato-soup Volkswagen Bug at Sherwood Forest, Maryland," 1963

me endlessly, and he was almost always angry at me. My mother and I didn't see eye to eye on much either, and I was glad to get away from Guilford Road for a while.

In Ocean City, I made friends with the other waitresses, all college girls, and found my first real boyfriend, a piano-playing fraternity boy named Jack. It was a great summer. Lots of sunshine, the ocean to swim in every day, the boardwalk to explore every night, and, best of all, no parents to lay down rules. The job itself was awful, the food worse, but for a summer at the ocean I was willing to tote trays.

I returned tan and happy and started my freshman year at the University of Maryland, a mile's walk from home and rather like grade thirteen. An amazing thing happened to me in college. I discovered I had a brain after all. I majored in studio art and minored in English, and, after completing the required torture of twelve credits of math and science, I spent my time doing what I loved best: reading, writing, drawing, and painting. I won a few prizes in the art department and published a couple of stories in the campus literary magazine. Hoping I was becoming a sophisticated intellectual at last, I started writing a novel about a tall, sensitive, misunderstood college girl. Although I never got past chapter three, I imagined myself becoming the J. D. Salinger of my generation and fantasized about publishing my stories in the *New Yorker.* In my senior year, my old friend Ann introduced me to Bill Hahn, and I fell in love. By the time I graduated in 1960, we were semi-engaged—no ring, no date set, but definitely thinking about spending the rest of our lives together.

That fall, I took a job as an art teacher at Greenbelt Junior High School, not a good career choice. I didn't like the petty routines, and I hated being an authority figure. I wanted to be one of the kids, and, in fact, was often mistaken for one of them. I looked so young a cafeteria worker asked me on my first day if I was a student or a teacher; if I'd said "student," my lunch would have been cheaper.

At the end of my year at Greenbelt, I told the principal I wasn't coming back. In the fall, I planned to begin graduate school in the University of Maryland English department. I'd had my fill of public school teaching.

That June, 1961, I went to Europe with three girlfriends. Violet Kelk, an old family friend who worked as a tour guide for Thomas Cook, helped plan our trip, and we spent almost three months traveling around Europe in a rented Volkswagen Beetle, relying on Arthur Frommer's *Europe on Five Dollars a Day* to find places to stay. It was probably the best summer of my life, the fulfillment of years of daydreaming about Rome and Pompeii and Paris and London. Everything I saw delighted me. Nothing disappointed me.

*

On October 7, 1961, I married Bill and started graduate school, hoping to earn a master's degree in English. After two years, Bill decided he wanted to go to law school, and, having done everything but write my thesis, I dropped out of graduate school to support us. All I found were several low-paying jobs; I worked for a couple months at the telephone company, another couple months at Hutzler's Department Store in Baltimore and then for a year at the Navy Federal Credit Union as a correspondence clerk. In 1965 I left the credit union to have my first baby. Katherine Sherwood Hahn was born on 18 August 1965. She was such delight I could hardly wait to have another one; thus Margaret Elizabeth Hahn was born on 11 May 1967.

Almost from the day they were born, I read to Kate and Beth. Through the picture books I borrowed from the library, I rediscovered my love of writing and drawing. While my daughters took their afternoon naps, I wrote and illustrated a number of picture books. Although Kate and Beth loved them, I wasn't able to find a publisher who shared the enthusiasm. Each time a book was rejected, I stuck it in a folder and started again. If one company didn't like a manuscript, what was the sense of sending it to anyone else?

During this time, we were living in a small brick house on Harvard Road in College Park, only a few blocks from my mother's house. While I wrote little books and played with Kate and Beth, the sixties ended and the seventies began. For a variety of reasons, all of them sad and depressing, my marriage began to fall apart, and, looking for a way to support myself, I enrolled in the Ph.D. program at the University of Maryland as a graduate assistant in the English department. At the age of thirty-four, I moved into university housing, just across Route One from College Park, and my daughters and I began life is a single-parent family. It was January 1971, and the campus was chaotic. The war raged in Vietnam, the National Guard occupied the

university every spring, all my friends' marriages were falling apart, and so was America. It was a hard time to find yourself responsible for two children.

Putting aside my picture books, I taught world literature, wrote seminar papers on John Milton, dreamed of illustrating Coleridge's poem "Christobel" for my dissertation, and read to Kate and Beth. In the summers, we drove to Vermont in my old Ford Falcon to visit my friend Ann and her family at Lake Bomoseen and then ventured farther north to New Hampshire and Maine, camping at Bar Harbor and other places. Each time we drove to New England, I looked for jobs at small colleges and public schools, but in the mid-seventies teaching positions were scarce.

Near the end of my four years in the Ph.D. program, John Robbins took me on as a freelance illustrator for his program *Cover to Cover,* a children's reading series airing on PBS television. Among my favorite projects were Joan Aiken's *Wolves of Willowby Chase,* Philippa Pearce's *Squirrel Wife,* Patricia Wrightson's *The Nargun and the Stars,* and Nina Bawden's *Carrie's War.*

John's television show broadened my knowledge of children's literature and helped me find a job in the Prince George's County Memorial Library System as a children's associate, a position which does not require a master of library science degree but demands a special knowledge of books. I was hired in 1975. At the time, I thought the job was temporary; in my spare time, I'd write my dissertation and find a college teaching position in New England.

However, that isn't the way it happened. As part of my orientation, I took a workshop from Helen Shelton, who was then the children's book selection officer for the library system. Helen's enthusiasm for juvenile literature was contagious, and her knowledge was impressive. After reading and discussing quantities of books, I began to write in my spare time—not a dissertation but a novel.

Although I thought a novel would take little time and effort, I spent almost a year working on the first version of what eventually became *The Sara Summer.* In 1976, I began sending the manuscript to publishing companies. Thanks to the how-to books in the library, I knew more about the process than I did in my easily discouraged picture-book stage. When the first editor sent my manuscript back, I stuck it in another envelope and mailed it to the next name on my list. Four times I sent Sara out, and four times she came back, accompanied by various rejections. Some were the dreaded "form letters," which begin "Dear Writer" and, after making mysterious references to the "needs" of their "present list," end with best wishes for placing your manuscript "elsewhere." Others were more personal, but no one offered to publish my book. Finally I mailed Sara to the fifth company, Clarion Books. After being passed from one reader to the next, the manuscript landed on James Giblin's desk. Jim read it and saw enough possibilities to mail it back with a letter telling me he was enclosing his staff's comments as well as his own. If I were willing to rewrite my novel, he would be willing to reread it.

Although the pages of criticism were daunting, I found myself agreeing with most of the comments and suggestions. My manuscript was indeed too episodic, and many of my "best" scenes added nothing to the story's continuity. Sitting down in front of my old government-surplus typewriter, I began the lengthy process of revising. Every time I mailed the manuscript to Jim, sure I'd improved it, he sent it back with more suggestions. It was like taking a correspondence course in novel writing.

Twelve years later, neither one of us now remembers how many times Sara traveled back and forth from Maryland to New York, but in the fall of 1978 Jim invited me to lunch to discuss the manuscript's progress. After a year of corresponding, I was eager to meet the mysterious editor who had so patiently read and reread my novel. Filled with anticipation and dread, I boarded the train in Baltimore. For years I'd fantasized about

having lunch with an editor in New York, and now that it was about to become a reality all I could think of was disaster. Suppose I knocked over a glass of water? Slurped my soup? Spilled something down the front of my dress? Said something incredibly stupid? Called him Mr. Giblet again as I'd once done on the telephone? Unfortunately, I was all too capable of doing any or all of those things, maybe even simultaneously.

By the time I reached the Clarion offices, having survived my first New York taxi ride, I was so nervous I could hardly tell the receptionist my name. Suppose I'd come on the wrong day? Suppose I'd misunderstood the time and I was late?

Fortunately, Jim put me at my ease right away. After getting through lunch without committing any blunders, I boarded the train for Baltimore with my manuscript tucked under my arm. One more rewrite, and Jim would offer me a contract. Of all the exciting things that have happened to me since I became a published writer, that day in New York remains a highlight.

I've worked with Jim ever since he and I suffered through *The Sara Summer* together. I consider him a

The author reading to her daughters Kate and Beth, c. 1968

friend as well as an editor, and I'll always be grateful to him for seeing some potential in my manuscript and working so patiently with me, an unknown writer. I hear many people complain about their editors. Listening to them makes me feel very fortunate. I knew nothing about Jim when I mailed him *The Sara Summer;* after four rejections, I chose Clarion from my list of children's publishers because I liked its name. It was indeed a lucky choice.

Not long after my second book was published, I married Norman Pearce Jacob. Considering Kate and Beth's stormy progress through adolescence, Norm took a brave step the day he said "I do." Although he was divorced, he had no children. Before he met me at a library retirement party, he lived a quiet life as the branch manager of the Hyattsville Public Library. In the evenings, he read and listened to recordings of the Gregorian chant. All too soon he was immersed in our chaotic household. While the phone rang constantly in the background, Kate and Beth waged clothing battles up and down the stairs and hallways of our Columbia town house and tried to drown out each other's rock music by turning up their radios. Norm gallantly took phone messages for the girls, helped with car pools, and gave them personal tape players to silence the roar of punk versus new wave.

Like me, he worried when they stayed out past curfew. Every now and then, he baked them special "super" cakes and then shuddered when they ate big gooey slices for breakfast. Looking at the artistic disarray of their bathroom and bedrooms, he once confessed he was learning more than he wanted to know about the domestic habits of teenage females.

Now both girls are away from home, and the house is very quiet. Kate attends the Art Institute in Chicago, and Beth is a student at the Pennsylvania Academy of Art in Philadelphia. They are both serious about their studies. As Kate once said, "If you wanted us to be engineers or lawyers, you shouldn't have given us all those art supplies. You encouraged us to be creative, and now we are."

And so they are. And I'm very proud of both of them. First my mother wanted to go to art school, then I wanted to go, and now, finally, Kate and Beth are actually there.

*

In this account of my life, I've revealed many of the sources of my books. My parents' history of loss and abandonment, my feelings about my senile grandmother, our family's brief homelessness, my loneliness, self-doubts, and insecurity, my years as a single parent, my father's emotional distance—all of these elements appear in my novels and give them a sadness readers often notice and sometimes ask about.

I can't keep my life out of my books. I might change events, make them sadder, scarier, more exciting, but emotionally my books are as honest as I can

With Norm Jacob at their wedding, Ellicott City, Maryland, 1982

make them; no matter how many supernatural turns my plot takes, I put my own feelings into every story I write. Flannery O'Connor once said that anyone who survives childhood has enough material to last the rest of his or her life. She was right about that. Never in adulthood are you so frightened, so angry, so eager for revenge, so vulnerable, so happy, so sad as you are when you're a child.

Although my books have been fairly successful, I still have trouble thinking of myself as a writer. When people ask me what I do, I usually tell them I'm a children's librarian. Saying I'm a writer sounds pretentious, even precarious or risky. To me, each book I complete is a gift. When I finish one, I worry I won't be able to write another. I keep my job at the library because it's my lifeline, my safety, my sure thing. What if a time comes when I can't face my word processor? What if someone asks the inevitable question "Are you still writing?" and I have to shake my head and admit it was merely a silly phase I went through once, an aberration, a whimsy, nothing to take seriously.

When I type "Chapter One," I'm excited by the story's possibilities but not sure I truly have a whole book's worth of ideas. My uncertainty arises from my inability to think ahead. How do I know what I'm going to write until I write it? Typically I begin a novel by imagining characters in a certain situation and then work out the plot as I go along, waiting for that magic moment when the narrator comes to life and begins to tell me the story. At that point, I'm in her place, experiencing everything that happens to her. One event leads to another, but not always in a logical order. To me, writing is like entering a forest and wandering off the path. I get lost in swamps, mired in quicksand, come to rivers too deep to cross, tumble into ravines, snag myself on brambles. In other words, I write and rewrite,

"In the parade to Judy's Bookstore, after winning the Northwest Pacific Children's Choice Award for **Wait till Helen Comes,** _Twin Falls, Idaho, 1989_

reorganize, cut, add, and fight my way out of the forest. If I'm lucky, I find the path again, wide and smooth, leading to a big sign that says "The End."

Once I have a beginning, a middle (the hardest part), and an end, I know I have a book. After revising the manuscript at least three or four times, I mail it to Jim and wait anxiously to hear his opinion. He usually asks for two and sometimes three rewrites, but they are never on the scale of _The Sara Summer_ revisions. He's very good at picking up inconsistencies and pointing out scenes where the action should be expanded or contracted. "What is Ashley thinking?" he may ask. "I need to know more about Molly's feelings at this point; is she afraid? angry? maybe a little of both?"

When I visit schools, I bring the seven manuscripts that went into the creation of _The Doll in the Garden,_ my ninth book. Holding up the pile of folders, I remind the class that the stack they see doesn't include all the changes I made on the computer before I printed each version. Although teachers love my "show-and-tell" display, I'm not sure how the kids feel. When I was eleven years old and preparing geography reports, when I was twenty-one or-two and writing short stories, even when I was in my thirties and working on seminar papers, I didn't take kindly to suggestions for revisions. Perhaps when I was younger, I was more arrogant, or maybe I was just plain lazy.

At my present age of fifty-two, I truly believe that revising is the most important step in writing a book. However, I admit that my word processor takes a lot of the tedium out of the process. Without my magical writing machine perhaps I would dread going over a manuscript six or seven times, but with the help of my insert and delete keys I don't mind it at all. Now, while I have more ideas than time, I'm working hard to write as many books as I can. Frustrating as it is to have a novel fizzle out after the third or fourth chapter, difficult as it is to rewrite the same scene dozens of times, painful as it is to see a reviewer pounce on the finished product, teeth bared, I truly love making words into stories.

Mary Downing Hahn contributed the following update to _SATA_ in 2005:

When I was about ten, I realized for the first time that I'd be sixty-three in the year 2000. I'd be old. Really old. Ancient. I pictured myself hobbling around with a cane, moaning and groaning and complaining about my endless aches and pains.

No, wait—my birthday was in December. I'd be sixty-two on the first of January, 2000. Subtracting that year didn't console me. Sixty two, sixty three—what was the difference? I'd still be watching the miracles of the new millennium from a wheelchair.

Why, I might even be dead!

Then and there, I went into a small depression, thinking of the fun I'd miss. It wasn't fair. But who was to blame? If I'd been the last born in my family instead of the first, I would have been nine years younger. Fifty-three instead of sixty-two—still too old. Way too old. My little sister and brother would be ancient, too.

As for my poor parents—my mathematical skills simply weren't sufficient to figure out how old they be in 2000. Nor did I want to think about it.

Well, as we all know, years fly past like calendar pages in old movies. As 2000 neared, some people bought gallons of water, dozens of candles, enough canned soup to fill a swimming pool, and hid in underground shelters fearing I'm not sure what—massive computer crashes, the end of the world, floods, fires, plagues. Not me. My only fear was dying in a tragic accident before 1 January 2000.

The new millennium began on schedule. Just as I'd anticipated, I was sixty-two. My hair was gray and I had more wrinkles than freckles, but I did not need a cane. I had no aches and pains. I still rode a bike and took long walks in the woods. Wouldn't that surprise the kid I used to be?

Actually the kid I used to be would be even more surprised by my becoming a writer.

When I was ten, I intended to be an artist when I grew up. Art was my best subject, my favorite subject. Although I loved to read almost as much as I loved to draw, I had no interest in writing—which in my experience meant long, hand-cramping, boring reports complete with deadly outlines and other tedious requirements such as neatness and perfect spelling and good penmanship and following directions. I wrote them, of course, but I didn't enjoy them. Nor did I receive A's—except for the cover; I was a B, sometimes a C, writing student. My teachers praised my artistic talent, but they never had much to say about my writing—unless you count negative comments such as "Please Follow Directions," "Poor Outline," "Sloppy handwriting," "Careless spelling," etc., etc.

Probably because I spent so much time reading, I began making up stories of my own. Instead of words, I used pictures to tell my stories. Drawing was easier than writing (it never made my hand or wrist hurt the way writing did) and it was much more fun.

I have a couple of yellowing drawing tablets full of mostly unfinished picture stories. My favorite was inspired by my father. Although he was born in New Zealand, he returned to England with his family when he was about seven years old. The Downings stayed there until 1915. Fearing England was doomed to be defeated by Germany, Grandfather decided to immigrate to America. With six sons and one daughter, ranging in age from thirteen to two, my grandparents boarded the _Lusitania_ for what would be her penultimate voyage. On her way back to England, the ship was torpedoed by the Germans, setting this country on its journey to World War I.

I never tired of hearing Dad's story of his voyage to America. It was the Downing family's watermark, a journey from wealth to poverty, an unfortunate reversal of the poor immigrant makes good saga. My grandfather came from a wealthy London family. He left England with a comfortable sum and set himself up in Maryland as a farmer, a vocation he'd pursued in New Zealand and England. Unfortunately Grandfather made a series of agricultural blunders and lost all his money. While he sat on the porch of a dilapidated farm house in Beltsville, reading and talking to fellow English exiles, the older boys, including my father, dropped out of school after completing the eighth grade and went to work to support the family.

My father retained his love of England and his citizenship, filling out his green card every November, keeping his accent, and speaking fondly of England, his lost Eden. His motto was "Once an Englishman, Always an Englishman." He knew by heart Gilbert & Sullivan's song from _H.M.S. Pinafore,_ "He is an Englishman." He took delight in confusing Americans by ordering spuds instead of potatoes, taking the lift instead of the elevator, filling his car with petrol instead of gas, asking for someone to check under the bonnet instead of the hood, and so on. He never failed to mention that the song we knew as "My Country 'Tis of Thee," was a blatant theft of "God Save the Queen."

Under Dad's influence, I became an ardent Anglophile—and I have a picture story to prove it. The first drawing shows a father reading a letter while his eager children look over his shoulder. Although I wrote nothing down, I can tell you exactly what that letter said:

Dear Mr. Downing,

We are delighted to inform you that you are the sole inheritor of Misty Cliffs Castle in England. Please come to England at once to claim your inheritance.

Sincerely yours,

[Signed by whoever would send such a letter]

You can't imagine how often I imagined that letter dropping into our mailbox at 4811 Guilford Road. We'd pack up at once and leave boring College Park forever and live in a castle in England where magic abounded and fairy folk haunted the woods and green hills.

I wasn't sure Mother would go along with this idea. Perhaps that's why the children in my story have no mother.

A series of pictures shows the family traveling by train and ship and finally arriving at a railway station in the English countryside. They are surrounded by suitcases and trunks labeled "Misty Cliffs," waiting for someone to pick them up and take them to their new home.

The next picture was my masterpiece—Misty Cliffs itself, a small castle drawn with great care. Although the pencil sketch is somewhat faded, the castle is clearly on the edge of a cliff. One small island breaks the surface of the sea. Oddly, a suburban style garage and a wishing well stand beside the castle. Write what you know, draw what you know.

I was very proud of that castle. Buildings challenged my artistic ability. Walls tended to lean, windows and doors were ill proportioned, and I had a poor grasp of perspective. I much preferred drawing people, especially children. My men resembled tall, gangling boys with precocious mustaches, and my women stumbled about on oddly shaped high-heeled shoes. I won't attempt to describe my cars and trains—or even my horses, save to say they were much worse than my dogs and cats.

Even though my story was inspired by my father's wish to return to England, it shows the influence of one of my favorite books. Two English children live in the castle, the son and daughter of the caretaker. The boy wears a patterned sweater, knee-length knickers, and argyle socks, my idea of English fashion. On his shoulder is a pet mouse. Remembering how much I loved *The Secret Garden,* I cannot help thinking of him as Dickon, the friend of mice, squirrels, birds, rabbits, and foxes.

In the next picture, Dickon and the American boy sit facing each other on a couch. A mouse perches on Dickon's shoulder; he offers another to his new friend. Hanging on the wall behind the boys is a framed motto: "Once an Englishman," it says, "always an Englishman."

Two or three more pictures suggest the island off the coast is a dangerous, mysterious place. Alas, the story ends with Dickon lying on his stomach, mouse on his shoulder, gazing at the island through binoculars.

Every time I look at this story, I'm tempted to finish it, not in pictures but in words. And that would surprise my ten-year-old self as much as my bicycle.

So how on earth did I become a writer instead of an artist?

*

I suppose the change from pictures to words began when I was about thirteen. Up till then, my stories had been adventures, the easiest sort of narrative to tell in pictures. In an adventure story, characters DO things—run, jump, swim, meet and fight enemies, find buried treasures, and so on. Think of a comic strip like "Spiderman." Even if the text were written in Japanese, you could follow the plot by looking at what Spiderman and his cohorts are doing.

But suppose the story teller wants to show what his characters are thinking and feeling? Suppose action is second place, peripheral even. Think of another comic strip: Snoopy lies motionless on the roof of his dog house. Words in balloons float over his head. What if those words were written in Japanese? You wouldn't have the slightest idea what was going on. In "Peanuts," it's the words that matter.

When expressing thoughts, feelings, and dialogue became more important to me than action, I realized I had a problem. I'd never thought of myself as a writer and neither had anyone else. I was artistic and I read well above grade level, but math continued to plague me. Frankly, I thought I was too stupid to write a book. I couldn't even outline a report until after I'd written it, proof I was backward. So how could I possibly become a writer?

Then the solution came to me. I could write *children's* books—and illustrate them myself like Robert McCloskey, whose "Homer Price" stories were among my favorites.

Surely children's books were easier to write than adults' books; they were shorter, for one thing. And they had plenty of pictures. In addition to *Homer Price,* Eleanor Estes' Moffat family books were illustrated, and so were Elizabeth Enright's Melendy family books. In fact, when I was a kid, books written for nine-to-twelve-year-olds were almost always illustrated, usually in black and white.

I began writing in secret, afraid to tell anyone what I was doing—not my teachers, not my friends, not even my mother—for fear they'd laugh at me.

At the same time, I began a diary. On the first page I wrote a typical kids' list of facts about myself:

Name—Mary Elizabeth Downing

Age—Almost fourteen

Birthday—December ninth

Favorite Animal—Dogs

Friend that moved away—Natalie Burdette

Friends—Mary and Sally Slayton, Ann Sines, Debby Hughes, Barbara Rogers

Grade—8th

Favorite Subjects—Art, Phys. Ed, Core and Math

Favorite Teacher—Mrs. Shank (Math)

Favorite outdoor Hobbies—Hiking, Hide and Go Seek, Tag, Bike Riding

Favorite Indoor Hobbies—Drawing, Writing, Reading, Listening to the Radio

Favorite Color—Blue

Pets—Binky, a cocker spaniel. Pete, a cat, ran away

Favorite Clothes—jeans, plaid shirts, sneakers

What I want to be when I grow up—A writer and illustrator

It's surprising to see math and physical education among my favorite subjects. Math can be explained by Mrs. Shank, my favorite teacher, the only one who made numbers understandable. But Phys. Ed? Usually it was even more humiliating than math. Eighth grade must have been a better year than most.

Although I haven't played hide and seek or tag for a while, I still hike and bike, and my indoor hobbies are much the same as they were when I was almost fourteen. My lovely dog Binky died over forty years ago, and Pete the cat never came back, but I share my home now with Oscar and Rufus, the best cats I've ever known. My favorite clothes are still jeans and sneakers—or running shoes as we now call them—but I wear T-shirts and sweatshirts more often than plaid shirts. My friend Natalie moved back to College Park, but she died when she was only twenty-seven years old; I still miss her. My friend Ann moved to Vermont forty years ago; I don't see her as often as I did when she lived next door, but we still consider each other our best and oldest friend. I've lost track of the other girls but hope they're all happily going on with their journeys.

And of course I did become a writer of children's books—but not an illustrator.

Things change, things remain the same.

Susan is the heroine of *Small Town Life,* my first book. She lives in a town much like College Park. The illustrations suggest she likes jeans and plaid shirts and sneakers—and sometimes sports a baseball cap. Her dark hair is jaw length and cut in bangs. She has freckles. She belongs to Girl Scouts and goes on a camping trip. She rescues a stray dog and brings it home. She hates chores. She quarrels with her younger siblings. In other words, she's just like I was.

No, not really. If you read *Small Town Life* side by side with my eighth grade diary, you'd see many differences. Susan is the girl I *wanted* to be, not the girl I was. In real life, I was a tall, shy, skinny, miserably self-conscious girl. I was what is politely called a late bloomer, meaning I was far less mature than most kids my age. I wanted life to stay the same: tree houses, bicycles, hide and seek. Not lipstick, home permanents, nylon stockings. What was so great about growing up? As far as I could see, kids had all the fun. Who wanted to vacuum, dust, wash dishes, do laundry, and fix meals? Growing up was absolutely boring. And it lasted a long time.

For inexplicable reasons, my friends couldn't wait to leave childhood behind. Their new attitude annoyed me. My stubborn immaturity annoyed them. I began to feel left out, even weird. I worried that something was wrong with me.

But Susan has no such problems. She's a leader—her friends do what she wants to do. She isn't weird. She isn't shy. Best of all, in my illustrations, she isn't any taller than anyone else.

In short, Susan is everything I wanted to be—my ideal self. In *Small Town Life,* I was retelling the story of my own life as it should have been—if only the world were fair.

That's why I write fiction. Reality isn't always to my liking. Why write a book about Abraham Lincoln? Everyone already knows the ending. He DIES. You can't change that.

Daughter Beth

It's much more fun to take a few details from here and there—things that happened to me, things that happened to my kids or my friends, things someone told me about—and mix them with lots of what ifs and supposes until they take on a life and a reality of their own, and you find yourself thinking, "Did I make that up or did it really happen?"

In other words, fiction writers can spend most of their adult lives daydreaming on paper—just so their imaginings are real enough for people to believe them.

*

I never finished *Small Town Life.* At the top of page 63, I wrote "Chapter Twelve, the Family Picnic." Under that is this sentence:

"Mom, can we go on a picnic?" Susan asked.

That's it. The rest of the composition book is blank.

What stopped me? Did I run out of ideas? Did I decide writing was too hard and I'd rather be an artist? Or did I simply get tired of Susan and her tomboyish ways?

I suspect all three had something to do with poor Susan's abandonment.

In the spring of eighth grade, my real life improved dramatically. Encouraged by my friend Anne, I joined the chorus of our school's production of *The Pirates of Penzance,* not as a sister or a cousin or an aunt like Anne, but as a pirate. Frankly I don't think I sang much better than I solved math problems or hit balls with bats, but Mrs. Hargraves was desperate for pirates and couldn't recruit enough boys. I took a deep breath and cast my lot with the pirates. Being part of a cast which included ninth graders, the elite of junior high, changed my outlook on everything, including becoming a teenager.

Thursday, May 15. 1952

Dear Diary,

We have been rehearsing for Mrs. Hargraves' Glee Club's operetta, The Pirates of Penzance. I am one of the pirate girls in it. I love it very much. It's about the biggest thing in my life now. Mrs. Hargraves really has some workers in it. Clarence especially. Without him, it would be a flop. He's wonderful! He knows everybody's part, he has the main role of Frederick, the Pirate's Apprentice, and he directs all the songs. I like him a lot. I wish I was in the ninth grade like him. He's a real nice boy. He has brown hair, big brown eyes, and a nice looking face. He has a good voice. He's going to get the medal for the best music pupil at the end of the year. I like him practically as much as Jerry now. Larry is very good as the Pirate King, Eddie is simply wonderful as Major General, you wouldn't think he was only in the ninth grade to hear him sing. Betty is really good as Mabel, the leading feminine role. Kay is all right as Mabel on the next night. But gosh, when she and Clarence sing a duet she drowns him out she's such a show-off and poor Clarence can't stand her. He likes Betty and I don't blame him.

By ninth grade, I was wearing lipstick and nylon stockings and hanging out in the record shop with Ann, Barbara, and Natalie, swooning over singers like Tony Bennett and Eddie Fisher and Johnny Ray (whose big hit was "The Little White Cloud That Cried"). I was embarrassed to remember the gawky, immature, bike riding dope I'd been in eighth grade. I wanted nothing more than to erase that weird girl from everyone's memory, including my own. Obviously, Susan was no longer my ideal self.

During my years at Northwestern High School, I wrote some bad love poetry which I showed to no one, and I kept a diary which I also showed to no one, but I shared my art with the whole school and soon became known as the class artist. I painted scenery for class plays, made posters for school activities, and worked on decorations for school dances. The theme of our senior prom was Undersea Fantasy; I dreamed up a pair of enormous fish made of chicken wire stuffed with tissue paper and spray painted silver. Like many things, my lopsided fish had looked much better on paper than they did in real life.

In my senior year, I won first prize for a fire prevention poster and entered the Scholastic Art Contest, receiving a gold key at the county level but failing to win anything at the regional level. My twelfth grade teacher gave me a B-minus on a short story but praised my art work; she even asked me to paint a watercolor of her family home in Virginia. Our beloved principal hung one of my seascapes in his office.

So at the end of my senior year when the Art Award was given, who do you think won it?

I was actually halfway out of my seat when my art teacher announced the winner. It was not my name he called. Humiliated and disappointed, I sank down in my chair while my friends murmured indignantly.

I hadn't known the winner had to belong to the Art Club. I'd never joined—because none of my friends had joined. And I didn't want to be in a club without them. So. . . .

But that was long ago—unless I think about it, and then it was yesterday and I am forever half way out of my seat to receive an award that went to someone else.

I entered the University of Maryland in the fall of 1956. The campus was a twenty-or thirty-minute walk from home. My parents had bought a house in College Park with that fact in mind. If the three Downing kids wanted to go to college, they'd save a ton of money on room and board. Most of my friends went to UMD for the same reason.

I majored in fine art and minored in English. To my surprise, I received B's in art and A's in English. My professors praised my writing instead of my drawing.

Pushing my self confidence to the limit, I enrolled in creative writing courses, wrote short stories and poetry, and was published twice in the campus literary magazine, *Expressions.* I remember the thrill of seeing my words in print for the first time, followed quickly by the breath-stopping realization that anyone who picked up the magazine could read my story. What if they hated it? What if it revealed something weird or stupid or unpleasant about me? I considered racing around campus, grabbing up every issue of *Expressions* and burning it. But there was just too much ground to cover. My story was out there and I'd have to live with it.

I don't think I'm alone in confessing I feel the same way about my books. Even when one is well received, I worry that the reviewer has made a mistake.

It's the bad reviews I remember. For example, *School Library Journal* had this to say about *The Dead Man in Indian Creek:* "With the abundance of good juvenile who-done-its available, this one is dead in the water." Although *Dead Man* received five Children's Choice Awards and has remained one of my most popular books, that review, like the art award I didn't receive, still hurts.

I graduated from the University of Maryland in 1960 with a B.A. in fine art and English. I taught art in a junior high school (the longest year of my life), spent a summer in Europe, got married, had two daughters, earned a master's degree in English, got divorced, went back to graduate school to pursue an elusive Ph.D., worked as a freelance artist for John Robbins' children's TV show *Cover to Cover,* and eventually ended up, sans Ph.D., as a children's associate librarian in the Prince George's County Memorial Library System.

If I'd taken the other job I was offered, proofreading for the IRS, I'm sure I would not be included in

Something about the Author because I would have gone mad and never written any books.

Before going to work at the library, I'd been one of those mothers who show up in the Children's Room every week and carry home a stack of picture books. I spent many happy hours reading Arnold Lobel, Maurice Sendak, and a host of others to my daughters Kate and Beth. Remembering my childhood ambition, I tried writing and illustrating my own picture books. Although Kate and Beth loved my efforts and never tired of hearing them, I failed to find a publisher who shared their enthusiasm. Easily discouraged, I gave up.

By the time I traded the English Department for the library, Kate and Beth were in grade school and reading Judy Blume instead of Arnold Lobel. Of course I read what they read, plus dozens more. I especially admired Katherine Paterson, Louise Fitzhugh, Betsy Byars, Penelope Lively, Helen Cresswell, Ursula Le Guin, and many others.

However, some authors (whose names I've forgotten) fell far short of the forenamed. It came to me that I could write as well, if not better, than some of these unmemorable authors. If they could get a book published, maybe I could too.

Instead of picture books, I tackled novels for older kids. Like many things that look easy—bowling, for instance—writing a book turned out to be much harder than I expected. In between working full time and taking care of my daughters, I typed and retyped, cursing my teenage self for thinking a typing class was less fun than ice skating lessons.

It took me a year to finish the manuscript. In 1976, I consulted *Writers' Market* for possible publishers and began mailing my big brown envelope to some of the same companies who had rejected my picture books in the early seventies.

That big brown envelope came back again and again, like the cat in the old folk song. Sometimes I wondered what the mailman thought it was.

The fifth publisher on my list was Clarion Books for Young People, then owned by Seabury Press. The editor, James Cross Giblin, asked for seven revisions before he accepted *The Sara Summer.* I learned a great deal about writing and editors that year. Never again would I think writers got it right the first time. Or the second time or the third time or—?

Now I can look back on twenty-six years of writing and hope for many more to come. Jim Giblin has edited all my books and has written many award winning books of his own. I will always be thankful to him for seeing potential in *The Sara Summer,* as well as in every manuscript I've sent him. I consider Jim a dear friend, as well as an astute editor and mentor. Without him, I'd be nearing retirement from the library, still vis-

iting schools and telling kids about other writers' books. Not a bad job—but not as much fun as the one I have now.

*

Like most writers, I've had my ups and downs, my disappointments and my successes, in life as well as writing. But I can't think of any other career I'd like better. Except maybe a fantasy I used to have of loading my daughters and my worldlies into a VW van and traveling around the country, home schooling Kate and Beth and entertaining audiences with story telling and puppet shows. Ah, for the life of a gypsy.

Actually, it's not too late, but I'd have to take my cats instead of my grown daughters.

Kate is a freelance writer in Los Angeles; among her published work is an account of her appearance on Hollywood Squares, recently published in the *Los Angeles Times.* *Newsweek* featured one of her humorous essays in "My Say," and *Dissent* ran an opinion piece. She also writes for several Internet sites, most notably *Behind the Chair,* a site for cosmetologists; Kate writes clever, informative articles about new beauty products. She's also a performer with a California stand-up com-

Daughter Kate

edy group. Beth lives in Manhattan. She teaches English and communication classes at Jersey City College. At one point, Beth was interested in becoming a children's book illustrator, but she now writes fiction for adults. She's had several short stories published. At the moment, she's looking for a home for her first novel, *The Lives of Animals.* I'm happy to say that both Kate and Beth are better writers than I am.

To sum it all up, I've never illustrated a published book, I've never learned to write an outline (which doesn't matter now—my editor doesn't require one). I still make up stories as I go along and am often surprised by the things my characters say and do. I still love to read (my current favorite book is *Jonathan Strange and Mr. Norrell*). I still write and rewrite, typing with two fingers as I always have. Sometimes I fail to finish a book, but I always keep the beginning in case I think of a good ending.

I'm pleased to say that this sometimes happens. Last fall, I finished a book I began about fifteen years ago. I kept returning to it, hoping to come up with a middle and an end (it had a great beginning). That book, *Witch Trap* will be published at long last in 2006.

At the present, my editor is reading my most recent manuscript, a ghost story called *Nothing but Trouble.* Like *The Old Willis Place,* the story centers around an unsolved mystery. I'm sure Jim will have a few suggestions.

While I wait to hear from Jim, I have two ongoing projects. "Sophie and the Graveyard Cats" is only a few pages long at the present, too new to talk about. Then there's "Closed for the Season," a sprawling mess of a manuscript, begun around the same time as *Witch Trap.* As Jim says, the characters are good, the setting is good, but the plot—well, it needs some work. Right now I'm not sure which one I'll finish first. Maybe I'll be inspired to write something else entirely.

Who knows? It could be "Small Town Life" or "The Strange Happenings at Misty Cliffs."

HARLOW, Joan Hiatt 1932-

Personal

Born July 25, 1932, in Malden, MA; daughter of Albert E. (a singer) and Marguerite (a registered nurse; maiden name, Small) Hiatt; married Richard Lee Harlow (a banker and auditor), August 17, 1951 (deceased, 2002); children: Deborah Balas, Lisa Harlow, Kristan Delphia, Scott, Jennifer Lichtenberg. *Ethnicity:* "English, Scots, and Welsh descent." *Education:* Stenotype Institute of Boston, certificate, 1951. *Hobbies and other interests:* Astronomy, traveling, history, swimming, music.

Addresses

Home—Venice, FL, and New Hampshire. *Agent*—c/o Author Mail, Margaret K. McElderry Books/Simon & Schuster, 1230 Avenue of the Americas, New York, NY 10020. *E-mail*—sevenjays@comcast.net.

Career

Children's book author. Redevelopment Authority, Wilmington, MA, administrative assistant, 1967-73; special-needs secretary of public schools in Littleton, MA, 1977-78; Institute of Children's Literature, instructor, 1981-2002.

Member

Society of Children's Book Writers, Author's Guild, Authors League of America, Westford Players (secretary and member of board of directors).

Joan Hiatt Harlow

Awards, Honors

Magazine Merit Award for fiction, Society of Children's Book Writers and Illustrators, 2000, for story "Si-Ling and the Dragon"; Disney Adventures Book Award, 2000, American Society for the Prevention of Cruelty to Animals Henry Bergh Companion Animals Award, Michigan Reading Association Readers' Choice Award, International Reading Association/Children's Book Council Children's Choice designation, Capitol Choice selection, Iowa Readers' Choice nomination, and Sunshine State Book Award, all 2002, and Sasquatch Reading Award nomination, 2003, all for *Star in the Storm;* Best Children's Book of the Year selection, Children's Book Committee at Bank Street College, William Allen White Children's Book Award nomination, and Rhode Island Reader's Choice nomination, all 2003, and Nutmeg Book Award nomination (CT), 2004, all for *Joshua's Song;* Best Children's Book of the Year selection, 2004, for *Shadows on the Sea.*

Writings

JUVENILE

(With daughter, Kristan Harlow) *Poems Are for Everything,* Christopher, 1973.
The Shadow Bear, Doubleday (New York, NY), 1980.
Star in the Storm, Margaret K. McElderry Books (New York, NY), 2000.
Joshua's Song, Margaret K. McElderry Books (New York, NY), 2001.
Shadows on the Sea, Margaret K. McElderry Books (New York, NY), 2003.
Thunder from the Sea. Margaret K. McElderry Books (New York, NY), 2004.
Midnight Rider, Margaret K. McElderry Books (New York, NY), 2005.

Also author of *The Wishing Sky, The Creatures of Sand Castle Key, The Dark Side of the Creek,* and *The Mysterious Dr. Chen,* Wright Group/McGraw-Hill. Contributor of stories and articles to periodicals, including *Cricket, Child Life, Ranger Rick's, Cobblestone, Humpty Dumpty's, ChickaDee, Your Big Backyard,* and *Young World.*

Adaptations

Shadows on the Sea was adapted for audiocassette by Recorded Books, 2003.

Work in Progress

Blown Away, a novel set in the Florida Keys that takes place during the 1935 Labor Day hurricane.

Sidelights

Joan Hiatt Harlow is the author of several novels for children that focus on the history of the author's native New England, including the award-winning adventure tale *Star in the Storm,* the Revolutionary War-era historical mystery *Midnight Rider,* and *Joshua's Song,* an historical novel set in Boston just after World War I. Taking place during World War II, Harlow's award-winning 2003 novel *Shadows on the Sea* finds fourteen-year-old Jill suspicious that a Nazi U-boat submerged off the Maine coast may be in contact with someone living near her grandmother's house, where Jill is spending the summer. The novel was praised by a *Publishers Weekly* contributor, who cited Harlow for her "excellent job of describing the hardships of war on those back home" in a mystery novel that "offers an enjoyable slice-of-life" portrait of a wartime childhood. Harlow includes an afterword to *Shadows on the Sea* that discusses the submarine and spy activity that actually took place along the northern New England coast.

Harlow's first novel, *Star in the Storm,* features Sirius, a large black dog with a white star on his chest who lives with Maggie's family in 1912 Newfoundland. When a new law bans all dogs except those used in sheep herding, Sirius risks being shot, so young Maggie hides her beloved dog in a cave. When a steamer runs into trouble offshore, Sirius is called upon to swim to the foundering ship with a rope, saving the passengers.

This 2003 novel draws readers back to the early years of World War II, as a teen is sent to live with her grandmother in Maine and becomes caught up in the suspicions running rampant in her new coastal community. (Cover illustration by Sammy J. Yuen.)

Debbie Carton, reviewing *Star in the Storm* for *Booklist,* wrote that "the relationship between the girl and her beloved dog is beautifully drawn." A *Horn Book* contributor found that "Maggie is a likable, self-reliant protagonist; and dog-lovers will revel in the many exploits of the gentle giant she loves so dearly." Renee Steinberg in *School Library Journal* noted that "Harlow's descriptive prose clearly evokes images of the Newfoundland coast and life in 1912, and she carefully incorporates folklore of the region into her story." *Star in the Storm* won the American Society for the Prevention of Cruelty to Animals' Henry Bergh Companion Animals Award, as well as a Disney Adventures book award and the Michigan Reading Association Readers' Choice Award.

Moving ahead a decade to 1929, *Thunder from the Sea* finds orphaned, thirteen-year-old Tom Campbell working at the Newfoundland home of childless couple Enoch and Fiona Murray. During a fishing trip with Enoch, a sudden storm comes up, and in the rough waters Tom sees a floundering Newfoundland pup. Rescuing the dog and naming his new friend Thunder, Tom gains the dog he always wanted, but is soon disheartened when another family, the Bosworths, attempt to part him from his new companion. Ultimately, several close encounters with danger and a shooting convince the Bosworths that Tom and Thunder should remain together, in a dog-and-boy story that *School Library Journal* contributor Shawn Brommer described as "fast paced," while *Booklist* reviewer Linda Perkins dubbed "nonstop action for dog lovers." *Joshua's Song* is set in 1918 Boston where young Joshua must quit school and earn a living after the death of his wealthy father during a flu epidemic. Working as a newsboy in the streets, he comes into conflict with a gang of young toughs who control newspaper distribution in downtown Boston. He also witnesses and describes the Great Molasses Flood, an event triggered by an explosion in a tank storing tons of molasses that killed twenty-one people. Chris Sherman, writing in *Booklist,* claimed that "even readers who don't usually like historical fiction will enjoy Harlow's vivid depiction of early-twentieth-century working-class life and conditions," while Sally Bates Goodroe concluded in *School Library Journal* that the author "skillfully integrates historical fact to make a colorful setting believable."

Harlow confessed to an interviewer with the *Lowell Sun* that writing children's books is "very easy, if you can think like a child," although she admits the craft itself requires passion, dedication, hard work, and the ability to deal with rejection. For Harlow, the pleasure of writing comes from " Escaping into another time realm with characters who wait patiently for my return. I love sharing this experience with children I've never met who enjoy my stories and feel affection for my characters. E-mails and letters from fans help me to realize how universal my books have become, and the responsibility that my stories may affect the lives of children. I want my books to portray courage, clean

Drawing on her interest in New England history, Harlow centers her story of a thirteen-year-old newspaper boy around a 1918 explosion that destroyed a Boston molasses storage facility. (Cover illustration by Larry Day.)

morals, good choices, and hope for the future." Her intense involvement has transformed many a family vacation into a research trip. "It's difficult not to get carried away at times," she once remarked. "I must be strange, because I really enjoy research!"

Biographical and Critical Sources

PERIODICALS

Booklist, January 1, 2000, Debbie Carton, review of *Star in the Storm,* p. 922; December 15, 2001, Chris Sherman, review of *Joshua's Song,* p. 731; September 15, 2003, Hazel Rochman, review of *Shadows on the Sea,* p. 231; August, 2004, Linda Perkins, review of *Thunder from the Sea,* p. 1934.

Horn Book, March, 2000, review of *Star in the Storm,* p. 195; July-August, 2004, Joanna Rudge Long, review of *Thunder from the Sea,* p. 452.

Kirkus Reviews, August 15, 2003, review of *Shadows on the Sea,* p. 1073.

Kliatt, May, 2004, John E. Boyd, review of *Shadows on the Sea* (audiobook), p. 55.

Library Journal, September, 2003, Cheri Estes Dobbs, review of *Shadows on the Sea,* p. 214

Lowell Sun (Lowell, MA), June 10, 1979, interview with Harlow.

New York Times Book Review, April 26, 1981, Karla Kuskin, review of *Shadow Bear,* p. 54.

Publishers Weekly, February 21, 2000, review of *Star in the Storm,* p. 88; August 27, 2001, review of *Star in the Storm,* p. 87; October 29, 2001, review of *Joshua's Song,* p. 64; September 15, 2003, review of *Shadows on the Sea,* p. 66; September 15, 2003, review of *Shadows on the Sea,* p. 66.

Sarasota Herald-Tribune Style, November, 2002, interview with Harlow, pp. 34-37.

School Library Journal, January, 1982, review of *Shadow Bear,* p. 64; April, 2000, Renee Steinberg, review of *Star in the Storm,* p. 134; November, 2001, Sally Bates Goodroe, review of *Joshua's Song,* p. 158; August, 2004, Gay Ann Loesch, review of *Shadows on the Sea* (audiobook), p. 76; September, 2004, Shawn Brommer, review of *Thunder from the Sea,* p. 207.

ONLINE

Joan Hiatt Harlow Web site, http://www.joanhiatt harlow.com (February 1, 2005).

*   *   *

HARMON, Dan
See HARMON, Daniel E(lton)

*   *   *

HARMON, Daniel E(lton) 1949-
(Dan Harmon)

Daniel E. Harmon

Personal

Born December 6, 1949, in Lexington, SC; son of Harvey J. (a law enforcement officer) and Mertie K. (a waitress) Harmon; married; wife's name Patricia C. (a social worker), August, 1976 (divorced, July, 2002); married June 6, 1997; second wife's name Sherie C. (a respiratory therapist); children: Courtney. *Education:* University of South Carolina, B.A. (journalism), 1972. *Religion:* Associate Reformed Presbyterian. *Hobbies and other interests:* Folk music, nautical history, correspondence chess.

Addresses

Office—Hornpipe Publications, P.O. Box 18428, Spartanburg, SC 29318. *E-mail*—d@danieleltonharmon.com.

Career

Author and editor. *Sandlapper: The Magazine of South Carolina,* Lexington, SC, assistant editor, 1971-73, associate editor and art director, 1989—; Dispatch-News, Lexington, reporter and editor, 1973-83; RPW Publishing Corp, Lexington, editor, 1983-97; freelance editor, beginning 1997.

Awards, Honors

Excellence in Technology Communications Award, Acer Group/Computer Museum, 1989; awards from Computer Press Association and South Carolina Press Association; various other press awards.

Writings

FOR CHILDREN

(Editor, under name Dan Harmon) Edwin P. Booth, *Martin Luther: The Great Reformer,* Barbour Publishers (Uhrichsville, OH), 1995.

(Under name Dan Harmon) *Civil War Generals,* Chelsea House Publishers (Philadelphia, PA), 1997.

The Tortured Mind: The Many Faces of Manic Depression, Chelsea House Publishers (Philadelphia, PA), 1998.

(Under name Dan Harmon) *Fighting Units of the American War of Independence,* Chelsea House Publishers (Philadelphia, PA), 1999.

(Under name Dan Harmon) *Life out of Focus: Alzheimer's Disease and Related Disorders,* Chelsea House Publishers (Philadelphia, PA), 1999.

(Under name Dan Harmon) *Anorexia Nervosa: Starving for Attention,* Chelsea House Publishers (Philadelphia, PA), 1999.

(With Tamela Hancock Murray; under name Dan Harmon) *More Clean Jokes for Kids,* Barbour Publishers (Uhrichsville, OH), 1999.

(Under name Dan Harmon) *Juan Ponce de Leon and the Search for the Fountain of Youth,* Chelsea House Publishers (Philadelphia, PA), 2000.

Nigeria: 1880 to the Present: The Struggle, the Tragedy, the Promise, Chelsea House Publishers (Philadelphia, PA), 2000.

Schizophrenia; Losing Touch with Reality, Chelsea House Publishers (Philadelphia, PA), 2000.

West Africa, 1880 to the Present: A Cultural Patchwork, Chelsea House Publishers (Philadelphia, PA), 2001.

The FBI, Chelsea House Publishers (Philadelphia, PA), 2001.

Jacques Cartier and the Exploration of Canada, Chelsea House Publishers (Philadelphia, PA), 2001.

Egypt: 1880 to the Present: Desert of Envy, Water of Life, Chelsea House Publishers (Philadelphia, PA), 2001.

La Salle and the Exploration of the Mississippi, Chelsea House Publishers (Philadelphia, PA), 2001.

The U.S. Armed Forced, Chelsea House Publishers (Philadelphia, PA), 2001.

(Under name Dan Harmon) *The Titanic,* Chelsea House Publishers (Philadelphia, PA), 2001.

The Attorney General's Office, Chelsea House Publishers (Philadelphia, PA), 2001.

Sudan: 1880 to the Present: Crossroads of a Continent in Conflict, Chelsea House Publishers (Philadelphia, PA), 2001.

Jolliet and Marquette: Explorers of the Mississippi River, Chelsea House Publishers (Philadelphia, PA), 2002.

Lord Cornwallis: British General, Chelsea House Publishers (Philadelphia, PA), 2002.

The Food and Drug Administration, Chelsea House Publishers (Philadelphia, PA), 2002.

The Environmental Protection Agency, Chelsea House Publishers (Philadelphia, PA), 2002.

Davy Crockett, Chelsea House Publishers (Philadelphia, PA), 2002.

Defense Lawyers, Chelsea House Publishers (Philadelphia, PA), 2003.

OTHER

(Editor, under name Dan Harmon) S. D. Gordon, *Life after Death,* Barbour Publishers (Uhrichsville, OH), 1998.

The Chalk Town Train, and Other Tales (first volume of "Harper Chronicles"), Trafford Publishing, 2001.

Bible Challenge: Small Facts from the Big Book, CrossAmerica Books, 2002.

(With others) *Taught to Lead: The Education of the Presidents of the United States,* Mason Crest Publishers, 2004.

Editor, *The Lawyer's PC,* 1983—.

Work in Progress

Biographies for "Amazing Americans" series; Volume 2 of the "Harper Chronicles."

Sidelights

Daniel E. Harmon told *Something about the Author:* "At about age thirteen, I determined to become a professional writer. School career counselors directed me to obtain a journalism degree, which led to ten agonizing years as a newspaper journalist after college. Although I hated the work, journalism matured my writing and taught me much about the publishing industry.

"Eventually, the Lord gave me more agreeable writing and editing work to do and, in 1994, opened the door to authoring books. After compiling several joke books and performing abridgement projects for Barbour Publishing, I was engaged by Chelsea House in 1997 to begin authoring educational books for different grade levels. The subjects were gloriously diverse, from history to foreign culture. Today I have the privilege of researching and writing books for several juvenile publishers.

"Meanwhile, as time permits, I relish crafting historical mystery short stories, the kind of writing I REALLY wanted to do from the very beginning, forty years ago. I continue to enjoy my long-term work on the editorial staff of *Sandlapper: The Magazine of South Carolina.* Since 1983, I've also edited *The Lawyer's PC,* a national technology newsletter now published by Thomson/West.

Biographical and Critical Sources

PERIODICALS

School Library Journal, February, 2001, Daniel Mungai, review of *Nigeria: 1880 to the Present: The Struggle, the Tragedy, the Promise,* p. 132; March, 2002, Genevieve Gallagher, review of *Egypt: 1880 to the Present: Desert of Envy, Water of Life,* p. 251; April, 2002, review of *Defense Lawyers,* p. 172; October, 2003, review of *The Environmental Protection Agency,* p. 43.

ONLINE

Daniel Harmon Web site, http://www.danieleltonharmon.com (January 3, 2005).

*   *   *

HASELEY, Dennis 1950-

Personal

Surname rhymes with "paisley"; born June 28, 1950, in Cleveland, OH; son of Robert Carl (a sales executive) and Margaret (an account supervisor; maiden name, Boigner) Haseley; married Claudia Eleanore Lament (a child psychoanalyst), October 12, 1986; children: Con-

Dennis Haseley

nor McMurray. *Education:* Oberlin College, A.B., 1972; New York University, M.S.W., 1982; attended New York University Psychoanalytic Institute. *Hobbies and other interests:* Tennis, skiing, running.

Addresses

Agent—c/o Wendy Schmalz Agency, Box 831, Hudson, NY 12534.

Career

Teacher and author. Worked variously as a professional fund raiser and community organizer. Jewish Board of Family and Children's Services, New York City, therapist, 1982-86; author of books for children, 1982–; private practice in psychotherapy, 1984–.

Member

Society of Children's Book Writers and Illustrators, Authors Guild.

Awards, Honors

The Old Banjo named among New York Public Library's Best Children's Books, Child Study Association's Children's Books of the Year, and as a Pick of the Lists by American Booksellers Association, all 1983; Parents' Choice Remarkable Book for Literature desig-

nation, Parents' Choice Foundation, 1983, for *The Scared One; The Kite Flier* chosen a Notable Book in the Field of Social Studies, National Council for Social Studies, and as a Pick of the Lists, American Booksellers Association, both 1986, and named among Child Study Association of America's Children's Books of the Year, 1987; *Shadows* chosen a Pick of the Lists by American Booksellers Association, and named among Library of Congress books of the year, both 1991; New York Foundation for the Arts fiction grant, 1994.

Writings

FOR CHILDREN

The Sacred One, illustrated by Deborah Howland, Warne (New York, NY), 1983.

The Old Banjo, illustrated by Stephen Gammell, Macmillan (New York, NY), 1983.

The Pirate Who Tried to Capture the Moon, illustrated by Sue Truesdell, Harper (New York, NY), 1984.

The Soap Bandit, illustrated by James Chambless-Rigie, Warne (New York, NY), 1984.

The Kite Flier, illustrated by David Wiesner, Aladdin Books (New York, NY), 1986.

The Cave of Snores, illustrated by Eric Beddows, Harper (New York, NY), 1987.

My Father Doesn't Know about the Woods and Me, illustrated by Michael Hays, Atheneum (New York, NY), 1988.

Ghost Catcher, illustrated by Lloyd Bloom, Harper (New York, NY), 1989.

The Thieves' Market, illustrated by Lisa Desimini, Harper-Collins (New York, NY), 1991.

Horses with Wings, illustrated by Lynn Curlee, HarperCollins (New York, NY), 1993.

Crosby, illustrated by Jonathan Green, Harcourt Brace (New York, NY), 1996.

A Story for Bear, illustrated by Jim LaMarche, Silver Whistle Books (New York, NY), 2002.

Photographer Mole, illustrated by Juli Kangas, Dial Books for Young Readers (New York, NY), 2004.

YOUNG-ADULT NOVELS

The Counterfeiter, Macmillan (New York, NY), 1987.

Shadows, illustrated by Leslie Bowman, Farrar, Straus (New York, NY), 1991.

Dr. Gravity, Farrar, Straus (New York, NY), 1992.

Getting Him, Farrar, Straus (New York, NY), 1994.

The Amazing Thinking Machine, Dial Books (New York, NY), 2002.

A Trick of the Eye, Dial Books (New York, NY), 2004.

Author's works have been translated into Chinese, French, and Spanish.

Two inventive brothers work out a machine they hope will help their overburdened mother while their father is gone in search of work during the Great Depression. (Cover illustration by Kazuhiko Sano.)

Adaptations

The Old Banjo was adapted as a filmstrip with cassette, Random House, 1986; *The Cave of Snores* was included in the video recording *Return to the Magic Library. Norbert, Snorebert* was produced by TVOntario (Chapel Hill, NC).

Sidelights

Psychotherapist Dennis Haseley has written extensively for children; his works include picture books as well as middle-grade and young-adult novels. Known for their unusual and imaginative subject matter, symbolism, and lyrical prose, Haseley's books have long captured the attention of reviewers. Among the most critically acclaimed are *The Old Banjo, Ghost Catcher,* and *Shadows.*

Haseley grew up in Brecksville, Ohio, where at the age of seven he wrote his first poem. While a student in high school and at Oberlin College, he renewed and developed his talent for writing, working with novelist and screenwriter William Goldman during a semester in

New York City. After graduation, Haseley published verse in literary magazines and came to the realization that children's books offered an opportunity for him to showcase his talent. His first book for children, 1983's *The Scared One,* is a prose poem picture book about the rites of passage of a timid young Native American boy who has been nicknamed the Scared One by his playmates. "It is gravely told, and touching" wrote a reviewer in the *Bulletin of the Center for Children's Books,* while a *Publishers Weekly* critic remarked that the story "resonates with the cadences of heroic legends."

Many of Haseley's picture books have caught the attention of reviewers. In *The Old Banjo,* which a *Publishers Weekly* critic termed a "sensitive ballad" and a "memorable story" and a *Booklist* reviewer called "a mystical, magical fantasy," a boy living on a Depression-era farm discovers some forgotten musical instruments that magically come alive. Describing the book—written by Haseley and illustrated by Stephen Gammell—George A. Woods concluded in the *New York Times Book Review* that "the combo of Mr. Haseley on words and Mr. Gammell on pencil have produced a modest piece that will strike a responsive chord in most readers." Likewise, *School Library Journal* contributor Ellen D. Warwick declared that "this beautiful book has something important to say about the nature of hope and the persistence of dreams."

In 1983's *The Pirate Who Tried to Capture the Moon,* a lonely, island-bound pirate captures all the ships that pass until he is himself captivated by the moon, an ending that a *Kirkus Reviews* contributor deemed "a satisfactory surprise." David Gale, writing in *School Library Journal,* noted that the text is "lyrical at times." Published the following year, Haseley's *The Soap Bandit* is, in the words of a *Publishers Weekly* critic, a "gentle allegory." Karla Kuskin, reviewing the book for the *New York Times Book Review,* commented on Halsley's inclusion of "imaginative and humorous touches." *The Soap Bandit* revolves around a mysterious stranger who steals all the soap from a quaint seaside town, changing the character of the inhabitants.

Many of Haseley's picture books deal with unusual subjects or are allegories. For example, *The Kite Flier* tells the tale of a man who is a stonemason by day and a kite maker by night. When his wife dies after their son is born, the man stops making kites until his son shows an interest in them. As the child grows, the father makes kites that symbolize his son's development. Years later, when his son is a young man ready to be launched into the world, he and his son make a special kite together and release it. While noting that the book's symbolism would be lost on a young readership, Maria B. Salvadore judged that "the book may have special appeal to an older audience" in her review for *School Library Journal.* Similarly, a *Booklist* critic predicted, "This quiet story is for the special reader; older children especially will respond to its formal language." With the picture book *Crosby,* Haseley returned to the subject of kites. This time, a lonely fatherless boy finds solace and freedom when he repairs and flies a broken kite. "It's a thoughtful, unusual picture book, more complex than most, and deserving of a close look," wrote a *Publishers Weekly* reviewer. A critic for *Kirkus Reviews,* while remarking that *Crosby* "is a strange story" for such young readers, also admitted that the book offers "an emotionally satisfying ending." Writing in *School Library Journal,* Judith Constantinides praised the book as "a feast for both the eye and the ear."

Another book by Haseley that commentators thought more appropriate for an older audience is *The Cave of Snores,* which concerns a shepherd's son who wishes that his father would not snore so loudly. Several critics praised Haseley's text, Karen K. Radtke writing in *School Library Journal* that the book's language "properly captures the tall-tale boastfulness of Arabian folklore." Tim Wynne-Jones of the Toronto *Globe and Mail* described *The Cave of Snores* as a "cleverly contrived coming-of-age allegory," and called Haseley's language "lyrical and bursting with life."

My Father Doesn't Know about the Woods and Me relates how a boy, walking in the woods with his father, feels like he is transformed into the animals he sees. This "possibility weaves a magic spell over readers and listeners," wrote David Gale in *School Library Journal.* Describing *My Father Doesn't Know about the Woods and Me* as a "magical story," a *Booklist* critic likewise remarked that the book "offers possibilities to tweak children's imaginations." Another fantasy by Halseley, *The Thieves' Market,* revolves around a group of thieves who open up a market outside a town where children come at night to choose their dreams. *Booklist* contributor Leone McDermott highly praised the metaphor of the market and the "eerie beauty" of the text, describing the work as "unusual and affecting" and "filled with insight and respect for children's inner lives." This is a story that "may intrigue the curious, the lovers of mystery and magic" remarked Shirley Wilton in *School Library Journal.*

Rona Berg, writing in the *New York Times Book Review,* called Haseley's 1989 storybook *Ghost Catcher* the author's "most ambitious and original work," a parable about "the pull of community and the power of love." The story tells of a solitary man called Ghost Catcher who has no shadow and so avoids forming relationships with the people of his Hispanic village. Be-

In **Crosby,** *Dennis Haseley's 1996 picture book, a young fatherless boy finds meaning in life when he takes up the challenge of kite flying. (Illustration by Jonathan Green.)*

cause he has no shadow, he can bring people back from the brink of death. When Ghost Catcher is tempted by curiosity to visit the land of shadows, he is trapped and must be rescued by the villagers who, through their compassion and efforts, show what it is to depend upon one another. "American children, used to a heavier does of realism or a lighter flight of fantasy, may find this story confusing," maintained Berg, who nonetheless concluded that *Ghost Catcher* can be read and enjoyed on several levels. A *Publishers Weekly* reviewer voiced similar comments, noting that while the book may be too difficult for some children, with its illustrations by Lloyd Bloom, it is still "an intriguing, thoughtful collaboration" and a "highly atmospheric parable."

If *Ghost Catcher* is steeped in fantasy, *Horses with Wings* is more down to earth. The book is based on an historical event: Leon Gambetta's balloon escape from besieged Paris during the Franco-Prussian War. Stephen Fraser, reviewing the book for *Five Owls,* praised *Horses with Wings* highly, declaring Haseley's work to be "nonfiction the way it should be: accessible, engaging, and alive." *Booklist* contributor Kay Weisman suggested that while "young children may miss the understated messages about war and peace" in the work, middle-school students could use the book as a discussion starter, and a critic for *Kirkus Reviews* called *Horses with Wings* "an interesting vignette, though the lack of a historical note is curious."

Although Haseley once admitted to *Something about the Author* that, after concentrating on picture books, "it was rather frightening to take on a novel," he has written several longer works for young adult readers. *The Counterfeiter* and *Dr. Gravity* are humorous treatments, while *Shadows* and *Getting Him* strike a more serious, responsive note. *The Counterfeiter* describes how would-be artist James falls in love with Heather, a cheerleader, and makes counterfeit currency in order to afford to take her on a date. James is a protagonist who "convincingly embodies the peculiar blend of frustration, cynicism and giddy optimism" characteristic of teens, according to a critic for *Publishers Weekly*. Reviewing *The Counterfeiter* for *School Library Journal,* Robert E. Unsworth noted that the book contains "lots of laughs and insight into the perplexities of adolescence."

With its focus on a man who releases townspeople from the force of gravity and faces weighty consequences, *Dr. Gravity* is a "rambling, old-fashioned novel" and "a graceful, carefully developed fantasy," according to a *Horn Book* contributor. Comparing the work to that of noted children's author Roald Dahl, Catherine M. Dwyer of *Voice of Youth Advocates* proclaimed that "Haseley has written a wonderful fantasy. *Dr. Gravity* is full of gentle humor and peopled with well-drawn characters." The *Horn Book* critic also maintained that "there is much humor in the story," adding that "Haseley's skilled use of description creates a convincing setting

for fantastic events." As Dwyer concluded, young readers "will love this tale."

Shadows, a short novel written for middle-grade readers, deals with subtle ideas. Young protagonist Jamie wonders about his absent father and learns about him through stories his grandfather tells by casting shadows on a wall. *Shadows* elicited high praise from Liz Rosenberg, who reviewed the book in the *New York Times Book Review.* Haseley, Rosenberg contended, "possesses an acute sense of childhood's pathos," putting his talent to good effect in this "beautifully written novel." Rosenberg added that the novel "combines realism and fantasy," and "is strong and powerfully appealing," a story "perfect for reluctant readers, as well as all those who love good books."

Set in a small Ohio town in the late 1950s, *Getting Him* is a story of revenge against an eccentric sixth grader named Harold who has accidentally injured the dog of another boy named Donald. Because precocious Harold, who is only eight years old, believes in the existence of extraterrestrials, Donald and several of his friends perpetrate an elaborate hoax involving "aliens." Citing the work as a combination science-fiction novel, fantasy, morality tale, and coming-of-age story, a *Publishers Weekly* commentator wrote that "Haseley creates a mysterious stark world of preadolescent confusion." In a *School Library Journal* review of *Getting Him,* Tim Rausch noted that while "readers may enjoy the details of the boys' prank and the mysterious elements of the plot," the book's characters, except for Harold, "are flat, stereotypical, and basically unlikable." A *Horn Book* contributor, on the other hand, described the novel as "a thoughtful, complex story with an intriguing plot and rich, believable characters."

Haseley's *A Story for Bear* has a fairy-tale quality in its story of a curious bear who watches a young woman reading in a cottage. Over the summer, the bear and the woman often come together over a book. When she leaves at the end of the summer, she leaves him some books. He keeps them with him as he hibernates, hearing her voice reading to him again. Critics praised the book for its sweet tone and message about words and reading together. In *Booklist,* Julie Cummins commended the artwork and concluded, "This gentle message about the power of words is a tender, wistful celebration of the pleasures of reading." Similarly, a reviewer for *Kirkus Reviews* described the book as a "tender, if unlikely, episode that affirms the value of both the written and the spoken word." In *Publishers Weekly,* a critic found some of the story's inconsistencies to be a weak point, but called *A Story for Bear* "wistful" and added that Jim LaMarche's "artwork conveys the bear and the woman in growing intimacy."

Photographer Mole is a light-hearted story of a mole who is the portrait photographer in his village. When he begins to feel that something is missing in his life, he leaves town only to return later with a wife. Critics enjoyed the story and were particularly taken with the old-fashioned illustrations by Juli Kangas. In *Publishers Weekly,* for example, a reviewer praised the book's "picturesque, old-fashioned English-village setting evoked in loving detail" and also cited its "nostalgic mood." In *Kirkus Reviews,* another critic was drawn to the atmosphere created by the illustrations, noting that they reflect "an era of cobblestone streets, rolling green hills, red clay-tiled roof cottages, and a menagerie of characters dressed in period clothing." Julie Roach, writing in *School Library Journal,* remarked that *Photographer Mole* will "strike just the right chord with readers," adding that the charming illustrations "make a nice accompaniment to the sweet and gentle text."

Art and history take on new meaning in Haseley's young-adult novel *Trick of the Eye.* Richard is a lonely young man who finds that he is able to enter works of art and interact with the subjects. As he begins to uncover some of his personal mysteries, he is also able to investigate the disappearance of various works of art from local galleries. Many critics found the narrative structure of *Trick of the Eye* to be too weak to carry such an unusual premise. In *Publishers Weekly,* for example, a reviewer noted that because the story is "elliptical in its storytelling and circuitous in its structure," it may engage some readers but "leave others confused or even bored." *School Library Journal* critic Connie Tyrell Burns questioned Halseley's storytelling and characterization, writing that "Minimally drawn characters and a weak plot that is puzzling and ambiguous gives this brooding tale limited appeal." Terry Glover, reviewing the novel for *Booklist,* was more attentive to the material than the "odd narrative structure." Roach observed that the unusual approach and some of the content may make the book more appropriate for older readers, "who will find it a fine introduction to art analysis alongside the well-woven mystery."

Haseley once commented: "I often start a story—whether for a picture book or a novel—with an image or metaphor that captures me. For instance, for *Dr. Gravity,* it was the idea of a town that could float. *Shadows* began when I came upon a reprinted nineteenth-century book instructing the reader how to make various hand shadows. *Crosby* grew from the images of a kite's tail made of old socks and scuffed shoes that looked like turtles. Starting with a key, evocative image, I try to reach in some way into my own experiences and emotions and build a story that becomes for the reader—and for me—something that's new."

Biographical and Critical Sources

PERIODICALS

Booklist, October 1, 1983, review of *The Old Banjo,* p. 294; October 1, 1986, review of *The Kite Flier,* p. 272; January 1, 1989, review of *My Father Doesn't Know*

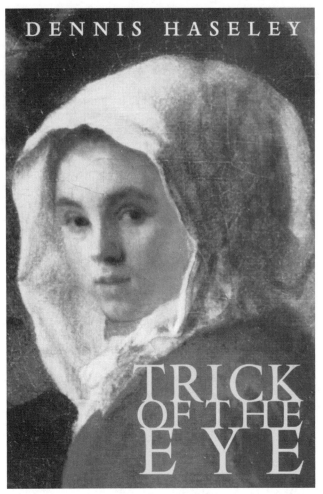

In this story about a twelve-year-old boy whose questions about his past are answered in the paintings he sees, Haseley's readers are drawn into a gothic-style mystery with an unexpected twist. (Cover illustration by Johannes Vermeer.)

about the Woods and Me, p. 788; March 15, 1991, review of *The Thieves' Market,* p. 1505; November 15, 1993, Kay Weisman, review of *Horses with Wings,* pp. 630-31; May 1, 2002, review of *A Story for Bear,* p. 1533; August, 2004, Terry Glover, review of *Trick of the Eye,* p. 1919.

Bulletin of the Center for Children's Books, January, 1984, review of *The Scared One,* p. 88.

Five Owls, September-October, 1993, Stephen Fraser, review of *Horses with Wings,* pp. 10-11.

Globe and Mail, May 30, 1987, Tim Wynne-Jones, review of *The Cave of Snores.*

Horn Book, March-April, 1993, review of *Dr. Gravity,* pp. 211-212; January-February, 1995, review of *Getting Him,* p. 59-60.

Kirkus Reviews, February 1, 1983, review of *The Pirate Who Tried to Capture the Moon,* p. 117; September 1, 1993, review of *Horses with Wings,* p. 54; August 1, 1996, review of *Crosby,* p. 1153; March 1, 2002, review of *A Story for Bear,* p. 335; May 1, 2004, review of *Photographer Mole,* p. 442.

New York Times Book Review, September 18, 1983, George A. Woods, review of *The Old Banjo,* p. 39; September

9, 1984, Karla Ruskin, review of *The Soap Bandit,* p. 43; October 20, 1991, Liz Rosenberg, review of *Shadows,* p. 53; April 26, 1992, Rona Berg, review of *Ghost Catcher,* p. 25.

Publishers Weekly, September 16, 1983, review of *The Scared One,* p. 125; October 14, 1983, review of *The Old Banjo,* p. 54; June 22, 1984, review of *The Soap Bandit,* p. 99; July 25, 1991, review of *Ghost Catcher,* p. 54; November 7, 1994, review of *Getting Him,* pp. 79-80; September 2, 1996, review of *Crosby,* p. 131; February 18, 2002, review of *A Story for Bear,* p. 96; April 26, 2004, review of *Trick of the Eye,* p. 67; July 5, 2004, review of *Photographer Mole,* p. 55.

School Library Journal, August, 1983, David Gale, review of *The Pirate Who Tried to Capture the Moon,* p. 51; November, 1983, review of *The Old Banjo,* p. 64; November, 1986, Maria B. Salvadore, review of *The Kite Flier,* p. 78; April, 1987, Tim Rausch, review of *The Cave of Snores,* pp. 82-3; October, 1987, Robert E. Unsworth, review of *The Counterfeiter,* pp. 138-139; October, 1988, David Gale, review of *My Father Doesn't Know about the Woods and Me,* p. 121; May, 1991, Shirley Wilton, review of *The Thieves' Market,* p. 78; September, 1996, Judith Constantinides, review of *Crosby,* p. 180; April, 2004, Connie Tyrell Burns, review of *Trick of the Eye,* p. 155; July, 2004, Julie Roach, review of *Photographer Mole,* p. 77.

Voice of Youth Advocates, December, 1992, Catherine M. Dwyer, review of *Dr. Gravity,* p. 292.*

*　　*　　*

HERALD, Kathleen
See PEYTON, Kathleen Wendy (Herald)

*　　*　　*

HIÇYILMAZ, Gaye 1947-

Personal

Born May 5, 1947, in Surbiton, Surrey, England; daughter of Harry (an engineer) and Dorothy (a teacher; maiden name, Hart) Campling; married Muzaffer Hiçyilmaz (a banker), 1970; children: Timur, Kubilay, Hulagu, Mewgu. *Education:* University of Sussex, B.A., 1969.

Addresses

Home—15 Kingsdowne Rd., Surbiton, Surrey KT6 6JL, England. *Agent*—Rosemary Bromley, Juvenalia, Avington, Winchester, Hampshire SO21 1DB, England.

Career

British Council teacher in Ankara, Turkey, c.1970s.

Awards, Honors

Whitbread Award shortlist, and *Guardian* Children's Book Award runner-up, both 1992, both for *Against the Storm; Guardian* Children's Book Award shortlist, Smarties Award shortlist, and Writer's Guild Children's Fiction Award, all 1993, all for *The Frozen Waterfall.*

Writings

Against the Storm, Viking Kestrel (London, England), 1990, Little, Brown (Boston, MA), 1992.
The Frozen Waterfall, Faber (London, England), 1993, Farrar, Straus (New York, NY), 1994.
Watching the Watcher, Faber (London, England), 1996.
And the Stars Were Gold, Orion (London, England), 1997.
Coming Home, Faber (London, England), 1998.
Smiling for Strangers, Orion (London, England), 1998, Farrar, Straus (New York, NY), 2000.
In Flame, Faber (London, England), 2000.
Girl in Red, Orion (London, England), 2000.
Pictures from the Fire, Orion (London, England), 2003.

Adaptations

Girl in Red was adapted as an audiobook, Bolida Audio, 2002.

Sidelights

Although born in England, author Gaye Hiçyilmaz spent several years living in Turkey with her Turkish husband, and her personal understanding of the culture and politics of Eastern Europe is woven throughout her highly praised novels for middle-grade and teen readers. Her first novel, *Against the Storm,* is characteristic of Hiçyilmaz's work: set in Turkey, where young Mehmet's family leaves their drought-stricken rural village and moves to a shanty town in the capital city of Ankara, hoping to find a better life, the book was praised by a *Publishers Weekly* reviewer who praised the author for presenting "a vivid and disturbing picture of poverty." Other novels by Hiçyilmaz include *Smiling for Strangers, The Frozen Waterfall,* and *Girl in Red.*

Like the protagonists in many of Hiçyilmaz's books, Selda, the leading character in *The Frozen Waterfall,* is a twelve-year-old Turkish girl who joins her father and brothers in Switzerland, where the family has moved to avoid racial tensions. The novel explores the new difficulties now facing Selda in a country where the people, customs, schools, and language are all unknown to her. A *Publishers Weekly* reviewer wrote that "hearts will go out to the heroine as she struggles to find a niche for herself," while Hazel Rochman noted in her *Booklist* review of *The Frozen Waterfall* that "the plot is dramatic; and the writing is sharp and lyrical."

Taking place in 1996, *Smiling for Strangers* is set in war-torn Bosnia and follows the travails of fourteen-year-old Nina Topic, a middle-class teen who flees from the violence that engulfed her family's home in Sarajevo and now spreads to the small town she lives in.

Forced to flee once more, Nina hopes that, with the help of some letters and a photograph, she can find refuge with a friend of her mother's, a woman believed to be living somewhere in Sussex, England. *School Library Journal* contributor Laura Scott praised Hiçyilmaz for her "beautiful writing and riveting characterizations," although she noted that many readers would require more background on the causes of Bosnian violence. "Nina emerges as psychologically complex, a tough and scarred heroine who may awaken readers to the price of war," maintained a *Publishers Weekly* critic, while in *Horn Book* a contributor wrote that in *Smiling for Strangers* "Hiçyilmaz reminds us repeatedly, without a trace of sentimentality, how much that is good and innocent is buried by war."

Considered a departure from her previous novels, *In Flame* focuses on a British teen whose move across England causes her family to suffer emotional upheaval. Fourteen-year-old Helen moves with her family to the coastal town of Pembroke after the death of her brother, Tom. Her mother wants to make a new start, but the family soon discovers that leaving the past behind is not as simple as moving one's home. Helen's younger brother continues to suffer emotional stress following the loss of his brother, and an encounter with a man named Christian leads to a gradual unveiling of disturbing secrets about the late Tom. A London *Guardian* reviewer found *In Flame* an "immensely satisfying" read, adding that Hiçyilmaz's "writing is delicate and pointed, the plotting exciting and the characters psychologically convincing."

Girl in Red also focuses on British teens, in this case Frankie, who lives with his single mother in a low-income housing project in Kent, and Emilia, the daughter of Rumanian immigrants. While the overweight, unathletic Frankie remains on the outside of most school social events, he becomes inspired with greater self-confidence after getting to know Emilia, a new student who enters school knowing very little English. His budding romance with Emilia soon forces Frankie into an open battle with his mother when the older woman rallies the neighborhood to reject Emilia's gypsy family and drive them from the area by inciting a race riot. Praising Hiçyilmaz for her sensitive portrayal of a young man coming of age, *Guardian* contributor Julia Eccleshare wrote that Frankie "observes and learns, moved by compassion . . . that leads him to reject the prejudice" he was raised with and make independent decisions based on his own sense of what is right. Emilia's story is continued in *Pictures from the Fire,* which finds the teen's family living at a refugee hostel. Emilia herself is confined to her room because of the belief that her shameful actions caused the riot that forced them from their Kent home. Now, through pictures, she attempts to sort out the events of her short life—from the family's flight from Bucharest hidden in a truck to her happiness at school, to the riot that forced them to leave Kent—and make the decisions that will shape her life as an independent young woman.

In her 2004 novel Gaye Hiçyilmaz continues the story begun in Girl in Red, *and finds Emilia attempting to make sense of her tragic life—and her captivity—through an illustrated journal.*

Biographical and Critical Sources

PERIODICALS

Booklist, April 15, 1992, Hazel Rochman, review of *Against the Storm,* p. 1522; October 1, 1994, Hazel Rochman, review of *The Frozen Waterfall,* p. 318; April 1, 2000, Hazel Rochman, review of *Smiling for Strangers,* p. 1451; July, 2000, Hazel Rochman, review of *Smiling for Strangers,* p. 2025.

Book Report, November-December, 1992, Gayle Berge, review of *Against the Storm,* p. 42; March-April, 1995, Susan Martin, review of *The Frozen Waterfall,* p. 37.

Guardian (London, England), June 20, 2000, Julia Eccleshare, review of *Girl in Red;* April 4, 2002, review of *In Flame.*

Horn Book, May-June, 1992, Hanna B. Zeiger, review of *Against the Storm,* p. 343; May, 2000, review of *Smiling for Strangers,* p. 314.

Kliatt, September, 2004, Pat Dole, review of *Girl in Red,* p. 60.

Publishers Weekly, May 11, 1992, review of *Against the Storm,* p. 73; August 1, 1994, review of *The Frozen*

Waterfall, p. 80; May 8, 2000, review of *Smiling for Strangers*, p. 222.
School Library Journal, May, 1992, Ellen D. Warwick, review of *Against the Storm*, p. 130; October, 1994, Ann W. Moore, review of *The Frozen Waterfall*, p. 142; June, 2000, Laura Scott, review of *Smiling for Strangers*, p. 146.
Times (London, England), March 10, 1990.*

*   *   *

HIRSCH, Odo
[A pseudonym]

Personal

Born in Melbourne, Australia. *Education:* Cambridge University, M.A. (political thought).

Addresses

Home—London, England. *Agent*—Allen & Unwin, 9 Atchinson St., Sidney, New South Wales 2065, Australia.

Career

Physician in Melbourne, Australia, and London, England; worked for Amnesty International in London, England, and in Eastern Europe; management consultant for McKinsey Consulting, beginning 1997. Author of books for adults and children.

Awards, Honors

National Children's Literature Award shortlist, Festival Awards for Literature, Book of the Year for Younger Readers shortlist, Australian Children's Book Council Book of the Year awards, 1998, and Patricia Wrightson Prize for Children's Literature, New South Wales Premier's Awards, 1999, all for *Antonio S. and the Mystery of Theodore Guzman;* honour book designation, Australian Children's Book Council Book of the Year Awards, 2002, for *Have Courage, Hazel Green!*

Writings

Antonio S. and the Mystery of Theodore Guzman, illustrated by Andrew McLean, Allen & Unwin (St. Leonards, New South Wales, Australia), 1997, illustrated by August Hall, Hyperion (New York, NY), 2001.
Bartlett and the Ice Voyage, illustrated by Andrew McLean, Allen & Unwin (St. Leonards, New South Wales, Australia), 1998, Bloomsbury Children's Books (New York, NY), 2002.
Bartlett and the City of Flames, illustrated by Andrew McLean, Allen & Unwin (St. Leonards, New South Wales, Australia), 1999, Bloomsbury Children's Books (New York, NY), 2003.

Hazel Green, illustrated by Andrew McLean, Allen & Unwin (St. Leonards, New South Wales, Australia), 1999, Bloomsbury Children's Books (New York, NY), 2003.
Something's Fishy, Hazel Green!, illustrated by Andrew McLean, Allen & Unwin (St. Leonards, New South Wales, Australia), 2000.
Frankel Mouse, illustrated by Ron Brooks, Allen & Unwin (St. Leonards, New South Wales, Australia), 2000.
Have Courage, Hazel Green!, illustrated by Andrew McLean, Allen & Unwin (St. Leonards, New South Wales, Australia), 2001.
Bartlett and the Forest of Plenty, illustrated by Andrew McLean, Allen & Unwin (St. Leonards, New South Wales, Australia), 2001, Bloomsbury Children's Books (New York, NY), 2004.
Yoss, Allen & Unwin (St. Leonards, New South Wales, Australia), 2001, Delacorte (New York, NY), 2004.
Frankel Mouse and the Bestish Lair, illustrated by Ron Brooks, Allen & Unwin (St. Leonards, New South Wales, Australia), 2002.
Pincus Corbett's Strange Adventure, Allen & Unwin (St. Leonards, New South Wales, Australia), 2002.
Think Smart, Hazel Green!, illustrated by Andrew McLean, Allen & Unwin (St. Leonards, New South Wales, Australia), 2003.
Bartlett and the Island of Kings, illustrated by Andrew McLean, Allen & Unwin (St. Leonards, New South Wales, Australia), 2003.

Sidelights

The pseudonymous Odo Hirsch is the author of such works as *Antonio S. and the Mystery of Theodore Guzman*, *Bartlett and the Ice Voyage*, *Hazel Green*, and *Yoss*. A native of Australia who now makes his home in London, England, Hirsch is a physician by training, and he once worked for Amnesty International. After completing a master's degree in political thought at Cambridge University, Hirsch became a management consultant and also began writing children's books. As he commented on the *Allen & Unwin Web site*, "For me, writing is great fun. I get to make up a world and I get to look at that world with freshness and curiosity." In his works, Hirsch explores the world of discovery available to children when creating their own reality. In *Antonio S. and the Mystery of Theodore Guzman*, for example, a boy discovers the magic of theater. Antonio, in a secret room in the rambling mansion where he lives, discovers a poster advertising a production of Shakespeare's *Hamlet* and becomes intrigued with the process of putting on a play. Encouraged by his magician father and professor mother, and guided by a mysterious neighbor, an elderly recluse named Theodore Guzman, Antonio and his friends set about creating and staging their own production. In a *Magpies* interview with Virginia Lowe, Hirsch commented that in *Antonio S. and the Mystery of Theodore Guzman* he "tries to capture certain elements of childhood—elements of inventiveness, discovery, learning, freshness. The book moves from a physical adventure . . . to an imaginative one." According to Geraldine Brennan in a *Times*

In Odo Hirsch's award-winning 1997 novel, the son of a magician father and a physician mother is introduced to the kind of magic wrought in the theatre after getting to know his mysterious neighbor. (Cover illustration by August Hall.)

Educational Supplement review, "Like the production, the story gets off to a slow start but gathers pace and deserves applause." *School Library Journal* contributor Ashley Larsen praised the novel, stating that "Antonio is fully developed as a clever, thoughtful, and creative boy," while in *Magpies* Kevin Steinberger hailed the book as "a rare junior novel of superb literary quality and classically engaging storytelling."

Hirsch's second children's novel, *Bartlett and the Ice Voyage,* is an adventure story populated with intrepid explorers and a busy young queen who rules seven countries. The tale, which a *Publishers Weekly* critic referred to as a "charming fantasy about the perils of desire," follows a quest set upon by the famous explorer Bartlett and his companion Jacques le Grand for an exotic fruit that the queen desires. The adventurers use their inventiveness, desperation, and perseverance in an attempt to grant the queen's request despite the machinations of petty courtiers who fuel the woman's impatience. Steinberger called *Bartlett and the Ice Voyage* "beautifully crafted with nary a word out of place," and *Booklist* critic Anne O'Malley stated that Hirsch

"blends sparkling wit with engaging characters and great pacing that follows through till the suspensefully timed end."

The dashing explorer and his sidekick make their second appearance in *Bartlett and the City of Flames.* In this novel Bartlett, Jacques, and their friend Gozo are taken prisoner by guards from the City of the Sun. The trio is directed to the royal palace where Gozo is mistaken for Prince Darian, who has been kidnapped by the mysterious beings from Underground. Bartlett and Jacques realize that they must locate the true prince to help free their companion, and the duo employ "generous measures of ingenuity, perseverance, and desperation in pursuit of a seemingly impossible task," noted a critic in *Kirkus Reviews.* Nicolette Jones, reviewing *Bartlett and the City of Flames* in the London *Sunday Times,* praised the author's "measured, self-delighting prose, with witty dialogue, successful jokes, surprises, a happy sprinkling of satire, and a gently didactic wishfulness about how people should behave better." "Well-paced action augmented by quirky characters and exotic settings make this sequel to *Bartlett and the Ice Voyage* a fast, enjoyable read," observed Corrina Austin in *School Library Journal.*

A forgotten city in the jungle is the setting for the third "Bartlett" tale, *Bartlett and the Forest of Plenty.* When Bartlett, Jacques, and Gozo enter the Forest of Plenty in search of adventure, they are pitted against a mystifying enemy who seeks to control their movements. The 2003 work *Bartlett and the Island of Kings* continues to follow the brave threesome, this time to a remote island ruled by a quartet of kings. While investigating a secretive figure who disappears seemingly at will, Bartlett, Jacques, and Gozo find themselves in peril when a towering volcano begins to erupt.The title character of *Hazel Green* is a determined girl with a formidable task: to revive the tradition of having children participate in her city's annual Frogg Day parade. She takes on the uncooperative parade organizer, Mr. Winkel, and is wrongfully accused of stealing the recipe for Chocolate Dippers by Mr. Volio, the pastry chef. Fortunately, Hazel has many people to vouch for her, including the mathematician Yak and Mrs. Gluck the floral arranger. According to *Booklist* reviewer Shelle Rosenfeld, Hirsch "has created an imaginative, outspoken protagonist for his charming tale," and a *Kirkus Reviews* contributor described Hazel as "a young mover-and-shaker who will stay with readers for a long time." *Magpies* reviewer Jo Goodman dubbed *Hazel Green* "delightful," and stated that "Hirsch deftly establishes a vivid cast of characters."

The resourceful, energetic Hazel returns in *Something's Fishy, Hazel Green!* After a pair of lobsters are stolen from Mr. Petrusca's store, Hazel attempts to find the culprit. Her only clue is a cryptic message, written in a secret code, that was left behind by the thief. Hirsch examines themes of discrimination and fairness in *Have*

Courage, Hazel Green!, and in *Think Smart, Hazel Green!,* he describes Hazel's efforts to help the neighborhood baker renew his bakery shop lease.

Hirsch has written for a young-adult audience as well as for younger readers. His novel *Yoss* concerns a fourteen-year-old boy who leaves his remote medieval village as part of a traditional rite of passage. Though Yoss is expected to return the following day, he decides to journey on, encountering a pair of ruffians who involve him in a crime. Yoss is later caught and enslaved by the merchant he robbed, and his harsh treatment while at the merchant's home strengthens his resolve to escape. Unlike some of Hirsch's other books, *Yoss* received a mixed reception from reviewers. A *Publishers Weekly* reviewer observed that the innocence of the novel's young protagonist "stands in marked contrast to the corruption he encounters at every turn, but he's also passive and a bit of a bore," and Connie Tyrell Burns, writing in *School Library Journal,* noted, "While much transpires in this coming-of-age tale that mixes fantasy, historical fiction, and adventure, the pace tends to be

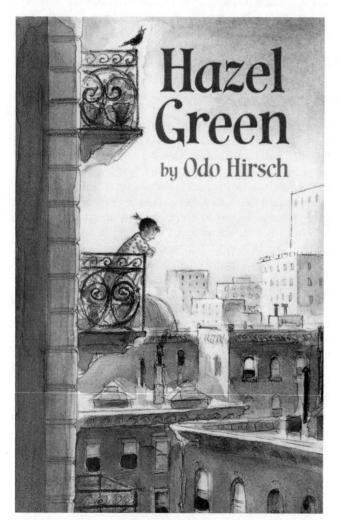

The protagonist of this 2000 Australian novel decides to take action to convince her city to allow young people to join the marchers in the city's festive Frogg Day parade. (Cover illustration by Andrew McLean.)

slow." More enthusiastic about the work, *Horn Book* contributor Susan P. Bloom remarked that "Hirsch provides plenty of action," and *Booklist* critic Jennifer Mattson praised the author's "vivid evocation of the disorienting universe Yoss enters and, eventually, leaves, both wiser and tougher than when he arrived."

Speaking to Lynne Babbage in *Reading Time,* Hirsch attributed his ability to write so well for children to being surrounded by a large extended family, and for his ability to look at the world through a child's eyes. That, and years of observing people and figuring out what makes them tick, have influenced his writing style. As Hirsch told Lowe in *Magpies,* "what one does with one's influences is to make them into a different mix, that's what makes it original and different."

Biographical and Critical Sources

PERIODICALS

Booklist, May 15, 2001, Carolyn Phelan, review of *Antonio S. and the Mystery of Theodore Guzman,* p. 1753; February 1, 2003, review of *Bartlett and the Ice Voyage,* pp. 994-995; June 1, 2003, Shelle Rosenfeld, review of *Hazel Green,* p. 1776; September 15, 2004, Jennifer Mattson, review of *Yoss,* p. 232.

Horn Book, September-October, 2004, Susan P. Bloom, review of *Yoss,* p. 585.

Kirkus Reviews, November 15, 2002, review of *Bartlett and the Ice Voyage,* p. 1694; June 15, 2003, review of *Hazel Green,* p. 859; November 1, 2003, review of *Bartlett and the City of Flames,* p. 1311; September 1, 2004, review of *Yoss,* p. 867.

Magpies, July, 1998, Virginia Lowe, interview with Hirsch, pp. 14-16, and Kevin Steinberger, review of *Bartlett and the Ice Voyage,* p. 32; March, 1999, Jo Goodman, review of *Hazel Green,* p. 32.

Publishers Weekly, March 12, 2001, review of *Antonio S. and the Mystery of Theodore Guzman,* p. 91; November 25, 2002, review of *Bartlett and the Ice Voyage,* p. 68; October 25, 2004, review of *Yoss,* pp. 48-49.

Reading Time, May, 1999, Lynne Babbage, interview with Hirsch, pp. 2-3.

School Librarian, summer, 1999, Beverly Mathias, review of *Antonio S. and the Mystery of Theodore Guzman,* p. 89.

School Library Journal, April, 2001, Ashley Larsen, review of *Antonio S. and the Mystery of Theodore Guzman,* p. 144; December, 2003, Corinna Austin, review of *Bartlett and the City of Flames,* p. 152; September, 2004, Connie Tyrrell Burns, review of *Yoss,* p. 208.

Sunday Times (London, England), June 4, 2000, Nicolette Jones, review of *Bartlett and the City of Flames,* p. 44.

Times Educational Supplement, March 5, 1999, Geraldine Brennan, "Dreams Meet Gritty Realism."

ONLINE

Allen & Unwin Web site, http://www.allen-unwin.com.au/ (January 5, 2005), interview with Hirsch.*

HOFF, Mary (King) 1956-

Personal

Born August 16, 1956; daughter of Harold and Delores (Reinecke) King; married Paul Hoff; chidlren: Tony, Kate, Daniel. *Education:* University of Wisconsin, B.S. 1978; University of Minnesota, M.A., 1984. *Hobbies and other interests:* Hiking, camping, reading, cooking, canoeing, gardening, knitting.

Addresses

Agent—c/o Author Mail, Creative Education, Inc., 123 South Broad St., Mankato, MN 56001.

Career

Writer. Free-lance communicator specializing in science and medical communication.

Writings

Our Endangered Planet: Atmosphere, Lerner Publications (Minneapolis, MN), 1995.
Living Together, Creative Education (Mankato, MN), 2003.
Pollination, Creative Education (Mankato, MN), 2003.
Mimicry and Camouflage, Creative Education (Mankato, MN), 2003.
Migration, Creative Education (Mankato, MN), 2003.
Metamorphosis, Creative Education (Mankato, MN), 2003.
Life at Night, Creative Education (Mankato, MN), 2003.
Handling Heat, Creative Education (Mankato, MN), 2003.
Coping with Cold, Creative Education (Mankato, MN), 2003.
Communication, Creative Education (Mankato, MN), 2003.
Swans, Creative Education (Mankato, MN), 2004.
Tigers, Creative Education (Mankato, MN), 2004.
Monkeys, Creative Education (Mankato, MN), 2004.
Polar Bears, Creative Education (Mankato, MN), 2004.
Koalas, Creative Education (Mankato, MN), 2004.

Also contributor to periodicals.

*   *   *

HOPE, Laura Lee
See STANLEY, George Edward

J-K

JORGENSEN, Norman 1954-

Personal
Born 1954, in Broome, Western Australia; partner's name Jan (a school librarian).

Addresses
Home—Perth, Australia *Agent*—c/o Author Mail, Simply Read Books, 74 Pease Ave., Verona NJ 07044.

Career
Author and bookseller.

Awards, Honors
Western Australia Premier's Book Award shortlist, 2002, and Children's Book Council of Australia Picture Book of the Year award and Notable Book for Young Readers designation, and Henry Berg Children's Book Award finalist, American Society for the Prevention of Cruelty to Animals, all 2003, all for *In Flanders Field.*

Writings

(With David Turton) *Ashe on Parade,* illustrated by Allan Langoulant, Thomas Catt (Victoria Park, Western Australia, Australia), 1992.

(With David Turton) *Ashe of the Outback,* illustrated by Allan Langoulant, Thomas Catt (Hamilton, Queensland, Australia), 1992, second edition, 1996.

(With David Turton) *The Great Escapes,* illustrated by Allan Langoulant, Thomas Catt (Hamilton, Queensland, Australia), 1993.

In Flanders Field, illustrated by Brian Harrison-Lever, Fremantle Arts Centre Press (Freemantle, Western Australia, Australia), 2002.

A Fine Mess!, Freemantle Arts Centre Press (Freemantle, Western Australia, Australia), 2004.

The Call of the Osprey, Freemantle Arts Centre Press (Freemantle, Western Australia, Australia), 2004.

Biographical and Critical Sources

PERIODICALS

CBCA Bulletin, May, 2002, "Showcasing Western Australia: Authors and Illustrators for Young People."

ONLINE

Aussie Reviews Online, http://www.aussiereviews.com/ (October 22, 2004), Sally Murphy, review of *In Flanders Field.**

*   *   *

JOSEPH, Patrick
See O'MALLEY, Kevin

*   *   *

KEENE, Carolyn
See STANLEY, George Edward

*   *   *

KELLER, Holly 1942-

Personal
Born February 11, 1942, in New York, NY; married Barry Keller (a pediatrician), June, 1963; children: Corey (daughter), Jesse (son). *Education:* Sarah Lawrence College, A.B., 1963; Columbia University, M.A., 1964; studied printmaking at Manhattanville College; studied illustration at Parsons School of Design. *Hobbies and other interests:* Tennis, travel.

Addresses
Home—West Redding, CT. *Agent*—c/o Author Mail, Greenwillow Press/William Morrow, 1350 Avenue of the Americas, New York, NY 10019.

Holly Keller

Career

Writer. Redding Board of Education, Redding, CT, member and vice chair, 1975-85.

Awards, Honors

Children's Book of the Year, Library of Congress, 1983, for *Ten Sleepy Sheep;* best book of the year, *School Library Journal,* 1984, for *Geraldine's Blanket;* Children's Choice and Child Study Association Children's Book of the Year, both 1987, both for *Goodbye, Max;* Notable Children's Trade Book in the Field of Social Studies, National Council for the Social Studies/Children's Book Council (NCSS/CBC), 1989, for *The Best Present;* Fanfare Honor Book, *Horn Book,* and Reading Rainbow Review Book, both 1991, both for *Horace;* Pick of the Lists, American Booksellers Association, 1991, for *The New Boy,* 1992, for *Island Baby,* and 1994, for *Geraldine's Baby Brother;* Notable Children's Trade Book in the Field of Social Studies, NCSS/CBC, 1994, for *Grandfather's Dream.*

Writings

FOR CHILDREN; SELF-ILLUSTRATED

Cromwell's Glasses, Greenwillow (New York, NY), 1982.
Ten Sleepy Sheep, Greenwillow (New York, NY), 1983.
Too Big, Greenwillow (New York, NY), 1983.

Geraldine's Blanket, Greenwillow (New York, NY), 1984.
Will It Rain?, Greenwillow (New York, NY), 1984.
Henry's Fourth of July, Greenwillow (New York, NY), 1984.
When Francie Was Sick, Greenwillow (New York, NY), 1985.
A Bear for Christmas, Greenwillow (New York, NY), 1986.
Lizzie's Invitation, Greenwillow (New York, NY), 1987.
Goodbye, Max, Greenwillow (New York, NY), 1987.
Geraldine's Big Snow, Greenwillow (New York, NY), 1988.
Maxine in the Middle, Greenwillow (New York, NY), 1989.
The Best Present, Greenwillow (New York, NY), 1989.
Henry's Happy Birthday, Greenwillow (New York, NY), 1990.
What Alvin Wanted, Greenwillow (New York, NY), 1990.
Horace, Greenwillow (New York, NY), 1991.
The New Boy, Greenwillow (New York, NY), 1991.
Furry, Greenwillow (New York, NY), 1992.
Island Baby, Greenwillow (New York, NY), 1992.
Harry and Tuck, Greenwillow (New York, NY), 1993.
Grandfather's Dream, Greenwillow (New York, NY), 1994.
Geraldine's Baby Brother, Greenwillow (New York, NY), 1994.
Rosata, Greenwillow (New York, NY), 1995.
Geraldine First, Greenwillow (New York, NY), 1996.
I Am Angela, Greenwillow (New York, NY), 1997.
Merry Christmas, Geraldine, Greenwillow (New York, NY), 1997.
Angela's Top-Secret Computer Club, Greenwillow (New York, NY), 1998.
Brave Horace, Greenwillow (New York, NY), 1998.
Jacob's Tree, Greenwillow (New York, NY), 1999.
What I See, Harcourt Brace (New York, NY), 1999.
A Bed Full of Cats, Harcourt Brace (New York, NY), 1999.
That's Mine, Horace, Greenwillow (New York, NY), 2000.
Geraldine and Mrs. Duffy, Greenwillow (New York, NY), 2000.
Cecil's Garden, Greenwillow (New York, NY), 2002.
Farfallina and Marcel, Greenwillow (New York, NY), 2002.
What a Hat!, Greenwillow (New York, NY), 2003.
The Hat, Harcourt (Orlando, FL), 2005.
Pearl's New Skates, Greenwillow (New York, NY), 2005.
To Sophie's Window, Greenwillow (New York, NY), 2005.

FOR CHILDREN; ILLUSTRATOR

Jane Thayer, *Clever Raccoon,* Morrow (New York, NY), 1981.
Melvin Berger, *Why I Cough, Sneeze, Shiver, Hiccup, and Yawn,* Crowell (New York, NY), 1983.
Roma Gans, *Rock Collecting,* Crowell (New York, NY), 1984.
Franklyn Mansfield Branley, *Snow Is Falling,* Crowell (New York, NY), 1986.
Franklyn Mansfield Branley, *Air Is All around You,* Harper & Row (New York, NY), 1986, revised edition, Crowell (New York, NY), 1986.

Patricia Lauber, *Snakes Are Hunters,* Crowell (New York, NY), 1988.

Franklyn Mansfield Branley, *Shooting Stars,* Crowell (New York, NY), 1989.

Patricia Lauber, *An Octopus Is Amazing,* Crowell (New York, NY), 1990.

Paul Showers, *Ears Are for Hearing,* Crowell (New York, NY), 1990.

Barbara Juster Ebensen, *Sponges Are Skeletons,* HarperCollins (New York, NY), 1993.

Patricia Lauber, *Be a Friend to Trees,* HarperCollins (New York, NY), 1994.

Wendy Pfeffer, *From Tadpole to Frog,* HarperCollins (New York, NY), 1994.

Patricia Lauber, *Who Eats What?: Food Chains and Food Webs,* HarperCollins (New York, NY), 1995.

Patricia Lauber, *You're Aboard Spaceship Earth,* HarperCollins (New York, NY), 1996.

Wendy Pfeffer, *What's It Like to Be a Fish?,* HarperCollins (New York, NY), 1996.

Stuart J. Murphy, *The Best Bug Parade,* HarperCollins (New York, NY), 1996.

Roma Gans, *Let's Go Rock Collecting,* HarperCollins (New York, NY), 1997.

Nola Buck, *Morning in the Meadow,* HarperCollins (New York, NY), 1997.

Wendy Pfeffer, *Sounds All Around,* HarperCollins (New York, NY), 1999.

Franklyn Mansfield Branley, *Snow Is Falling,* revised edition, HarperCollins (New York, NY), 1999.

Anne Rockwell, *Growing like Me,* Silver Whistle (San Diego, CA), 2001.

Paul Showers, *Hear Your Heart,* HarperCollins (New York, NY), 2001.

Sidelights

Author/illustrator Holly Keller is noted for her penchant for creating animal protagonists, which she draws in a minimalist, flat, cartoon style. While her picture books are entertaining to read, they also have a message, dealing with issues ranging from adoption to fitting in, from sibling relationships to saying farewell to a beloved pet. Keller's endearing characters, many of whom appear in several volumes, include Geraldine, a plucky piglet who is featured in *Geraldine's Blanket, Geraldine's Big Snow, Geraldine's Baby Brother, Geraldine First,* and *Merry Christmas, Geraldine.* Horace, another beloved character and a personal favorite of Keller's, is a whimsical young leopard adopted into a family of tigers whose adventures play out in *Horace,* as well as in *Brave Horace* and *That's Mine, Horace.* A rambunctious possum named Henry is featured in *Too Big, Henry's Fourth of July,* and *Henry's Happy Birthday.* Other popular and award-winning picture-book titles from Keller include *Ten Sleepy Sheep, Goodbye, Max, The Best Present,* and *What a Hat!* She has also expanded her writing repertoire to include several chapter books featuring a young girl named Angela, who stars in *I Am Angela* and *Angela's Top-Secret Computer Club.*

Keller was born in 1942, in New York City, and was a fan of reading from an early age. Drawing also quickly became an early form of self-entertainment; one of Keller's early projects was copying all the bird illustrations from a book by noted American naturalist illustrator John James Audubon. A school project, translating *Little Red Riding Hood* into Latin and illustrating it, also served as a sort of preview of things to come for Keller, however, when she attended Sarah Lawrence College, she ultimately traded the study of art for a degree in history. At Columbia University, she continued her history studies by earning a master's degree, even though she retained her love of drawing and painting. Married in 1963, Keller soon became the mother of two children and found herself living in rural Connecticut.

When the time became available, Keller began taking classes in printmaking, and her instructor encouraged her to consider trying her hand at children's book illustration. After taking a course in illustration at the Parsons School of Design, she put together a portfolio of her works and submitted it to an editor at Greenwillow Press in 1981. Given an assignment to turn one set of drawings into a story within a week, Keller sat down and wrote her first picture book, *Cromwell's Glasses,* the tale of a young rabbit's anxiety at receiving his first pair of spectacles. Carolyn Noah, reviewing Keller's debut for the *School Library Journal,* noted that "this brief tale thoughtfully treats the difficulties that glasses present to a young child," and concluded that the book would make "a serviceable addition to storytime collections." Already in place with this first book was Keller's characteristic cartoon-style black ink drawings filled in with watercolor, as well as her positive treatment of a difficult childhood issue.

The follow-up to *Cromwell's Glasses, Ten Sleepy Sheep* features a little boy who cannot fall asleep; when he tries counting sheep things get worse because the animals throw a giant party in his room. A critic for *Kirkus Reviews* called the book "neatly done" and "lightly whimsical," while Margery Fisher, writing in *Growing Point,* dubbed it an "elegantly produced picture-book." *Ten Sleepy Sheep* was voted a Library of Congress Children's Book of the Year and firmly established Keller in her new career as a picture-book author and illustrator.

Keller's picture books have continued to win kudos from readers and critics alike. *Too Big* introduces Henry, a possum who encounters new-brother problems when baby Jake comes home from the hospital. Each time he tries to join in with Jake's activities—from sucking on a bottle to putting on a diaper—Henry is met by the statement, "You're too big." Finally Henry begins to realize that he is too big for babyish things, and a new bike christens his role as official older brother in a book that is "both touching and funny," according to Sarah Wintle in the *Times Literary Supplement.*

In *Henry's Fourth of July* the possum has a great time at a Fourth of July picnic, running a sack race and watching the fireworks. *Booklist* reviewer Ilene Cooper

Keller uses both prose and artwork to tell a story about a young boy who gets himself into problems when he lays claim to another friend's toy in **That's Mine, Horace.**

called the book a "happy introduction" for young readers to the national holiday. Henry reappears in *Henry's Happy Birthday,* this time fearing that his fifth birthday is going to be a disaster, especially when his mother insists he wear a shirt and tie to his own party. After munching on cake and receiving a present he has been hoping for, Henry decides the party wasn't so bad after all. Elizabeth S. Watson noted in *Horn Book* that *Henry's Happy Birthday* is an "appealing and refreshingly honest approach to the traditional birthday party story."

Keller introduces readers to a likeable young piglet named Geraldine in *Geraldine's Blanket.* Reaching a more mature age, like Henry, Geraldine takes some convincing but finally realizes that her security blanket needs to be reworked into a more socially acceptable product: like new dresses for her dolls. A *Kirkus Reviews* contributor called Geraldine "a piglet with aplomb," and praised Keller's "deft, spare, pink-and-gold cartoon" illustrations. In *Booklist* Cooper described *Geraldine's Blanket* as a "novel look at a familiar problem, and one that may provide a solution for some families." *Geraldine's Big Snow* finds the piglet bursting with anticipation while awaiting for the first snow of the season. "Geraldine may be a pig," commented Janet Hickman in a review of the book for *Language Arts,* "but her experience with waiting out a weather forecast

will be familiar to young children wherever snow falls." Writing in *School Library Journal,* Trev Jones dubbed *Geraldine's Big Snow* "fresh, appealing, and perfectly delightful."

Geraldine finds herself with a new baby brother named Willie in tow in *Geraldine's Baby Brother,* which like Keller's *Too Big,* explores sibling rivalry. Harriett Fargnoli observed in *School Library Journal* that the "expressive pig's appeal remains timeless," while a *Kirkus* reviewer noted that the "whimsical line drawings add to the overall charm" of Keller's "wise, funny, accepting little book."

Willie also makes an appearance in *Geraldine First,* doing his best to live up to his responsibility as an annoying little brother by mimicking everything Geraldine says and does. *School Library Journal* contributor Virginia Opocensky commented that Keller successfully captures a familiar sibling problem with "understated humor and a satisfying denouement," and also noted that the author's "marvelously minimalist pen-and-watercolor drawings [extend] the story beyond the words." An overlarge Christmas tree picked by Geraldine is the focus of *Merry Christmas, Geraldine,* a book that prompted *Booklist* reviewer Carolyn Phelan to dub

Keller's illustrations "beguiling" and declare that "fans of the series will enjoy watching this assertive heroine plow through every obstacle."

Her own experience meeting a child troubled by the knowledge that she was adopted inspired Keller to create her popular and award-winning picture book *Horace*. A spotted leopard-cub adoptee, Horace feels out of place with his new family—striped tigers all—especially when all his striped cousins arrive at Horace's first birthday party. "I think *Horace* and *Geraldine's Blanket* are my two favorites," Keller once explained to *Something about the Author* of her books. "I like Geraldine because she's really me, and *Horace* because it's a gentle and nice story, one of the better ones I've done." Cooper agreed in her *Booklist* review, writing that while adopted children can identify with Keller's "gentle story," *Horace* also has appeal for children "who simply feel like the odd one out." Anna Biagioni Hart, writing in *School Library Journal,* called "Keller's use of appealing animal characters in a fictional tale . . . a welcome approach" to the difficult issue of adoption.

Horace returns in *Brave Horace,* in which he comes unglued in anticipation of going to his friend's monster-movie party, and *That's Mine, Horace,* in which he lays claim to a toy truck he "found" on the playground and sticks to his story that it now belongs to him even after his good friend Walter claims to have lost just such a toy. "This sensitive and entertaining picture book is just right for young children," noted Phelan in her *Booklist* review of *Brave Horace,* while *School Library Journal* contributor Jody McCoy called the book a "boon for timid youngsters." Noting that "Keller raises ethical issues that will be easily grasped by young readers," a *Horn Book* contributor praised *That's Mine, Horace* as a picture book containing a "perfectly paced, dramatic story with appealing illustrations and a satisfying resolution."

In addition to her books featuring Henry, Horace, and the irrepressible Geraldine, Keller has earned high marks for her many standalone picture books. Her *Goodbye, Max* is the story of the death of a pet; *The Best Present* presents a tale of a hospitalized grandmother; *The New Boy* focuses on what it is like to feel un-welcomed by students at a new school; *Grandfather's Dream* is a Vietnamese tale about a grandfather's wisdom; and *What a Hat!* illustrates that true tolerance means respecting the harmless quirks of others.

Keller's picture book *Cecil's Garden* focuses on a three rabbits who quibble about what seeds to plant in their garden plot until one of their numbers—Cecil—realizes that disagreement like this, which cause great arguments, usually have simple solutions. *Booklist* contributor Gillian Engberg called *Cecil's Garden* a "sunny story about cooperation," while in *Publishers Weekly* a reviewer noted that Keller's illustrations "possess a sophisticated color sensibility even as they play up the . . . comedy" in a succession of silly arguments. Also featuring animal characters, *Farfallina and Marcel* finds a caterpillar and a gosling becoming fast friends, even after they both transform into a more mature phase of life. Calling the book a "deceptively simple story of friendship," a *Publishers Weekly* reviewer dubbed Keller's work "perfectly paced," while in *Christian Century* a critic praised *Farfallina and Marcel* as "quietly dramatic and beautifully illustrated," noting that Keller effectively intertwines the rhythms of nature with the strong bonds of true friendship.

In addition to writing and illustrating her own picture books, Keller has also created artwork for stories by other writers, such as Paul Showers, Wendy Pfeffer, and Anne Rockwood. While she initially limited her own writing to short picture-book texts, Keller has expanded into the easy-reader chapter-book format with *I Am An*

Keller has contributed her cheerful portraits of young children to books by a number of authors such as Franklyn M. Branley's 1986 picture book **Snow Is Falling.**

Keller explores the boundaries of true friendship and finds that there are none in her gentle picture book **Farfallina and Marcel.**

gela and *Angela's Top-Secret Computer Club.* The first book details five episodes in the life of feisty Angela. including playing softball at camp, visiting the zoo with her Scout troop, creating a class exhibit, and becoming a dog walker. *Booklist* contributor Stephanie Zvirin noted that in *I Am Angela* "there's always some goofy complication in the goings-on to ensure laughs." In *Angela's Top-Secret Computer Club,* after someone breaks in to the school's computer system and misprints all the student report cards, Angela and her computer-whiz friends are called on to solve the mystery before total chaos ensues. In her *Booklist* review, Kay Weisman called *Angela's Top-Secret Computer Club* an "upbeat

mystery" and wrote that Keller's entertaining illustrations combine with her creation of an "intrepid heroine" in a book that "hits just the right note" with novice readers.

Biographical and Critical Sources

BOOKS

Authors of Books for Young People, 3rd edition, Scarecrow Press (Metuchen, NJ), 1990.

Children's Books and Their Creators, Houghton Mifflin (Boston, MA), 1995, pp. 363-364.

Children's Literature Review, Volume 45, Gale (Detroit, MI), 1997, pp. 43-61.

PERIODICALS

Booklist, June 15, 1984, Ilene Cooper, review of *Geraldine's Blanket,* p. 1484; April 1, 1985, Ilene Cooper, review of *Henry's Fourth of July,* p. 1120; February 11, 1991, Ilene Cooper, review of *Horace,* p. 1130; March 15, 1992, p. 1388; May 15, 1997, Stephanie Zvirin, review of *I Am Angela,* p. 1575; Carolyn Phelan, review of *Merry Christmas, Geraldine,* September 1, 1997, p. 139; Carolyn Phelan, review of *Brave Horace,* March 1, 1998, p. 1140; August 19, 1998, Kay Weisman, review of *Angela's Top-Secret Computer Club,* p. 1140; February 15, 2000, Gillian Engberg, review of *Snow Is Falling,* p. 1115; August, 2000, Gillian Engberg, review of *That's Mine, Horace,* p. 2147; March 1, 2001, Hazel Rochman, review of *Growing like Me,* p. 1284; February 1, 2002, Gillian Engberg, review of *Cecil's Garden,* p. 947; September 15, 2002, Hazel Rochman, review of *Farfallina and Marcel,* p. 240; September 15, 2003, Ilene Cooper, review of *What a Hat!,* p. 246.

Bulletin of the Center for Children's Books, July, 1990, p. 269; March, 1998, p. 247.

Christian Century, December 13, 2003, review of *Farfallina and Marcel,* p. 25.

Growing Point, March, 1984, Margery Fisher, review of *Ten Sleepy Sheep,* p. 4220.

Horn Book, May-June, 1990, p. 326; November-December, 1990, Elizabeth S. Watson, review of *Henry's Happy Birthday,* p. 729; November-December, 1994, p. 720; November-December, 1995, p. 734; May-June, 1996, p. 325; July-August, 1998, p. 475; March-April, 1999, p. 193; July, 2000, review of *That's Mine, Horrace,* p. 437; September, 2001, review of *Growing like Me,* p. 615; November-December, 2003, Susan Dove Lempke, review of *What a Hat!,* p. 731.

Kirkus Reviews, September 1, 1983, review of *Ten Sleepy Sheep,* p. J150; March 1, 1984, review of *Geraldine's Blanket,* pp. J5-J6; April 15, 1993, p. 531; August 15, 1994, p. review of *Geraldine's Baby Brother,* 1131; July 15, 1995, p. 1025; February 15, 1998, p. 269; March 15, 1999, p. 452; December 15, 2001, review of *Cecil's Garden,* p. 1759; August 1, 2003, review of *What a Hat!,* p. 1019.

Language Arts, January, 1989, Janet Hickman, review of *Geraldine's Big Snow,* pp. 65-66.

Publishers Weekly, April 5, 1991, p. 145; April 26, 1993, p. 77; March 23, 1998, p. 98; March 12, 2001, review of *Growing like Me,* p. 88; December 24, 2001, review of *Cecil's Garden,* p. 64; July 29, 2002, review of *Farfallina and Marcel,* p. 71; October 6, 2003, review of *What a Hat!,* p. 84.

School Library Journal, March, 1982, Carolyn Noah, review of *Cromwell's Glasses,* p. 136; February, 1989, Trev Jones, review of *Geraldine's Big Snow,* p. 72; August, 1990, pp. 143-144; April, 1991, Anna Biagioni Hart, review of *Horace,* p. 97; November, 1991,

p. 100; November, 1992, p. 72; August, 1994, Harriett Fargnoli, review of *Geraldine's Baby Brother,* p. 133; May, 1996, Virginia Opocensky, review of *Geraldine First,* p. 93; April, 1998, Jody McCoy, review of *Brave Horace,* p. 102; June, 1998, pp. 111-112; May, 2000, Kay Bowles, review of *Snow Is Falling,* p. 160; June, 2000, Marianne Saccardi, review of *That's Mine, Horace,* p. 116; April, 2001, Judith Constantinides, review of *Growing like Me,* p. 134; March, 2002, Karen Scott, review of *Cecil's Garden,* p. 190; October, 2002, Maryann H. Owen, review of *Farfallina and Marcel,* p. 114; October, 2003, Leanna Manna, review of *What a Hat!,* p. 128.

Times Literary Supplement, September 30, 1983, Sarah Wintle, review of *Too Big,* p. 1050.

Tribune Books (Chicago, IL), September 13, 1992, p. 7.*

*　　*　　*

KEY, Samuel M.
See DE LINT, Charles (Henri Diederick Höefsmit)

*　　*　　*

KING, Stephen Michael

Personal

Born in Sydney, Australia; married; two children.

Addresses

Home—Australia. *Agent*—c/o Author Mail, Scholastic Australia, P.O. Box 579, Gosford, New South Wales 2250, Australia.

Career

Author, illustrator, and book designer. Worked as a children's library assistant; Walt Disney Studios, Surry Hill, Australia, illustrator, beginning 1990; Scholastic Australia, book designer.

Awards, Honors

Family Therapy Association Award, and Crichton Award shortlist, both 1996, both for *The Man Who Loved Boxes;* Children's Book Council of Australia (CBCA) Book of the Year for Young Readers shortlist, 1997, for *Beetle Soup;* CBCA Picture Book of the Year Award shortlist, 1998, for *The Little Blue Parcel,* 1999, for *Henry and Amy,* and 2001, for *The Pocket Dogs;* Australian Publishers Association Design Award shortlist, 2002, for *Emily Loves to Bounce;* KOALA/Young Australian Best Book Award (YABBA) for picture book, 2002, and Books I Love Best Yearly Award shortlist, 2003, both for *The Pocket Dogs;* YABBA shortlist, 2003, for *Henry and Amy.*

Writings

SELF-ILLUSTRATED

A Special Kind of Love, Scholastic (New York, NY), 1995.

The Man Who Loved Boxes, Scholastic Australia (Gosford, New South Wales, Australia), 1996.

Beetle Soup: Australian Stories and Poems for Children, Scholastic (New York, NY), 1996.

Patricia, Scholastic Australia (Gosford, New South Wales, Australia), 1997.

Henry and Amy (Right-Way-Round and Upside Down), Walker (New York, NY), 1998.

The Startling Secret of Successful Riddling, Scholastic Australia (Gosford, New South Wales, Australia), 1998.

The Little Blue Parcel, Scholastic Press (Gosford, New South Wales, Australia), 1998.

Rat's Lucky Day, and Rat Goes Fishing, Scholastic Australia (Gosford, New South Wales, Australia), 1999.

Rat and the Rud Cap, and Rat and the Big Stink, Scholastic Australia (Gosford, New South Wales, Australia), 1999.

Amelia Ellicott's Garden, Scholastic Australia (Gosford, New South Wales, Australia), 2000.

Emily Loves to Bounce, Scholastic (New York, NY), 2000.

The Pocket Dogs, Scholastic Australia (Gosford, New South Wales, Australia), 2000, Scholastic Press (New York, NY), 2001.

Where Does Thursday Go?, Clarion Books (New York, NY), 2001.

Jack's Owl, Scholastic Australia (Gosford, New South Wales, Australia), 2001.

Milli, Jack, and the Dancing Cat, Philomel Books (New York, NY), 2004.

Mutt Dog, Scholastic Australia (Gosford, New South Wales, Australia), 2004.

Author's works have been translated into several languages.

Adaptations

King's books have been adapted as a play produced by the Patch Theatre Company.

Sidelights

Australian author and illustrator Stephen Michael King has created a number of award-winning picture books for the younger set, among them *Millie, Jack, and the Dancing Cat, Emily Loves to Bounce, Where Does Thursday Go?,* and *The Pocket Dogs.* A *Publishers Weekly* reviewer stated that *Milli, Jack, and the Dancing Cat* "is likely to delight readers" with its story of a "small gaggle of eccentric characters" who unleash their creativity in a variety of ways. Linda Ludke, writing in *School Library Journal,* dubbed the book a "charming story that celebrates imagination and individuality," while *Booklist* reviewer Gillian Engberg had praise for King's "exhuberant illustrations" using "scribbly ink lines and bright watercolor washes."

Another of King's children's stories, *Emily Loves to Bounce,* utilizes a rhyming text to tell the story of a playful little girl named Emily. "Through the rhyming text and King's vibrant ink and watercolour illustration, the reader feels Emily's energy and enthusiasm," commented Kathryn McNaughton in a review for *Resource Links.* A *Publishers Weekly* critic wrote that although the "narrowly focused picture book might not stand up to repeated readings, most children will enjoy a glimpse into Emily's colorful, imaginative, and very active world," and warned: "don't be surprised if your listeners begin bounding right along." Another whimsical work, *The Pocket Dogs,* finds mini-canines Biff and Buff tucked inside the pockets of their owner whenever he goes for a walk. When one pocket comes unraveled Bifff is deposited on the floor of the local grocery store, and a search for his unaware owner ensues. Noting that the book will "strike a chord with young readers" who count losing sight of parents among their biggest fears, *Booklist* contributor Carolyn Phelan wrote that *The Pocket Dogs* is "well-conceived and told with rhythm and humor."

Biographical and Critical Sources

PERIODICALS

Booklist, June 1, 1999, Hazel Rochman, review of *Henry and Amy (Right-Way-Round and Upside Down),* p. 1842; February 1, 2001, Carolyn Phelan, review of *The Pocket Dogs,* p. 1051; March 1, 2002, Carolyn Phelan, review of *Where Does Thursday Go?,* p. 1139; March 1, 2004, Gillian Engberg, review of *Milli, Jack, and the Dancing Cat,* p. 1196.

Kirkus Reviews, January 15, 2003, review of *Emily Loves to Bounce,* p. 143; March 1, 2004, review of *Milli, Jack, and the Dancing Cat,* p. 224.

Publishers Weekly, May 27, 1996, review of *A Special Kind of Love,* p. 77; April 19, 1999, review of *Henry and Amy,* p. 71; April 2, 2001, review of *The Pocket Dogs,* p. 63; December 9, 2002, review of *Emily Loves to Bounce,* p. 82; May 10, 2004, review of *Milli, Jack, and the Dancing Cat,* p. 58.

Resource Links, June, 2003, Kathryn McNaughton, review of *Emily Loves to Bounce,* p. 5.

School Library Journal, June, 2001, Lisa Gangemi Krapp, review of *The Pocket Dogs,* p. 132; April, 2002, Kathleen Kelly MacMillan, review of *Where Does Thursday Go?,* p. 100; March, 2003, Lisa Dennis, review of *Emily Loves to Bounce,* p. 196; April, 2004, Linda Ludke, review of *Milli, Jack, and the Dancing Cat,* p. 116.

ONLINE

Scholastic Australia Web site, http://www.scholastic.com/au/ (February 16, 2005), "Stephen Michael King."*

KOLLER, Jackie French 1948-

Personal

Born March 8, 1948, in Derby, CT; daughter of Ernest James (an electrical engineer) and Margaret (Hayes) French; married George J. Koller (president of a hospital), July 11, 1970; children: Kerri Mercier, Ryan, Devin. *Education:* University of Connecticut, B.A., 1970.

Addresses

Agent—Ginger Knowlton, Curtis Brown Ltd., 10 Astor Place, New York, NY.

Career

Writer.

Member

Society of Children's Book Writers and Illustrators.

Awards, Honors

Best Books for Young Adults designation, American Library Association (ALA), for *The Primrose Way* and *The Falcon;* ALA Notable Book designation, Pick of the Lists designation, American Booksellers Association, and Teachers' Choice designation, International Reading Association (IRA), all for *A Place to Call Home;* Books for the Teen Age designation, New York Public Library, for *Nothing to Fear, If I Had One Wish . . . , The Last Voyage of the Misty Day,* and *The Primrose Way;* IRA Teachers' Choice designation and Young Adults' Choice designations, both for *Nothing to Fear;* Recommended Books for Reluctant Readers designation, Young Adult Library Services Association (YALSA), for *If I Had One Wish . . .* and *The Last Voyage of the Misty Day;* International Honor Book designation, Association of School Librarians, Honor Book designation, Bank Street College Children's Book Committee, and Blue Ribbon designation, *Bulletin of the Center for Children's Books,* all for *No Such Thing.*

Writings

FOR CHILDREN

Impy for Always, illustrated by Carol Newsom, Little, Brown (Boston, MA), 1989.

Mole and Shrew, illustrated by Stella Ormai, Atheneum (New York, NY), 1991.

Fish Fry Tonight!, illustrated by Catharine O'Neill, Crown (New York, NY), 1992.

Mole and Shrew Step Out, illustrated by Stella Ormai, Atheneum (New York, NY), 1992.

The Dragonling, illustrated by Judith Mitchell, Archway Minstrel (New York, NY), 1996.

Jackie French Koller

A Dragon in the Family, illustrated by Judith Mitchell, Archway Minstrel (New York, NY), 1996.

No Such Thing, illustrated by Betsy Lewin, Boyds Mills Press, 1997.

Dragon Quest, Archway Minstrel (New York, NY), 1997.

Mole and Shrew, All Year Through, illustrated by John Beder, Random House (New York, NY), 1997.

Dragons of Krad, Archway Minstrel (New York, NY), 1997.

Dragon Trouble, Archway Minstrel (New York, NY), 1997.

Dragons and Kings, illustrated by Judith Mitchell, Archway Minstrel (New York, NY), 1998.

One Monkey Too Many, illustrated by Lynn Munsinger, Harcourt (New York, NY), 1999.

Bouncing on the Bed, illustrated by Anna Grossnickle Hines, Orchard (New York, NY), 1999.

Nickommoh! A Narragansett Thanksgiving Celebration, illustrated by Marcia Sewall, Atheneum (New York, NY), 1999.

The Promise, illustrated by Jacqueline Rogers, Knopf (New York, NY), 1999.

Mole and Shrew Are Two, illustrated by Anne Reas, Random House (New York, NY), 2000.

Mole and Shrew Have Real Jobs to Do, illustrated by Anne Reas, Random House (New York, NY), 2001.

Mole and Shrew Find a Clue, illustrated by Anne Reas, Random House (New York, NY), 2001.

Baby for Sale, illustrated by Janet Pederson, Marshall Cavendish (New York, NY), 2002.

Horace the Horrible: A Knight Meets His Match, illustrated by Jackie Urbanovic, Marshall Cavendish (New York, NY), 2003.

Seven Spunky Monkeys, illustrated by Lynn Munsinger, Harcourt (Orlando, FL), 2005.

Contributor of poems and short fiction to periodicals, including *Cobblestone, Spider,* and *Ladybug;* short fiction anthologized in in *Time Capsule,* edited by Don Gallo, Bantam, 1999.

FOR YOUNG ADULTS

Nothing to Fear, Harcourt (New York, NY), 1991.
If I Had One Wish . . . , Little, Brown (Boston, MA), 1991.
The Last Voyage of the Misty Day, Atheneum (New York, NY), 1992.
The Primrose Way, Harcourt (New York, NY), 1992.
A Place to Call Home, Atheneum (New York, NY), 1995.
The Falcon, Atheneum (New York, NY), 1998.
Someday, Orchard Books (New York, NY), 2002.

"KEEPERS" SERIES; FOR YOUNG ADULTS

A Wizard Named Nell, Aladdin (New York, NY), 2003.
The Wizard's Apprentice, Aladdin (New York, NY), 2003.
The Wizard's Scepter, Aladdin (New York, NY), 2004.

Adaptations

Several of Koller's books have been adapted as audiobooks by Recorded Books, including *The Dragonling,* 2002, and *A Wizard Named Nell,* 2004.

Sidelights

Children's book author Jackie French Koller has spent her life immersed in stories: listening as her mother read to her when she was a child; conjuring up make-believe adventures to entertain herself as a schoolgirl; and developing a lifetime habit of avid reading. As an adult, she has entertained legions of readers, transforming the history of her native New England into young adult novels such as *Someday* and *The Primrose Way;* conjuring up fantastic adventures in her "Keeper" trilogy as well as in her books *The Dragonling, Dragon's Quest,* and *Dragon Trouble,* about the friendship between a boy and a young dragon; and translating her love of young children into picture books that depict affectionate families and loyal friendships.

Born and raised in Connecticut, Koller developed the ability to entertain and amuse herself early on. "I developed a vivid imagination and was forever pretending," she recalled in an interview for *Authors and Artists for Young Adults.* "I would dream up great adventures for my siblings and friends to act out, and I, of course, was always the star, the hero, or, one might say, the main character, for as I look back now I can see that those early games of pretend were my first attempts at creating stories." To survive her teen years she took solace in books and nature, hiking in the woods near her home or diving into a book and losing herself in the story and characters, leaving all the pain of the real world behind.

Although she first contemplated a career in art, as a student at the University of Connecticut Koller studied interior design. She met George J. Koller her junior year, and the two were married in 1970. When her husband went on to graduate school, Koller supported him by working in the insurance industry. She began to write for children while raising her three children, and her first book, *Impy for Always,* was published in 1989.

Koller's first novel for older readers, *Nothing to Fear,* focuses on an Irish immigrant family living in poverty in New York City during the Great Depression of the 1930s. The only family income is what Danny can make shining shoes and what his mother earns doing laundry, and when his father leaves town to seek work, Danny becomes the man of the house. Pregnant and weary, his mother loses her laundress jobs and Danny begins begging for food. The family finally gains relief, ironically, by helping a sick and hungry stranger who appears at their doorstep. While *Voice of Youth Advocates* contributor Rosemary Moran described the story as "in turn depressing and enriching," *School Library Journal* reviewer Ann Welton commended *Nothing to Fear* and added that Koller's "interesting supporting characters will hold readers' attention." A critic in *Kirkus Reviews* dubbed *Nothing to Fear* an "involving account of the Great Depression . . . conjuring an entire era from the heartaches and troubles of one struggling family."

The Primrose Way tells of a sixteen-year-old girl, Rebekah Hall, who comes to live with her Puritan father in seventeenth-century Massachusetts. While pretending that she is converting the local Native Americans, Rebekah befriends Qunnequawese, the chief's niece. Their friendship awakens a cultural understanding between the two teens, and Rebekah's interest in the Native-American way of life makes her question the Puritan salvation. Her problems worsen as she falls in love with the tribe's holy man, Mishannock. Reviewing the novel, Esther Sinofsky wrote in the *Voice of Youth Advocates* that *The Primrose Way* is a "beautiful story" of a young woman's search for identity highlighted by "carefully researched" scenes depicting early New England. A *Kirkus Reviews* critic praised Koller's creation of a vivid landscape that "successfully de-romanticizes the early settlers' struggles," while *School Library Journal* contributor Barbara Chatton remarked that the "carefully researched book incorporates authentic language in a readable text."

Koller introduces readers to fifteen-year-old Anna O'Dell in *A Place to Call Home.* In this novel, the teen returns home from school to discover that her infant brother, Casey, alone and screaming. Anna's alcoholic mother is later discovered to have drowned in a lake, a suicide. Determined to keep her five-year-old sister, Mandy, and Casey with her, Anna shows her intelligence, strength, and determination to fight for her family, according to Hazel Moore in *Voice of Youth Advocates.* Carolyn Noah, writing in *School Library Journal,* called *A Place to Call Home* an "eloquent depiction of impoverishment and courage," adding that the novel contains a "fast paced" and "compelling" story laced with "satisfying social values."

In *The Falcon* Koller uses a journal format to reveal a secret about Luke, the novel's principal protagonist. Luke's self-destructive behavior lands him in a psychiatric hospital, where he must overcome a deep emotional scar on his way to recovery. "Koller's portrayal of a foolhardy teen who feels invincible is incredibly well drawn," asserted *School Library Journal* contributor Alison Follos, the critic adding that Luke's "past seeps out surreptitiously, adding powerful impact to an already interesting life." Writing in *Booklist*, reviewer Roger Leslie maintained that "Luke's strong voice comes through quite believably," while *Kliatt* contributor Paula Rohrlick called *The Falcon* an "involving and often suspenseful tale."

Based on a true story, *Someday* follows a teen who loses her childhood roots when her hometown in a Massachusetts river valley is flooded to create the Quabbin Reservoir. Taking place during the 1930s, the coming-of-age novel finds fourteen-year-old Cecelia Wheeler

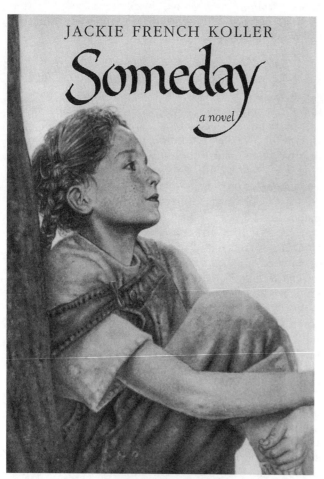

Based on a true story and taking place in 1938, Koller's 2002 novel finds a young teen learning that her hometown, with all its memories, is about to be flooded to create a reservoir. (Cover illustration by Jason Cockcroft.)

forced to say goodbye to her best friend, adjust to life in her new home in Chicago, and also encounter first love in the form of Mr. Parker, a handsome young reservoir employee who lodges at the Wheeler homestead. In *School Library Journal* Beth L. Meister called *Someday* "a moving and well-plotted story about the end of an era," while Diane Foote wrote in her *Booklist* review that Koller creates a "heartbreaking account" of a teen's transition in which "scenes of the town's dismantling are truly harrowing." A *Kirkus* reviewer described the novel as "a perceptive picture of small-town life" and noted that Koller's "readers will understand how emotional ties to a place can define who you are." Koller moves from historical fiction to fantasy with her "Keepers" series: *A Wizard Named Nell, The Wizard's Apprentice,* and *The Wizard's Scepter.* The series draws readers into the kingdom of Eldearth, which is threatened by the dark forces of the evil Lord Graieconn. When the ageing imperial wizard of Eldearth begins to wilt in his role as Keeper of the Light and protector of the realm, a search for a successor begins. While wizards have always been old men, young Princess Arnelle believes that she may be the one destined to fulfil a prophecy and take up the role of Keeper of the Light. To prove her worthiness to apprentice to the imperial wizard she undertakes a quest fraught with danger, joined by her friend Owen. Praising *A Wizard Named Nell,* Susan L. Rogers wrote in *School Library Journal* that Koller has created "a fast-moving and easy-to read" novel that features a "steadfast and admirable heroine."

In addition to novels for older readers, Koller has also penned a number of well-received picture books for children. In *No Such Thing* Howard has just moved with his family into a new home. Unable to fall sleep because he is certain that there is a monster under his bed, Howard summons his mother over and over in a futile attempt to convince her. Meanwhile, a little monster under Howard's bed cannot get to sleep because he is certain there is a boy on top of his bed, and he is also unable to convince his reassuring mother. "Any child who has been convinced of the presence of a monster at bedtime will feel vindicated by [this] satisfying story," maintained a *Kirkus Reviews* critic, dubbing the story "irresistible."

The counting books *One Monkey Too Many* and *Seven Spunky Monkeys* center on the adventures of vacationing monkeys. *Horn Book* reviewer Marilyn Bousquin, in a review of *One Monkey Too Many,* praised Koller's "infectious, rollercoaster rhythm," while *School Library Journal* contributor Lauralyn Persson wrote that "the infectious rhythm of the text never falters. . . . Spilling, breaking, dropping, and crashing have never been this much fun."

Other picture books by Koller include *Horace the Horrible: A Knight Meets His Match,* in which a robust knight widely praised for his dragon-slaying abilities meets his match when babysitting his young niece, the

In the first part of a series that takes place in Eldearth, Princess Arenelle is determined to undertake the traditional quest demanded of those who hope to be apprentice wizards, and she finds an ally in the form of an orphaned boy named Owen. (Cover illustration by Rebecca Guay.)

young and homesick Princess Minuette. Praising the quirky watercolor and pencil illustrations by Jackie Urbanovic, *School Library Journal* contributor Laurie Edwards called *Horace the Horrible* "a rollicking, humorous tale" about two equally stubborn characters as well as an upbeat choice for story hour. Koller also depicts a test of wills in *Baby for Sale,* in which young Peter decides that it's time for his toddler sister Emily to find a new home after she throws his new cap into the toilet. While Peter attempts to convince a succession of neighbors of Emily's good qualities, her toddler antics gradually win him over in what Rosalyn Pierini praised as a "sweet, recognizable family story" in her *School Library Journal* review.

Koller lives on ten acres of mountaintop land in Western Massachusetts in a house she shares with her husband and Labrador retriever. "It amazes me that I'm actually a published author," she noted on her Web site, adding that, even with dozens of books in print, "sometimes I still have to pinch myself."

Biographical and Critical Sources

BOOKS

Authors and Artists for Young Adults, Volume 28, Gale (Detroit, MI), 1999.

PERIODICALS

Booklist, October 15, 1995, Merri Monks, review of *A Place to Call Home,* p. 396; April 15, 1998, Roger Leslie, review of *The Falcon,* p. 1436; June 1, 2002, Diane Foote, review of *Someday,* p. 1723; September 1, 2002, Lauren Peterson, review of *Baby for Sale,* p. 136; October 1, 2003, Eva Mitnick, review of *A Wizard Named Nell,* p. 321.

Bulletin of the Center for Children's Books, March, 1991, p. 168; April, 1992, Zena Sutherland, review of *The Last Voyage of the Misty Day,* p. 211; March, 1997, p. 237.

Horn Book, March-April, 1999, Marilyn Bousquin, review of *One Monkey Too Many,* p. 194.

Kirkus Reviews, March 1, 1991, review of *Nothing to Fear,* September 15, 1992, review of *The Primrose Way,* p. 1189; January 1, 1997, review of *No Such Thing,* p. 60; May 1, 2002, review of *Someday,* p. 659; August 1, 2002, review of *Baby for Sale,* p. 1134; October 1, 2003, review of *Horace the Horrible,* p. 1226.

Kliatt, July, 1998, Paula Rohrlick, review of *The Falcon;* November, 2003, Sherri F. Ginsberg, review of *Someday,* p. 52.

Publishers Weekly, December 30, 1996, p. 67; April 19, 1999, review of *One Monkey Too Many,* p. 72; July, 2002, review of *Someday,* p. 80; August 12, 2002, review of *Baby for Sale,* p. 299.

School Library Journal, May, 1991, Ann Welton, review of *Nothing to Fear,* p. 93; June, 1992, p. 116; September, 1992, Barbara Chatton, review of *The Primrose Way,* p. 278; October, 1995, Carolyn Noah, review of *A Place to Call Home,* p. 155; June, 1997, p. 95; May, 1999, Lauralyn Persson, review of *One Monkey Too Many,* p. 92; July, 2002, Beth L. Meister, review of *Someday,* p. 122; September, 2002, Rosalyn Pierini, review of *Baby for Sale,* p. 196; October, 2003, Cheryl Preisendorfer, review of *Someday,* p. 90; November, 2003, Laurie Edwards, review of *Horace the Horrible,* p. 104, and Susan L. Rogers, review of *A Wizard Named Nell,* p. 142; June, 2004, MaryAnne Karre, review of *A Wizard Named Nell* (audio version), p. 73.

Teacher Librarian, April, 2004, Helen Moore, review of *A Wizard Named Nell,* p. 10.

Voice of Youth Advocates, October, 1991, Rosemary Moran, review of *Nothing to Fear,* p. 228; December, 1992, Esther Sinofsky, review of *The Primrose Way,* p. 280; February, 1996, Hazel Moore, review of *A Place to Call Home,* p. 373.

ONLINE

Jackie French Koller's Author Page, http://www.geocities.com/˜jackiekoller (February 1, 2005).*

KRAFT, Betsy Harvey 1937-

Personal

Born May 21, 1937, in Indianapolis, IN; daughter of Robert Sidney (a professor) and Helen (a librarian; maiden name, Porter) Harvey; married Michael Baker Kraft (a special projects director), November 28, 1970; children: Katherine Porter. *Education:* DePauw University, B.A., 1959; Brown University, M.A., 1961.

Addresses

Home—Washington, DC. *Agent*—c/o Author Mail, Clarion Books, 215 Park Ave., New York, NY 10003.

Career

Worked as children's book editor in New York, NY, for Macmillan, Bobbs-Merrill, and Dutton, 1962-68; writer. Director of education for energy trade association.

Writings

Coal, Franklin Watts (New York, NY), 1976.
Careers in the Energy Industry, Franklin Watts (New York, NY), 1977.
Oil and Natural Gas, Franklin Watts (New York, NY), 1978.
Mother Jones: One Woman's Fight for Labor, Clarion Books (New York, NY), 1995.
Sensational Trials of the Twentieth Century, Scholastic, Inc. (New York, NY), 1998.
Theodore Roosevelt: Champion of the American Spirit, Clarion Books (New York, NY), 2003.

Sidelights

Nonfiction author Betsy Harvey Kraft has translated her interest in the rise in industry during the early twentieth century—and the factors that powered that industry—into a series of books for young people. Stemming from her interest in the energy field are her first two books: *Coal* and *Careers in the Energy Industry,* both published by Franklin Watts. In a somewhat related book, *Mother Jones: One Woman's Fight for Labor* profiles the Irish-American immigrant who, in middle age, took on the battle against unscrupulous employers during the formative years of the U.S. labor movement. Praising the work, a *Publishers Weekly* reviewer noted that Kraft presents a balanced view of her subject, showing Jones' rise to power as a labor activist, but also profiling the woman's "blatant self-promotion and her scattered but costly defeats." Kraft's second biography, *Theodore Roosevelt: Champion of the American Spirit,* focuses on one of the era's most colorful, as well as powerful characters: the twenty-sixth president of the United States. Unlike most biographies, however, Kraft focuses on the human side of the president, weaving recollections of friends and family into a legacy that included a concern for conservation, strong-minded efforts to conform big business to the law of the land, and Roosevelt's receipt

Betsey Harvey Kraft presents a fact-filled biography of the enigmatic man who rose from governor of New York to become the twenty-sixth U.S. president in Theodore Roosevelt: Champion of the American Spirit. (Photograph courtesy of the Library of Congress.)

of a Nobel Peace Prize for his diplomatic work during the war between Russia and Japan. Praising Kraft's biography as "richly illustrated" with letters, news clippings, and cartoons, as well as with the late president's correspondence with his children, *School Library Journal* critic Ginny Gustin added that *Theodore Roosevelt* allows readers a "fascinating glimpse into the public and private life and the wide range of accomplishments of a major figure in American history." Writing in *Booklist,* Carolyn Phelan referred to Kraft's work as a "handsome biography," noting that it succeeds as "an informative and entertaining introduction to one of America's most dynamic presidents."

Kraft told *Something about the Author:* "The children's books I have published are the result of my interest in the energy field. I also enjoy the world of children's fiction, especially picture books and stories for the seven-to eleven-year-old age group. And, like every other author who has ever threaded paper into a typewriter, I am working on an adult novel—which happens to have one of the energy industries as a background."

Biographical and Critical Sources

PERIODICALS

Booklist, October 15, 2003, Carolyn Phelan, review of *Theodore Roosevelt: Champion of the American Spirit,* p. 402.
Horn Book, November-December, 2003, Betty Carter, review of *Theodore Roosevelt,* p. 766.
Publishers Weekly, May 8, 1995, review of *Mother Jones: One Woman's Fight for Labor,* p. 297; June 23, 2003, review of *Theodore Roosevelt,* p. 69.
School Library Journal, December, 2003, Ginny Gustin, review of *Theodore Roosevelt,* p. 170.*

L

Larrick, Nancy 1910-2004

OBITUARY NOTICE— See index for *SATA* sketch: Born December 28, 1910, in Winchester, VA; died of pneumonia November 14, 2004, in Winchester, VA. Educator, editor, and author. The founder of the International Reading Association, Larrick was a champion of literacy who also wrote and edited books that promoted better reading skills for children. After completing her undergraduate work at Goucher College in 1930, she became a public school teacher in Winchester, Virginia, finishing her master's degree at Columbia University in 1937. As an eighth-grade English teacher, Larrick was very involved in her students' home lives, and she learned that the more parents were active in their children's education the better readers their kids became. This discovery would influence her beliefs in education for the rest of her life. During World War II, she worked as an education director for the U.S. Treasury Department, and after the war she became involved in publishing as an editor for *Young America Readers*. Larrick's next job was at the publisher Random House, where she was education director in the children's book department from 1952 until 1959. Having earned her doctorate in education from New York University in 1955, she later joined the faculty at Lehigh University in Bethlehem, Pennsylvania in 1964 as an adjunct professor, retiring in 1979. Much of her time after leaving Random House, however, was spent writing and editing books. Larrick began publishing books with her cowritten *Printing and Promotion Handbook* (1949; third edition, 1966). She was best known, though, for her books that offered guidance to parents and teachers in helping their kids to read. Among these works are *A Parent's Guide to Children's Reading* (1958; fourth edition, 1975), *A Teacher's Guide to Children's Books* (1960), and *A Parent's Guide to Children's Education* (1963). As an editor, Larrick published over a dozen poetry anthologies for children, including *You Come Too: Poetry of Robert Frost* (1959), *Piping Down the Valleys Wild* (1967), and *Crazy to Be Alive in Such a Strange World* (1977). Noticing that too much of children's literature being published and promoted was written by white authors, she emphasized that teachers should bring more minority-written stories to the attention of their students. She also founded the International Reading Association, an organization that now has chapters in about one hundred countries. Widely recognized by her colleagues for her success in promoting literacy, Larrick received many honors in her lifetime, including being named to the Reading Hall of Fame in 1977 and being named to the list of "Seventy Women Who Have made a Difference in the World of Books" by the Women's National Book Association in 1987.

OBITUARIES AND OTHER SOURCES:

PERIODICALS

Chicago Tribune, November 22, 2004, Section 1, p. 12.
New York Times, November 21, 2004, p. A33.
Washington Post, November 27, 2004, p. B4.

* * *

LASKY, Kathryn 1944-
(Kathryn Lasky Knight, E. L. Swann)

Personal

Born June 24, 1944, in Indianapolis, IN; daughter of Marven (a wine bottler) and Hortense (a social worker) Lasky; married Christopher G. Knight (a photographer and filmmaker), May 30, 1971; children: Maxwell, Meribah. *Education:* University of Michigan, B.A., 1966; Wheelock College, M.A., 1977. *Religion:* Jewish. *Hobbies and other interests:* Sailing, skiing, hiking, reading, movies.

Addresses

Home—7 Scott St., Cambridge, MA 02138. *Agent*—Jed Mattes, 175 West 73rd St., New York, NY.

Career

Writer.

Awards, Honors

Boston Globe/Horn Book Award, 1981, for *The Weaver's Gift;* Notable Books designation, American Library Association (ALA), 1981, for *The Night Journey* and *The Weaver's Gift;* National Jewish Book Award, Jewish Welfare Board Book Council, and Sydney Taylor Book Award, Association of Jewish Libraries, both 1982, both for *The Night Journey;* Notable Book designation, *New York Times,* and Best Books for Young Adults designation, ALA, both 1983, both for *Beyond the Divide;* Newbery Honor Book, and Notable Books designation, both ALA, both 1984, and both for *Sugaring Time;* Best Books for Young Adults designation, ALA, 1984, for *Prank;* Notable Books designation, ALA, 1985, for *Puppeteer;* Best Books for Young Adults designation, ALA, 1986, for *Pageant;* "Youth-to-Youth Books: A List for Imagination and Survival" citation, Pratt Library's Young Adult Advisory Board, 1988, for *The Bone Wars;* Golden Trilobite Award, Paleontological Society, 1990, for *Traces of Life: The Origins of Humankind;* Parenting Reading Magic Award, 1990, for *Dinosaur Dig;* Edgar Award nominee for Best Juvenile Mystery, 1992, for *Double Trouble Squared;* Sequoyah Young Adult Book Award, 1994, for *Beyond the Burning Time;* National Jewish Book Award and Notable Books designation, ALA, both 1997, both for *Marven of the Great North Woods;* John Burroughs Award for Outstanding Nature Book for Children, and Editor's Choice designation, *Cricket* magazine, both 1998, both for *The Most Beautiful Roof in the World: Exploring the Rainforest Canopy;* Western Heritage Award, National Cowboy Hall of Fame, and Edgar Award nominee, both 1999, both for *Alice Rose and Sam.* In 1986, Lasky won the *Washington Post/Children's Book Guild Nonfiction Award* for her body of work; she is also the recipient of several child-selected awards.

Writings

FOR CHILDREN

(With Lucy Floyd) *Agatha's Alphabet,* Rand McNally, 1975.

I Have Four Names for My Grandfather, illustrated with photographs by husband, Christopher G. Knight, Little, Brown (Boston, MA, 1976.

Tugboats Never Sleep, illustrated with photographs by Christopher G. Knight, Little, Brown (Boston, MA), 1977.

Tall Ships, illustrated with photographs by Christopher G. Knight, Scribner (New York, NY), 1978.

My Island Grandma, illustrated by Emily McCully, Warne (New York, NY), 1979, illustrated by Amy Schwartz, Morrow (New York, NY), 1993.

The Weaver's Gift, illustrated with photographs by Christopher G. Knight, Warne (New York, NY), 1981.

Dollmaker: The Eyelight and the Shadow, illustrated with photographs by Christopher G. Knight, Scribner (New York, NY), 1981.

The Night Journey, illustrated by Trina Schart Hyman, Warne (New York, NY), 1981.

Jem's Island, illustrated by Ronald Himler, Scribner (New York, NY), 1982.

Sugaring Time, illustrated with photographs by Christopher G. Knight, Macmillan (New York, NY), 1983.

Beyond the Divide, Macmillan (New York, NY), 1983.

(With son, Maxwell B. Knight) *A Baby for Max,* illustrated with photographs by Christopher G. Knight, Scribner (New York, NY), 1984.

Prank, Macmillan (New York, NY), 1984.

Home Free, Macmillan (New York, NY), 1985.

Puppeteer, illustrated with photographs by Christopher G. Knight, Macmillan (New York, NY), 1985.

Pageant, Four Winds Press (New York, NY), 1986.

Sea Swan, illustrated by Catherine Stock, Macmillan (New York, NY), 1988.

The Bone Wars, Morrow (New York, NY), 1988.

Traces of Life: The Origins of Humankind, illustrated by Whitney Powell, Morrow (New York, NY), 1989.

Dinosaur Dig, illustrated with photographs by Christopher G. Knight, Morrow (New York, NY), 1990.

Fourth of July Bear, illustrated by Helen Cogancherry, Morrow (New York, NY), 1991.

Surtsey: The Newest Place on Earth, illustrated with photographs by Christopher G. Knight and Sigurdur Thoraisson, Hyperion (New York, NY), 1992.

Think like an Eagle: At Work with a Wildlife Photographer, illustrated with photographs by Christopher G. Knight and Jack Swedberg, Little, Brown (Boston, MA), 1992.

I Have an Aunt on Marlborough Street, illustrated by Susan Guevara, Macmillan (New York, NY), 1992.

The Solo, illustrated by Bobette McCarthy, Macmillan (New York, NY), 1993.

The Tantrum, illustrated by Bobette McCarthy, Macmillan (New York, NY), 1993.

Monarchs, illustrated with photographs by Christopher G. Knight, Harcourt (San Diego, CA), 1993.

(With daughter, Meribah Knight) *Searching for Laura Ingalls: A Reader's Journey,* illustrated with photographs by Christopher G. Knight, Macmillan (New York, NY), 1993.

Lunch Bunnies, illustrated by Marylin Hafner, Little, Brown (Boston, MA), 1993.

Memoirs of a Bookbat, Harcourt (San Diego, CA), 1994.

Beyond the Burning Time, Blue Sky Press/Scholastic (New York, NY), 1994.

Cloud Eyes, illustrated by Barry Moser, Harcourt (San Diego, CA), 1994.

The Librarian Who Measured the Earth, illustrated by Kevin Hawkes, Little, Brown (Boston, MA), 1994.

Days of the Dead, illustrated by Christopher G. Knight, Hyperion (New York, NY), 1994.

Pond Year, illustrated by Mike Bostok, Candlewick (Cambridge, MA), 1995.

She's Wearing a Dead Bird on Her Head!, illustrated by David Catrow, Hyperion (New York, NY), 1995.

The Gates of the Wind, illustrated by Janet Stevens, Harcourt (San Diego, CA), 1995.

A Journey to the New World: The Diary of Remember Patience Whipple, Mayflower, 1620, Scholastic (New York, NY), 1996.

True North: A Novel of the Underground Railroad, Blue Sky Press/Scholastic (New York, NY), 1996.

A Brilliant Streak: The Making of Mark Twain, illustrated by Barry Moser, Harcourt (San Diego, CA), 1996.

The Most Beautiful Roof in the World: Exploring the Rainforest Canopy, illustrated with photographs by Christopher G. Knight, Harcourt (San Diego, CA), 1997.

Marven of the Great North Woods, illustrated by Kevin Hawkes, Harcourt (San Diego, CA), 1997.

Hercules: The Man, the Myth, the Hero, illustrated by Mark Hess, Hyperion (New York, NY), 1997.

Grace the Pirate, illustrated by Karen Lee Schmidt, Hyperion (New York, NY), 1997.

Shadows in the Dawn: The Lemurs of Madagascar, illustrated with photographs by Christopher G. Knight, Harcourt (San Diego, CA), 1998.

Dreams in the Golden Country: The Diary of Zipporah Feldman, a Jewish Immigrant Girl, Scholastic (New York, NY), 1998.

Sophie and Rose, illustrated by Wendy Anderson Helperin, Candlewick Press (Cambridge, MA), 1998.

Alice Rose and Sam, Hyperion (New York, NY), 1998.

Show and Tell Bunnies, illustrated by Marylin Hafner, Candlewick Press (Cambridge, MA), 1998.

The Emperor's Old Clothes, illustrated by David Catrow, Harcourt (San Diego, CA), 1999.

Star Split, Hyperion (New York, NY), 1999.

Elizabeth I, Red Rose of the House of Tudor, Scholastic (New York, NY), 1999.

First Painter, illustrated by Rocco Baviera, DK Ink (New York, NY), 2000.

The Journal of Augustus Pelletier: The Lewis and Clark Expedition, Scholastic (New York, NY), 2000.

Lucille's Snowsuit, Crown Publishers (New York, NY), 2000.

Marie Antoinette, Princess of Versailles, Scholastic (New York, NY), 2000.

Science Fair Bunnies, Candlewick Press (Cambridge, MA), 2000.

Vision of Beauty: The Story of Sarah Breedlove Walker, illustrated by Nneka Bennett, Candlewick Press (Cambridge, MA), 2000.

Born in the Breezes: The Seafaring Life of Joshua Slocum, illustrated by Walter Lyon Krudop, Orchard (New York, NY), 2001.

Christmas after All: The Great Depression Diary of Minnie Swift, Scholastic (New York, NY), 2001.

Interrupted Journey: Saving Endangered Sea Turtles, photographs by Christopher G. Knight, Candlewick (Cambridge, MA), 2001.

Starring Lucille, illustrated by Marylin Hafner, Alfred A. Knopf (New York, NY), 2001.

Jahanara: Princess of Princesses, Scholastic (New York, NY), 2002.

Mary, Queen of Scots, Queen without a Country, Scholastic (New York, NY), 2002.

(With Jane Kamine) *Mommy's Hands,* Hyperion (New York, NY), 2002.

Porkenstein, illustrated by David Jarvis, Blue Sky Press (New York, NY), 2002.

A Time for Courage: The Suffragette Diary of Kathleen Bowen, Scholastic (New York, NY), 2002.

Before I Was Your Mother, Harcourt (San Diego, CA), 2003.

Home at Last, Scholastic (New York, NY), 2003.

Hope in My Heart, Scholastic (New York, NY), 2003.

Lucille Camps In, illustrated by Marilyn Hafner, Alfred A. Knopf (New York, NY), 2003.

The Man Who Made Time Travel, Melanie Kroupa Books (New York, NY), 2003.

A Voice of Her Own: The Story of Phillis Wheatley, Slave Poet, Candlewick Press (Cambridge, MA), 2003.

An American Spring, Scholastic (New York, NY), 2004.

Blood Secret, HarperCollins (New York, NY), 2004.

Charles Darwin, Candlewick Press (Cambridge, MA), 2004.

Humphrey, Albert, and the Flying Machine, illustrated by John Manders, Harcourt (San Diego, CA), 2004.

Kazunomiya: Prisoner of Heaven, Scholastic (New York, NY), 2004.

Love That Baby!: A Book about Babies for New Brothers, Sisters, Cousins, and Friends, illustrated by Jennifer Plecas, Candlewick Press (Cambridge, MA), 2004.

"STARBUCK FAMILY" SERIES; MIDDLE-GRADE FICTION

Double Trouble Squared, Harcourt (San Diego, CA), 1991.

Shadows in the Water, Harcourt (San Diego, CA), 1992.

A Voice in the Wind, Harcourt (San Diego, CA), 1993.

"GUARDIANS OF GA'HOOLE" SERIES; MIDDLE-GRADE FICTION

The Capture, Scholastic (New York, NY), 2003.

Burning, Turtleback, 2004.

The Rescue, Scholastic (New York, NY), 2004.

The Siege, Scholastic (New York, NY), 2004.

The Shattering, Scholastic (New York, NY), 2004.

FOR ADULTS; AS KATHRYN LASKY KNIGHT, EXCEPT AS NOTED

Atlantic Circle (nonfiction), illustrated with photographs by Christopher G. Knight, Norton (New York, NY), 1985.

Trace Elements (novel), Norton (New York, NY), 1986.

The Widow of Oz (novel), Norton (New York, NY), 1989.

Mortal Words (novel), Simon & Schuster (New York, NY), 1990.

Mumbo Jumbo (novel), Simon & Schuster (New York, NY), 1991.

Dark Swan (novel), St. Martin's Press (New York, NY), 1994.

(Under pseudonym E. L. Swann) *Night Gardening* (mystery novel), Hyperion (New York, NY), 1998.

Contributor to periodicals, including *Horn Book, New York Times Book Review,* and *Sail.*

Adaptations

Sugaring Time was adapted as a filmstrip by Random House/Miller-Brody, 1984, for audiocassette, 1986, and for videocassette, 1988.

Work in Progress

A second mystery novel.

Sidelights

Called "a remarkably versatile writer" by *Booklist* reviewer Ilene Cooper, Kathryn Lasky is an American author of fiction, nonfiction, and picture books who is noted for her success in several genres. A prolific writer, Lasky is the creator of contemporary fiction, historical fiction, informational books, and picture books that incorporate both fictional and nonfictional elements. Lasky aims her work at an audience ranging from preschool to high school-aged readers, but most often addresses her books to middle graders and older teenage readers; she is also the author of fiction and nonfiction for adults. Lasky's books range from humorous picture books and light middle-grade fiction to extensively researched informational books and thought-provoking novels for young adults on such serious subjects as slavery, censorship, and anti-Semitism.

In her nonfiction, the author characteristically explores science, nature, and arts and crafts as well as both familiar and unfamiliar aspects of world and American history. Lasky's nonfiction encompasses a wide range of subjects, including the origin of humankind, the gathering of maple sugar, the life cycle of the monarch butterfly, the story of American sailing ships, and the wonders of the Belize rainforest. In addition, Lasky has written biographies of ancient and contemporary scientists and such well-known figures as Queen Elizabeth I and Mark Twain. In her fiction, Lasky usually features strong-willed, free-thinking female protagonists whose experiences, often centered around historical, ethnic, or moral issues, strengthen the character's independence and self-reliance; several of her novels reflect the author's Jewish heritage. Lasky is the creator of the "Starbuck Family" series, a popular trilogy of mystery/adventure stories for middle-graders about a family with two sets of twins who communicate telepathically and become involved in cases set in London, Florida, and New Mexico. In addition, she is the reteller of the legends of Hercules and Robin Hood and has written several books—both fiction and nonfiction—based on her own experiences and those of her family. Lasky often collaborates on her books with her husband, photographer Christopher G. Knight.

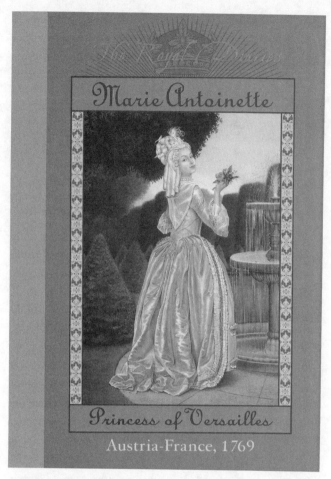

Writing in the form of a diary, Kathryn Lasky creates a fictional chronicle that captures the thoughts, feelings, and day-to-day life of the thirteen-year-old girl who, as eventual queen of France, will one day meet a tragic fate. (Cover illustration by Tim O'Brien.)

Lasky is praised for exploring topics not often covered in books for the young and for explaining them in an accessible, enjoyable manner. She is also acknowledged for her well-developed characterizations—both in her fiction and nonfiction—and for her narrative skill, and noted for providing young readers with strong storylines, even in her informational books. Lasky favors clear, concise language with vivid imagery that is often called poetic; writing in *Booklist,* Ilene Cooper stated, "Few authors are as eloquent as Lasky." She is considered a writer of unusual, effective books that reveal their author's enthusiasm for her subjects. In an essay in *Twentieth-Century Young Adult Writers,* Linda Garrett commented that Lasky "has made and continues to make an impact on young-adult literature. Her well-researched books provide a thorough, accurate picture of whatever theme is being presented. Her use of lyrical language captures the moods as well as facts leaving the reader with [in Lasky's words] 'a sense of joy—indeed celebration' of the world in which they live." Carol Hurst of *Carol Hurst's Children's Literature Newsletter* added, "I'm always impressed when an author can move from one genre to another with competence, but Kathy Lasky does so with such ease and skill that I am more than impressed, I'm awed."

Born in Indianapolis, Indiana, Lasky is the descendant of a family who escaped from czarist Russia to avoid religious persecution; their exodus forms the basis of her novel *The Night Journey*. She is the daughter of social worker Hortense Lasky and Marven Lasky, a wine bottler whose boyhood experience of being sent to a logging camp in the Minnesota woods are recounted by Lasky in the picture book *Marven of the Great North Woods.*

Lasky was a storyteller from an early age; she once explained, "When I was growing up, I was always thinking up stories—whether I wrote them down or not didn't seem to matter. I was a compulsive story-maker. I was fiercely private about these early stories—never really sharing them with anybody. I always wanted to be a writer, but on the other hand it seemed to lack a certain legitimacy as a profession. It was enjoyable, not reliable, and you were your own boss. This all seemed funny. It was only when I began to share my writing with my parents (and much later my husband) and sensed their responsiveness that I began to think that it was OK to want to be a writer."

Despite her love of telling stories, as a child, Lasky was labeled a reluctant reader. "The truth is," she stated on her Web site, "I didn't really like the kind of books they had you reading at school—the 'See Dick, See Jane' books. So I made a voluntary withdrawal from reading in school. But I loved the books my mom was reading to me, books like *Peter Pan* and *The Wonderful Wizard of Oz.*"

Lasky first realized that she could become a writer when she was about ten years old. She and her family, which also included an older sister, were driving at night in their convertible. The top was down and, Lasky recalled on her Web site, "The sky looked so interesting—you couldn't see the stars because of these woolly clouds. And I said it looked like a sheepback sky. My mom turned around and said, 'Kathryn, you should be a writer.' When my mom said that, I thought, 'Wow, maybe I will be.'"

Although Lasky is well respected as an author of informational books, she claims that as a young reader she was not a fan of the genre. As she stated on her Web site, "I didn't like nonfiction as a kid—the nonfiction books were really dry back then. But then I realized that you can make the characters in nonfiction as fascinating as those in fiction."

In *Horn Book*, Lasky described how she employed her research techniques as a seventh-grader in writing a report on the Pleistocene Age due the next morning. "First," the author recalled, "I went to the dictionary and looked up a definition. Webster really had a knack for providing material for desperate seventh-graders.

Then I would proceed to the *World Book Encyclopedia.* If I was feeling very scholarly, I would persevere and take on the Mount Everest of research—*Encyclopedia Brittanica.*" Mostly, though, Lasky would move to the final step in her research: "Bursting into my sister's room, I would fling myself on her bed and in anguish cry, "Quick, I need a first sentence about the Pleistocene Age!' Sometimes I would get one from her and sometimes she'd tell me to get out." As a last resort, Lasky would go to her mother, who would "toss off opening sentences like a comedy writer searching for one-liners. Like all seventh-graders, I considered the quality of my mother's thoughts stupid, boring, and embarrassing. I would roll my eyes and groan and wish that Ozzie and Harriet were my real parents." Lasky attended a private all-girls school in Indianapolis, which she felt did not particularly suit her; later, she drew on her experiences in the autobiographical novel *Pageant,* a humorous coming-of-age story about Sarah Benjamin, a Jewish teenager in a Christian girls' school who learns what she really wants from life. After finishing high school, Lasky attended the University of Michigan as an English major; after receiving her degree, she became a teacher and began writing seriously in her spare time. In 1971, she married Christopher Knight, whose youthful experiences kayaking and camping with his father and grandfather form the basis for the novel *Jem's Island.* The couple had two children: Max, whose desire for a baby sister inspired the photo-essay *A Baby for Max,* and Meribah, who shares her name with the title character of the young-adult novel *Beyond the Divide* and who collaborated with her mother on *Searching for Laura Ingalls,* the story of her family's journey to the settings of the "Little House" books by Laura Ingalls Wilder.

In 1975, Lasky published her first book for children, the colorful concept book *Agatha's Alphabet.* Her second work, *I Have Four Names for My Grandfather,* was published the following year. A picture book, *I Have Four Names for My Grandfather* depicts Tom and his grandfather fishing, planting flowers, and looking at a train, among other activities; Tom concludes that although his grandfather has four names—Poppy, Pop, Grandpa, and Gramps—he is always the same grandfather to him. The first of Lasky's books to be illustrated by her husband, *I Have Four Names for My Grandfather* also introduces one of the author's major themes: intergenerational bonding. Barbara S. Wertheimer of *Children's Book Review Service* noted "the sensitivity and depth of feeling within the text," while Andd Ward of *School Library Journal* wrote that the strength of the book "lies in the compatibility of the text with the abundant photographs."

Lasky's first work to win a major award is *The Weaver's Gift,* a photo-essay that won the *Boston Globe/Horn Book* Award for juvenile nonfiction in 1982. In this book, Lasky and Knight spotlight weaver Carolyn Frye, a Vermont woman who raises sheep and converts their wool to finished products; the author and photographer document Frye's hard work and artistry while demonstrating how sheared wool becomes a child's blanket. Writing in *Interracial Books for Children*, Jan M. Goodman stated that *The Weaver's Gift* "is a rare find," adding that the text is "extremely well-written and factual and shows deep appreciation and respect for a woman and her trade." A critic for *Kirkus Reviews* noted that while "there have been other juvenile introductions to this basic sequence, . . . they are dull or feeble in comparison."

In 1981, Lasky published *The Night Journey,* a young-adult novel that is highly respected as a work of Jewish literature. Based on a true story, the novel outlines how a nine-year-old girl orchestrates her family's escape from religious persecution in czarist Russia. The girl grows up to become Nana Sachie, great-grandmother to thirteen-year-old Rachel, who learns this piece of family history during their afternoons together; Sachie finishes the tale, which is filled with excitement, shortly before her death. Calling *The Night Journey* "a story to cherish," Ilene Cooper noted in *Booklist* that it "has so many aspects that each person will come away with his own idea of what makes the book memorable." Peter Kennerley concluded in a review for *School Librarian:*

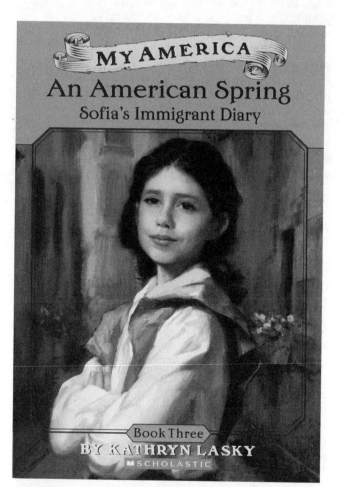

This 2004 work continues ten-year-old Italian immigrant Sofia Monari's story of life in her adopted country, as she tells of her family's move to North Boston, where they become shopkeepers. (Cover illustration by Glenn Harrington.)

"I believe this to be a satisfying novel, if not without blemish, and I recommend it strongly."

Sugaring Time, a photo-essay also illustrated by Knight, was named a Newbery honor book in 1984. The volume outlines the activities of the Lacey family during the month of March, the period they call "sugaring time," on their Vermont farm. Lasky and Knight portray the hard work—and the pleasure—involved in turning maple sugar into maple syrup while providing young readers with a sense of the seasons and the value of the earth. Alice Naylor of *Language Arts* called Lasky's text "a model of good exposition," while Martha T. Kane wrote in *Appraisal* that "You can almost hear the crunch of snow beneath the horses' feet, the sweet maple sap dripping into the buckets, and the roar of the fire in the sugarhouse. . . . Lasky involves *all* the reader's senses in her memorable description of the collection and processing of maple sap in a small sugarbush in Vermont."

One of Lasky's most critically acclaimed novels for young adults is *Beyond the Divide.* Set in the mid-1800s, the story outlines the journey of fourteen-year-old Meribah Simon, an Amish girl who travels with her father from Pennsylvania to California by wagon train during the Gold Rush. Meribah's trek to California is an ordeal: her father dies after one of his wounds becomes infected; a friend is raped and commits suicide; and Meribah, now left alone, struggles to survive in the wilderness. Rescued by a group of Yahi Indians, Meribah learns to understand them and to appreciate their lifestyle; at the end of the novel, she decides to go back to a fertile valley she had seen from the wagon train and make a life for herself.

Calling *Beyond the Divide* an "elegantly written tour de force," Ilene Cooper commented that Lasky has written a "quintessential pioneer story, a piece so textured and rich that readers will remember it long after they've put it down." Dick Abrahamson, reviewing the novel for the *English Journal,* called *Beyond the Divide* "one of the finest historical novels I've read in a long time. It certainly ought to be considered for the Newbery Award." Writing in *Language Arts,* M. Jean Greenlaw concluded that the major strength of the book is that it "is a magnificent story. The westward movement is an integral part of American history and nature, and this book is the most gripping account of that time I have ever read," Linda Garrett of *Twentieth-Century Children's Writers* added that the novel "is so realistic it would be easy to believe that *Beyond the Divide* is directly from a diary of a young girl going West."

Lasky's *Traces of Life: The Origins of Humankind* is an informational book that outlines the history of evolution. In this work, the author, who has had a longtime interest in paleontology, attempts to determine the moment at which humanity as we know it began to exist. She discusses evolution and the science of paleoanthropology while presenting biographical information about several notable scientists. *Voice of Youth Advocates* contributor Shirley A. Bathgate said that Lasky "combines research and creativity in yet another excellent book"; the critic concluded, "Younger young-adult readers will find the book both easy and fun to read." *Traces of Life* received the Golden Trilobite Award from the Paleontological Society in 1990. Lasky also received consistently favorable reviews for *Monarchs,* an informational book that describes the cycle of the migrating monarch butterfly. In recreating the monarch's journey from Maine to Mexico, Lasky and Christopher Knight blend scientific facts with information about adults and children involved with preserving the monarch and its environment. Susan Oliver of *School Library Journal* noted that *Monarchs* "strikes a perfect balance between science and humanity"; the critic added that "the diversity of the people who care about conserving the beauty and mystery of nature makes it a truly compelling book." Betsy Hearne concluded in the *Bulletin of the Center for Children's Books* that Lasky "has trimmed her prose for an action-packed nature narrative that crosses cultural as well as geographic boundaries."

The Librarian Who Measured the Earth is an informational picture book about Eratosthenes, the Greek scholar who became the head librarian of the famous library in Alexandria, Egypt, and was the first person to determine and document the size of the earth. Using a technique she calls "responsible imagining," Lasky combines existing information about Eratosthenes and his times with what Joanne Schott of *Quill and Quire* called "some reasonable assumptions" about her subject's early life and personality. Schott called *The Librarian Who Measured the Earth* a "beautiful picture-book biography" in which "Eratosthenes comes across as an individual rather than just another name from the history books." Anne Lundin of the *Five Owls* posed the question: "How many counting books count in a whole language program? After a while, the numbers themselves are pretty familiar, and the challenge is to find a book that explores mathematics and geography from a more human scale, as a quest to answer the mysteries of life. Here it is." Describing herself as "a rather nonnumerate soul and a naturalist," Lundin concluded, "For someone like me, [this book] shakes the sky. I am proud to associate with the librarian Eratosthenes, who goads me to ask my own questions."

One of Lasky's most well-received picture-book biographies is *Marven of the Great North Woods,* a vignette from her father's childhood. As a ten year old, Marven Lasky was sent to a logging camp in the Minnesota north woods to avoid the influenza epidemic that hit his hometown of Duluth in 1918. At first, Marven finds this new world to be foreign—for example, there was no kosher food at the camp—but he adjusts to his situation and forms warm friendships with the lumberjacks, especially Jean Louis, a French Canadian who is the biggest man in the camp. Calling *Marven of the Great North Woods* a story of "courage inspired by familial affection and the unexpected kindness of strangers," a critic in

Publishers Weekly predicted, "Thanks to Lasky's considerable command of language and narrative detail, readers will linger over" the descriptions in the book. Roger Sutton of *Horn Book* called the work "both invigorating and cozy" and noted that the text, though long for a picture book, is "fully eventful." In her newsletter, Carol Hurst concluded that Lasky "makes the extraordinary adventure possible and [Kevin Hawkes's] paintings combine with her writing to show wonder and tenderness." *Marven of the Great North Woods* won the National Jewish Book Award in 1997.

Lasky has a particular fascination with American author Samuel Langhorne Clemens, who wrote as Mark Twain: the subject of the picture book biography *A Brilliant Streak: The Making of Mark Twain,* he also appears as a major character in *Alice Rose and Sam,* a story for middle graders. In *A Brilliant Streak,* Lasky recounts Clemens's life until he takes on his famous pseudonym at age thirty. The author details Twain's Missouri childhood and his experiences as a steamboat pilot, prospector, and reporter as well as a humorist and social commentator; in addition, Lasky provides a sense of how Twain's life and personality are reflected in his works. Stephanie Zvirin of *Booklist* predicted that after reading *A Brilliant Streak,* "Children will definitely want to find out more about Clemens," while a critic in *Kirkus Reviews* concluded that Twain's "successes are the source of one colorful anecdote after another, which Lasky taps and twirls into an engaging narrative that glimmers with its own brand of brilliance."

Set in Virginia City, Nevada, during the 1860s, *Alice Rose and Sam* describes how twelve-year-old Alice Rose, a newspaperman's daughter, joins forces with reporter Samuel Clemens to solve a murder and expose a plot by a group of Confederate vigilantes called the Society of Seven. "Ultimately," noted Jennifer A. Fakolt of *School Library Journal,* Alice Rose and Clemens "end up teaching one another valuable lessons about life and truth." Calling the book an "open-throttled page-turner," a critic for *Kirkus Reviews* concluded that fans of Karen Cushman's *The Ballad of Lucy Whipple* and Kathleen Karr's *Oh, Those Harper Girls!* "have a plucky new heroine to admire," while a reviewer for *Publishers Weekly* called *Alice Rose and Sam* a "view of American history teeming with adventure and local color." *Alice Rose and Sam* won the Western Heritage Award and was nominated for an Edgar Allan Poe award in 1999.

Another historical figure featured in one of Lasky's books is John Harrison, whose story is told in *The Man Who Made Time Travel.* When the English Parliament offered a multi-million dollar reward in 1707 for anyone who could accurately measure longitude in a way that would aid in sea navigation, Harrison devoted more than three decades of his life to solving the problem. A *Publishers Weekly* reviewer found that "Lasky gets off to a bumpy start," but when the story begins to focus on Harrison, the author's "prose becomes clear and

Lasky has authored many works for the picture-book crowd, including **Mommy's Hands,** *which illustrates the loving bond between mother and daughter. (Cover illustration by Darcie LaBrose.)*

compelling." Carolyn Phelan of *Booklist* remarked that "the text makes absorbing reading both for its sidelights on history and for the personal drama portrayal." Critics noted that the illustrations by Kevin Hawkes bring visual appeal to the book. In *School Library Journal,* Dona Ratterree wrote that because of Hawkes's artwork, the book's "clear science, and its compelling social commentary, this title is not to be missed."

Vision of Beauty: The Story of Sarah Breedlove Walker profiles America's first self-made female African-American millionaire. Walker made her fortune in the hair-care-products industry and was a civil rights pioneer. In *Black Issues Book Review,* Merce Robinson and Kelly Ellis praised the book for its inspiring portrayal of Walker. The noted that Lasky demonstrates that Waker's vision was not "beauty for its sake alone, but that the tools of beauty could be used by black

women to inspire self-confidence." *Booklist*'s Marta Segal deemed the biography "engaging," noting that "Walker's feminism and work for civil rights are described in terms that will make sense to young readers."

Lasky created a series character with Lucille, a piglet who struggles with everyday challenges common to younger readers. Lasky adds humor to the "Lucille" books to keep the tone light and accessible. In *Lucille Camps In,* Lucille is left at home while her father and siblings go on a camping trip, so she decides to camp in her living room. Gillian Engberg of *Booklist* described the book as "an endearing, realistic story in short sentences and simple language a new reader can handle." In *School Library Journal,* Martha Topol observed that the "family dynamics are great—supportive while allowing for individuality." In *Lucille's Snowsuit,* the pig is delighted that school is canceled because of snow, but then she has difficulty getting into her snow-suit so she can go out and play. Todd Morning remarked in *Booklist* that "the best pages in the book focus on Lucille's struggles to put on her suit." A *Publishers Weekly* contributor, however, was disappointed in the story, deeming it "disappointingly plodding and predictable," although the illustrations are "spirited." Regarded by critics as endearing and touching, Lasky's *Mommy's Hands*—coauthored with Jane Kamine—is told by three toddlers who describe why they love their mommy's hands. The story relates the many things mommies do with their hands that amaze and comfort their children. Maryann H. Owen praised the book for its "affectionate tribute to every mother whose gentle touch has helped to mold her child." Similarly, GraceAnne A. DeCandido of *Booklist* called the book a "tender and affectionate series of tete-a-tetes." In *Kirkus Reviews,* a critic commented on the way the authors approach the story with a "gentle give-and-take," concluding, "Reading this cozy tale is rather like being enveloped by a mother's warm embrace."

In 2003, Lasky began a series of fantasy novels for young adults called "Guardians of Ga'Hoole." The series is about a community of owls in a world that is partially fictionalized and partially based on facts about owls. The first installment, *The Capture,* tells the story of a baby owl, Soren, who is knocked out of his nest too soon. When he is scooped up by another owl and taken to an orphanage, Soren soon realizes that he is in a military training camp where the captives are being brainwashed. Thanks to new friends, he is able to escape. Francisca Goldsmith of *Booklist* noted that Lasky's owlish world inspires "big questions about human social psychology and politics along with real owl science." In *Kliatt,* Erin Lukens Darr commended the educational value of the novel, as Lasky uses "a combination of scientific and creative vocabulary," adding that *The Capture,* "would be a good language arts complement to the study of owls." In contrast, a reviewer for *Publishers Weekly* found the story to be "unevenly paced" and often "encumbered by excessive detail," although the characters are "likable."

Lasky once told *Something about the Author* (SATA): "I write directly from my own experiences." In an article for *Horn Book* on writing nonfiction, she stated that as a writer she searches "for the story among the truths, the facts, the lies, and the realities. . . . I have always tried hard to listen, smell, and touch the place that I write about—especially if I am lucky enough to be there." She continued, "I have a fascination with the inexact and the unexplainable. I try to do as little explaining as possible, but I try to present my subject in some way so it will not lose what I have found to be or suspect to be its sacred dimension." The author concluded, "In my books I am not concerned with messages, and I really do not care if readers remember a single fact. What I do hope is that they come away with a sense of joy—indeed celebration–about something they have sensed in the world in which they live."

Regarding her fiction, much of which reflects her extensive research, Lasky stated on her Web site, "I want young readers to come away with a sense of joy about life. I want to draw them into a world where they're really going to connect with the characters." In another article for *Horn Book,* Lasky claimed: "I can't stand doing the same thing twice. I don't want to change just for the sake of change. But the whole point of being an artist is to be able to get up every morning and reinvent the world."

Biographical and Critical Sources

BOOKS

Twentieth-Century Young Adult Writers, edited by Laura Standley Berger, Gale (Detroit, MI), 1994, pp. 371-373.

PERIODICALS

Appraisal, winter, 1984, Martha T. Kane, review of *Sugaring Time,* pp. 34-35.
Black Issues Book Review, November, 2000, Merce Robinson and Kelly Ellis, review of *Vision of Beauty: The Story of Sarah Breedlove Walker,* p. 80.
Booklist, July, 1983, Ilene Cooper, review of *Beyond the Divide,* p. 1402; November 15, 1982, Ilene Cooper, review of *Jem's Island,* p. 446; January 15, 1986, Ilene Cooper, review of *Home Free,* pp. 758-759; November 15, 1981, Ilene Cooper, review of *The Night Journey,* pp. 439-440; April, 1998, Stephanie Zvirin, review of *A Brilliant Streak: The Making of Mark Twain,* p. 1317; August 21, 2000, Marta Segal, review of *Vision of Beauty,* p. 2032; September 15, 2000, Todd Morning, review of *Lucille's Snowsuit,* p. 249; June 1, 2002, GraceAnne A. DeCandido, review of *Mommy's Hands,* pp. 1740-1741; March 1, 2003, Carolyn Phelan, review of *The Man Who Made Time Travel,* p. 1196; July, 2003, Gillian Engberg, review of *Lucille Camps In,* p. 1897; September 15, 2003, Francisca Goldsmith, review of *The Capture,* p. 240.
Bulletin of the Center for Children's Books, November, 1993, Betsy Hearne, review of *Monarchs,* pp. 88-89.
Carol Hurst's Children's Literature Newsletter, winter, 1999, "Featured Author: Kathryn Lasky," p. 4.
Children's Book Review Service, November, 1976, Barbara S. Wertheimer, review of *I Have Four Names for My Grandfather,* p. 22.
English Journal, January, 1984, Dick Abrahamson, "To Start the New Year off Right," pp. 87-89.
Five Owls, February, 1995, Anne Landis, review of *The Librarian Who Measured the Earth,* pp. 61-62.
Horn Book, June, 1983, Karen Jameyson, review of *Sugaring Time,* p. 323; September-October, 1985, Kathryn Lasky, "Reflections on Nonfiction," pp. 527-532; November-December, 1991, Kathryn Lasky, "Creativity in a Boom Industry," pp. 705-711; November-December, 1997, Roger Sutton, review of *Marven of the Great North Woods,* p. 670.

Interracial Books for Children Bulletin, Volume 12, numbers 4-5, 1981, Jan M. Goodman, review of *The Weaver's Gift,,* p. 38.

Kirkus Reviews, March 1, 1981, review of *The Weaver's Gift,* p. 286; March 1, 1998, review of *Alice Rose and Sam,* p. 341; April 1, 1998, review of *A Brilliant Streak: The Making of Mark Twain,* p. 497; March 15, 2002, review of *Mommy's Hands,* pp. 416-417.

Kliatt, September, 2003, Erin Lukens Darr, review of *The Capture,* p. 26.

Language Arts, January, 1984, M. Jean Greenlaw, review of *Beyond the Divide,* pp. 70-71; September, 1984, Alice Naylor, review of *Sugaring Time,* p. 543.

Publishers Weekly, October 6, 1997, review of *Marven of the Great North Woods,* p. 83; February 16, 1998, review of *Alice Rose and Sam,* p. 212; August 21, 2000, review of *Lucille's Snowsuit,* p. 73; March 17, 2003, review of *The Man Who Made Time Travel,* p. 77; July 7, 2003, review of *The Capture,* p. 72.

Quill and Quire, October, 1994, Joanne Schott, "The One Who . . . ," p. 46.

School Librarian, June, 1983, Peter Kennerley, review of *The Night Journey,* p. 144.

School Library Journal, November, 1976, Andd Ward, review of *I Have Four Names for My Grandfather,* p. 48; September, 1993, Susan Oliver, review of *Monarchs,* p. 244; May, 1998, Jennifer A. Fakolt, review of *Alice Rose and Sam,* p. 145; July, 2002, Maryann H. Owen, review of *Mommy's Hands,* p. 94; April, 2003, Dona Ratterree, review of *The Man Who Made Time Travel,* p. 184; July, 2003, Martha Topol, review of *Lucille Camps In,* p. 100.

Voice of Youth Advocates, June, 1990, Shirley A. Bathgate, review of *Traces of Life: The Origin of Humankind,* pp. 126-127.

ONLINE

Kathryn Lasky Web site, http://www.kathrynlasky.com (January 5, 2005).*

*   *   *

LASKY KNIGHT, Kathryn
See LASKY, Kathryn

*   *   *

LASSITER, Rhiannon 1977-

Personal

Born February 9, 1977, in London, England; daughter of Mary Hoffman (a writer) and Stephen Barber. *Education:* Attended Oxford University.

Addresses

Home—Oxford, England. *Agent*—c/o Author Mail, Simon & Schuster, 1230 Avenue of the Americas, New York, NY 10020. *E-mail*—rhiannon@rhiannonlassiter.com.

Career

Writer and Web designer.

Writings

FOR YOUNG ADULTS

The Supernatural, Barron's (Hauppage, NY), 1999.
Waking Dream, Macmillan (London, England), 2002.
Super Zeroes, Oxford University Press (London, England), 2005.

"HEX" TRILOGY; FOR YOUNG ADULTS

Hex, Macmillan (London, England), 1998, Simon & Schuster (New York, NY), 2002.

Rhiannon Lassiter sets her sci-fi novel in twenty-fourth-century London, as a small band of street-smart kids discover that children with a gene that gives them computer-like powers are being hunted down and exterminated by the powerful European Federation. (Cover illustration by Paul Young.)

Ghosts, Macmillan (London, England), 2001, Simon & Schuster (New York, NY), 2002.
Shadows, Simon & Schuster (New York, NY), 2002.

"RIGHTS OF PASSAGE" SERIES; FOR YOUNG ADULTS

Outland, Oxford University Press (Oxford, England), 2003.
Borderland, Oxford University Press (Oxford, England), 2004.
Shadowland, Oxford University Press (Oxford, England), 2005.

OTHER

(Editor with Mary Hoffman) *Lines in the Sand: New Writing on War and Peace,* Disinformation Company (New York, NY), 2003.

Contributor of book reviews to periodicals, including London *Daily Telegraph.*

Sidelights

British writer Rhiannon Lassiter became a published author at an early age, perhaps influenced by growing up around her mother, children's author Mary Hoffman, and Hoffman's circle of publishing insiders. Lassiter, an avid reader, and began trying her hand at writing at age fourteen; she submitted work for publication when she was sixteen, and although she did not get published at that time, editors encouraged her to try again. Not surprisingly, Lassiter was thrilled when her first book, the young-adult fantasy novel *Hex,* was published by Macmillan when she was only nineteen years old. The first part of Lassiter's futuristic fantasy trilogy, the novel also marked its author's emergence as a popular YA writer. The "Hex" trilogy takes place in twenty-fourth-century London. Hexes are people who have been born with the ability to interface directly with computers. As yet, the full force of their powers is unknown, but the European Federation is threatened by them and is determined to destroy them completely. For this reason, most Hexes do not even survive childhood. A group of young Hexes who have evaded capture band together with Raven as their leader. In the first installment in the series, *Hex,* Raven and her brother, Wraith, set about finding their sister who was adopted at an early age. They succeed in locating her and almost abandon their plan to take her back with them when it appears she is happily placed in a loving home. When they discover that she has been kidnaped by the government, however, they know they do not have much time to save her from extermination. Sally Estes, reviewing the novel in *Booklist,* commented that "the action is nonstop" and dubbed *Hex* "a good start for this noir thriller series." The second book in the trilogy, *Shadows,* finds the group of Hexes in league with another anti-government faction intent upon taking down the arm of the government responsible for destroying Hexes. Although Raven is captured, she escapes and finds her powers even

In this 1999 sequel to **Hex** *the ragtag mutant band, led by fifteen-year-old Raven, encounter danger when they join up with an underground group trying to stop the Federation's efforts to eliminate Hex children like them from the planet. (Cover illustration by Mark Gerber.)*

stronger. *School Library Journal* reviewer Ronni Krasnow declared Raven "about as strong a female protagonist as there is," while also noting that the same insecurities and flaws are present within her clique as there are in ordinary teenagers' circles. Krasnow praised the novel as "fast-paced" and "engaging," noting that Lassiter "shows considerable skill in drawing readers into her world of tomorrow."

The final book in the "Hex" trilogy is *Ghosts.* In this book Raven and the others save a pair of siblings whose mother passed on to them a computer file just before she died. The file contains critical information about the Hexes and their future, and reveals that the group now faces dangers from the government and the world's computer system. In *School Library Journal,* Molly S. Kinney remarked that "the strength of the characters, their willingness to fight, their survival instinct, and goodness ring true, even if everything is a little glossed over." Praising the "Hex" trilogy as "tautly plotted and exciting to the max," *Booklist* reviewer Estes concluded that series conclusion *Ghosts*. "will satisfy readers."

In an online interview for *Achuka*, Lassiter discussed how she came to write the "Hex" trilogy, noting that she first thought up the story "when I was seventeen and wrote most of it when I was eighteen. It was accepted for publication shortly after my nineteenth birthday." "I wanted to set 'Hex' in London because it's a city I know well but when I started writing . . . I came up with an image of a city with incredibly high buildings where the heights were gleaming and beautiful and the depths hidden from sight. It occurred to me quite soon that the two ideas were complementary and from that was created a London which had swallowed its own history, building on top of the ancient parts of the city in an effort to progress."

In addition to penning fantasy fiction, Lassiter has teamed up with her mother to edit *Lines in the Sand: New Writing on War and Peace,* a book containing writings about war. Intended to shed light on the war in Iraq and its impact on people at a personal level, this book features the work of numerous children's authors, poets, and artists. Topics include the Crusades, the Holocaust, and revolutionary violence occurring in Nigeria, and Kosovo. Hazel Rochman, reviewing *Lines in the Sand* for *Booklist,* wrote that while some of the material is a little heavy-handed, much of it is less propaganda and more storytelling. The critic added that the most effective entries "bring the suffering close to home," and cited the work as a useful springboard for discussion "both in and out of the classroom." All profit from the sale of *Lines in the Sand* were earmarked for UNICEF.

Biographical and Critical Sources

PERIODICALS

Booklist, January 1, 2002, Sally Estes, review of *Hex,* p. 842; April 15, 2002, Sally Estes, review of *Ghosts,* p. 1395; February 1, 2004, Hazel Rochman, review of *Lines in the Sand: New Writings on War and Peace,* p. 968.
Kliatt, March, 2002, Susan Cromby, review of *Hex,* p. 24.
School Library Journal, April, 2002, Ronni Krasnow, review of *Shadows,* p. 152; January, 2003, Molly S. Kinney, review of *Ghosts,* p. 140.

ONLINE

Achuka.co.uk, http://www.achuka.co.uk/ (February 3, 2005), interview with Lassiter.
Rhiannon Lassiter Home Page, http://www.rhiannon lassiter.com (February 3, 2005).*

LESTER, Julius (Bernard) 1939-

Personal

Born January 27, 1939, in St. Louis, MO; son of W. D. (a minister) and Julia (Smith) Lester; married Joan Steinau (a researcher), 1962 (divorced, 1970); married Alida Carolyn Fechner, March 21, 1979 (divorced, 1993); married Milan Sabatini, August 17, 1995; children: (first marriage) Jody Simone, Malcolm Coltrane; (second marriage) Elena Milad Grohmann (stepdaughter), David Julius; (third marriage) Lian Amaris Brennan (stepdaughter). *Education:* Fisk University, B.A., 1960.

Addresses

Agent—c/o Author Mail, Dial Press, Dell Publishing, 1540 Broadway, New York, NY 10036. *E-mail*—lester@ judnea.umass.edu.

Career

Educator, historian, folklorist, writer, and performer. Professional musician and singer, c. 1960s, recording with Vanguard Records; Newport Folk Festival, Newport, RI, director, 1966-68; WBAI-FM, New York, NY, producer and host of live radio show, 1968-75; WNET-TV, New York, NY, host of live television program *Free Time,* 1971-73; University of Massachusetts-Amherst, professor of Afro-American studies, 1971-88, professor of Near Eastern and Judaic Studies, 1982-2003, acting director and associate director of Institute for Advanced Studies in Humanities, 1982-84, adjunct professor in English and history departments, 1988-2003, professor emeritus, beginning 2004. Lecturer, New School for Social Research (now New School University), 1968-70; writer-in-residence, Vanderbilt University, 1985.

Awards, Honors

Newbery Honor Book citation, 1969, and Lewis Carroll Shelf Award, 1970, both for *To Be a Slave;* Lewis Carroll Shelf Award, 1972, and National Book Award finalist, 1973, both for *Long Journey Home: Stories from Black History;* Lewis Carroll Shelf Award, 1973, for *The Knee-high Man and Other Tales;* honorable mention, Coretta Scott King Award, 1983, for *This Strange New Feeling,* and 1988, for *Tales of Uncle Remus: The Adventures of Brer Rabbit;* Parents' Choice Story Book award, 1987, for *The Tales of Uncle Remus,* and 1990, for *Further Tales of Uncle Remus;* Reading Magic Award, 1988, for *More Tales of Uncle Remus; Boston Globe/Horn Book* award, American Library Association (ALA) Notable Book, and Caldecott Honor Book, all 1995, all for *John Henry;* ALA Notable Book, 1996, for *Sam and the Tigers.* Distinguished Teacher's Award, 1983-84; Faculty Fellowship Award for Distinguished Research and Scholarship, 1985; National Professor of the Year Silver Medal Award, Council for Advancement and Support of Education, 1985; Massachusetts State

Professor of the Year and Gold Medal Award for National Professor of the Year, Council for Advancement and Support of Education, both 1986; Distinguished Faculty Lecturer, 1986-87.

Writings

FOR CHILDREN

(Editor, with Mary Varela) *Our Folk Tales: High John, The Conqueror, and Other Afro-American Tales,* illustrated by Jennifer Lawson, privately printed, 1967.

To Be a Slave, illustrated by Tom Feelings, Dial (New York, NY), 1969.

Black Folktales, illustrated by Tom Feelings, R. W. Baron (New York, NY), 1969, reprinted, Grove Press (New York, NY), 1992.

Long Journey Home: Stories from Black History, Dial (New York, NY), 1972.

The Knee-high Man and Other Tales, illustrated by Ralph Pinto, Dial (New York, NY), 1972.

This Strange New Feeling, Dial (New York, NY), 1982, published as *A Taste of Freedom: Three Stories from Black History,* Longman (London, England), 1983.

The Tales of Uncle Remus: The Adventures of Brer Rabbit (also see below), illustrated by Jerry Pinkney, Dial (New York, NY), 1987.

More Tales of Uncle Remus: Further Adventures of Brer Rabbit, His Friends, Enemies, and Others (also see below), illustrated by Jerry Pinkney, Dial (New York, NY), 1988.

How Many Spots Does a Leopard Have? and Other Tales, illustrated by David Shannon, Scholastic (New York, NY), 1990.

Further Tales of Uncle Remus: The Misadventures of Brer Rabbit, Brer Fox, Wolf, the Doodang, and Other Creatures (also see below), illustrated by Jerry Pinkney, Dial (New York, NY), 1990.

The Last Tales of Uncle Remus (also see below), illustrated by Jerry Pinkney, Dial (New York, NY), 1994.

John Henry, illustrated by Jerry Pinkney, Dial (New York, NY), 1994.

The Man Who Knew Too Much: A Moral Tale from the Baila of Zambia, illustrated by Leonard Jenkins, Clarion (New York, NY), 1994.

Othello (young-adult novel), Scholastic (New York, NY), 1995.

Sam and the Tigers: A New Retelling of Little Black Sambo, illustrated by Jerry Pinkney, Dial (New York, NY), 1996.

What a Truly Cool World, illustrated by Joe Cepeda, Scholastic (New York, NY), 1998.

Black Cowboy, Wild Horses: A True Story, illustrated by Jerry Pinkney, Dial (New York, NY), 1998.

From Slave Ship to Freedom Road, illustrated by Rod Brown, Dial (New York, NY), 1998.

When the Beginning Began: Stories about God, the Creatures, and Us, illustrated by Emily Lisker, Silver Whistle/Harcourt Brace (San Diego, CA), 1998.

Uncle Remus: The Complete Tales (includes *The Tales of Uncle Remus, More Tales of Uncle Remus, Further Tales of Uncle Remus,* and *The Last Tales of Uncle Remus*), illustrated by Jerry Pinkney, Phyllis Fogelman Books (New York, NY), 1999.

Shining, illustrated by John Clapp, Harcourt Brace (San Diego, CA), 2000.

Pharaoh's Daughter (young-adult novel), Silver Whistle/Harcourt (San Diego, CA), 2000.

Albidaro and the Mischievous Dream, illustrated by Jerry Pinkney, Phyllis Fogelman Books (New York, NY), 2001.

Ackamarackus: Julius Lester's Sumptuously Silly Fantastically Funny Fables, illustrated by Emilie Chollat, Scholastic (New York, NY), 2001.

The Blues Singers: Ten Who Rocked the World, illustrated by Lisa Cohen, Hyperion (New York, NY), 2001

When Dad Killed Mom (young-adult novel), Silver Whistle/Harcourt (San Diego, CA), 2001.

Why Heaven Is Far Away, illustrated by Joe Cepeda, Scholastic (New York, NY), 2002.

The Old African, illustrated by Jerry Pinkney, Dial (New York, NY), 2004.

Let's Talk about Race, illustrated by Karen Barbour, HarperCollins (New York, NY), 2005.

The Day of Tears, 2005.

Lester has recorded his "Uncle Remus" tales as *The Tales of Uncle Remus, More Tales of Uncle Remus, Further Tales of Uncle Remus* and *Last Tales of Uncle Remus,* both Recorded Books, 2003.

OTHER

(With Pete Seeger) *The 12-String Guitar as Played by Leadbelly: An Instructional Manual,* Oak (New York, NY), 1965.

The Angry Children of Malcolm X, Southern Student Organizing Committee (Nashville, TN), 1966.

(Editor, with Mary Varela) Fanny Lou Hamer, *To Praise Our Bridges: An Autobiography,* KIPCO, 1967.

The Mud of Vietnam: Photographs and Poems, Folklore Press (New York, NY), 1967.

Look out Whitey! Black Power's Gon' Get Your Mama!, Dial (New York, NY), 1968.

Search for the New Land: History as Subjective Experience, Dial (New York, NY), 1969.

Revolutionary Notes, R. W. Baron (New York, NY), 1969.

(Editor) *The Seventh Son: The Thoughts and Writings of W. E. B. DuBois,* two volumes, Random House (New York, NY), 1971.

(Compiler, with Rae Pace Alexander) *Young and Black in America,* Random House (New York, NY), 1971.

Two Love Stories, Dial (New York, NY), 1972.

(Editor) Stanley Couch, *Ain't No Ambulances for No Nigguhs Tonight* (poems), R. W. Baron (New York, NY), 1972.

(With David Gahr) *Who I Am* (photopoems), Dial (New York, NY), 1974.

All Is Well: An Autobiography, Morrow (New York, NY), 1976.

Do Lord Remember Me (adult novel), Holt (New York, NY), 1984.

Lovesong: Becoming a Jew (autobiographical), Holt (New York, NY), 1988.

Falling Pieces of the Broken Sky, Arcade (New York, NY), 1990.

And All Our Wounds Forgiven, Arcade (New York, NY), 1994.

The Autobiography of God (novel), St. Martin's Press (New York, NY), 2004.

On Writing for Children and Other People, Dial (New York, NY), 2004.

Contributor of essays and reviews to numerous magazines and newspapers, including *New York Times Book Review, New York Times, New Republic, Nation, Katallagete, Democracy,* and *Village Voice.* Associate editor, *Sing Out,* 1964-70; contributing editor, *Broadside of New York,* 1964-70.

Lester's works have been translated into eight languages.

Sidelights

In addition to his work as a respected educator, historian, and performer, Julius Lester has had a long career as a writer, and many of the books he has published since the late 1960s have been penned for younger readers. Through his efforts to reintroduce American children to traditional folk tales, Lester has made a lasting contribution to the field of children's literature through his many focusing on African-American history and culture. An outspoken advocate of books for black children that are penned by black authors, Lester has also advocated for a re-visioning of children's literature. As he once noted in *Publishers Weekly,* too much of children's literature is out date and has no relevance to young people living in modern society.

In books such as *To Be a Slave, Long Journey Home: Stories from Black History,* and *This Strange Feeling,* as well as in his many retellings of the "Uncle Remus" stories, Lester has helped to preserve the history of black Americans, often focusing on black experience in the rural Deep South, especially during slavery and the Reconstruction period following the U.S. Civil War. Throughout, he has been acclaimed for his blend of realistic detail, dialogue, and storytelling—all contributing to important historical knowledge about African Americans. Through his historical work he illustrates themes central to black history and the civil rights movement of the twentieth century, such as oppression and racism, and ultimately hopes to politicize young readers; according to Eric Foner and Naomi Lewis in the *New York Review of Books,* Lester's goal is to provide readers with "a sense of history which will help shape their lives and politics." Despite this serious intent, Lester also reveals his lighthearted side in books such as *Ackamarackus: Julius Lester's Sumptuously Silly Fantastically Funny Fables,* which features a

quirky assortment of animal characters in a book characterized by what *Booklist* reviewer GraceAnne A. DeCandido described as "rampant silliness" and an "inventive" text. Praising the storyteller's lighthearted approach, Wendy Lukehart noted in *School Library Journal* that Lester manages to weaves "pithy morals brimming with wisdom and wit" within his "alliterative language" and "turns of phrase that dance off the tongue."

As he wrote in an article for *School Library Journal,* Lester "grew up during a time when racial segregation and discrimination in the North and South were as common as dandelion fluff." He was born in St. Louis, Missouri in 1939, the son of a Methodist minister, and his family relocated to Kansas City, Kansas, when Lester was two years old. In Kansas He experienced a combustible world in which black men and boys were lynched for even looking at a white woman. "In such a world, childhood was a luxury my parents could not have afforded for me even if they had known how," he wrote. As a contrast to the violence of the times, the sermons and stories of his father brought him into contact with black traditions, and the soothing rhythms and expressions common to the black population of Nashville, where he and his family moved in 1954. Summers spent on his grandmother's farm in rural Arkansas allowed Lester to also experience rural speech patterns and learn a wealth of new stories.

Enjoying music and reading as a child, Lester found in books an escape from reality, and at a young age he became an avid reader of Western and mystery novels despite his limited access to libraries. Eventually turning to the adult books in his father's library, he was particularly struck by a biography of early twentieth-century civil rights leader W. E. B. DuBois. Another significant inspiration was a comment his father made in response to an advertisement offering to trace one's family tree. When his father told Lester to throw it away, the boy asked why his father was uninterested in the family history. As Lester later wrote in *School Library Journal,* his father simply laughed and told him that he knew where they came from: "'Our family tree ends in a bill of sale. Lester is the name of the family that owned us.'" Lester recalls the incident as "one of the defining moments of my life," and added: "So much of my writing has been dedicated to putting faces to the bills of sale."

Lester graduated in 1960 from Nashville's Fisk University with a degree in English and moved to New York City the following year. In the mid-1960s he joined the Student Non-Violent Coordinating Committee (SNCC), at a time when the group advocated that blacks assume a more militant stance to fight racism. As head of the SNCC's photo department, he traveled to North Vietnam during the Vietnam War to document the effects of U.S. bombing missions, and went on to write several adult books on political themes.

In New York City Lester was encouraged to embark upon a publishing career when the editor of his book *Look out, Whitey! Black Power's Gon' Get Your Mama* was impressed with his writing. As Lester explained to *Something about the Author,* "She asked if I had ever thought about writing children's books. I had not. she asked if I would like to meet the children's book editor. I said yes and told the children's book editor about my idea of using the words from former slaves to tell the story of slavery." The result was 1969's *To Be a Slave,* as well as *Black Folktales.*

Runner-up for the Newbery Medal, *To Be a Slave* is an historical narrative based on quotes from slave testimonies. Praised for bringing to light "tremendously moving documents" by John Howard Griffin in the *New York Times Book Review, To Be a Slave* was described by *Bulletin of the Center for Children's Books* reviewer Zena Sutherland as "moving and explicit" in its description of slavery from "capture to auction, from servitude to freedom." Evelyn Geller remarked in *School Library Journal* that Lester's book "quietly lays bare the shame of American history while making slavery, suffering, and resistance part of [a] black child's heritage."*Black Folktales* features tales featuring both human and animal characters drawn from African legends and slave narratives. "Although these tales have been told before, . . . Lester brings a fresh street-talk language . . . and thus breathes new life into them," wrote John A. Williams in a review of the book for the *New York Times Book Review.*

Lester has continued to produce books that reflect his interests in African-American history, folklore, and politics. *The Knee-high Man and Other Tales* collects six black folk tales, including those of the famous Brer Rabbit, that feature humor and political satire. In one story, "The Farmer and the Snake," Ethel Richard noted in the *New York Times Book Review* that "the lesson is that kindness will not change the nature of a thing—in this case, the nature of a poisonous snake to bite." Lester's four compilations of "Uncle Remus" tales—*The Tales of Uncle Remus, More Tales of Uncle Remus, Further Tales of Uncle Remus,* and *The Last Tales of Uncle Remus*—separate that stock figure from the Uncle Tom stereotype and make him accessible to modern readers.

Originally compiled by newspaperman Joel Chandler Harris between 1876 and 1918 and narrated by the fictional Uncle Remus in an approximation of nineteenth-century Southern black dialect, these stories featuring the quick-minded Brer Rabbit have African roots: folklorists have long noted similarities between the quick-witted rabbit and Anansi, the spider trickster of West Africa, and Wakaima, the hare trickster of the continent's west coast. Lester has been praised for retelling these tales in a contemporary idiom without losing the bite of the original. A *Kirkus Reviews* critic dubbed the four-volume collection "a landmark retelling," while Betsy Hearne concluded in a review of *The Last Tales*

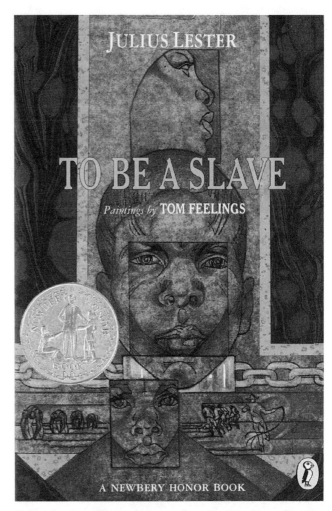

Julius Lester collects writing and transcripts that reflect the feelings and experiences of slaves, those who were born into slavery as well as those who remembered their former life in Africa. (Cover illustration by Tom Feelings.)

of *Uncle Remus* for *Bulletin of the Center for Children's Books* that "respect is a key word here. That's what Lester shows for the largest body of African-American folklore collected in this country. You can't get any more respectful of a cultural tradition than recharging the elements that helped it survive and that affirm its kinship with other peoples of the world."

More folktales are served up by Lester in *How Many Spots Does a Leopard Have? and Other Tales,* which includes ten African stories and two tales with traditional Jewish roots. Intended for children of all ages, "the stories in this collection are as rich, various, and intriguing as the titles," according to Susan Perren in *Quill & Quire.* In *Sam and the Tigers: A New Retelling of Little Black Sambo* Lester takes on the now-controversial story of the African lad whose trick caused a group of hungry tigers to turn into butter. With his politically sensitive retelling readers can, according to Rayma Turton in *Magpies,* "enjoy this new version for what it is—a joyous romp with a true storyteller's pattern."

Retellings of a different sort are contained in Lester's award-winning picture-book collaborations with illustrator Jerry Pinkney. *John Henry, Black Cowboy, Wild Horses,* and *The Old African.* Lester takes on the legendary steel-drivin' man in *John Henry,* a tall tale that "bursts to life," according to Elizabeth Bush in the *Bulletin of the Center for Children's Books.* Jack Zipes commented in the *New York Times Book Review* that "Lester's eloquent prose . . . incorporates light, humorous remarks and sayings," and the book as a whole suggests "that we still have a lot to learn from folk heroes, even if they may not have existed."

In *Black Cowboy, Wild Horses,* Lester turns his historian's eye to the story of Bob Lemmons, one of many unheralded slaves who became cowboys and helped build the American West. In doing so he creates a picture book for older readers that is "rich with simile and metaphor," according to *Booklist* contributor Michael Cart. Noting the "spirit of freedom" reflected in Lester's text, a reviewer for *Publishers Weekly* described *Black Cowboy, Wild Horses* as "notable for the light it sheds on a fascinating slice of Americana."

In the picture book *From Slave Ship to Freedom Road* Lester traces the history and effects of slavery in America. Working with illustrator Rod Brown, he sets forth the entire 250 years of black history in America, from the arrival of the first slave ships to Emancipation. "This is a powerful book, and it is an important one," commented Shirley Wilton in *School Library Journal.* A retelling of the Creation story from a black point of view is the subject of *What a Truly Cool World,* and a companion volume titled *Why Heaven Is Far Away* contains an adaptation of two folk tales. Lester focuses on the characteristics all humans share in *Let's Talk about Race.* The author uses the metaphor of a story to describe an individual, then explains a person's race "as just one of many chapters" in that story, according to *School Library Journal* reviewer Mary Hazelton. Encouraging interaction with young listeners by explaining that people are all pretty much the same under their skin, he uses what Hazelton described as a nonthreatening and "engaging tone" that helps children "to appreciate a common spiritual identity." Praising Lester's direct approach and "lighthearted" tone, a *Kirkus* reviewer noted that *Let's Talk about Race* "speaks to a child's concrete understanding of the world." In addition to writing for young children, Lester has produced several novels for adults as well as original fiction for young-adults readers. *When Dad Killed Mom* is the story of two children who must deal with family violence. The book is narrated by twelve-year-old Jeremy and his fourteen-year-old sister, Jenna, each of whom tell the story in alternating chapters. After learn-

Lester joins with artist Rod Brown in producing the 1998 work **From Slave Ship to Freedom Road,** *creating an inspiring and sensitive text to accompany Brown's visual history of the slave experience.*

A brutal murder haunts siblings Jeremy and Jenna, creating problems at school as well as at home, as each searches for answers and deals with the aftermath of the family tragedy in a different way.

ing that their psychologist father has shot and killed their mother, the two try to understand the tragedy, in the process gradually revealing family secrets—such as a dead child from a former marriage, the death of a younger sibling, and a romantic affair—that may have triggered the awful event. While several reviewer noted the book's melodramatic quality, *Horn Book* critic Deborah Z. Porter praised the story as "undeniably gripping" while a *Publishers Weekly* critic described Lester's depiction of the emotional state of Jeremy and Jenna as "subtly and credibly done." Francisca Goldsmith, writing in *School Library Journal,* praised the skills Lester demonstrates in *When Dad Killed Mom:* "excellent research, a willingness to confront and present controversial topics, . . . and insight on how young people's concerns do not necessarily match those of their elders."

Some of Lester's novels for older, more sophisticated readers often draw on literature and history. With *Othello* he adapts William Shakespeare's play, making Iago, Othello, and Emilia African immigrants living in England, resetting the Moor in London and making the issue of race more central to the action. In the process he creates "a wonderful achievement," according to

Margaret Cole in *School Library Journal,* while Nancy Menaldi-Scanlan added in the same periodical that *Othello* serves as a useful touchstone in discussions of "the assimilation of race and of varying approaches" to Shakespeare's dramas.

Returning to biblical themes, Lester tells the story of Moses from a fresh point of view in *Pharaoh's Daughter.* As all Hebrew boys are being killed under the command of Ramses the Great, Moses's older sister, Almah, saves her infant brother. Educated and independent-minded, Almah leads Meryetamun, Ramses' daughter, to rescue Moses in the bulrushes. Meeting Almah, Ramses is struck by the young woman because she resembles his dead wife, and soon the pharaoh proclaims that she is, in fact, his daughter. As Almah takes the place of Meryetamun, Meryetamun becomes drawn to Hebrew society; meanwhile, Almah grows immersed in the Egyptian court and becomes a priestess. Growing to manhood, Moses is torn between his Hebraic roots and the Egyptian lifestyle he enjoys as a grandson of the pharaoh.

Told from the alternating viewpoint of Almah and Moses, *Pharaoh's Daughter* is a "stunning blend of imagination and research," according to *Horn Book* contributor Mary M. Burns, while Barbara Scotto praised the book in *School Library Journal* as a "rich and fascinating retelling" of a much-told tale. *Booklist* reviewer Ilene Cooper noted that Lester "writes with verve and obvious pleasure" and introduces readers to a "strong cast of characters who struggle with life-and-death issues, physical and philosophical."

Lester's interest in rejuvenating and restoring traditional stories and classic themes in ways that will interest newer generations of readers is a result of his strong belief in the ability of books to change young people's lives for the better. "What children need are not role models but heroes and heroines," he told an audience of the New England Library Association in a speech reprinted in *Horn Book.* "A hero is one who is larger than life. Because he or she is superhuman, we are inspired to expand the boundaries of what we had thought was possible. We are inspired to attempt the impossible, and in the attempt, we become more wholly human. . . . The task of the hero and heroine belongs to us all. That task is to live with such exuberance that what it is to be human will be expanded until the asphyxiating concepts of race and gender will be rendered meaningless, and then we will be able to see the rainbow around the shoulders of each and every one of us, the rainbow that has been there all the while."

Biographical and Critical Sources

BOOKS

Children's Literature Review, Gale (Detroit, MI), Volume 2, 1976, Volume 41, 1997.
Lester, Julius, *All Is Well,* Morrow (New York, NY), 1976.

Lester, Julius, *Lovesong: Becoming a Jew,* Holt (New York, NY), 1988.

St. James Guide to Young-Adult Writers, edited by Tom Pendergast and Sara Pendergast, St. James Press (Detroit, MI), 1999.

Twentieth-Century Children's Writers, 3rd edition, edited by Tracy Chevalier, St. James Press (Detroit, MI), 1989, pp. 575-576.

PERIODICALS

Black Issues Book Review, September, 2001, Khafre Abif, review of *The Blues Singers: Ten Who Rocked the World,* p. 76.

Booklist, October 14, 1994, Hazel Rochman, review of *The Man Who Knew Too Much: A Moral Tale from the Baila of Zambia,* p. 4342; November 1, 1995, p. 494; June 1, 1996, p. 1727; January, 1997, p. 768; February 15, 1998, p. 1009; May 1, 1998, Michael Cart, review of *Black Cowboy, Wild Horses,* p. 1522; April 1, 2000, Ilene Cooper, review of *Pharaoh's Daughter,* p. 1474; July, 2000, Hazel Rochman, review of *From Slave Ship to Freedom Road,* p. 2025; February 1, 2001, GraceAnne A. DeCandido, review of *Ackamarackus: Julius Lester's Sumptuously Silly Fantastically Funny Fables,* p. 1056; June 1, 2001, Marta Segal, review of *When Dad Killed Mom,* p. 1862, Stephanie Zvirin, review of *The Blues Singers,* p. 1870; October 1, 2002, John Green, review of *Why Heaven Is Far Away,* p. 345; October 1, 2004, Hazel Rochman, review of *On Writing for Children and Other People,* p. 321; November 15, 2004, Hazel Rochman, review of *The Autobiography of God,* p. 562.

Book World, September 3, 1972, William Loren Katz, review of *Long Journey Home,* p. 9.

Bulletin of the Center for Children's Books, April, 1969, Zena Sutherland, review of *To Be a Slave,* pp. 129-130; May, 1982; February, 1994, Betsy Hearne, review of *The Last Tales of Uncle Remus,* pp. 179-180; October, 1994, Elizabeth Bush, review of *John Henry,* p. 54; February, 1998, p. 212; May, 1998, p. 327.

Horn Book, March-April, 1984, Julius Lester, "The Beechwood Staff," pp. 161-169; September-October, 1988, Mary M. Burns, review of *More Tales of Uncle Remus,* pp. 639-640; January-February, 1996, Julius Lester, "John Henry," pp. 28-31; September-October, 1996, p. 536; July-August, 1998, p. 477; July-August, 2000, Mary M. Burns, review of *Pharaoh's Daughter,* p. 460; May-June, 2001, Deborah Z. Porter, review of *When Dad Killed Mom,* p. 330.

Kirkus Reviews, January 1, 1994, review of *The Last Tales of Uncle Remus,* p. 70; November 15, 1997, p. 1709; May 1, 1998, p. 661; September 15, 2002, review of *Why Heaven Is Far Away,* p. 1393; October 1, 2003, review of *Shining,* p. 1226; October 15, 2004, review of *On Writing for Children and Other People,* p. 1009; December 15, 2004, review of *Let's Talk about Race,* p. 1204.

Magpies, March, 1997, Rayma Turton, review of *Sam and the Tigers: A New Retelling of Little Black Sambo,* p. 27.

New York Review of Books, April 20, 1972, Eric Foner, and Naomi Lewis, review of *Long Journey Home: Stories from Black History,* pp. 41-42.

New York Times Book Review, November 3, 1968, John Howard Griffin, review of *To Be a Slave,* p. 7; November 9, 1969, John A. Williams, review of *Black Folktales,* 10, 12; May 24, 1970, Julius Lester, "Black and White: An Exchange," pp. 1, 34, 36, 38; February 4, 1973, Ethel Richard, review of *The Knee-high Man and Other Tales,* p. 8; May 17, 1987; November 13, 1994, Jack Zipes, "Power Rangers of Yore," p. 30; November 19, 1996, p. 34.

Publishers Weekly, February 23, 1970, Julius Lester, "The Kinds of Books We Give Our Children: Whose Nonsense?," pp. 86-88; February 12, 1988, Barry List, "Julius Lester," pp. 67-68; December 1, 1997, p. 54; April 6, 1998, review of *Black Cowboy, Wild Horses,* p. 77; April 1, 2000, review of *Pharaoh's Daughter,* p. 1474; October 2, 2000, review of *Albidaro and the Mischievous Dream,* p. 81; February 12, 2001, Sally Lodge, "Working at His Creative Peak" (interview), p. 180; May 14, 2001, review of *The Blues Singers,* p. 81, review of *When Dad Killed Mom,* p. 83; December 22, 2003, review of *Shining,* p. 60; October 25, 2004, review of *The Autobiography of God,* p. 28.

Quill & Quire, December, 1989, Susan Perren, review of *How Many Spots Does a Leopard Have? And Other Tales,* p. 24.

School Librarian, May, 1988, Irene Babsky, review of *The Tales of Uncle Remus,* p. 72.

School Library Journal, Mary, 1969, Evelyn Geller, "Julius Lester: Newbery Runner-Up"; April, 1995, Margaret Cole, review of *Othello: A Novel,* p. 154; November, 1997, p. 41; February, 1998, Shirley Wilton, review of *From Slave Ship to Freedom Road,* pp. 119-120; June 1998, p. 113; August, 1998, p. 43; June, 2000, Barbara Scotto, review of *Pharaoh's Daughter,* p. 148; November, 2000, review of *Albidaro and the Mischievous Dream,* p. 126; March, 2001, Wendy Lukehart, review of *Ackamarackus,* p. 214; May, 2001, Francisca Goldsmith, review of *When Dad Killed Mom,* p. 155; June, 2001, Tim Wadham, review of *The Blues Singers,* p. 138; January, 2002, Julius Lester, "The Way We Were," pp. 54-58; October, 2002, Miriam Lang Budin, review of *Why Heaven Is Far Away,* p. 118; November, 2003, Anna DeWind Walls, review of *Shining,* p. 105; February, 2004, Nancy Menaldi-Scanlan, review of *Othello,* p. 83; March, 2004, Casey Rondini, review of *The Last Tales of Uncle Remus,* p. 86; October, 2004, Alison Follos, review of *On Writing for Children and Other People,* p. 202; December, 204, Ginny Gustin, review of *The Blues Singers,* p. 61; January, 2005, Mary Hazelton, review of *Let's Talk about Race,* p. 112.

Voice of Youth Advocates, April, 1998, p. 43; June, 1999, Kathleen Beck, review of *When the Beginning Began,* p. 194.

ONLINE

Scholastic Author Studies Home Page, http://www2.scholastic.com/ (November 27, 2002), "Julius Lester's Biography," and "Julius Lester's Interview Transcript."

University of Massachusetts-Amherst Web site, http://www.umass.edu/ (November 27, 2002), "Julius Lester."*

LONDON, Jonathan (Paul) 1947-
(Jonathan Sherwood)

Personal

Born March 11, 1947, in Brooklyn, NY; son of Harry and Anne (Sittenreich) London; married first wife, JoAnn (divorced May, 1974); married Maureen Weisenberger (a registered nurse), March 21, 1976; children: (second marriage) Aaron, Sean. *Education:* San Jose State University, B.A., 1969, M.A., 1970; Sonoma State University, teaching certificate for grades K-12, 1985. *Hobbies and other interests:* Hiking, backpacking, kayaking, cross-country skiing.

Addresses

Home and office—P.O. Box 537, Graton, CA 95444. *Agent*—Barbara Kouts, P.O. Box 560, Bellport, NY 11713.

Career

Freelance laborer, dancer, child counselor, display installer, 1979—; children's writer, 1989—. American Booksellers Association, panelist for Children's Book Council, 1993.

Member

Amnesty International, Wilderness Society.

Awards, Honors

Ina Coolbrith Circle Award for Poetry, 1979; Parent-Teacher Association (PTA) scholarship, 1984; Teachers' choice selection, International Reading Association (IRA), 1993, for *Thirteen Moons on Turtle's Back;* American Booksellers for Children (ABC) award, 1993, for *The Eyes of Grey Wolf;* Best Book awards, *Child* magazine, for *Like Butter on Pancakes* and *Dream Weaver;* Best books of the year designation, *School Library Journal,* 1995, for *Like Butter on Pancakes* and 1996, for *Red Wolf Country;* Best Book citation, *Time* magazine, 1996, for *Fireflies, Fireflies, Light My Way;* Parent's Choice Gold Award, 1997, for *Ali: Child of the Desert; The Owl Who Became the Moon, Where's Home?,* and *Ice Bear and Little Fox* named Bankstreet College children's literature choices; "Froggy" series named IRA/Children's Book Council children's choices.

Writings

(With Joseph Bruchac) *Thirteen Moons on Turtle's Back: A Native American Year of Moons,* illustrated by Thomas Locker, Philomel Books (New York, NY), 1992.

The Lion Who Had Asthma, illustrated by Nadine Bernard Westcott, Albert Whitman (Morton Grove, IL), 1992.

Froggy Gets Dressed, illustrated by Frank Remkiewicz, Viking (New York, NY), 1992.

Gray Fox, illustrated by Robert Sauber, Viking (New York, NY), 1993.

(With Lanny Pinola) *Fire Race: A Karuk Coyote Tale,* illustrated by Sylvia Lang, Chronicle Books (Boston, MA), 1993.

The Owl Who Became the Moon, illustrated by Ted Rand, Dutton (New York, NY), 1993.

Into This Night We Are Rising, illustrated by G. Brian Karas, Viking (New York, NY), 1993.

Voices of the Wild, illustrated by Wayne McCloughlin, Crown (New York, NY), 1993.

The Eyes of Gray Wolf, illustrated by Jon Van Zyles, Chronicle Books (Boston, MA), 1993.

Hip Cat (picture book), illustrated by Woodleigh Hubbard, Chronicle Books (Boston, MA), 1993.

A Koala for Katie: An Adoption Story, illustrated by Cynthia Jabar, Albert Whitman (Morton Grove, IL), 1993.

Let's Go, Froggy!, illustrated by Frank Remkiewicz, Viking (New York, NY), 1994.

Liplap's Wish, illustrated by Sylvia Long, Chronicle Books (Boston, MA), 1994.

Condor's Egg, illustrated by James Chaffee, Chronicle Books (Boston, MA), 1994.

Honey Paw and Lightfoot, illustrated by Jon Van Zyles, Chronicle Books (Boston, MA), 1994.

Froggy Learns to Swim, illustrated by Frank Remkiewicz, Chronicle Books (Boston, MA), 1995.

The Sugaring-off Party, illustrated by Gilles Pelletier, Dutton (New York, NY), 1995.

Like Butter on Pancakes, illustrated by G. Brian Karas, Viking (New York, NY), 1995.

Master Elk and the Mountain Lion, illustrated by Wayne McCloughlin, Crown (New York, NY), 1995.

Where's Home (young adult novel), Viking (New York, NY), 1995.

Jackrabbit, illustrated by Deborah Kogan Ray, Crown (New York, NY), 1996.

Froggy Goes to School, illustrated by Frank Remkiewicz, Viking (New York, NY), 1996.

The Village Basket Weaver, illustrated by George Crespo, Dutton (New York, NY), 1996.

Red Wolf Country, illustrated by Daniel San Souci, Dutton (New York, NY), 1996.

What Newt Could Do for Turtle, illustrated by Louise Voce, Candlewick Press (Cambridge, MA), 1996.

Fireflies, Fireflies, Light My Way, illustrated by Linda Messier, Viking (New York, NY), 1996.

Let the Lynx Come In, illustrated by Patrick Benson, Candlewick Press (Cambridge, MA), 1996.

I See the Moon and the Moon Sees Me, illustrated by Peter Fiore, Viking (New York, NY), 1996.

Ali, Child of the Desert, illustrated by Ted Lewin, Lothrop, Lee & Shepard Books (New York, NY), 1997.

Old Salt, Young Salt, illustrated by Todd L. W. Doney, Lothrop, Lee & Shepard Books (New York, NY), 1997.

If I Had a Horse, illustrated by Brooke Scudder, Chronicle Books (Boston, MA), 1997.

Phantom of the Prairie: Year of the Black-footed Ferret, illustrated by Barbara Bash, Sierra Club Books for Children (San Francisco, CA), 1997.

Little Red Monkey, illustrated by Frank Remkiewicz, Dutton (New York, NY), 1997.

Dream Weaver, illustrated by Rocco Baviera, Silver Whistle/Harcourt (San Diego, CA), 1997.

Puddles, illustrated by G. Brian Karas, Viking (New York, NY), 1997.

Moshi Moshi, illustrated by Yoshi Miyake, Millbrook Press (New York, NY), 1998.

At the Edge of the Forest, illustrated by Barbara Firth, Candlewick Press (Cambridge, MA), 1998.

Froggy's First Kiss, illustrated by Frank Remkiewicz, Viking (New York, NY), 1998.

Hurricane!, illustrated by Henri Sorensen, Lothrop, Lee & Shepard Books (New York, NY), 1998.

Tell Me a Story (autobiography), photographs by Sherry Shahan, Richard C. Owens (New York, NY), 1998.

The Candystore Man, illustrated by Malcolm Brown, Lothrop, Lee & Shepard Books (New York, NY), 1998.

Ice Bear and Little Fox, illustrated by Daniel San Souci, Dutton (New York, NY), 1998.

Wiggle, Waggle, illustrated by Michael Rex, Silver Whistle/Harcourt (San Diego, CA), 1999.

Froggy Plays Soccer, illustrated by Frank Remkiewicz, Viking (New York, NY), 1999.

Froggy's Halloween, illustrated by Frank Remkiewicz, Viking (New York, NY), 1999.

Baby Whale's Journey, illustrated by Jon Van Zyles, Chronicle Books (Boston, MA), 1999.

Shawn and Keeper and the Birthday Party, illustrated by Renée Williams-Andriani, Dutton (New York, NY), 1999.

What Do You Love?, illustrated by Karen Lee Schmidt, Harcourt Brace (New York, NY), 2000.

Snuggle Wuggle, illustrated by Michael Rex, Silver Whistle (San Diego, CA), 2000.

Who Bop, illustrated by Henry Cole, HarperCollins (New York, NY), 2000.

Shawn and Keeper: Show and Tell, illustrated by Renée Williams-Andriani, Dutton (New York, NY), 2000.

Panther: Shadow of the Swamp, illustrated by Paul Morin, Candlewick Press (Cambridge, MA), 2000.

Mustang Canyon, illustrated by Daniel Van Souci, Candlewick Press (Cambridge, MA), 2000.

Froggy Goes to Bed, illustraaed by Frank Remkiewicz, Viking (New York, NY), 2000.

Froggy Bakes a Cake, illustrated by Frank Remkiewicz, Grosset & Dunlap (New York, NY) 2000.

Froggy's Best Christmas, illustrated by Frank Remkiewicz, Viking (New York, NY), 2000.

Froggy Eats Out, illustrated by Frank Remkiewicz, Viking (New York, NY), 2001.

Froggy Takes a Bath, illustrated by Frank Remkiewicz, Viking (New York, NY), 2001.

(With Aaron London) *White Water,* illustrated by Jill Kastner, Viking (New York, NY), 2001.

Where the Big Fish Are, illustrated by Adam Gustavson, Candlewick Press (Cambridge, MA), 2001.

Sun Dance, Water Dance, illustrated by Greg Couch, Dutton (New York, NY), 2001.

Park Beat: Rhymin' Through the Seasons, illustrated by Woodleigh Marx Hubbard, HarperCollins (New York, NY), 2001.

Gone Again Ptarmigan, illustrated by Jon Van Zyle, National Geographic Society (Washington, DC), 2001.

Crocodile: Disappearing Dragon, illustrated by Paul Morin, Candlewick Press (Cambridge, MA), 2001.

Crunch Munch, illustrated by Michael Rex, Red Wagon Books (New York, NY), 2001.

Count the Ways, Little Brown Bear, illustrated by Margie Moore, Dutton (New York, NY), 2002.

Zack at School, illustrated by Jack Medoff, Scholastic (New York, NY), 2002.

What the Animals Were Waiting For, illustrated by Paul Morin, Scholastic (New York, NY), 2002.

Loon Lake, illustrated by Susan Ford, Chronicle Books (San Francisco, CA), 2002.

Froggy Plays in the Band, illustrated by Frank Remkiewicz, Viking (New York, NY), 2002.

Froggy Goes to the Doctor, illustrated by Frank Remkiewicz, Viking (New York, NY), 2002.

When the Fireflies Come, illustrated by Terry Widener, Dutton (New York, NY), 2003.

Giving Thanks, illustrated by Gregory Manchess, Candlewick Press (Cambridge, MA), 2003.

Froggy's Baby Sister, illustrated by Frank Remkiewicz, Viking (New York, NY), 2003.

"Eat!" Cried Little Pig, illustrated by Delphine Durand, Dutton (New York, NY), 2003.

Zack at the Dentist, illustrated by Jack Medoff, Scholastic (New York, NY), 2004.

Froggy's Day with Dad, illustrated by Frank Remkiewicz, Viking (New York, NY), 2004.

Sled Dogs Run, illustrated by Jon Van Zyle, Walker (New York, NY), 2005.

Froggy's Sleepover, illustrasted by Frank Remkiewicz, Viking (New York, NY), 2005.

Do Your ABC's, Little Brown Bear, illustrated by Margie Moore, Dutton (New York, NY), 2005.

A Truck Goes Rattley Bumpa, illustrated by Denis Roche, Holt (New York, NY), 2005.

Contributor of poems and short stories to periodicals, including *Cricket, Us Kids, Child Life,* and *Short Story International.* Also author of *In a Season of Birds: Poems for Maureen,* sometimes under the pseudonym Jonathan Sherwood.

London's work has been translated into Spanish, German, Greek, Dutch, Danish, French, Japanese, Chinese, and Korean.

Adaptations

Froggy Gets Dressed and *Honey Paw and Lightfoot* were featured on the PBS television program *Storytime; Hip Cat* and *Thirteen Moons on Turtle's Back* were featured on *Reading Rainbow; What Newt Could Do for Turtle* was adapted for television and broadcast in Great British and Germany.

Sidelights

Jonathan London is a poet-turned-children's book writer whose picture books reproduce the natural world for young readers. In books such as *Gray Fox, The Eyes of Grey Wolf, Condor's Egg, Master Elk and the Mountain*

Lion, Crocodile: Disappearing Dragon, and many others, London tells fictionalized but unsentimental stories of animals in their natural habitats, tales of survival and the interconnection of all nature. In other picture books, especially the "Froggy" series, London's animals take on anthropomorphic and humorous traits. Humans figure in London's storybooks as well, with warm family stories such as *The Sugaring-off Party,* tales of adventure such as *Old Salt, Young Salt* and *Hurricane!,* and rhyming, playful, everyday enjoyments such as *Like Butter on Pancakes, Puddles,* and *I See the Moon and the Moon Sees Me.* London's love of jazzy rhyming schemes and his sense of humor have also led to books that feature the cadences of hip-hop and jazz, such as *Hip Cat* and *The Candystore Man.* Since embarking on his career as a children's writer in 1989, London has proven himself to be a prolific author, turning out several titles each year. In his first decade as a published writer he penned roughly fifty picture books as well as a juvenile novel, *Where's Home?,* and he has shown no signs of slowing. Critics have often praised his poet's eye and ear, lauding London's "spare, lyrical text," as Marianne Saccardi did in a *School Library Journal* review of *The Owl Who Became the Moon.* London's infectious humor has also been noted by many reviewers, particularly in his "Froggy" books, all illustrated by Frank Remkiewicz. The reader "will surely laugh out loud," commented a critic for *Publishers Weekly* in a review of *Froggy Gets Dressed.* A versatile and engaging writer for children, London blends bouncy, alliterative verse rhythms and clear, understated prose to create books for young children that make a difference.

Born in Brooklyn, New York, in 1947, London graduated from California's San Jose State University with an M.A. in 1970. His studies were in the social sciences, but it was poetry that captured his imagination. After graduation, London spent several years traveling around the world, encountering other cultures and ways of living. He began writing poetry, meanwhile earning a living in a variety of ways, from a day laborer to dancer and child counselor. With the birth of two sons after his second marriage, London returned to college to earn a teaching certificate, but soon he felt the draw of another creative impulse. Telling stories to his own young sons, London began to wonder if writing children's books might not be a viable option and a way to put his poetic voice to use.

The first children's book London wrote, *The Owl Who Became the Moon,* was actually his fourth book to be published, and was inspired by a bedtime fantasy he told his son Sean at age two. This tale about a young boy riding on a train at night who watches and listens to the animals in their wilderness homes was told in verse and announced an abiding interest in nature that many of London's books portray in one way or another. "With spare elegance, London celebrates both the beauty of nighttime—and the power of the train," noted a reviewer for *Publishers Weekly.*

The "Froggy" stories had their inspiration in the demand of London's other son, Aaron, for a tale. "The image of a frog dressing in winter clothes so he can play in the snow struck my funny bone," the author once told *Something about the Author* (*SATA*), "and my kids' funny bones, too!" In *Froggy Gets Dressed,* Froggy wakes up one morning to discover a snow-filled world. Jumping out of bed to go frolic, he is summoned back by his mother to put on some warm clothes. London uses sound effects such as "zoop," "zup," and "zip" for the action of putting on various articles of clothing. Ultimately the poor frog is embarrassed in front of his playmates when his mother yells to tell him he has forgotten his underwear. A reviewer for the *Horn Book Guide* noted that the text "has many wonderful sound effects" as well as "plenty of repetition to enhance the silliness of the story."

London serves up more Froggy action in his further adventures of the rambunctious amphibian. Froggy and his father go for a bike trip in *Let's Go, Froggy!,* in which "humor, delightful sound effects, and bright, enthusiastic illustrations make the book appealing," according to a *Horn Book* contributor. The frog takes to water in *Froggy Learns to Swim* and overcomes nervousness to finally enjoy his first day of school in *Froggy Goes to School. Booklist*'s Hazel Rochman concluded that "children will laugh at [Froggy's] innocence

In the rollicking text of his 2001 picture book Crunch Munch *Jonathan London describes the many different ways animals from cats to bird eat their evening meal. (Illustration by Michael Rex.)*

Children's universal fear of the family physician is addressed in London's comical **Froggy Goes to the Doctor,** *although with London's young amphibian as a patient Dr. Mugwort may have met his match. (Illustration by Frank Remkiewicz.)*

and sympathize with his jitters," in this schooldays tale. Froggy becomes the Frog Prince in *Froggy's Halloween,* only to be chased by Princess Frogolina, who wants to plant a kiss on his cheek. Then, in *Froggy's First Kiss,* Valentine's Day provides Froggy and Frogolina the perfect venue for amphibious amours. Froggy has some trouble preparing for his doctor's visit in *Froggy Goes to the Doctor;* he forgets to put on underwear and to brush his teeth—much to the doctor's displeasure when she looks in his mouth and gets a whiff of his breath. And that's not the end of poor Dr. Mugwort's torments with Froggy: he also shouts into her stethoscope and kicks her in the face when she tests his reflexes. London has even had his frog take to the football field in *Froggy Plays Soccer,* another hilarious romp with Froggy and friends.

More animals with seeming human traits appear in *Liplap's Wish, What Newt Could Do for Turtle, Hip Cat,* and *Count the Ways, Little Brown Bear.* The first title is a "wonderful, sensitive story about children's

feelings of sadness and loss after the death of a loved one," according to Martha Gordon in *School Library Journal.* London employs a young rabbit named Liplap who has lost his grandmother and finds little solace in busying himself in building a snowman. "This sympathetic book will help comfort generations of grieving children," Gordon concluded. Friendship and sharing are explored in *What Newt Could Do for Turtle,* a "delightful" story, according to a critic in *Kirkus Reviews.* A cat of very different stripes is presented in the bebopping *Hip Cat,* about the ultimately cool feline Oobie-do John who goes to San Francisco to become a famous sax-playing jazzcat. "Playful and optimistic, this story of dreams—and persistence rewarded—is the cool cat's meow," according to a *Publishers Weekly* reviewer.

Count the Ways, Little Brown Bear features a mama and baby bear spending a lazy day together, playing games, reading books, and picking apples. Through it all, the baby bear demands to know how much his mother loves him. She replies with reference to things around them, such as "I love you more than you love two green apples plus two red apples." However, until the end of the book, when she declares that she loves him "more than all the stars in the sky," the little brown bear always declares that it is "not enough." The "text is sweet and succinct," commented a *Publishers Weekly* contributor, but it also helps young children to learn about counting, addition, and subtraction.

Animals in their natural habitats are depicted in a bevy of books by London detailing life in the wild. *Booklist*'s Emily Melton, in a review of *Gray Fox*, noted that the "beauty and the cruelty of nature, the dangers posed to wild animals by humans, the invincibility of the animal spirit, and the reassuring cycle of life and death are all part of this book about Gray Fox." A similar title, *The Eyes of Gray Wolf*, brought praise from the reviewer for *Publishers Weekly* who noted that "words pour out, as fierce as the arctic cold or as luminous as the yellow moon" in this tale of the leader of a wolf pack who has lost his mate.

In *Voices of the Wild*, a dozen different animals describe—in first person—their wariness of a lone kayaker breaching their northern habitat. *Kirkus Reviews* called this a "quietly lyrical book that effectively evokes the experience of observing these wilderness creatures with respect, and without disturbing them." In *Condor's Egg*, London "gives eloquent testament to the first pair of California condors to return to the wild since 1987," according to *Publishers Weekly*. Susan Dove Lempke, reviewing *Condor's Egg* in *Bulletin of the Center for Children's Books*, observed that London "does not romanticize the birds, which are after all vultures, but they are individuated and majestic-looking in flight. . . . The text is spare but poetically evokes the lives of the condors in the wild."

London looks at the life cycle of an elk in *Master Elk and the Mountain Lion*, in which a young calf grows to become a strong bull and defeats the leader or master of the herd, then defends the herd against an old enemy, the mountain lion. Janice Del Negro noted in a *Booklist* review that the elk's life was "effectively narrated and evocatively described." The life of a grizzly bear is narrated in *Honey Paw and Lightfoot*, a "combination of fun and learning" that makes an "eloquent" if "implicit plea for wilderness preservation," according to *Booklist*'s Mary Harris Veeder. Another such plea for preservation comes in *Red Wolf Country*, a "spare and lyrical story" according to Susan S. Verner in *Bulletin of the Center for Children's Books*, which takes the reader through a year in the life of a pair of this endangered species, native to the southeastern United States. *Mustang Canyon* follows a newborn mustang colt, whom London calls "Little Pinto," as he and his herd of wild horses attempt to survive such challenges as strange stallions, low-flying planes, and river rapids. "The words are spare, immediate, and informative," Gillian Engberg wrote in *Booklist*, and the book is "a must for cowboy wannabes." Plus, commented a *Kirkus Reviews* contributor, "Young readers should not miss the sense of community and family these 'wild' horses must have to survive in their harsh but beautiful land."

A change of pace for London is the 1995 juvenile novel *Where's Home*, the story of a Detroit teenager and his father who go to San Francisco and there become homeless. Abandoned by a mentally ill mother, young Aaron is left to sort things out when his father takes to the bottle and loses his job. The pair hitchhike their way west only to be arrested on charges of vagrancy in San Francisco. Out of jail and in a shelter, Aaron and his father begin to learn lessons from the other people gathered there. Reviewing the novel in *School Library*

With sun-drenched watercolors by illustrator Daniel San Souci, London's **Mustang Canyon** *finds three-week-old Little Pinto forced to travel with his mustang herd in search of much-needed water.*

Journal, Cindy Darling Codell called the work "lyrical, yet also spare," and noted that it "threads together incidents of love and loss, fire and friendship, and symbolism."

Turning his attention and his lyrical voice to human subjects, London has created a batch of heartwarming and humorous tales for young children that speak of everything from family relations to ethnic differences in tales that teach without being didactic. In *The Sugaring-off Party,* London presents nothing less than the history of a French-Canadian family as condensed in the vital moment of sugaring-off in the maple syrup process. "London's evocative text perfectly re-creates the thrill and excitement of this coming-of-spring ritual," observed Ann W. Moore in *School Library Journal. I See the Moon and the Moon Sees Me* is a "charmingly adapted nursery favorite," according to *Kirkus Reviews,* while *Like Butter on Pancakes* and *Puddles* both celebrate the simple things in life for a little boy, using onomatopoeic phrasing to tickle little funny bones. "London catalogues a glorious array of the delights of muddy weather," commented *School Library Journal*'s Marcia Hupp in reviewing *Puddles.* More singing rhymes fill the pages of *The Candystore Man,* a be-bop picture book reminiscent of London's *Hip Cat.* In this tale, the man behind the soda fountain serves up "ice cream and candy with flair," according to Adele Greenlee in *School Library Journal.*

Narrative tales are recounted in such books as *Ali, Child of the Desert, Hurricane!, At the Edge of the Forest, Moshi Moshi, What the Animals Were Waiting For,* and *The Waterfall.* Saharan cultures are examined in the first title, in which young Ali experiences a rite of passage when a sandstorm separates him from his father on their way to a market. "The theme of a young boy proving himself to his father and achieving manhood is a universal one," noted Janice Del Negro in the *Bulletin of the Center for Children's Books,* "and this strongly plotted title communicates that theme quite successfully." Another storm figures in *Hurricane!,* which recounts an incident from the author's childhood, while *At the Edge of the Forest* tells the story of a sheep farmer's son and a battle with coyotes. "London knows just how to kindle the audience's concern and stoke his drama," commented a reviewer for *Publishers Weekly* on this title. "Author and artist soften a harsh reality without blunting it."

London returns to Africa for *What the Animals Were Waiting For.* A Masai boy named Tepi is waiting, too, although he does not know for what. As he herds his family's livestock, he watches the local wildlife, including giraffes, elephants, and zebras. They all seem to be waiting for something, but every time he asks his grandmother what that something might be, she tells him that he will see eventually. Then a storm comes, ending the dry season—also called the Months of Hunger—and Tepi sees, as the animals all stampede off into the rain and his neighbors go out and dance in celebration as

well. This "poetic telling of how nature's cycle affects animals and humans is well structured and emotionally resonant," Margaret Bush wrote in *School Library Journal. Booklist*'s Carolyn Phelan also commented on London's poetic voice: "Rhythmic with repeated phrases and studded with sensory details, London's telling is simple yet vivid," she declared.

In *Moshi Moshi,* an "exuberant picture book," according to Grace Anne A. DeCandido in *Booklist,* an American boy reluctantly joins his older brother on a visit to Japan. By the end of the summer, reluctance has changed to enthusiasm. Brothers again figure in *The Waterfall,* when siblings and their parents set off on a camping trip up a creek. Eventually they navigate a tricky bit of terrain up the side of a steep waterfall. A contributor to *Kirkus Reviews* called this book a "poetic appreciation of the beauty of nature and respect for its awesome forces."

Sun Dance Water Dance and *When the Fireflies Come* particularly showcase London's background as a poet. Both books celebrate old-fashioned children's summers, the former with a poem about a trip to go swimming in a river on a hot summer day, the latter with a prose tale about ice cream, baseball, and of course fireflies. But even *When the Fireflies Come* has more than a hint of poetry in it. A *Kirkus Reviews* contributor described London's prose in that book as "image-rich [and] impressionistic," while a *Publishers Weekly* critic noted that it "appeals to all five senses."

In all of his books, London blends his poetic voice with concerns about nature and how we are connected with it. In his career this children's author has created a body of work that entertains as it teaches. But for London, such an achievement is as natural as a walk in the woods. As he once explained to *SATA:* "This act of writing, for me, is a part of my celebration of life, a way to give back a little for all that I have been given."

Biographical and Critical Sources

BOOKS

London, Jonathan, *Count the Ways, Little Brown Bear,* Dutton (New York, NY), 2002.
London, Jonathan, *Froggy Gets Dressed,* Viking (New York, NY), 1992.
London, Jonathan, *Tell Me a Story* (autobiography), photographs by Sherry Shahan, Richard C. Owens (New York, NY), 1998.

PERIODICALS

Booklist, March 1, 1992, Karen Hutt, review of *Thirteen Moons on Turtle's Back: A Native American Year of Moons,* p. 1281; January 15, 1993, Kay Weisman, review of *The Owl Who Became the Moon,* p. 922, Emily Melton, review of *Gray Fox,* p. 922; January 15, 1993, Emily Melton, review of *Gray Fox,* p. 922; November 1, 1993, Janice Del Negro, review of *Voices of the Wild,* p. 523; March 15, 1995, Mary Harris Veeder, review of *Honey Paw and Lightfoot,* p. 1335; April 1, 1995, Janice Del Negro, review of *Like Butter on Pancakes,* p. 1428; December 15, 1995, Janice Del Negro, review of *Master Elk and the Mountain Lion,* p. 709; January 1, 1996, Hazel Rochman, review of *Red Wolf Country,* p. 847; June 1, 1996, Hazel Rochman, review of *Froggy Goes to School,* p. 1735; July, 1996, Kay Weisman, review of *Jackrabbit,* p. 1830; November 1, 1998, GraceAnne A. DeCandido, review of *Moshi Moshi;* April 15, 2000, Stephanie Zvirin, review of *Shawn and Keeper Show-and-Tell,* p. 1555; January 1, 2001, Ellen Mandel, review of *Panther: Shadow of the Swamp,* p. 963, Carolyn Phelan, review of *Gone Again Ptarmigan,* p. 963; June 1, 2001, Gillian Engberg, reviews of *White Water* and *Froggy Eats Out,* p. 1892; December 1, 2001, Carolyn Phelan, review of *Crocodile: Disappearing Dragon,* p. 646; May 15, 2002, Carolyn Phelan, review of *What the Animals Were Waiting For,* p. 1602; August 1, 2002, review of *Mustang Canyon,* p. 1136; December 1, 2002, Gillian Engberg, review of *Mustang Canyon,* p. 675; January 1, 2003, Catherine Andronik, review of *Froggy Goes to the Doctor,* p. 908.

Bulletin of the Center for Children's Books, February, 1993, review of *The Owl Who Became the Moon,* p. 183; October, 1994, Susan Dove Lempke, review of *Condor's Egg,* p. 55; June, 1996, Susan S. Verner, review of *Red Wolf Country,* p. 344; February, 1997, review of *What Newt Could Do for Turtle,* p. 213; June, 1997, Janice Del Negro, review of *Ali, Child of the Desert,* p. 365.

Five Owls, January-February, 1993, review of *Froggy Gets Dressed,* p. 59; September-October, 1994, review of *Liplap's Wish,* p. 10.

Horn Book, spring, 1993, review of *Froggy Gets Dressed,* p. 37; fall, 1994, review of *Let's Go, Froggy!,* p. 280.

Kirkus Reviews, January 15, 1992; April 1, 1993, p. 460; October 1, 1993, review of *Voices of the Wild,* p. 1276; December 1, 1995, review of *I See the Moon and the Moon Sees Me,* p. 1704; June 15, 1995, pp. 858-59; November 15, 1996, review of *What Newt Could Do for Turtle,* p. 1671; April 15, 1997, p. 643; April 1, 1998, p. 497; February 1, 1999, review of *The Waterfall;* November 15, 2001, review of *Count the Ways, Little Brown Bear,* p. 1613; August 1, 2002, review of *Froggy Goes to the Doctor,* p. 1135; May 1, 2003, review of *When the Fireflies Come,* p. 679.

Publishers Weekly, August 3, 1992, review of *Froggy Gets Dressed,* p. 70; December 28, 1992, review of *The Owl Who Became the Moon;* August 16, 1993, review of *The Eyes of Gray Wolf,* p. 102; October 3, 1994, review of *Condor's Egg,* p. 68; August 16, 1993, review of *Hip Cat,* p. 102; July 20, 1998, review of *The Candystore Man,* p. 219; August 17, 1998, review of *At the Edge of the Forest,* p. 72; November 19, 2001, review of *Count the Ways, Little Brown Bear,* p. 66; June 11, 2001, reviews of *Sun Dance Water Dance*

and *White Water,* p. 85; June 24, 2002, review of *Froggy Goes to the Doctor,* p. 59; April 28, 2003, review of *When the Fireflies Come,* p. 69; November 10, 2003, review of *"Eat!" Cried Little Pig,* p. 60; January 5, 2004, review of *Giving Thanks,* p. 60.

Quill and Quire, March, 1995, review of *The Sugaring-off Party,* p. 78; June, 1998, review of *Dream Weaver,* p. 58.

School Library Journal, February, 1993, Marianne Saccardi, review of *The Owl Who Became the Moon,* p. 76; August, 1993, Carolyn Polese, review of *Fire Race: A Karuk Coyote Tale,* p. 159; November, 1994, Martha Gordon, review of *Liplap's Wish,* p. 84; January, 1995, Ann W. Moore, review of *The Sugaring-off Party,* p. 89; August, 1995, Cindy Darling Codell, review of *Where's Home,* pp. 154-155; March, 1996, Joy Fleishhacker, review of *Red Wolf Country,* p. 178; June, 1996, Judith Constantinides, review of *Fireflies, Fireflies Light My Way,* p. 104; May, 1997, Marcia Hupp, review of *Puddles,* p. 104; July, 1998, Margaret Bush, review of *Dream Weaver,* pp. 78-79; October, 1998, Adele Greenlee, review of *The Candystore Man,* p. 107; June, 1999, Gale W. Sherman, review of *Wiggle, Waggle,* p. 100; May, 2000, Susan M. Moore, review of *Snuggle Wuggle,* p. 148; June, 2000, Elizabeth O'Brien, review of *Froggy Goes to Bed,* p. 119; September, 2000, Maura Bresnahan, review of *Shawn and Keeper Show-and-Tell,* p. 204; October, 2000, review of *Froggy's Best Christmas,* p. 61; December, 2000, Susan Hepler, review of *What Do You Love?,* p. 114; January, 2001, Arwen Marshall, review of *Panther,* p. 119; April, 2001, Meghan R. Malone, review of *Crunch Munch,* p. 117; May, 2001, Robin L. Gibson, review of *Park Beat: Rhymin' through the Seasons,* and Sue Sherif, review of *Gone Again Ptarmigan,* p. 128; June, 2001, Diane Olivo-Posner, review of *White Water,* p. 125; July, 2001, Lisa Dennis, review of *Sun Dance Water Dance,* p. 85; November, 2001, Cathie E. Bashaw, review of *Crocodile,* p. 129; April, 2002, Gay Lynn Van Vleck, review of *Count the Ways, Little Brown Blair,* p. 116; May, 2002, Margaret Bush, review of *What the Animals Were Waiting For,* p. 121; September, 2002, Shawn Brommer, review of *Loon Lake,* pp. 199-200; August, 2003, Ruth Semrau, review of *Mustang Canyon,* p. 138; December, 2003, Linda M. Kenton, review of *"Eat!" Cried Little Pig,* p. 119, Andrea Tarr, review of *Froggy's Baby Sister,* p. 119; January, 2004, Maryann H. Owen, review of *Giving Thanks,* p. 100; June, 2004, Holly T. Sneeringer, review of *Froggy's Day with Dad,* p. 114.

* * *

LOTTRIDGE, Celia Barker 1936-

Personal

Born April 1, 1936, in Iowa City, IA; daughter of a professor and a teacher; married a serviceman (divorced); children: one son. *Education:* Stanford University, B.A. (modern European history), 1957; Columbia University, M.L.S., 1959; University of Toronto, B.Ed, 1975.

Addresses

Home—42 Vermont Ave., Toronto, Ontario M6G 1X9, Canada. *E-mail*—celialottridge@yahoo.com.

Career

Writer and storyteller. Children's librarian in San Diego, CA; lower-school librarian at Dalton School, New York, NY; librarian in Rhode Island, 1965-72; Toronto School Board, teacher-librarian. Children's Book Store, Toronto, book buyer, 1977-90. Regina Public Library, Regina, Saskatchewan, Canada, writer-in-residence, 1991; Parent-Child Mother Goose program, director. Member of founding board, Storyteller's School of Toronto.

Member

Writers Union, Canadian Children's Book Centre, Canadian Society of Children's Authors, Illustrators, and Performers, Storytellers of Canada, Storytellers School of Toronto.

Awards, Honors

Mr. Christie Award in English Illustration, 1989, and second runner-up, Amelia Frances Howard-Gibbon award, and Elizabeth Mrazik-Cleaver award, both 1990, all for *The Name of the Tree;* Book of the Year, Canadian Library Association, and Honor Book for Canada designation, International Board on Books for Youth, and Geoffrey Bilson Award, all 1993, all for *Ticket to Curlew;* IODE Toronto Award, 1993, for *Ten Small Tales;* Violet Downey Award, 1997, for *Wings to Fly;* Ruth Schwartz Award, 1998, for *Music for the Tsar of the Sea;* Mr. Christie Award, 2002, for *The Little Rooster and the Diamond Button.*

Writings

FOR CHILDREN

Gerasim and the Lion, illustrated by Joanne Page, Bright Star Bookstores (Erin, Ontario, Canada), 1979.

(With Ariadna Ochrymovych) *The Juggler,* North Winds Press (Richmond Hill, Ontario, Canada), 1985.

(With Susan Horner) *Prairie Dogs,* Grolier (Toronto, Ontario, Canada), 1985, bound with *Bighorn Sheep,* by Bill Ivy, 1985, reprinted, Grolier (Danbury, CT), 1999.

(With Susan Horner) *Mice,* Grolier (Toronto, Ontario, Canada), 1986.

One Watermelon Seed (picture book), illustrated by Karen Patkau, Stoddart (Toronto, Ontario, Canada), 1986.

(Reteller) *The Name of the Tree: A Bantu Tale,* illustrated by Ian Wallace, Groundwood Books (Toronto, Ontario, Canada), 1989, Margaret K. McElderry Books (New York, NY), 1990.

(Reteller) *Ten Small Tales,* illustrated by Joanne Fitzgerald, Margaret K. McElderry Books (New York, NY), 1990, reprinted, Groundwood Books (Toronto, Ontario, Canada), 2005.

(Editor) *The American Children's Treasury,* Key Porter (Toronto, Ontario, Canada), 1991.

Ticket to Curlew (novel), illustrated by Wendy Wolsak-Frith, Groundwood Books (Toronto, Ontario, Canada), 1992, published as *Ticket to Canada,* Silver Burdett, 1996.

Something Might Be Hiding (picture book), illustrated by Paul Zwolak, Groundwood Books (Toronto, Ontario, Canada), 1994.

(Reteller) *Music for the Tsar of the Sea: A Russian Wonder Tale,* illustrated by Harvey Chan, Groundwood Books (Toronto, Ontario, Canada), 1995, Groundwood Books (Buffalo, NY), 1998.

The Wind Wagon (novel), illustrated by Daniel Clifford, Silver Burdett Press, 1995.

(Compiler) *Letters to the Wind: Classic Stories and Poems for Children,* Key Porter (Toronto, Ontario, Canada), 1995, published as *American Stories and Poems for Children,* 2001.

Wings to Fly (novel), illustrations by Mary Jane Gerber, Groundwood Books (Toronto, Ontario, Canada), 1997.

(Adaptor) Sandra Carpenter-Davis, compiler, *Bounce Me, Tickle Me, Hug Me: Lap Rhymes and Play Rhymes from around the World,* Parent-Child Mother Goose Program (Toronto, Ontario, Canada), 1997.

(Reteller) *The Little Rooster and the Diamond Button: A Hungarian Folktale,* illustrated by Joanne Fitzgerald, Groundwood Books (Toronto, Ontario, Canada), 2001.

Berta, a Remarkable Dog (novel), illustrated by Elsa Myotte, Groundwood Books (Toronto, Ontario, Canada), 2002.

(Reteller) *Stories from the Life of Jesus: Stories from the Bible,* illustrated by Linda Wolfsgruber, Groundwood Books (Toronto, Ontario, Canada), 2004.

(Reteller) *Stories from Adam to Ezekiel; Retold from the Bible,* illustrated by Gary Clement, Groundwood Books (Toronto, Ontario, Canada), 2004.

Several of Lottridge's books have been translated into French and published in braille editions.

OTHER

(Compiler with Alison Dickie) *Mythic Voices: Reflections in Mythology* (textbook with teacher's guide), Nelson Canada (Scarborough, Ontario, Canada), 1990.

(With Gail de Vos and Merle Harris) *Telling Tales: Storytelling in the Family,* second, expanded edition, University of Alberta Press (Edmonton, Alberta, Canada), 2003.

Adaptations

The Juggler was adapted as a sound recording, CNIB (Toronto, Ontario, Canada), 1987; *Mythic Voices* was adapted as a sound recording, Alberta Education (Edmonton, Alberta, Canada), 1992; *Ticket to Curlew* was adapted as a sound recording, Library Services Branch of British Columbia (Vancouver, British Columbia, Canada), 1994.

Sidelights

Celia Barker Lottridge writes novels that focus on life in her adopted country of Canada, where she settled permanently in the mid-1970s. A former librarian, she has worked as a storyteller for several years, and several of her books, such as *The Little Rooster and the Diamond Button: A Hungarian Folktale* and *The Name of the Tree: A Bantu Tale*, present her favorite folk stories. Lottridge has created both picture books and longer, novel-length works geared for readers in the early elementary grades, and has also collected shorter stories in the anthologies *The American Children's Treasury* and *Letters to the Wind*. For older readers, she has also written longer novels, including *Ticket to Curlew* and *Wings to Fly*, which recount life in rural Canada at the turn of the twentieth century. "Lottridge is particularly adept at evoking time and place," noted Jennifer Sullivan in *Canadian Review of Materials*, praising *Wings to Fly* for featuring "independent and resourceful women" as protagonists.

Born in Iowa City in 1936, Lottridge and her family moved frequently due to her father's transient career as a college professor, and by age twelve she could count seven towns in the United States that she had, at one time or another, called home. She credits these moves with broadening her perspective on people and places, as well as with transforming her into "an avid reader," as she recalled to Dave Jenkinson in *Canadian Review of Materials*. "I gave up really working at making friends when I was going on ten, but books were always there, so reading, and the people in books, were very important to me."

After graduating from high school, Lottridge attended Stanford University and graduated with a degree in modern European history in 1957. Two years later, she earned her master of library science degree at Columbia University. Married to a man in the U.S. Navy, she soon found herself moving again, this time to San Diego, where she got a job as a children's librarian before transferring to a library position in a private school in New York City when her husband's career brought the couple back to the East Coast. When Lottridge and her husband divorced in the early 1970s, she decided to move with her six-year-old son to Toronto, where her brother lived, and she has remained there ever since.

Becoming an accredited teacher-librarian, Lottridge worked for the Toronto School Board for a year, then found a job at a local bookstore, where she was quickly promoted to book buyer. After a few years Lottridge began to combine her work at the store with storytelling

In **Ten Small Tales: Stories from around the World** *Celia Barker Lottridge gathers magical stories that draw on many cultures, such as the tale of a monkey who cannot get too many bananas. (Illustration by Joanne Fitzgerald.)*

Lottridge's retelling of the Hungarian tale **The Little Rooster and the Diamond Button** *finds a farmyard animal fighting the will of a king to keep his sparkly treasure. (Illustration by Joanne Fitzgerald.)*

and writing, and her first published work, *Gerasim and the Lion,* was released in 1979. She helped to form the Storyteller's School of Toronto to promote storytelling in the city's schools, and in the 1980s she began to take writing seriously as a way to supplement her income as a single parent. In addition to producing the nature books *Mice* and *Prairie Dogs,* she retold foreign-language folk tales for English-speaking readers, publishing several works under a pseudonym.

The Name of the Tree was the first book where, as the author later recalled to Jenkinson, "I just said, 'I'll write this book myself.'" The story, based on a tale Lottridge recalled from her own childhood, finds a lack of rain forcing Africa's animals to search for a new source of water. Full of much-needed liquid, the fruit of a tall tree might suffice, but it can only be had if the animals formally request the tree to release its fruit. To properly address the tree, the animals must learn the tree's name. *Quill & Quire* contributor Michele Landsberg had lavish praise for *The Name of the Tree,* declaring that "Lottridge's subtlety and skill as a storyteller reverberate on every page," making the book "a joy to read aloud." Landsberg further commended Lottridge's storytelling skills, citing the tale's "delectable rhythm, just the right amount of repetition, gentle suspense, and deftly underplayed humor."

Other books by Lottridge that have their basis in spoken stories are *Something Must Be Hiding,* about moving to a new town and coping with feelings of not fitting in; *Music for the Tsar of the Sea,* a tale of a Russian minstrel whose music brings both bounty and problems when it pleases a powerful sea spirit; and *Ten Small Tales,* a collection of folk that proved to be favorites at Lottridge's own storytelling programs. "I'm mainly interested in putting into print stories that aren't already easily available and usually ones that I've told a lot so that I have a real feeling for the story," the author explained to Jenkinson. *Ten Small Tales* includes several lesser-known folk tales—such as a Malaysian tiger story and a Khanti fairy tale of a mouse sailing in a walnut shell—which *Horn Book* critic Sarah Ellis noted would be "welcome in a world that contains too many lush editions of 'Goldilocks.'" Reviewing *Ten Small Tales* Julie Corsaro declared in *Booklist* that "Lottridge knows what little ones like in their folklore: simple and direct storylines, rhythmic rhyme and repetition . . . plenty of action, and a reassuring ending."

Several of Lottridge's retellings, as well as original stories such as *Berta, a Remarkable Dog,* feature animal characters. In *The Little Rooster and the Diamond Button,* folk story and farmyard collide when a rooster living with a poor old woman scratches around the dusty farmyard and discovers a sparkling diamond button instead of the typical bug, worm, or seed. When the button is snatched from the beak of the rooster by a greedy sultan who is passing by on his way to his palace, the rooster pursues the thief, crowing loudly. When the sultan attempts to drown the noisy bird, the rooster drinks up all the water; when the sultan tries roasting, the bird releases the water and puts out the cooking fire. Other attempts by the sultan at ridding himself of the button's rightful owner also fail in a story that has parallels in tales from many lands, as Lottridge notes in a special note to readers of her book. Dubbing *The Little Rooster and the Diamond Button* "a perfect read-aloud," *Resource Links* contributor Linda Ludke cited the author's "wonderfully constructed text" and "lyrical refrains," while Be Astengo commented in *School Library Journal* that "young audiences will clamor for this tale over and over again." *Berta, a Remarkable Dog,* Lottridge's beginning chapter book, focuses on a farm-dwelling Dachshund who mothers chicks, piglets, and even a young lamb. The work was praised by *Resource Links* reviewer Veronica Allen for its "lively style" and "soothing quality," while in *Booklist* Carolyn Phelan cited the book's "appealing" and detailed story of life on a farm.

In 1991, while working as writer-in-residence at the public library in Regina, Saskatchewan, Lottridge began what has become one of her most well-known books, the award-winning novel, *Ticket to Curlew.* The book, which was published in the United States as *Ticket to Canada,* tells the story of Sam Ferrier, a pre-teen growing up in the Alberta prairie around the turn of the twentieth century. Based on Lottridge's father's memories of his years spent on an Alberta farm, the novel brings to life an era where things moved at a much slower pace. "For children," Lottridge noted in her interview, "I think that what brings historical fiction alive is a character in the book they feel akin to or have empathy with. Then they can experience the historical part of it. They're not just reading it as: 'Well this happened here back then.'"

A sequel to *Ticket to Curlew,* titled *Wings to Fly,* takes place in 1918, and focuses on Sam's younger sister, twelve-year-old Josie, as she tries to adjust to the isolation of living on the prairie. When British couple Mr. and Mrs. Graham and their daughter Margaret move into a nearby sod house, Josie's hopes of finding a friend rise when she discovers that Margaret is her age. Unfortunately, Margaret is less than friendly, leaving Josie hurt and confused until her imagination is captured by the exploits of a daring female pilot. "In *Wings to Fly,* the rigors of prairie life are made real," Jennifer Sullivan declared in *Canadian Review of Materials,* "from the influenza epidemic and winter storms that ravage the small community, to the patriarchal society that confines women to the home." Sullivan also praised the novel for depicting the coming-of-age of its young protagonist and for "painting an interesting picture of a society on the verge of reform" in the wake of World War I. *Quill & Quire* reviewer Barbara Greenwood called Lottridge's story "appealing" and "well-written" and her characters "fully developed," concluding that the plot of *Wings to Fly* "will keep readers turning the pages."

Biographical and Critical Sources

PERIODICALS

Booklist, March 15, 1994, Julie Corsaro, review of *Ten Small Tales,* p. 1368; February 1, 1996, Carolyn Phelan, review of *Ticket to Canada,* p. 932; August, 1996, Hazel Rochman, review of *Something Might Be Hiding,* p. 1908; January 1, 1999, Kathy Broderick, review of *Music for the Tsar of the Sea,* p. 882; May 1, 2002, Carolyn Phelan, review of *Berta, a Remarkable Dog,* p. 1526.

Canadian Book Review Annual, 1997, p. 516.

Canadian Children's Literature, Volume 47, 1987, p. 96; spring, 1996, p. 45.

Canadian Review of Materials, January, 1988, p. 7; November, 1994, p. 208.

Five Owls, May-June, 1990, p. 85.

Horn Book, March, 1990, p. 85; January-February, 1994, Sarah Ellis, review of *Ten Small Tales,* pp. 112-114.

Junior Bookshelf, August, 1987, p. 164.

Kirkus Reviews, April 1, 1994, review of *Ten Small Tales,* pp. 481-482.

Publishers Weekly, February 28, 1994, review of *Ten Small Tales,* p. 88.

Quill & Quire, July, 1980, p. 57; December, 1985, p. 27; June, 1986, p. 28; October, 1989, Michele Landsberg, review of *The Name of the Tree,* p. 13; October, 1993, p. 37; June, 1995, p. 58; June, 1997, Barbara Greenwood, review of *Wings to Fly,* p. 66.

Resource Links, December, 2001, Linda Ludke, review of *The Little Rooster and the Diamond Button,* p. 7; June, 2002, Veronica Allan, review of *Berta, a Remarkable Dog,* p. 14.

School Librarian, May, 1988, p. 53.

School Library Journal, March, 1990, p. 209; June, 1994, p. 122; June, 1996, p. 104; August, 1995, p. 125; January, 2002, Be Astengo, review of *The Little Rooster and the Diamond Button,* p. 120.

Times Educational Supplement, August 21, 1987, p. 17.

ONLINE

Canadian Review of Materials Online, http://www.umanitoba.ca/cm/ (June 4, 1999), Dave Jenkinson, "Celia Lottridge"; (January 16, 1998) Jennifer Sullivan, review of *Wings to Fly.*

CANSCAIP Web site, http://www.canscaip.org/ (January 19, 2005), "Celia Barker Lottridge."*

LUND, Deb

Personal

Married Karl Olsen (a vocalist); children: Kaj (son), Sandra, Jean (son). *Education:* Bachelor degrees in music and elementary education, library endorsement; M.A. (applied liberal studies).

Addresses

Agent—Marcia Wernick, Sheldon Fogelman Agency, Inc., 10 East 40th St., New York, NY 10016. *E-mail*—deb@deblund.com.

Career

Writer. Formerly worked as a music teacher, classroom teacher, librarian, and school director. Speaker at conferences, schools, and libraries.

Writings

Play and Pray: Toddler Prayers, illustrated by Joni Oeltjenbruns, Morehouse Pub. (Harrisburg, PA), 2002.

Dinosailors, illustrated by Howard Fine, Harcourt (San Diego, CA), 2003.

Me and God: A Book of Partner Prayers, illustrated by Carolyn Digby Conahan, Morehouse Pub. (Harrisburg, PA), 2003.

Deb Lund

Little children beginning to question where they came from will benefit from a reading of Deb Lund's reassuring **Tell Me My Story, Mama,** *illustrated with watercolors by Hiroe Nakata.*

Tell Me My Story, Mama, illustrated by Hiroe Nakata, HarperCollins (New York, NY), 2003.

All Day Long: A Book of Partner Prayers, illustrated by Carolyn Digby Conahan, Morehouse Pub. (Harrisburg, PA), 2004.

All Aboard the Dinotrain, Harcourt (Orlando, FL), 2005.

Sidelights

A former music and classroom teacher, as well as a librarian and founding director of a home-school support program, Deb Lund is the author of several children's books, among them *Dinosailors,* and *Tell Me My Story, Mama.* Described as "a lovely choice for children" according to *Booklist* critic Gillian Engberg, *Tell Me My Story, Mama* offers readers a mother's account of pregnancy and her fond memories of the excitement and anticipation leading up to her daughter's birth. Covering everything from the trip to the hospital and the actual birth to the new parents' love at first glimpse of their newborn infant, Lund provides readers with a "warmhearted and compassionate" tale according to a *Kirkus Reviews* critic. The reviewer recommended *Tell Me My Story, Mama* as a book that is "ideal for sharing with expectant siblings, who will appreciate this subtle reminder of their own individuality." "The shelf of new baby books may be crowded, but it's well worth making room for this graceful, gently funny entry" added a *Publishers Weekly* reviewer.

Prehistoric creatures take to the high seas in Lund's *Dinosailors,* which finds a group of bulky dinosaurs clambering weightily aboard ship, only to encounter a bad storm and realize that perhaps they were meant to be landlubbers after all. Praising Lund's entertaining, rhyming text, a *Publishers Weekly* contributor wrote that "young salts and dinosaur devotees will likely be happy to sign on for a cruise with this boisterous bunch," while in *Booklist* Stephanie Zvirin praised Lund's "happy-go-lucky tale" in which "the rhythm and the wordplay are the fun." Teaming up with illustrator Howard Fine again, Lund continues her dino adventures in *All Aboard the Dinotrain,* which carries readers on a train trip that features a turn toward the unexpected along with the fun.

Lund enjoys working with students, teachers, librarians, and others who care about writing and children's books. She also performs with the "Basics," a family music group that promotes the arts, diversity and imagination, and lives with her family on an island in the Pacific Northwest.

Biographical and Critical Sources

PERIODICALS

Booklist, September 1, 2003, Stephanie Zvirin, review of *Dinosailors,* p. 129; April 1, 2004, Gillian Engberg, review of *Tell Me My Story, Mama,* p. 1369.

Childhood Education, mid-summer, 2004, Kristen Snyder, review of *Dinosailors,* p. 274.

Kirkus Reviews, September 15, 2003, review of *Dinosailors,* p. 1177; March 1, 2004, review of *Tell Me My Story, Mama,* p. 226.

Publishers Weekly, September 8, 2003, review of *Dinosailors,* p. 75; March 1, 2004, review of *Tell Me My Story, Mama,* p. 67.

School Library Journal, September, 2003, Steven Engelfried, review of *Dinosailors,* p. 184; February, 2004, Heide Piehler, review of *Tell Me My Story, Mama,* p. 118.

ONLINE

Deb Lund Web site, http://www.deblund.com (February 16, 2005).

M

MENDES, Valerie 1939-

Personal
Born 1939, in Buckinghamshire, England; children: Sam Mendes (a film and theatre director). *Education:* Attended North London Collegiate School; University of Reading, degree (English and philosophy; with double honors).

Addresses
Home—The Cloister, Wytham Abbey, Wytham, Oxford OX2 8QB, England. *Office*—Wordwise, 37 Elmthrope Rd., Wolvercote, Oxford OX2 8PA, England. *Agent*—Philippa Milnes-Smith, LAW Ltd., 14 Vernon St., London W14 ORJ, England. *E-mail*—valerie@mendes. demon.co.uk.

Career
Writer and editor. Marshall Cavendish, commissioning editor and journalist, c. 1960s; Oxford University Press, Oxford, England, children's book editor; editor for various other publishers; Wordwise (editorial consultancy), Oxford, founder, 1990-2004.

Writings

Tomasina's First Dance, illustrated by Heather Calder, Little, Brown (Boston, MA), 1992.
Look at Me Grandma!, illustrated by Claire Fletcher, Chicken House (New York, NY), 2001.
Girl in the Attic, Simon & Schuster (London, England), 2002.
Coming of Age, Simon & Schuster (London, England), 2003.
Lost and Found, Simon & Schuster (London, England), 2004.
The Drowning, Simon & Schuster (London, England), 2005.

Valerie Mendes

Also author of nonfiction series of educational books for Ladybird publishers. Contributor to periodicals.

Work in Progress
Louisa, an historical novel for young adults set in 1939.

Sidelights
British author Valerie Mendes has been writing since the young age of six. Retaining her passion for writing and books while attending college, she graduated to a succession of writing and editing jobs with publishers. After encouragement while working as a commissioning editor and journalist for London publisher Marshall Cavendish during the 1960s, Mendes began to take her own writing seriously, and published her first book for children, *Tomasina's First Dance,* in 1992. After found-

ing her own editorial consultancy business, she gradually was able to write full time, and has produced such well-received books as *Girl in the Attic, Coming of Age,* and *Lost and Found.*

Praising *Lost and Found,* a young-adult novel that focuses on the connection between three Oxford residents, Philippa Boston wrote in the *Oxford Times* that Mendes "is a mistress of plot-weaving, skillfully introducing characters at a comfortable speed . . . and never patronizing" her teen readership.Mendes's second published picture book, *Look at Me, Grandma!,* is the story of a young boy named Jamie, whose grandma has come to watch him while his mother is at the hospital giving birth to a new baby. A *Publishers Weekly* reviewer described the book as "curious" in that Mendes "combines fantasy elements with a conventional story of a new sibling," while a *Kirkus* reviewer wrote that the author "nicely weaves together the triumphs of acquiring new skills with new-sibling jitters."

From her beginning in picture books, Mendes moved to writing novels for older readers, and her 2002 title *Girl*

in the Attic, has been followed by several other critically praised titles. *Girl in the Attic,* finds thirteen-year-old Nathan Fielding none too happy about his newly separated mother's decision to move to Cornwall, a move that separates Nathan from his best friend, Tom, as well as from his father. However, when he discovers a new friend in a girl named Rosalie, he is drawn into her life, as well as into her family's mysteries in a novel that London *Daily Telegraph* contributor Rebecca Abrams dubbed "beautifully written" and John McLay described in *Carousel* as "sometimes tense, sometimes atmospheric. . . . a sound read."

Coming of Age also finds a child dealing with a disrupted family and a new location. Sixteen-year-old Amy, who has been traumatized by witnessing her mother's violent accidental death, now reacts to her widowed father's new girlfriend by fleeing to Italy, hoping to reconnect with her mother's memory and the truth about her life. While *School Librarian* reviewer Anne Harvey noted that Amy's "new-found power and ruthlessness towards her father" is unsettling, the critic nonetheless praised *Coming of Age* as a "gripping story" containing

By telling the story of how she misses her own little brother, Grandma helps Jamie look at the birth of a new baby sister with excitement rather than trepidation in Mendes' **Look at Me, Grandma!,** *illustrated by Claire Fletcher.*

"exquisite descriptions" of Italy. Also enthusiastic about Mendes' fiction, Kit Spring wrote in the London *Observer* that the "tantalising tale unfolds in an atmospheric and engaging" fashion. Mendes' fourth novel, *The Drowning,* also features a sixteen year old, in this case Jenna, whose plans to dance professionally in London are put on hold when a fatal accident tears her Cornish family apart.

Mendes commented to *Something about the Author:* "People often ask me why I choose to write for children. It's a stony path. When you are trying to get a first novel accepted, you have to be able to withstand fierce criticism and often walls of impenetrable silence from busy publishers. There are no short cuts, no hiding places but—when you get it right—joy that knows no bounds.

"Why do I chose to write for children? My answer always is: I don't choose it, it chooses me. And I feel most blessed that it does."

Biographical and Critical Sources

PERIODICALS

Carousel, autumn, 2002, John McLey, review of *Girl in the Attic.*

Childhood Education, summer, 2002, Heather J. B. Artbuckle, review of *Look at Me, Grandma!,* p. 239.

Daily Telegraph (London, England), January 4, 2003, Rebecca Abrams, review of *Girl in the Attic,* p. 15.

Entertainment Weekly, April 28, 2000, p. 102.

Kirkus Reviews, November 1, 2001, review of *Look at Me, Grandma!,* p. 1533.

Observer (London, England), May 25, 2003, Kit Spring, review of *Coming of Age.*

Oxford Times, July 18, 2003, Philippa Boston, interview with Mendes; June 4, 2004, Philippa Boston, review of *Lost and Found.*

Publishers Weekly, November 12, 2001, review of *Look at Me, Grandma!,* p. 59.

School Librarian, autumn, 2003, Anne Harvey, review of *Coming of Age.*

School Library Journal, December, 2001, Catherine Threadgill, review of *Look at Me, Grandma!,* p. 106.

Times Educational Supplement, June 25, 2004, Adèle Geras, review of *Lost and Found.*

*   *   *

MILLS, Adam
See STANLEY, George Edward

*   *   *

MURPHY, Stuart J. 1942-

Personal

Born 1942, in Rockville, CT; married Nancy Kolanko; children: Randall, Kristin. *Education:* Rhode Island

Stuart J. Murphy

School of Design, B.F.A., 1964; graduate, Harvard Business School management program. *Hobbies and other interests:* Sketching, Italian language.

Addresses

Home—Boston, MA; and Tuscany, Italy. *Agent*—c/o Author Mail, HarperCollins Publishers, 1350 Avenue of the Americas, New York, NY 10019.

Career

Education research consultant and author of children's books. Art director, *The Art Gallery* magazine, 1964-67; designer and art director, Ginn and Company (educational publishers), 1967-80; co-founder and president of Ligature, Inc. (educational research and development firm), 1980-92; freelance writer, consultant, and lecturer, beginning 1992. Served on board of trustees, Rhode Island School of Design, on committee on museum education for the Art Institute of Chicago, and Harvard University Graduate School of Education arts advisory council; served on board of governors, Northwestern University Library Council.

Awards, Honors

Xerox Social Service Leave, 1973; Mary Alexander Award, Chicago Book Clinic, 1992; W. A. Dwiggins Award, Bookbuilder of Boston, 1993; Top-Ten Nonfiction Series for Young Children listee, *Booklist,* 1999, for "MathStart" series; Bank Street College of Education Best Children's Book of the Year designation, 2003, for *Slugger's Car Wash;* Oppenheim Toy Portfolio Gold Sea, and *Science Books and Film* Best Book designation, both 2004, both for *Less than Zero.*

Writings

"MATHSTART" SERIES

The Best Bug Parade, illustrated by Holly Keller, HarperCollins (New York, NY), 1996.

Give Me Half!, illustrated by G. Brian Karas, HarperCollins (New York, NY), 1996.

Ready, Set, Hop!, illustrated by Jon Buller, HarperCollins (New York, NY), 1996.

A Pair of Socks, illustrated by Lois Elhert, HarperCollins (New York, NY), 1996.

Get up and Go!, illustrated by Diane Greenseid, HarperCollins (New York, NY), 1996.

Too Many Kangaroo Things to Do!, illustrated by Kevin O'Malley, HarperCollins (New York, NY), 1996.

The Best Vacation Ever, illustrated by Nadine Bernard Westcott, HarperCollins (New York, NY), 1997.

Divide and Ride, illustrated by George Ulrich, HarperCollins (New York, NY), 1997.

Every Buddy Counts, illustrated by Fiona Dunbar, HarperCollins (New York, NY), 1997.

Betcha!, illustrated by S. D. Schindler, HarperCollins (New York, NY), 1997.

Elevator Magic, illustrated by G. Brian Karas, HarperCollins (New York, NY), 1997.

Just Enough Carrots, illustrated by Frank Remkiewicz, HarperCollins (New York, NY), 1997.

Lemonade for Sale, illustrated by Tricia Tusa, HarperCollins (New York, NY), 1998.

Circus Shapes, illustrated by Edward Miller, HarperCollins (New York, NY), 1998.

A Fair Bear Share, illustrated by John Speirs, HarperCollins (New York, NY), 1998.

The Greatest Gymnast of All, HarperCollins (New York, NY), 1998.

Animals on Board, HarperCollins (New York, NY), 1998.

The Penny Pot, HarperCollins (New York, NY), 1998.

Henry the Fourth, illustrated by Scott Nash, HarperCollins (New York, NY), 1999.

Jump, Kangaroo, Jump!, illustrated by Kevin O'Malley, HarperCollins (New York, NY), 1999.

Super Sand Castle Saturday, illustrated by Julia Gorton, HarperCollins (New York, NY), 1999.

Rabbit's Pajama Party, HarperCollins (New York, NY), 1999.

Spunky Monkeys on Parade, HarperCollins (New York, NY), 1999.

Room for Ripley, HarperCollins (New York, NY), 1999.

Beep Beep, Vroom Vroom, HarperCollins (New York, NY), 2000.

Pepper's Journal, HarperCollins (New York, NY), 2000.

Dave's Down-to-Earth Rock Shop, HarperCollins (New York, NY), 2000.

Game Time, HarperCollins (New York, NY), 2000.

Let's Fly a Kite, HarperCollins (New York, NY), 2000.

Monster Musical Chairs, HarperCollins (New York, NY), 2000.

Captain Invincible and the Space Shapes, illustrated by Remy Simard, HarperCollins (New York, NY), 2001.

Dinosaur Deals, illustrated by Kevin O'Malley, HarperCollins (New York, NY), 2001.

Missing Mittens, illustrated by G. Brian Karas, HarperCollins (New York, NY), 2001.

Probably Pistachio, illustrated by Marsha Winborn, HarperCollins (New York, NY), 2001.

Seaweed Soup, HarperCollins (New York, NY), 2001.

The Shark Swimathon, HarperCollins (New York, NY), 2001.

Bigger, Better, Best!, illustrated by Murphy, 2002.

Bug Dance, illustrated by Christopher Santoro, HarperCollins (New York, NY), 2002.

One—Two—Three—Sassafrass!, illustrated by John Wallace, HarperCollins (New York, NY), 2002.

Racing Around, illustrated by Mike Reed, HarperCollins (New York, NY), 2002.

Safari Park, illustrated by Steve Bjorkman, HarperCollins (New York, NY), 2002.

Sluggers' Car Wash, illustrated by Barney Saltzberg, HarperCollins (New York, NY), 2002.

100 Days of Cool, illustrated by John Bendall-Brunello, HarperCollins (New York, NY), 2003.

Three Little Firefighters, illustrated by Bernice Lum, HarperCollins (New York, NY), 2003.

Coyotes All Around, illustrated by Steve Bjorkman, HarperCollins (New York, NY), 2003.

Double the Ducks, illustrated by Valerie Petrone, HarperCollins (New York, NY), 2003.

The Grizzly Gazette, illustrated by Steve Bjorkman, HarperCollins (New York, NY), 2003.

Less than Zero, illustrated by Frank Remkiewicz, HarperCollins (New York, NY), 2003.

The Sundae Scoop, illustrated by Cynthia Jabar, HarperCollins (New York, NY), 2003.

Hamster Champ, illustrated by Pedro Martin, HarperCollins (New York, NY), 2004.

It's about Time, illustrated by John Speirs, 2004.

Leaping Lizards, illustrated by Adinolfi, 2004.

More or Less, illustrated by David T. Wenzel, 2004.

Polly's Pen Pal, illustrated by Remy Simard, HarperCollins (New York, NY), 2004.

Same Old Hankie, illustrated by Steve Bjorkman, 2004.

Earth Day-Hooray!, illustrated by Renee Andriani, 2004.

A House for Birdie, illustrated by Edward Miller, HarperCollins (New York, NY), 2004.

Mighty Maddie, illustrated by Bernice Lum, HarperCollins (New York, NY), 2004.

Tally O'Malley, illustrated by Cynthia Jabar, HarperCollins (New York, NY), 2004.

Treasure Map, illustrated by Tricia Tusa, HarperCollins (New York, NY), 2004.

Also author of *Elementary Mathematics,* Silver Burdett Ginn, *Integrated Mathematics 1-3,* McDougal Littel, and *The Fat Firm,* McGraw Hill.

Sidelights

Stuart J. Murphy is an education consultant whose "MathStart" books for HarperCollins have helped kick-start a new approach in teaching math skills. At more than fifty titles strong, the series is graded in three levels and aimed at young children. Murphy's idea is to present math concepts such as comparing, counting, matching, sequencing, fractions, adding, and subtracting, among dozens of others, in the context of stories. His stories deal with circuses, vacations, birthdays, shopping, gymnastics, food, and just about any other situation that a young child will encounter in real life. The math concepts are also presented visually through diagrams and illustrations. "I think that most people understand things best when they can see them," Murphy once told *Something about the Author (SATA)*. "It's often better to draw a map then to try and explain where you're going to meet someone. Family trees help to show how people are related to one another. And graphs are usually the easiest way to demonstrate comparisons between two or more things. . . . I also found that stories helped kids to see how math is used in everyday, real-life situations. . . . This is how 'MathStart' was born."

Murphy served a long apprenticeship before inaugurating his popular math series. Graduating from the Rhode Island School of Design in 1964, he served as the art director for the magazine *The Art Gallery* for three years before joining the textbook company Ginn and Company as a designer. In 1971 he became art director for Ginn, a position he held until 1980. In that year he co-founded Ligature, Inc., an educational research and development firm that worked with publishers to conceptualize and prepare high quality books for U.S. schools. During these years he worked on social studies projects as well as math books.

Combining his background in visual arts with his work in educational publishing and research, Murphy began working on the books that would become "MathStart." He took as his starting point two principles: first, that many kids are visual learners, and second, that students do not study math the same way they experience it. That is to say that while they study mathematics in terms of word problems or operations symbols and numbers, they experience it directly by telling time, buying things, keeping score, and hundreds of other real-life situations. Murphy put these two principles together and come up with the concept for his narrative and visual approach to teaching math. When he pitched the idea to HarperCollins, they contracted an initial three, then twenty-four books in the series, later expanding it to sixty-three.

Written on three levels from preschool through second grade and up, "MathStart" deals with beginning math concepts such as counting, comparing, and ordering in Level 1; in Level 2 basic math skills such as adding and subtracting are introduced; and in Level 3 multiplying and dividing are demonstrated. As Ian Elliot noted in *Teaching K-8*, "It's easy to see why Murphy is so successful in getting young children turned on to math." Elliot pointed out the "lively but simple story lines," "delightful illustrations," and "visual representations of the math that's involved."

The first three books in the series were some four years in the making, and covered each of the three levels in the "MathStart" program. *The Best Bug Parade* is aimed at Level 1, *Give Me Half!* is geared for Level 2, and *Ready, Set, Hop!* at Level 3. *The Best Bug Parade* deals with size comparisons, with a red ladybug parade marshal as a constant referent, while a sibling squabble over pizza is the story line in *Give Me Half!* and two frogs debate their estimated length of jump in *Ready, Set, Hop!* Reviewing the first title in *School Library Journal*, Diane Nunn noted that concepts such as long/short and big/bigger/biggest "are presented by an assortment of cheery insects marching through a colorful environment of flowers and grass," and concluded that "teachers and parents will all find this a useful book, and youngsters will be attracted to the lively illustrations." Reviewing *Give Me Half!*, Carolyn Phelan noted in *Booklist* that it is "one of the few math concept books with realistic dialogue, authentic emotions, and genuine humor."

While the initial "MathStart" books did not impress all reviewers, critical reception improved as the series continued. Reviewing the next three books in the series—*A Pair of Socks, Get up and Go*, and *Too Many Kangaroo Things to Do*—for *School Library Journal*, Marsha McGrath noted that each "focuses on a simple math concept: matching, time lines, or multiplication." McGrath went on to comment, "Bright hues of acrylic paint and collage are used in the cartoon illustrations" while the end pages provide "helpful hints about using the books to teach additional concepts." *Booklist* reviewer Carolyn Phelan felt that Murphy's *A Pair of Socks* might be the only picture book story "told from the point of view of a sock." Phelan also commented, "Short, snappy rhymes and Elhert's brilliantly colored collage illustrations combine to make this tale from the MathStart series an entertaining book."

Publication of six further titles came in 1997: *Every Buddy Counts, The Best Vacation Ever*, and *Divide and Ride*, followed by *Just Enough Carrots, Elevator Magic*, and *Betcha!* Reviewing the first three titles in *School Library Journal*, Christine A. Moesch pointed out that they dealt with concepts such as counting, collecting data, and dividing, and concluded that the books present students with an "entertaining approach to progressive levels of math concepts." *Booklist* reviewer Hazel Rochman, reviewing the same three books, remarked that "these stories use everyday situations and lively line-and-watercolor illustrations to teach math concepts at various levels of difficulty." Noting in particular *Divide and Ride* as "the most sophisticated in math and story," Rochman felt that kids "of all ages will be drawn into the story" of how eleven children at the carnival need to divide up into twos and threes and fours for various rides.

Rochman also had praise for Murphy's second group of 1997 titles, noting that *Betcha!* "is a real winner that will entertain kids with the buddy story and the causal dialogue and with Schindler's bright, active pictures of two boys having fun in the city." Commenting on how the boys in *Betcha!* play at estimating the number of people on the bus as they ride to the city and the number of jellybeans in a window display, a writer for *Kirkus Reviews* noted that all the while readers would be introduced to concepts and techniques such as "rounding off and how to count a small number and apply that to the great, uncounted whole through the use of multiplication, fractions, and simple geometry." The same reviewer concluded that "Murphy's success is in beveling the sharp, unforgiving reputation of math and in showing how numbers can be toyed with."

The new millennium saw the introduction of broader math concepts into the series. In *Treasure Map,* Murphy explores a basic understanding of mapping. When a group of kids find a map that leads to a time capsule, they work together to follow the map to its treasure. Although Lauren Peterson wrote in her review for *Booklist* that "The mapping concepts are not presented as effectively as they could have been," she concluded that the book offers teachers and parents a good start for teaching these ideas. Similarly, a *Kirkus Reviews* contributor remarked that the activities in the back of the book are useful, but "as a stand-alone story, this one is weak."

Another unexpected subject is presented in *Earth Day-Hooray!* Here, the Save the Planet Club hosts a can drive to make money recycling so they can plant flowers in a local park. As Murphy teaches about conservationism and teamwork, he also teaches about sorting and place value. A *Kirkus Reviews* critic declared this book a "marvelous addition to the series," making spe-

Counting from 1 to 100 is the challenge to readers of **100 Days of Cool,** *in which savvy teacher Mrs. Lopez challenges students to devise one hundred cool things they can do, one each day, with the coolest party ever waiting at the end. (Illustration by John Bendall-Brunello.)*

cial note of the "excellent activity suggestions." Kay Weisman of *Booklist* wrote that this would be a "good choice for jazzing up a routine math lesson or as a springboard for Earth Day activities."

Traditional counting concepts provide the basis of *100 Days of Cool* and *Sluggers' Car Wash*. *100 Days of Cool* is about a class who tries to meet the challenge of staying "cool" for one hundred days. As they come to school in sunglasses, sequins, dyed hair, and other looks, they also decorate their bikes and form volunteer groups. As the days pass, Murphy reinforced counting ideas with a number line and comments from kids about fractions. In *Booklist*, Rochman praised the "lively classroom scenario," and noted that the "play and socializing dramatize the math." Gloria Koster, in a review for *School Library Journal*, wondered about the age-appropriateness of the book, commenting that it offers "reinforcement for one-by-one counters, [but] it won't dazzle children who are ready to investigate numbers in groups." Even less impressed was a *Kirkus Reviews* contributor who warned that the "cool/school wordplay wears thin quickly" and the "efforts of the group aren't particularly novel."In *Sluggers' Car Wash*, a baseball team earns money for new team shirts by holding a car wash. One player, CJ, is in charge of the money, but his teammates make sure he gets as soaked as the rest of them at day's end. As CJ takes customers' money and makes change, readers learn counting and keeping track of sums as the team approaches their goal. Phelan, writing in *Booklist*, was impressed by the variety of concepts presented in this simple story, commenting that learning to make change is a confusing task for many adults. A reviewer for *Kirkus Reviews* also noted that "lots of math/money games can be spun off from this story."

Double the Ducks and *The Sundae Scoop* offer lighthearted stories for young readers that are learning the basics of subtraction, multiplication, and combinations. In *Double the Ducks* a young farm boy must feed his five ducks with three bags of food, four bundles of hay, and only two hands. When he discovers that his ducks have invited friends, he realizes he must now feed twice as many ducks. Rochman commented in *Booklist* that this story makes "preschoolers' first steps into addition and multiplication more fun," while a *Kirkus* reviewer concluded that "Readers will delight in all the fun they're having on the farm while they're learning some new math." *The Sundae Scoop* is about a picnic where a group of kids are making sundaes. The ingredients they have enable them to make eight kinds of sundaes, but after the sprinkles are spilled, the caramel is tipped, and the chocolate ice cream melts the possibilities decrease. "Murphy easily folds the math concepts into a lively story that will capture young readers," wrote Helen Rosenberg in *Booklist*. A *Kirkus Reviews* contributor remarked that "Murphy plays the concept like a slide trombone," increasing and decreasing the number of sundae possibilities for the picnic.

Captain Invincible and the Space Shapes uses an outer space setting for a story about three-dimensional shapes. Captain Invincible and his dog, Comet, use various three-dimensional shapes from their spaceship to solve problems they encounter on their journey through space. According to Shelley Townsend-Hudson of *Booklist*, "The story gives the math lesson an out-of-this-world appeal." Wanda Meyers-Hines of *School Library Journal* concluded that the "reinforcement strategies and activities are very good," and deemed the book a "good choice as a read-aloud or for independent reading."The "MathStart" series has continued at the primary level, with twenty-seven titles that have earned general praise from reviewers, teachers, and students alike. Reviewing the first group of 1998 titles—*Circus Shapes, A Fair Bear Share,* and *Lemonade for Sale,* a *Publishers Weekly* contributor praised Murphy's "disarmingly chipper stories," a writer for *Kirkus Reviews* describing *Lemonade for Sale* as a "lively entry" demonstrating the use of bar graphs. The same reviewer called the series "a winning way to make some basic concepts and techniques less intimidating." Reviewing the 1999 entries—*Henry the Fourth* and *Jump, Kangaroo, Jump!, Booklist* critic John Peters felt that the former title has "the more complex story line," but that both titles follow "a winning formula." Writing in *School Library Journal*, Jane Claes reviewed a further 1999 addition to the series, *Super Sand Castle Saturday*. "Murphy does a good job of imparting the math lesson while delivering a natural story," Claes noted.

Murphy expounded on his methodology and writing technique in a *Booklist* interview. Noting that "most people don't see math as part of their daily lives," he explained that the driving force behind his "MathStart" series is "to draw kids into a story based on their own experiences sorting socks, rushing to get ready for school, fighting for a fair share of a pizza." He explained that his books begin with a concept and that he then searches his mind for a story to fit. "For example, I wanted to do a book on division. I was looking for a model in the daily experiences of children, but I kept coming up with things that were more like fractions. Then I remembered going to the carnival with my kids." At the carnival, Murphy and his children always had the problem of how they were going to divide up to go on rides, and employing this in his story *Divide and Ride,* he provided a very realistic approach to the concept of division.

In an interview for *TeachingBooks.net,* Murphy revealed his vision and motivation for the work he does. "One of the things that's really important to me is helping our kids become more fluent in the language of mathematics," he explained. "Children are visual learners, and I really want to make sure that kids understand that math is relevant to their lives." Talking about the approach he takes to his work, he added, "I've spent a lot of my life in classrooms talking with real kids—we talk about what they're having for lunch, we talk about what their favorite things are—all of those kinds of things that

In his "MathStart" books, which include **Lemonade for Sale,** *Murphy shows young readers that math is part of the fun in daily life. (Illustration by Tricia Tusa.)*

kids really care about, and then I find ways to build them into my stories. And that's what MathStart is—it's pictures, words and math—pictures, words and math coming together to tell a story."

Murphy, a trained artist, also oversees the early versions of artwork, supplying roughs for the artists to work from. His end-of-the-book suggestions for further reading and extended activities come from his own experience and are also added to and checked by three teachers in the field. Finally, each title is tested in the field with children's workshops at schools. Murphy remarked that kids in these workshops "end up having so much fun giggling and participating and explaining their work that I almost have to remind them that this is math."

"The 'MathStart' series is designed to help children become more fluent in the language of mathematics," Murphy concluded in *SATA,* "be more comfortable with match concepts, and make math part of their system of communication. By presenting math concepts in stories, supporting those stories with high-quality illustrations and carefully constructed math diagrams, and providing easy-to-accomplish activities that extend the learning of the story at the end of each book, children will realize that math can be easy—and fun!"

Biographical and Critical Sources

PERIODICALS

Booklist, May 1, 1996, Carolyn Phelan, review of *Give Me Half!,* p. 1510; October 1, 1996, Carolyn Phelan, review of *A Pair of Socks,* p. 355; February 1, 1997, Hazel Rochman, review of *The Best Vacation Ever,* p. 943; April 1, 1997, interview with Murphy, p. 1347; October 1, 1997, Hazel Rochman, review of *Betcha!,* p. 336; April 15, 1999, John Peters, reviews of *Henry the Fourth* and *Jump, Kangaroo, Jump!,* p. 1534; November 15, 2001, Shelley Townsend-Hudson, review of *Captain Invincible and the Space Shapes,* p. 578; January 1, 2003, Helen Rosenberg, review of *The Sundae Scoop,* p. 899; February 1, 2003, Carolyn Phelan, review of *Sluggers' Car Wash,* p. 999; March 15, 2003, Hazel Rochman, review of *Double the Ducks,* p. 1328; January 1, 2004, Kay Weisman, review of *Earth Day-Hooray!,* p. 868; April 1, 2004, Hazel Rochman, review of *100 Days of Cool,* p. 1367; September 1, 2004, Lauren Peterson, review of *Treasure Map,* pp. 127-128.

Bulletin of the Center for Children's Books, May, 1996, Elizabeth Bush, review of *The Best Bug Parade,* p. 310.

Kirkus Reviews, September 15, 1997, review of *Betcha!,* p. 1460; November 15, 1998, review of *Lemonade for Sale,* p. 1711; July 15, 2002, review of *Sluggers' Car Wash,* p. 355; November 15, 2002, review of *The Sundae Scoop,* p. 1700; December 1, 2002, review of *Double the Ducks,* p. 1770; January 1, 2004, review of *100 Days of Cool,* p. 39; January 15, 2004, review of *Earth Day-Hooray!,* p. 87; August 1, 2004, review of *Treasure Map,* p. 746.

Publishers Weekly, January 19, 1998, review of *Circus Shapes,* pp. 379-380.

School Library Journal, June, 1996, Diane Nunn, review of *The Best Bug Parade,* pp. 106-107; June, 1996, JoAnn Rees, review of *Ready, Set, Hop!,* pp. 117-118; December, 1996, Marsha McGrath, review of *A Pair of Socks,* p. 116; March, 1997, Christine A. Moesch, review of *The Best Vacation Ever,* pp. 179-180; July, 1999, Jane Claes, review of *Super Sand Castle Saturday,* p. 88; October, 2001, Wanda Meyers-Hines, review of *Captain Invincible and the Space Shapes,* p. 144; March, 2004, Gloria Koster, review of *100 Days of Cool,* p. 198.

Teaching K-8, January, 1998, Ian Elliot, "Murphy's Magical MathStart," pp. 43-44.

ONLINE

Stuart J. Murphy Web site, http://www.stuartjmurphy.com (April 23, 2005).

TeachingBooks.net, http://www.teachingbooks.net/ (February 3, 2005).

*   *   *

MYERS, Walter M.
See MYERS, Walter Dean

*   *   *

MYERS, Walter Dean 1937-
(Walter M. Myers)

Personal

Born Walter Milton Myers, August 12, 1937, in Martinsburg, WV; son of George Ambrose and Mary (Green) Myers; raised from age three by Herbert Julius (a ship-

ping clerk) and Florence (a factory worker) Dean; married (marriage dissolved); married Constance Brendel, June 19, 1973; children: (first marriage) Karen, Michael Dean; (second marriage) Christopher. *Education:* Attended City College of the City University of New York; Empire State College, B.A., 1984.

Addresses

Home—2543 Kennedy Blvd., Jersey City, NJ 07304.

Career

New York State Department of Labor, New York, NY, employment supervisor, 1966-70; Bobbs-Merrill Co., Inc. (publisher), New York, NY, senior trade books editor, 1970-77; full-time writer, beginning 1977. Teacher of creative writing and black history on a part-time basis in New York, NY, 1974-75; worked variously as a post-office clerk, inter-office messenger, and a interviewer at a factory. *Military service:* U.S. Army, 1954-57.

Member

PEN, Harlem Writers Guild.

Awards, Honors

Council on Interracial Books for Children Award, 1968, for *Where Does the Day Go?;* Children's Book of the Year, Child Study Association of America (CSAA), 1972, for *The Dancers;* Notable Book designation, American Library Association (ALA), 1975, and Woodward Park School Annual Book Award, 1976, both for *Fast Sam, Cool Clyde, and Stuff;* Best Books for Young Adults designation, ALA, 1978, for *It Ain't All for Nothin',* and 1979, for *The Young Landlords;* Coretta Scott King Award, 1980, for *The Young Landlords;* Best Books for Young Adults designation, ALA, 1981, and Notable Children's Trade Book in the Field of Social Studies designation, National Council for Social Studies/Children's Book Council, 1982, both for *The Legend of Tarik;* runner-up, Edgar Allan Poe Award, and Best Books for Young Adults designation, ALA, 1982, both for *Hoops;* Parents' Choice Award, Parents' Choice Foundation, 1982, for *Won't Know till I Get There,* 1984, for *The Outside Shot,* and 1988, for *Fallen Angels;* New Jersey Institute of Technology Authors Award, 1983, for *Tales of a Dead King;* Coretta Scott King Award, 1985, for *Motown and Didi;* Children's Book of the Year, CSAA, 1987, for *Adventure in Granada;* Parents' Choice Award, 1987, for *Crystal;* New Jersey Institute of Technology Authors Award and Best Books for Young Adults designation, ALA, 1988, Coretta Scott King Award, 1989, and Children's Book Award, South Carolina Association of School Librarians, 1991, all for *Fallen Angels;* Notable Book and Best Books for Young Adults designations, ALA, both 1988, both for *Me, Mop, and the Moondance Kid;* Notable Book designation, ALA, 1988, and Newbery Medal Honor Book designation, ALA, 1989, both for

Scorpions; Parents' Choice Award, 1990, for *The Mouse Rap;* Golden Kite Award Honor Book, and Jane Addams Award Honor Book, both 1991, and Coretta Scott King Award, and Orbis Pictus Award Honor Book, both 1992, all for *Now Is Your Time! The African-American Struggle for Freedom;* Parents' Choice Award, 1992, for *The Righteous Revenge of Artemis Bonner; Boston Globe/Horn Book Award* Honor Book, 1992, and Coretta Scott King Award Honor Book, and Newbery Medal Honor Book, both 1993, all for *Somewhere in the Darkness;* Jeremiah Ludington Award, Educational Paperback Association, 1993, for "18 Pine St." series; CRABberry Award, 1993, for *Malcolm X: By Any Means Necessary;* Margaret A. Edwards Award, ALA/*School Library Journal,* 1994, for contributions to young adult literature; Coretta Scott King Award, 1997, for *Slam!; Boston Globe/Horn Book Award* Honor Book designation, 1997, for *Harlem: A Poem;* several child-selected awards.

Writings

FICTION; FOR CHILDREN AND YOUNG ADULTS

Fast Sam, Cool Clyde, and Stuff, Viking (New York, NY), 1975.
Brainstorm, photographs by Chuck Freedman, F. Watts (New York, NY), 1977.
Mojo and the Russians, Viking (New York, NY), 1977.
Victory for Jamie, Scholastic (New York, NY), 1977.
It Ain't All for Nothin', Viking (New York, NY), 1978.
The Young Landlords, Viking (New York, NY), 1979.
The Golden Serpent, illustrated by Alice and Martin Provensen, Viking (New York, NY), 1980.
Hoops, Delacorte (New York, NY), 1981.
The Legend of Tarik, Viking (New York, NY), 1981.
Won't Know till I Get There, Viking (New York, NY), 1982.
The Nicholas Factor, Viking (New York, NY), 1983.
Tales of a Dead King, Morrow (New York, NY), 1983.
Motown and Didi: A Love Story, Viking (New York, NY), 1984.
The Outside Shot, Delacorte (New York, NY), 1984.
Sweet Illusions, Teachers & Writers Collaborative, 1986.
Crystal, Viking (New York, NY), 1987, reprinted, HarperTrophy (New York, NY), 2001.
Scorpions, Harper (New York, NY), 1988.
Me, Mop, and the Moondance Kid, illustrated by Rodney Pate, Delacorte (New York, NY), 1988.
Fallen Angels, Scholastic (New York, NY), 1988.
The Mouse Rap, HarperCollins (New York, NY), 1990.
Somewhere in the Darkness, Scholastic (New York, NY), 1992.
Mop, Moondance, and the Nagasaki Knights, Delacorte (New York, NY), 1992.
The Righteous Revenge of Artemis Bonner, HarperCollins (New York, NY), 1992.
The Glory Field, Scholastic (New York, NY), 1994.
Darnell Rock Reporting, Delacorte (New York, NY), 1994.

Shadow of the Red Moon, illustrated by Christopher Myers, Scholastic (New York, NY), 1995.
Sniffy Blue, Ace Crime Detective: The Case of the Missing Ruby and Other Stories, illustrated by David J. A. Sims, Scholastic (New York, NY), 1996.
Slam!, Scholastic (New York, NY), 1996.
The Journal of Joshua Loper: A Black Cowboy, Atheneum, 1999.
The Journal of Scott Pendleton Collins: A World War II Soldier, Normandy, France, 1944, Scholastic (New York, NY), 1999.
Monster, illustrated by Christopher Myers, HarperCollins (New York, NY), 1999.
The Blues of Flats Brown, illustrated by Nina Laden, Holiday House (New York, NY), 2000.
145th Street: Short Stories, Delacorte Press (New York, NY), 2000.
Patrol: An American Soldier in Vietnam, illustrated by Ann Grifalconi, HarperCollins (New York, NY), 2001.
The Journal of Biddy Owens and the Negro Leagues, Scholastic (New York, NY), 2001.
Three Swords for Granada, illustrated by John Speirs, Holiday House (New York, NY), 2002.
Handbook for Boys: A Novel, illustrated by Matthew Bandsuch, HarperCollins (New York, NY), 2002.
A Time to Love: Stories from the Old Testament, illustrated by Christopher Myers, Scholastic (New York, NY), 2003.
The Beast, Scholastic (New York, NY), 2003.
The Dream Bearer, HarperCollins (New York, NY), 2003.
Shooter, HarperTempest (New York, NY), 2004.
Southern Fried, St. Martin's Minotaur (New York, NY), 2004.

Creator and editor of "18 Pine Street" series of young adult novels, Bantam, beginning 1992. Work represented in anthologies, including *What We Must SEE: Young Black Storytellers,* Dodd, 1971, and *We Be Word Sorcerers: Twenty-five Stories by Black Americans.*

"ARROW" SERIES

Adventure in Granada, Viking (New York, NY), 1985.
The Hidden Shrine, Viking (New York, NY), 1985.
Duel in the Desert, Viking (New York, NY), 1986.
Ambush in the Amazon, Viking (New York, NY), 1986.

JUVENILE NONFICTION

The World of Work: A Guide to Choosing a Career, Bobbs-Merrill, 1975.
Social Welfare, F. Watts (New York, NY), 1976.
Now Is Your Time! The African-American Struggle for Freedom, HarperCollins (New York, NY), 1992.
A Place Called Heartbreak: A Story of Vietnam, illustrated by Frederick Porter, Raintree (Austin, TX), 1992.
Young Martin's Promise (picture book), illustrated by Barbara Higgins Bond, Raintree (Austin, TX), 1992.
Malcolm X: By Any Means Necessary, Scholastic (New York, NY), 1993.

One More River to Cross: An African-American Photograph Album, Harcourt (New York, NY), 1995.

Turning Points: When Everything Changes, Troll Communications (Matwah, NJ), 1996.

Toussaint L'Ouverture: The Fight for Haiti's Freedom, illustrated by Jacob Lawrence, Simon & Schuster (New York, NY), 1996.

Amistad: A Long Road to Freedom, Dutton (New York, NY), 1998.

At Her Majesty's Request: An African Princess in Victorian England, Scholastic (New York, NY), 1999.

Malcolm X: A Fire Burning Brightly, illustrated by Leonard Jenkins, HarperCollins (New York, NY), 2000.

The Greatest: Muhammad Ali, Scholastic (New York, NY), 2001.

Bad Boy: A Memoir, HarperCollins (New York, NY), 2001.

USS Constellation: Pride of the American Navy, Holiday House (New York, NY), 2004.

I've Seen the Promised Land: The Life of Dr. Martin Luther King, Jr., illustrated by Leonard Jenkins, HarperCollins (New York, NY), 2004.

Antarctica: Journeys to the South Pole, Scholastic (New York, NY), 2004.

PICTURE BOOKS

(Under name Walter M. Myers) *Where Does the Day Go?*, illustrated by Leo Carty, Parents Magazine Press, 1969.

The Dragon Takes a Wife, illustrated by Ann Grifalconi, Bobbs-Merrill, 1972.

The Dancers, illustrated by Anne Rockwell, Parents Magazine Press, 1972.

Fly, Jimmy, Fly!, illustrated by Moneta Barnett, Putnam (New York, NY), 1974.

The Black Pearl and the Ghost; or, One Mystery after Another, illustrated by Robert Quackenbush, Viking (New York, NY), 1980.

Mr. Monkey and the Gotcha Bird, illustrated by Leslie Morrill, Delacorte (New York, NY), 1984.

The Story of the Three Kingdoms, illustrated by Ashley Bryan, HarperCollins (New York, NY), 1995.

How Mr. Monkey Saw the Whole World, illustrated by Synthia Saint James, Bantam (New York, NY), 1996.

Harlem: A Poem, illustrated by Christopher Myers, Scholastic (New York, NY), 1997.

POETRY

Brown Angels: An Album of Pictures and Verse, HarperCollins (New York, NY), 1993.

Remember Us Well: An Album of Pictures and Verse, HarperCollins (New York, NY), 1993.

Glorious Angels: A Celebration of Children, HarperCollins (New York, NY), 1995.

Angel to Angel: A Mother's Gift of Love, HarperCollins (New York, NY), 1998.

Blues Journey, illustrated by Christopher Myers, Holiday House (New York, NY), 2003.

Here in Harlem: Poems in Many Voices, Holiday House (New York, NY), 2004.

OTHER

Contributor of articles and fiction to books and to periodicals, including *Alfred Hitchcock Mystery Magazine, Argosy, Black Creation, Black World, Boy's Life, Ebony, Jr.!, Espionage, Essence, McCall's, National Enquirer, Negro Digest,* and *Scholastic;* also contributor of poetry to university reviews and quarterlies.

Adaptations

The Young Landlords was made into a film by Topol Productions. *Mojo and the Russians* was made into a videorecording by Children's Television International, Great Plains National Instructional Television Library, 1980. Demco Media released videos of *Fallen Angels* and *Me, Mop, and the Moondance Kid* in 1988, *Scorpions* in 1990, and *The Righteous Revenge of Artemis Bonner* in 1996. *Darnell Rock Reporting* was released on video in 1996. *Harlem: A Poem* was released as a combination book and audio version in 1997. *Scorpions* was adapted as a sound recording in 1998.

Sidelights

Called "one of today's most important authors of young adult literature" by Rudine Sims Bishop in *Presenting Walter Dean Myers* and "a giant among children's and young adult authors" by Frances Bradburn in the *Wilson Library Bulletin,* Walter Dean Myers is regarded as one of the best contemporary American writers for children and teens. An author of African-American descent, he is credited with helping to redefine the image of blacks in juvenile literature.

A number of African-American writers emerged in the 1960s and 1970s who sought to provide more realistic storylines and more well-rounded portrayals of black characters than those by previous authors. As a member of this group, which also includes Alice Childress, Lucille Clifton, Eloise Greenfield, Virginia Hamilton, and Sharon Bell Mathis, Myers distinguished himself by bringing both humor and poignancy to his work as well by creating books with special appeal to boys; in addition, he is considered the only prominent male writer of the group to have consistently published books of quality. A versatile and prolific author, Myers has written realistic and historical fiction, mysteries, adventure stories, fantasies, nonfiction, poetry, and picture books for a diverse audience of young people. Although he is praised for his contributions to several genres, he is perhaps best known as the writer of books for readers in junior high and high school that range from farcical, lighthearted stories for younger teens to powerful, moving novels for older adolescents. Myers stresses the more positive aspects of black urban life in his works; often setting his stories in his boyhood home of Harlem, he is acknowledged for depicting the strength and dignity of his characters without downplaying the harsh realities of their lives.

Although he features both young men and women as protagonists, Myers is noted for his focus on young black males. His themes often include the relationship

The African American who helped lead a nation toward racial equality is profiled in Myers's **I've Seen the Promised Land: The Life of Martin Luther King, Jr.,** *illustrated by Leonard Jenkins.*

between fathers and sons as well as the search for identity and self-worth in an environment of poverty, drugs, gangs, and racism. Although his characters confront difficult issues, Myers stresses survival, pride, and hope in his works, which are filled with love and laughter and a strong sense of possibility for the future of their protagonists. Lauded for his understanding of the young, Myers is acclaimed as the creator of believable, sympathetic adolescent characters; he is also praised for creating realistic dialogue, some of which draws on rap music and other aspects of black culture. Calling Myers "a unique voice," Rudine Sims Bishop said that Myers has become "an important writer because he creates books that appeal to young adults from many cultural groups. They appeal because Myers knows and cares about the things that concern his readers and because he creates characters that readers are happy to spend time with." R. D. Lane noted in the *African American Review* that the author "celebrates children by weaving narratives of the black juvenile experience in ways that reverse the effects of mediated messages of the black experience in public culture. . . . Myers's stratagem is revolutionary: the intrinsic value to black youth of his lessons stands priceless, timeless, and class-transcendent." In her entry in *Dictionary of Literary Biography,* Carmen Subryan concluded, "Myers's books demonstrate that writers can not only challenge the minds of black youths but also emphasize the black experience in a nondidactic way that benefits all readers."

Born Walter Milton Myers in Martinsburg, West Virginia, Myers lost his mother, Mary Green Myers, at age two, during the birth of his younger sister Imogene. Since his father, George Ambrose Myers, was struggling economically, Walter and two of his sisters were informally adopted by family friends Florence and Herbert Dean; Myers has written about surrogate parenting in several of his stories, including *Won't Know Till I Get There* and *Me, Mop, and the Moondance Kid.*

The Deans moved their family to Harlem when Myers was about three years old. He recalled in *Something about the Author Autobiography Series (SAAS),* "I loved Harlem. I lived in an exciting corner of the renowned Black capital and in an exciting era. The people I met there, the things I did, have left a permanent impression on me." When he was four years old Myers was taught to read by his foster mother; his foster father sat the boy on his knee and told him what Myers called "endless stories" in *SAAS.* The author wrote in *Children's Books and Their Creators,* "Somewhere along the line I discovered that books could be part of a child's world, and by the time I was nine I found myself spending long hours reading in my room. The books began to shape new bouts of imagination. Now I was one of 'The Three Musketeers' (always the one in the middle), or participating in the adventures of Jo's boys. John R. Tunis brought me back to sports, and I remember throwing a pink ball against the wall for hours as I struggled through baseball games that existed only in the rich arena of invention."

When not reading, Myers enjoyed playing sports, especially stickball, baseball, and basketball; baseball provides the background for three of the author's most popular young-adult novels: *Hoops, The Outside Shot,* and *Slam!* At school, Myers enjoyed classwork but found that a speech impediment caused him some difficulty. His fellow classmates would laugh at him and, as a result, he would fight back; consequently, he was often suspended from school. When Myers was in fifth grade, as he recalled in *SAAS,* "a marvelous thing happened." Made to sit at the back of the class for fighting, he was reading a comic book during a math lesson when the teacher, Mrs. Conway, caught him. Mrs. Conway, who was known for her meanness, surprised Walter by saying that if he was going to read, he might as well read something decent and brought him a selection of children's books; Myers remembered Asbjornsen and Moe's *East of the Sun and West of the Moon,* a collection of Norwegian folktales, as a turning point in his appreciation of literature. Mrs. Conway also required her students to read aloud in class. In order to avoid some of the words that he had trouble speaking, she suggested that Walter write something for himself to read. The poems that he wrote for class—which deliberately skirted problematic consonants—were Myers's first literary attempts.

After completing an accelerated junior high school program, Myers attended Stuyvesant High School, a school for boys that stressed academic achievement. Although he struggled somewhat due to the school's focus on science, Myers met another influential teacher, Bonnie Liebow, who interviewed each of her students and made up individualized reading lists for them; Myers's list included works by such European authors as Emile Zola and Thomas Mann. Liebow also told Myers that he was a gifted writer, and he began thinking of writing as a career.

He wrote every day, sometimes skipping school to sit in a tree in Central Park to read or work on his writing. However, at age sixteen Myers began to feel frustrated. Although he won a prize for an essay contest and was awarded a set of encyclopedias for one of his poems, he realized that writing "had no practical value for a Black child." He recalled: "These minor victories did not bolster my ego. Instead, they convinced me that even though I was bright, even though I might have some talent, I was still defined by factors other than my ability." In addition, Myers was depressed by the fact that he would not be able to attend college due to his family's financial status. Consequently, he wrote in *SAAS,* he began "writing poems about death, despair, and doom" and began "having doubts about everything in my life."

When not writing or working odd jobs, Myers hung out in the streets: "I was steeped in the mystique of the semi-hoodlum," he recalled in *SAAS.* He acquired a stiletto and acted as a drug courier; he also became a target for one of the local gangs after intervening in a fight between three gang members and a new boy in the neighborhood. Finally, influenced by the war poems of British writer Rupert Brooke, Myers joined the army at age seventeen in order to, as he wrote in *SAAS,* "hie myself off to some far-off battlefield and get killed. There, where I fell, would be a little piece of Harlem."

Myers's army experience was less than the glorious adventure promised by the poetry he had read; he went to radio-repair school and spent most of his time playing basketball. "I also learned several efficient ways of killing human beings," he wrote in *SAAS.* In *Presenting Walter Dean Myers,* the author told Bishop, "I learned something about dying. I learned a lot about facilitating the process, of making it abstract." He developed a strong antiwar attitude that would later become part of his young-adult novel *Fallen Angels,* the story of a young black soldier in Vietnam. After three years in the army, he returned to his parents, who had moved to Morristown, New Jersey. After a brief period, he moved back to Harlem, where he took an apartment and began to work at becoming a professional writer. In what he recalled as his "starving artist period" in *SAAS,* Myers wrote poetry and read books about the Bohemian life by such authors as George Orwell and André Gide; he also lived on two dollars a week from unemployment compensation and lost fifty pounds. Finally, after a friend suggested that he take the civil service exam, Myers got a job with the post office, a job that lasted

One of Myers' most popular novels, this 1994 work traces several generations of an African-American family, beginning with Muhammad Bilal's childhood in Africa and ending centuries later with a family pilgrimage to the plantation where Bilal began his new life as a slave.

only a few months. He also married Joyce, a woman he called "wonderful, warm, beautiful, religious, caring" in *SAAS.* Even after becoming a father—two of his three children, Karen and Michael, are from his first marriage—Myers continued to try to live a romantic lifestyle. While working odd jobs in a factory and an office, he played bongos with a group of jazz musicians, some of whom were into heroin and cocaine, and wrote jazz-based poetry, some of which was published in Canada. He also began to be published in African-American magazines such as the *Negro Digest* and the *Liberator* as well as in men's magazines such as *Argosy* and *Cavalier.* "I also," Myers recalled in *SAAS,* "drank too much and ran around too much." Eventually, his marriage collapsed.

In 1961, Myers enrolled in a writing class with author Lajos Egri, who told him that he had a special talent. A few years later, he attended City College of the City University of New York as a night student, but dropped out. At a writer's workshop at Columbia University led by novelist John Oliver Killens, Killens recommended Myers for a new editorial position at the publishing house Bobbs-Merrill. Myers got the job and became an acquisitions editor. In 1968, he entered a contest for black writers sponsored by the Council on Interracial Books for Children. The manuscript Myers submitted was selected as the first-prize winner in the picture book category; in 1969, it was published by Parents' Magazine Press as *Where Does the Day Go?* The book features Steven, a small black boy whose father takes him and a group of children of various races for an evening walk in the park. When Steven wonders where the day goes, his friends each provide imaginative opinions of their own. Finally, Steven's dad explains that the day and night are different, just like people, and that the times of day are caused by the rotation of the Earth. "Integration, involvement, and togetherness are all deftly handled," noted Mary Eble in *School Library Journal,* while Zena Sutherland, Dianne L. Monson, and May Hill Arbuthnot claimed in *Children and Books* that the story has "other strong values in addition to its exploration of the mystery of night and day." The critics noted that *Where Does the Day Go?* "explains natural phenomena accurately, and it presents an exemplary father."

After the publication of his first book, Myers changed his name from Walter Milton Myers to, as he wrote in *SAAS,* "one that would honor my foster parents, Walter Dean Myers." He also remarried, and he and his wife Connie had a son, Christopher, an artist who has illustrated several of his father's works. In 1972, Myers published *The Dragon Takes a Wife,* a picture book that was viewed by several critics as controversial. The story features Harry, a lonely dragon who cannot fight, and Mabel May, the African-American fairy who helps him. In order to acquire a wife, Harry must defeat a knight in battle. When Mabel May turns into a dragon to show Harry how to fight, Harry falls in love with her, defeats the knight, and wins her hand, not to mention a good job at the post office.

Myers received mixed reviews for *The Dragon Takes a Wife.* For example, a critic in *Kirkus Reviews* called it "pointless intercultural hocus-pocus," while Nancy Griffin of the *New York Times Book Review* praised it as "the funniest, most-up-to-the-minute fairy tale of 1972." Some readers were angered by the fact that Mabel May is black and speaks in hip lingo; they were also concerned that this character appears in a fairy tale for young children. *The Dragon Takes a Wife* was banned by some libraries; Myers also received hate mail from disgruntled adult readers of the book.

In 1975, Myers published his first novel for young adults, *Fast Sam, Cool Clyde, and Stuff.* Set in a Harlem neighborhood much like the one in which its author grew up, the story describes a group of young teens who take a positive approach to living in a difficult environment. The story is narrated by eighteen-

year-old Stuff, who recalls the year that he was thirteen and formed a sort of anti-gang, the Good People, with his best friends Fast Sam and Cool Clyde plus five other boys and girls from the neighborhood. The Good People have several hilarious adventures, including one where Sam and Clyde—who is dressed as a girl—win a dance contest. However, they also deal with such problems as mistaken arrest and the deaths of one of their fathers and a friend who has turned to drugs. The children survive, both through their inner strength and the fellowship of their friends, who are dependable and respectful of one another.

Writing in *English Journal,* Alleen Pace Nilsen called *Fast Sam, Cool Clyde, and Stuff* "a rich, warm story about black kids in which Myers makes the reader feel so close to the characters that ethnic group identification is secondary." Paul Heins of *Horn Book* noted that "the humorous and ironic elements of the plot give the book the flavor of a Harlem *Tom Sawyer* or *Penrod.*" *Fast Sam, Cool Clyde, and Stuff* continues to be one of Myers's most popular works, especially among middle graders and junior high school students.

In 1977, after being fired from his job as a senior editor for Bobbs-Merrill due to a dispute with a company vice president, Myers became a full-time writer. *It Ain't All for Nothin',* a young-adult novel published the next year, is considered the first of the author's more serious, thought-provoking works. The novel features twelve-year-old Tippy, a motherless Harlem boy who has been living with his loving, principled grandmother since he was a baby. When she goes into a nursing home, Tippy moves in with his father Lonnie, an ex-con who makes his living by stealing and who beats his son viciously. Lonely and afraid, Tippy begins drinking whiskey. When Lonnie and his pals rob a store, he coerces Tippy into participating. Bubba, a member of the group, is shot; in order to save Bubba and save himself, Tippy calls the police and turns in his father. At the end of the novel, Tippy goes to live with Mr. Roland, a kind man who has befriended him. *It Ain't All for Nothin'* was praised by Steven Matthews in *School Library Journal* as "a first-rate read," and by a critic in *Kirkus Reviews* as "like Tippy—a winner." Although questioning "how many children are really going to 'drop a dime' on their father?," Ashley Jane Pennington concluded in her review in *Interracial Books for Children Bulletin* that *It Ain't All for Nothin'* "is a devastating book which needed to be written." In 1984, Myers published *Motown and Didi: A Love Story,* a highly praised sequel that features two of the novel's peripheral characters. A romance between two Harlem teens, *Motown and Didi* includes a strong antidrug message as well as the theme that love can conquer all.

In 1988 Myers published *Scorpions* and *Fallen Angels,* two novels for young people that are considered among his best. In *Scorpions* twelve-year-old Jamal lives in Harlem with his mother and younger sister. He is approached to take the place of his older brother Randy, who is in jail for killing a man, as the leader of his gang, the Scorpions. At first, Jamal refuses; however, he is fascinated with the gun that Randy's friend Mack gives him and is searching for a way to help his family raise the money for Randy's appeal. Jamal and his best friend Tito, a sensitive Puerto Rican boy, join the Scorpions, who are dealing cocaine. During a confrontation, Jamal is defended by Tito, who uses the gun Mack had given Jamal to kill to protect his friend. Marcus Crouch, in the *Junior Bookshelf,* wrote that Myers "writes with great power, capturing the cadences of black New York, and keeps a firm hold on his narrative and his emotions. He is a fine story-teller as well as a social critic and, I suspect, a moralist." Writing in the *Bulletin of the Center for Children's Books,* Roger Sutton noted that Myers's "compassion for Tito and Jamal is deep; perhaps the book's seminal achievement is the way it makes us realize how young, in Harlem and elsewhere, twelve years old really is."

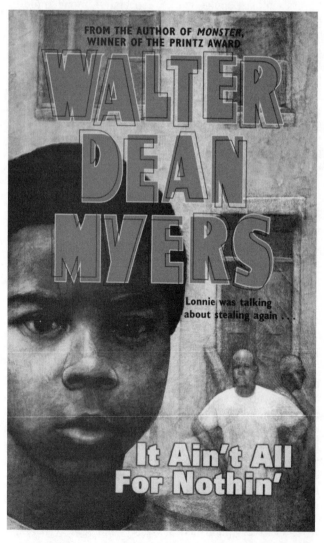

In Walter Dean Myers' powerful 1978 coming-of-age novel a teen must make a difficult choice: whether to follow his father into a life of petty crime or reject him and likely lose his dad's love. (Cover illustration by Joel P. Johnson.)

Fallen Angels describes the horrors of the Vietnam War from the perspective of Richie Perry, a seventeen-year-old African American who has joined the U.S. Army as a way to make life easier for his mother and younger brother in Harlem. During the course of a year, Richie experiences fear and terror as he fights in the war; he burns the bodies of American soldiers because they cannot be carried and—with a rifle at his head—shoots a North Vietnamese soldier in the face; finally, after being wounded twice, he is sent home. Underscoring the novel, which includes rough language and gallows humor, is a strong antiwar message; Myers also addresses such issues as racial discrimination within the service and the conditions faced by the Vietnamese people. Calling Myers "a writer of skill, maturity, and judgment," Ethel L. Heins maintained in *Horn Book* that, "With its intensity and vividness in depicting a young soldier amid the chaos and the carnage of war, the novel recalls Stephen Crane's *The Red Badge of Courage.*" W. Keith McCoy, writing in *Voice of Youth Advocates,* commented that "Everything about this book rings true," while Mary Veeder, writing in Chicago's *Tribune Books,* noted that *Fallen Angels* "may be the best novel for young adults I've read this year."

Myers wrote *Fallen Angels* as a tribute to his brother Sonny, who was killed on his first day as a soldier in Vietnam; he also based much of the book on his own experience in the U.S. Army. In discussing both *Fallen Angels* and *Scorpions* with Kimberly Olson Fakih in *Publishers Weekly,* Myers called these books "a departure" and "very serious, probing work." He concluded: "Not that the others didn't address serious issues, too, but the new ones were more difficult to write." In 1993, Myers published *A Place Called Heartbreak: A Story of Vietnam,* a well-received biography of Colonel Fred V. Cherry, an Air Force pilot and African American who was held as a prisoner of the North Vietnamese for nearly eight years.

In addition to his fiction, Myers has written several highly praised informational books for children and young people in which he characteristically outlines the fight for freedom by people of color; he has also written biographies of such figures as Toussaint L'Ouverture, Martin Luther King, and Malcolm X. *Now Is Your Time! The African-American Struggle for Freedom* is one of Myers's most well regarded works of nonfiction. In this book, the author recounts the history of black Americans through both overviews and profiles of individuals. "What happens," wrote a critic in *Kirkus Reviews,* "when a gifted novelist chooses to write the story of his people? In this case, the result is engrossing history with a strong unifying theme, the narrative enriched with accounts of outstanding lives." Michael Dirda, writing in the *Washington Post Book World,* added that Myers "writes with the vividness of a novelist, the balance of a historian, and the passion of an advocate. He tells a familiar story and shocks us with it all over again." Writing in *Voice of Youth Advocates,*

Kellie Flynn noted that *Now Is Your Time!* "is alive and vital—with breathing biographical sketches and historic interpretations like rabbit punches."

With *Amistad: A Long Road to Freedom* Myers tells the dramatic story of the captive Africans who mutinied against their captors on the slave ship *Amistad* in the late 1830s. The book recounts the hellish journey on the ship and the forced landing in Connecticut as well as the landmark trial and the struggle of the West Africans to return home. Writing in *Booklist*, Hazel Rochman stated, "The narrative is exciting, not only the account of the uprising but also the tension of the court arguments about whether the captives were property and what their rights were in a country that banned the slave trade but allowed slavery." Gerry Larson added in a review for *School Library Journal* that, "With characteristic scholarship, clarity, insight, and compassion, Myers presents readers with the facts and the moral and historical significance of the *Amistad* episode."

A longtime collector of historical photographs and documents depicting the lives and culture of African Americans, Myers has used his own art to illustrate several of his informational books. The photos and letters from the author's collection have also inspired several of his works, including volumes of original poetry on black children and mothers and the biography *At Her Majesty's Request: An African Princess in Victorian England.* Published in 1999, this work reconstructs the life of Sarah Forbes Bonetta, a child of royal African descent who became a goddaughter of Queen Victoria as well as a British celebrity. Saved from a sacrificial rite in Dahomey by English sea captain Frederick E. Forbes, orphaned Sarah—named after her rescuer and his ship— was brought to England as a gift for Queen Victoria from the Dahomian king who slaughtered her family. Victoria provided the means for Sarah—nicknamed Sally—to be educated as a young woman of privilege in a missionary school in Sierra Leone. Sally, who often returned to England to visit her benefactor, grew up to marry a West African businessman, a marriage arranged by Buckingham Palace; she named her first-born child Victoria. Eventually returning with her husband to Africa, Sally taught in missionary schools until she died of tuberculosis at the age of thirty-six.

Working from a packet of letters he discovered in a London bookstore, Myers tells Sally's story, which he embellishes with quotes from Queen Victoria's diary, newspapers, and other memoirs of the time. A critic in *Kirkus Reviews* commented, "This vividly researched biography will enthrall readers, and ranks among Myers's best writing." Calling *At Her Majesty's Request* a "fascinating biography" and a "moving and very humane portrait of a princess," a reviewer in *Publishers Weekly* concluded that Myers "portrays a young woman who never truly belongs."

The Blues of Flats Brown is a children's picture book about a dog who flees to Memphis and has a hit record, angering his former owner, the mean A. J. Grubbs, who

follows him on to New York. "Myers's shaggy fantasy has the slow-and-easy pacing of a lazy Southern afternoon," wrote a *Publishers Weekly* reviewer. "Myers beautifully conveys the blues' unique roots and the way the music bestows comfort, catharsis, and healing," said Shelle Rosenfeld in *Booklist*.

Myers's second book about Malcolm X, *Malcolm X: A Fire Burning Brightly,* focuses on the stages of Malcolm's life and contains Leonard Jenkins's artwork, "full-color montage illustrations, in acrylic, pastel, and spray paint . . . like mural art, with larger-than-life individual portraits set against the crowded streets and the swirl of politics," wrote *Booklist* contributor Rochman, who noted that nearly every page contains a quote from speeches or writings. Myers chronicles Malcolm's childhood, his time in the Charlestown State Prison, his conversion to Islam, leadership of the Black Muslims, and ultimate break with Black Muslim leader Elijah Muhammad, and his pilgrimage to Mecca prior to his assassination in 1965.

In *The Greatest: Muhammad Ali,* Myers documents the life of the boxer born Cassius Clay from his childhood in segregated St. Louis to his Olympic win in 1960 and his success as a world-class athlete. Myers then relates Clay's commitment as a Black Muslim and his political activism as a conscientious objector during the Vietnam War. Myers also reports on Ali's major fights against Sonny Liston, Joe Frazier, and George Foreman. *Horn Book* contributor Jack Forman felt the book "is more portrait of Ali's character and cultural impact than a narrative of his life." "This is finally a story about a black man of tremendous courage," wrote Bill Ott in *Booklist*, "the kind of universal story that needs a writer as talented as Myers to retell it for every generation." Khafre K. Abif added in *Black Issues Book Review* that Myers "inspires a new generation of fans by exposing the hazards Ali faced in boxing, the rise of a champion, and now his battle against Parkinson's disease."

In *Bad Boy: A Memoir,* Myers begins with an account of his childhood, then takes the reader through his adolescence—during which he often skipped school and sometimes made deliveries for drug dealers—and to his beginnings as a writer. Rochman said, "The most beautiful writing is about Mama: how she taught him to read, sharing *True Romance* magazines." "The author's growing awareness of racism and of his own identity as a black man make up one of the most interesting threads," wrote Miranda Doyle in *School Library Journal.* Myers' "voice and heart are consistently heard and felt throughout," concluded a *Horn Book* contributor.

Myers's nonfiction title *USS Constellation* relates the entire story of the famous ship, from construction to war victories to encounters with slave ships to crew training. The book is complemented by first-person accounts, along with illustrations and charts. Carolyn Phelan, writing in *Booklist,* praised this "well-re-

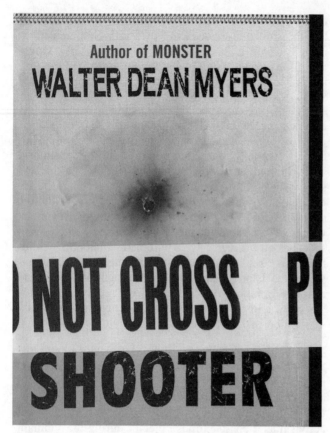

Reflecting modern newspaper headlines, Myers' 2004 novel contains interviews, journal entries, and other reports that follow three troubled high schoolers whose problems culminate in a stunning school tragedy. (Cover illustration by Robert Beck.)

searched" volume, adding that it is a "unique addition to American history collections." In *Publishers Weekly,* a reviewer praised Myers book as a"meticulously researched, fast-flowing chronicle," and applauded the book for offering "a larger view of the shaping of America." Betty Carter, writing in *Horn Book,* noted that the first-person accounts "lend authenticity while personalizing events." The novel *Shooter* focuses on the events leading up to and following a school shooting that many reviewers compared to the real-life and well-publicized Columbine school tragedy that had occurred months prior to *Shooter*'s publication. The novel is told through a unique narrative approach: the book consists of police reports, news articles, a journal, and other "real-life" documentation of the event. For its dark subject matter and its unique narration, *Shooter* has often been compared with *Monster.* Of *Shooter,* Lauren Adams wrote in *Horn Book* that Myers's "exacting look at the many possible players and causes in the events makes for a compelling story." A *Publishers Weekly* reviewer praised the author for his handling of a controversial subject in which "no one is completely innocent and no one is entirely to blame." The reviewer concluded, "Readers will find themselves racing through the pages, then turning back to pore over the details once more."

"Children and adults," wrote Myers in *SAAS,* "must have role models with which they can identify"; therefore in his writing he has attempted to "deliver images upon which [they] could build and expand their own worlds." In an interview with Roger Sutton for *School Library Journal,* Myers noted that writing about the African-American experience is fraught with complexity and difficulties. "Very often people want more from books than a story," the author explained; "they want books to represent them well. This is where I get the flak."

Commenting on the question of writing primarily for a black audience, Myers stated: "as a black person you are always representing the race. . . . So what you have to do is try to write it as well as you can and hope that if you write the story well enough, people won't be offended." Myers sees an element of racism in the notion that black authors must write about "black subjects" for a primarily black audience. Likewise, he views the controversy surrounding the question of whether whites should write about the black experience as "a false issue." "I think basically you need to write what you believe in."

Writing in *SAAS,* Myers stated that he feels the need to show young blacks "the possibilities that exist for them that were never revealed to me as a youngster; possibilities that did not even exist for me then." He continued: "As a Black writer I want to talk about my people. . . . I want to tell Black children about their humanity and about their history and how to grease their legs so the ash won't show and how to braid their hair so it's easy to comb on frosty winter mornings. The books come. They pour from me at a great rate. . . . There is always one more story to tell, one more person whose life needs to be held up to the sun."

In an interview in *Teaching and Learning Literature,* he noted: "What I do with whatever art I have is to try to communicate the human experience." He works to communicate this experience to "my sons, my son's sons, daughters, the next generation, and that is what life is about. We are the ones that have the gift of story, the gift of passing it on." Writing in *Children's Books and Their Creators,* Myers concluded: "What I do with my books is to create windows to my world that all may peer into. I share the images, the feelings and thoughts, and, I hope, the delight."

Biographical and Critical Sources

BOOKS

Bishop, Rudine Sims, *Presenting Walter Dean Myers,* Twayne, 1991.
Dictionary of Literary Biography, Volume 33: *Afro-American Fiction Writers after 1955,* Gale (Detroit, MI), 1984, pp. 199-202.
Something about the Author Autobiography Series, Gale (Detroit, MI), 1986, pp. 143-156.

PERIODICALS

African American Review, spring, 1988, R. H. Lane, "Keepin It Real: Walter Dean Myers and the Promise of African-American Children's Literature," p. 125.

Black Issues Book Review, May, 2001, Khafre K. Abif, review of *The Greatest: Muhammad Ali,* p. 80.

Booklist, February 15, 1998, Hazel Rochman, "Some Versions of *Amistad,* " p. 1003; February 15, 2000, Hazel Rochman, review of *Malcolm X: A Fire Burning Brightly,* p. 1103; March 1, 2000, Shelle Rosenfeld, review of *The Blues of Flats Brown,* p. 1242; January 1, 2001, Bill Ott, review of *The Greatest,* p. 952; May 1, 2001, Hazel Rochman, review of *Bad Boy: A Memoir,* p. 1673; July, 2004, Carolyn Phelan, review of *USS Constellation,* p. 1841.

Bulletin of the Center for Children's Books, July-August, 1988, review of *Scorpions,* p. 235.

English Journal, March, 1976, Alleen Pace Nilsen, "Love and the Teenage Reader," pp. 90-92.

Horn Book, August, 1975, Ethel L. Heins, review of *Fallen Angels,* pp. 503-504; July-August, 1988, Paul Heins, review of *Fast Sam, Cool Clyde, and Stuff,* pp. 388-389; May, 2000, review of *Malcolm X: A Fire Burning Brightly,* p. 336; January, 2000, Jack Forman, review of *The Greatest,* p. 115; July, 2001, review of *Bad Boy,* p. 473; May-June, 2004, Lauren Adams, review of *Shooter,* p. 335; July-August, 2004, Betty Carter, review of *USS Constellation,* p. 469.

Interracial Books for Children Bulletin, Volume 10, number 4, 1979, Ashley Jane Pennington, review of *It Ain't All for Nothin',* p. 18.

Junior Bookshelf, August, 1990, Marcus Crouch, review of *Scorpions,* pp. 190-191.

Kirkus Reviews, March 1, 1972, review of *The Dragon Takes a Wife,* p. 256; October 15, 1978, review of *It Ain't All for Nothin',* p. 1143; October 1, 1991, review of *Now Is Your Time!,* p. 1537; December 15, 1998, review of *At Her Majesty's Request: An African Princess in Victorian England,* p. 1802.

New York Times Book Review, April 19, 1972, Nancy Griffin, review of *The Dragon Takes a Wife,* p. 8; October 21, 2001, Kermit Frazier, review of *Bad Boy,* p. 31.

Publishers Weekly, February 26, 1988, "Walter Dean Myers," p. 117; February 8, 1999, review of *At Her Majesty's Request,* p. 215; January 24, 2000, review of *The Blues of Flats Brown,* p. 311; March 22, 2004, review of *Shooter,* p. 87; June 28, 2004, review of *USS Constellation,* p. 52.

School Librarian, August, 1990, Allison Hurst, review of *Fallen Angels,* pp. 118-119.

School Library Journal, April 15, 1970, Mary Eble, review of *Where Does the Day Go?,* p. 111; October, 1978, Steven Matthews, review of *It Aint' All for Nothin',* p. 158; May, 1998, Gerry Larson, review of *Amistad: A Long Road to Freedom,* p. 158; March, 2000, Karen James, review of *The Blues of Flats Brown,* p. 210; May, 2001, Miranda Doyle, review of *Bad Boy,* p. 169; December, 2001, Kathleen Baxter, review of *The Greatest,* p. 39.

TALL, September-October, 1998, Ellen A. Greever, "Making Connections in the Life and Works of Walter Dean Myers," pp. 42-54.

Tribune Books (Chicago, IL), November 13, 1988, Mary Veeder, "Some Versions of *Fallen Angels,* " p. 6.

Voice of Youth Advocates, August, 1988, W. Keith McCoy, review of *Fallen Angels,* p. 133; February, 1992, Kellie Flynn, review of *Now Is Your Time!,* p. 398.

Washington Post Book World, March 8, 1992, Michael Dirda, review of *Now Is Your Time!,* p. 11.

Wilson Library Bulletin, January, 1993, Frances Bradburn, review of *The Righteous Revenge of Artemis Bonner,* p. 88.*

N

NAMIOKA, Lensey 1929-

Personal

Born June 14, 1929, in Peking, China; immigrated to United States, 1938; daughter of Yuen Ren (a linguist) and Buwei (a physician and writer; maiden name, Yang) Chao; married Isaac Namioka (a mathematician), September 9, 1957; children: Aki, Michi. *Education:* Attended Radcliffe College, 1947-49; University of California, Berkeley, B.A., 1951, M.A., 1952. *Hobbies and other interests:* Music ("prefer to make it myself badly than to hear it performed superbly").

Addresses

Home—2047 23rd Avenue E., Seattle, WA 98112. *Agent*—Ruth Cohen, Box 2244, La Jola, CA 92038-2244.

Career

Wells College, Aurora, NY, instructor in mathematics, 1957-58; Cornell University, Ithaca, NY, instructor in mathematics, 1958-61; Japan Broadcasting Corporation, broadcasting monitor, beginning 1969. American Mathematical Society, translator, 1958-66.

Member

Authors Guild, Authors League of America, Mystery Writers of America, Society of Children's Book Writers and Illustrators, PEN (USA West), Seattle Free Lances.

Lensey Namioka

Awards, Honors

Washington State Governor's Writers Award, 1976, for *White Serpent Castle,* 1996, for *April and the Dragon Lady;* runner-up, Edgar Allan Poe Award, 1982, and American Library Association (ALA) Best Book designation, 1993, both for *Village of the Vampire Cat;* ALA Best Book designation, 1990, for *Island of the Ogres;* Certificate of Merit, *Parenting* magazine, 1994, for *The Coming of the Bear;* Parents' Choice recognition, 1995, for *Yang the Third and Her Impossible Family;* Parents' Choice Gold Medal, 2000, for *Yang the Eldest and His Odd Jobs;* Washington State Governor's Writers Award, and ALA Best Book designation, both 2000, and California Young Reader Medal, 2004, all for *Ties That Bind, Ties That Break.*

Writings

FICTION FOR YOUNG ADULTS

The Samurai and the Long-nosed Devils, McKay (New York, NY), 1976, reprinted, Tuttle (Boston, MA), 2004.

White Serpent Castle, McKay (New York, NY), 1976, reprinted, Tuttle (Boston, MA), 2004.

Valley of the Broken Cherry Trees, Delacorte (New York, NY), 1981, reprinted, Tuttle (Boston, MA), 2005.

Village of the Vampire Cat, Delacorte (New York, NY), 1981, reprinted, Tuttle (Boston, MA), 2005.

Who's Hu?, Vanguard (New York, NY), 1981.

The Phantom of Tiger Mountain, Vanguard (New York, NY), 1986.

Island of Ogres, Harper (New York, NY), 1989.

The Coming of the Bear, HarperCollins (New York, NY), 1992.

Yang the Youngest and His Terrible Ear, illustrated by Kees de Kiefte, Joy Street (Boston, MA), 1992.

April and the Dragon Lady, Browndeer Press (San Diego, CA), 1994.

The Loyal Cat, illustrated by Aki Sogabe, Browndeer Press (San Francisco, CA), 1995.

Yang the Third and Her Impossible Family, illustrated by Kees de Kiefte, Little, Brown (Boston, MA), 1995.

Den of the White Fox, Harcourt Brace (San Diego, CA), 1997.

The Laziest Boy in the World, Holiday House (New York, NY), 1998.

Yang the Second and Her Secret Admirers, Little, Brown (Boston, MA), 1998.

Ties That Bind, Ties That Break, Delacorte (New York, NY), 1999.

Yang the Eldest and His Odd Job, Little, Brown (Boston, MA), 2000.

The Hungriest Boy in the World, Holiday House (New York, NY), 2001.

An Ocean Apart, a World Away, Delacorte (New York, NY), 2002.

Half and Half, Delacorte (New York, NY), 2003.

OTHER

(Translator) Buwei Y. Chao, *How to Order and Eat in Chinese,* Vintage (New York, NY), 1974.

Japan: A Traveler's Companion, Vanguard (New York, NY), 1979.

China: A Traveler's Companion, Vanguard (New York, NY), 1985.

Also author of plays included in *Center Stage,* edited by Donald Gallo. Contributor of travel and humor articles to magazines and newspapers.

Sidelights

Lensey Namioka worked primarily as a mathematics instructor before beginning her career as a published writer in the mid-1970s. Namioka's works, as she once told *Something about the Author (SATA),* "draw heavily" on her "Chinese cultural heritage and on [her] husband's Japanese cultural heritage." Namioka is perhaps best known for her series of exciting, adventure-mystery books about two sixteenth-century Japanese samurai warriors and for her humorous, juvenile novels about a family of Chinese immigrants living in Seattle.

Namioka's first book for young readers, *The Samurai and the Long-nosed Devils,* is set in sixteenth-century Japan and introduces Konishi Zenta and Ishihara Matsuzo. They are young, freelance samurai warriors, or *ronin,* and must wander to find work. When they gain employment as the bodyguards of Portuguese missionaries, Zenta and Matsuzo must solve a murder mystery to save their employers. As their investigation progresses, the two ronin find themselves enmeshed in a web of political intrigue. Zena Sutherland, writing in the *Bulletin of the Center for Children's Books* commented that Namioka's debut "has a lively plot with an abundance of derring-do." Adventures continue in *White Serpent Castle,* as Zenta and Matsuzo must confront the ghost of a white serpent as they investigate another mystery. According to Sada Fretz in *Kirkus Reviews,* the "solution . . . folds in on itself like . . . origami." Namioka includes historical notes and bibliographies in both *The Samurai and the Long-nosed Devils* and *White Serpent Castle.*

Zenta and Matsuzo continue their adventures in *Valley of the Broken Cherry Trees.* Expecting to see the beautiful cherry trees of the famed valley, the two currently unemployed samurai are shocked to find destruction: a number of trees have been mutilated. As they investigate to determine who has harmed the trees, they once again find themselves in the middle of a power struggle. A critic in *Bulletin of the Center for Children's Books* reported that the author "evokes the place and period vividly." Paul Heins, reviewing *Valley of the Broken Cherry Trees* for *Horn Book,* noted that the "narrative, which develops an elaborate plot, is threaded with mystery, intrigue, action, and suspense."

When Zenta and Matsuzo arrive at a familiar village to visit an elderly tea master in *Village of the Vampire Cat,* they discover another mystery: a vampiric feline appears to be killing young women. Zenta and Matsuzo investigate the murders and prove that the vampire cat is neither a vampire nor a cat. They also participate in the Japanese tea ceremony. As Betsy Fuller McGuckin asserted in *School Library Journal,* Namioka's characters "offer all the mystery and contradiction of human nature." According to Sutherland in *Bulletin of the Center for Children's Books,* "the period details, the mores, and the customs are smoothly integrated."

In *Island of Ogres,* another samurai, Kajiro, is sent to an island to spy on its commander. Kajiro is mistakenly identified as Zenta, who is already hiding on the island, having fallen in love with the commander's wife. Matsuzo's challenge in this story is to help Zenta. As Chris-

Tao Ailin, a Chinese teen who has reached marriage age, battles foot binding, an arranged marriage, and the other traditional ways of her family in Namioka's powerful coming-of-age tale, set in 1911. (Cover illustration by Michael Frost.)

tine Behrmann wrote in *School Library Journal,* Namioka's storyline is "byzantine" and "appearance versus reality permeates the plot." According to Behrmann, readers who follow the shifting perspectives and "elliptical style" so appreciated by Namioka's fans "will be rewarded."

In *The Coming of the Bear* Zenta and Matsuzo are taken prisoner on the island of the Ainu, a race of round-eyed people that still live on the island of Hokkaido. Nevertheless, they manage to solve the mystery of a killer bear while also preventing a war between Ainu and Japanese settlers. This book, according to Lola H. Teubert in the *Voice of Youth Advocates,* will "bring to the reader romance, adventure, cunning, mystery . . . and insight into a vanishing culture." John Philbrook dubbed *The Coming of the Bear* "a real page-turner" in his *School Library Journal* review.

Namioka's first work of young-adult fiction set in contemporary times, *Who's Hu?,* was published in 1981. This novel follows Emma, a Chinese teenager who must decide whether to follow Chinese ways or those of the Americans she meets in her new home in the Boston area. Emma is led to believe that appearances, and fitting in, are more important in this culture than academic excellence; she must discover what she herself values. Malinda Sinaiko, writing in *School Library Journal,* noted that "an entertaining education in Chinese customs and culture vs. the American way of life" is included in the plot.

Similarly, *April and the Dragon Lady* is a novel about a girl coming to terms with her Chinese cultural heritage and contemporary American expectations at the same time. Chinese-American April Chen must balance her plans to go away to college with her responsibilities to her grandmother, the "dragon lady." She must also weigh the respect she has for her family with her decision to see a white boyfriend. "This is a well told story, believable and engaging," wrote Linda Palter in the *Voice of Youth Advocates.* "Sparked by Namioka's own experiences as an Asian-American, April's first person narrative rings true," concluded Sharon Korbeck in *School Library Journal.*

Yang the Youngest and His Terrible Ear and *Yang the Third and Her Impossible Family* are part of a series of humorous novels about a family of Chinese musicians who have recently immigrated to Seattle. In *Yang the Youngest and His Terrible Ear* tone-deaf Yang Yingtao has a difficult time performing in the family quartet and prefers to exercise his natural athletic talent in baseball games. He develops a friendship with a white boy, and they begin to introduce each other to their different norms, customs, and prejudices. According to Nancy Vasilakis in *Horn Book,* Namioka "explores issues of diversity, self-realization, friendship, and duty with sensitivity and a great deal of humor." In *Yang the Third and Her Impossible Family* Yingmei, or Mary, gradually comes to terms with the embarrassment cultural differences bring her. Hazel Rochman, reviewing the novel for *Booklist,* remarked upon the "uproarious scenes of cross-cultural awkwardness," and concluded that children will understand Namioka's message: "that we are all 'ethnic.'"

The Hungriest Boy in the World is a humorous cautionary tale for young readers. A boy named Jiro has a bad habit of putting anything and everything in his mouth. When he inadvertently swallows a hunger monster, he literally eats everything, including quilts and fish guts. Jiro's problem is resolved when the monster is tricked into leaving Jiro's body and entering a puppet. *Horn Book* reviewer Jennifer M. Brabander found the artwork by Aki Sogabe perfectly suited to the story, writing that "the humor of Namioka's matter-of-fact tone is reflected in Sogabe's illustrations." Similarly, Gillian Engberg wrote in *Booklist* that the "silly, farcical story is spiced with images kids will love," and added that the book is good for reading aloud. Namioka's humor was also appreciated by *School Library Journal* reviewer Grace Oliff, who commented that *The Hungriest Boy in the World* "is told economically but with wit and humor."- *Ties That Bind, Ties That Break* explores themes of cultural conflict and political unrest. Ailin is a young woman in 1920s China who is expected to prepare herself for marriage and a traditional family life. Unwilling to take the road expected of her, Ailin rebels and her journey of independence eventually takes her to America. Although the transition is a difficult one, in the end she is rewarded with happiness and self-respect. Shelle Rosenfeld, reviewing the novel for *Booklist*, praised Namioka's depiction of the complicated heroine, commenting specifically that the "characters have exceptional depth." Rosenfeld also praised the author's "lyrical, descriptive prose" and the accomplishment of a book that is "emotionally and historically illuminating."

Namioka reunites her readers with some of the characters from *Ties That Bind, Ties That Break* in *An Ocean Apart, a World Away,* where young Yanyan is bent on making her own way despite the tradition and culture of 1920s China. Her dream is to become a doctor, not a wife, and her wealthy parents are willing to support her decision, but when Yanyan develops feelings toward one of her brother's friends, however, she questions her original plan. Because the man she loves is a political rebel, and life with him would be dangerous, she ultimately turns down his request to run away together and heads to America to attend school at Cornell University. The second half of the book follows Yanyan as she adapts to her new life. She faces challenges emotionally, socially, and academically, including the opportunity to enter into a traditional Chinese marriage, but eventually gets her footing.Reviewing *An Ocean Apart, a World Away*, Olivia Durant in *Kliatt* applauded Namioka for creating a "captivating story of a strong female character in a nontraditional role, smoothly weaving in aspects of Chinese culture and history." According to Lori Atkins Goodson in the *Journal of Adolescent and Adult Literacy*, "Namioka gives a lively history lesson—She wraps these historic elements around the tale of a typical teenager trying to find her own place in the world." Paula Rohrlick, writing in *Kliatt*, found Yanyan to be much more than a typical teenager, remarking that Namioka's "tale of a resolute early feminist and of cultural differences will appeal to fans of historical fiction and of feisty female protagonists." While the romance, setting, and strong heroine "contribute to the book's appeal," wrote Kathleen Isaacs in *School Library Journal*, "its special strength is the voice of its narrator."

Supported by her father in leaving China to obtain a college education in the United States, Yanyan is again confronted with a choice between the old and new ways when her Chinese boyfriend wants her to become a traditional-style wife.

Biographical and Critical Sources

PERIODICALS

Booklist, April 15, 1995, Hazel Rochman, review of *Yang the Third and Her Impossible Family,* p. 1500; May 15, 1999, Shelle Rosenfeld, review of *Ties That Bind, Ties That Break,* p. 1697; April 1, 2001, Gillian Engberg, review of *The Hungriest Boy in the World,* p. 1479.

Bulletin of the Center for Children's Books, January, 1977, Zena Sutherland, review of *The Samurai and the Long-nosed Devils,* pp. 78-79; June, 1980, review of *Valley of the Broken Cherry Trees,* p. 197; June, 1981, Zena Sutherland, review of *Village of the Vampire Cat,* p. 200.

Horn Book, June, 1980, Paul Heins, review of *Valley of the Broken Cherry Trees,* pp. 307-308; July-August, 1992, Nancy Vasilakis, review of *Yang the Youngest and His Terrible Ear,* pp. 452-453; May, 2001, Jennifer M. Brabander, review of *The Hungriest Boy in the World,* p. 313.

Journal of Adolescent and Adult Literacy, May, 2003, Lori Atkins Goodson, review of *An Ocean Apart, a World Away,* p. 701.

Kirkus Reviews, October 15, 1976, Sada Fretz, review of *White Serpent Castle,* p. 1146.

Kliatt, July, 2002, Paula Rohrlick, review of *An Ocean Apart, a World Away,* p. 13; May, 2004, Olivia Durant, review of *An Ocean Apart, a World Away,* p. 21.

Publishers Weekly, July 8, 2002, review of *An Ocean Apart, a World Away,* p. 50.

School Library Journal, May, 1981, Betsy Fuller McGuckin, review of *Village of the Vampire Cat,* p. 76; February, 1982, Malinda Sinaiko, review of *Who's Hu?,* p. 79; March, 1989, Christine Behrmann, review of *Island of the Ogres,* p. 200; March, 1992, John Philbrook, review of *The Coming of the Bear,* p. 240; April, 1994, Sharon Korbeck, review of *April and the Dragon Lady,* p. 152; April, 2001, Grace Oliff, review of *The Hungriest Boy in the World,* p. 119; July, 2002, Kathleen Isaacs, review of *An Ocean Apart, a World Away,* pp. 123-1224.

Voice of Youth Advocates, October, 1992, Lola H. Teubert, review of *The Coming of the Bear,* p. 227; June, 1994, Linda Palter, review of *April and the Dragon Lady,* pp. 87-88.*

*　　*　　*

NEUSCHWANDER, Cindy 1953-

Personal

Born October 27, 1953, in San Diego, CA; daughter of Max (a teacher) and Carol (a homemaker) Grazda; married Bruce Neuschwander (a C.F.O.), May 26, 1973; children: Tim, Seth. *Education:* Willamette University, B.A., 1975; Stanford University, M.A., 1976. *Religion:* Christian *Hobbies and other interests:* Travel, skiing, beach bodysurfing.

Addresses

Office—c/o Frederiksen Elementary School, 7243 Tamarack Dr., Dublin, CA 94568.

Career

Teacher and writer. Frankfurt International School, Oberursel, Germany, teacher, 1989-92; American Community School, London, England, teacher, 1992-93; Tracy Unified School District, Tracy, CA, teacher, 1993-96; Dublin Unified School District, Dublin, CA, teacher, 1996—.

Member

Society of Children's Book Writers and Illustrators, National Council of Teachers of Mathematics.

Writings

Sir Cumference and the First Round Table: A Math Adventure, illustrated by Wayne Geehan, Charlesbridge (Watertown, MA), 1997.

Cindy Neuschwander

Amanda Bean's Amazing Dream: A Mathematical Story, Scholastic (New York, NY), 1998.

Sir Cumference and the Dragon of Pi: A Math Adventure, illustrated by Wayne Geehan, Charlesbridge (Watertown, MA), 1999.

Sir Cumference and the Great Knight of Angleland: A Math Adventure, illustrated by Wayne Geehan, Charlesbridge (Watertown, MA), 1999.

88 Pounds of Tomatoes, illustrated by Terry Sirrell, Scholastic (New York, NY), 2001.

The Chocolate Champs, illustrated by Cristina Ong, Scholastic (New York, NY), 2002.

Sir Cumference and the Sword in the Cone, illustrated by Wayne Geehan, Charlesbridge (Watertown, MA), 2003.

Mummy Math: An Adventure in Geometry, illustrated by Bryan Langdo, Henry Holt (New York, NY), 2005.

Sidelights

An elementary school teacher by profession, Cindy Neuschwander has penned several educational children's books that take an unusual approach to an often intimidating subject. Titled to attract even the most math-averse student, *Sir Cumference and the Sword in the Cone: A Math Adventure* and *Sir Cumference and the First Round Table: A Math Adventure* revisit the classic tale of King Arthur and the Sword in the Stone while creating scenarios with a strong math angle. In the pun-laden *Sir Cumference and the Sword in the Cone,* for example, Radius, the son of Sir Cumfrence and his wife, the Lady Di of Ameter, joins his youthful friend Vertex in a quest for Edgecalibur in order to win the favor of the king. Featuring humorous, brightly colored illustrations by Wayne Geehan, "the books can be used to support educational initiatives such as multiple intelligences, and students who are strong in verbal/linguistic areas will appreciate the integration of literature into their math lesson" stated Christine E. Carr in *School Library Journal.*

Neuschwander once told *Something about the Author:* "I am a native Californian. I was born in San Diego, but have lived in many places, including Germany, England, Austria, Switzerland, Hawaii, and the East

Sir Vertex and Lady Di are among the cast of geometrically inclined characters that inhabit Neuschwander's entertaining **Sir Cumfrence and the Sword in the Cone,** *which focuses on the hunt for the magical sword Edgecaliber. (Cover illustration by Wayne Geehan.)*

Coast. I received a B.A. in international studies from Willamette University and an M.A. in education from Stanford University. I have been teaching since 1976, both at the high school and elementary school levels.

"I currently teach third grade in Dublin, California, where I'm a mathematics education specialist. I also enjoy reading children's literature. An interest in both of these areas led me to write children's stories with mathematics-based themes.

"In 1992, while living in England, I began working on my first book, *Sir Cumference and the First Round Table.* Prior to submitting it for publication, I took a writing class through the University of California at Berkeley. Since then I have had several other books published, including *Amanda Bean's Amazing Dream* and *Sir Cumference and the Dragon of Pi.*

"In my spare time, I enjoy activities with my family. I have been married to my husband, Bruce, for more than twenty-five years. We have two sons: Tim, a medical doctor, and Seth, a college student and part-time firefighter.

"My family and I also enjoy traveling. The entire family has spent time on five of the earth's seven continents. Only Australia and Antarctica remain unvisited. We love to ski in the winter and body surf and backpack in the summer. We are active in our local church and are a committed Christian family."

Biographical and Critical Sources

PERIODICALS

Booklist, September 15, 1998, review of *Amanda Bean's Amazing Dream: A Mathematical Story,* p. 239.
Childhood Education, winter, 2003, review of *Sir Cumference and the Sword in the Cone: A Math Adventure,* p. 91.
Kirkus Reviews, July 1, 1998, p. 970.
School Library Journal, September, 1998, p. 178; February, 2002, Nancy A. Gifford, review of *Sir Cumference and the Great Knight of Angleland: A Math Adventure,* p. 125; February, 2004, Christine E. Carr, review of *Sir Cumference and the Sword in the Cone,* p. 136; September, 2004, review of *Sir Cumference and the First Round Table: A Math Adventure,* p. 58.
Teaching Children Mathematics, April, 2004, review of *Sir Cumference and the Sword in the Cone,* p. 430.

*   *   *

NOLAN, Han 1956-

Personal

Born August 25, 1956, in Birmingham, AL; married September 12, 1981; children: three (adopted). *Education:* University of North Carolina at Greensboro, B.S.,

1979; Ohio State University, M.S. (dance), 1981. *Hobbies and other interests:* Reading, hiking, running, swimming, "I love to move and be outside."

Addresses

Agent—c/o Author Mail, Harcourt Brace & Company, 525 B St., Suite 1900, San Diego, CA 92101-4495. *E-mail*—han@hannolan.com.

Career

Writer. Teacher of dance, 1981-84. Hollins University, Roanoke, VA, writer-in-residence, 2002, visiting associate professor, 2004-05.

Member

Society of Children's Book Writers and Illustrators, Author's Guild.

Awards, Honors

People's Choice Award and National Book Award nominee, both 1996, both for *Send Me down a Miracle;* Books for the Teen Age, New York Public Library, 1994, for *If I Should Die before I Wake,* 1996, for *Send Me down a Miracle,* and 1997, for *Dancing on the Edge;* National Book Award, 1997, and Best Books for Young Adults, American Library Association (ALA), 1998, both for *Dancing on the Edge;* Best Books for Young Adults, ALA, 2002, for *Born Blue.*

Writings

If I Should Die before I Wake, Harcourt (San Diego, CA), 1994.
Send Me down a Miracle, Harcourt (San Diego, CA), 1996.
Dancing on the Edge, Harcourt (San Diego, CA), 1997.
A Face in Every Window, Harcourt (San Diego, CA), 1999.
Born Blue, Harcourt (San Diego, CA), 2001.
When We Were Saints, Harcourt (San Diego, CA), 2003.

Sidelights

The 1997 winner of the National Book Award for her young adult novel, *Dancing on the Edge,* Han Nolan speaks directly to teenage readers in a voice at once empathic and down-home humorous. Through her novels, Nolan has captured a wide and loyal readership with her themes of tolerance and understanding, and with her youthful protagonists who discover—in the course of her books—who they are and what they want. "I'm always searching for the truth in my stories," Nolan commented in an interview on the *Harcourt Books Web site.* "That truth has led me to the characters that I have created."

Unlike many authors of books for young adults, with Nolan there was no serendipity in determining the audience for whom she chose to write. From the beginning of her career she set out to write novels for young readers. "Young people inspire me, my own children especially, but young people in general,"she stated in the Harcourt interview. "I like their spirit and their energy and all the growing and changing and exploring and questioning that is going on inside them." Nolan's books have dealt with neo-Nazis, religious zealotry, and the lies a family promulgates to supposedly protect its members. Her characters are young men and women on the cusp, emerging into an uncertain adulthood from shaky adolescence. They are young people who must learn to stand up for themselves—to throw off the influences of adults and peers and find their own center in a turbulent universe.

The next to youngest of five children, Nolan and the rest of her family moved several times during her childhood. Friends and neighborhoods changed, but a constant in the family was a love of books and the arts. Like the rest of her family, she loved reading from an early age. "One of my favorites books as a child was *Harriet the Spy,*" Nolan stated on her Web site. "I wanted to be a spy, so I started spying on my family, especially my older sister. It turned out I was a terrible spy because I kept getting caught, but I kept a spy notebook, just like Harriet. I quickly gave up on the spying, but writing thoughts and stories in a notebook has been a habit for me ever since."

Upon graduation from high school, Nolan attended the University of North Carolina at Greensboro to major in dance. After graduating in 1979, she entered a master's program in dance at Ohio State University, where she met her future husband, who was working on his doctorate in classics. In 1981 she graduated, married, and began teaching dance. When the couple wanted to start a family several years later, Nolan also opted for a career change. "I decided to return to my first love, writing," she noted on her Web site. "Soon after that we adopted three children and I knew for sure that staying home and writing instead of dancing was the best decision for me."

Thus began Nolan's literary career. She studied not only markets, but every book on writing technique that she could get her hands on. She wrote stories and sent some out with no success. Then she tackled lengthier projects, writing a mystery that won some attention with a publisher but was not purchased. Nonetheless, there was encouragement in the fact that an editor had taken an interest in her work. She joined or formed writers' groups wherever she happened to be living. She began another mystery, but one of the characters was stubbornly going off on her own, dreaming about the Holocaust.In addition to Nolan's subconscious at work, there were also contemporary events impinging. She discovered that a Ku Klux Klan group was active in a neighboring town, and that hate crimes were being reported. In her debut novel, *If I Should Die before I Wake,* Nolan recast the stubborn character from her mystery novel as Hilary Burke, a young neo-Nazi who

is lying in a coma in a Jewish hospital. Hilary's family has a history: her father died years before, his death caused, so Hilary believes, by a Jew, and her Bible-thumping mother temporarily abandoned her. She has found a home with a group of neo-Nazis; her boyfriend is the leader of the group. Hilary now lies in a hospital as a result of a motorcycle accident. In her coma, she sees another patient, an elderly Jewish woman named Chana, in her room. Chana is a Holocaust survivor, but to Hilary she is sarcastically labeled "Grandmaw." Suddenly Hilary spins back in time, trading places with Chana, becoming herself the persecuted young girl in Poland. She experiences firsthand the horrors of the Holocaust: her father is shot; she lives in the ghetto for a time; she escapes with her grandmother from the ghetto only to be captured, tortured, and sent to Auschwitz-Birkenau. Hilary intermittently drifts back to real time and the hospital, and by the novel's end, "has come back from her own near-death experience as well as Chana's to be a more understanding, tolerant person," as Susan Levine explained in *Voice of Youth Advocates.*

The first review Nolan read—or actually had read to her by her husband over the phone while attending a writer's conference—questioned the taste of the book. This was shattering enough for Nolan to later warn off a would-be purchaser of her first novel at the conference. Most reviewers, however, responded positively to this first effort. Roger Sutton, writing in the *Bulletin of the Center for Children's Books,* commented that Nolan is forthright in dealing with her material, "and her graphic descriptions of camp life have a morbid interest that teeters on exploitation but comes down on the side of the truth." *Booklist* critic Mary Harris Veeder stated that Nolan's "first novel has great strengths and weaknesses." Among the latter, Veeder felt, are the time-travel episodes and certain contemporary characterizations. "Chana's story, however, is brilliantly rendered," Veeder noted, and "carries memorable emotional impact." A *Kirkus Reviews* critic remarked that "Nolan's first novel is ambitious indeed," and concluded that "the book as a whole is deeply felt and often compelling."

Nolan was already 100 pages into her next novel by the time of publication of *If I Should Die before I Wake.* She admitted on her Web site that she wrote *Send Me down a Miracle* because she "was homesick for the South, where I was born and where all my relatives lived." In the work, Nolan follows the fortunes of fourteen-year-old Charity Pittman as she battles for a sense of self in her hometown of Casper, a fictional locale inspired by the small southern towns of Nolan's childhood. Charity feels trapped at home with her younger sister Grace and preacher father now that her mother has left them. Her father's stern interpretation of Christianity has chased away Charity's mother, but soon Charity is attracted to the cosmopolitan Adrienne Dabney, who has returned from New York to her family home, where she sets about trying a deprivation experiment. For three weeks Adrienne locks herself away in her inherited home, without visitors, light, or food. Emerging from the experiment, she says that Jesus has visited her, sitting in the chair in her living room. This proclamation splits the small town asunder: Charity and many others believe in the chair and its miraculous powers; Charity's father calls it all blasphemy, warning that Adrienne is evil incarnate. Caught between the prickly father whom she loves and Adrienne, who has taken her on as a friend and fellow artist, Charity must finally learn to make up her own mind. When her father comes to destroy the chair, Charity is there to stand up to him.

"The dichotomy of professing one's faith and actually living it is interestingly portrayed throughout this novel," commented Jana R. Fine in a *School Library Journal* review of *Send Me down a Miracle*. Fine also noted that readers are brought into the "heart of a young girl" who learns to meld her religious background with compassion and forgiveness. A critic in *Kirkus Reviews* called the novel a "busy, hilarious, tragic story," and concluded that "readers will be dizzied by the multiple subplots and roller-coaster highs and lows" in this story of a small town. *Booklist* reviewer Ilene Cooper remarked that Nolan's "plot is intricate, sharp, and invigorating." Award committees agreed with the reviewers: *Send Me down a Miracle* was nominated for the National Book Award in 1996.

Nolan's next book, *Dancing on the Edge,* was inspired by her own adopted children. The book's protagonist, Miracle McCloy, was so named because she was delivered after her mother was killed in an accident. Her spiritualist grandmother Gigi calls it "the greatest miracle to ever come down the pike," but Miracle herself is not convinced. She feels like a misfit, hardly special at all. Ten years old, she lives in Alabama with her father, Dane, a one-time child prodigy who now sits around in his bathrobe in the basement all day, and with Dane's mother, Gigi, who spends her time with matters of the occult. When Dane suddenly disappears one day, Gigi tells Miracle that her father has "melted." Gigi and Miracle then go to live with Opal, Gigi's ex-husband, where Miracle finds some stability in the form of her gruff grandfather who buys her a bicycle and starts her in dancing lessons. Dance proves to be a momentary salvation for Miracle, something that actually makes her feel as special as everyone always says she is. But when she starts imitating her grandmother's occult fancies, casting spells and making love potions for her classmates, troubles arise. Accused of being a phony by another student, Miracle sets herself on fire and is committed to a mental hospital.

The second part of *Dancing on the Edge* details Miracle's therapy and recovery as she slowly accepts the facts of her life. "Nolan skillfully discloses" the nature of her cast of offbeat characters, a *Kirkus Reviews* critic noted, calling the novel "intense" and "exceptionally well-written." Miriam Lang Budin, writing in *School*

Library Journal, dubbed *Dancing on the Edge* an "extraordinary novel," and concluded that "Nolan does a masterful job of drawing readers into the girl's mind and making them care deeply about her chances for the future." Again award committees agreed. *Dancing on the Edge* was nominated for a National Book Award, the first time an author had been nominated for that prestigious award two years in a row. And 1997 proved to be Nolan's year: her novel won the award and was commended by the panel of judges as "a tale of chilling reality."

Nolan published *A Face in Every Window* in 1999. On her Web site, the author remarked that facets of her own life are reflected in the novel. "When I was younger, people moved in and out of my family's home, staying for a while and then moving on. Sharing their home was a way for my parents to share the love they had for us and for each other; they simply passed it on to anyone who needed it."

Described by a *Publishers Weekly* critic as a "sometimes outlandish, often poignant exploration of a chaotic household," *A Face in Every Window* is narrated by teenager James Patrick O'Brien, known to everyone

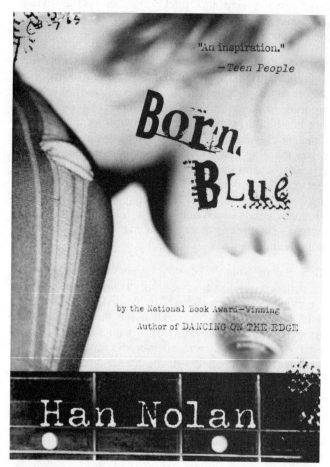

"An inspiration."
—Teen People

Born Blue

by the National Book Award-Winning Author of DANCING ON THE EDGE

Han Nolan

In Nolan's 2001 novel a girl travels a difficult road, moving from her drug-addicted parents through several foster families, and as a troubled teen finds her only comfort in singing the blues music she listened to as a child. (Cover photograph by A. Hoffman/Photonica.)

as JP. After his grandmother dies, JP is left to care for his mentally ill father and his emotionally fragile mother. Determined to give her family a fresh start, JP's mother moves them to a ramshackle farmhouse in Pennsylvania, which she won in an essay contest. The dwelling is soon filled with an odd collection of musicians, artists, and misfits that Mam has invited into her home, fulfilling her dream of being welcomed by "a face at every window." JP, though, is disturbed by the situation and withdraws into his room. Gradually, he comes to know the strangers as individuals and begins to accept them as his new "family."

"Only a writer as talented as Nolan could make this improbable story line and bizarre cast of characters not only believable but also ultimately uplifting, intriguing, and memorable," noted *Booklist* contributor Frances Bradburn in a review of *A Face in Every Window.* According to the critic in *Publishers Weekly,* Nolan "delivers a profound and heartwarming message about the various manifestations of love."*Born Blue* follows the grim life of Janie, the abused daughter of a heroin-addicted mother who ends up lonely and neglected in a foster home. Janie, who is white, takes solace in her friendship with her African-American foster brother Harmon, who introduces Janie to the soulful blues music of Etta James and Billie Holiday. Her fascination with black culture grows so strong, in fact, that she later changes her name to Leshaya. Janie's biological mother, Mama Linda, remains a disruptive presence in her daughter's life; at one point she kidnaps the girl and sells her to a drug dealer. The instability and disruptions have devastating consequences. As Claire Rosser observed in *Kliatt,* "When Janie becomes an adolescent, she tries to satisfy her endless hunger with drugs and sex, sabotaging every promising relationship, abandoning her own newborn baby." Janie's salvation appears to be her magnificent singing voice. She eventually joins a blues band and develops a romantic interest in a gifted songwriter. But Janie grows careless, wastes her talent, and betrays her friends. "When she's used up everyone she knows," wrote Lauren Adams in a *Horn Book* review of *Born Blue,* "she seeks Mama Linda once more and finds her dying of AIDS; finally Leshaya confronts herself as the mirror image of her mother."

Born Blue "is raw, rough, and riveting," stated Alison Follos in *School Library Journal.* "The writing is superb; like the blues, it bores down through the soul, probing at unpleasant truths and wringing out compassion." According to a reviewer in *Publishers Weekly,* as readers reach the novel's conclusion "they will have gained an understanding of the tragic heroine's fears, desires and warped perception of family, but Janie herself remains hauntingly elusive, adding to the impact of the book." Gillian Engberg, reviewing *Born Blue* in *Booklist,* stated that "with themes of race, talent, family, love, control, and responsibility, the novel asks essential questions about how to reclaim oneself and build a life."Nolan's decision to write *When We Were Saints* was influenced by several factors. The author explained

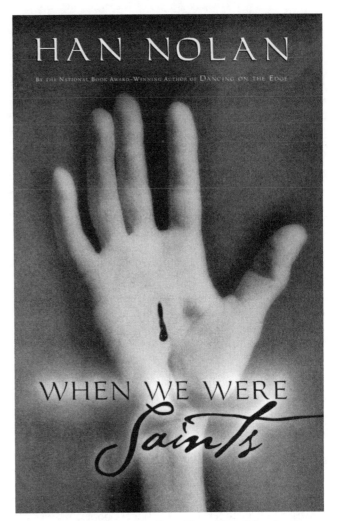

Fourteen-year-old Archie Caswell, saddened by the departure of a friend and by his grandpa's death, becomes caught up in a new friend's belief that the two children are saints destined for spiritual greatness. (Cover photograph by Alex Howe.)

on her Web site that she had long been interested in the Middle Ages, stained glass, and cathedrals, and that she had spent considerable time researching those subjects. After attending a conference where she met a number of young people concerned with religious issues, she decided upon the direction the book would take: "I decided that what I really wanted was to explore what it would be like for a young person today to experience the deeply spiritual life that someone in the Middle Ages might have experienced. Is it even possible today to have those kinds of experiences?"

When We Were Saints concerns fourteen-year-old Archie Caswell, a naïve southern farm boy whose grandfather declares on his deathbed, "Young man, you are a saint!" Archie starts to believe those words after meeting a beautiful, charismatic newcomer named Claire, whose strange religious rituals both intrigue and confuse Archie. When Claire convinces Archie that they have been called by God to make a pilgrimage to the Cloisters Museum in New York City, he steals his grandfather's truck so the pair can journey north. "Nolan's novel of spiritual exploration is both exceptionally grounded and refreshingly open," remarked *Horn Book* contributor Lauren Adams, and *School Library Journal* reviewer Joel Shoemaker described *When We Were Saints* as "powerfully written" and "outstanding in terms of the intensity of the experience described." A *Publishers Weekly* critic praised Nolan's skillful portrayal of Archie, but stated that Clare's character "is what keeps the pages turning; audience members are left to ponder whether she is truly a Christ figure or an emotionally disturbed teen bent on self-destruction."

Asked in the *Harcourt Books Web site* interview what drives her to write, Nolan responded, "I like the creative process. I like exploring lives so different from my own and I like the way I learn so much about these other worlds and about myself when I write."

Biographical and Critical Sources

BOOKS

St. James Guide to Young-Adult Writers, 2nd edition, St. James Press (Detroit, MI), 1999.

PERIODICALS

ALAN Review, winter, 1998.
Booklist, April 1, 1994, Mary Harris Veeder, review of *If I Should Die before I Wake,* p. 1436; March 15, 1996, Ilene Cooper, review of *Send Me down a Miracle,* p. 1263; October 1, 1997, Ilene Cooper, review of *Dancing on the Edge,* p. 331; November 1, 1999, Frances Bradburn, review of *A Face in Every Window,* p. 525; May 1, 2001, Stephanie Zvirin, review of *Send Me Down a Miracle,* p. 1611; September 15, 2001, Gillian Engberg, review of *Born Blue,* p. 217; October 1, 2003, Ilene Cooper, review of *When We Were Saints,* p. 330.
Bulletin of the Center for Children's Books, April, 1994, Roger Sutton, review of *If I Should Die before I Wake,* pp. 267-268; July, 1996, p. 382; December, 1997, pp. 135-136.
English Journal, review of *Dancing on the Edge,* p. 124.
Horn Book, January-February, 2002, Lauren Adams, review of *Born Blue,* pp. 82-83; January-February, 2004, Lauren Adams, review of *When We Were Saints,* p. 87.
Kirkus Reviews, March 1, 1994, review of *If I Should Die before I Wake,* p. 308; March 15, 1996, review of *Send Me down a Miracle,* p. 451; August 1, 1997, review of *Dancing on the Edge,* p. 1227; October 1, 2003, review of *When We Were Saints,* p. 1228.
Kliatt, July, 1996, p. 15; July, 2003, Claire Rosser, review of *Born Blue,* pp. 24-25; September, 2003, Claire Rosser, review of *When We Were Saints,* pp. 9-10.
Publishers Weekly, January 31, 1994, p. 90; August 18, 1997, p. 94; November 24, 1997, p. 14; November 1, 1999, review of *A Face in Every Window,* p. 85; October 8, 2001, review of *Born Blue,* p. 66; October 20, 2003, *When We Were Saints,* p. 55.
School Library Journal, April, 1994, pp. 152-153; April, 1996, Jana R. Fine, review of *Send Me down a Miracle,* p. 157; September, 1997, Miriam Lang Budin, review of *Dancing on the Edge,* p. 223; January, 1998, "Nolan Wins 1997 National Book Award," p. 22; November, 2001, Alison Follos, review of *Born Blue,* p. 162; November, 2003, Joel Shoemaker, review of *When We Were Saints,* p. 144.
Voice of Youth Advocates, June, 1994, Susan Levine, review of *If I Should Die before I Wake,* p. 88; June, 1996, p. 99; June, 1997, p. 86.

ONLINE

Han Nolan Web site, http://www.hannolan.com (January 6, 2005).
Harcourt Books Web site, http://www.harcourtbooks.com/ (January 6, 2005), interview with Nolan.

*   *   *

NOLEN, Jerdine 1953-

Personal

Born April 6, 1953, in Crystal Springs, MS; daughter of Eugene (Sr.) and Eula (Lee) Nolen; married Anthony L. Harold (an administrator and educator), May 27, 1988; children: Matthew, Jessica. *Education:* Northeastern Illinois University, B.A. (special education), 1975; Loyola University, M.Ed., 1981.

Addresses

Home—Ellicott City, MD. *Agent*—Kia Neri, c/o Harcourt Children's Books, 617B St., San Diego, CA 92101; Janet Ross, c/o HarperCollins Children's Books, 1350 Avenue of the Americas, New York, NY 10019.

Career

Educator and writer. James Weldon Johnson Elementary School, New Orleans, LA, special education teacher, 1974-75; Chicago Public Schools, Chicago, IL, special education teacher, 1975-76, learning disabilities resource teacher, 1986-87; Martin Luther King Experimental Laboratory School, Evanston, IL, elementary education teacher, 1976-85; Baltimore County Public schools, Baltimore, MD, special education teacher, 1987-94, English/language arts specialist, 1994-96, Title I and family involvement specialist, 1996—. Arabesque Ladies' Clothing Boutique, Evanston, buyer and window designer, 1980-87; teacher in Maryland middle schools, 1987-94.

Member

National Council of Teachers of English, Society of Children's Book Writers and Illustrators, Authors Guild, Maryland State Teachers Association, Chicago Reading Round Table, Baltimore Writers Alliance, Black Literary Umbrella (cofounder), Delta Kappa Gamma (Xi Chapter).

Jerdine Nolen

Awards, Honors

Notable Book citation, American Library Association, for *Harvey Potter's Balloon Farm.*

Writings

Harvey Potter's Balloon Farm, illustrated by Mark Buehner, HarperCollins (New York, NY), 1994.

Raising Dragons, illustrated by Elise Primavera, Harcourt/Silver Whistle (San Diego, CA), 1998.

In My Momma's Kitchen, illustrated by Colin Bootman, Lothrop, Lee & Shepard (New York, NY), 1999.

Irene's Wish, illustrated by Martin Matje, Harcourt/Silver Whistle (San Diego, CA), 2000.

Big Jabe, illustrated by Kadir Nelson, Lothrop, Lee & Shepard (New York, NY), 2000.

Plantzilla, illustrated by David Catrow, Harcourt/Silver Whistle (San Diego, CA), 2002.

Max and Jax in Second Grade, illustrated by Karen Lee Schmidt, Harcourt/Silver Whistle (San Diego, CA), 2002.

Thunder Rose, illustrated by Kadir Nelson, Harcourt/Silver Whistle (San Diego, CA), 2003.

Lauren McGill's Pickle Museum, illustrated by Debbie Tilley, Harcourt/Silver Whistle (San Diego, CA), 2003.

Plantzilla Goes to Camp, illustrated by David Catrow, Harcourt/Silver Whistle (San Diego, CA), 2005.

Hewitt Anderson's Great Big Life, illustrated by Kadir Nelson, Simon & Schuster (New York, NY), 2005.

Contributor of stories and readings to books, including *Talk That Talk,* Simon & Schuster, 1989; *People We Know,* Harcourt Brace, 1991; *Places We Know,* Harcourt Brace, 1991; and *ENGLISH in Charge,* Scott Foresman. Contributor of stories and poems to *Ebony, Jr!* and *American Poetry Review.*

Adaptations

Disney adapted *Harvey Potter's Balloon Farm* for film as a *Wonderful World of Disney* made-for-television movie titled *Balloon Farm.*

Sidelights

Jerdine Nolen is an educator as well as the author of the popular picture books *Harvey Potter's Balloon Farm* and *Raising Dragons,* both of which chronicle marvelous and exuberant goings-on down on the farm. The two tales are told from the point of view of an African-American girl, and the language of the texts blends southern patois, rural colloquialisms, and big-hearted humor. *Harvey Potter's Balloon Farm* was the recipient of a number of awards and made first-time author Nolen something of an immediate success when her book was featured on the Columbia Broadcasting System (CBS) *Morning News* and in elementary classrooms around the United States.

Regarding her beginnings, Nolen once told *Something about the Author (SATA):* "While my mother was pregnant with me, she went South to care for her own mother, who was ill. That is how I came to be born in Crystal Springs, Mississippi." After the death of her grandmother four months later, Nolen's family returned to the North, where young Nolen was raised in Chicago with her five sisters and two brothers. Because of her family's strong Southern roots, Nolen felt like an outsider while growing up in the Midwest, and her Southern cultural heritage has found its way into several of her children's books.

Her family, with its use of both Northern and Southern dialect, influenced not only Nolen's ear for speech patterns, but her sense of humor as well. She was also influenced by the work of the writers, poets, and musicians whose works she discovered, from Paul Laurence Dunbar, Zora Neale Hurston, and Dr. Seuss to Kenneth Patchen, Paul Simon, and Nina Simone. "Growing up in such a large family, I had to have a good sense of humor—to make up for a lack of space," the author once told *SATA.* "My sisters and brothers were pretty funny, too—but my father said I was 'right witty.'" Because of her upbringing and her imaginative nature, Nolen developed an early love of words, and published her first poem—a Thanksgiving verse—in her school paper as a second grader. "It was printed on pink paper," Nolen reminisced to *SATA,* "and I still remember the joy I felt to see my name in print."

Nolen's love of words took her to Northeastern Illinois University, where she majored in special education, and then, after teaching several years, to Loyola University, where she earned a master's degree in education in

1981. She worked as an elementary and special education teacher in New Orleans, Louisiana, and Chicago, Illinois, before taking up duties at the Baltimore County Public Schools, where she has become an English and language arts specialist and a Title I specialist. (Title I is a federally sponsored entitlement program for schools with student poverty rates of fifty percent or higher.) All the while, she has been writing: for her students, for textbooks, and for her own personal enjoyment. Nolen's first book, *Harvey Potter's Balloon Farm,* grew out of a 1984 classroom assignment. While teaching a first-and-second-grade combination class as part of a six-member team, she conducted a unit on money. As Nolen recalled to *SATA:* "We taught the students what money was, what it looked like, and we explored what it was for. For a culminating activity, each of the six classrooms were turned into stores within a single community. There was a bakery, a movie theater, a popcorn store, a book store, a food store, and a balloon farm. Some products were: balloons, wind socks (made from paper), small kites, and antique balloons made from paper maché. That summer, as I was scrubbing the tiles in my shower, I got the first line of what later developed into *Harvey Potter's Balloon Farm:* 'Harvey Potter was a very strange fellow indeed.' At the time I was writing that line, I had no idea that Harvey Potter was strange because he grew balloons. That was a delightful surprise. I guess there really is no wasted motion in the universe."

In her wildly popular **Harvey Potter's Balloon Farm** *Jerdine Nolen weaves a magical tale of a quirky farmer who cultivates an unusual crop, but keeps his growing methods a secret. (Cover illustration by Mark Buehner.)*

Harvey Potter is a farmer who grows multi-colored balloons atop long sturdy stalks lined up in resemblance to a corn field. His balloons are grown to order, shaped like clowns, monsters, and animals. When a young African-American girl decides to figure out how Harvey creates his balloon magic, she secretly watches Harvey dance at night in his field with his magic stick. Soon denounced by a jealous farmer and threatened by government inspectors, Harvey's future looks grim, but all turns out fine in the end; he retains his ranking as a government-certified balloon farmer. The little girl grows up to become a balloon farmer as well, but in her case the balloons are a root crop.

Horn Book's Ann A. Flowers called *Harvey Potter's Balloon Farm,* "an excellent story" with the added attraction of Mark Buehner's "vivid, air-brushed illustrations of balloons with expressive faces in every size, color, and shape." Flowers also noted Nolen's "lively and unusual" narration of the imaginative tale, an observation shared by other critics. A *Kirkus Reviews* critic noted that "Nolen's writing has an oral lilt to it," and described the book as containing a "wonderfully appealing premise, skillfully developed." *Booklist* reviewer Mary Harris Veeder thought that "Nolen's 'true truth' style contrasts delightfully with the pictures of Harvey's crop." Writing in *School Library Journal,* Kathleen Whalin commented that *Harvey Potter's Balloon Farm* is "the best sort of fantasy—imaginative, inventive, and believable." Whalin concluded, "This title should sail into every library shelf. May Nolen grow a bumper crop of books."

Nolen published her second picture book, *Raising Dragons,* in 1998. Again she places her story in a rural setting and features a young African-American girl. Instead of balloons, however, in *Raising Dragons* the focus is an egg that is discovered near the young girl's farm. When it hatches, out pops a tiny dragon whom the girl proceeds, quite nonchalantly, to name Hank. "As I touched skin to scale, I knew I was his girl and he was my dragon," the girl comments. Her parents are more conservative about such matters and at first do not care for Hank. Their opinions change, however, when Hank starts helping out by sowing Pa's seeds and rescuing Ma's wilting crop of tomato plants. Hank ultimately grows to the size of a barn, and becomes a genuine full-grown, flying, fire-breathing dragon able to pop a whole field of corn with a single fiery breath. Soon forced by public opinion to flee to the volcanic island where other such creatures live, Hank leaves behind a special present for his human buddy: a wheelbarrow full of dragon eggs ready for the hatching.

Reviewing *Raising Dragons,* a *Kirkus Reviews* critic remarked that "Nolen unearths some unique livestock in this tale of a farmer's daughter who braves her parents' skepticism to hatch and raise a flying, fire-breathing dragon" and summarized the picture book as a "fresh and cheery tall tale, told in an appropriately matter-of-fact tone." Susan P. Bloom, building on the favorable

In Nolen's modern-day Paul Bunyan tale Thunder Rose, *a young girl shocks her parents by her abilities, which includes being able to tame the weather and speak in complete sentences as an infant. (Illustration by Kadir Nelson.)*

mix of text and artwork, remarked in *Horn Book* that "Nolen's chimerical text meets its match in [Elise] Primavera's imaginative and bold acrylic and pastel illustrations." Bloom went on to point out that "author and artist both reach their peak when Hank's enthusiastically planted corn crop overflows," inspiring "the first dragon-popped popcorn anybody ever saw or tasted." A reviewer for *FamilyFun* remarked that "the whole fantastical tale is told with an engaging mix of matter-of-factness and awe," while a contributor to *Working Mother* wrote: "Seldom is a story so fanciful told in a voice so plain and true." The *Working Mother* critic went on to call *Raising Dragons* "a lovely book about nurturing, accepting differences, and embracing magic," while a *Publishers Weekly* reviewer dubbed it an "enchanting blend of the real and unreal." The author's understated tone, in the opinion of the same reviewer, "adds a layer of humor" when contrasted to the very unusual circumstances happening in the book. This same reviewer concluded that "youngsters will hanker to go on this journey; it will set their imagination soaring."

Soaring imaginations have continued to be Nolen's stock and trade. In addition, she has written humorous and homey tales, such as *In My Momma's Kitchen.* The book is a celebration of African-American families and mothers and fathers, told through a story of a family's year as witnessed by events in the heart of the family's home: the kitchen. Reviewing the picture book in *Booklist,* Hazel Rochman felt that though its depiction is "idyllic (not a hint of a quarrel or disagreement in this family)," Nolen's work is still "a great place to start kids telling stories of a special place at home." A reviewer for *Publishers Weekly* noted that Nolen's

"subtle details add color and depth to the proceedings," and concluded that "art and text work together to transport readers to a place where abundant love and sweet memories are staples of daily fare."

In *Big Jabe* Nolen presents an original tall tale about a special young man who does wonderful things for the slaves on the Plenty Plantation. "Part Moses, part John Henry" is how *Booklist*'s Rochman described Nolen's hero. Found floating in a basket on the river as an infant, Jabe soon grows to gigantic proportions and has the strength of fifty men. He helps his people with hard labor and also in bad times helps them to disappear. Rochman felt that "Nolen dramatizes the strength of community and of story" with *Big Jabe,* while a reviewer for *Publishers Weekly* remarked that "folklore and history give an uncommonly rich patina to this freshly inspiring original tale set in slave times." The same reviewer called the book an "eloquent tale" that "empower[s] the audience to confront an unbearable history and come away with hope." And a contributor for *Horn Book* concluded, "This powerful story will be particularly effective shared aloud."

In *Plantzilla,* "Nolen delivers another picture book with a far-out premise and plenty of heart," observed a *Publishers Weekly* reviewer. When third-grader Mortimer Henryson gets permission to care for his class's unusual plant at his home over summer vacation, trouble ensues: the plant grows uncontrollably, moves about on its own, and develops a taste for fresh meat, a development coincidental with the disappearance of the family's Chihuahua. Nolen tells her story through a series of letters from Mortimer and his mom to Mr. Lester, the boy's science teacher, and according to *Booklist* contributor Lauren Peterson, much of the humor in the work comes from "the contrast between Mortimer's glowing reports of life with Plantzilla and frantic communications from Mortimer's mother." As the summer goes along, Plantzilla thrives under the boy's tender care and proves itself to be a valuable family member. "Readers, plant-lovers or otherwise, will find this vegetative visitor taking root in their affections," noted a critic writing in *Kirkus Reviews*.

In *Irene's Wish* a little girl gets her wish to spend more time with her father when he swallows seeds and turns into a tree, while a different young girl's obsession with pickles is at the heart of *Lauren McGill's Pickle Museum*. And in *Max and Jax in the Second Grade*, the eponymous twin alligators want to start off the summer right with a fishing trip and sleepover, but after Max's specially ordered lure fails to help him catch a fish, he uses his sister's homemade bait to land a rainbow trout. "Nolen shows a gift for straightforward dialogue that leaves readers feeling enchanted without being otherworldly," wrote *School Library Journal* contributor Louie Lahana, while a critic in *Kirkus Reviews* stated that Max and Jax "have plenty to offer, such as an example of harmony in the household, and the real gift: generosity." An African-American girl possessing extraordinary gifts is the protagonist of *Thunder Rose*, another tall tale penned by Nolen. Born on a stormy night, tiny but confident Rose astonishes her parents by rolling lightning into a ball, lifting a cow over her head, building a thunderbolt from scrap iron, halting a stampede, and inventing barbed wire. When tornadoes threaten the family ranch, Rose displays her gentler side, transforming the twisters into rain clouds by singing a lullaby. Rose "shows a reflective bent that gives her more dimension than most tall-tale heroes," stated a critic in *Kirkus Reviews*. Although a contributor in *Publishers Weekly* felt that Nolen's "packed plot slows the rhythms of her fun writing style," *Booklist* reviewer GraceAnne A. DeCandido called *Thunder Rose* "exuberant" and a "terrific read-aloud." In the words of *School Library Journal* critic Andrea Tarr, *Thunder Rose* is "a wonderful tale of joy and love, as robust and vivid as the wide West."

Loosely based on the story "Jack and the Beanstalk," *Hewitt Anderson's Great Big Life* concerns a brave but diminutive boy born into a family of giants. The J. Carver Worthington Andersons pride themselves on their heritage, because every member of their family has been a giant. However, that tradition ends when Hewitt comes along. In fact, Hewitt's tiny stature actually worries his loving parents; the small child often falls between the floorboards or gets lost in his enormous bed sheets. Hewitt's size has its advantages, though: he comes to the rescue when his father grows fearful after climbing a tall beanstalk, and Hewitt also assists his parents after they become trapped in a locked house. Reviewing *Hewitt Anderson's Great Big Life*, a *Kirkus Reviews* contributor concluded: "Nolen writes, as always, with a distinctive mix of humor and formality."

Despite her whimsical tall tales and humorous realistic snippets for young readers, Nolen explained to an interviewer for *Publishers Weekly:* "I'm really a very down-to-earth person." Stories are within each of us, the author contends, just waiting to get out. It is a matter of perseverance and hanging on to one's dreams that brings the stories out. "When I get in a writing jam, I ask myself, 'So, then what happens?' Your imagination won't let you down." Sage advice from a writer who typically autographs her books with the words, "Hold fast to your dreams as you would your balloons."

Biographical and Critical Sources

PERIODICALS

Booklist, April 15, 1994, Mary Harris Veeder, review of *Harvey Potter's Balloon Farm,* p. 1541; April, 1998, Stephanie Zvirin, review of *Raising Dragons,* p. 1334; February 15, 1999, Hazel Rochman, review of *In My Momma's Kitchen,* p. 1077; April 1, 2000, Hazel Rochman, review of *Big Jabe,* p. 1478. June 1, 2002, review of *Max and Jax in Second Grade,* Kathy Broderick, p. 1724; October 15, 2002, Lauren Peterson, review of *Plantzilla,* p. 413; October 15, 2003, Brian Wilson, review of *Plantzilla* (audiobook review), p. 445; November 1, 2003, GraceAnne A. DeCandido, review of *Thunder Rose,* p. 505.

Christian Science Monitor, May 28, 1998, Karen Carden, review of *Raising Dragons,* p. B7.

Entertainment Weekly, April 8, 1994, Leonard S. Marcus, review of *Harvey Potter's Balloon Farm,* p. 69.

FamilyFun, May, 1998, review of *Raising Dragons,* p. 116.

Horn Book, July-August, 1994, Ann A. Flowers, review of *Harvey Potter's Balloon Farm,* pp. 442-443; March-April, 1998, Susan P. Bloom, review of *Raising Dragons,* p. 217; July, 2000, review of *Big Jabe,* p. 440.

Kirkus Reviews, March 15, 1994, review of *Harvey Potter's Balloon Farm,* p. 401; March 1, 1998, review of Raising Dragons, p. 343; March 1, 2002, review of *Max and Jax in Second Grade,* p. 342; July 15, 2002, review of *Plantzilla,* p. 1040; May 1, 2003, review of *Lauren McGill's Pickle Museum,* p. 681; September 15, 2003, review of *Thunder Rose,* p. 1180; December 15, 2004, review of *Hewitt Anderson's Great Big Life,* p. 1206.

New York Times, December 1, 1994, Christopher Lehmann-Haupt, review of *Harvey Potter's Balloon Farm,* p. B2.

New York Times Book Review, September 11, 1994, p. 32.

People, November 28, 1994, review of *Harvey Potter's Balloon Farm,* p. 47.

Publishers Weekly, April 11, 1994, review of *Harvey Potter's Balloon Farm,* p. 65; July 4, 1994, "Flying Starts," pp. 36-41; March 9, 1998, review of *Raising Dragons,* p. 67; April 12, 1999, review of *In My Momma's Kitchen,* p. 75; April 17, 2000, review of *Big Jabe,* p. 79; May 7, 2001, review of *In My Momma's Kitchen,* p. 249; February 11, 2002, review of *Max and Jax in Second Grade,* p. 187; August 12, 2002, review of *Plantzilla,* p. 300; April 14, 2003, review of *Lauren McGill's Pickle Museum,* p. 70; October 6, 2003, review of *Thunder Rose,* p. 84.

School Library Journal, May, 1994, Kathleen Whalin, review of *Harvey Potter's Balloon Farm,* p. 102; April, 1998, Faith Brautigan, review of *Raising Dragons,* p. 106; May, 1999, Tom S. Hurlburt, review of In *My Momma's Kitchen,* p. 94; June, 2000, Ellen A. Greever, review of *Big Jabe,* p. 122; April, 2002, Louie Lahana, review of *Max and Jax in Second Grade,* p. 118; July, 2003, Eve Ortega, review of *Lau-ren McGill's Pickle Museum,* pp. 102-103; September, 2003, Andrea Tarr, review of *Thunder Rose,* p. 186.

Smithsonian, November, 1998, p. 26.

Working Mother, June 19, 1998, review of *Raising Dragons,* p. 62.

ONLINE

Jerdine Nolen Web site, http://www.jerdinenolen.com (January 7, 2005).*

O

O'MALLEY, Kevin 1961-
(Patrick Joseph)

Personal

Born 1961; married; wife's name Dara; children: Connor, Noah.

Addresses

Home—Baltimore, MD. *Agent*—c/o Author Mail, Walker & Company, 104 Fifth Ave., New York, NY 10011. *E-mail*—komalley@comcast.net.

Career

Author and illustrator.

Writings

Let's Sing about America, Troll Associates (Mahwah, NJ), 1993.

Who Killed Cock Robin?, Lothrop, Lee & Shepard (New York, NY), 1993.

The Box, Stewart, Tabori & Chang (New York, NY), 1993.

There Was a Crooked Man, Little Simon (New York, NY), 1995.

Roller Coaster, Lothrop, Lee & Shepard Books (New York, NY), 1995.

Carl Caught a Flying Fish, Simon & Schuster Books for Young Readers (New York, NY), 1996.

Velcome, Walker & Co. (New York, NY), 1997.

Leo Cockroach—Toy Tester, Walker and Co. (New York, NY), 1999.

Bud, Walker & Co. (New York, NY), 2000.

Humpty Dumpty Egg-Splodes, Walker & Co. (New York, NY), 2001.

Little Buggy, Harcourt (San Diego, CA), 2002.

Mount Olympus Basketball, Walker & Co. (New York, NY), 2003.

Little Buggy Runs Away, Gulliver Books (San Diego, CA), 2003.

Straight to the Pole, Walker & Co. (New York, NY), 2003.

Lucky Leaf, Walker & Co. (New York, NY), 2004.

Captain Raptor and the Moon Mystery, Walker & Co. (New York, NY), 2005.

Once upon a Cool Motorcycle Dude, Walker & Co. (New York, NY), 2005.

ILLUSTRATOR

Joanne Oppenheim, *Row, Row, Row Your Boat,* Bantam (New York, NY), 1993.

John Schindel, *What's for Lunch?,* Lothrop, Lee & Shepard (New York, NY), 1994.

Ellen B. Jackson, *Cinder Edna,* Lothrop, Lee & Shepard (New York, NY), 1994.

JoAnn Vandine, *Run! Run!,* Mondo Pub. (Greenvale, NY), 1995.

Judy Finchler, *Miss Malarkey Doesn't Live in Room 10,* Walker & Co. (New York, NY), 1995.

Stuart J. Murphy, *Too Many Kangaroo Things to Do!,* HarperCollins (New York, NY), 1996.

Robert Kraus, *Big Squeak, Little Squeak,* Orchard Books (New York, NY), 1996.

David A. Adler, *Chanukah in Chelm,* Lothrop, Lee & Shepard (New York, NY), 1997.

Dan Harder, *Colliding with Chris,* Hyperion Books for Children (New York, NY), 1997.

Phyllis Root, *Rosie's Fiddle,* Lothrop, Lee & Shepard (New York, NY), 1997.

Jonathan London, *The Candystore Man,* Lothrop, Lee & Shepard (New York, NY), 1998.

Franklyn Mansfield Branley, *The Planets in Our Solar System,* HarperCollins (New York, NY), 1998.

Betty Ren Wright, *Pet Detectives!,* BridgeWater Books (Mahwah, NJ), 1999.

Michael O. Tunnell, *Halloween Pie,* Lothrop, Lee & Shepard (New York, NY), 1999.

Debbie Dadey, *King of the Kooties,* Walker & Co. (New York, NY), 1999.

Stuart J. Murphy, *Jump, Kangaroo, Jump,* HarperCollins (New York, NY), 1999.

Ellen A. Kelley, *The Lucky Lizard,* Dutton Children's Books (New York, NY), 2000.

Judy Finchler, *Testing Miss Malarkey,* Walker & Co. (New York, NY), 2000.

Judy Finchler, *Miss Malarkey Won't Be in Today,* Walker & Co. (New York, NY), 2000.

Joseph E. Wallace, *Big and Noisy Simon,* Hyperion Books for Children (New York, NY), 2001.

Stuart J. Murphy, *Dinosaur Deals,* HarperCollins (New York, NY), 2001.

John W. Stewigh, *Making Plum Jam,* Hyperion Books for Children (New York, NY), 2002.

Gordon Snell, *Twelve Days: A Christmas Countdown,* HarperCollins (New York, NY), 2002.

Judy Finchler, *You're a Good Sport, Miss Malarkey,* Walker & Co. (New York, NY), 2002.

Judy Finchler, *Miss Malarkey's Field Trip,* Walker & Co. (New York, NY), 2004.

ILLUSTRATOR; UNDER NAME PATRICK JOSEPH:

Kathryn Heling, *Mouse Makes Magic: A Phonics Reader,* Random House (New York, NY), 2002.

Kathryn Heling, *Mouse Makes Words: A Phonics Reader,* Random House (New York, NY), 2002.

Kathryn Heling, *Mouse's Hide-and-Seek Words: A Phonics Reader,* Random House (New York, NY), 2003.

Sidelights

Baltimore, Maryland-based author and illustrator Kevin O'Malley began drawing as a child, inspired by the illustrations in Maurice Sendak's groundbreaking children's book *Where the Wild Things Are.* A prolific author and artist who experiments in a variety of mediums and styles in his illustrations, O'Malley has contributed artwork to numerous books by authors such as Judy Fincher, Michael O. Tunnell, and David A. Adler. O'Malley has also created original titles such as *Lucky Leaf, Straight to the Pole, Lucky Leaf,* and *Little Buggy Runs Away,* all of which feature humor and an upbeat ending.

Described as a "simple story" about forgiveness by *Booklist* reviewer Gillian Engberg, *Little Buggy Runs Away* finds a young beetle known as Little Buggy determined to run away from home after a fight with Big Buggy. However, despite the help of two friendly ants, the outside world—and a scary lightning storm—proves too intimidating, and Little Buggy eventually learns to put his small disagreement into perspective and decides to return home. home. "Children will easily recognize the bugs' roiling emotions, which O'Malley expertly captures in his characters' faces, and the supporting cast's humorous asides, printed in dialogue bubbles, will elicit some giggles" commented Engberg. "O'Malley's wise decision to start the story after Little Buggy has run away allows youngsters to identify with the diminutive hero's feelings rather than his circumstances," noted a *Publishers Weekly* critic, adding that the author/illustrator's "Slick visuals, broad humor and . . . warm-hearted portrayal of helpful friends" make Little Buggy a likeable hero for the read-aloud crowd.

In **Miss Malarkey's Field Trip** *author/illustrator Kevin O'Malley joins co-author Judy Finchler in recounting the confusion that ensues when a new teacher takes her energetic class on a trip to a nearby science center.*

A lesson in sticktoitiveness illustrated in comic-book fashion, complete with dialogue balloons and digitized color blocks, *Lucky Leaf* finds a young video gamester shooed out of doors on a fall day by his parents. Accompanied by the family dog, the boy soon links up with a group of friends who have met the same fate. After a period of boredom, the group decides that a lone leaf hanging in an otherwise bare tree will bring good luck to whichever boy catches it when it falls. Noting that "there's more going on in the pictures than O'Malley's text would indicate," a *Kirkus* reviewer wrote that video-game fans will "feel right at home in the comic-book format." Predicting that the book's graphic design will attract even reluctant readers, a *Publishers Weekly* contributor concluded that with *Lucky Leaf* "O'Malley delivers another triumph for the kids who have to be dragged kicking and screaming away from their action figures and video games."

Biographical and Critical Sources

PERIODICALS

Booklist, May 1, 2003, Gillian Engberg, review of *Mount Olympus Basketball,* p. 1594; November 15, 2003,

Gillian Engberg, review of *Little Buggy Runs Away,* p. 602; September 15, 2004, Ilene Cooper, review of *Miss Malarkey's Field Trip,* p. 248.

Childhood Education, summer, 2003, Amy Livengood, review of *You're a Good Sport, Miss Malarkey,* p. 245.

Kirkus Reviews, August 15, 2003, review of *Little Buggy Runs Away,* p. 1077; October 1, 2003, review of *Straight to the Pole,* p. 1228; July 1, 2004, review of *Miss Malarkey's Field Trip,* p. 628; August 15, 2004, review of *Lucky Leaf,* p. 810.

Publishers Weekly, October 27, 2003, review of *Little Buggy Runs Away,* p. 67; November 3, 2003, review of *Straight to the Pole,* p. 73; October 4, 2004, review of *Lucky Leaf,* p. 87.

School Library Journal, May, 2003, Marge Loch-Wouters, review of *Mount Olympus Basketball,* p. 126; November, 2003, Joy Fleishhacker, review of *Straight to the Pole,* and Grace Oliff, review of *Little Buggy Runs Away,* p. 112; March, 2004, Andrew Medlar, review of *Mount Olympus Basketball,* p. 67; April, 2004, review of *Straight to the Pole,* p. 26, and *Mount Olympus Basketball,* p. 39.

ONLINE

Embracing the Child Web site, http://www.embracingthe child.org/ (October 23, 2004), "Kevin O'Malley."

Kevin O'Malley Bookpage, http://www.mywebpages. comcast.net/komalley/ (October 23, 2004).

Underdown.org, http://www.underdown.org/ (October 23, 2004), interview with O'Malley.*

*　　*　　*

ONYEFULU, Ifeoma 1959-

Personal

Name is pronounced "Ee-for-ma Oh-yefulu"; born March 31, 1959, in Onitsha, Nigeria; daughter of Emmanuel (a lawyer) and Emily (a businesswoman; maiden name, Ekwensi) Onyefulu; married Roger Malbert (an exhibition organizer), June 6, 1988; children: Emeka, Ikenna (sons). *Education:* London College of Higher Education, Higher National Diploma, 1984. *Religion:* Church of England.

Addresses

Home—15 Bickerton Rd., London N19 5JU, England. *Agent*—c/o Author Mail, Frances Lincoln, 4 Torriano Mews, Torriano Ave., London NW5 2RZ, England.

Career

Photographer and author. *Caribbean Times,* London, England, staff photographer, 1986-87; freelance writer and photographer, beginning 1987.

Ifeoma Onyefulu

Writings

PICTURE BOOKS; AND PHOTOGRAPHER

A Is for Africa: An Alphabet in Words and Pictures, Cobblehill Books (New York, NY), 1993.

Emeka's Gift: An African Counting Story, Cobblehill Books (New York, NY), 1995.

Ogbo: Sharing Life in an African Village, Cobblehill Books (New York, NY), 1996, published as *One Big Family: Sharing Life in an African Village,* Frances Lincoln (London, England), 1996.

Chidi Only Likes Blue: An African Book of Colors, Cobblehill Books (New York, NY), 1997.

Grandfather's Work: A Traditional Healer in Nigeria, Millbrook Press (Brookfield, CT), 1998, published as *My Grandfather Is a Magician: Work and Wisdom in an African Village,* Frances Lincoln (London, England), 1998.

Ebele's Favourite: A Book of African Games, Frances Lincoln (London, England), 1999.

A Triangle for Adaora: An African Book of Shapes, Dutton's Children's Books (New York, NY), 2000.

Saying Good-bye: A Special Farewell to Mama Nkwelle, Millbrook Press (Brookfield, CT), 2001.

Here Comes Our Bride! An African Wedding Story, Frances Lincoln (New York, NY), 2004.

Contributor of photographs to *West Africa* magazine.

Sidelights

Ifeoma Onyefulu is a Nigerian expatriate living in England who has successfully introduced English-speaking audiences to the range and variety of village life in her homeland through her picture books for young readers. Illustrated with her own photographs, Onyefulu's books have been praised as useful additions to classroom libraries for the lessons they teach about the universality of some experiences, as well as for offering a rarely seen depiction of African village life. The brightly colored photographs she includes in books such as *A Is for Africa, Grandfather's Work: A Traditional Healer in Nigeria,* and *A Triangle for Adaora: An African Book of Shapes* evoke the important relationships between the people in her stories and also illustrate the customs and realities of everyday life in contemporary Africa.The first of Onyefulu's concept books, *A Is for Africa* provides an overview of Nigerian village life while also reviewing the alphabet for young English speakers. Chris Powling, writing in *Books for Keeps,* compared the visual impact of *A Is for Africa* to "stepping from a darkened room straight into noon sunshine, so bright and needle-sharp are the author's photographs." Onyefulu selects traditional, African objects and artifacts to exemplify each letter, observed Roger Sutton, the critic adding in the *Bulletin of the Center for Children's Books,* that in *A Is for Africa* such objects "are simply explained and provide good material for a lapsitting visit."

Like *A Is for Africa,* the counting book *Emeka's Gift* contains a brightly lit visual tribute to Nigerian village life that some critics have found enchanting. The simple story finds a young boy setting off to buy his grandmother a birthday gift. Along the way to the market Emeka encounters two friends and three women; having reached his destination, he finds four brooms, five hats, and so forth up to ten, but despairs because he does not have enough money to buy any of the items he sees. He goes to his grandmother and tells her what happened, only to be told that he himself is the best gift she could ever receive. *Emeka's Gift* was praised as "a wonderful multidimensional story with universal appeal" by Barbara Osborne Williams in *School Library*

Professional photographer Ifeoma Onyefulu introduces pre-readers to the many variations of life and culture that exist on the plateau continent in her 1992 picture book **A Is for Africa.**

Journal. In *Booklist* Mary Harris Veeder wrote that Onyefulu's book succeeds in its aim of teaching Western children about Nigerian life because the "nice balance between difference and sameness" allows American children to relate to scenes such as of children playing even if they don't recognize the rules of the game. A reviewer for *Junior Bookshelf* praised Onyefulu for avoiding sentimentality in the telling of her story, displaying instead "honest observation and understanding." The result is "an outstanding counting book."

Other simple math concepts are explored in *A Triangle for Adaora,* which *School Library Journal* contributor Tammy K. Baggett dubbed "a unique approach to learning about shapes." Onyefulu's story focuses on the quest of two young children, Ugo and his cousin Adaora, to find a triangle shape somewhere in their small village. Of course, the triangle is the last shape they encounter: circles, squares, rectangles, and diamonds are encountered, hidden in the everyday objects all around them. *Booklist* contributor Susan Dove Lempke praised the book's "lush color photographs" and noted that *A Triangle for Adaora* successfully doubles as "a concept book and . . . an early social studies book."

Sarah Mear, a reviewer for *School Librarian,* described *Chidi Only Likes Blue* as "a book of colours with a difference." In this story, narrator Nneka introduces readers to a spectrum of colors available in her Nigerian village while trying to convince her brother Chidi that blue—his favorite—is not the only color of beauty. Praising the book as "a quality non-fiction text," Roy Blatchford added in his *Books for Keeps* review that *Chidi Only Likes Blue* "achieves that singular aim of fiction: allowing the reader to climb inside a character's skin and see life from her point of view." Praising the author's characteristic deeply hued photographs, Elizabeth Bush wrote that young readers "will certainly be charmed by the luminous range of tones that sets Nneka's world aglow" in her review for the *Bulletin of the Center for Children's Books.*

In addition to concept books, Onyefulu has created several highly praised books that detail specific aspects of African village life as seen from a child's perspective. *Ebele's Favourite* explains ten games commonly played by children in Nigeria, and also includes detailed directions for interested readers. In *Ogbo: Sharing Life in an African Village* she tells the story of Nigerian age-sets through the eyes of six-year-old Obioma. An *ogbo,* or age-set, is a tradition practiced by some Nigerian villages in which each person is grouped together with all those born within a few years of each other. As each ogbo ages its members are given different responsibilities in service to the community. "As each group is shown working and playing together, readers get a first-hand look at customs" common to Nigerian villagers, noted Loretta Kreider Andrews in *School Library Journal.* Obioma's mother's ogbo ensures the river is kept free of litter; her father's age-set votes on how to get electricity to the village; her uncle's builds houses

for those who cannot afford to build their own. "Keep this title in mind when Kwanzaa next comes around or any time you want a little lesson in cooperation," advised Bush in her review of *Ogbo* for the *Bulletin of the Center for Children's Books.*

Onyefulu's book *Grandfather's Work: A Traditional Healer in Nigeria* introduces the variety of work available to Nigerian villagers, including doctor, lawyer, and artisan, while also taking a close look at the narrator's grandfather's work as a healer. Calling the study of native healing "fascinating," Christine A. Moesch added in the *School Library Journal* that *Grandfather's Work* leaves "readers hungry for more information on the use of various herbs and roots in healing." An author's note at the end explains that modern Western researchers have investigated the use of some of the traditional herbs grandfather uses and found evidence for their healing properties. "With its possibilities for many cross-curricular uses, the book is a natural for the classroom," concluded Maeve Visser Knoth in *Horn Book.* Through books such as *Here Comes Our Bride! An African Wedding Story* and *Saying Good-bye: A Special Farewell to Mama Nkwelle* Onyefulu illustrates the universality of many human customs, including courtship, marriage, and death. *Saying Good-bye* was Onyefulu's way of honoring the passing of her grandmother, a Nigerian dancer and the matriarch of her village, at 102 years of age. Narrated by Onyefulu's youngest son, Ikenna, the book follows the two-week ritual celebration of the deceased woman's life, and, according to *Horn Book* reviewer Anita L. Burkam, serves as "a valuable cross-cultural resource" while also "providing natural explanations of customs that may seem strange to Westerners." A young boy named Ekinadose provides young readers with a window onto a different African tradition in *Here Comes Our Bride!,* as he explains the visits, gift-giving, and other activities surrounding a young couple who have both a traditional ceremony and a church wedding. "Kids will enjoy learning about the Nigerian ritual while they recognize the universal excitement of wedding pagentry" and family festivities, noted *Booklist* contributor Hazel Rochman, while in *Horn Book* Kitty Flynn commended Onyefulu for prefacing *Here Comes the Bride!* with "a helpful introduction outlining the customs" involving the families of the bride and groom.

Onyefulu once told *Something about the Author:* "I love people very much, and having grown up in Nigeria where one is never alone, this type of hunger for company comes naturally. Therefore, my interest in people has increased since I left my country." Noting her love of photography, she added that it has been important to her to "document . . . the everyday life of people, especially Africans, as we have been portrayed by the media as poor people, constantly in need of the West for everything." She decided to create her first book, *A Is for Africa,* "in order to show the African way of life not often seen in the West and in children's books."

The crisp, colorful photographs in Onyefulu's Here Comes Our Bride *highlight her story about a young Nigerian boy who anticipates being part of the festive wedding ceremony of his uncle Osaere.*

Biographical and Critical Sources

PERIODICALS

Booklist, August, 1993, p. 2067; June 1-15, 1995, Mary Harris Veeder, review of *Emeka's Gift,* p. 1779; April 15, 1996, p. 1444; September 15, 1997, Susan Dove Lempke, review of *Chidi Only Likes Blue,* p. 243; March 1, 2001, Susan Dove Lempke, review of *A Triangle for Adaora: An African Book of Shapes,* p. 1284; May 1, 2001, Hazel Rochman, review of *Saying Good-bye: A Special Farewell to Mama Nkwelle,* p. 1687; September 1, 2004, Hazel Rochman, review of *Here Comes Our Bride! An African Wedding Story,* p. 128.

Books for Keeps, September, 1993, Chris Powling, review of *A Is for Africa,* p. 40; November, 1997, Roy Blatchford, review of *Chidi Only Likes Blue,* p. 24.

Bulletin of the Center for Children's Books, September, 1994, Roger Sutton, review of *A Is for Africa,* pp. 19-20; April, 1996, Elizabeth Bush, review of *Ogbo,* pp.

274-275; November, 1997, Elizabeth Bush, review of *Chidi Only Likes Blue,* p. 95.

Horn Book, September, 1993, p. 627; January-February, 1999, Maeve Visser Knoth, review of *Grandfather's Work,* pp. 83-84; January, 1999, Maeve Visser Knoth, review of *Grandfather's Work,* p. 83; July, 2001, Anita L. Burkam, review of *Saying Good-bye,* p. 474; September-October, 2004, Kitty Flynn, review of *Here Comes Our Bride!,* p. 607.

Junior Bookshelf, August, 1995, review of *Emeka's Gift,* p. 130.

Kirkus Reviews, August 15, 1999, p. 1077.

Library Talk, November, 1993, p. 50.

Publishers Weekly, June 28, 1993, p. 75.

School Librarian, November, 1993, p. 150; November, 1997, Sarah Mear, review of *Chidi Only Likes Blue,* p. 187.

School Library Journal, August, 1993, p. 160; July, 1995, Barbara Osborne Williams, review of *Emeka's Gift,* p. 74; April, 1996, Loretta Kreider Andrews, review of *Ogbo,* p. 127; January, 1999, Christine A. Moesch, review of *Grandfather's Work,* p. 100; December, 2000, Tammy K. Baggett, review of *A Triangle for Adaora,* p. 135; July, 2001, Genevieve Ceraldi, review of *Saying Good-bye,* p. 97.

ONLINE

Jubilee Books Web site, http://www.jubileebooks.co.uk/ (February 1, 2005), "Ifeoma Onyefulu."*

* * *

ORENSTEIN, Denise Gosliner 1950-

Personal

Born April 14, 1950, in New York, NY; daughter of Bertram J. (a physician) and Julia (an interior designer; maiden name, Kotler) Gosliner; married (divorced); one child. *Education:* Bennington College, B.A., 1972; Brown University, M.A., 1973.

Addresses

Home—5330 Belt Rd., Washington, DC 20015. *Office*— American University, Department of Literature, 237 Battelle-Tompkins, 4400 Massachusetts Ave. N.W., Washington, DC 20016-8047. *E-mail*—denise@american.edu.

Career

Bethel Receiving Home (orphanage), Bethel, AK, director, 1971; school teacher in villages in AK, 1973-74; Sheldon Jackson College, Sitka, AK, professor of English and education, 1973-74; U.S. Department of Health, Education, and Welfare, Washington, DC, program officer, 1975-79; Central Virginia Child Development Association, Charlottesville, executive director, 1979-82; Human Growth Foundation, Chevy Chase, MD, executive director, 1982—. American University, Washington, DC, instructor in writing, beginning 1987, and director of M.F.A. program in creative writing. President, Thomas Jefferson Child Advocacy Committee, 1979-82; affiliated with Centaur Management Consultants.

Awards, Honors

Distinguished Faculty Award, American University Office of Multicultural Affairs, 2003; Outstanding Teacher Award, American University, 2004.

Writings

When the Wind Blows Hard, illustrated by Linda Strauss Edwards, Addison-Wesley (Reading, MA), 1982.
Unseen Companion, Katherine Tegen Books (New York, NY), 2003.

Work represented in anthologies, including *Stories for Free Children,* McGraw, 1982. Contributor of stories and articles to periodicals, including *Ms.*

Sidelights

Writer and educator Denise Orenstein is the author of the children's books *When the Wind Blows Hard* and *Unseen Companion,* both of which take place in rural Alaska, where Orenstein spent much of her early career. Her first novel, *When the Wind Blows Hard,* is based on her experiences as a teacher in native Alaskan villages and focuses on a young girl whose loneliness after her divorced mother moves to a remote town is ultimately cured through a new friendship.

In Orenstein's young-adult novel *Unseen Companion* the lives of four Alaskans intersect when they come into contact with a mixed-race teen named Dove Alexie. The boy is a prisoner at the Bethel jail and is apparently being battered. When Alexie goes missing, his absence is noticed by Lorraine, who delivers food to the jail, as well as by Annette, who works as a part-time jail bookkeeper. Edgar and Thelma remember Alexie from school, and are left wondering when the teen arrives at jail beaten and then disappears without a trace.

In Denise Gosliner Orenstein's coming-of-age novel, several teens in a remote Alaskan town react differently to the disappearance of an injured boy, although all suspect that foul play was involved. (Cover illustration by Craig Harris.)

When Annette and the others attempt to get to the truth of the matter, jail officials deny the corruption taking place, and even go so far at to deny any knowledge of the missing boy. Orenstein alternates between the four narrators, each portraying Alexie in a different light and providing readers with varying perspectives that incorporate racial issues unique to Alaska. *School Library Journal* critic Vicki Reutter praised the novel as "a multifaceted, compelling glimpse into Alaskan bush life," while a *Booklist* reviewer commented that "Exceptionally strong characters and a background of unusual cultural conflict distinguish Orenstein's stark, kaleidoscopic novel" Praising *Unseen Companion* as a "gritty, tightly written" story, a *Kirkus* reviewer also cited the author for her present-tense narration and her "complex and fully realized characters."

Biographical and Critical Sources

PERIODICALS

Booklist, October 15, 2003, Carolyn Phelan, review of *Unseen Companion,* p. 409; January 1, 2004, review of *Unseen Companion,* p. 780.

Kirkus Reviews, July 15, 2003, review of *Unseen Companion,* p. 966.

Publishers Weekly, November 24, 2003, review of *Unseen Companion,* p. 66.

School Library Journal, January, 2004, Vicki Reutter, review of *Unseen Companion,* p. 134.

P

PAOLINI, Christopher 1983(?)-

Personal

Born c.1983. *Education:* Home schooled.

Addresses

Agent—Writer's House, 21 West 26th St., New York, NY 10010.

Writings

Eragon (first volume in "Inheritance" trilogy), Paolini International (Livingston, MT), 2002, revised edition, Alfred A. Knopf (New York, NY), 2003.

Adaptations

Eragon was adapted as an audiobook read by Gerald Doyle, Books on Tape, 2003; film rights to the novel were purchased by Fox 2000 and a film planned for release in 2005.

Work in Progress

Eldest, a sequel to *Eragon* and the second volume in the "Inheritance" trilogy.

Sidelights

The publication of Christopher Paolini's first novel by New York-based publisher Alfred A. Knopf received more than its share of press, the reason being that the author was still a teenager. Paolini's novel, *Eragon,* the first book of a projected trilogy, quickly topped the bestseller charts.

Eragon takes place in Alagaësua, where a fifteen-year-old boy named Eragon lives on his family's farm with his uncle and cousin. Eragon discovers what he thinks is a blue gemstone covered with white veins, but the object is, in fact, a dragon egg. When a beautiful blue dragon emerges from the egg, the teen names her Saphira.

For over a century an evil king that rules Alagaësua took pains to destroy the Dragon Riders; now, by bonding with the mythical beast, Eragon becomes one of these forbidden riders. The evil King Galbatorix kills the boy's family and charges his dark servants with capturing Eragon and Saphira. Now hunted by these dark servants, the boy and dragon become travelers, and are joined by an old storyteller named Brom. During the adventures the travelers encounter, Eragon matures, and gains an understanding of love, loss, and the evil that is present in his world as he is pulled into the struggle between the king and the resistance forces of the Varden. Together, the boy, dragon, and wise old man draw on a combination of magic and traditional methods to protect and defend themselves from humanoid warriors. Paolini, who was home schooled by his mother, began writing *Eragon* at age fifteen, after earning his GED, because he was not yet ready to attend college and had time to kill. He finished the first draft of his novel within a year, and the second draft consumed another year. As Paolini noted on the *Eragon Web site:* "I started this book when I was fifteen, after several failed attempts composing other stories. It has been an incredible learning experience, and not only in writing. The greatest lesson it taught me was that clear writing is a direct result of clear thinking. Without one you cannot have the other."

Paolini's parents, who own a small publishing company, helped the teen edit the lengthy novel, and then printed 10,000 copies of the book. Turning down a full scholarship to attend Reed College in Portland, Oregon, Paolini and his parents took *Eragon* on the road. Dressed in medieval costume to reflect his novel's fantasy elements, the teen visited schools, libraries, bookstores, and fairs around the country, reading from his novel and promoting it at book signings, The Paolinis also placed *Eragon* in Montana book stores, where a

Written when its author was still in high school, this 2003 novel by Christopher Paolini draws readers into a saga that begins when Alageëlian teen Eragon finds a stone with magical powers. (Cover illustration by John Jude Palencar.)

copy was purchased by the stepson of Florida novelist Carl Hiaasen, while the Hiaasen family was in Montana on a fly-fishing trip. Hiaason called his editor at Alfred E. Knopf and suggested that the publisher might want to look at *Eragon*. They did and published a second edition, after doing some more editing of the book's length. In addition to climbing the bestseller charts, the novel was adapted as an audiobook and a film based on *Eragon* was scheduled for production in 2005.

Paolini drew on his knowledge of the history of modern fantasy, which he noted on his Web site has roots in "Teutonic, Scandinavian, and Old Norse history." He invented an Elven language based on Old Norse for his book; "all the Dwarf and Urgal words, however, are of my own invention," he added. The scenic area around Livingston, Montana, where the author lives, was also an inspiration for his story, which was described as a "solid, sweeping epic fantasy" by a *Kirkus Reviews* contributor. *Booklist* reviewer Sally Estes wrote that Paolini's "lush tale is full of recognizable fantasy elements and conventions. But the telling remains constantly fresh and fluid." *Kliatt* contributor Michele Winship noted that, in creating *Eragon*, the young au-

thor "takes a little Tolkien, a little McCaffrey, a coming-of-age quest, and combines them with some wicked good storytelling."

While both readers and critics enjoyed *Eragon*, some noted that the book nonetheless shows signs of being written by a first-time novelist. *School Library Journal* reviewer Susan L. Rogers felt that "sometimes the magic solutions are just too convenient for getting out of difficult situations," but noted that fans of J. R. R. Tolkien's "Lord of the Rings" trilogy would find much in the novel that is familiar. *New York Times Book Review* contributor Liz Rosenberg cited what she saw as faults in the story, including clichés and "B-movie dialogue." While the book's "plot stumbles and jerks along, with gaps in logic and characters dropped, then suddenly remembered, or new ones invented at the last minute," Rosenberg added that "*Eragon*, for all its flaws, is an authentic work of great talent. The story is gripping; it may move awkwardly, but it moves with force. The power of *Eragon* lies in its overall effects— in the sweep of the story and the conviction of the storyteller. Here, Paolini is leagues ahead of most writers, and it is exactly here that his youth is on his side." While also noting Paolini's debt to Tolkien's work, a *Publishers Weekly* reviewer called *Eragon* "an auspicious beginning to both career and series."

Biographical and Critical Sources

PERIODICALS

Booklist, August 15, 2003, Sally Estes, review of *Eragon,* p. 1981.
Christian Science Monitor, August 7, 2003, Yvonne Zipp, "Teen Author Wins Readers Book by Book."
Kirkus Reviews, July 15, 2003, review of *Eragon,* p. 967.
Kliatt, September, 2003, Michele Winship, review of *Eragon,* p. 10.
New York Times Book Review, November 16, 2003, Liz Rosenberg, review of *Eragon.*
Publishers Weekly, July 21, 2003, review of *Eragon,* p. 196.
School Library Journal, September 1, 2003, Susan L. Rogers, review of *Eragon,* p. 218; February, 2004, Francisca Goldsmith, review of *Eragon* (audiobook), p. 76.
Writer, March, 2004, interview with Paolini, p. 66.

ONLINE

Eragon Web site, http://www.randomhouse.com/teens/eragon/ (February 1, 2005).
Powells.com, http://www.powells.com/ (July 31, 2003), David Welch, "Philip Pullman, Tamora Pierce,a nd Christopher Paolini Talk Fantasy Fiction" (interview).*

*   *   *

PARKER, Barbara Keevil 1938-

Personal

Born May 17, 1938, in Tacoma, WA; daughter of William H. and Jean (Durkee) Keevil; married Duane F.

Barbara Keevil Parker

Parker (a minister), June 11, 1960; children: Stacy, Pamela, Jon. *Education:* University of Puget Sound, B.A., 1960; Kansas State University, M.S., 1973, Ph.D., 1976. *Hobbies and other interests:* Travel, toy trains, collecting German nutcrackers.

Addresses

Home—Everett WA. *Agent*—c/o Author Mail, Lerner Publications, 241 First Ave. North, Minneapolis, MN 55401. *E-mail*—bkeevil5@aol.com.

Career

Therapist, educator, and writer. Rhode Island College Department of Economics and Management, Center for Economic Education, coordinator, 1976-78; curriculum consultant, 1978-79; Salve Regina College, Newport, RI, graduate instructor in health services administration, 1981-82; Employee Education and Training, Rhode Island Hospital, Providence, manager, 1979-84; Wesley Homes, Atlanta, GA, director of education, 1985-91; coordinator of employee assistance program, 1987-91; Covenant Counseling Institute, Snellville, GA, therapist and director of education, 1991-94; Interfaith Counseling Center, therapist, 1995-98. Freelance writer, beginning 1986; Institute of Children's Literature, West Redding, CT, writing instructor, beginning 2000.

Member

Society of Children's Book Writers and Illustrators, American Association of Marriage and Family Therapists.

Awards, Honors

Parchment and Quill Award, Georgia Society of Healthcare and Training, 1986, 1992; Distinguished Achievement Award, American Society of Healthcare Education and Training 1991.

Writings

FOR CHILDREN

Christian Celebrations, Pockets of Learning, 1998.
The Lord Is My Shepherd, Pockets of Learning, 1998.
The Good Samaritan, Pockets of Learning, 1998.
North American Wolves, Carolrhoda Books (Minneapolis, MN), 1998.
Susan B. Anthony: Daring to Vote, Millbrook Press (Brookfield, CT), 1998.
(With Duane F. Parker) *Miguel de Cervantes,* Chelsea House Publishers (Philadelphia, PA), 2003.
Giraffes, Carolrhoda Books (Minneapolis, MN), 2004.
Cheetahs, Lerner Publication Co. (Minneapolis, MN), 2005.
(With Dwayne F. Parker) *Canada Lynx,* Lerner Publication Co. (Minneapolis, MN), 2005.

OTHER

Healthcare Education: A Guide to Staff Development, 1986.

Contributor to periodicals, including *Grit, Your Big Backyard, Cogniz, Boys' Quest, Collector Editions, Aim,* and various professional journals.

Sidelights

Barbara Keevil Parker is the author of several children's books, including *North American Wolves* and *Susan B. Anthony: Daring to Vote.* Inspired by Parker's interest in wildlife and the outdoors, *North American Wolves* introduces elementary-grade readers to the everyday world of wild wolves, including their physiology, their habits, and their unique behavior, which includes instinctive territoriality, hunting strategies, and communication techniques. Clear photos depicting the sometimes maligned and controversial animals accompany the text so young researchers can more clearly visualize the topics under discussion. Characterizing the book's introduction as "dramatic," Stephanie Zvirin added in a review of the book for *Booklist* that the author quickly "gets down to business, clearly and informatively."

Parker told *Something about the Author:* "I live in the Pacific Northwest and grew up a country girl. We lived on a small lake, and I spend many hours on the lake swimming, fishing, and canoeing, and an equal number of hours hiking in the woods, building secret camps, and learning to appreciate nature.

"In high school, I was deeply involved in journalism—editing the yearbook and writing for the school paper. I changed direction in college and majored in speech and drama with the goal of teaching in that area. Fortunately, I minored in English and American literature, because that's where I found my first teaching job.

"Marriage right after college took me to Evanston, Illinois, where my husband was attending school at Garrett Theological Seminary. During his graduate school years I taught school, and delivered our first child. From Evanston, we moved to Kansas, where two more children were born. Here, when our children were young, I took my first stab at writing children's books. The publishers rejected them. Then I got busy teaching preschool, middle school, and high school. I put aside my writing.

"When all the children were in school, I needed something new for me. I decided to go to graduate school. As a graduate assistant in adult education, I discovered I could write and publish articles about my work. I also studied marriage and family therapy and spent a year at the Menninger Foundation doing an internship in counseling.

"After another move I started my Rhode Island career in a fascinating job at a college. As coordinator of the Center for Economic Education, I collaborated with a local puppeteer to write a play called *Dollars and Sense.* Armed with puppets and a portable stage, I traveled to schools throughout the state presenting a puppet show to elementary children to get them thinking about basic

In Parker's **North American Wolves** *readers learn the truth about this much-maligned creature, and discover how wolves are being saved from extinction in their ever-shrinking natural habitat. (Photograph by Rick McIntyre.)*

economic concepts. Later I moved away from children to become director of education at a hospital. Here I wrote my first book, published in 1986, about developing courses for use in a hospital setting. In the meantime, we moved to Atlanta, Georgia. Emory University offered a class called Writing for Children, and I enrolled.

"I love animals so one of my early stories was about a wolf. I mailed it to a publisher. They wrote back that they didn't take fiction. Would I be interested in writing a nonfiction book on wolves? Of course I said yes! However, when I sent the manuscript to them, they rejected it. Brokenhearted, I paced around the house and finally mustered up enough courage to call them to ask what was wrong. 'Boring presentation,' they said. 'Well if I can rewrite it and make it more exciting, would you still be interested?' I asked. They agreed. A few months later I had my first children' book contract.

"After ten years in Georgia, we moved back to New England to be near children and grandchildren. New England was home for eight years. In addition to my writing career, I was a marriage and family therapist.

"My husband and I enjoy several hobbies, travel being one of them. We also love toy trains and German nutcrackers. Scattered throughout our houses we have two hundred nutcracker eyes staring at us year-round.

"From my window, I can watch the wind and sun play games on the nearby water. Mt. Baker towers above the hills and water, wearing its gleaming white snow cover year-round. Seeing nature in action right outside my window provides inspiration and an abundance of story ideas. I write every weekday, usually in the morning, however, when I get deep into a manuscript, time stops and I get lost in my writing."

Biographical and Critical Sources

PERIODICALS

Booklist, June 1, 1998, Ilene Cooper, review of *Susan B. Anthony: Daring to Vote,* p. 1758; December 1, 1998, Stephanie Zvirin, review of *North American Wolves,* p. 681.

*　　*　　*

PELL, Ed(ward) 1950-
(Bob Boudelang)

Personal

Born April 5, 1950, in Baltimore, MD.

Addresses

Home—NJ. *Agent*—c/o Author Mail, Capstone Press, 151 Good Counsel Dr., P.O. Box 669, Mankato, MN 56002. *E-mail*—espvent@bellatlantic.net.

Career

Writer, journalist, and marketing consultant. ESP Ventures (marketing consultant firm), Morristown, NJ, president.

Awards, Honors

Jesse H. Neal Business Journalism Competition award, 1989; American Society of Business Press Editors award, 1995.

Writings

Maryland ("Land of Liberty" series), Capstone Press (Mankato, MN), 2003.
Connecticut ("Land of Liberty" series), Capstone Press (Mankato, MN), 2003.
Indiana ("Land of Liberty" series), Capstone Press (Mankato, MN), 2003.
John Winthrop: Governor of the Massachusetts Bay Colony, Capstone Press (Mankato, MN), 2004.

Author of online column "Equal Time with Bob Boudelang, Angry American Patriot," for *Democratic Under ground.com.* Contributor to periodicals, including *Simply the Best, Internet Publishing, NJ Savvy Living,* and *Prehistoric Times.*

Biographical and Critical Sources

PERIODICALS

School Library Journal, August, 2004, Kathleen Simonetta, review of *The Salem Witch Trials,* p. 133.

ONLINE

DemocraticUnderground.com, http://www.democraticunder ground.com/bob/ (August 12, 2004).*

*　　*　　*

PEYTON, K. M.
See PEYTON, Kathleen Wendy (Herald)

*　　*　　*

PEYTON, Kathleen Wendy (Herald) 1929-
(Kathleen Herald, K. M. Peyton, a joint pseudonym)

Personal

Born August 2, 1929, in Birmingham, England; married Michael Peyton (a commercial artist and cartoonist), 1950; children: Hilary, Veronica. *Education:* Attended

Kingston School of Art; Manchester Art School, A.T.D. *Hobbies and other interests:* Riding, walking in the mountains, airplanes, sailing, horseback riding, music.

Addresses

Home—Chelmsford, England *Agent*—c/o Author Mail, Oxford University Press, Great Clarendon St., Oxford OX2 6DP, England.

Career

Art teacher at high school in Northampton, England, 1952-56; writer, beginning 1956.

Member

Society of Authors.

Awards, Honors

American Library Association Notable Book designation, 1963, for *Sea Fever*, 1969, for *Flambards in Summer*, 1971, for *Pennington's Last Term* and *The Beethoven Medal*, and 1972, for *A Pattern of Roses*; *New York Herald Tribune* book award, 1965, for *The Maplin Bird*; Carnegie Medal, 1969, for *The Edge of the Cloud*; *Guardian* book award, 1970, for *Flambards, The Edge of the Cloud*, and *Flambards in Summer*; *Prove Yourself a Hero* named a Best Books for Young Adults, 1979.

Writings

JUVENILE; UNDER NAME KATHLEEN HERALD

Sabre, the Horse from the Sea, illustrated by Lionel Edwards, A. & C. Black (London, England), 1947, reprinted, Macmillan (London, England), 1963.
The Mandrake: A Pony, illustrated by Lionel Edwards, A. & C. Black (London, England), 1949.
Crab the Roan, illustrated by Peter Biegel, A. & C. Black (London, England), 1953.

JUVENILE; WITH HUSBAND, MICHAEL PEYTON, UNDER JOINT PSEUDONYM K. M. PEYTON

North to Adventure, Collins (London, England), 1959, Platt & Munk (New York, NY), 1965.
Stormcock Meets Trouble, Collins (London, England), 1961.
The Hard Way Home, illustrated by R. A. Branton, Collins (London, England), 1962, revised edition, Goodchild, 1986, published as *Sing a Song of Ambush*, Platt & Munk (New York, NY), 1964.

JUVENILE; UNDER NAME K. M. PEYTON

Windfall, illustrated by Victor G. Ambrus, Oxford University Press (Oxford, England), 1962, published as *Sea Fever*, World Publishing, 1963.

Brownsea Silver, Collins (London, England), 1964.
The Maplin Bird, illustrated by Victor G. Ambrus, Oxford University Press (Oxford, England), 1964, World Publishing, 1965, reprinted with a new introduction, Gregg (Boston, MA), 1980.
The Plan for Birdsmarsh, illustrated by Victor G. Ambrus, Oxford University Press (Oxford, England), 1965, World Publishing, 1966.
Thunder in the Sky, illustrated by Victor G. Ambrus, Oxford University Press (Oxford, England), 1966, World Publishing, 1967, reprinted, Bodley Head (London, England), 1985.
Flambards (first book in "Flambards" series; also see below), illustrated by Victor G. Ambrus, Oxford University Press (Oxford, England), 1967, World Publishing, 1968, reprinted Oxford University Press, 2004.
Fly-by-Night, uncredited illustration by Michael Peyton, Oxford University Press (Oxford, England), 1968, World Publishing, 1969, published in *Three in One Pony Stories*, Red Fox (London, England), 1999.
The Edge of the Cloud (second book in "Flambards" series; also see below), illustrated by Victor G. Ambrus, World Publishing, 1969, reprinted, Oxford University Press (Oxford, England), 1999.
Flambards in Summer (third book in "Flambards" series; also see below), illustrated by Victor G. Ambrus, Oxford University Press (Oxford, England), 1969, World Publishing, 1970, reprinted, Oxford University Press, 1999.
Pennington's Seventeenth Summer (also see below), uncredited illustration by Michael Peyton, Oxford University Press (Oxford, England), 1969, World Publishing, 1970, published as *Pennington's Last Term*, Crowell (New York, NY), 1971.
The Beethoven Medal (also see below), uncredited illustration by Michael Peyton, Oxford University Press (Oxford, England), 1971, Crowell (New York, NY), 1972.
A Pattern of Roses, uncredited illustration by Michael Peyton, Oxford University Press (Oxford, England), 1972, Crowell (New York, NY), 1973 reprinted, Oxford University Press, 2001.
Pennington's Heir (also see below), uncredited illustration by Michael Peyton, Oxford University Press (Oxford, England), 1973, Crowell (New York, NY), 1974.
The Team, uncredited illustration by Michael Peyton, Oxford University Press (Oxford, England), 1975, Crowell (New York, NY), 1976.
The Right-Hand Man, Oxford University Press (Oxford, England), 1977.
Prove Yourself a Hero, Oxford University Press (Oxford, England), 1977, Philomel Books (New York, NY), 1978, reprinted, Oxford University Press, 2000.
A Midsummer Night's Death, Oxford University Press (Oxford, England), 1978, Philomel Books (New York, NY), 1979.
Marion's Angels, Oxford University Press (Oxford, England), 1979.
The Flambards Trilogy (contains *Flambards, The Edge of the Cloud*, and *Flambards in Summer*), Puffin Books, 1980.

Flambards Divided (fourth book in "Flambards" series), Oxford University Press (Oxford, England), 1981, Philomel Books (New York, NY), 1982, reprinted, 1999.

Dear Fred, Bodley Head (London, England), 1981.

Going Home, illustrated by Chris Molan, Philomel Books (New York, NY), 1982.

Who, Sir? Me, Sir?, Philomel Books (New York, NY), 1983, 2nd edition revised by Diane Mowat, Oxford University Press (Oxford, England), 2000.

Free Rein, Philomel Books (New York, NY), 1983.

The Last Ditch, Oxford University Press (Oxford, England), 1983.

Pennington: A Trilogy (contains *Pennington's Seventeenth Summer, The Beethoven Medal,* and *Pennington's Heir*), Oxford University Press (Oxford, England), 1984.

Frogett's Revenge, illustrated by Leslie Smith, Oxford University Press (Oxford, England), 1985, illustrated by Maureen Bradley, Puffin Books (New York, NY), 1987.

The Sound of Distant Cheering, Bodley Head (London, England), 1986.

Downhill All the Way, Oxford University Press (Oxford, England), 1988.

Plain Jack, uncredited illustration by Michael Peyton, Hamish Hamilton (London, England), 1988.

Skylark, Oxford University Press (Oxford, England), 1989.

Darkling, 1990.

The Boy Who Wasn't There, Doubleday (New York, NY), 1992.

Poor Badger, 1992.

The Wild Boy and Queen Moon, Doubleday (New York, NY), 1993.

The Swallow Tale, Doubleday (New York, NY), 1995.

Swallow Summer, Doubleday (New York, NY), 1996.

Swallow the Star, Doubleday (New York, NY), 1997.

The Pony That Went to Sea, Hamish Hamilton (London, England), 1997.

Unquiet Spirits, Scholastic (New York, NY), 1997.

Firehead, Scholastic (New York, NY), 1998.

Snowfall, Houghton Mifflin (Boston, MA), 1998.

Horses, illustrated by Michael Langham Rowe, Oxford University Press (Oxford, England), 2000.

Blind Beauty, Dutton Children's Books (New York, NY), 2001.

Stealaway, illustrated by David Wyatt, Macmillan (London, England), 2001, Cricket Books (Chicago, IL), 2004.

Pony in the Dark, Young Corgi (London, England), 2001.

Small Gains, David Fickling Books (London, England), 2003.

Greater Gains, David Fickling Books (London, England), 2005.

Adaptations

The Right-Hand Man was adapted as an Australian film in 1987.

Sidelights

Publishing her first novel at the age of eighteen, and continuing her prolific writing career—sometimes in collaboration with her husband, writer and illustrator Michael Peyton—under the name K. M. Peyton, Kathleen Wendy Peyton pens stories that deal with the problems young people face while growing into adulthood. Praising such novels as the Carnegie Medal-winning *The Edge of the Cloud* as well as the books *Blind Beauty, The Beethoven Medal,* and *The Maplin Bird,* a *Junior Bookshelf* reviewer declared that "few writers deal more convincingly with the exquisite agony of growing up than Peyton."

Peyton's love of horseback riding, sailing, music, and flying is reflected in many of her books, and reviewers have praised the vivid descriptions of such activities as one of the best features of Peyton' books. In his *A Sense of Story: Essays on Contemporary Writing for Children,* John Rowe Townsend commented that Peyton "has, among many other gifts, the unusual one of writing extremely well about *movement*: about the way people move with and through and against the elements, in

Unhappy in her new home, which includes a difficult-to-like stepfather, Tessa focuses her can-do spirit on training an ugly horse named Buffoon to compete in an upcoming horse show. (Cover illustration by Pete Kelly.)

boats, on horseback, and—in the *Flambards* novels—in those frail, wind-buffeted early aircraft." For many years the Peytons lived close to nature and to the sea, making their home on an estuary in Essex, England. Noting this fact, *Junior Bookshelf* contributor Marcus S. Crouch wrote that Peyton "knows the sea, the creeks and the saltings, as well as the villages and the ports." Several of Peyton's stories, such as *The Maplin Bird, The Plan for Birdsmarsh, Thunder in the Sky,* and *Sea Fever,* take advantage of this background. Margaret Meek wrote in a review of *The Maplin Bird* for *School Librarian and School Library Review* that "the estuary scenery and details of seafaring are skillfully woven into the texture of the relationships" that unfold in Peyton's story. Just as Peyton's stories about sailing are not solely limited to descriptions of boating, critics have noted that her books about horses are balanced by their attention to the personal problems of their young protagonists. In *Blind Beauty,* for example, a troubled, horse-crazy pre-teen named Tessa comes to terms with the problems in her life and her relationships with her difficult parents through her determination to train an ungainly horse limited potential and failing eyesight to qualify to race in the Grand National. Praising the novel in *Publishers Weekly,* a reviewer wrote that Peyton's "distinctively cadenced prose . . . keeps the narrative galloping at a cracking pace," while *School Library Journal* reviewer Barbara Wysocki described Tessa as "an impulsive, independent, horse-loving teen with twenty-first-century problems. Appraising *Fly-by-Night,* Peyton's story about a young girl who raises a horse in her lower middle-class home, Crouch commented in his *The Nesbit Tradition: The Children's Novel in England, 1945-70* that when the plot-line turned its focus on the personal struggles of its "young heroine, ponies quickly disappeared and [Peyton] . . . wrote a serious social novel." The story's protagonist, Ruth, a *Young Readers' Review* critic further asserted, "is a fine creation. She is a likeable, intense girl whose heart is in the right place. The way she meets her problems is completely realistic." The reviewer concluded that *Fly-by-Night* is a "beautifully written horse story." Other books involving horses and the teens who love them include *Stealaway,* which draws elements of mystery and the supernatural into its plot. In the novel, Nicky's horse-trainer mother gets a job at the stable of an isolated Scottish castle that has a centuries-old past which includes regional wars, the unsolved murder of a child, and the theft of a prize stallion. Along with her new friend Jed, Nicky finds herself drawn into the castle's past when the stable's new stallion is threatened and a ghostly white pony haunts the premises. Reviewing the book for *School Library Journal,* Kelley Rae Unger dubbed *Stealaway* "a good choice for horse lovers and mystery aficionados alike." A mistreated pony is the subject of *Poor Badger,* a book for younger readers that focuses on a young girl's efforts to find the pony a loving home and features "a veritable encyclopedia of how not to care for a pony," according to a *Publishers Weekly* contributor. Like *Blind Beauty* a teen's belief in the potential of a lackluster horse is the focus of *Darkling,* which finds

K. M. Peyton is perhaps best known for horse stories, such as this 2001 novel that combines a girl's love of horses with a haunted Scottish castle and a mysterious curse. (Cover illustration by David Wyatt.)

Jenny's dedication to a wild colt paying off in a conclusion that features both an exciting horserace sequence and a budding romance.

While Peyton often pens stories about horses that are aimed at a pre-teen readership, she has also strayed into other subjects. In fact, the first three "Flambards" novels—*Flambards, The Edge of the Cloud,* and *Flambards in Summer*—are considered her most acclaimed books. Winner of the *Guardian* Award for Fiction in 1970, the first three volumes of the series follow the life of Christina, an orphan who lives in the crumbling English mansion Flambards along with her uncle Russell, a crippled yet domineering man whose only concerns are hunting, horses, and making certain his two sons carry on his Edwardian lifestyle. However, Will, the younger son, loves airplanes more than horses, and has no desire to be part of a social class that believes horses should be treated better than servants. Christina, who, as one *Times Literary Supplement* reviewer described, "loves hunting but hates the mindless world of the hunters," marries Will after discovering that they have similar beliefs, and the couple flee to London. Peyton's ability to highlight the shifting class landscape during the early twentieth century through characters such as Will and Uncle Russell makes *Flambards* an "important novel," according to *Washington Post Book World* contributor Madeline L'Engle.

Becoming a pilot for the Royal Air Force after World War I breaks out, Will is shot down and killed in Europe. *Flambards in Summer* relates how Christina, now a twenty-one-year-old widow, returns to the mansion and attempts to restore new life to Flambards. Following their *Guardian* award, the Peytons continued their popular series with *Flambards Divided,* which finds Christina facing the repercussions of her decision to marry "beneath her" after she weds Dick, a former stable hand at the mansion. The newlyweds' life together represents the rise of a new social class, as well as a threat to class traditions; and they are ignored socially by the local gentry.

Another of Peyton's well-known characters is Patrick Pennington, who first appears in *Pennington's Last Term.* Pamela T. Cleaver, reviewing the novel for the *Children's Book Review,* dubbed it "a rare, marvelous book." Peyton's "seventeen-year-old rebel, hating his last year at school, arrogant and surly, butting his head against authority," is "a totally believable teenager," Cleaver added. Pennington has a talent for playing the piano, and it is this ability that eventually redeems him in the eyes of his elders. In novels such as *The Beethoven Medal* and *Pennington's Heir,* Peyton's protagonist matures: Pennington marries Ruth, the leading character in *Fly-by-Night,* and the couple have a baby. Although Ruth and Pennington suffer some setbacks, such as Pennington's brief term in jail for striking a policeman, their ability to grow as people helps them overcome many obstacles successfully.Because Peyton usually sets her books in the twentieth century, the novel *Snowfall* serves as a bit of a departure. In addition to the absence of horses, the book was characterized by *Booklist* reviewer Frances Bradburn as "a delightful Victorian romance novel for teens." Based on a true incident, the novel finds sixteen-year-old Charlotte, who has been raised by her grandfather, promised in marriage to her grandfather's colleague, an assistant vicar who the young woman has few positive feelings for. Convincing her grandfather to allow her one last holiday prior to her wedding, Charlotte conspires with her older brother Ben to join a mountaineering party planned for the Swiss Alps. In the company of Ben and his handsome college friends, Charlotte visits the home of Milo, a well-connected young man of questionable values, where she is quickly swept off her feet and into the arms of more than one available young man. While noting that Charlotte's behavior does not reflect appropriate Victorian manners, Bradburn maintained that the young woman still conforms to the social "constraints of the era." Somewhat critical of the novel, a *Publishers Weekly* contributor maintained that *Snowfall* also reflects Victorian society in its "cliched" characterizations of Jews and people of "'low' birth.

Peyton has published numerous novels with her husband, Michael, under the pseudonym K. M. Peyton, including this 1994 novel about a teen rebelling against the stuffiness of Victorian society. (Cover illustration by Elizabeth Sayles.)

While some reviewers have taken issue with Peyton's tendency to resolve her stories with happy endings—the author was said to have a "strong but romantic heart" by one *Times Literary Supplement* critic—Townsend noted that several of her books "deal with large themes" and feature "excellent plots" featuring "great pace and certainty." With regard to Peyton's depiction of adolescents, John W. Conner cited *Pennington's Last Term* as proof that the author "understands the emotional turbulence" of the teenaged years. In general, Peyton has been characterized by critics like *New Statesman* contributor Naomi Lewis as "a strong, trenchant, curiously unsentimental novelist," and the Peyton's books have continued to be reissued, steadily winning new fans throughout her long career.

The purpose of all her writing, Peyton once asserted in *The Thorny Paradise: Writers on Writing for Children,* is solely to entertain, and not to convey any particular moral message. "When a writer knows he has a juvenile audience," she explained, "a certain responsibility is inevitably felt, but to think that he can 'con' his audience into what might be called correct attitudes [is an effort that] must be doomed to failure."

Biographical and Critical Sources

BOOKS

Blishen, Edward, _The Thorny Paradise: Writers on Writing for Children,_ Kestrel Books (London, England), 1975.
Children's Literature Review, Volume 3, Gale (Detroit, MI), 1978.
Crouch, Marcus S., _The Nesbit Tradition: The Children's Novel in England, 1945-70,_ Benn (London, England), 1972.
Townsend, John Rowe, _A Sense of Story: Essays on Contemporary Writing for Children,_ Longman (London, England), 1971.

PERIODICALS

Booklist, September 15, 1998, Frances Bradburn, review of _Snowfall,_ p. 221.
Chicago Tribune Book World, December 29, 1968; May 9, 1971.
Children's Book News, March-April, 1969; September-October, 1970.
Children's Book Review, October, 1971; February, 1973; spring, 1974.
Children's Literature in Education, July, 1972; November, 1972.
English Journal, November, 1971; November, 1972.
Junior Bookshelf, November, 1964; December, 1966; June, 1969; October, 1971; February, 1974.
Kirkus Reviews, August 15, 2004, review of _Stealaway,_ p. 811.
New Statesman, November 3, 1967.
New York Times Book Review, July 10, 1966.
Publishers Weekly, May 11, 1990, review of _Darkling,_ p. 261; January 20, 1992, review of _Poor Badger,_ p. 65; September 14, 1998, review of _Snowfall,_ p. 69; January 29, 2001, review of _Blind Beauty,_ p. 90.
School Librarian and School Library Review, March, 1965.
School Library Journal, March, 2001, Carol Schene, review of _Blind Beauty,_ p. 255; August, 2004, Barbara Wysocki, review of _Blind Beauty_ (audiobook), p. 77; December, 2004, Kelley Rae Unger, review of _Stealaway,_ p. 117.
Spectator, November 1, 1969; November 13, 1971.
Times Literary Supplement, December 9, 1965; November 30, 1967; October 3, 1968; April 3, 1969; October 16, 1969; November 30, 1970; November 3, 1972; December 5, 1975; September 29, 1978; September, 17, 1982; March 29, 1985; August 16, 1985.
Use of English, spring, 1972.
Washington Post Book World, November 11, 1979; February 12, 1984.
Young Readers' Review, December, 1968; May, 1969.

*   *   *

PRUETT, Candace (J.) 1968-

Personal

Born March 31, 1968, in Denver, CO; daughter of Corwin Alexander (a realtor, broker, and appraiser) and Carol J. (a city manager) Brown; married Bart W. Pruett (a sales manager), June 4, 1994; children: Morgan, Benjamin. _Ethnicity:_ "Caucasian." _Education:_ University of Colorado, B.A.. _Politics:_ Republican. _Religion:_ Lutheran.

Addresses

Home—Nunn, CO. _Office_—Poudre Valley Health System, 1024 South Lemay Ave., Fort Collins, CO 80524. _E-mail_—cjp2@pvhs.org.

Career

Writer, registered nurse, and consultant. Poudre Valley Health System, Fort Collins, CO, human resources consultant and nurse recruiter, 1993—. Project Self-Sufficiency, counselor; mentor for International Telementor program.

Member

American Nurses Association, Colorado Nurses Association (vice president of District 9), Northern Colorado Nurses Coalition.

Writings

A Visit with My Uncle Ted, Elderberry Press (Oakland, OR), 2003.

Work in Progress

Two other children's books focused on increasing interest in nursing: _My Mommy Is Special_ and _I Made a New Friend Today._

R

RAKE, Jody 1961-
(Jody Sullivan)

Personal

Born November 21, 1961, in Hollywood, CA; daughter of J. Gordon and Jacqueline (a homemaker, maiden name Dente) Brown; married Scott Byrum, June 19, 1989 (divorced, March, 1998); married Andrew Rake (a computer graphics animator), February 16, 2002; children: Jeffrey Byrum, Justine Byrum. *Ethnicity:* "Caucasian." *Education:* College of San Mateo, A.A., 1981; San Francisco State University, B.A. (zoology), 1987; Mesa College, certificate in technical writing, 1994. *Politics:* Republican. *Religion:* Christian. *Hobbies and other interests:* Antique collecting, hiking, traveling, trivia, movies.

Addresses

Home—7813-60 Tommy Dr., San Diego, CA 92119. *E-mail*—raked@sbcglobal.net.

Career

Freelance writer and proofreader, 1999—; Capstone Press, Mankato, MN, consultant, beginning 1999.

Member

Southwest Marine Educators Association.

Writings

UNDER NAME JODY SULLIVAN

Cheetahs: Spotted Speedster, Bridgestone Books (Mankato, MN), 2003.
Beavers: Big-toothed Builders, Bridgestone Books (Mankato, MN), 2003.

Jody Rake

Deer: Graceful Grazers, Capstone Press (Mankato, MN), 2003.
Georgia, Capstone Press (Mankato, MN), 2003.
Hawaii, Capstone Press (Mankato, MN), 2003.
Parrotfish, Capstone Press (Mankato, MN), 2006.
Crabs, Capstone Press (Mankato, MN), 2006.
Sea Anemones, Capstone Press (Mankato, MN), 2006.
Sea Stars, Capstone Press (Mankato, MN), 2006.

Also author of informational booklets, teacher's guides, and other educational materials for SeaWorld. Contributor of articles to periodicals, including *Satlink,* and

Christian Classroom. Editor of newsletter for Southwest Marine Educators Association, 1998-2002.

Work in Progress

Beagles, Dalmatians, Pugs, and *St. Bernards,* for Capstone Press.

Sidelights

Writing under the pen name Jody Sullivan, Jody Rake is the author of several nonfiction children's books, including *Beavers: Big-toothed Builders* and *Cheetahs: Spotted Speedsters,* both part of the "Wild World of Animals" series. *Booklist* reviewer Stephanie Zvirin enjoyed the clear and colorful photographs in *Cheetahs* and also noted that the "'fast facts' scattered through the book" provide a lively format for readers. In addition to continuing to write nonfiction titles that draw on her interest and training in the sciences, Rake produced many educational materials for SeaWorld and has also been a scientific consultant to Capstone Press's "Ocean Life" series.

Rake told *Something about the Author:* "I took the scenic route toward becoming an author. It wasn't the first job that came to mind. Never in my life have I demonstrated any talent for creative writing. I came to San Diego in 1989 with a degree in zoology and a desire to work with animals. I got a job at SeaWorld, but because my practical experience was in child care and education, I was hired by the education department. I was confident that I would eventually work my way into the mammal department. In the course of my job, I was given some writing assignments, and discovered the art of nonfiction writing. I discovered that the education department had a science writer. I thought that sounded very cool, and then and there I did some serious reevaluation.

"I went back to school and earned a certificate in technical writing. I landed an internship with the aforementioned science writer, and within six months attained a permanent position as a science writer. For ten years I wrote numerous nonfiction publication for SeaWorld, mostly about marine animals. I eventually began doing some freelance projects at home, and gradually, the urge to quit my job and stay home with my children grew into an overwhelming pull. My last day at SeaWorld was September 5, 2003, and I've been a freelance writer and editor ever since.

"As a mother of an elementary student, I often help gather research materials for reports and projects. While the Internet is amazing and useful, it is no substitute for quality books. Sometimes I find that resources are limited, outdated, too high-level, or otherwise unable to support the state and national teaching standards. It is a goal of mine to help contribute to the body of resources that help teachers fulfill these standards.

"My advice for aspiring writers? Read! Read much and often. There is no better way to learn how to write. I also recommend identifying what type of writer you are: fiction or nonfiction? Do you have a story to tell? Are the words just bursting out of you? Or are you better suited at expressing information? Try writing both ways—which one comes more naturally? In either case, pick a topic you are passionate about, otherwise you'll struggle. Always develop the gifts you are given—don't waste your time trying to be something you're not."

Biographical and Critical Sources

PERIODICALS

Booklist, January 1, 2003, Stephanie Zvirin, review of *Groundhogs: Woodchuck, Marmots, and Whistle Pigs,* p. 900.
School Library Journal, April, 2003, Susan Oliver, review of *Woodchucks, Marmots, and Whistle Pigs,* p. 154.

*   *   *

RATHMANN, Peggy 1953-
(Margaret Crosby)

Personal

Born March 4, 1953, in St. Paul, MN; married John Wick. *Education:* University of Minnesota, B.A. (in psychology); studied art at American Academy (Chicago, IL), Atelier Lack (Minneapolis, MN), and Otis Parson's School of Design. *Hobbies and other interests:* Flying kites, walks on the beach, chess.

Addresses

Agent—c/o Author Mail, Putnam/Berkeley Publicity Department, 200 Madison Ave., New York, NY 10016.

Career

Children's book writer and illustrator, 1991—.

Member

International Sociological Association, American Sociological Society.

Awards, Honors

Most Promising New Author mention, *Publishers Weekly* Cuffies Awards, 1991, for *Ruby the Copycat;* Notable Children's Book, American Library Association, 1994, for *Good Night, Gorilla;* Chicago Public Library, Best Books of the Year list, 1995, *School Library Journal*'s Best Books of 1995 list, and Caldecott Medal, 1996, all for *Officer Buckle and Gloria.*

Writings

SELF-ILLUSTRATED, UNLESS OTHERWISE NOTED

Ruby the Copycat, Scholastic (New York, NY), 1991.
Good Night, Gorilla, Putnam (New York, NY), 1994.
Officer Buckle and Gloria, Putnam (New York, NY), 1995.

*In author/illustrator Peggy Rathmann's award-winning
1995 picture book* Officer Buckle and Gloria, *a helpful policeman is upstaged by his canine partner while teaching
street safety to school kids.*

Ten Minutes till Bedtime, Putnam (New York, NY), 1998.
The Day the Babies Crawled Away, Putnam (New York,
NY), 2003.

ILLUSTRATOR

Barbara Bottner, *Bootsie Barker Bites,* Putnam (New York,
NY), 1992.

Sidelights

Peggy Rathmann pulled a hat trick with her first children's book, *Ruby the Copycat,* turning an embarrassing personal incident into a well-received story and
earning the "most promising new author" distinction in
the 1991 Cuffies Awards. Her second self-illustrated
book, *Good Night, Gorilla,* was an American Library
Association Notable Children's Book. And with her
third title, *Officer Buckle and Gloria,* Rathmann walked
off with the Caldecott Medal in 1996. Not bad for someone who got into children's books only to curry favor
with her nieces.

In her Caldecott acceptance speech, as reported in *Horn
Book,* Rathmann explained the genesis of her writing/
illustrating career. "I was vacationing with my two
nieces. The girls were three and five years old, and as
far as I could tell, they didn't like me nearly enough."
One day on a car trip the nieces both wanted to sit in
front next to another aunt. "Now, this aunt cannot help

that she is extremely attractive, intelligent, and pleasant
to be around. *I* wanted to sit next to her, too." But there
was only room for one, so the younger niece was sent
howling to the back seat with Rathmann. "She glow-
ered at me; I was the booby prize." In desperation,
Rathmann pulled out her sketch pad and began drawing
a story "that starred my niece and me as extremely attractive people with good personalities and high IQs. It
worked." It was also the start of an award-winning
career. According to Diane Roback and Shannon
Maughan in *Publishers Weekly,* Rathmann creates "characters with built-in kid appeal: a copycat, a girl who
bites, a young gorilla who slips the keys away from the
zookeeper." Roback and Maughan also noted that while
Rathmann's books may be "spare in text," they are
"long on action, much of it related through her cleverly
expressive pictures."

Rathmann was born in St. Paul, Minnesota in 1953, one
of five children. She started her illustrating career in the
seventh grade, designing campaign posters for her older
brother's successful bid for student council. After graduation from Mounds View High School in New Brigh-
ton, Minnesota, she attended several colleges before
settling down at the University of Minnesota where she
took a degree in psychology. Rathmann once said that
she "wanted to teach sign language to gorillas, but after
taking a class in signing, I realized what I'd rather do
was draw pictures of gorillas." There followed various
career plans from commercial artist to fine artist, but
meanwhile she continued to work on the picture book
she had begun with her nieces, a book that became
"endless," as she described it in her Caldecott acceptance speech. "A whopping 150 pink-and-purple
pages. . . . The book had everything—except conflict
and a plot."

A publisher's rejection and a subsequent tip from a
published writer sent Rathmann back to school, this
time to a children's book-writing and illustration class.
It was there that she began an assignment on an embarrassing incident in her life that led to her first published
book. The teacher of this class suggested that students
develop a story idea from the worst or most embarrassing thing they knew about themselves. At first Rathmann was unsuccessful, but as her classmates began
presenting *their* stories, she developed the "overwhelming compulsion to swipe" the embarrassing incidents of
other students, as she confessed in her Caldecott acceptance speech. Eventually she decided that this very tendency toward copying was the shameful thing she could
use for the assignment which eventually turned into the
book *Ruby the Copycat.* "Since then, all of my books
have been based on embarrassing secrets," Rathmann
said in her Caldecott speech.

Ruby the Copycat, a book that *Kirkus Reviews* dubbed
"a solid debut," tells the story of a new girl in class
named Ruby who tries to act just like the popular girl,
Angela. Ruby's poem is almost exactly like Angela's;
Ruby was a flower girl in a wedding, just like Angela.

Initially, the popular girl finds such adulation flattering, but ultimately it is flat out irritating. Ruby even copies the painted nails of the teacher, Miss Hart, who finally takes Ruby in hand and lets her know it is okay to be herself. In fact, the kindly teacher advises her that is the only way she will really fit in and win friends. So Ruby shows off her hopping ability, and the other kids soon are copying her. This feat even wins Angela's friendship.

Martha Topol, reviewing *Ruby the Copycat* in *School Library Journal,* called it a "book with a strong story and complementary illustrations that addresses the philosophical question of individuality vs. conformity" and dubbed the book "a small gem." Other critics noted the originality of Rathmann's artwork and how integrally it fits in and helps develop the story. Ilene Cooper, writing in *Booklist* commented that Rathmann's "colorful artwork adds new bits of humor to the text," and a *Publishers Weekly* reviewer asserted that her "expressively illustrated, quirky and individualistic first book" would help inspire confidence in children and teach them "not to take skills . . . for granted."

Rathmann followed up this success with the illustrations for Barbara Bottner's *Bootsie Barker Bites,* and then with her own story, *Good Night, Gorilla,* inspired by another classroom assignment and aided by a childhood memory. The writing and illustrating, however, were not the matter of a quick study session. The initial draft of the manuscript had value, but everyone who read it found the ending problematic. It took two years and ten more trial endings to put together the final manuscript for *Good Night, Gorilla,* which went on to win an American Library Association Notable Book citation in 1994. This book relies heavily on pictures to convey story; words are limited to a bubbled "Good night," as the keeper of a zoo makes his rounds, tucking in the various animals he cares for. Little does the zookeeper know that the gorilla in the first cage has lifted his keys and is setting free the animals in back of him, and that they are all following the zookeeper home to the cozy security of a surrogate "parent."

Deborah Stevenson, writing in the *Bulletin of the Center for Children's Books,* noted both the story and pictorial value of *Good Night, Gorilla* in her review. She noted that Rathmann's lines are "rounder here than in her previous work," while her animal characters are drawn with "a cheerful simplicity of mien" and her palate "relies on a twilit glow of pink and green that lends a gentle circus flavor to the proceedings." *Booklist* critic Ilene Cooper noted that the author/illustrator's "jaunty four-color artwork carries the story and offers more with every look," while a *Kirkus Reviews* contributor dubbed the book "delightful" and *Horn Book* reviewer Ann A. Flowers called it "an outstanding picture book." Considering the effect of both picture and story, Jan Shepherd Ross in *School Library Journal* concluded that *Good Night, Gorilla* is "a clever, comforting bedtime story."

"There's a funny thing that happens between words and pictures," Rathmann said in her interview for *Publishers Weekly,* explaining that she learned the symbiotic nature of the two in her classes at Otis Parsons. She also learned that neither can exist without the other. In fact, it was yet another class assignment that led to *Officer Buckle and Gloria* and her Caldecott Medal. "The assignment was to write and illustrate a story which could not be understood by reading the text alone," she related in her Caldecott acceptance speech. "I did it because the teacher told us to, but in the process I discovered that this challenge was the very definition of a picture book. Officer Buckle was the words, Gloria was the pictures, and neither could entertain or enlighten without the other."

Employing the acrobatic and clowning talents of her own family dog, Rathmann wrote and illustrated a story about a school safety officer and the dog who makes him fabulously popular for a time. Officer Buckle knows more about safety than just about anybody in the town of Napville, but he is a tremendous bore when he gives assemblies to impart his safety tips. One day, though, the Napville Police Department buys a police dog with the improbable name of Gloria. Buckle begins taking Gloria with him to his demonstrations and, behind his back, the jolly dog performs a series of skillful acrobatic tricks, much to the amazement and amusement of the audience. Suddenly, Officer Buckle is much in demand, and things go along wonderfully until the policeman sees a video of his performance on the television news and understands that the cheers have been for Gloria, and not for him. Outraged, Officer Buckle refuses to visit any more schools, and when Gloria goes on her own, she is a bomb. In fact, the two need each other, and when they return to the stage, they present a final safety tip: "Always stick with your buddy."

Deborah Stevenson, writing in the *Bulletin of the Center for Children's Books,* noted that *Officer Buckle and Gloria* "is at heart the old story of the importance of friendship, but the safety tips . . . and the rest of the plot devices give it a fresh twist." Indeed, Rathmann spent much time and money on the 101 safety tips posted throughout the book. With deadlines approaching and more tips needed, Rathmann offered her nieces and nephews $25 apiece for any safety tips that made it past her editor. "The response was very expensive," she recalled in her Caldecott acceptance speech. Though many such tips are quite humorous, Stevenson went on to note that the illustrations are "the lifeblood" of the book: "scratchy-edged watercolors in a luminous palette." Carolyn Phelan, writing in *Booklist,* commented that "the deadpan humor of the text and slapstick wit of the illustrations make a terrific combination." Kathie Krieger Cerra, reviewing the book for *Five Owls,* noted especially how Rathmann's illustrations "move beyond the story and enrich it," and concluded that *Officer Buckle and Gloria* "is a book that children return to repeatedly, for there is much to be discovered in the illustrations and the language." A *Publishers Weekly* reviewer asserted that Rathmann "brings a lighter-than-air comic touch to this outstanding, solid-as-a-brick picture book," and *Horn Book*'s Ann A. Flowers called it "a glorious picture book." In *Ten minutes till Bedtime* a father announces to his son that he has ten minutes until he has to go to bed. As the boy begins to prepare, his pet hamster welcomes a hamster family that arrives in time for the bedtime tour. The baby hamsters wear numbers one through ten, and they all watch the boy go through his routine. Thanks to the numbered hamsters, children can practice counting forward and backward as the boy's father counts down the time to bed. A reviewer for *Publishers Weekly* praised the book as a "captivating series of mini-plots," concluding, "If Rathmann has her way, young slumberers will be counting hamsters, not sheep, as they drift off to sleep." David J. Whitin, reviewing the book for *Teaching Children Mathematics,* found that the book is better suited as a bedtime read than as a group storytime selection because of the small numbers on the hamsters backs and the task of finding them all. Barbara Bader, writing in *Horn Book,* commented that while *Ten Minutes till Bedtime* "hasn't the one-two punch of its predecessors," nonetheless it contains the "Rathmann sense of small-fry mischief" and the book's ending, a "mad scramble to exit as the countdown comes to a final ringing close, is the essence of explosive fun."

The Day the Babies Crawled Away relates the story of a well-meaning little boy who sets about rounding up five babies who crawl away to follow butterflies while their parents are distracted during a picnic. He quickly realizes that returning the babies to their parents is not simple task, and when he finally reunites each infant with its parents, he is one exhausted little hero. The illustrations in this book are a departure from Rathmann's usual art; here she uses silhouettes against a changing sky to create excitement and to reflect the closing of the day. According to Susan Dove Lempke in *Horn Book,* the illustrator's choice of technique "isolates the important parts of the tale, highlighting each gesture and detail Rathmann wants us to see." To ensure that readers can always locate the boy, Rathmann puts him, fittingly, in a firefighter's hat, making him easy to find in each picture and adding to his role as rescuer. McClelland also praised Rathmann's illustrations, noting that "the babies and their adventures are rendered in stunning, sharply detailed "silhouette." A *Publishers Weekly* contributor made the point that in this "rollicking rhyming tale," parents are never cast as neglectful, but instead the focus is on the "sleepy, baby-wrangling hero." A *School Library Journal* reviewer deemed the light-hearted book "inspired silliness," while Kate McClelland, also writing for the same periodical, dubbed *The Day the Babies Crawled Away* "fanciful."

Hard at work on further picture books, Rathmann is still tongue-in-cheek about her achievements. As she said in her *Publishers Weekly* interview, "To be frank, I like making these books so I can crack myself up." And at last report, her nieces seem to like her a lot better now.

Those last few minutes until the lights go out are made to fly when a youngster finds his home invaded by a tour-bus full of on-the-clock hamsters in Rathmann's fun-filled **Ten Minutes till Bedtime.**

A young do-gooder finds himself bested by a five fast-crawling infants when he attempts to catch up with the babies as they escape from unattentive parents during a group picnic.

Biographical and Critical Sources

PERIODICALS

Booklist, November 15, 1991, Ilene Cooper, review of *Ruby the Copycat,* p. 631; July, 1994, Ilene Cooper, review of *Good Night, Gorilla,* p. 1956; November 1, 1995, Carolyn Phelan, review of *Officer Buckle and Gloria,* p. 471; October 15, 1998, Stephanie Zvirin, review of *Ten Minutes till Bedtime,* p. 428.

Bulletin of the Center for Children's Books, May, 1994, Deborah Stevenson, review of *Good Night, Gorilla,* p. 299; October, 1995, Deborah Stevenson, review of *Officer Buckle and Gloria,* p. 66.

Five Owls, March-April, 1996, Kathie Krieger Cerra, review of *Officer Buckle and Gloria,* pp. 85-86.

Horn Book, July-August, 1994, Ann A. Flowers, review of *Good Night, Gorilla,* pp. 443-444; July, 1994, Ilene Cooper, review of *Good Night, Gorilla,* p. 1956; November-December, 1995, Ann A. Flowers, review of *Officer Buckle and Gloria,* pp. 736-737; July-August, 1996, Peggy Rahtmann, Caldecott Medal Acceptance speech, pp. 424-427; September-October, 1998, Barbara Bader, review of *Ten Minutes till Bedtime,* pp. 598-599; Sepvember-October, 2003, Susan Dove Lempke, review of *The Day the Babies Crawled Away,* p. 600.

Kirkus Reviews, November 15, 1991, review of *Ruby the Copycat,* p. 1474; April 15, 1994, review of *Good Night, Gorilla,* p. 562; July, 1994, Ilene Cooper, review of *Good Night, Gorilla,* p. 1956; November-December, 1995, Ann A. Flowers, review of *Officer Buckle and Gloria,* pp. 736-737; September 15, 2003, review of *The Day the Babies Crawled Away,* p. 1181.

Publishers Weekly, November 8, 1991, review of *Ruby the Copycat,* p. 64; February 20, 1995, p. 125; July 17, 1995, review of *Officer Buckle and Gloria,* p. 229; June 15, 1998, review of *Ten Minutes till Bedtime,* p. 58; September 22, 2003, review of *The Day the Babies Crawled Away,* p. 102.

School Library Journal, January, 1992, Martha Topol, review of *Ruby the Copycat,* p. 96; July, 1994, Jan Ross Shepherd, review of *Good Night, Gorilla,* p. 87; September, 1995, Lisa S. Murphy, review of *Officer Buckle and Gloria,* p. 185; November, 2003, Kate McClelland, review of *The Day the Babies Crawled Away,* p. 113; April, 2004, review of *The Day the Babies Crawled Away,* p. S26.

Teaching Children Mathematics, April, 2000, David J. Whitin, review of *Ten Minutes till Bedtime,* p. 532.*

*   *   *

ROTTMAN, S(usan) L(ynn) 1970-

Personal

Born July 12, 1970, in Albany, GA; married Arthur E. Wickberg (member of U.S. Air Force); children: Arthur "Paul" Wickberg.. *Education:* Colorado State University, B.A. (English), and secondary teacher certification, 1992. *Hobbies and other interests:* White-water rafting, swimming, downhill skiing, watching sit-coms.

Addresses

Agent—c/o Author Mail, Viking, Penguin Putnam, 375 Hudson St., New York, NY 10014.

Career

Educator and author. Widefield School District Number Three, Colorado Springs, CO, English teacher, 1993-96, 1998—; Deer Creek Schools, Edmond, OK, English teacher, 1996-98.

Awards, Honors

Oklahoma Book Award, young adult/children's category, and Books for the Teen Age citation, New York Public Library, both 1998, and Best Books for Young Adults designation, Young Adult Library Services Association (YALSA), 1999, all for *Hero;* Quick Pick for Reluctant Readers, YALSA, 1999, for *Rough Waters.*

Writings

Hero, Peachtree (Atlanta, GA), 1997.
Rough Waters, Peachtree (Atlanta, GA), 1998.
Head above Water, Peachtree (Atlanta, GA), 1999.

S. L. Rottman

Stetson, Viking (New York, NY), 2002.
Shadow of a Doubt, Peachtree (Atlanta, GA), 2003.
Slalom, Viking (New York, NY), 2004.

Sidelights

S. L. Rottman's first novel, *Hero,* garnered considerable attention as a moving account of a young man's transformation from a troublemaking outsider to one who has learned to give and receive help from others. The novel "had me laughing out loud on page three and nearly crying several times thereafter," wrote Cynthia L. Blinn in a *Voice of Youth Advocates* review of the book, published in 1997.

Hero centers on Sean, a fifteen year old who has learned to mistrust all adults based on his experience with his own parents: his alcoholic mother is both physically and emotionally abusive, while his father's presence is known only through a monthly support check. During a week's suspension from school for fighting, Sean breaks curfew for a fourth time and is sentenced to a week of community service on World War II veteran Dave Hassler's farm. There, as Mr. Hassler helps Sean express and work through his feelings of abandonment and neglect, the teen learns that hard work has its rewards in

increased self-confidence. "Sean is a likable loner— tough as nails—with a survivor's sense of humor," remarked a reviewer for *Publishers Weekly,* adding that Rottman's "message is a powerful one for adolescents." While some reviewers contended that Rottman avoids an easy ending, Sean comes to terms with a school bully as well as a trying family situation; "Through Sean [Rottman] gives readers a convincing and difficult protagonist and a fresh perspective on what it means to be a hero," observed Carolyn Lehman in *School Library Journal.*

Stetson focuses on a seventeen-year-old boy who has lived with his alcoholic father since his mother left years ago and now works at a salvage yard, where he has befriended his Vietnam veteran boss. Stetson wants to be the first in his family to graduate from high school, but some misguided pranks bring him dangerously close to suspension. His personal plans change, however, when a fourteen-year-old girl arrives at his home and proves to be his sister, Kayla. Critics applauded Rottman's unforced portrayal of social issues in *Stetson,* as well as the author's portrayal of realistic relationships throughout the novel. A *Kirkus* reviewer wrote that "in this novel of broken dreams turned to new possibilities, Rottman delivers a believable story with characters that ring true." Delia Fritz, reviewing the book for *School Library Journal,* noted that while "the writing can be repetitive, . . . this may be a consequence of the narrator's humdrum attitude toward life," and concluded that readers will most likely be "cheering him on to the end." Paula Rohrlick, reviewing *Stetson* in *Kliatt,* also found the title character to be a worthy protagonist. She described him as a "clever, talented, sensitive teen," and declared Stetson "a character teens will admire and embrace."

Considered by several reviewers to be an equally strong protagonist, Shadow got his nickname when he was small because he was always trailing right behind his older brother, Daniel. As Rottman's novel *Shadow of a Doubt* opens, Shadow is fifteen, and Daniel has been gone for seven years, having left as a young teen and devastating Shadow's family in the process. When Daniel now calls home out of the blue with the news that he has been arrested for a murder he did not commit, Shadow's parents must wrestle with the emotional, social, and legal issues, leaving their younger son feeling abandoned. Luckily, Shadow turns to friends on the school debate team to help him through a trying time.

In *Kliatt,* Rohrlick commented that Rottman "excels at realistically depicting teens struggling with family issues," and predicted that readers of *Shadow of a Doubt* "will eagerly turn the pages." A critic for *Kirkus Reviews* was also impressed with the novel's depiction of family relationships, noting that the story is "thoughtful and forgiving of the large and small weaknesses of parents and children." In *Booklist,* Shelle Rosenfeld also praised Rottman's portrayal of family dynamics and dubbed the book a "thought-provoking novel" featuring a "three-dimensional, introspective protagonist." *School Library Journal* reviewer Lynn Evarts remarked that Shadow is evidence of Rottman's ability to create consistently believable male characters and added that "the unusual plot gives the book its strength and appeal, and the realistic ending adds to its credibility and message."

Set in a ski town, *Slalom* is the story of Sandro, who has been reared by his single mother, Tiffany. As a young woman, Tiffany had a brief affair with Alessandro, an Italian race skier, and became pregnant. Because Alessandro had moved on by the time Tiffany discovered she was with child, she decided to move to the ski town where they met, sure the skier would one day return. When that day comes, Sandro—also a talented skier at age seventeen—is not the romantic his mother is. As he struggles to deal with the emotions surrounding the return of his father, Sandro also deals with the demands of being part of his school's competitive ski team, as well as with a new romance. Reviewing *Slalom* in *Kliatt*, Rohrlick concluded that "Rottman's skill at describing teenagers struggling with family issues . . . will keep readers turning the pages." Diane Foote, writing in *Booklist*, praised the excitement generated by the ski theme, predicting that Rottman's "jam-packed storyline will keep the interest of kids who prefer to read by the fire."

Rottman once told *Something about the Author:* "The first story I remember writing (that I liked) was when I was in the sixth grade. I continued to write for my own enjoyment through high school, and received a creative writing scholarship from Colorado State University for a short story. I never dreamed I would sell my first novel before I turned thirty. . . . Although I was born in Georgia and have lived in Oklahoma, I consider Colorado my true home."

Biographical and Critical Sources

PERIODICALS

Booklist, November 15, 2003, Shelle Rosenfeld, review of *Shadow of a Doubt*, p. 593; September 1, 2004, Diane Foote, review of *Slalom*, p. 110.

Kirkus Reviews, February 15, 2002, review of *Stetson*, p. 264; October 1, 2003, review of *Shadow of a Doubt*, p. 1230; September 15, 2004, review of *Slalom*, p. 919.

Kliatt, March, 2002, Paula Rohrlick, review of *Stetson*, p. 12; November, 2003, Paula Rohrlick, review of *Shadow of a Doubt*, p. 10; September, 2004, Paula Rohrlick, review of *Slalom*, p. 16.

Publishers Weekly, August 18, 1997, review of *Hero*, p. 93.

School Library Journal, December, 1997, review of *Hero*, p. 130; April, 2002, Delia Fritz, review of *Stetson*, p. 156; January, 2004, Lynn Evarts, review of *Shadow of a Doubt*, p. 134.

Voice of Youth Advocate, December, 1997, Cynthia L. Blinn, review of *Hero*, p. 320.*

S

SANDER, Heather L. 1947-

Personal

Born December 4, 1947, in Saskatoon, Saskatchewan, Canada; daughter of William and Audrey Walker; married Eugene Sander (a college teacher), June 28, 1969; children: Ian, Ronald. *Ethnicity:* "Scottish." *Education:* University of Saskatchewan, B.A., 1967, Dip.Ed., 1969; University of Victoria, M.A., 1985.

Addresses

Agent—c/o Author Mail, Orca Book Publishers Ltd., P.O. Box 5626, Station B, Victoria, British Columbia, Canada V8R 6S4. *E-mail*—gandh.sander@shaw.ca.

Career

Writer and school councillor. Victoria School District, Victoria, British Columbia, Canada, elementary school councillor, 1987—.

Member

British Columbia School Counsellors' Association; Victoria Writers' Association.

Writings

Robbie Packford: Alien Monster, Orca Book Publishers (Victoria, British Columbia, Canada), 2003.
Make Mine with Everything ("Robbie Packford" series), Orca Book Publishers (Custer, WA), 2004.
Whatever Happened to My Dog Cuddles? ("Robbie Packford" series), Orca Book Publishers (Custer, WA), 2004.

Sidelights

A native of western Canada, Heather L. Sander is the author of a series of humorous children's books that includes *Robbie Packford: Alien Monster* and its sequels, *Make Mine with Everything* and *Whatever Happened to My Dog Cuddles?* In the series opener, sixth grader Robbie does not want to believe that his new friend is really an alien from the planet Kerbosky, but the fantastic chain of events that unfolds in *Robbie Packford: Alien Monster* forces him to face the unearthly reality. Robbie is transformed into an reptilian-looking creature with amazing powers after being exposed to a secret formula belonging to this now-questionable "friend," and soon finds himself aboard a space shop and enlisted in a crusade to save planet Kerbosky from nasty killer robots. Noting that the "killer-robots-conquer-the-world plot has been used countless times," *School Library Journal* reviewer Elaine E. Knight nonetheless credited Sander for adding "a touch of wry humor as Robbie continually tries to balance his human and monster nature." Teresa Hughes, reviewing *Robbie Packford: Alien Monster* for *Resource Links,* stated that although Sander's novel "is short enough for the reluctant reader who is intimidated by larger novels," the humorous space adventure is "still interesting and funny."

Sander told *Something about the Author:* "I've researched my career as a kid's writer for a long time. First I was a kid. Then I had them. When they grew up and were more or less unavailable for research, they produced grandchildren. (Hooray!) In the meantime, by a clever scheme, I managed to get paid by the public school system to continue my research as a teacher and elementary school counselor where I could invite children into my office or wander through classes at silent reading time and quiz kids at will as to what they were reading. In a recent values exercise, a lot of Grade Six boys rated good books at the bottom of their list, so I'm still working on that one.

"I've always been a fantasy and science-fiction fan since you don't have to be bound by the laws of physics and if you get tired of one planet you can try another. My science-fiction reading passion fell neatly between two other reading periods in my childhood; horses, where I wished I could have my own and keep it in the backyard, and archaeology, where I dreamed of sailing across the Pacific in a papyrus boat like Thor Heyerdahl. I started with Tom Swift and graduated to Isaac Asimov. As an adult, reading *HitchHiker's Guide to the Galaxy* in one go while sick at home with a high fever was a mind-altering experience. I've never been the same since.

"*Robbie Packford: Alien Monster,* for kids aged eight through twelve, considers the following important question: What would happen if that new kid in your class was actually telling the truth when he said he was an alien?"

Biographical and Critical Sources

PERIODICALS

Canadian Review of Materials, October 1, 2004, Mary Thomas, review of *Make Mine with Everything.*
Resource Links, December, 2003, Teresa Hughes, review of *Robbie Packford: Alien Monster,* p. 20.
School Library Journal, September, 2004, Elaine E. Knight, review of *Robbie Packford: Alien Monster,* p. 217.

Ntozake Shange

*   *   *

SHANGE, Ntozake 1948-

Personal

Name pronounced "En-to-zaki Shong-gay" born Paulette Linda Williams; October 18, 1948, in Trenton, NJ; name changed 1971; daughter of Paul T. (a surgeon) and Eloise (a psychiatric social worker and educator) Williams; married second husband, David Murray (a musician), July, 1977 (divorced); children: Savannah. *Education:* Barnard College, B.A. (with honors), 1970; University of Southern California, Los Angeles, M.A., 1973, and graduate study. *Hobbies and other interests:* Playing the violin.

Addresses

Home—231 North Third St., No. 119, Philadelphia, PA 19106. *Office*—Department of Drama, University of Houston, University Park, 4800 Calhoun Rd., Houston, TX 77004.

Career

Writer, performer, and teacher. Faculty member in women's studies, California State College, Sonoma Mills College, and the University of California Extension, 1972-75; associate professor of drama, University of Houston, beginning in 1983; artist-in-residence, New Jersey State Council on the Arts; creative writing instructor, City College of New York. Lecturer at Dou-

glass College, 1978, and at many other institutions, such as Yale University, Howard University, Detroit Institute of Arts, and New York University. Dancer with Third World Collective, Raymond Sawyer's Afro-American Dance Company, Sounds in Motion, West Coast Dance Works, and For Colored Girls Who Have Considered Suicide (Shange's own dance company); has appeared in Broadway and off-Broadway productions of her own plays, including *For Colored Girls Who Have Considered Suicide/When the Rainbow Is Enuf* and *Where the Mississippi Meets the Amazon.* Director of several productions, including *The Mighty Gents,* produced by the New York Shakespeare Festival's Mobile Theatre, 1979, *A Photograph: A Study in Cruelty,* produced in Houston's Equinox Theatre, 1979, and June Jordan's *The Issue* and *The Spirit of Sojourner Truth,* 1979. Has given many poetry readings.

Member

Actors Equity, National Academy of Television Arts and Sciences, Dramatists Guild, PEN American Center, Academy of American Poets, Poets and Writers Inc., Women's Institute for Freedom of the Press, New York Feminist Arts Guild, Writers' Guild.

Awards, Honors

NDEA fellow, 1973; Off-Broadway Award, *Village Voice,* Outer Critics Circle Award, Audience Development Committee Award, *Mademoiselle* Award, and Antoinette Perry, Grammy, and Academy award nominations, all 1977, all for *For Colored Girls Who Have Considered Suicide/When the Rainbow Is Enuf;* Frank Silvera Writers' Workshop Award, 1978; *Los Angeles Times* Book Prize for Poetry, 1981, for *Three Pieces;* Guggenheim fellowship, 1981; Medal of Excellence, Columbia University, 1981; Off-Broadway Award, 1981, for *Mother Courage and Her Children;* Nori Eboraci Award, Barnard College, 1988; Lila Wallace-*Reader's Digest* Fund writer's award, 1992; Paul Robeson Achievement Award, 1992; Arts and Cultural Achievement Award, National Coalition of 100 Black Women, Inc. (Pennsylvania chapter), 1992; Living Legend Award, National Black Theatre Festival, 1993; Claim Your Life Award, WDAS-AM/FM, 1993; Pew fellowship in fiction, 1993-94; City of Philadelphia Literature Prize, 1994; Black Theatre Network Winona Fletcher award, 1994; Monarch Merit Award, National Council for Culture and Art, Inc.; Pushcart Prize.

Writings

FOR CHILDREN

Whitewash (picture book), illustrated by Michael Sporn, Walker (New York, NY), 1997.

Float like a Butterfly (picture book), illustrated by Edel Rodriguez, Hyperion (New York, NY), 2002.

Daddy Says (young-adult novel), Simon & Schuster (New York, NY), 2003.

Ellington Was Not a Street (picture book), illustrated by Kadir Nelson, Simon & Schuster (New York, NY), 2004.

PLAYS

For Colored Girls Who Have Considered Suicide/When the Rainbow Is Enuf: A Choreopoem (first produced in New York, NY, 1975; produced off-Broadway, then on Broadway, 1976), Shameless Hussy Press (San Lorenzo, CA), 1975, revised edition, Macmillan (New York, NY), 1976.

Boogie Woogie Landscapes (also see below; first produced in New York, NY, 1976), St. Martin's Press (New York, NY), 1978.

A Photograph: A Study of Cruelty (poem-play; first produced off-Broadway, 1977; revised as *A Photograph: Lovers in Motion* [also see below] and produced in Houston, TX, 1979), Samuel French (New York, NY), 1981.

(With Thulani Nkabinde and Jessica Hagedorn) *Where the Mississippi Meets the Amazon,* first produced in New York, NY, 1977.

From Okra to Greens: A Different Kinda Love Story; A Play with Music and Dance (first produced in New York, NY, at Barnard College, 1978), Samuel French, 1985.

Spell #7: A Geechee Quick Magic Trance Manual (also see below; produced on Broadway, 1979), published as *Spell #7: A Theatre Piece in Two Acts,* Samuel French (New York, NY), 1981.

Black and White Two-dimensional Planes, first produced in New York, NY, 1979.

(Adapter) Bertolt Brecht, *Mother Courage and Her Children,* first produced off-Broadway, 1980.

Three Pieces: Spell #7; A Photograph: Lovers in Motion; Boogie Woogie Landscapes, St. Martin's Press (New York, NY), 1981.

Three for a Full Moon [and] *Bocas,* first produced in Los Angeles, CA, 1982.

(Adapter) Willy Russell, *Educating Rita,* first produced in Atlanta, GA, 1982.

Three Views of Mt. Fuji, first produced at the Lorraine Hansberry Theatre, 1987.

The Love Space Demands: A Continuing Saga (produced in London, England, 1992), St. Martin's Press (New York, NY), 1991.

Contributor to *Love's Fire: Seven New Plays Inspired by Shakespearean Sonnets,* Morrow (New York, NY), 1998. Author of play *Mouths* and operetta *Carrie,* both produced in 1981. Has written for a television special starring Diana Ross.

POETRY

Melissa & Smith, Bookslinger (St. Paul, MN), 1976.

Natural Disasters and Other Festive Occasions (prose and poems), Heirs International (San Francisco, CA), 1977.

Nappy Edges, St. Martin's Press (New York, NY), 1978.

A Daughter's Geography, St. Martin's Press (New York, NY), 1983.

From Okra to Greens: Poems, Coffee House Press (St. Paul, MN), 1984.

Ridin' the Moon in Texas: Word Paintings (responses to art in prose and poetry), St. Martin's Press (New York, NY), 1987.

I Live in Music (poem), edited by Linda Sunshine, illustrated by Romare Bearden, Stewart, Tabori & Chang (New York, NY), 1994.

The Sweet Breath of Life: A Poetic Narrative of the African-American Family, Atria (New York, NY), 2004.

NOVELS

Sassafrass (novella), Shameless Hussy Press (San Lorenzo, CA), 1976.

Sassafrass, Cypress & Indigo, St. Martin's Press (New York, NY), 1982.

Betsey Brown, St. Martin's Press (New York, NY), 1985.

Liliane: Resurrection of the Daughter, St. Martin's Press (New York, NY), 1994.

OTHER

See No Evil: Prefaces, Essays, and Accounts, 1976-1983, Momo's Press (San Francisco, CA), 1984.

If I Can Cook/You Know God Can (essays), Beacon Press (Boston, MA), 1998.

Ntozake Shange's play **For Colored Girls Who Have Considered Suicide/When the Rainbow Is Enuf** *had its first Broadway production in 1976, a year after it was published.*

(Editor) *The Beacon Best of 1999: Creative Writing by Women and Men of All Colors,* Beacon Press (Boston, MA), 1999.

Also author of *Some Men* (poems in a pamphlet that resembles a dance card), 1981. Work represented in anthologies, including *"May Your Days Be Merry and Bright" and Other Christmas Stories by Women,* edited by Susan Koppelman, Wayne State University Press (Detroit, MI), 1988; *Breaking Ice: An Anthology of Contemporary African American Fiction,* edited by Terry McMillan, Penguin Books (New York, NY), 1990; *Yellow Silk: Erotic Arts and Letters,* edited by Lily Pond and Richard Russo, Harmony Books (New York, NY), 1990; *Daughters of Africa: An International Anthology,* edited by Margaret Bushby, Pantheon (New York, NY), 1992; *Erotique noire-Black Erotica,* edited by Miriam DeCosta-Willis, Reginald Martin, and Roseann P. Bell, Anchor (New York, NY), 1992; *Resurgent: New Writing by Women,* edited by Lou Robinson and Camille Norton, University of Illinois Press (Champaign, IL), 1992; and *Wild Women Don't Wear No Blues: Black Women Writers on Love, Men, and Sex,* edited by Marita Golden, Doubleday (New York, NY), 1993. Author of preface to *Plays by Women, Book Two: An International Anthology,* Ubu Repertory Theater

Publications (New York, NY), 1994. Contributor to periodicals, including *Black Scholar, Third World Women, Ms.,* and *Yardbird Reader.*

Adaptations

A musical-operetta version of Shange's novel *Betsey Brown* was produced by Joseph Papp's Public Theater in 1986.

Sidelights

An accomplished poet and novelist, Ntozake Shange is best known for her play *For Colored Girls Who Have Considered Suicide/When the Rainbow Is Enuf.* A unique blend of poetry, music, dance and drama called a "choreopoem," it was still being produced around the country decades after its debut in 1975 on Broadway. In the 1990s Shange expanded her writing and began publishing books for children and young adults, such as *Daddy Says* and *Ellington Was Not a Street.*

Born to a surgeon and an educator, Ntozake Shange—originally named Paulette Williams—was raised in a black middle-class family. Breaking out on her own after college proved difficult, as one by one, the roles she chose for herself—including war correspondent and jazz musician—were dismissed by her parents as "no good for a woman," she told Stella Dong in a *Publishers Weekly* interview. She chose to become a writer because "there was nothing left." Frustrated and hurt after separating from her first husband, Shange attempted suicide several times before focusing her rage against the limitations society imposes on black women. While earning a master's degree in American studies from the University of Southern California, she took the African name meaning "she who comes with her own things" and she "who walks like a lion." Since then she has sustained a triple career as an educator, a performer/director in New York and Houston, and a writer whose works draw heavily on her experiences and the frustrations of being a black female in America.

Writing dramatic poetry became Shange's way to express her dissatisfaction with the role of black women in society. Joining with musicians and the choreographer-dancer Paula Moss, she created improvisational works comprised of poetry, music, and dance that were performed in bars in San Francisco and New York. When Moss and Shange moved to New York City, they presented *For Colored Girls Who Have Considered Suicide* at a Soho jazz loft, the Studio Rivbea. Director Oz Scott saw the show and with his help the work was performed in bars on the Lower East Side. Impressed by one of these, producer Woodie King, Jr., joined Scott to stage the choreopoem off-Broadway at the New Federal Theatre, where it ran successfully from November 1975, to the following June. Then Joseph Papp became the show's producer at the New York Shakespeare Festival's Anspacher Public Theatre. From there, it moved to the Booth Theatre uptown.

In *For Colored Girls Who Have Considered Suicide,* poems dramatized by female dancers recall encounters with classmates, lovers, rapists, abortionists, and latent killers. The women survive the abuses and disappointments put upon them by the men in their lives and come to recognize in each other, dressed in the colors of Shange's personal rainbow, the promise of a better future. In unison, at the end, they declare, "i found god in myself / and i loved her / . . . fiercely." "The poetry," stated Marilyn Stasio in *Cue,* "touches some very tender nerve endings. Although roughly structured and stylistically unrefined, this fierce and passionate poetry has the power to move a body to tears, to rage, and to an ultimate rush of love."

A similar work, *Spell #7: A Geechee Quick Magic Trance Manual,* concerns nine characters in a New York bar who discuss the racism black artists contend with in the entertainment world. At one point, the all-black cast appears in overalls and minstrel-show blackface to address the pressure placed on the black artist to fit a stereotype in order to succeed.

Shange's poetry books, like her theater pieces, are distinctively original; she takes many liberties with the conventions of written English, using nonstandard spell-

ings and punctuation. While some reviewers maintained that these innovations present unnecessary obstacles to readers, Shange justified her use of "lower-case letters, slashes, and spelling" to Claudia Tate in *Black Women Writers at Work,* noting: "I like the idea that letters dance. . . . I need some visual stimulation, so that reading becomes not just a passive act and more than an intellectual activity, but demands rigorous participation." She also takes liberties with the conventions of fiction writing in such novels as *Sassafrass, Cypress & Indigo* and *Liliane: Resurrection of the Daughter.* A mix of verse, incantations, letters, and spells, *Sassafrass, Cypress & Indigo* focuses on sisters who find different ways to cope with their love relationships, while in *Liliane* a woman undergoes psychoanalysis in an attempt to better understand the events of her life, particularly her mother's decision to abandon the family for a white man when Liliane was a child. Shange "offers a daring portrait of a black woman artist re-creating herself out of social and psychological chaos," remarked Kelly Cherry in the *Los Angeles Times Book Review.*

In 1997 Shange published *Whitewash,* her first picture book for young readers. Based on actual events, *Whitewash* concerns an African-American girl, Helene-Angel, and her brother, Mauricio, who are the victims of a ra-

Shange's poem "Ellington Was Not a Street," which recalls her inner-city childhood and close-knit family, was written in 1983 and published as a picture book in 2004, with illustrations by Kadir Nelson.

cial attack by a white gang. The thugs beat Mauricio and cover Helene-Angel's face with white paint. In the days after the assault, the pair are so upset that they refuse to leave their home, until Helene-Angel's classmates visit and offer their support. Jennifer Ralston, writing in *School Library Journal*, called the work "powerful," and a *Publishers Weekly* reviewer observed that Shange's "characters speak in tones of shock and pain that clearly convey the seriousness of the issues here."

Boxing great Muhammad Ali is the subject of the 2002 picture book *Float like a Butterfly*. In an interview with Clarence V. Reynolds in *Black Issues Book Review*, Shange said she approached the work with great enthusiasm: "Ali came to dinner at [my] house when I was teenager, and I saw quite a different man from the macho man that everybody else saw. Not only was he impressive and intelligent, he was surprisingly soft-spoken. This project gave me a chance to honor him." The story follows Ali through his childhood in the segregated South, his gold medal performance at the 1960 Olympics, his reign as heavyweight boxing champion, and his conversion to Islam. In *Float like a Butterfly*, Shange "has masterfully captured the unique cadence of Ali's voice as she offers an unabashedly positive story that will leave kids cheering," remarked *Booklist* contributor John Green.

The young-adult novel *Daddy Says* "fills a niche by portraying African-American girls in a western context," observed a critic in *Kirkus Reviews*. Published in 2003, the novel takes place on an East Texas ranch, where sisters Lucie-Marie and Annie Sharon are coping with the death of their mother, a rodeo champion, and their father's relationship with his new girlfriend. To regain her father's attention, Annie Sharon attempts to ride the same horse that killed her mother, a risky decision that places her own life in danger. *Daddy Says* received mixed reviews. In *Publishers Weekly* a critic wrote that while "the story provides enough action to keep pages turning, . . . the heart-felt moments are too few," and *School Library Journal* contributor Carol A. Edwards stated, "Despite strong characters and a lively setting, this novel is disjointed and unsatisfying, which is a shame, since Shange is clearly capable of portraying rivalry and competitive spirit realistically." *Ellington Was Not a Street*, a 2004 picture book, "is a paean to Shange's family home and the exciting men who gathered there," noted Ilene Cooper in *Booklist*. The family's illustrious visitors included musicians Duke Ellington and Dizzy Gillespie, actor Paul Robeson, activist W. E. B. DuBois, and Dr. Kwame Nkrumah, the former president of Ghana. The text of the story is taken from Shange's poem "Mood Indigo," found in her 1983 collection, *A Daughter's Geography;* according to a *Kirkus Reviews* critic, "The poetic text is spare, with only a few words on each spread, but they match the majesty of the scene." Reviewing *Ellington Was Not a Street*, a reviewer in *Ebony* called the work a "heartfelt homage to [a] community of artists and innovators," while a *Publishers Weekly* reviewer deemed it an "elegiac tribute to a select group of African-American men who made important contributions to twentieth-century culture."

Biographical and Critical Sources

BOOKS

African-American Writers, 2nd edition, Scribner (New York, NY), 2001.

Betsko, Kathleen, and Rachel Koenig, editors, *Interviews with Contemporary Women Playwrights,* Beech Tree Books, 1987.

Contemporary Dramatists, 6th edition, St. James Press (Detroit, MI), 1999.

Contemporary Literary Criticism, Gale (Detroit, MI), Volume 8, 1978, Volume 25, 1983, Volume 38, 1986, Volume 74, 1993, Volume 26, 2000.

Contemporary Poets, 7th edition, St. James Press (Detroit, MI), 2001.

Dictionary of Literary Biography, Gale (Detroit, MI), Volume 38: *Afro-American Writers after 1955: Dramatists and Prose Writers,* 1985; Volume 249: *Twentieth-Century American Dramatists,* Third Series, 2002.

Drama for Students, Volume 2, Gale (Detroit, MI), 1997.

Encyclopedia of World Biography Supplement, Volume 23, Gale (Detroit, MI), 2003.

Tate, Claudia, editor, *Black Women Writers at Work,* Continuum (New York, NY), 1983.

PERIODICALS

African American Review, spring, 1992; summer, 1992.

American Black Review, September, 1983; March, 1986.

Back Stage, June 30, 1995, Ira J. Bilowit, "Twenty Years Later, Shange's 'Colored Girls' Take a New Look at Life," pp. 15-16.

Black Issues Book Review, November-December, 2002, Clarence V. Reynolds, "For Colored Girls Who Have Considered Fairy Tales," review of *Float like a Butterfly,* p. 42; March-April, 2003, review of *Daddy Says,* p. 66; November-December, 2004, Patricia Spears Jones, review of *The Sweet Breath of Life: A Poetic Narrative of the African-American Family,* p. 46.

Black Scholar, March, 1979; March, 1981; December, 1982; July, 1985; winter, 1996, p. 68; summer, 1996, p. 67.

Booklist, April 15, 1987; May 15, 1991; January 1, 1998, Alice Joyce, review of *If I Can Cook/You Know God Can,* pp. 759-76; October 15, 1999, Vanessa Bush, review of *The Beacon Best of 1999: Creative Writing by Women and Men of All Colors,* p. 1837; June 1, 2001, Joanne Wilkinson, review of *Betsey Brown,* p. 1837; September 1, 2002, John Green, review of *Float like a Butterfly,* p. 131; February 15, 2004, Ilene Cooper, review of *Ellington Was Not a Street,* p. 1070; October 15, 2004, Janet St. John, review of *The Sweet Breath of Life,* p. 382.

Chicago Tribune, October 21, 1982.

Chicago Tribune Book World, July 1, 1979; September 8, 1985.

Christian Science Monitor, September 9, 1976; October 8, 1982; May 2, 1986.

Cue, June 26, 1976.

Ebony, March, 2004, review of *Ellington Was Not a Street,* p. 28.

Entertainment Weekly, March 10, 1995, p. 65; March 20, 1998, Carmela Ciuraru, review of *If I Can Cook/You Know God Can,* p. 84.

Essence, November, 1976; May, 1985, "Ntozake Shange Talks with Marcia Ann Gillespie," pp. 122-123; June, 1985; August, 1991; December, 2004, Douglas Danoff, review of *The Sweet Breath of Life,* p. 134.

Horizon, September, 1977.

Horn Book, November-December, 2002, Peter D. Sieruta, review of *Float like a Butterfly,* p. 781.

Kirkus Reviews, September 1, 2002, review of *Float like a Butterfly,* p. 1320; December 1, 2002, review of *Daddy Says,* p. 1773; November 15, 2003, review of *Ellington Was Not a Street,* p. 1364.

Kliatt, January, 1989.

Library Journal, May 1, 1987; January, 1998, Wendy Miller, review of *If I Can Cook/You Know God Can,* p. 130; October 15, 1999, Louis J. Parascandola, review of *The Beacon Best of 1999,* p. 70; September 1, 2004, Doris Lynch, review of *The Sweet Breath of Life,* pp. 155-156.

Los Angeles Times, October 20, 1982; June 11, 1985; July 28, 1987.

Los Angeles Times Book Review, August 22, 1982; October 20, 1982; January 8, 1984; July 29, 1984; June 11, 1985; July 19, 1987; December 18, 1994, p. 12.

New Statesman, October 4, 1985; May 19, 1995, p. 37.

Newsweek, June 14, 1976; July 30, 1979.

New York Daily News, July 16, 1979.

New Yorker, June 14, 1976; August 2, 1976; January 2, 1978.

New York Times, June 16, 1976; December 22, 1977; June 4, 1979; June 8, 1979; July 16, 1979; July 22, 1979; May 14, 1980; June 15, 1980; September 3, 1995, Andrea Stevens, "*For Colored Girls* May Be for the Ages," p. H5.

New York Times Book Review, June 25, 1979; July 16, 1979; October 21, 1979; September 12, 1982; May 12, 1985; April 6, 1986; January 1, 1995, p. 6; October 15, 1995, p. 36; February 25, 1996, p. 32.

New York Times Magazine, May 1, 1983.

Publishers Weekly, May 3, 1985; November 14, 1994, p. 65; January 1, 1996, p. 69; November 3, 1997, review of *Whitewash,* p. 85; September 20, 1999, review of *The Beacon Best of 1999,* p. 65; September 16, 2002, review of *Float like a Butterfly,* p. 68; November 25, 2002, review of *Daddy Says,* p. 68; December 22, 2003, review of *Ellington Was Not a Street,* p. 59; August 2, 2004, review of *The Sweet Breath of Life,* p. 66.

Saturday Review, February 18, 1978; May/June, 1985.

School Library Journal, October, 2002, Ajoke' T. I. Kokodoko, review of *Float like a Butterfly,* p. 152; February, 2003, Carol A. Edwards, review of *Daddy Says,* p. 148; October, 2003, Jennifer Ralston, review of *Whitewash,* p. 98; January, 2004, Mary N. Oluonye, review of *Ellington Was Not a Street,* p. 122.

Time, June 14, 1976; July 19, 1976; November 1, 1976.

Times (London, England), April 21, 1983.

Times Literary Supplement, December 6, 1985; April 15-21, 1988.

Variety, July 25, 1979.

Village Voice, August 16, 1976; July 23, 1979; June 18, 1985.

Voice Literary Supplement, August, 1991; September, 1991.

Washington Post, June 12, 1976; June 29, 1976; February 23, 1982; June 17, 1985.

Washington Post Book World, October 15, 1978; July 19, 1981; August 22, 1982; August 5, 1984; February 5, 1995, p. 4.

Wilson Library Bulletin, October, 1990.

World Literature Today, summer, 1995, p. 584.

ONLINE

Voices from the Gaps Web site, http://voices.cla.umn.edu/ (January 10, 2005), "Ntozake Shange."*

*   *   *

SHERWOOD, Jonathan
See LONDON, Jonathan (Paul)

*   *   *

STANLEY, George Edward 1942-
(M. T. Coffin, Franklin W. Dixon, a house pseudonym, Laura Lee Hope, a house pseudonym, Carolyn Keene, a house pseudonym, Adam Mills, Stuart Symons)

Personal

Born July 15, 1942, in Memphis, TX; son of Joseph (a farmer) and Cellie (a nurse; maiden name, Lowe) Stanley; married Gwen Meshew (a Slavic specialist), June 29, 1974; children: James Edward, Charles Albert Andrew. *Education:* Texas Tech University, B.A., 1965, M.S., 1967; University of Port Elizabeth, South Africa, D.Litt., 1974. *Politics:* Democrat. *Religion:* Baptist.

Addresses

Home—5527 Eisenhower Dr., Lawton, OK 73505. *Office*—Department of English, Foreign Languages, Cameron University, 2800 West Gore, Lawton, OK 73505. *Agent*—Susan Cohen, Writers House, Inc., 21 West 26th St., New York, NY 10010. *E-mail*—georges@cameron.edu.

Career

East Texas State University, Commerce, instructor in English as a foreign language, 1967-69; University of Kansas, Lawrence, instructor in English as a foreign

George Edward Stanley

language, 1969-70; Cameron University, Lawton, OK, instructor, 1970-73, assistant professor, 1973-76, associate professor, 1976-79, professor of African and Middle-Eastern languages, 1979—, chairman of department of English, Foreign Languages, and Journalism, 1984-2000. Fulbright lecturer at University of Chad, 1973. Director, annual Writers of Children's Literature Conference co-sponsored by Cameron University and the Society of Children's Book Writers; member of faculty, Institute of Children's Literature, Redding Ridge, CT, 1986-92; member of faculty, Writer's Digest School, Cincinnati, OH, 1992-99.

Member

Mystery Writers of America, Society of Children's Book Writers and Illustrators, Modern Language Association, Middle East Studies Association, American Association of Teachers of Arabic, American Association of Teachers of Turkic Languages, African Language Teachers Association, American Association of Teachers of Persian, American Institute for Yemeni Studies, Syrian Studies Association, National Council of Less-Commonly Taught Languages.

Awards, Honors

Distinguished Faculty Award, Phi Kappa Phi, 1974; Member of the Year Award, Society of Children's Book Writers, 1979; Oklahoma Writers Hall of Fame, 1994.

Writings

FICTION; FOR CHILDREN

Mini-Mysteries, Saturday Evening Post Co. (Indianapolis, IN), 1979.
The Crime Lab, illustrated by Andrew Glass, Avon (New York, NY), 1980.
The Case of the Clever Marathon Cheat, Meadowbrook (Minnetonka, MN), 1985.
The Ukrainian Egg Mystery, Avon (New York, NY), 1986.
The Codebreaker Kids!, Avon (New York, NY), 1987.
The Italian Spaghetti Mystery, Avon (New York, NY), 1987.
(Under house pseudonym Laura Lee Hope) *The New Bobbsey Twins: The Case of the Runaway Money,* Simon & Schuster (New York, NY), 1987.
The Mexican Tamale Mystery, Avon (New York, NY), 1988.
(Under house pseudonym Laura Lee Hope) *The Bobbsey Twins: The Mystery on the Mississippi,* Simon & Schuster (New York, NY), 1988.
The Codebreaker Kids Return, Avon (New York, NY), 1989.
Hershell Cobwell and the Miraculous Tattoo, Avon (New York, NY), 1991.
Rats in the Attic: And Other Stories to Make Your Skin Crawl, Avon (New York, NY), 1994.
Happy Deathday to You: And Other Stories to Give You Nightmares, Avon (New York, NY), 1995.
Snake Camp ("Road to Reading" series), Golden Books (New York, NY), 2000.
Ghost Horse ("Road to Reading" series), Golden Books (New York, NY), 2000.
(Under house pseudonym Carolyn Keene) *The Mystery in Tornado Alley* ("Nancy Drew" series), Simon & Schuster (New York, NY), 2000.
(Under house pseudonym Franklin W. Dixon) *The Case of the Psychic's Vision* ("Hardy Boys" series), Simon & Schuster (New York, NY), 2003.
(Under house pseudonym Franklin W. Dixon) *The Mystery of the Black Rhino* ("Hardy Boys" series), Simon & Schuster (New York, NY), 2003.
(Under house pseudonym Franklin W. Dixon) *The Secret of the Soldier's Gold* ("Hardy Boys" series), Simon & Schuster (New York, NY), 2003.
(Under house pseudonym Carolyn Keene) *Danger on the Great Lakes* ("Nancy Drew" series), Simon & Schuster (New York, NY), 2003.
(Under house pseudonym Franklin W. Dixon) *One False Step* ("Hardy Boys" series), Simon & Schuster (New York, NY), 2005.
(Under house pseudonym Carolyn Keene) *The Secret of the Library Clock* ("Nancy Drew" series), Simon & Schuster (New York, NY), 2005.

"SCAREDY CATS" SERIES

The Day the Ants Got Really Mad, Simon & Schuster (New York, NY), 1996.

There's a Shark in the Swimming Pool!, Simon & Schuster (New York, NY), 1996.

Mrs. O'Dell's Third-Grade Class Is Shrinking, Simon & Schuster (New York, NY), 1996.

Bugs for Breakfast, Simon & Schuster (New York, NY), 1996.

Who Invited Aliens to My Slumber Party?, Simon & Schuster (New York, NY), 1997.

The New Kid in School Is a Vampire Bat, Simon & Schuster (New York, NY), 1997.

A Werewolf Followed Me Home, Simon & Schuster (New York, NY), 1997.

The Vampire Kittens of Count Dracula, Simon & Schuster (New York, NY), 1997.

"SPINETINGLERS" SERIES; UNDER PSEUDONYM M. T. COFFIN

Billy Baker's Dog Won't Stay Buried!, Avon (New York, NY), 1995.

Where Have All the Parents Gone?, Avon (New York, NY), 1995.

Check It out and Die!, Avon (New York, NY), 1995.

Don't Go to the Principal's Office, Avon (New York, NY), 1996.

The Dead Kid Did It!, Avon (New York, NY), 1996.

Pet Store, Avon (New York, NY), 1996.

Escape from the Haunted Museum, Avon (New York, NY), 1996.

The Curse of the Cheerleaders, Avon (New York, NY), 1997.

Circus F.R.E.A.K.S, Avon (New York, NY), 1997.

"THIRD GRADE DETECTIVES" SERIES

The Clue of the Left-handed Glove, illustrated by Salvatore Murdocca, Aladdin (New York, NY), 1998, published as *The Clue of the Left-handed Envelope,* 2000.

The Puzzle of the Pretty Pink Handkerchief, illustrated by Salvatore Murdocca, Aladdin (New York, NY), 1998.

The Mystery of the Hairy Tomatoes, illustrated by Salvatore Murdocca, Aladdin (New York, NY), 2001.

The Cobweb Confession, illustrated by Salvatore Murdocca, Aladdin (New York, NY), 2001.

The Secret of the Green Skin, illustrated by Salvatore Murdocca, Aladdin (New York, NY), 2003.

The Case of the Dirty Clue, Aladdin (New York, NY), 2003.

The Mystery of the Wooden Witness, Aladdin (New York, NY), 2004.

The Case of the Sweaty Bank Robber, Aladdin (New York, NY), 2004.

The Mystery of the Stolen Statue, Aladdin (New York, NY), 2004.

"KATIE LYNN COOKIE COMPANY" SERIES

The Secret Ingredient, illustrated by Linda Dockey Graves, Random House (New York, NY), 1999.

Frogs' Legs for Dinner, illustrated by Linda Dockey Graves, Random House (New York, NY), 2000.

The Battle of the Bakers, illustrated by Linda Dockey Graves, Random House (New York, NY), 2000.

Bottled Up!, illustrated by Linda Dockey Graves, Random House (New York, NY), 2001.

Wedding Cookies, illustrated by Linda Dockey Graves, Random House (New York, NY), 2001.

"ADAM SHARP" SERIES

Adam Sharp, the Spy Who Barked, illustrated by Guy Francis, Golden Books (New York, NY), 2002, published as *The Spy Who Barked,* Random House (New York, NY) 2003.

Adam Sharp, London Calling, illustrated by Guy Francis, Golden Books (New York, NY), 2002, published as *London Calling,* Random House (New York, NY), 2003.

Swimming with Sharks, illustrated by Guy Francis, Random House (New York, NY), 2003.

Operation Spy School, illustrated by Guy Francis, Random House (New York, NY), 2003.

The Riddle of the Stolen Sand, illustrated by Salvatore Murdocca, Aladdin (Ne York, NY), 2003.

Moose Master, illustrated by Guy Francis, Random House (New York, NY), 2004.

Code Word Kangaroo, illustrated by Guy Francis, Random House (New York, NY), 2004.

"TWIN CONNECTION" SERIES; UNDER PSEUDONYM ADAM MILLS

Hot Pursuit, Ballantine (New York, NY), 1989.

On the Run, Ballantine (New York, NY), 1989.

Right on Target, Ballantine (New York, NY), 1989.

Secret Ballot, Ballantine (New York, NY), 1989.

Dangerous Play, Ballantine (New York, NY), 1989.

Skyjack!, Ballantine (New York, NY), 1989.

High-Tech Heist, Ballantine (New York, NY), 1989.

Cold Chills, Ballantine (New York, NY), 1989.

NONFICTION; FOR CHILDREN

Wild Horses, illustrated by Michael Langham Rowe, Random House (New York, NY), 2001.

Geronimo: Young Warrior, illustrated by Meryl Henderson, Aladdin (New York, NY), 2001.

Andrew Jackson, Young Patriot, Aladdin (New York, NY), 2003.

Mr. Rogers: Young Friend and Neighbor, Aladdin (New York, NY), 2004.

Harry S Truman, Aladdin (New York, NY), 2004.

A Primary Source History of the United States, eight volumes, Gareth-Stevens (Milwaukee, WI), 2005.

RADIO PLAYS

The Reclassified Child, British Broadcasting Corporation (London, England), 1974.

Another Football Season, British Broadcasting Corporation (London, England), 1974.

Better English, British Broadcasting Corporation (London, England), 1975.

OTHER

Writing Short Stories for Young People, Writer's Digest (Cincinnati, OH), 1987.

Also author of "Mini-Mystery Series," a monthly short story in *Child Life Mystery and Science Fiction,* 1977—. Contributor of short stories under pseudonym Stuart Symons to *Espionage.* Also contributor of articles, stories, and reviews to scholarly journals and popular magazines for adults and children, including *Texas Outlook, English Studies in Africa, Linguistics, Bulletin of the Society of Children's Book Writers, Darling, Women's Choice, Children's Playmate, Health Explorer, Junior Medical Detective,* and *Jack and Jill.*

Work in Progress

Crazy Horse: Young Sioux Warrior, for Simon & Schuster; *Leonardo da Vinci: Young Artist,* for Simon & Schuster; *Framed* ("Nancy Drew" series), for Simon & Schuster; *Heroes and Villains of the American Revolution,* for Scholastic; *Pioneers of the American West,* for Scholastic.

Sidelights

An extraordinarily prolific writer, George Edward Stanley has also found time to travel and teach, drawing many of the plots for his books from his diverse experiences and natural curiosity. In addition to penning numerous books under his own name, Stanley has also published under several pseudonyms, including the well-known house pseudonyms Carolyn Keene and Franklin W. Bramley, the fictitious authors of the perennially popular "Nancy Drew" and "Hardy Boys" novels, respectively.

"When I was growing up in the small town of Memphis, Texas, in the late 1940s and early 1950s, I discovered that I had two passions: mysteries and movies,"- Stanley once told *Something about the Author.* "I read all the mysteries in the public library and went to all the Saturday afternoon matinees, mainly to see the serials. There were two movie houses in Memphis and I would walk to town several times a week just to see the new movie posters. Since I was allowed to go to the movies only on Saturday afternoons, I missed a lot of the great films of those years, but have since been able to buy video tapes of most of the ones that I never got to see and can now watch them anytime I want to! (I also collect movie posters!). Two of my favorite movies from that period are *The Bat* and *Home Sweet Homicide,* because they both have mystery writers as the main characters.

"As I grew older, my interests broadened, of course, and I began studying foreign languages. (Actually, I have always liked anything 'foreign.') In college, I ma-jored in French and Portuguese and minored in German, and I went the route of the typical college professor as far as writing is concerned: I began writing very esoteric articles about linguistics that I doubt many people read.

"When it came time to work on my doctorate, I decided to follow another one of my dreams: going to Africa. I went to South Africa, to the University of Port Elizabeth, to research the problems the Xhosa have learning English and Afrikaans. Following my work in South Africa, I accepted a Fulbright professorship to the University of N'Djamena in Chad, Central Africa. It was there that I began writing fiction (something else I had always wanted to do) and I sold my first radio play to the British Broadcasting World Service in London.

"I grew up reading mysteries and wanting to write mysteries. I never got over Nancy Drew, the Dana Girls, or the Hardy Boys. If Nancy Drew had been a forensic scientist, I might be in a different occupation today. But she wasn't and that's why I created Dr. Constance Daniels, head of the Forensic Science laboratory of the Bay City Police Department. Dr. Daniels first appeared in *Child Life* magazine. Later, I introduced a new, younger character in the series, Marie-Claire Verlaine, and moved the locale to Paris, but the forensic science solutions remained. If I had known someone like Dr. Daniels, or Marie-Claire, when I was studying biology, chemistry, and physics, I might have excelled in science."

Inspired, in part, by these life experiences, Stanley has continued to author books for younger readers. In *The Codebreaker Kids* he introduces readers to three enterprising kids who start a business encoding and decoding messages for would-be spies. In what *School Library Journal* reviewer Elaine Knight called an "off-the-wall but very funny spy mystery," the three friends become enmeshed in both sides of tricky situations. Diane Roback's review for *Publishers Weekly* found the humor far-fetched, but the inclusion of real codes good for the reader in "this fast-paced caper" with "Dinky's careful instructions for using them" a fine embellishment.

Reviewers gave *The Italian Spaghetti Mystery* higher marks for mystery than humor. Blair Christolon, writing in *School Library Journal,* found the plot of a private school headmistress and her students'—cum summer performers—search for Mr. Spaghetti Man and his spaghetti-making secret to be "evenly paced and the conclusion clever," despite "primitive sound effects" and "corny" humor. Writing again for *Publishers Weekly,* Diane Roback declared the book—a sequel to Stanley's *The Ukrainian Egg Mystery*—"wacky." *Hershell Cobwell and the Miraculous Tattoo* places a series of crazy events in a different context, illustrating the lengths to which one boy goes to get attention and approval from his peers. A reviewer in *Booklist* dubbed it "a cautionary tale, filled with zestful humor."

Reviewers have often commented upon Stanley's skill in writing books that are not only engaging, but are also very easy for young readers to complete by themselves, and his "Third Grade Detectives" series is a good example. Mr. Merlin was once a spy, but now he teaches third grade and leads his class in solving simple mysteries. Readers can follow the clues through each short, illustrated chapter book, attempting to solve the mystery before the characters do, and there are also simple codes and riddles for the reader to decipher as well. The types of mysteries that the children solve vary widely, including some actual crimes. The puzzle of the series' first book, *The Clue of the Left-handed Envelope,* though, is not so serious. This time, the class's job is to figure out who sent classmate Amber Lee a secret admirer letter. They succeed, with the assistance of Mr. Merlin's helpful friend, Dr. Smiley, a forensic scientist working in a police lab. The second book of the "Third Grade Detectives" series, *The Puzzle of the Pretty Pink Handkerchief,* finds the children trying to discover who trespassed in Todd's treehouse and left the titular pink handkerchief there. Todd is also the victim in *The Cobweb Confession,* when his baseball card collection disappears. Todd's friend Noelle is at the center of other volumes, including *The Mystery of the Hairy Tomatoes,* in which her dog is wrongly accused of digging in Mrs. Ruston's vegetable garden. The two work together on solving serious, adult crimes in the volumes *The Case of the Sweaty Bank Robber* and *The Mystery of the Stolen Statue.*

In *The Case of the Dirty Clue,* Mr. Merlin's students want to know who ran over Misty's brand new bike. The bike is covered with their best clue: an unusual red soil, left there by the car that hit it. With Mr. Merlin's help, they discover that this type of soil comes from Arizona, leading them to the offending car and its driver. Critics also praised this entry in the series; *School Library Journal* contributor Andrea Tarr noted the "believable characters and . . . fast-paced plot," while *Booklist*'s Hazel Rochman thought that "as always in this series . . . readers will enjoy the puzzles and the forensics." Continuing the "Third Grade Detectives" series, *The Cobweb Confession* also shares another feature common to many of Stanley's books: children overcoming their fears, particularly of creepy-crawly animals. This theme reappears in the non-series book *Snake Camp.* Stevie's parents send him to "Viper" camp, thinking that Viper is a computer program. But it isn't: the camp features real snakes—and Stevie *hates* snakes. By the end of the book, though, one of the reptiles has stolen Stevie's heart and becomes his pet. "The plot is decidedly contrived," Hazel Rochman commented in *Booklist,* "but the hissing, slimy, scaly stuff is fun."

"There was a long period of time in my life when I wrote only one short story a month," Stanley once recalled to *SATA.* "Looking back on that period now, I can't honestly tell you why that's all I did, but it was, and I was perfectly satisfied. It filled my need to be a

Part of Stanley's "Third-Grade Detectives" series **The Mystery of the Hairy Tomatoes** *finds the sleuths on the trail of the true marauder in Mrs. Ruston's garden after they find several long yellow hairs on one of the plants. (Illustration by Salvatore Murdocca.)*

published writer, but the need then probably wasn't as great as it has since become, and I think that's a normal development. We develop into writers. For some of us it's absolutely necessary that we take it easy and let ourselves evolve into writers. I used to wonder how some of my friends wrote several different stories and books at the same time. I thought I'd never be able to do that, but I was able, and I am able.

"As I developed, I got to the point where I began getting ideas for other stories and other series and other characters. I'd been working long enough with some of my editors that I felt quite comfortable in suggesting these new ideas to them. Some of them were accepted. Some weren't. Some even became the basis for entire magazines. At one time, I had seven series running at the same time (some stayed longer in the magazines than others), but soon the evolutionary process took over and I got to the point where I wanted to write books, too."

One area Stanley explored was the story meant to be read aloud. In the case of *Rats in the Attic: And Other*

Stories to Make Your Skin Crawl, the best place for reading is suggested to be a campfire. Reviewer Larry Prater predicted in *Kliatt* that "middle schoolers will . . . revel in the soft-core gore and mayhem" of the stories, which involve kids who flirt with danger and the supernatural and pay dearly.

Stanley also shared his views about the role of an children' book author. "Writing for young people carries with it a great responsibility. Some young person is actually going to read what you've written and be influenced by it. Keeping this in mind can be helpful because it makes you want to put your best foot forward and produce not only something that you'll be proud of, but something that the young reader will never forget, whether it carries a lesson for life or simply recounts an exciting adventure.

"It's very important that you perceive yourself as a young person; this is one of the secrets of writing for them. You have to live what he is living and feel what he is feeling. You have to understand a young person's emotions, fears, disappointments, triumphs. You have to understand what it means to score that soccer goal or not to score it. You have to understand what it means to make one hundred percent on a spelling quiz. You have to understand what it means not to understand math. You have to understand what it means not to be able to play football, either because you're too small or because your parents won't let you. You have to understand what it means to have to wait for Christmas or a birthday party. You almost have to become the character you're writing about.

"One of the great things about writing for young people is that they're interested in learning about everything. This can't help but inspire the writer to reach greater heights. You want to teach them, to entertain them, to make them read what you've written. It's quite mind-boggling, frankly, when they come up to you and tell you that they really enjoy reading your stories.

"I very much dislike a lot of what is being written today for children. I think most children are looking for something that will excite them and carry them off to other worlds. They can see enough realism on the nightly news to last them a lifetime. Give them something they can look forward to, something that will stir their sense of adventure and make them want to become the best in whatever they finally end up doing. But don't forget to make them laugh!"

Stanley combines adventure and the required dose of humor in his "Scaredy Cat" series, which includes *The Day the Ants Got Really Mad.* Intended for children of early-grade-school age, the book tells how Michael, a boy about the same age, copes with the discovery that his family's home is built on the world's largest anthill. Maura Bresnahan, in her review for *School Library Journal,* wrote that Stanley's informative story about ants "combines humor and a semi-scary situation" in a way "children will find immensely entertaining."

"I spend my spare time reading, learning new languages, watching foreign films, and just trying to keep my head above the water," Stanley explained. "My wife tells me that I can't relax; actually, I'm relaxing when I'm busy. It's when I'm not busy that I start getting uptight!"

Snake-hating Stevie Marsh finds himself in a problematic situation when he signs up for Camp Viper thinking that it will focus on the Viper computer game in Stanley's amusing **Snake Camp.** *(Illustration by Jared Lee.)*

Biographical and Critical Sources

PERIODICALS

Booklist, March 15, 1991, review of *Hershell Cobwell and the Miraculous Tattoo;* April 1, 1996, p. 1366; December, 2000, Hazel Rochman, review of *Snake Camp,* p. 727; May 1, 2003, Stephanie Zvirin, review of *The Secret of the Green Skin,* pp. 1529-1530; February 1, 2004, Hazel Rochman, review of *The Case of the Dirty Clue,* p. 977.
Kirkus Reviews, July 15, 1999, p. 1139.

Kliatt, May, 1995, Larry W. Prater, review of _Rats in the Attic: And Other Stories to Make Your Skin Crawl,_ pp. 18-19.

Library Journal, April 1, 1987, p. 145.

Publishers Weekly, January 16, 1987, Diane Roback, review of _The Italian Spaghetti Mystery,_ p. 74; May 8, 1987, Diane Roback, review of _The Codebreaker Kids,_ p. 71.

School Library Journal, August, 1986, Maura Bresnahan, review of _The Day the Ants Got Really Mad,_ p. 130; June-July, 1987, Blair Christolon, review of _The Italian Spaghetti Mystery,_ p. 101; September, 1987, Elaine E. Knight, review of _The Codebreaker Kids,_ p. 183; June, 1997, p. 101; March, 2001, Maura Bresnahan, review of _Ghost Horse,_ p. 205; March, 2003, John Sigwald, review of _The Riddle of the Stolen Sand,_ pp. 207-208; August, 2003, Pat Leach, review of _The Secret of the Green Skin,_ p. 144; January, 2004, Andrea Tarr, review of _The Case of the Dirty Clue,_ p. 107.

ONLINE

George Stanley's Home Page, http://www.cameron.edu/~georges (January 26, 2005).

* * *

SUEN, Anastasia

Personal

Female.

Addresses

Home—TX. _Agent_—c/o Author Mail, Harcourt International, 6277 Sea Harbor Dr., Orlando, FL 32887. _E-mail_—asuen@asuen.com.

Career

Writer and educator. University of North Texas, instructor in children's literature; Southern Methodist University, teacher of story structure; instructor affiliated with Creative Habits Workshop (online course). Lecturer and presenter at conferences. Member of Rosen Publishing reading advisory board; poetry consultant for Sadlier-Oxford; former director of Seminars in Children's Literature. Moderator of cw-biz (online chat group for children's writers). Founder, Writer's Roundtable Conference.

Member

Society of Children's Book Writers and Illustrators (advisor).

Writings

Man on the Moon, illustrated by Benrei Huang, Viking (New York, NY), 1997.

Baby Born, illustrated by Chih-wei Chang, Lee & Low Books (New York, NY), 1998.

Window Music, illustrated by Wade Zahares, Viking (New York, NY), 1998.

Delivery, illustrated by Wade Zahares, Viking (New York, NY), 1999.

Toddler Two, illustrated by Winnie Cheon, Lee & Low Books (New York, NY), 2000.

Air Show, illustrated by Cecco Mariniello, Henry Holt (New York, NY), 2001.

Make a Turkey, illustrated by Kurt Nagahori, Lee & Low (New York, NY), 2002.

Raise the Roof!, illustrated by Elwood H. Smith, Viking (New York, NY), 2003.

Picture Writing: A New Approach to Writing for Kids and Teens (nonfiction), Writer's Digest Books (Cincinnati, OH), 2003.

Subway, illustrated by Karen Katz, Viking (New York, NY), 2004.

Splish, Splash!, Sadlier-Oxford (New York, NY), 2004.

Fractals: The Art of Math, Celebrations Press (Parsippany, NJ), 2004.

Remarkable Robots, Celebration Press (Parsippany, NJ), 2004.

Finding a Way: Six Historic U.S. Routes, Celebration Press (Parsippany, NJ), 2005.

Red Light, Green Light, illustrated by Ken Wilson-Max, Harcourt (Orlando, FL), 2005.

Ice Cream Money, illustrated by Farah Aria, Lee & Low (New York, NY), 2005.

Mysterious Magnets, Celebration Press (Parsippany, NJ), 2005.

Pencil Talk and Other School Poems, illustrated by Susie Lee Jin, Lee & Low (New York, NY), 2005.

Wetlands, Celebration Press (Parsippany, NJ), 2005.

Several of Suen's titles have been translated into Spanish.

"PETER'S NEIGHBORHOOD" SERIES:

Willie's Birthday (based on characters by Ezra Jack Keats), illustrated by Allan Eitzen, Viking (New York, NY), 2001.

Hamster Chase (based on characters by Ezra Jack Keats), illustrated by Allan Eitzen, Viking (New York, NY), 2001.

The Clubhouse (based on characters by Ezra Jack Keats), illustrated by Allan Eitzen, Viking (New York, NY), 2002.

Loose Tooth (based on characters by Ezra Jack Keats), illustrated by Allan Eitzen, Viking (New York, NY), 2002.

The Red Cross, PowerKids Press (New York, NY), 2002.

"HELPING ORGANIZATION" SERIES; NONFICTION:

ASPCA: The American Society for the Prevention of Cruelty to Animals, PowerKids Press (New York, NY), 2002.

UNICEF: United Nations Children's Fund, PowerKids Press (New York, NY), 2002.

Doctors without Borders, PowerKids Press (New York, NY), 2002.

Habitat for Humanity, PowerKids Press (New York, NY), 2002.

The Peace Corps, PowerKids Press (New York, NY), 2002.

"SPORTS HISTORY" SERIES:

The Story of Soccer, PowerKids Press (New York, NY), 2002.

The Story of Hockey, PowerKids Press (New York, NY), 2002.

The Story of Football, PowerKids Press (New York, NY), 2002.

The Story of Figure Skating, PowerKids Press (New York, NY), 2002.

The Story of Basketball, PowerKids Press (New York, NY), 2002.

The Story of Baseball, PowerKids Press (New York, NY), 2002.

Sidelights

Educator and writer Anastasia Suen is the author of numerous children's books that range from toddler board books to elementary-grade readers to nonfiction. Her titles, which include the picture books *Subway, Window Music,* and *Raise the Roof!,* often feature rhyming texts, while interesting facts are explored in nonfiction books such as *The Red Cross,* from the "Helping Organizations" series, and and *The Story of Baseball,* one of several titles in the "Sports History" series. Reviewing the "Sports History" series, *Booklist* contributor John Peters maintained that Suen's choice of "popular topics and [the] inviting look of this series may tempt reluctant or below-grade-level readers to give it a try."

Praising Suen's simple, rhyming text in *Subway,* a *Publishers Weekly* contributor noted that the author "turns city life into one big happy hub-bub" in her description of a young girl's ride downtown. Margaret R. Tassia was equally enthusiastic in her *School Library Journal* review, noting that the book's rhyming text "captures the feel of her journey and a repeated refrain invites readers to participate" in the storytelling process. *Window Music,* which focuses on the view of the world as seen from the window of a fast-moving trains, was described by a *Publishers Weekly* contributor as a "magical excursion" that features a rhythmic text reminiscent of "music with several movements."With illustrations by Elwood H. Smith, Suen's picture book *Raise the Roof!* follows a man, a woman, and the loyal family dog as the trio go about the task of building their own house. From pouring the concrete—with the family pooch operating the concrete mixer—to sawing, hammering, measuring, and plumbing, the book follows the home-building process from start to finish. Praising Suen's "concise, catchy verse," as well as Smith's

Anastasia Suen's 2003 picture book **Raise the Roof** *finds everyone in the family drafted into aiding with home construction tasks, although some helpers are best kept away from dangerous power tools. (Illustration by Elwood H. Smith.)*

"retro-cartoon style" illustrations, *Horn Book* reviewer Lauren Adams cited the book for its "fresh charm and . . . easy sense of humor." Although a *Publishers Weekly* critic was less enthusiastic, dubbing the book "cheery but tepid," in *Kirkus Reviews* a critic commented suggested that *Raise the Roof!* be shared with "emergent readers to give them deeper appreciation for what goes into putting up those walls."

Suen's *The Clubhouse,* a book included in Viking's "Easy-to-Read" series, adapts characters created by late author Ezra Jack Keats, including a young boy named Peter who lives in an inner-city neighborhood. One day Peter and his friends stumble upon an old pile of wood in a vacant lot and decide that it has potential to become a clubhouse. Other books in the series includes *Loose Tooth,* which finds Peter hoping his loose tooth won't fall out until after his class picture is taken, while the neighborhood gang tracks down a classroom pet on the lam in *Hamster Chase.* In *Booklist* Sally R. Dow praised the series as "action-packed" while Laura Scott described *Loose Tooth* as a "satisfying" story that "celebrates friendship."

Biographical and Critical Sources

PERIODICALS

Booklist, November, 1, 1997, Carolyn Phelan, review of *Man on the Moon,* p. 477; September 1, 1999, Kay Weisman, review of *Delivery,* p. 144; June 1, 2001, Carolyn Phelan, review of *Air Show,* p. 1886; April

15, 2002, Hazel Rochman, review of *The Clubhouse,* p. 1409; May 15, 2002, John Peters, review of *The Story of Baseball,* p. 1598; June 1, 2002, Hazel Rochman, review of *The Red Cross,* p. 1728; February 15, 2003, Todd Morning, review of *Raise the Roof!,* p. 1077; February 1, 2004, Gillian Engberg, review of *Subway,* p. 982; April 1, 2004, Isabel Schon, review of *Historia de los Deportes,* p. 1376.

Horn Book, March-April, 2003, Lauren Adams, review of *Raise the Roof!,* p. 206.

Kirkus Reviews, December 15, 2002, review of *Raise the Roof!,* p. 1857; January 15, 2004, review of *Subway,* p. 89.

Publishers Weekly, November, 10, 1997, review of *Man on the Moon,* p. 73; September, 21, 1998, review of *Window Music,* p. 83; September 13, 1999, review of *Delivery,* p. 82; November 6, 2000, review of *A, B, C, Easy as 1, 2, 3,* p. 93; December 16, 2002, review of *Raise the Roof!,* p. 65; February 2, 2004, review of *Subway,* p. 75.

School Library Journal, January, 2001, JoAnn Jonas, review of *Toddler Two,* p. 110; March, 2001, Sally R. Dow, review of *Willie's Birthday,* p. 220; April, 2001, Lisa Smith, review of *Hamster Chase,* p. 123; March, 2002, Blair Christolon, review of *The Story of Soccer,* p. 222; March, 2002, Kathleen Simonetta, review of *Habitat for Humanity,* p. 222; April, 2002, Elizabeth Stumph, review of *ASPCA: The American Society for the Prevention of Cruelty to Animals,* p. 141; April, 2002, Laura Scott, review of *Loose Tooth,* p. 124; August, 2002, Holly T. Sneeringer, review of *The Clubhouse,* p. 170; February, 2003, Lisa Dennis, review of *Raise the Roof!,* p. 123; February, 2004, Margaret R. Tassia, review of *Subway,* p. 124.

ONLINE

Anastasia Suen Web site, http://www.asuen.com (February 14, 2005).

*　　*　　*

SULLIVAN, Jody
See RAKE, Jody

*　　*　　*

SWANN, E. L.
See LASKY, Kathryn

*　　*　　*

SYMONS, Stuart
See STANLEY, George Edward

SZEKERES, Cyndy 1933-

Personal

Surname is pronounced "*zeck*-er-es"; born October 31, 1933, in Bridgeport, CT; daughter of Stephen Paul (a toolmaker) and Anna (Ceplousky) Szekeres; married Gennaro Prozzo (an artist), September 20, 1958; children: Marc, Christopher. *Education:* Pratt Institute, certificate, 1954.

Addresses

Home—P.O. Box 280, RFD 3, Putney, VT O5346.

Career

Illustrator and writer. Artwork has appeared on calendars and greeting cards.

Writings

FOR CHILDREN; SELF-ILLUSTRATED

Long Ago (collection of calendar art), McGraw Hill (New York, NY), 1976.

A Child's First Book of Poems, Golden Books (New York, NY), 1981, published as *Cyndy Szekeres' ABC,* Golden Books (New York, NY), 1983.

Puppy Too Small, Golden Books (New York, NY), 1984.

Scaredy Cat!, Golden Books (New York, NY), 1984.

Thumpity Thump Gets Dressed, Golden Books (New York, NY), 1984.

Baby Bear's Surprise, Golden Books (New York, NY), 1984.

Cyndy Szekeres' Counting Book 1 to 10, Golden Books (New York, NY), 1984.

Suppertime for Frieda Fuzzypaws, Golden Books (New York, NY), 1985.

Hide-and-Seek Duck, Golden Books (New York, NY), 1985.

Nothing-to-Do Puppy, Golden Books (New York, NY), 1985.

Good Night, Sammy, Golden Books (New York, NY), 1986.

Puppy Lost, Golden Books (New York, NY), 1986.

Sammy's Special Day, Golden Books (New York, NY), 1986.

Little Bear Counts His Favorite Things, Golden Books (New York, NY), 1986.

Melanie Mouse's Moving Day, Golden Books (New York, NY), 1986.

(Compiler) *Cyndy Szekeres' Book of Poems,* Western Publishing (Racine, WI), 1987.

(Compiler) *Cyndy Szekeres' Mother Goose Rhymes,* Golden Books (New York, NY), 1987.

Cyndy Szekeres

(Compiler) *Cyndy Szekeres' Book of Fairy Tales,* Golden Books (New York, NY), 1988.

Good Night, Sweet Mouse, Golden Books (New York, NY), 1988.

Cyndy Szekeres' Favorite Two-Minute Stories, Golden Books (New York, NY), 1989.

Things Bunny Sees, Western Publishing (Racine, WI), 1990.

What Bunny Loves, Western Publishing (Racine, WI), 1990.

Cyndy Szekeres' Nice Animals, Western Publishing (Racine, WI), 1990.

Cyndy Szekeres' Hugs, Western Publishing (Racine, WI), 1990.

Puppy Learns to Share, Western Publishing (Racine, WI), 1990.

Ladybug, Where Are You?, Western Publishing (Racine, WI), 1991.

(Compiler) *Cyndy Szekeres' Favorite Fairy Tales,* Western Publishing (Racine, WI), 1992.

(Compiler) *Cyndy Szekeres' Favorite Mother Goose Rhymes,* Western Publishing (Racine, WI), 1992.

Fluffy Duckling, Western Publishing (Racine, WI), 1992.

Teeny Mouse Counts Herself, Western Publishing (Racine, WI), 1992.

Cyndy Szekeres' Colors, Western Publishing (Racine, WI), 1992.

Kisses, Western Publishing (Racine, WI), 1993.

Little Puppy Cleans His Room, Western Publishing (Racine, WI), 1993.

Cyndy Szekeres' Baby Animals, Western Publishing (Racine, WI), 1994.

Cyndy Szekeres' I Am a Puppy, Western Publishing (Racine, WI), 1994.

Cyndy Szekeres' Christmas Mouse, Western Publishing (Racine, WI), 1995.

Cyndy Szekeres' Giggles, Western Publishing (Racine, WI), 1996.

Yes, Virginia, There Is a Santa Claus, Scholastic (New York, NY), 1997.

Cyndy Szekeres' I Love My Busy Boook, Western Publishing (Racine, WI), 1997.

The Mouse That Jack Built, Scholastic (New York, NY), 1997.

The Deep Blue Sky Twinkles with Stars, Scholastic (New York, NY), 1998.

I Can Count 100 Bunnies: and So Can You!, Scholastic (New York, NY), 1998.

Kisses, Golden Books (New York, NY), 1998.

A Very Merry Mouse Country Christmas: an Advent Calendar, Scholastic (New York, NY), 1998.

Cyndy Szekeres' Learn to Count, Funny Bunnies, Scholastic (New York, NY), 2000.

Wilbur Bunny's Funny Friends A to Z, Scholastic (New York, NY), 2001.

"TOBY" SERIES; SELF-ILLUSTRATED

Toby!, Little Simon (New York, NY), 2000.

Toby's Alphabet Walk, Little Simon (New York, NY), 2000.

Toby's Rainbow Clothes, Little Simon (New York, NY), 2000.

Toby Counts His Marbles Little Simon (New York, NY), 2000.

Toby's Flying Lesson Little Simon (New York, NY), 2000.

Toby's Holiday Hugs and Kisses, Little Simon (New York, NY), 2000.

Toby's New Brother, Little Simon (New York, NY), 2000.

Toby's Please and Thank You, Little Simon (New York, NY), 2001.

Toby's Good Night, Little Simon (New York, NY), 2001.

Toby's Dinosaur Halloween, Little Simon (New York, NY), 2001.

Santa Toby's Busy Christmas, Little Simon (New York, NY), 2001.

Do You Love Me? Little Simon (New York, NY), 2001.

I Can Do It! Little Simon (New York, NY), 2001.

"TINY PAW LIBRARY" SERIES; SELF-ILLUSTRATED

A Busy Day, Golden Books (New York, NY), 1989.

The New Baby, Golden Books (New York, NY), 1989.

Moving Day, Golden Books (New York, NY), 1989.

A Fine Mouse Band, Golden Books (New York, NY), 1989.

A Mouse Mess, Western Publishing (Racine, WI), 1990.

ILLUSTRATOR

Sam Vaughan, *New Shoes,* Doubleday (New York, NY), 1961.

Jean Latham and Bee Lewi, *When Homer Honked,* Macmillan (New York, NY), 1961.

Marjorie Flack, *Walter, the Lazy Mouse,* Doubleday (New York, NY), 1963.

Evelyn Sibley Lampman, *Mrs. Updaisy,* Doubleday (New York, NY), 1963.

Phyllis Krasilovsky, *Girl Who Was a Cowboy,* Doubleday (New York, NY), 1965.

(With others) Alvin Tresselt, editor, *Humpty Dumpty's Storybook,* Parents Magazine Press (New York, NY), 1966.

Edward Ormondroyd, *Michael, the Upstairs Dog,* Dial (New York, NY), 1967.

Nancy Faulkner, *Small Clown and Tiger,* Doubleday (New York, NY), 1968.

Kathleen Lombardo, *Macaroni,* Random House (New York, NY), 1968.

Peggy Parrish, *Jumper Goes to School,* Simon & Schuster (New York, NY), 1969.

Adelaide Holl, *Moon Mouse,* Random House (New York, NY), 1969.

Barbara Robinson, *Fattest Bear in the First Grade,* Random House (New York, NY), 1969.

John Peterson, *Mystery in the Night Woods,* Scholastic (New York, NY), 1969.

Joy Lonergan, *Brian's Secret Errand,* Doubleday (New York, NY), 1969.

Patsy Scarry, *Little Richard,* McGraw Hill (New York, NY), 1970.

P. Scarry, *Waggy and His Friends,* McGraw Hill (New York, NY), 1970.

Kathryn Hitte, *What Can You Do without a Place to Play?,* Parents Magazine Press (New York, NY), 1971.

Lois Myller, *No! No!,* Simon & Schuster (New York, NY), 1971.

Patsy Scarry, *Little Richard and Prickles,* McGraw Hill (New York, NY), 1971.

Betty Jean Lifton, *Good Night, Orange Monster,* Atheneum (New York, NY), 1972.

Mary Lystad, *James, the Jaguar,* Putnam (New York, NY), 1972.

Betty Boegehold, *Pippa Mouse,* Knopf (New York, NY), 1973.

Adelaide Holl, *Bedtime for Bears,* Garrard (Champaign, IL), 1973.

Patsy Scarry, *More about Waggy,* McGraw Hill (New York, NY), 1973.

Miriam Anne Bourne, *Four-Ring Three,* Coward (New York, NY), 1973.

Mary Lystad, *The Halloween Parade,* Putnam (New York, NY), 1973.

Kathy Darling, *Little Bat's Secret,* Garrard (Champaign, IL), 1974.

Robert Welber, *Goodbye, Hello,* Pantheon (New York, NY), 1974.

Julia Cunningham, *Maybe, a Mole,* Pantheon (New York, NY), 1974.

Albert Bigelow Paine, *Snowed-in Book,* Avon (New York, NY), 1974.

Jan Wahl, *The Muffletumps' Christmas Party,* Follett (Chicago, IL), 1975.

Jan Wahl, *The Muffletumps' Storybook,* Follett (Chicago, IL), 1975.

Carolyn S. Bailey, *A Christmas Party,* Pantheon (New York, NY), 1975.

Betty Boegehold, *Here's Pippa Again!,* Knopf (New York, NY), 1975.

Jan Wahl, *The Clumpets Go Sailing,* Parents Magazine Press (New York, NY), 1975.

Jan Wahl, *The Muffletumps' Halloween Scare,* Follett (Chicago, IL), 1977.

Jan Wahl, *Doctor Rabbit's Foundling,* Pantheon (New York, NY), 1977.

Tony Johnston, *Night Noises, and Other Mole and Troll Stories,* Putnam (New York, NY), 1977.

Mary D. Kwitz, *Little Chick's Story,* Harper (New York, NY), 1978.

Jan Wahl, *Who Will Believe Tim Kitten?,* Pantheon (New York, NY), 1978.

Adelaide Holl, *Small Bear Builds a Playhouse,* Garrard (Champaign, IL), 1978.

Judy Delton, *Brimhall Comes to Stay,* Lothrop (New York, NY), 1978.

Marjorie W. Sharmat, *The 329th Friend,* Four Winds Press (New York, NY), 1979.

Tony Johnston, *Happy Birthday, Mole and Troll,* Putnam (New York, NY), 1979.

Catherine Hiller, *Argentaybee and the Boonie,* Coward (New York, NY), 1979.

Jan Wahl, *Doctor Rabbit's Lost Scout,* Pantheon (New York, NY), 1979.

Betty Boegehold, *Pippa Pops Out!,* Knopf (New York, NY), 1979.

Betty Boegehold, *Hurray for Pippa!,* Knopf (New York, NY), 1980.

Patsy Scarry, *Patsy Scarry's Big Bedtime Storybook,* Random House (New York, NY), 1980.

Polly B. Berends, *Ladybug and Dog and the Night Walk,* Random House (New York, NY), 1980.

Marci Ridion, *Woodsey Log Library,* four volumes, Random House (New York, NY), 1981.

Margo Hopkins, *Honey Rabbit,* Golden Books (New York, NY), 1982.

Marci McGill, *The Six Little Possums: A Birthday ABC,* Golden Press (New York, NY), 1982.

Marci McGill, *The Six Little Possums and the Baby Sitter,* Golden Press (New York, NY), 1982.

Marci McGill, *The Six Little Possums at Home,* Golden Press (New York, NY), 1982.

Marci McGill, *The Six Little Possums: Pepper's Good and Bad Day,* Golden Press (New York, NY), 1982.

Clement C. Moore, *The Night before Christmas,* Golden Books (New York, NY), 1982.

Selma Lanes, selector, *A Child's First Book of Nursery Tales,* Golden Books (New York, NY), 1983, published as *Cyndy Szekeres' Book of Nursery Tales,* 1987.

Tony Johnston, *Five Little Foxes and the Snow,* HarperCollins (New York, NY), 1987.

Betty Boegehold, *Here's Pippa!,* Knopf (New York, NY), 1989.

Margaret Wise Brown, *Whispering Rabbit,* Western Publishing (Racine, WI), 1992.

Ole Risom, *I Am a Kitten,* Western Publishing (Racine, WI), 1993.

Beatrix Potter, *The Tale of Peter Rabbit,* Western Publishing (Racine, WI), 1993.

(And compiler) *A Small Child's Book of Cozy Poems,* Scholastic (New York, NY), 1999.

(And compiler) *A Small Child's Book of Prayers,* Scholastic (New York, NY), 1999.

Also illustrator of Albert Bigelow Paine's "Hollow Tree" series, three volumes, Avon, 1973, and of calendars and "My Workbook Diary"series, 1973-75.

OTHER

(Editor) Joyce Segal, *It's Time to Go to Bed,* Doubleday (Garden City, NY), 1979.

Work in Progress

More books in the "Tiny Paw Library" series.

Sidelights

Cyndy Szekeres is a well-known illustrator of both her own children's books and those of such writers as Betty Boegehold, Patsy Scarry, and Jan Wahl. Szekeres began drawing at an early age and soon showed promise. As she later recalled in *Something about the Author* (*SATA*): "I can't remember a time when I didn't draw. I was the artist in the family, an aptitude inherited from my father who never had a chance to develop his talent."

A child of the late-Depression era, Szekeres drew on paper bags flattened and trimmed by her father, a toolmaker. Although she continued drawing throughout adolescence and her young-adult life, she harbored few illusions about actually working as an artist. "I assumed that I was headed for a job in a factory and probably marriage," she told *SATA.*

Before Szekeres graduated from high school, however, her father learned that advertising might prove a lucrative and fulfilling career for her. Though she did not plan to become a commercial artist, she enrolled at Pratt Institute at her father's urging. "I had no intention of embarking on a career in advertising," she related to *SATA.* "I had my heart set on becoming an illustrator."

Szekeres won admittance to Pratt and studied there until earning her certificate in 1954. Upon leaving the school, she discovered that few career opportunities existed for budding illustrators, so she obtained commercial work as a designer at display houses serving prominent New York City department stores. "Then I did children's fashion illustration for the Saks Fifth Avenue department store, requiring overly well-groomed, coiffed children wearing perfectly fit clothing," Szekeres told *SATA.* "This interrupted the way I usually drew children and I didn't appreciate the influence. It caused me to focus more keenly on anthropomorphic animals and I eventually decided (later on, after several books) to illustrate these animals only."

Marriage to a fellow artist in 1958 changed Szekeres' career plans. Her husband encouraged her to continue working at becoming an illustrator and gradually her luck began to turn for the better. In 1959, the publishing house Doubleday, which had been maintaining a file of Szekeres' department-store works, contacted her with a request that she produce illustrations for Sam Vaughan's *New Shoes,* a book for children. By this time Szekeres was pregnant with her first child, but she nonetheless accepted the Doubleday offer. The results were a success.

In the ensuing years, though her family grew, Szekeres assumed a considerable pace illustrating various children's books. In 1969, for instance, she provided drawings for five works, including Adelaide Holl's *Moon Mouse,* and in the next two years she illustrated five more books, including Patsy Scarry's *Little Richard*—Szekeres' first full-color work—*Waggy and His Friends,* and *Little Richard and Prickles.*

In 1981 Szekeres signed an exclusive contract with Western Publishing, and as of 1996, more than fourteen million copies of her books had been sold. Her success has also been confirmed by reviewers, who have noted that her books, which often feature animals with childlike personalities, are illustrated with attractive, bright artwork brimming with ingenious details.

Working beyond the parameters of Western Publishing, Szekeres has continued to build a respected list of self-illustrated works while continuing to provide illustrations for the texts of others. Among popular books in the latter category are *A Small Child's Book of Prayers* and *A Small Child's Book of Cozy Poems.* Szekeres acted as editor and compiler of both of these books in addition to illustrating them. Reviewing *A Small Child's Book of Cozy Poems, Booklist* critic Hazel Rochman praised Szekeres' "gentle, domestic line-and-watercolor pictures of animals in old-fashioned dress," and indeed such animals have become something of a trademark of this author-illustrator.

Illustrating her own texts, such as *The Deep Blue Sky Twinkles with Stars,* Szekeres displays her full talents for anthropomorphic tales and warm, feel-good settings. "There is a very detailed, three dimensional anthropomorphic world, up there in my head," Szekeres once told *SATA.* "It has been there since I could read. Now, characters rattle around in my brain, tumble out and run around my desk. When I am pleased with my work it is because I listened to them! When I am disappointed it is because I tried to please and accommodate others. There is a fine line between the two."

Booklist critic Ellen Mandel praised the world Szekeres creates in *The Deep Blue Sky Twinkles with Stars,* commenting on the "sunny, spring colors of golden chicks, tawny bunnies, pink blossoms, and green grass" in this "inviting bedtime tale." A contributor to *Publishers Weekly* called the same book a "sprightly tale of a woodland bunny family getting ready to call it a day." More bunnies take center stage in *Learn to Count, Funny Bunnies,* a rhyming board book. Kristina Aaronson, reviewing the title in *School Library Journal,* felt that "children will love the rhythm of the story, the amusing illustrations, and the small size of the book."

An "energetic young mouse"—as a contributor for *Publishers Weekly* described the protagonist—stars in Szekeres's "Toby" series, board books with an educational intent. Numbers, the alphabet, colors, feelings, and manners are just some of the topics covered in this "spunky series" of concept books, according to the *Publishers Weekly* critic, who further commented that the author's "spirited artwork offers winsome particulars." In the series Toby prefers being busy to being bored, and his adventures include pretending to be a dinosaur, learning to fly, and helping with Christmas preparations. Toby received such popularity among young readers that in 2001, a stuffed toy based on the character was released to toy and book stores; Simon & Schuster also released coloring pages on their Web site for story hours and for children who want to color their own versions of Toby's adventures.

Among Szekeres' influences is another luminary of children's literature: Richard Scarry. "I am proud to have had Richard Scarry as my mentor," Szekeres once told *SATA.* "I never met him," she said, but "we've exchanged letters that began with his encouragement. He said, 'If you're not having fun, you're not doing it right.' Sometimes, it is so hard. I was trained as a child to be obedient. It stuck! It takes discipline and conviction to be true to oneself and one's labors, to remember they should produce a smile! Encouragement is paramount. Mine, from special editors, art directors my ever-patient agent Marilyn Marlow and another most important mentor, my husband, Gennaro Prozzo (a fine artist) of forty-three years."

Biographical and Critical Sources

BOOKS

Pendergast, Sara, and Tom Pendergast, *St. James Guide to Children's Writers,* 5th edition, St. James Press (Detroit, MI), 1999.
Ward, Martha E., and Dorothy A. Marquardt, *Illustrators of Books for Young People,* 2nd edition, Scarecrow Press (Metuchen, NJ), 1979.

PERIODICALS

Booklist, January 1, 1985, p. 643; December 1, 1985, p. 577; March 1, 1992, p. 1287; February 1, 1997, p. 949; February 15, 1998, Ellen Mandel, review of *The Deep Blue Sky Twinkles with Stars,* pp. 1020-1021; January 1, 1999, p. 891; February 1, 1999, Hazel Rochman, review of *A Small Child's Book of Cozy Poems,* p. 976.
Junior Literary Guild, April, 1973; September, 1974; March, 1975.
Publishers Weekly, September 26, 1977, p. 137; September 19, 1980; October 30, 1981, p. 63; March 26, 1982; June 22, 1984, p. 99; August 12, 1988, p. 455; June 15, 1992, p. 101; January 20, 1997, pp. 400-401; January 12, 1998, p. 58; January 12, 1998, review of *The Deep Blue Sky Twinkles with Stars,* p. 58; February 22, 1999, p. 97; June 5, 2000, review of *Toby!,* p. 92; January 22, 2001,"Toby,", p. 184; May 14, 2001, p. 84.
School Library Journal, April, 1985, p. 83; March, 1986, p. 153; April, 1997, p. 118; October, 1997, p. 48; March, 1998, p. 188; February, 1999, p. 89; April, 1999, p. 126; May, 2000, Kristina Aaronson, review of *Learn to Count, Funny Bunnies,* p. 156.

Autobiography Feature

Cyndy Szekeres

Cyndy Szekeres contributed the following autobiographical essay to *SATA:*

I am Cyndy. I do not know why, but I am different because I do not think and see things like anybody else, but that's all right. I realized this at the age of five. Even so, unwanted differences separated me from my peers. My playmate, not by choice, by geography, was the girl next door. I didn't really enjoy her company but wasn't required to cross the street or travel any forbidden distance to play. Her mother's tulip beds fascinated me. Dozens of uniform red-cupped petals held black stamens resembling burnt matches. These were surrounded by a burst of yellow that seemed to be hand painted. My memories of that time, the thirties, evoke visions of wonderful details in the gardens and fields that framed each home around our town.

We lived in Fairfield, Connecticut, bordering Bridgeport, an industrial town that was filled to over-flowing with Italian, Romanian, Slovanian, and Hungarian neighborhoods. My grandparents lived in Bridge-port, along with other immigrants attracted by jobs and the great need for an unskilled labor force.

The first few miles within Fairfield were the sub-urbs for factory workers; further in were homes, afflu-ent choices of pioneering commuters to New York City, and the stately mansions of the area businessmen. Our house sat on old farmland. In the thirties, this land had been quickly covered with modest one-and two-family dwellings.

Our neighbors were Hungarian immigrants their offspring. Each family maintained a sense of pride and competition over the flowers and vegetables they raised, their grape arbors and the wine they produced from them, and the chickens and geese that put a bird on the table every Sunday and feather quilts on each bed.

My father was first-generation American, but he identified with the ethnic standards of his immigrant parents. We lived like Hungarians, part of a tightly knit family consisting of his parents (my grandparents), his two brothers and two sisters (my aunts and uncles), and their families. Our activities and sociabilities were fo-cused in this group.

My mother's father came to America from Lithua-nia with his wife in the early 1900s. He died during the influenza epidemic in 1917, when she was nine, the oldest of four daughters. Her mother, who spoke little English, raised these children as best she could. The goal for the young in such families was to quit school when the law allowed, and go to work . . . and so they did . . . my mother, my father, and some of my aunts and uncles. As family life was structured with a patriar-chal head, my father's side received more of our attention.

My father was a toolmaker. My mother also worked in a factory on the assembly line. Happy preschool memories were days spent with my paternal grandmother. She did housecleaning and laundry for New York commuters. Gramma focused on her tasks with a sense of pleasure and accomplishment, traits then instilled in me. She would hum a tune or whistle, in an odd way, not really knowing any tunes or how to whistle for that matter. Why? "Because it makes work nice." Today, I play tapes, classical or Gershwin . . . "because it makes work nice." An exceptional cook, baking was Gramma's special treat for us all. "Come, *feeum* (that's 'dear one' in Hungarian), watch this so you can do it." A pinch of this, a handful of that, every-thing was measured by sight. Mixing was an art, too, resulting in delectable *kalacs, pogacsa, kifli,* and *fanks* (that's bread, biscuits, pastry, and donuts). I am an in-spired cook, and if there is anything that I do well, it is to Gramma's credit.

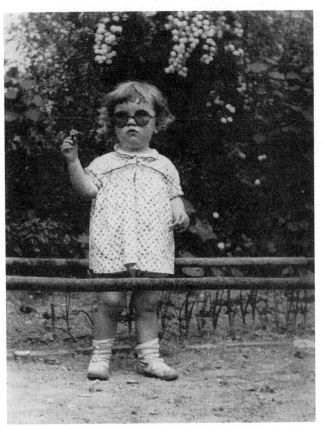

"Me, in 1935; it is a snowberry I am holding. I remember inspecting these!"

My brother was my father's namesake. We called him Junior. He was two years older than I and obliged to take me everywhere. This hardly pleased either of us. I was curious about things that neither he nor his friends had any patience for: Did a buttercup's yellow reflec-tion on the chin mean that one liked butter? Would picking dandelions make you wet the bed? Did babies really grow under cabbage leaves? (I checked them regularly!)The playthings I liked most came from sweat equity. Brown paper bags cut open made good drawing paper. The thin cardboard used for bakery boxes was stiff enough for paper dolls. I made a lot of them and filled a shoe box with "designer dresses."

Junior had loftier thoughts. Floating through space was one of them. A borrowed bed sheet and some clothesline rope became a parachute. I cheered him on. An assisting friend spread the "chute" on the ground behind the garage, throwing the clothesline ties up and over the roof, where my brother climbed to wrap it around his waist and jump. Our father arrived in time to stop the scheduled flight. Back then, one's attempted adventures weren't corrected and explained. One was more likely to get yelled at and whacked on the behind . . . a confusing message, as we'd been encouraged to "make" own play. Everybody else was occupied with the busy labor of self-sustenance.

That included raising chickens for eggs abd meat. Vegetables came from our own garden. My brother and

I were expected to keep it weed free, so I had lots of opportunity to study leaves and bugs. From our garden harvest, my mother canned what we didn't use fresh. In the fall, we gathered peach and strawberries at "pick your own" farms, grapes and blackberries from the fields. With these she added to the bounty on the shelves in our cellar . . . preserves! Along with the vegetables, we had enough to last till the next summer, when it was time to start all over again. As we grew older, the care of our chickens was added to our duties. I collected eggs, but only if the nests weren't occupied. My brother kept the barn clean. On Saturday the feed man would come, in an open-backed truck that seemed to carry the rainbow. Cracked corn and mash had been bagged in fifty-to one-hundred-pound sacks made out of cotton printed fabrics . . . calicoes, checks, stripes and flowers . . . enough cloth for a skirt or blouse, or an eight-year-old's dress. "No, not that one; those two, way down at the bottom." This proved to be more popular with sewing mothers than the feed man! There were plain white bags, too. These could be bleached free of lettering and sewn together for pillowcases and sheets. This was a part of the efficient life-style that was common where we lived in the forties. The pride of doing it well prevailed.

School brought pleasures and problems to me. Our teachers, none of whom were Hungarian, favored the few students who weren't with privileges and attention. They let the rest of us know that we were, somehow, inferior. If that wasn't bad enough, I had the misfortune of being left-handed, considered a fault at that time and meant to be corrected. I'd be sent to the back of the class to practice O's with my right hand, outcast from the group learning perfect penmanship. To this day, I half-write, mostly print. An advantage of this punishment came much later. One of my freelance jobs was painting decorative murals for a commercial interior decorator. He designed showrooms for accessory manufacturers in the garment district of Manhattan. My work began when the space was almost finished, bringing me an audience of tenants anxious to move in. Working on a vertical with an outstretched arm is tiring. I credit my unhappy grade school exercises with being able to switch hands and continue painting. My viewer's reactions were more positive than former classmates' taunts. During the last two years in grade school, we had a drawing class! An art teacher traveled to all of the surrounding town schools. She came to ours twice a month. We spent winters at the windows, drawing street scenes. In the spring we would be sent out to fill the mop pails with flowers picked from the roadsides and reluctant gardens. To draw this was an easy effort for me, and I finished too soon, volunteering my assistance to nearby classmates who didn't like to draw. This was managed without notice, until our work was hung in front of the class. "Why do so many of these pictures look alike, Cynthia Szekeres?" My creative appetite won no sympathy.

Twice a month a music teacher came to our school. She introduced us to opera. We learned Bizet's *Carmen* and Gounod's *Faust,* the story, the dialogue, and the musical score. Miracle of miracles, when we had mastered each one, we were bussed to the matinee performance at the Metropolitan Opera House in New York City (two hours away). The beauty of sounds, sights, costumes, and atmosphere was overwhelming! Here was my first witnessed illustrated tale, not from the books I read, with too few, too meager pictures, but the opera! That's when life really began for me. I saw what inspiration and talent could achieve . . . something more than I had ever known. I knew why I was different. I could and would go beyond mop pails filled with goldenrod and lilacs, teachers who looked down at my kind. I already had my focus, art. But here, I knew that there was more to learn and to aspire for.

When it came, in 1941, the war was vague and far away . . . just a headline of ships sunk, battles fought. However, as Bridgeport's factories took on night shifts, making parts for planes and other wartime supplies, air raid practice began in earnest. In school, at the sound of the alarm, we would huddle under our desks; at home, the place to be was under the kitchen table. I worried about Hitler and Mussolini; all of the kids in my school did. We would plot their downfall for that day when they surely would come seek us out. Why, I didn't know.

"With Gramma," 1937

During the war years, I came of age to handle a two-wheeled bike. "Victory bikes" were all that were available. They required less use of precious metals and rubber and were made skinnier than the usual models; they were similar to today's ten-speeds, except for the gears.

Getting my bike was equivalent to sprouting wings! Now, old enough to pick and choose my friends, I could explore with them the places we liked. Nearby Fairfield University, in the forties, had acres of groomed rolling hills, ponds, and idyllic landscaping. I felt compelled to draw what I saw. Long Island Sound, with beaches only two miles away, or the undeveloped pine forest near the parkway, these were both good places to bike with a peanut butter and jelly sandwich and the urge to sit and contemplate the world at large.The special thing made accessible to me, with a bike, was the library. The books weren't particularly memorable; I had no guide, even in high school, where factory workers' kids were singled out for the less challenging classes. At the library, a spot of color in the corner of the room caught my eye . . . a low, round table covered with picture books. I had two of my own from younger years, but was surprised that so many more existed. The idea of words with pictures set well with me, as words have always formed pictures in my head. I studied all of these books and more, as I became a baby-sitter in high school, then a playground instructor during summer vacations from art school. I enjoyed young children and had an empathy for their curiosities and discoveries. This was to be a permanent, committed connection, a bond. I would carry the convictions from this experience into art school and beyond.

Why I was accepted, I'll never know, but from 1951 to 1954 I attended Pratt Institute in Brooklyn, New York. What a shock . . . students with a more sophisticated education, some came from art high schools, some had years of private instruction. I felt tossed to the wolves! All that I brought with me were stamina and determination. That meant something, because by the end of the first term, one third of the freshman class had left. This was hard work! I had many memorable and nurturing teachers who helped me to hang in there. One was Richard Lindner, who taught me to "see," retain details in my memory, draw from my feelings and experience, and define my point of view. I thrived on his encouragement. I was learning to speak through pictures Once again, I had wings!'

It was a fruitful time at Pratt. Some notable illustrators were also students at that time: Arnold Lobel, his future wife, Anita Kempler, and Tomie de Paola. Tomie was a good friend. To me, his most praiseworthy accomplishment (not in his books) was introducing me to Gennaro "Jerry" Prozzo, a fellow artist whom I came to love.

Jerry worked at night in the post office. He painted and etched during the day. I was amused by the thought that someone really had asked me to "come up and see my etchings." Because of his work schedule, our dating

"My father, mother, brother, and me, in 1938"

was during the daytime, trips to museums and the Central Park Zoo, where we each filled sketchbooks with pictures of animals. I drew the children who watched them.

Graduating from Pratt in 1954, I was armed with a portfolio crammed with proof that I could render the alphabet in a flawed Caslon; utilize scratchboard, pen and ink, watercolors, and gouache; and imitate David Stone Martin, Ben Shahn, and a variety of illustrators for adult works and advertising. Rounding this out were two books I had illustrated and written as class projects and some samples of the things I liked to draw. With the exception of my own drawings, this portfolio was a disaster . . . ill advised. After a few appointments of showing it to art directors, and a lot of good advice, I threw most of my samples away and spent my time filling another portfolio with samples of who I was and what I had to "say." Even so, the work that I was looking to do was only available to the more experienced. Freelance illustrating would have to wait. I needed to earn a living, bring in a weekly paycheck that would pay the bills.

My first job was with Timely Service, a display house in Brooklyn, New York. I painted and dressed motorized figures destined for holiday windows . . . too many Santa Clauses with fiberglass beards for a hot summer's work!

In 1955 I succeeded in getting a job in New York City with a very small ad agency, doing pasteups and mechanicals. A year of this then qualified me to become an assistant to the art director for a magazine . . . dare I say? . . . *True Confessions*.

I learned a lot about printing and production. I continued to show my portfolio, now methodically visiting every children's book publisher in the city. My interest in children, and enjoyment of speaking with pictures, gave me the incentive to want to do books. The details in nature that I always enjoyed should be a part of it; how, I wasn't certain. I visited libraries and began to read children's books again. A friend gifted me with an unillustrated copy of Kenneth Grahame's *The Wind in the Willows*. Wouldn't this be a joy to work on? How naive I was! When I found Ernest Shepard's, then Arthur Rackham's, version of this wonderful story, I was filled with pleasure by the beauty of their successes, and dismayed in realizing how far away I was from such an accomplishment. However, some publishers on seeing my work would say, "We really like it, come back when you have something published." ???????? Catch-22!

My work at the magazine didn't require the allotted time spent there each day, but there was an obligation to appear to be busy. I worked on more portfolio samples, concentrating on preschool boys and girls. Baby-sitting familiarities made this a comfortable choice. When developed, these characters were put through their paces . . . laughing, crying, tumbling over, running around. Some of these sketches were used on interoffice notes. Somebody sent them to the publisher of *Parents* magazine who also produced *Humpty Dumpty* magazine for children. The art director of *Humpty Dumpty* called and asked me to do a story! One story led to many, soon on a monthly basis. It was time to take the plunge and freelance.

Maintaining my stamina and determination, I lacked self-confidence. If you really put yourself in your work, to show it in a portfolio is much, I imagine, like flashing. One indifferent art director could wipe me out. I'd spend days in despair, with no creative juices, feeling worthless. The job market was booming then, 1957, and placement agencies were prolific. Discouraged, I went to one, ready to give up and find full-time pasteup work again. What I found was that such places can be very enthusiastic and full of praise for one with abilities to qualify for full-time work of any kind. This boost to my lagging ego was very invigorating! Since there were many of these offices, I must confess that whenever I was down, like some who in need seeks therapy, I would visit another job agency. It kept me going for quite a while. Saks Fifth Avenue needed a children's fashion illustrator. It wasn't *Wind in the Willows,* but I needed work. They liked the kids that I drew, except "they're a bit too rumpled . . . if you could comb their hair and clean them up. . ." I did this and was kept busy for three years, doing fashion ads for the *New York Times*. Children's clothing held little interest with me and for fun, when I could, I would surround them with animals and birds.

Other fashion work came along, then some advertising, window display, and the aforementioned murals. I continued to submit my work to publishers.

*

In 1958 Jerry Prozzo and I were married. He became the occasional boost that I needed, guiding and encouraging me. More than that, marriage was a wonderful thing. I was nurtured and found fulfilling pleasure in being able to nurture. Every day was like Sunday, the best of times! We never stopped visiting museums and zoos. I was beginning to enjoy drawing animals more than people. This was probably due to being required to clean up my rumpled characters.One day in 1959, Doubleday publishers called me! They had been keeping a file of my Saks Fifth Avenue ads and wanted me to illustrate a book that they thought my work would be suitable for. It was *New Shoes* by Sam Vaughan, a story about a little girl who was going to get new shoes. Great! One of my weaknesses was feet. But I managed with high spirits, as good things were to come in clumps . . . I was pregnant! I became a children's book illustrator and a mother at the same time. Marco Prozzo was born on April 15, 1960. There was an advantage here: I never knew what it was like not to handle two things (motherhood and books) at the same time.

I just did it, with less sleep, and less time than I would have preferred for books; parenting was priority. Doing a book is a lot like being pregnant. You nurture it for months and, suddenly, it's on its own.

Marco grew quickly into a wonderful little boy. By his first birthday he was talking in sentences! The deceptive thing about a child under three with a considerable vocabulary is that you assume that he can reason, having the words and all. We became a very verbal family. We learned from him, and he from us. Baby books didn't cover this. An extra measure of patience had to be developed by all parties. He especially loved books, and we brought them home from the library by the shopping bagful. Marco was inspired to make up his own stories. These he would dictate to his father every night. I wish that we still had them. Living in a six-room railroad flat with one (count, one!) small closet, we did succeed in holding on to favorite toys, drawings, and books. Marco was a joy. Every day was filled with learning and wondering. He is thirty-one years old now, and his brother is going on twenty-nine, but whenever I write or illustrate I always have one of them on each knee, as preschool siblings, showing me the way.

One book led to another, and I didn't have to show my portfolio anymore. An abundance of children's books were being published in the sixties. This gave opportunity to a novice like me to accumulate experience, grow, and develop. Some manuscripts lacked strength and focus. Not the choicest of projects, these

The author in high school, 1948

were allotted to me. The illustrations had to give the story what it lacked, glue the pieces together, provide a clarity. Reviews were an extra reward, after these efforts: "The story is weak, but the illustrations serve it well."

Jerry became an art teacher in the parochial schools of Brooklyn, grammar schools, high schools. He also taught adult night classes. We explored the creative possibilities with children together. I helped him to plan classes and he continued to encourage and guide me through the forming of my own style. In the beginning, I never thought that I had one; as I look back, it was with me all along. Illustrating is communicating. To do it successfully, one needs strong convictions, an empathy and understanding of one's audience, the ability to take criticism and direction (heeding the perspective of others and knowing when it's right), something to give, and the need to give it. Mix this all up and put it forth with clarity and a distinctive but honest (not manipulated) point of view . . . Jerry helped me to do this. He still does!

Jerry exceeded in the challenge of parenting and maintaining careers. Concentrating his creative energies on etching, he exhibited and sold work in area shows and local galleries. A hands-on father, he did diapering, bathing, walking the floor or mopping it; we shared

alike.September 2, 1962, our son Christopher was born. I was just finishing the art for a reprint of Marjorie Flack's *Walter, the Lazy Mouse,* for Doubleday. The almost-completed cover was brought with me to the hospital. When we decided on his name, I turned the art upside down and rendered "Christopher" into the grass. Any book that I finished and signed during pregnancy has a plus after my name, as I was more than myself at the time.

Christopher was a happy, enjoyable baby, too. As he grew, it was apparent that he had preferences and interests unlike those of his brother. Not as verbal, he was dexterous and enjoyed using his hands, making things. How fascinating! I had thought that babies were all alike. Watching him showed me that each was a unique human being. Parents shouldn't try to bend or mold babies to what they could be. Loving our children, we are happily obliged to guide them along their chosen ways, pick them up when they fall, show them, tell them, and be there for them always.

Our sons did have in common a voracious curiosity about everything, hearty appetites for facts. We enthusiastically accommodated them, with the knowledge we could glean, the knowledge that they wanted . . . "No, they aren't just 'choo-choo' trains, that one's an open-topped hopper. Here comes a tank car, a refrigerator car, and there's the caboose!" "This is a beetle . . . it has six legs. See, this spider has eight!" I cannot believe what I allowed myself to pick up and touch for the sake of their interests!

From our fifth-floor walk-up in Brooklyn Heights, we made daily outings to a playground half a mile from home. It overlooked lower Manhattan and the Statue of Liberty, which our sons were in the habit of "waving back" at. We strolled on a promenade above ships in port and a network of railroad cars moving goods. On weekends we explored Prospect Park, Central Park, the zoos, and all of the museums.

Christopher was barely two and Marco was four when we first visited the Museum of Natural History. They had a general knowledge of the anatomy of living beings and their skeletal structures, and a smattering of the fact that there was a "long ago," when things were different. While they are very popular today, in the sixties no one paid attention to the dinosaurs. Marco ran ahead of us, into the main exhibit hall where "they" were . . . Christopher was close behind. I still hold the vision of two small boys, awestruck by what they saw. We stayed in that room for an hour, inspecting everything. Other special events instilled in my mind the gestures and expressions of their wonder. All of the feelings our sons experienced, which showed in their gestures and facial expressions, reappear in my work. . . laughing, crying, running, and jumping through the pages; they are there.

*

The largest room in our apartment became our combined studios plus substitute backyard. We worked, the boys played, and their friends joined them. As my work became more noticeable to them, they complained, "Why can't we draw like that?" I explained that I had years of practice; however, what I had lost was the ability to draw as freely and beautifully as youngsters of their age and, maybe, they could help me. Most of the stories I illustrated involved young ones in a home environment. It stands to reason these homes would have pictures they drew hanging on the walls. When I had completed an interior illustration, I drew two blank pieces of paper taped to the walls of the interior . . . three, if a friend was over. I sat them down with the illustration and colored pencils and asked them to do what I couldn't: a child's drawing on those pieces of paper. There was much pride and concentration in these efforts! One of my favorite "assisted works" is in *What Can You Do without a Place to Play?* I rendered a brick wall and requested some graffiti on it from Marco and his friends who were busy playing Monopoly on the floor near my desk. They did a wonderful' job!Until the late sixties, my finished work was done in pen and ink. It was easier to reproduce and I had reasoned that finished drawings "are supposed to be in ink." Polly Berends, a Random House editor, gave me a story by Adelaide Holl, *Moon Mouse.* I brought her a few pencil

sketches of the possible character and she suggested that the finishes should be in pencil. I found that my work is fuller and richer in pencil. As a "lefty" I am more in control, not working to accommodate wet ink under a busy hand. I had my doubts about pencil finishes, but she saw me through the work with much encouragement, and I put my pens away for good! Another suggestion that she made was to concentrate on what it was that I did best: anthropomorphic animals. I have never regretted following that advice. All of my work, to this point, had been black and white with overlays of one to three colors. In the projects that followed, I worked in full color. This was done in a multimedia way. I would draw the finish in pencil, paint over it in gouache, and add finishing touches in colored pencil. This method suits me well and I am content to maintain it.

My first full-color works were stories by Patsy Scarry; *Little Richard* (who was a rabbit child) and *Waggy* (a toy dog). These were both successful and led to sequels. The publisher of this series was Albert Leventhal at American Heritage. When I had finished, he asked me what else I would like to do. I told him about calendar ideas I had, defining each month with an anthropomorphic illustration. No sketches, written propos-

Cyndy in her studio, 1981

als, executive meetings considered. He told me to go ahead and do it! There is a great rush of confidence and competence that surges forth after such a remark, implying trust and faith. It can go a long way, and it did. The calendar was well received and I continued to do one, yearly, for five years. The last was for our country's bicentennial year, 1976. History books for the young never helped them understand the very basic differences of time past. I attempted to remedy that by showing life as it was two hundred years ago . . . what homes were like, food, clothing, playtime, light and heat, personal grooming. I did this with my usual animal characters; as I look back at it, not the right choice. These life-style differences were a human reality and should have been shown as such. But this calendar did well, too, in spite of my misgivings. Then, American Heritage merged with McGraw-Hill. I was told the calendar was book-worthy and that I should put myself to the task of writing one!

I had never considered myself a writer. Writers had to be qualified, have degrees, work their way up through "writing type" jobs, didn't they? I felt like I had cotton in my mouth. Words wouldn't come. I shouldn't be allowed to do this, should I? The facts had already been gathered for the calendar and only needed to be sorted and clarified in simple, sequential order. With a lot of help from my friends, I overcame self-doubt. *Long Ago* was published in 1977. In the seventies, I had been accepted as a client of Curtis Brown, Ltd., and Marilyn Marlow became my agent. It is difficult and confusing to speak up for needs and rights when you barely know what they are, even if you indeed deserve them. It was a relief and of great benefit to me when Marilyn took on this task. She has been most supportive and effective. Book work didn't always consume all of my time, so the need for income prompted me to illustrate for children's magazines and greeting cards. The cards gave me the opportunity to develop and experiment with all kinds of animal characters. I enjoyed creating single, simple thoughts with them.

Our family made the move to bucolic Vermont in 1974. Jerry and I had visited the state when we were first married and vowed we would someday make it our home. We have a house in the woods, surrounded by research! Our sons have grown and are gone. Marco is a very talented photographer. He gravitated back to New York City. One of his jobs had him on the scaffold surrounding the face on the Statue of Liberty when she was being cleaned. He got to kiss on the lips the lady he waved to as a child! Christopher is an electrical engineer and computer programmer. We are exceedingly proud of both boys/men. Chris lives nearby with his wife Monica, and their new baby girl, our first grandchild She is old enough to stop chewing on page corners and look at the pictures in a book. It is fulfilling to give her my books, but, I must admit, I am most preoccupied in enjoying her as another special little life in our family to delight and to wonder over. Gramma's joy, Nina Prozzo!

"Big jump—1990—Jerry and I"

Nineteen eighty-one was the start of my commitment to work exclusively for Western Publishing. Each year, for ten years, I have continued to reaffirm this. I explore my own ideas, try a variety of formats, and become involved with promotion. In 1984 I began a series of twelve board books for the very young. I became an author/artist in earnest, as I also wrote them. Years and books go by like constant "pregnancies." I am comfortable with the convictions and the inspirations I have gleaned in all of this time. Selma Lanes, my editor, gives me perspective and constructive criticism . . . and challenges.

Nina, and any child that I look at, memories of my own childhood, they all play a part in the books that lie ahead of me. It is, indeed, all right to be me! The size and the allover fuzziness of a very young animal are actual features; the roly-poly proportions are, too. The visual message is: very young, almost infant animal child . . . however, another translation is "cute." The latter is never my intention when I draw; is simply a part of what happens. Anthropomorphism serves a noble cause. A blond child is always who it appears to be, the features and colorings are there, and final. A mouse in overalls can be every child, any kind . . . big, small, dark, light. This allows a visual way of saying, "This book is for you, reader . . . about you." There are no specific definitions that will prevent the young reader from becoming the character.Over the years all of what is me has found its my into my work . . . the awareness of Nature's beauty in a tulip bed, the pride-and-pleasure work ethic that my grandmother enjoyed, the response of children as I sat and read to them, teachers, editors, and friends that kept me going . . . most of all a loving family that continues to grow.

I have enjoyed illustrating because there is much to explore and share, and I am compelled to do this. My few experiences with writing make the quest all the richer. Aspiring authors and illustrators should consider the purpose they wish to serve. A means to earn a living is not enough; find reason and inspiration!

Cyndy Szekeres contributed the following update to *SATA* in 2005: Illustration and motherhood came to me simultaneously. I was often asked, "How do you manage parenting and a career?"

The answer is, you do what you have to do.

I've nursed an infant, held in my right arm, as I drew with my left hand. I rocked a cradle with my big toe, as I drew with my left hand. As my happy son crawled around the room, I sat, undisturbed, in his playpen . . . where I drew with my left hand.

Time goes by. Now two sons in school come home with latchkey friends. They spend hours playing monopoly, managing hotels and buying property. Where does this take place? Not on the kitchen table or in their rooms, but in our studio that used to be a living room, on the floor nestled around me at my desk, where I drew with my left hand.

A problem with two young sons observing my work: "Wow! Why can't we draw like you do? Our pictures are no good!"

"Oh yes they are!" I say. "The very best work is done by children who don't try to copy or please, but focus on what they see and feel."

"You have to help me."

In my illustrations, in an animals' home, I drew papers taped to the walls, blank papers. "I cannot do childrens' drawings as well as children can. You do it!" . . . and they did, in every book thereafter, until, now grown, my grandchildren do it, with pride and joy and healthy esteem.

I do preliminary sketches on tracing paper. As it is transparent, I can layer bits and pieces, changing positions and sizes of things. Better yet, on a character's

"Marco, his dog Jax, Jerry, me, Monica holding Nina, and Chris," 1991

"Me and my wonderful grandchildren, Emmett and Nina Prozzo"

of feelings and thoughts coming to life. The anthropomorphic world, much alive in my head, is filled with events and characters that are constantly evolving and changing. Sometimes, this world spills over, out of my head, down my arm and on to paper and I watch this happen, as an observer, not a creator.

Emotions are profound events. Laughing or crying will dictate gesture, posture and expression . . . in images or words. Staying true to the animal, but applying enough human qualities to understand special feelings and responses in each personality . . . this is what I work for.

Often when I meet illustrators, I observe that they resemble the characters that they draw. Do they make faces in the mirror, as I do? . . . or does the daily routine of face-washing, hair-combing, tooth-brushing imprint their particular proportions into each creature they create?

*

I have a big, bright studio filled with books and collectibles (doll chairs and mice) and work tables that I share with Nina and Emmett, our grandchildren. They each have their special place in which to create. I continue to multitask, now with words . . . calling out some color-mixing thoughts to Emmett and cajoling Nina, who is fussing over an image. With my foot, I stroke our dog, Frieda Fuzzypaws, who wants a belly rub . . . as I draw with my left hand.

Writing my own stories, I still find it hard, after dozens of books, to call myself an author. While inspired by activities in the anthropomorphic world in my head, as words tumble out and sentences form, I am haunted with guilt . . . I am not qualified to do this . . . I only studied art. No degrees in writing or litera-

face, I can rearrange and reposition the eyes, try different expressions, lengthen or shorten arms and legs. I top my decision with a clean sheet and draw the adjusted finish. I may redraw and rearrange such a choice a dozen or more times before transferring the accepted image to illustration board. I then paint with gouache, an opaque water color; use colored pencils, pastels . . . anything that gets me where I want to go.

When our sons had grown and gone, we became "empty nesters" and work time then involved me and our cat. Hot summer evenings were spent at my desk, a new, larger one—big enough for me, my work and a browsing cat.

The lamp light attracts a small cloud of insects. One of them senses the puddles of water (paint) and drops down for a drink. With a fat, wet brush I surround him with a liquid ring. He forgets he can fly and checks the circle for a walk-away opening. The cat then decides it is time for batting practice and I must reclaim my work.

Now, the cat is in kitty heaven and we have a small dog who insists on her share of attention and affection. As for the insects, a few unfortunates have expired, drying in the paint, to become a permanent part of my illustrations. I can imagine a tiny insect ghost exclaiming, "I've been published!"

Soon the image wasn't enough. I was encouraged to write what I illustrate, and with the help and encouragement of friends and editors, I eventually found the word to be a wonderful new paint brush.

Random thoughts:

"Where do you get your ideas?" . . . A popular question.

An idea is not like an ingredient for a cake. It cannot be found on a shelf in the marketplace, nor will it show up in a basket, behind a magic door. It is a sense

Cyndy Szekeres

ture . . . where do I get the colossal nerve to write? Then, I look down at the page, see the need to embellish or clarify, and I become engrossed with appetizing thoughts and everything is all right.

This is not much different than illustrating—sketches, layers, over and over again, until it comes to life. I read my efforts out loud. If I stumble over a word or a phrase, I know something is wrong—it needs tweaking. As with images, I redo the words, again and again and again, until it reads smoothly.

So, author/illustrator. . . . Here I am . . . my books, my book. It's like having a baby! "Morning sickness" most definitely! "I can not do this." "Oh, yes I can!" "Blegh!" Next, the first kick. "It's alive!" Then, labor, much labor, "aagh!" and finally birth!

How awesome to see the book all put together. What fell out of my head is now pictures and words on pages, a cover. First step: reviews. "Please, if you don't approve of anthropomorphic animals, don't review my book. It isn't fair." After only one of those (ouch!), now comes praise or constructive critiques. "Hey, that's my kid you're talking about!" Next comes the response from the reader transformed into sales. Then, almost immediately, I'm "pregnant" again!

Author/illustrator . . . first the pen . . . then the brush . . . in my left hand.

T

TUNNELL, Michael
See TUNNELL, Michael O('Grady)

*   *   *

TUNNELL, Michael O('Grady) 1950-
(Michael Tunnell)

Personal

Born June 14, 1950, in Nocona, TX; son of Billie Bob Tunnell and Mauzi Chupp; legally adopted by Grady and Trudy Chupp (maternal grandparents); married Glenna Maurine Henry (a librarian); children: Heather Anne Wall, Holly Lyne Argyle, Nikki Leigh, Quincy Michael. *Education:* University of Utah, B.A., 1973; Utah State University, M.Ed., 1978; Brigham Young University, Ed.D., 1986. *Politics:* Democrat. *Religion:* Church of Jesus Christ of Latter-day Saints (Mormon). *Hobbies and other interests:* Reading, photography, travel.

Addresses

Home—579 North 900 East, Orem, UT 84097. *Office*—210K McKay Building, Brigham Young University, Provo, UT 84602. *E-mail*—mike_tunnell@byu.edu.

Career

Uintah School District, Vernal, UT, sixth-grade teacher, 1973-75; Wasatch School District, Heber City, UT, teacher and library/media specialist, 1976-85; Arkansas State University, Jonesboro, assistant professor of elementary education, 1985-87; Northern Illinois University, DeKalb, assistant professor of language arts and children's literature, 1987-92; Brigham Young University, Provo, UT, associate professor of elementary education, 1992-97, professor of teacher education, 1997—. Children's book writer, 1993—.

Michael O. Tunnell

Member

International Reading Association, American Library Association (member of Newbery Award committee, 1990), National Council of Teachers of English (board member and treasurer, Children's Literature Assembly, 1992-94; member of board of directors and chair of Poetry Award committee, 1995-97), Society of Children's Book Writers and Illustrators.

Awards, Honors

American Booksellers Pick of the Lists designation, and Association of Mormon Letters Award in Children's Literature, both 1993, both for *Chinook!* and *Beauty and the Beastly Children;* Association of Mormon Letters Award in Children's Literature, 1993, for *The Joke's on George;* Parents' Choice Gold award, and Cooperative Children's Book Center Choice, both 1996, Notable Children's Trade Book in the Field of Social Studies, Children's Book Council/National Council for the Social Studies (CBC/NCSS), New York Public Library Books for the Teen Age listee, Distinguished Title designation, Public Library Association, Notable Books for a Global Society designation, International Reading Association (IRA), Notable Books in the Language Arts designation, National Council of Teachers of English (NCTE), and Nonfiction Honor listee, *Voice of Youth Advocates,* all 1997, and Carter G. Woodson Honor Book Award, NCSS, Utah Children's Informational Book Award Master List, 1997-98, and Maine Student Book Award Master List, all 1997-98, all for *The Children of Topaz;* Parents' Choice Gold Award, and *Child* magazine Best Book designation, both 1997, Notable Children's Trade Book in the Field of Social Studies Selector's Choice designation, CBC/NCSS, Notable Children's Book designation, American Library Association, Notable Books in the Language Arts, NCTE, Teachers' Choice designation, IRA, *Parent's Guide* Outstanding Achievement in Picture Books designation, and *Storytelling World* Honor Award, all 1998, and numerous state Master List inclusions, 1997-2001 all for *Mailing May;* Parent's Choice Recommended Book designation, 1998, and Utah Children's Book Award Master List inclusion, 1999, both for *School Spirits;* Notable Books for a Global Society designation, International Reading Association, 2002, for *Brothers in Valor;* Parent's Choice Recommended Book designation, 2004, for *Wishing Moon.*

Writings

FOR CHILDREN

Chinook!, illustrated by Barry Boot, Tambourine (New York, NY), 1993.

The Joke's on George, illustrated by Kathy Osborn, Tambourine (New York, NY), 1993.

Beauty and the Beastly Children, illustrated by John Emil Cymerman, Tambourine (New York, NY), 1993.

(With George W. Chilcoat) *The Children of Topaz: The Story of a Japanese-American Internment Camp Based on a Classroom Diary,* Holiday House (New York, NY), 1996.

Mailing May, illustrated by Ted Rand, Greenwillow (New York, NY), 1997.

School Spirits, Holiday House (New York, NY), 1997.

Halloween Pie, illustrated by Kevin O'Malley, Lothrop, Lee, & Shepard (New York, NY), 1999.

Brothers in Valor: A Story of Resistance, Holiday House (New York, NY), 2001.

Wishing Moon, Dutton (New York, NY), 2004.

OTHER

The Prydain Companion: A Reference Guide to Lloyd Alexander's Prydain Chronicles, Greenwood (Westport, CT), 1989, revised, Holt (New York, NY), 2003.

(With James S. Jacobs) *Lloyd Alexander: A Bio-Bibliography,* Greenwood (Westport, CT), 1992.

(Editor with Richard Ammon) *The Story of Ourselves: Teaching History through Children's Literature,* Heinemann (London, England), 1993.

(With James S. Jacobs) *Children's Literature, Briefly,* Merrill/Prentice Hall (New York, NY), 1996, revised edition, Merrill/Prentice Hall (Upper Saddle River, NJ), 2004.

(With Daniel L. Darrigan and James S. Jacobs) *Children's Literature: Engaging Teachers and Children in Good Books,* Merrill/Prentice Hall (Upper Saddle River, NJ), 2002.

Contributor of articles and short stories to children's magazines, including *Cricket* and *Spider,* and of chapters and articles to professional books and journals, including *Reading Teacher, Language Arts, Horn Book, Children's Literature in Education, School Library Journal, Reading Improvement, Book Links, Social Education, New Advocate,* and *Journal of Educational Research.* Book reviewer for several publications, including *Booklist.*

Sidelights

Michael O. Tunnell is the author of several picture books, including the award-winning *Mailing May,* and of nonfiction works and novels for middle-grade readers. A professor of children's literature at Brigham Young University, Tunnell thoroughly knows the terrain of which he writes, yet when he came to creating his own stories and novels, it was as if he were in uncharted territory. "I discovered critiquing someone else's work is an entirely different process than creating your own stories," Tunnell once told *Something about the Author (SATA).* "Perhaps I was simply too close to my own work, which made applying what I thought I knew about quality literature difficult. In any case, I had a lot to learn (and the learning has just begun!) about the creative process. I guess writers are born perhaps more than they are made. (I feel the same way about teachers.) So, part of the challenge has been to find and cultivate any spark of literary creativity with which I might have been blessed."

Born in Texas, Tunnell was raised in Canada by his grandparents, and his love affair with books started at a young age. "My grandmother . . . would read to me every day," the author recalled. "Fairy tales, comic books, and wonderful picture books like *Caps for Sale* and *Mike Mulligan and His Steam Shovel.* I soon discovered that books were the world's best teachers and entertainers. I grew up wanting to spend my life working with books." He was at college studying for a career in law when he rediscovered this early commitment. Working part-time for an automobile dealer in Salt Lake City, Utah, he was sent to deliver a car to a customer at a nearby elementary school. "The second I walked through the school doors, I was flooded with the strangest feelings. I remembered my favorite books and my magical childhood years. The next day I changed my major to education. Since then, I've completed several degrees, all relating to reading, children's literature, and teaching." A classroom teacher and media specialist for several years, Tunnell eventually wound up teaching children's literature at the university level.

Tunnell's love of books and language encouraged him to try writing short stories as a child, and in his twenties he wrote his first novel, one that was rejected by over twenty publishers. Tunnell then channeled his literary efforts into educational books and journal articles, though his desire to write children's books remained strong.

In 1993 he published *Chinook!,* his first picture book. For the work, Tunnell harkened back to some of his own childhood memories of growing up in Alberta, Canada, and the warm, dry wind—the chinook—that blows off the eastern slopes of the Rocky Mountains. The result is a book of original tales narrated by old-timer Andrew Delaney McFadden to two ice-skating children. Out ice-fishing, McFadden pulls the children into his boat that sits on top of the ice, warning them about the possible dangers of being stranded far from shore should the weather suddenly change because of a chinook. He relates the story of one such chinook which swept down in 1888 and quickly melted the ice, explaining why he prefers to sit in a boat while ice fishing on a frozen lake. Other tales follow as McFadden gives these newly arrived siblings a taste for Western weather: tomato seeds sprouting in February; apple blossoms and fruit in winter. A cautionary tale, *Chinook!* was dubbed a "fine picture-book debut with some nicely understated tall tales" by a *Kirkus Reviews* contributor. "Few tall tales focus so intently on weather," Deborah Abbott concluded in her *Booklist* review, "and this one, with its flamboyant shift from winter to summer, radiates a gentle warmth."

The Joke's on George, Tunnell's second picture book, again employs historical situations in an amusing manner. Taken from the eighteenth-century journals of Rembrandt Peale, the book deals with an incident involving Peale's father, painter and museum keeper Charles Willson Peale, and George Washington. Visiting Peale's Philadelphia museum, the president—renowned for his courtesy to all—is fooled by one of Peale's trompe l'oeil paintings. He politely bows to two children on a staircase, but oddly they make no reaction, no response. Only when the children in question turn out to be paintings on a wall does President Wash-

ington realize that he has been fooled. Deborah Stevenson, writing in the *Bulletin of the Center for Children's Books,* called *The Joke's on George* "an entertaining tale that shows Washington in a different light," and added that the book could lead to "some entertaining artistic discussions." A critic in *Kirkus Reviews* described the book as "a delightful vignette" and a "handsome, entertaining glimpse of times past."

Tunnell turns a traditional fairy tale on its head with his what-if rendition of the Beauty and the Beast. In *Beauty and the Beastly Children* he imagines what might have happened after Beauty married the Beast. Beast—aka Auguste—regresses to ale drinking and darts while Beauty gives birth to rather horrid beast-like triplets. Auguste finally accepts his parental responsibilities, however, and helps to bring the unruly children around. When he does, the witch lifts the spell on the children, and finally there is a "a happily ever after" ending. Tunnell related his tale in "colloquial, sassy prose," according to Susan Hepler in *School Library Journal.*

Returning to history for inspiration, Tunnell relates the actual story of a girl sent by parcel post to visit her grandmother in 1914. With a mailing label and fifty-three cents worth of stamps stuck to her coat—she is luckily under the fifty-pound parcel-post limit—May sets off one morning for her visit. Her cousin Leonard mans the train's mail car, so she accompanies him on the journey. Seventy-five miles later, having passed through the mountainous terrain of Idaho, she arrives safely at her grandmother's.

Mailing May earned high critical praise. Carolyn Phelan noted in *Booklist:* "Told in the first person from May's point of view, the story has a folksy quality and a ring of truth that will hold children's interest beyond the central anecdote." Applauding the "childlike understated quality" of Tunnell's story, Betsy Groban observed in the *New York Times Book Review* that *Mailing May* "is a heartwarming period piece based on a true incident, lovingly told, beautifully illustrated and extremely well produced in an oversized format." Pat Mathews concluded in the *Bulletin of the Center for Children's Books* that "May tells the story of her bygone journey with homespun perfection, so stamp this one 'First Class' and make a special delivery to a story-time in your area."

Determined to achieve historical accuracy when compiling *Mailing May,* Tunnell not only rode on the rail line which May followed, and but also found and interviewed May's son—May herself died in 1987. Additionally, he used a two-page account of the trip written by May's cousin Leonard, the postal clerk in charge of the girl on her trip in February of 1914. However, for his nonfiction book on Japanese-American internment during World War II, *The Children of Topaz,* the research was much more extensive. There was library work and also the tracking down of primary sources. "I was privileged to run on to the story of Lillian 'Anne'

Yamauchi Hori and her third-grade class, who were interned during World War II in the Japanese-American relocation camp at Topaz, Utah. These children and their young teacher appear in no history textbooks, yet they are the ones who experienced firsthand the fallout of decisions made by well-known personalities such as Franklin Delano Roosevelt. Their illustrated class diary, an integral part of *The Children of Topaz,* helps us see and feel the effects of war hysteria and prejudice on a personal level." Tunnell and his coauthor, George Chilcoat, located the widower of the teacher as well as several of the men who, as boys, had been interned in the camp and interviewed them for the book. Female students were harder to track down because of name changes with marriage. After publication of the book however, several of the other former students contacted Tunnell and in 1996 a reunion of the class was held in Berkeley, California. "Fifteen of the twenty-three Japanese-American students, now in their sixties, attended," Tunnell recalled to *SATA.* "It was one of the most moving experiences of my life."

About a third of the class diary was used in *The Children of Topaz;* each entry is further annotated by "well-researched commentaries explaining the children's allusions, expanding upon the diary text, and placing events in socio-historical perspective," according to reviewer John Philbrook in *School Library Journal.* "Here readers are exposed to nine-year-olds writing as it happened," Philbrook concluded. *Booklist*'s Hazel Rochman noted that "the primary sources have a stark authority; it's the very ordinariness of the children's concerns that grabs you as they talk about baseball, school, becoming Scouts and Brownies." A critic in *Kirkus Reviews* commented that "Tunnell and Chilcoat provide a valuable, incisive, comprehensive text," while Elizabeth Bush concluded in a review for the *Bulletin of the Center for Children's Books* that "the ingenuous testimony left by Yamauchi's third-graders may make the Topaz story accessible to an audience slightly younger" than those for whom other such internment books have been written. Tunnell's first novel for young readers, *School Spirits,* likewise deals with history. Set in a small town in 1958, the book is a ghost story; its writing thus combined two of Tunnell's favorite themes: history and fantasy. *School Spirits* tells the story of Patrick, whose father has just become principal of Craven Hill School, a castle-like building and scene to the twentieth-century gothic tale Tunnell weaves. Though reluctant to move, Patrick quickly becomes involved in the new town, becoming friends with Nairen, the girl next door, and encountering the ghost of Barney Dawe, whose disappearance in 1920 has gone unexplained. Patrick and Nairen soon take up the investigation, which involves researching in the town library and time-traveling down a tube-like school fire escape. Molly S. Kinney observed in *School Library Journal* that "this fast-paced story" has "solid writing and doesn't rely on buckets of blood or hacked bodies to entice readers." Writing in *Booklist,* Susan Dove Lempke noted that "the 1958 setting is a change of pace from contemporary horror tales."

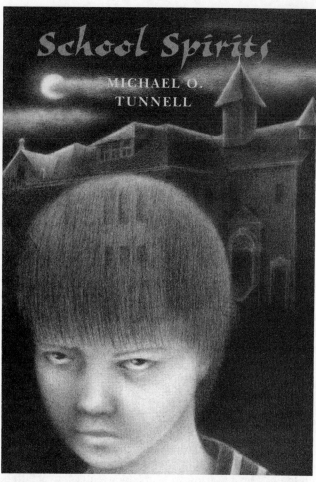

Tunnell's 1997 mystery centering around a schoolboy's disappearance finds friends Patrick and Narien determined to solve the decades old crime in the hopes that it will let a young ghost go to its rest. (Cover illustration by Barbara J. Roman.)

In Tunnell's 1999 picture book *Halloween Pie,* a group of frightening cemetery creatures, including a banshee, a ghost, a ghoul, a skeleton, a vampire, and a zombie, steal a freshly baked pumpkin pie from Old Witch's house. What they don't know is that Old Witch has cast a spell on the treat, and after the six fall asleep, they are transformed into the ingredients Old Witch needs to bake another pie. Though a *Publishers Weekly* reviewer felt that *Halloween Pie* "provides only tame surprises," *Booklist* critic Kay Weisman believed that the creatures "are just creepy enough to delight children who beg for a scary story."

Brothers in Valor: A Story of Resistance examines a little-known slice of history: the methods by which German youth actively opposed Adolf Hitler and the Nazi Party during the 1930s and 1940s. Based on a true story, the novel follows Rudi Ollenik, Helmuth Hubener, and Karl Schneider, three friends from the Mormon church in Hamburg who become increasingly disturbed by the persecution of the Jews. After war breaks out, Hubener illegally obtains a shortwave radio and the trio begin to monitor BBC broadcasts. They also create and distribute a series of flyers critical of Hitler's policies. In 1942 the boys are arrested, tortured, and put on trial; Hubener is executed, while the others receive prison sentences. In *Brothers in Valor* Tunnell "convincingly demonstrates the pervasiveness of Nazi propaganda," noted a contributor in *Publishers Weekly.* "The research, however, feels stitched together and the characters are underdeveloped, with the result that suspense never builds." Hazel Rochman, reviewing the work in *Booklist,* offered a contrasting opinion, stating that the author "does an excellent job of dramatizing the ordinariness of the boys, their teasing friendship and mounting terror, the sense of what it was like to be young at that time."

In 2003, Tunnell reworked his 1989 publication, *The Prydain Companion: A Reference Guide to Lloyd Alexander's Prydain Chronicles,* so that it would appeal to younger fans of the perennially popular novel series. In Alexander's foreword to the book, he calls Tunnell "a friendly guide who well knows the country and its inhabitants." Reviewing the book for *Voice of Youth Advocates,* Hillary Crew wrote that *The Prydain Companion* "should provide much pleasure and interest to Alexander fans and serve as a rich resource for discussions with young people and for those teaching and studying children's literature."

Tunnell's young-adult fantasy novel *Wishing Moon* was described as a "captivating original sequel to 'Aladdin'" by a *Kirkus Reviews* contributor. In the work, fourteen-year-old Aminah, an orphan who survives by begging on the streets of al-Kal'as, ventures to the royal palace to ask Princess Badr for work. The disdainful princess, the wife of Aladdin, responds by tossing an old lamp at Aminah's head, not recognizing that the lamp contains magical powers. Aminah learns how to summon the genie, who must grant her three wishes each time the moon is full, yet surprisingly Aminah uses the genie's powers to improve not only her own life but the lives of the poor. In time, Princess Badr realizes her mistake and uses every method at her disposal to recover the lamp, creating a perilous situation for Aminah. *Wishing Moon* received generally strong reviews. Claire Rosser, writing in *Kliatt,* praised the author's style, remarking, "The desert, the bazaars, the narrow streets are described vividly by Tunnell, to make an exotic story." *School Library Journal* contributor Miriam Lang Budin called the work "a satisfying fairy-tale elaboration," and *Booklist* reviewer Anne O'Malley applauded the "strong, suspenseful plot worthy of the Arabian Nights." In fact, Tunnell visited the Middle East and engaged in other sorts of research in order to accurately recreate the ninth-century Arab world in which this story is set.

Whether he is writing a picture book, an information book, or a novel, Tunnell approaches each project with enthusiasm. As he once told *SATA:* "I enjoy trying my hand at the various genres and formats of literature. The economy required by the picture-book format

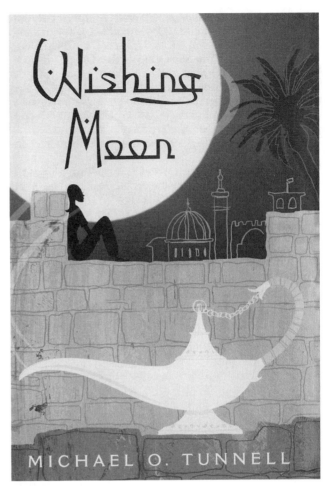

Aminah, a fourteen-year-old orphan, learns to trust the expression "Be careful what you wish for" after becoming the owner of a magic lamp that allows her to change her life in Tunnell's 2004 novel. (Cover illustration by Jo Tronc.)

makes that sort of writing a challenge. Naturally, non-fiction books demand careful attention to factual detail, but the biggest challenge is writing nonfiction with flair. . . . The novel, however, I find the most challenging. Writing novels requires sustained imaginative output unlike picture or informational books. Creating and developing believable characters who are doing things worth reading about for one hundred pages or more is difficult yet extremely fulfilling business."

Biographical and Critical Sources

PERIODICALS

Booklist, October 1, 1993, p. 349; August 15, 1993, Deborah Abbott, review of *Chinook!,* p. 1524; December 15, 1993; July, 1996, Hazel Rochman, review of *The Children of Topaz,* p. 1818; August, 1997, Carolyn Phelan, review of *Mailing May,* p. 1908; February 15, 1998, Susan Dove Lempke, review of *School Spirits,* p. 1012; September 15, 1999, Kay Weisman, review of *Halloween Pie,* p. 270; May 1, 2001, Hazel Rochman, review of *Brothers in Valor: A Story of Resistance*, p. 1676; August, 2004, Anne O'Malley, review of *Wishing Moon*, p. 1921; September 15, 2004, Jennifer Mattson, "You Say Genies, I Say Djinni," p. 233.

Bulletin of the Center for Children's Books, October, 1993, Deborah Stevenson, review of *The Joke's on George*, p. 60; September, 1996, Elizabeth Bush, review of *The Children of Topaz*, pp. 34-35; October, 1997, Pat Mathews, review of *Mailing May*, p. 69.

Horn Book, July-August, 1993, p. 451; September-October, 1997, p. 564.

Kirkus Reviews, February 15, 1993, review of *Chinook!*, p. 235; July 1, 1993, review of *The Joke's on George*, p. 867; December 15, 1995, review of *The Children of Topaz*, p. 1777; June 15, 1997, p. 958; May 15, 2004, review of *Wishing Moon*, p. 499.

Kliatt, May, 2004, Claire Rosser, review of *Wishing Moon*, p. 14.

New York Times Book Review, Betsy Groban, review of *Mailing May,* March 15, 1998, p. 24.

Publishers Weekly, March 15, 1993, p. 87; July 12, 1993, p. 80; June 9, 1997, p. 45; December 8, 1997, review of *School Spirits*, p. 72; September 27, 1999, review of *Halloween Pie*, p. 47; May 28, 2001, review of *Brothers in Valor*, p. 89.

School Library Journal, June, 1993, pp. 91-92; January, 1994, Susan Hepler, review of *Beauty and the Beastly Children*, p. 100; August, 1996, John Philbrook, review of *The Children of Topaz*, pp. 161-162; March, 1998, Molly S. Kinney, review of *School Spirits*, p. 224; July, 2004, Miriam Lang Budin, review of *Wishing Moon*, p. 113.

Voice of Youth Advocates, December, 1996, p. 292; August, 1997, p. 167.

W

WADSWORTH, Ginger 1945-

Personal
Born May 7, 1945, in San Diego, CA; daughter of Hal G. (a writer) and Dorothea A. (an art teacher) Evarts; married Bill Wadsworth (an accountant and financial advisor for an engineering firm), June 4, 1967; children: two sons. *Education:* University of California, Davis, B.A., 1967. *Politics:* Democrat. *Hobbies and other interests:* Gardening with California native plants, hiking, camping, bird watching, photography, travel, reading.

Addresses
Home and office—2 Fleetwood Court, Orinda, CA 94563-4004. *E-mail*—plumepal@aol.com.

Career
Elementary school teacher and teacher's aide in Walnut Creek and Orinda, CA, 1982-86; writer, 1986—. Former owner of a book store in Napa, CA. Active volunteer with local library.

Member
Society of Children's Book Writers and Illustrators, Authors Guild, Western Writers of America, Women Writing the West, Audubon Society, Nature Conservancy, Yosemite Association, John Burroughs Association, California Historical Society.

Ginger Wadsworth

Awards, Honors
Notable Children's Trade Book in the Field of Social Studies, National Council for the Social Studies/ Children's Book Council (NCSS/CBC), Best Book in Social Studies, Social Studies Librarians International (SSLI), and Distinguished Book designation, Association of Children's Librarians of Northern California, all 1990, all for *Julia Morgan, Architect of Dreams;* Nature Books for Young Readers selection, John Burroughs Association, 1992, for *John Muir, Wilderness Protector;* Best Book in Science (secondary), SSLI, 1992, for *Rachel Carson, Voice for the Earth;* Notable Children's Trade Book in the Field of Social Studies, NCSS/CBC, 1994, for *Along the Santa Fe Trail: Marion Russell's Own Story,* and 2004, for *Benjamin Banneker, Pioneering Scientist;* third-place award for illustrated nonfiction, New York Book Show, 1997, and Books for the Teen Age designation, New York Public Library, 1998, both for *John Burroughs, the Sage of Slabsides;* Spur Award for juvenile nonfiction, Western Writers of America,

Distinguished Book designation, Association of Children's Librarians of Northern California, Will Award finalist, Women Writing the West, and finalist for PEN Center Literary Award, all 2004, all for *Words West: Voices of Young Pioneers.*

Writings

JUVENILE BIOGRAPHIES

Julia Morgan, Architect of Dreams, Lerner Publications (Minneapolis, MN), 1990.

Rachel Carson, Voice for the Earth, Lerner Publications (Minneapolis, MN), 1992.

John Muir, Wilderness Protector, Lerner Publications (Minneapolis, MN), 1992.

(Adaptor) *Along the Santa Fe Trail: Marion Russell's Own Story,* illustrated by James Watling, Albert Whitman (Morton Grove, IL), 1993, published in *Explore, Invitations to Literacy,* Houghton (Boston, MA), 1996.

Susan Butcher, Sled Dog Racer, Lerner Publications (Minneapolis, MN), 1994.

Laura Ingalls Wilder: Storyteller of the Prairie, Lerner Publications (Minneapolis, MN), 1997.

John Burroughs, The Sage of Slabsides, Clarion Books (New York, NY), 1997.

Laura Ingalls Wilder ("On My Own" series), illustrated by Shelly O. Haas, Carolrhoda Books (Minneapolis, MN), 2000.

(Editor) *Words West: Voices of Young Pioneers,* Clarion Books (New York, NY), 2003.

Benjamin Banneker: Pioneering Scientist ("On My Own" series), illustrated by Craig Orback, Carolrhoda Books (Minneapolis, MN), 2003.

The Wright Brothers, Lerner Publications (Minneapolis, MN), 2004.

Cesar Chavez ("On My Own" series), Carolrhoda Books (Minneapolis, MN), 2005.

Annie Oakley, Lerner Publications (Minneapolis, MN), 2006.

Author's books have been translated into Japanese, Korean, Chinese, and Danish.

OTHER

Tomorrow Is Daddy's Birthday, illustrated by Maxie Chambliss, Caroline House/Boyds Mills Press (Honesdale, PA), 1994.

Giant Sequoia Trees, photographs by Frank J. Staub, Lerner Publications (Minneapolis, MN), 1995.

One on a Web: Counting Animals at Home, illustrated by James M. Needham, Charlesbridge (Watertown, MA), 1997.

Desert Discoveries, illustrated by John Carrozza, Charlesbridge (Watertown, MA), 1997.

Tundra Discoveries, illustrated by John Carrozza, Charlesbridge (Watertown, MA), 1999.

One Tiger Growls: A Counting Book of Animal Sounds, illustrated by James M. Needham, Charlesbridge (Watertown, MA), 1999.

River Discoveries, illustrated by Paul Kratter, Charlesbridge (Watertown, MA), 2002.

Wooly Mammoths, Carolrhoda Books (Minneapolis, MN), 2006.

Contributor to *Writers in the Kitchen,* compiled by Tricia Gardella, Boyds Mills Press, 1998; *Idiot's Guide to Publishing Children's Books,* Alpha Books, 2001; and *ABC's of Writing for Children.* Elizabeth Koehler-Pentacoff, compiler, Quill Driver Books, 2003.

Adaptations

Rachel Carson: Voice for the Earth was adapted as an audiobook, Audio Bookshelf, 1996.

Sidelights

Ginger Wadsworth is, as she has pointed out, "a third-generation writer." Not only was her father, Hal G. Evarts, Jr., a writer, but so was his father before him, and all three generations have sought to capture aspects of the American West in their prose. Biographies form the core of Wadsworth's published work, and most of these concern either prominent Western figures or environmentalists, and sometimes—as in the case of naturalist John Muir—both.

The subject of Wadsworth's first book, *Julia Morgan, Architect of Dreams,* is most famous for her design of Hearst Castle, the San Simeon, California, playground for newspaper magnate William Randolph Hearst and his many celebrity guests during the early twentieth century. This structure alone constituted the work of a lifetime—"Morgan devoted 27 years to creating a setting for [Hearst's] life," explained Cathy Simon in the *New York Times Book Review*—but Morgan also managed to design some seven hundred other buildings, ranging from churches to libraries to private residences. Working as she did in the early years of the twentieth century, Morgan was a ground-breaking figure for women in the field of architecture, but she did not tend to be outspoken about her abilities. In fact, she was reserved about disclosing the facts of her life, which may be why the first biography of her, Sara Holmes Boutelle's *Julia Morgan, Architect,* did not appear until 1988, some thirty years after Morgan's death. Wadsworth's book followed two years later, and distinguished itself as "a lively read," in the words of Deborah Stevenson in the *Bulletin of the Center for Children's Books.* "It should be an inspiration," wrote Rosilind von Au in *Appraisal,* "to young women who feel called to scientifically oriented careers, such as architecture, where women are not in great number."

Rachel Carson, Voice for the Earth examines the life of the woman whose books *Silent Spring* and *The Sea around Us* are credited with spawning the environmental movement of the late twentieth century. Carolyn

Phelan, writing in *Booklist,* commented favorably on "Wadsworth's competent research, writing, and source notes." *Appraisal* contributor Kathryn L. Harvis called *Rachel Carson* "a well-done, laudatory effort by an author who obviously has done her homework." Comparing Wadsworth's effort to other biographies, *School Library Journal* contributor Pat Katka maintained that it "stands up well" and "is more visually appealing than most."

Long before Carson, there was John Muir, who founded the Sierra Club and started the movement to conserve the nation's vast natural resources in the 1800s. Wadsworth's biography, *John Muir, Wilderness Protector,* is "far superior to any series biographies about the naturalist," wrote Judith Walker in *Appraisal,* "and one can sense the author's respect and admiration for Muir." The book was particularly timely, Walker noted, given "the resurgence of interest in the environmental movement" during the 1990s. Kathleen Odean in *School Library Journal* called *John Muir* a "readable biography," and also noted its timeliness: "With the increasing interest in environmental issues, this inspiring story should have wide appeal."

In contrast to her earlier books, Wadsworth takes a slightly different approach in *Along the Santa Fe Trail: Marion Russell's Own Story.* The book is an adaptation of a pioneer's diary, written when Russell was eighty years old. As Julie Corsaro noted in *Booklist,* whereas Russell herself wrote from the perspective of an adult, Wadsworth utilizes the viewpoint of the seven-year-old Marion. The book, Corsaro concluded, "deserves a place in large regional or pioneer [library] collections." Pioneer children are also the subject of another of Wadsworth's books, *Words West: Voices of Young Pioneers.* This book, intended for middle-grades students, mixes excerpts from the journals, diaries, and letters of children who traveled westward with their families together with Wadsworth's own explanations of the subject. The text is accompanied by period photographs and engravings, as well as maps and an extensive bibliography. Critics praised the volume for presenting so vividly the experience of being a young pioneer, with its delights as well as its perils—at its best, riding in a wagon across the prairie, watching the scenery go by by day and singing around a campfire by night, was much more fun than sitting in a schoolroom for the young travelers. "This book will be a valuable addition to large collections of Western history because of its unique primary-source material," Ginny Gustin concluded in *School Library Journal.* A *Kirkus Reviews* contributor also praised *Words West,* noting Wadsworth's "clear prose and . . . passion for her subject" and calling the finished result "a model of fine history writing."

In *Laura Ingalls Wilder: Storyteller of the Prairie* Wadsworth profiles a much more famous pioneer woman. The facts of the biography, several reviewers noted, will be familiar to anyone who has read Wilder's novels, which chronicle her story in a fictionalized form.

Nonetheless, Wilder leaves out a painful chapter about her loss of an infant baby boy, which Wadsworth reports. Pat Mathews, writing in the *Bulletin of the Center for Children's Books,* maintained that the book is "a fine contribution to any biography collection," with its Little House addresses, bibliography, map called "Laura's Tracks," sources, index, and "twelve readable chapters." Adele Greenlee, writing in *School Library Journal,* also praised *Laura Ingalls Wilder* as a "readable biography."

Wadsworth has also written other well-received biographies. *Susan Butcher, Sled Dog Racer* describes an athlete who, like Julia Morgan, competed as a woman in a man's world, in Butcher's case, the grueling Iditarod sled-dog race through Alaska and Canada. *John Burroughs, the Sage of Slabsides* tells the life story of a figure who occupied a place similar, in the history of American naturalism, to that of John Muir. John Burroughs, whose woodland hideaway in New York was called Slabsides, rejected the urban life of the late nineteenth and early twentieth centuries, and yet some of the era's most distinguished figures—President Theodore Roosevelt, poet Walt Whitman, and automaker Henry Ford—became his friends. Wadsworth's biography, observed Marilyn Fairbanks in *School Library Journal,* is "written with a familiar, almost intimate tone." *Horn Book* reviewer Mary M. Burns called it "an accessible, respectable, and respectful treatment . . . aimed at young nature buffs, for whom little else about this significant individual is readily available." A *Kirkus Reviews* commentator called Wadsworth's book

Through actual documents, Wadsworth allows readers to experience the hardships, challenges, joys, and sense of adventure that captured the imagination of the American nation during the nineteenth century. (Cover illustration by G. E. Anderson.)

"a capable biography," noting that it "offers a good sense of Burroughs's gregarious personality."

Wadsworth has also written fiction and other works for a younger audience. Her picture book *Tomorrow Is Daddy's Birthday* introduces a young narrator named Rachel, who is so excited about the gift she plans to give her father that she cannot resist telling everyone she knows. Patricia Pearl Dole, writing in *School Library Journal*, called the book "an enjoyable story of family giving and sharing." *One Tiger Growls: A Counting Book of Animal Sounds* is also geared for young children, but not quite as young as the usual counting-book audience. Twenty animals are presented, from one tiger growling, through llamas um-m-m-m-m-ming and sea lions ork-ork-orking, all the way to twenty frogs ribbiting. Each two-page spread features a single animal, depicted realistically in its natural habitat, and Wadsworth's inclusion of a paragraph detailing scientific facts about the animal represented makes the book a potentially useful teaching tool. "There's not enough information for report writers," Kay Weisman commented in *Booklist*, but the book is perfect for "sophisticated browsers who may be almost ready for research."

Tundra Discoveries and *River Discoveries* also share information about wildlife with young listeners and readers. The former book follows various Arctic inhabitants, including caribou, musk oxen, foxes, lemmings, and ground squirrels, through a year, month by month. Watercolor paintings depict the animals going about their lives, while graphs on each page visually display information about the weather in that month, such as the number of hours of daylight versus darkness and the average temperature. The book's "attractive visuals together with the focused facts will engage many young naturalists," thought *Booklist* reviewer Ellen Mandel. *River Discoveries* uses a similar format, but only takes readers through a single day, rather than an entire year in the life of a waterway. The animals featured in this volume live both in the river—catfish, trout, river otters, water beetles—and near it—blackbirds, raccoons, mountain lions, and moose, for example. As in *Tundra Discoveries*, each page of *River Discoveries* features a question, such as "How does this trout keep from floating downriver with the currents?," to help keep children engaged. Overall, "the book offers children an attractive, informative introduction to riparian ecology," Catherine Andronik concluded in *Booklist*, and, as Barbara L. McMullin commented in a review for *School Library Journal*, it is one that "is equally effective as a read-aloud or for research."

Biographical and Critical Sources

BOOKS

Wadsworth, Ginger, *River Discoveries*, illustrated by Paul Kratter, Charlesbridge (Watertown, MA), 2002.

PERIODICALS

Appraisal, spring-summer, 1991, Rosilind Von Au, review of *Julia Morgan, Architect of Dreams*, pp. 49-50; autumn, 1992, Kathryn L. Harvis, review of *Rachel Carson, Voice for the Earth*, pp. 38-39; winter, 1993, Judith A. Walker, review of *John Muir*, pp. 52-53.

Booklist, June 1, 1992, Carolyn Phelan, review of *Rachel Carson, Voice for the Earth*, p. 1761; August, 1992, Mary Romano, review of *John Muir, Wilderness Protector*, pp. 2003; January 15, 1994, Julie Corsaro, review of *Along the Santa Fe Trail*, p. 928; March 15, 1997, Carolyn Phelan, review of *John Burroughs, the Sage of Slabsides*, p. 1241; February 1, 1999, Kay Weisman, review of *One Tiger Growls: A Counting Book of Animal Sounds*, p. 978; September 1, 1999, Ellen Mandel, review of *Tundra Discoveries*, p. 136; September 15, 2002, Catherine Andronik, review of *River Discoveries*, p. 230.

Bulletin of the Center for Children's Books, December, 1990, Deborah Stevenson, review of *Julia Morgan, Architect of Dreams*, p. 104; May, 1997, review of *John Burroughs, the Sage of Slabsides*, pp. 336-37; September, 1997, Pat Mathews, review of *Laura Ingalls Wilder: Storyteller of the Prairie*, p. 30.

Horn Book, July-August, 1992, Ellen Fader, review of *Rachel Carson, Voice for the Earth*, pp. 471-472; July-August, 1997, Mary M. Burns, review of *John Burroughs, the Sage of Slabsides*, pp. 478-479.

Journal of Adolescent and Adult Literacy, November, 2004, review of *Words West: Voices of Young Pioneers*, p. 268.

Kirkus Reviews, July 1, 1992, p. 856; February 1, 1997, review of *John Burroughs, the Sage of Slabsides*, p. 229; February 15, 1997, p. 307; July 1, 2002, review of *River Discoveries*, p. 964; October 1, 2003, review of *Words West*, p. 1232.

New York Times Book Review, March 17, 1991, Cathy Simon, review of *Julia Morgan, Architect of Dreams*, p. 27.

Publishers Weekly, August 9, 1993, review of *Along the Santa Fe Trail*, p. 479; February 1, 1999, review of *One Tiger Growls*, p. 83.

School Library Journal, February, 1991, Jeanette Larson, review of *Julia Morgan, Architect of Dreams*, p. 101; July, 1992, Pat Katka, review of *Rachel Carson, Voice for the Earth*, p. 88; September, 1992, Kathleen Odean, review of *John Muir, Wilderness Protector*, p. 271; December, 1993, Sally Bates Goodroe, review of *Along the Santa Fe Trail*, p. 108; June, 1994, pp. 142-143; November, 1994, Patricia Pearl Dole, review of *Tomorrow Is Daddy's Birthday*, p. 92; April, 1997, Adele Greenlee, review of *Laura Ingalls Wilder: Storyteller of the Prairie*, p. 162; May, 1997, Marilyn Fairbanks, review of *John Burroughs, the Sage of Slabsides*, p. 151; May, 2000, Kathleen Simonetta, review of *Laura Ingalls Wilder*, p. 165; August, 2002, Barbara L. McMullin, review of *River Discoveries*, p. 181; December, 2003, Ginny Gustin, review of *Words West*, p. 175.

ONLINE

Ginger Wadsworth Home Page, http://www.gingerwadsworth.com (December 23, 2004).

WAGNER, Michele R. 1975-

Personal

Born September 8, 1975, in San Diego, CA; daughter of Richard Henry and Barbara (an escrow officer; maiden name, Wilson) Cecelski; married Mark S. Wagner (an engineering lab supervisor) August 2, 1997; children: Gwendolyn. *Ethnicity:* "Caucasian." *Education:* California State University, San Marcas, B.A. (English), 1997. *Politics:* Republican Conservative. *Religion:* Reformed Presbyterian.

Addresses

Agent—c/o Author Mail, Gareth Stevens, Inc., 330 West Olive St., No. 100, Milwaukee, WI 53212-1068.

Career

Writer and editor. Greehaven Press, San Diego, CA, editor and proofreader, 1998-2001.

Writings

At Issue: How Should Prisons Treat Their Inmates?, Greenhaven Press (San Diego, CA), 2000.

Sweden, Gareth Stevens Pub. (Milwaukee, WI), 2001, expanded with text by Vimala Alexander as *Welcome to Sweden,* 2002.

Michele R. Wagner

Haiti, Gareth Stevens (Milwaukee, WI), 2002, expanded with text by Katharine Brown as *Welcome to Haiti,* 2003.

Sidelights

Michele R. Wagner told *Something about the Author:* "I have always been more comfortable reading than writing. While studying for my English degree, I chose a literature emphasis over writing. Writing books to educate children has been a step toward finally crossing that line and trying something different. I have enjoyed my forays into the world of writing and hope that as my confidence in my writing grows, so will my collection of work."

Biographical and Critical Sources

PERIODICALS

School Library Journal, February, 2002, Blair Christolon, review of *Sweden,* p. 151; February, 2003, Be Astengo, review of *Sri Lanka,* p. 160.*

*   *   *

WELLINGTON, Monica 1957-

Personal

Born June 17, 1957, in London, England; daughter of Roger (a business executive) and Diana (Guerin) Wellington; children: Lydia. *Education:* University of Michigan, B.F.A., 1978; additional study at New York School of Visual Arts, 1986. *Hobbies and other interests:* Travel, ballet, sewing, quilting.

Addresses

Home—243 West 70th St., No.7F, New York, NY 10023. *E-mail*—monicaaw@earthlink.net.

Career

Artist; freelance writer and illustrator of children's books, 1987—. Teacher at School of Visual Arts, New York, NY, 1994—. Formerly worked in antique galleries and at the Victoria and Albert Museum, London, England.

Writings

SELF-ILLUSTRATED

Molly Chelsea and Her Calico Cat, Dutton (New York, NY), 1988.

All My Little Ducklings, Dutton (New York, NY), 1989.

Monica Wellington

Seasons of Swans, Dutton (New York, NY), 1990.
The Sheep Follow, Dutton (New York, NY), 1992.
Mr. Cookie Baker, Dutton (New York, NY), 1992.
Night Rabbits, Dutton (New York, NY), 1995.
Baby in a Buggy, Dutton (New York, NY), 1995.
Baby in a Car, Dutton (New York, NY), 1995.
Baby at Home, Dutton (New York, NY), 1997.
Baby Goes Shopping, Dutton (New York, NY), 1997.
Night House, Bright House, Dutton (New York, NY), 1997.
Night City, Dutton (New York, NY), 1998.
Bunny's Rainbow Day, Dutton (New York, NY), 1999.
Bunny's First Snowflake, Dutton (New York, NY), 2000.
Squeaking of Art: The Mice Go to the Museum, Dutton (New York, NY), 2000.
Apple Farmer Annie, Dutton (New York, NY), 2001.
Firefighter Frank, Dutton (New York, NY), 2002.
Crêpes by Suzette, Dutton (New York, NY), 2004.
Zinnia's Flower Garden, Dutton (New York, NY), 2005.

Apple Farmer Annie has been translated into Spanish.

ILLUSTRATOR

Alhambra G. Deming, *Who Is Tapping at My Window?,* Dutton (New York, NY), 1988.
Virginia Griest, *In Between,* Dutton (New York, NY), 1989.
Arnold Shapiro, *Who Says That?,* Dutton (New York, NY), 1991.
Debra Leventhal, *What Is Your Language?,* Dutton (New York, NY), 1994.

Steve Metzger, *The Little Snowflake,* Scholastic (New York, NY), 2003.
Steve Metzger, *Little Snowflake's Big Adventure,* Scholastic (New York, NY), 2005.

Sidelights

The work of author and illustrator Monica Wellington is heavily influenced by memories of her childhood. Born in London, England, she had lived in England, Germany, and Switzerland before reaching the age of seven. As Wellington once told *Something about the Author* (*SATA*), "I think my early childhood has a big influence on my books. In Switzerland we lived close to a small town. We were surrounded by mountains, woods, lakes, orchards, fields, and farms. . . . In my books, I find myself doing pictures of these kinds of places." In fact, the natural world plays a prominent role in each of Wellington's picture books for young children, which include *Night Rabbits, Seasons of Swans,* and *The Sheep Follow.*

Wellington fell in love with art early. "I always loved to draw as a child. I recently found some of the first pictures I did when we were living in Europe and they are not that different from what I am doing now! I still like to do pictures full of color, of the same things!" Despite her creative streak, however, Wellington did not decide to become a children's book illustrator until she was in her late twenties.

In the meantime, she and her family relocated to the United States, although they still continued to travel and Wellington lived in four states while going to junior high and high school. After high-school graduation, she enrolled at the University of Michigan's School of Art, where she studied pottery, painting, and printmaking. After college, she moved back to England for several years, studying the decorative arts and working in a London antique gallery specializing in English porcelain as well as in the ceramics department of the Victoria and Albert Museum. Despite her interest in the decorative arts, Wellington eventually realized that she needed to do something more creative. A move to New York City in 1981 marked her change to a career as a freelance artist.

"For about three years I worked in a pottery studio," Wellington recalled of her first years in New York. "Then gradually I started to do more painting projects. The more pictures I did, because of the style and images that were developing, the more I thought of doing children's books. I kind of wandered into the field and then was struck by how much I absolutely loved doing this. I had finally found the perfect outlet for my creative energy."

In 1986 Wellington studied under noted illustrator Bruce Degen at the School of Visual Arts, which prompted her to bring her portfolio to publishers. One of the pictures in Wellington's portfolio, a proposed illustration for a poem by writer Alhambra G. Deming, had been a class assignment. That picture eventually was expanded into Wellington's first picture book, Deming's *Who Is Tapping at My Window?*, which a *Publishers Weekly* reviewer deemed the work of "a seasoned illustrator rather than a first-time artist."

Who Is Tapping at My Window was quickly followed by several more books, including *All My Little Ducklings,* which Wellington both wrote and illustrated. Tracing the typical day of an average duckling, Wellington's pictures show the little creatures engaged in such pursuits as visiting nearby farmyard animals, floating on the pond, and nosing around the local beehive, all accompanied by a simple text filled with words that elicit the sounds of the ducks' activities: "Scurry Hurry Plunk / Flipping Dipping Splatter Splash / Paddle in the Pond." The idea for *All My Little Ducklings* came from a German song Wellington recalled from her childhood: "Alle meine Entchen." "'All my little ducklings, swimming in the sea, heads are in the water, tails are to the sun,'—I took this image as a starting point and it grew into a book about a day in the life of this family of ducks," the author/illustrator explained. Ellen Fader, writing in *Horn Book,* praised the "graceful story," noting that Wellington's illustrations "are bright and clear, pruned of unnecessary detail," while Ilene Cooper described the ducklings as "winsome" in her review for *Booklist,* and predicted that the author's choice of words "will help instill a love of language in young ears."

Seasons of Swans also features feathered protagonists; Wellington's story of the cycle of nature revolves around a family of swans as they nest, lay eggs, and hatch their young, called cygnets. By autumn, the young swans have learned to swim and fish, and are ready to leave their parents' nest and make their own home before winter falls. *School Library Journal* contributor Danita Nichols praised the book's colorful and "uncluttered" illustrations, as well as Wellington's "spare and precise prose," which Nichols deemed a match for the straightforward drawings.

In *The Sheep Follow* youngsters witness what happens when a flock of sheep are left to their own devices while their shepherd takes a nap. Following first a butterfly, then a cat, pigs, rabbits, and a succession of other animals, the silly sheep eventually arrive back at the pasture in which the young shepherd is finally awakening. "The stylized graphic art and simple narration insure the book's success with the toddler set," maintained Nancy Seiner in *School Library Journal.* Deborah Abbott of *Booklist* commented on the "sprightly outdoor scenes" and "buoyant simplicity" of the book, concluding, "Be prepared to read this again and again."

Traveling animals are also a feature of *Night Rabbits,* as frisky white bunnies come out to play when the sun sets and the countryside is quiet. While they have to watch for predators—an owl and fox are also out and about in the rabbit's vicinity—the pair find much to do and eat before returning to their cozy burrow for another nap until dusk. *Booklist* reviewer Lauren Peterson praised Wellington's simple, unadorned prose, calling it "rich" and "poetic" and hailing the inclusion of "sensory images, onomatopoeia, and rhyme." "Totally charming and uncynical," observed a *Kirkus Reviews* critic, adding, "Wellington's simplicity is a stand-out."

The world of the night is also the backdrop for *Night House, Bright House,* and *Night City.* In the first, a group of ten mice hunting for something to nibble on meets up with the family tabby cat. The ensuing chase is watched by household objects, which come to life at night and offer helpful, rhyming commentary. "Some of the rhymes are wildly funny to read aloud," noted a *Kirkus Reviews* critic, who maintained that many would be adopted by young listeners for use in their own homes. "The art," added a *Publishers Weekly* reviewer,

Author and illustrator Monica Wellington presents an interactive introduction to the art museum as readers join a rodent field trip in her energetic picture book Squeaking of Art: The Mice Go to the Museum.

Featuring the author's bright, graphic artwork, **Apple Farmer Annie** *describes the many tasks that must be undertaken to bring fresh fruit to market, and also creates a healthy appetite for apple pie, apple cider, and apple sauce!*

"is inventive and diverting," while adults have the further pleasure of recognizing "playful knockoffs of well-known paintings." *Night City* highlights the bustle of activity occurring late at night in a large city while a little girl sleeps soundly at home. "The text imparts plenty of information, offering windows on new worlds for children," noted a *Kirkus Reviews* critic, who commented favorably on Wellington's "congenially depicted scenes."

In addition to picture books, Wellington has also created a series of board books for toddlers, including *Baby in a Buggy, Baby at Home,* and *Baby Goes Shopping,* all of which feature brightly colored, graphic illustrations that reviewers have compared to the work of author-illustrator Eric Carle. A *Publishers Weekly* critic lauded Wellington's illustrations as "pack[ing] a punch," while Darla Remple in *School Library Journal* noted how the simple shapes are "positioned jauntily" against

colorful backgrounds in these "appealing" books for youngsters under two.In *Squeaking of Art: The Mice Go to the Museum,* a group of ten mice tour an imaginary museum, passing through a number of galleries, each with its own theme. Dozens of masterpieces, including portraits, landscapes, and still lifes, hang on the gallery walls, all reproduced by Wellington in her recognizable style. *Booklist* contributor Michael Cart called the work a "clever, beautifully realized introduction to the world of art." In *School Library Journal,* Wendy Lukeheart observed that when "shared one-on-one with a child, Wellington's age-appropriate questions and playful approach to art work both as model and motivation for visiting a museum."

Apple Farmer Annie follows the efforts of an orchard keeper as she harvests her crop, prepares treats such as apple cider and apple muffins, and sells her wares at the market. "The illustrations seem to step right out of a coloring book with simple shapes, objects, and bright crayon-box colors," noted Pamela K. Bomboy in *School Library Journal. Booklist* critic Marta Segal also praised Wellington's artwork, remarking that her paintings, "bright, colorful, and detailed, have a pleasant, childlike quality."A day in the life of a rescue worker is the subject of *Firefighter Frank.* According to a critic in *Kirkus Reviews,* "this tribute to this challenging profession is sure to inspire children who dream of one day wearing the uniform." *Crêpes by Suzette* is an "original and appealing concept book that mixes art appreciation with a travelogue," in the words of *School Library Journal* reviewer Lauralyn Persson. Published in 2004, *Crêpes by Suzette* tells the story of a friendly street vendor who encounters a host of characters as she wheels her pushcart through the parks and along the boulevards of Paris, France. Though some critics felt the plot lacks depth, others applauded the author/illustrator's inventive design work, especially her use of mixed-media collage. "Wellington uses . . . photographs of Parisian streets, storefronts, parks and apartment buildings (with faces of real children peeking out) as a vibrant backdrop,"

noted a critic in *Publishers Weekly,* and she augments the photographs with a variety of materials, including maps, tickets, stamps, and postcards, as well as her own colorful illustrations. "The dense visuals make for delightful exploration," remarked *Booklist* reviewer Terry Glover.

Wellington has more than twenty books to her credit; she has both written and illustrated the vast majority of them. On her Web site, Wellington described her approach to creating a new work: "I usually start a book visually, with an idea of pictures I want to paint. I usually start making sketches before I even write any words at all. Both the pictures and words go through many revisions, and I am often still working on the final words after I finish the pictures." Although the development process can be difficult at times, Wellington observed, it is also enjoyable and fulfilling. "Going through the different stages of making a book is quite a bit of work, but it is also enormously satisfying," she commented. "I spend my days doing exactly what I love to do, and it is very gratifying that my work goes out into the world and is shared with other people. I feel incredibly lucky."

A trip to Paris is in store for readers of **Crêpes by Suzette,** *as Wellington combines her own photographs of the city with her brightly colored original art.*

Biographical and Critical Sources

PERIODICALS

Booklist, April 15, 1989, Ilene Cooper, review of *All My Little Ducklings,* p. 1473; February 1, 1992, Deborah Abbott, review of *The Sheep Follow,* p. 1042; October 15, 1992, p. 443; April 15, 1995, Lauren Peterson, review of *Night Rabbits,* p. 8; June 1, 1995, Hazel Rochman, review of *Baby in a Car* and *Baby in a Buggy,* p. 1780; February 1, 1997, Hazel Rochman, review of *Night House,* p. 949; September 1, 1997, Hazel Rochman, review of *Baby at Home* and *Baby Goes Shopping,* p. 136; July, 1998, Michael Cart, review of *Night City,* p. 1879; February 1, 1999, Ilene Cooper, review of *Bunny's Rainbow Day,* p. 983; February 15, 2000, Michael Cart, review of *Squeaking of Art,* p. 1116; October 15, 2000, Connie Fletcher, review of *Bunny's First Snowflake,* p. 448; December 15, 2000, Gillian Engberg, review of *Squeaking of Art: The Mice Go to the Museum,* p. 811; September 1, 2001, Marta Segal, review of *Apple Farmer Annie,* p. 118; January 1, 2004, Terry Glover, review of *Crêpes by Suzette,* p. 883.

Childhood Education, spring, 1993, Joan M. Hildebrand, review of *Mr. Cookie Baker,* p. 174.

Horn Book, May, 1989, Ellen Fader, review of *All My Little Ducklings,* pp. 366-367.

Kirkus Reviews, April 1, 1989, p. 556; December 15, 1991, p. 1600; February 15, 1995, review of *Night House,*

Bright House, p. 234; November 15, 1996, review of *Night House, Bright House,* p. 1677; May 1, 1998, review of *Night City,* p. 666; September 1, 2002, review of *Firefighter Frank,* p. 1323; January 15, 2004, review of *Crêpes by Suzette,* p. 90.

Publishers Weekly, February 26, 1988, review of *Who Is Tapping at My Window?,* p. 194; February 13, 1995, review of *Night Rabbits,* p. 77; July 3, 1995, review of *Baby in a Buggy* and *Baby in a Car,* p. 59; December 16, 1996, review of *Night House, Bright House,* p. 58; March 8, 2004, review of *Crêpes by Suzette,* p. 72.

School Arts, October, 2004, Ken Marantz, review of *Crêpes by Suzette,* p. 66.

School Library Journal, October 1990, Danita Nichols, review of *Seasons of Swans,* p. 104; March, 1992, Nancy Seiner, review of *The Sheep Follow,* p. 225; January, 1993, p. 88; March, 1995, p. 189; September, 1995, p. 188; June, 1997, Darla Remple, review of *Baby at Home,* p. 102; May, 2000, Wendy Lukeheart, review of *Squeaking of Art,* p. 165; October, 2000, Lisa Smith, review of *Bunny's First Snowflake,* p. 142; August, 2001, Pamela K. Bomboy, review of *Apple Farmer Annie,* p. 197; January, 2003, Linda M. Kenton, review of *Firefighter Frank,* pp. 114-115; March, 2004, Lauralyn Persson, review of *Crêpes by Suzette,* p. 186.

ONLINE

Monica Wellington Home Page, http://www.monica wellington.com (January 10, 2005).

Illustrations Index

(In the following index, the number of the *volume* in which an illustrator's work appears is given *before* the colon, and the *page number* on which it appears is given *after* the colon. For example, a drawing by Adams, Adrienne appears in Volume 2 on page 6, another drawing by her appears in Volume 3 on page 80, another drawing in Volume 8 on page 1, and so on and so on. . . .)

YABC

Index references to *YABC* refer to listings appearing in the two-volume *Yesterday's Authors of Books for Children,* also published by Thomson Gale. *YABC* covers prominent authors and illustrators who died prior to 1960.

Illustrations Index

Illustrations Index

Illustrations Index

Illustrations Index

Illustrations Index

Author Index

The following index gives the number of the volume in which an author's biographical sketch, Autobiography Feature, Brief Entry, or Obituary appears.

This index includes references to all entries in the following series, which are also published by The Gale Group.

YABC—*Yesterday's Authors of Books for Children: Facts and Pictures about Authors and Illustrators of Books for Young People from Early Times to 1960*
CLR—*Children's Literature Review: Excerpts from Reviews, Criticism, and Commentary on Books for Children*
SAAS—*Something about the Author Autobiography Series*

Author Index

Author Index

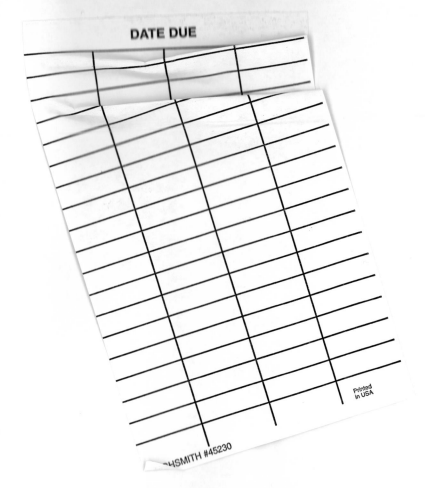

DATE DUE

Printed
in USA

HSMITH #45230